RALPH WALDO EMERSON

Ralph Waldo Emerson

SELECTED JOURNALS
1841–1877

Lawrence Rosenwald, editor

THE LIBRARY OF AMERICA

RALPH WALDO EMERSON: SELECTED JOURNALS 1841–1877
Volume compilation, notes, and chronology copyright © 2010 by
Literary Classics of the United States, Inc., New York, N.Y.

Published in the United States by Library of America.
Visit our website at www.loa.org.

This paper meets the requirements of
ANSI/NISO Z39.48–1992 (Permanence of Paper).

Distributed to the trade in the United States
by Penguin Random House Inc.
and in Canada by Penguin Random House Canada Ltd.

Library of Congress Control Number: 2009935641
ISBN 978–1–59853–068–1

Second Printing
The Library of America—202

Manufactured in the United States of America

Ralph Waldo Emerson: Selected Journals
is published with support from

THE GOULD FAMILY FOUNDATION

and is kept in print by a gift from

THE BERKLEY FOUNDATION

to the Guardians of American Letters Fund,
established by The Library of America
to ensure that every volume in the series
will be permanently available.

Ralph Waldo Emerson: Selected Journals
is dedicated to the memory of

RICHARD POIRIER
(1925–2009)

a founder and chairman of The Library of America
whose engagement with the work of Emerson
as a reader, critic, and teacher was lifelong.

The Library of America wishes to thank the editors of The Journals and Miscellaneous Notebooks of Ralph Waldo Emerson (Harvard University Press, 1960–1982): Linda Allardt, Ruth H. Bennett, Ronald A. Bosco, George P. Clark, Merrell R. Davis, Alfred R. Ferguson, William H. Gilman, Harrison Hayford, David W. Hill, Glen M. Johnson, Ralph H. Orth, J. E. Parsons, A. W. Plumstead, Merton M. Sealts, Jr., and Susan Sutton Smith. The present edition is greatly indebted to their scholarship.

Contents

from

Journal G

1841

6 July 1841.

Ah ye old ghosts! ye builders of dungeons in the air! why do I ever allow you to encroach on me a moment; a moment to win me to your hapless company? In every week there is some hour when I read my commission in every cipher of nature, and know that I was made for another office, a professor of the Joyous Science, a detector & delineator of occult harmonies & unpublished beauties, a herald of civility, nobility, learning, & wisdom; an affirmer of the One Law, yet as one who should affirm it in music or dancing, a priest of the Soul yet one who would better love to celebrate it through the beauty of health & harmonious power.

My trees teach me the value of our circumstance or limitation. I have a load of manure, & it is mine to say whether I shall turn it into strawberries, or peaches, or carrots. I have a tree which produces these golden delicious cones called Bartlett pears, & I have a plant of strong common sense called a potato. The pear tree is certainly a fine genius but with all that wonderful constructive power it has, of turning air & dust yea the very dung to Hesperian fruit, it will very easily languish & bear nothing, if I starve it, give it no southern exposure, & no protecting neighborhood of other trees. How differs it with the tree planter? He too may have a rare constructive power to make poems or characters, or nations perchance but though his power be new & unique if he be starved of his needful influences, if he have no love, no book, no critic, no external call, no need or market for that faculty of his, then he may sleep through dwarfish years and die at last without fruit.

I copy from a fragment of Edward's "Certificate of Departure" from Liverpool these fugitive shadows—1826 Aug 31

Edward B Emerson native of Boston Aged 21 years, height 5 feet, 10; light hair, blue eyes, sharp nose; *from* London; going *to* New York, in the ship Cincinnatus

Colombe prefers to take work of Edmund Hosmer by the job, "for the days are damn long."

Sunday.

If I were a preacher, I should carry straight to church the remark Lidian made today, that "she had been more troubled by piety in her *help* than with any other fault." The girls that are not pious, she finds kind & sensible, but the church members are scorpions, too religious to do their duties, and full of wrath & horror at her if she does them.

Every man has had one or two moments of extraordinary experience, has met his soul, has thought of something which he never afterwards forgot, & which revised all his speech, & moulded all his forms of thought.

I resent this intrusion of *alterity*. That which is done, & that which does, is somehow, I know not how, part of me. The Unconscious works with the Conscious,—tells somewhat which I consciously learn to have been told. What I am has been conveyed secretly from me to another whilst I was vainly endeavoring to tell him it. He has heard from me what I never spoke.

If I should or could record the true experience of my late years, I should have to say that I skulk & play a mean, shiftless, subaltern part much the largest part of the time. Things are to be done which I have no skill to do, or are to be said which others can say better, and I lie by, or occupy my hands with something which is only an apology for idleness until my hour comes again. Thus how much of my reading & all my labor in house or garden seems mere waiting: any other could do it as well or better. It really seems to me of no importance,—so little skill enters into these works, so little do they mix with my universal life,—what I do, whether I hoe, or turn a grindstone, or copy manuscript, or eat my dinner. All my virtue consists in my consent to be insignificant which consent is founded on my faith in the great Optimism, which will justify itself to me at last.

The worst feature of our biography is that it is a sort of double consciousness, that the two lives of the Understanding & of the Soul which we lead, really show very little relation to each other, that they never meet & criticize each other, but one prevails now, all buzz & din, & the other prevails then, all infinitude & paradise, and with the progress of life the two discover no greater disposition to reconcile themselves.

—

> "When nature is forsaken by her lord be she ever so great she doth not survive." Veeshnoo Sarma

Too feeble fall the impressions of our sense upon us to make us artists. Every touch should thrill: now 'tis good for life not for poetry. It seems as if every man ought to be so much an artist that he could report in conversation what has befallen him.

It would seem that in Athens they gave themselves the luxury of bare feet.

—

The Church aerates my good neighbors & serves them as a somewhat stricter & finer ablution than a clean shirt or a bath or a shampooing. The minister is a functionary & the meetinghouse a functionary: they are one and when they have spent all their week in private & selfish action the Sunday reminds them of a need they have to stand again in social & public & ideal relations—beyond neighborhood,—higher than the town-meeting,—to their fellow men. They marry, & the minister who represents this high Public, celebrates the fact; their child is baptized & again they are published by his intervention. One of their family dies, he comes again, & the family go up publicly to the Church to be publicised or churched in this official sympathy of mankind. It is all good as far as it goes. It is homage to the Ideal Church, which they have not;—which the actual Church so foully misrepresents. But it is better so than nohow. These people have no fine arts, no literature, no great men to boswellize, no fine speculation to entertain their family board or their solitary toil with. Their talk is of oxen & pigs & hay & corn & apples. Whatsoever liberal aspirations they at any time have, whatsoever spiritual experiences, have looked this way, and the church is their fact for such things. It has not been discredited in their eyes as books, lectures, or living men of genius have been. It is still to them the accredited symbol of the religious Idea. The Church is not to be defended against any spiritualist clamoring for its reform, but against such as say it is expedient to shut it up & have none, thus much may be said. It stands in the history of the present time as a high school for the civility & mansuetude of the people. Do you not suppose that it is some benefit to a young villager who comes out of the woods of New Hampshire to Boston & serves his apprenticeship in a shop & now opens his own store to hang up his name in bright gold letters a foot long? His father could not write his name: it is only lately that he could: the name is mean & unknown: now the sun shines on it: all men, all women, fairest eyes read it. It is a fact in the great city. Perhaps he shall be successful & make it wider known: shall leave it greatly brightened to his son. His son may be head of a party: Governor of the state: a poet: a powerful thinker: & send the knowledge of this name over the habitable earth. By all these suggestions, he is at least made responsible & thoughtful by this public relation of a seen & aerated name.

—

Let him hope infinitely with a patience as large as the sky. Nothing is so young & untaught as time.

Cities of men are like the perpetual succession of shells on the beach.

This world is a palace whose walls are lined with mirrors.

—

All is for thee but thence results the inconvenience that all is against thee which thou dost not make thine own. Victory over things is the destiny of man; of course until it be accomplished it is the war & insult of things over him. He may have as much time as he pleases, as long as he likes to be a coward, & a disgraced person, so long he may delay to fight, but there is no escape from the alternative. I may not read Schleiermacher or Plato, I may even rejoice that Germany & Greece are too far off in time & space than that they can insult over my ignorance of their works, I may even have a secret joy that the heroes & giants of intellectual labor, say for instance these very Platos & Schleiermachers are dead & cannot taunt me with a look: my soul knows better: they are not dead: for the nature of things is alive and that passes its fatal word to me that these men shall yet meet me and shall yet tax me line for line, fact for fact with all my pusillanimity.

—

Shall I write a sincerity or two? I who never write anything else, except dulness? And yet all truth is ever the new morn risen on noon. But I shall say that I think no persons whom I know could afford to live together *on their merits.* Some of us or of them could much better than others live together, but not by their power to command respect, but because of their easy genial ways; that is, could live together by aid of their weakness & inferiority.

Understand that the history of modern improvements is good as matter of boast only for the twelve or twenty or two hundred who made them, not for those who adopted them & said *We.* The smallest sign of moral force in any person countervails all the models in Quincy Hall. The inventor may indeed show his model as sign of a moral force of some sort, but not the user.

I only need to meet one agreeable person,—boy or man or woman to make my journey a happy one. But lately it has been my misfortune to meet young men with a certain impudence on their brow, & who speak & answer with that offensive assumption that what I say I say to fill up the time & not that I mean anything. Not so with that fair & noble boy whom I saw at Nantasket, & whom all good auguries attend! I suppose there was never a noble youth or maid who did not find such joy in loving, that their eyes always rest on some individual (perhaps personally unknown to them, but whose fame had penetrated their solitude,) for whose sake they wished to exist and whom they thanked for existing.

Ascending souls sing a paean. We will not exhort but study the natural history of souls & congratulate one another on the admirable harmonies.

Rich, say you? Are you rich? how rich? rich enough to help any body? rich enough to succor the friendless, the unfashionable, the eccentric, rich enough to make the Canadian in his wagon, the itinerant travelling with his written paper which recommends him to the Charitable, the Italian foreigner with his few broken words of English, the ugly lame pauper hunted by overseers from town to town, even the poor insane or half insane wreck of man or woman feel the noble exception of your presence & your house from the general bleakness & stoniness;—to make such feel that they were greeted with a voice that made them both remember & hope. What is vulgar but to refuse the claim? what is gentle but to allow it?

Be calm, sit still in your chair, though the company be dull & unworthy. Are you not there? There then is the choir of your friends; for subtle *influences* are always arriving at you from them, & you represent them, do you not? to all who stand here.

It is not a *word* that "I am a gentleman & the king is no more" but is a fact expressed in every passage between the king and a gentleman.

He is very young in his education who needs distinguished men in order to see grand traits. If there is grandeur in you, you will detect grandeur in laborers & washerwomen. And very fine relations are always established between a clear spirit and all the bystanders. Do you think there is no tie but your dollar between you & your landlord or your merchant? Have these made no distinction between their customers or guests?

C. writes that her imaginary persons are nearly as vivid & as much society as real persons.

With our faith that every man is a possessed person, having that admirable Prompter at his ear, is it not a little superfluous to go about to reason with a person so advised?

We treat him as a detachment.

Do people expect the world to drop into their mouths like a peach?

I wish I could see a child go to school or a boy carrying a basket without a feeling of envy but now I am so idle that every body shames me.

The Metamorphosis of nature shows itself in nothing more than this that there is no word in our language that cannot become typical to us of nature by giving it emphasis. The world is a Dancer; it is a Rosary; it is a Torrent; it is a Boat; a Mist; a Spider's Snare; it is what you will; and the metaphor will hold, & it will give the imagination keen pleasure. Swifter than light the World converts itself into that thing you name & all things find their right place under this new & capricious classification. There is no thing small or mean to the soul. It derives as grand a joy from symbolizing the Godhead or his Universe under the form of a moth or a gnat as of a Lord of Hosts. Must I call the heaven & the earth a maypole & country fair with booths or an anthill or an old coat in order to give you the shock of pleasure which the imagination loves and the sense of spiritual greatness? Call it a blossom, a rod, a wreath of parsley, a tamarisk-crown, a cock, a sparrow, the ear instantly hears & the spirit leaps to the trope; and hence it is that men of eloquence like Chatham have found a Dictionary very suggestive reading when they were disposed to speak.

The doctrine of Necessity or Destiny is the doctrine of Toleration but every moment whilst we think of this offending person that he is ridden by a devil & go to pity him comes in our sensibility to persuade us that the person is the devil, then the poison works, the devil jumps on *our* neck, & back again wilder on the other; jumps from neck to neck, & the kingdom of hell comes in.

The AGE

What is the reason to be given for this extreme attraction which persons have for us but that they are the Age, they are the results of the Past, they are the heralds of the Future? They indicate,—these witty blushing figures of the only race in which there are individuals or change,—how far on the Fate has got & what it is driving at.

Well now we have some fine figures in the great group & many who promise to be fine. I think the nobility of the company or Period is always to be estimated from the depth of the ideas. Here is great variety & great richness of mysticism which when it shall be taken up as the garniture of some profound genius will appear as the rich & appropriate decoration of his robes whilst now that it forms the sole thought of some poor Come-outer or Swedenborgian it disgusts. But how many mysticisms of alchemy, magic, second sight & the like, can a grand genius like Leibnitz, Newton, or Milton dispose of amongst his shining parts, & be never the worse.

Motley assemblage on the planet; no conspiring as in an anthill. Every one his own huckster to the ruin of the rest for aught he cares: In perspective one may find symmetry & unconscious furtherance.

I am describing my platoon & call it the Age. Milton & Dante describe theirs & call it Heaven & Hell.

In describing ages it is still this personal picture, we do not think peas will be greener or steel smoother but men may be radiant. As soon as a man gets his suction hose down into the great deep he belongs to no age but is Eternal Man.

And as soon as there is elevation of thought we leave The Times.

I will add to the portrait of Osman that he was never interrupted by success; he had never to look after his fame & his compliments, his claps & editions. In very sooth shall I not say that one of the wisest men I have known was one who begun life as fool, at least, with a settled reputation of being underwitted.

"To me men are for what they are
They wear no masks with me."

When I was praised I lost my time, for instantly I turned round to look at the work I had thought slightly of, & that day I made nothing new.

—

Superlative

The greatest wit, the most space. It is the little wit that is always in extremes & sees no alternative but revelry or daggers. Hurry is for slaves.

The poet writes fable, but I read truth in it: he rages or rests, he trifles now, & now is grand, but I remain single & firm, taking one even sense from the whole.

We are to each other results. As your perception or sensibility is exalted, you see the genesis of my action, & of my thought, you see me in my debt & fountains, & to your eye instead of a little pond of the water of life, I am a rivulet fed by rills from every plain & height in nature & antiquity & deriving a remote origin from the foundation of all things.

—

When you are possessed of the principle it is equally easy to make four or forty thousand applications of it. A great man will be content to have only written a letter or any the slightest composition demonstrating his perception of the reigning Idea of his time, & will leave to more mercantile men the multiplication of examples.

Genius unsettles everything. It is fixed, (is it?) that after the reflective age arrives, there can be no quite rustic & united man born? Yes quite fixed. Ah this unlucky Shakspeare! and ah this hybrid Goethe! Make a new rule, my dear, can you not? and tomorrow Genius shall stamp on it with his starry sandal.

Then it is very easy to write as Mr Pericles writes. Why, I have been reading the books he read before he wrote his Dialogue, & I have traced him in them all & know where he got the things you most admire. Yes and the turnip grows in the same soil with the strawberry; knows all the nourishment that gets, and feeds on the very same itself; yet is a turnip still.

All histories, all times equally furnish examples of the spiritual economy; so does every kitchen & hencoop. But I may choose then to use those which have got themselves well written. The annals of Poland would be as good to a philosopher as those of Greece, but these last are well composed.

Portableness

The meaner the type by which a spiritual law is expressed, the more pungent it is, & the more lasting in the memories of men, just as we value most the smallest box or case in which any needful utensil can be carried.

—

Humoring.

I weary of dealing with people each cased in his several insanity. Here is a fine person with wonderful gifts but mad as the rest and madder &, by reason of his great genius, which he can use as weapon too, harder to deal with. I would gladly stand to him in relation of a benefactor as screen & defence to me thereby having him at some advantage & on my own terms —that so his frenzy may not annoy me. I know well that this wish is not great but small, is mere apology for not treating him frankly & manlike: but I am not large man enough to treat him firmly & unsympathetically as a patient, and if treated equally & sympathetically as sane, his disease makes him the worst of bores.

Quarrels are not composed on their own grounds, but only by the growth of the character which subverts their place & memory. We form in the life of a new idea new relations to all persons; we have become new persons & do not inherit the wars or the friendships of that person we were.—If the misunderstanding could be healed, it would not have existed, added L.

—

I remember when a child in the pew on Sundays amusing myself with saying over common words as "black," "white," "board," &c twenty or thirty times, until the word lost all meaning & fixedness, & I began to doubt which was the right name for the thing, when I saw that neither had any natural relation, but all were arbitrary. It was a child's first lesson in Idealism.

Measure

So many promising youths & never a finished man. 'Tis strange; but this masterpiece is a result of such an extreme delicacy, that the most unobserved flaw in the boy will neutralize the most aspiring genius & spoil the work.

How readily we join certain persons in our thought. Among my friends I couple particular names as naturally as I say apples & pears.

There are people who when they are mutually avoiding each other are sure to meet.

When each the other shall avoid
Shall each by each be most enjoyed.

27 Aug. How noble in secret are the men who have never stooped nor betrayed their faith! The two or three rusty perchance wearisome souls who could never bring themselves to the smallest composition with society rise with grandeur in the background like statues of the gods, whilst we listen in the dusty crowd to the adroit flattery & literary politics of those who stoop a little. If these also had stooped a little, then had we no examples, our ideas had been all unexecuted: we had been alone with the mind.

The solitary hours—who are their favorites? who cares for the summer fruit, the sopsavines that are early ripe by help of the worm at the core? Give me the winter apple, the russetin & pippin cured & sweetened by all the heat & all the frost of the year.

In regard to Hedge I suppose we all feel alike that we care very little what he says, provided only that he says it well. What he establishes with so much ingenuity today, we know he will demolish with equal ingenuity tomorrow not valuing any position or any principle, but only the tactics or method of the fight. Intellectual play is his delight, the question is indifferent. He is a warrior, & so only there be war, he is not scrupulous on which side his aid is wanted. In his oration there was universal attack, chivalry all round the field, but he cut up all so fast & with right good will that he left himself no ground to stand on, universal offence but no power of retreat or resistance in him, so that we agreed it was a triumphant success for his troop but no sincerity, a devastation & no home. It was the profoundness of superficiality, the most universal & triumphant seeming. The sentence which began with an attack on the conservatives ended with a blow at the reformers: the first clause was applauded by one party & the other party had their revenge & gave their applause before the period was closed.

It is not to be denied that the pious youth who in his closet espouses some rude & harsh reform such as Antislavery or the abstinence from animal food, lays himself open to the witty attacks of the intellectual man; is partial; & apt to magnify his own: yes, & the prostrate penitent also, he is not comprehensive, he is not philosophical in those tears & groans. Yet I feel that under him & his partiality & exclusiveness is the earth & sea and all that in them is, and the axis around which the eternal universe revolves, passes through his body there where he stands while the outcast that affects to pity his narrowness & chains, is a wanderer, free as the unloved and the unloving are free and independent on the state just as bachelors & beggars are homeless, companionless, useless. The heart detects immediately, whether the head find it out or not, whether you exist for purposes of exhibition or are holden by all the force of God to the place you occupy & the thing you do. This abuse of the conservative to win the reformer, & abuse of the reformer to win the conserver may deceive the head but not the heart. The heart knows that it is the fear & love of Beacon street which got this bottle green flesh fly, and that only the love & the terror of the Eternal God begets the Angel which it waiteth for.

There is no depth to the intellectual pleasure which this speculation gives. But let in one of those men of love in the shade there, whom you affect to compassionate, & you shall feel instantly how shallow all this entertainment was, for he shall exercise your affection as well as your thought & confront you with the realities that analyse Heaven & Hell.

Long ago I said, I have every inch of my merits allowed me, & was sad because my success was more than I deserved,—sad for others who had less. Now the beam trembles, & I see with some bitterness the slender claims I can make on fortune & the inevitable parsimony with which they will be answered.

When we are old, we have not an assurance that we are wanted. We need a continual reinforcement of compliments to certify us.

—

I saw a young man who had a rare gift for pulpit eloquence: his whole constitution seemed to qualify him for that office and to see & hear him produced an effect like a strain of music: not what he said but the pleasing efflux of the spirit of the man through his sentences & gesture, suggested a thousand things, and I enjoyed it as I do painting or poetry, & said to myself, "Here is creation again." I was touched & taken out of my numbness & unbelief & wished to go out & speak & write all things. After months I heard the favored youth speak again. Perhaps I was critical, perhaps he was cold. But too much praise I fancied had hurt him, had given to his flowing gesture the slightest possible fixedness; to his glowing rhetoric an artful return; it was later in the season yet the plant was all in flower still & no signs of fruit. Could the flowers be barren or was an artificial stimulus kept upon the plant to convert all the leaves & fruitbuds to flowers? We love young bachelors & maidens but not old bachelors & old maids. It seemed to me that I had seen before an example of the finest graces of youthful eloquence hardened by the habit of haranguing into grimace. It seemed that if instead of the certainty of a throng of admirers the youth had felt assured every Sunday that he spoke to hunger & debt, to lone women & poor boys, to grief & to the friends of some sick or insane or felonious person, he would have lopped some of these redundant flowers, & given us with all the rest one or two plain & portable propositions. Praise is not so safe as austere exactors. And of all teachers of eloquence the best is a man's own penitence & shame.

—

Aug. 31.

I know not why Landor should have so few readers. His book seems to me as original in its form as in its substance. He has no dramatic, no epic power but he makes sentences, which though not gravitation & electricity is still vegetation. After twenty years I still read his strange dialogues with pleasure not only sentences but page after page the whole discourse. I regret his love of obscenity, it is so gratuitous & defying. Before a well dressed company he plunges his jewelled fingers in a swill-tub as if to notice the more accurately the whiteness of his hands & the jewels on his ring. Afterward he washes them in water, he washes them in wine, but from his freaks you are never secure. I do not like his dogmatism though I separate it easily from his genius. What he says of Wordsworth is true of himself, that he delights to throw a clod of dirt on the table, & cry Gentlemen, there is a better man than any of you. Bolivar, Mina, & General Jackson will never be greater men than Washington or Scipio, but a man may love a paradox without losing either his wit or his honesty. I think he loves truth & justice & wit everywhere. I think him capable of appreciating character. He has not drawn the interest of his page from circumstance: he loves fine clothes but only on fine persons. He loves to draw the portrait of a man who never said anything good & never did anything ill. Rarer, higher than our interest in intellect is our interest in character. Who are the persons who without being public men or literary men or rich men or active men have a certain salutary omnipresence in all our life's history almost giving permanence & their own quality to the planet? A moral force but wholly unmindful of the catechism, intellectual but scornful of books it is the light of day and not the sovereign but sovereignty. Landor loves all his own advantages, is not insensible to beauty of his watch seal or the Turk's head on his umbrella, values his pedigree, his acres, the syllables of his name, & yet with his ostentation rejoices that he is so rich he can spare them all and draws his own portrait in the character of a village schoolmaster & a sailor and highly enjoys the victory of character over fortune. Not only the picture of Normanby but the whimsical selection of heroes in his gallery prove this taste. A sort of Earl Peterborough in literature his eccentricity is too decided not to have diminished his greatness. He has capital stock enough to have furnished fifty good authors yet has written no good book.

I value a book which like this or Montaigne proves the existence of a literary world. What boundless leisure, what original jurisdiction, what new heavens & new earth. The old constellations have set, new & brighter have arisen; we have eaten lotus, we have tasted nectar. O that the dream might last! There is no man in this age who so truly belongs to this dispensation as Landor. To the reformer this appears luxury; well, when he has quite got his new views through, when he sees how he can mend the old house, we will quit this entertainment. Until then, leave us the land where Horace & Ovid, Erasmus & Scaliger, Isaak Walton & Ben Jonson, Dryden & Pope had their whole existence.

In the afternoon we came unto a land
In which it seemed always afternoon

But consider O Reformer ere you denounce the House of Fame & the land whose intoxications Homer & Milton, Plato & Shakspear have partaken that a shade of uncertainty still hangs over all that is actual. Alas that I must hint to you that poverty is not an unmixed good, that Labor may easily exceed. The sons of the rich have finer forms & in some respects a better organization than the sons of the laborer. The Irish population in our towns, is the most laborious but neither the most moral nor the most intelligent: the experience of the colleagues of Brook Farm was unanimous, 'We have no thoughts.'

Landor's position in the Republic of Letters is that of a noble: There is no such independent criticism in England as this, unless we can add the names of Coleridge & Carlyle. But Landor discriminates the faults also of his favorites. He judges from an elevated point but not from the highest. Some of his attempts at definition are very unlucky.

—

Well for us that we cannot make good apologies. If I had skill that way, I should spend much of my time at that. Not being able, I leave it with nature who makes the best; meantime I am doing something new, which crowns the apology.

Whitewashing

We embellish involuntarily all stories, facts, & persons. In nature there is no emphasis. By detaching & reciting a fact, we already have added emphasis to it & begun to give a wrong impression, which is inflamed by the new point given every time it is told. All persons exist to society by some shining trait of beauty or utility they have. We borrow the proportions of the man from that one fine feature we see, & finish the portrait symmetrically; which is false; for the rest of his body is small or deformed. I see a person who makes a fine public appearance & conclude thence the perfection of his private character on which this is based but he has

I had occasion in 1835 to inquire for the facts that befel on the Nineteenth April 1775. Dr. R. carried me to Abel Davis & Buttrick & Master Blood. The Doctor carried in his mind what he wished them to testify & extorted where he could their assent to his forewritten History. I who had no theory was anxious to get at their recollections but could learn little. Blood's impression plainly was that there was no great courage exhibited, except by a few. I suppose we know how brave they were by considering how the present inhabitants would behave in the like emergency. No history is true but that which is always true. It is plain that there is little of "*the 2 o'clock-in-the-morning courage*," which, Napoleon said, he had known few to possess.

The thoughts of which the Universe is the celebration, are, no doubt, as readily & thoroughly denoted in the nature & habits of animals and in those of plants as in Men. The words *dog* & snake & crocodile are very significant to us.

At Cambridge, the last Wednesday I met twenty members of my college class & spent the day with them. Governor Kent of Maine presided, Upham, Quincy, Lowell, Gardner, Loring, Gorham, Motte, Wood, Blood, Cheney, Withington, Bulfinch, Reed, Burton, Stetson, Lane, Angier, Hilliard, Emerson, (Farnsworth), Dexter. It was strange how fast the company returned to their old relation and the whole mass of college nonsense came back in a flood. They all associated perfectly, were an unit for the day—men who now never meet. Each resumed his old place. The change in them was really very little in 20 years although every man present was married & all but one fathers. I too resumed my old place & found myself as of old a spectator rather than a fellow. I drank a great deal of wine (for me) with the wish to raise my spirits to the pitch of good fellowship, but wine produced on me its old effect, & I grew graver with every glass. Indignation & eloquence will excite me, but wine does not. One poor man came whom fortune had not favored, & we carried round a hat, & collected $115.00 for him in two minutes.

Almost all these were prosperous men, but there was something sad and affecting in their prosperity. Very easy it was to see that each owed his success to some one trait or talent not supported by his other properties. There is no symmetry in great men of the first or of the tenth class. Often the division of talents is very minute. One man can pronounce well; another has a voice like a bell and the "orotund tone." Edward Everett's beautiful elocution & rhetoric had charms for the dull. I remember C. J. in my class who said "he did not care what the subject was, he would hear him lecture on Hebrew or Persian." There is this pleasure in a class meeting: Each has been thoroughly measured & known to the other as a boy, and they are not to be imposed upon by later circumstances & acquisitions. One is a governor of a state, one is a President of a college, one is President of a senate, two or three are Bank Presidents.—They have removed from New Hampshire or from Massachusetts or from Vermont into the state where they live.—Well all these are imposing facts in the new neighborhood, in the imaginations of the young men among whom they come; but not for us. When they come into the presence of either of their old mates, off goes every disguise, & the boy meets the boy as of old. This was ludicrously illustrated in the good story Wood told us of his visit to Moody in his office among his clients at Bangor. "How are you, Moody," with a slap on the back. "How do you do, sir," with a stare & a civil but formal bow. "Sir you have the advantage of me." "Yes and I mean to keep it. But I am in no hurry. Go on with your business. I will sit here & look at this newspaper until your client is gone." M. looked up every now & then from his bond & his bondsman but could not recollect the stranger. By & by they were left alone. "Well" said Wood "And you have not found me out?" "*Hell!*" cried Moody with the utmost prolongation of accent, "it's Wood!"

What you owe to me—you will vary the phrase but I shall still recognize my thought. But what you say from the same Idea, will have to me also the expected unexpectedness which belongs to every new work of nature.

Amongst us only the face is well alive: the trunk & limbs have an inferior & subsidiary life seeming to be only supporters to the head. The head is finished, the body only blocked. Now & then in a Southerner, we see a body which is also alive, as in young E. So is it with our manners & letters.

A beautiful woman varies her dress with her mood, as our lovely Walden Pond wears a new weather each time I see it, and all are so comely that I can prefer none. But there must be agreement between the mood & the dress. Vain & forgotten are the fine things if there is no holiday in the eye.

A great man conquers, not because he hits on some new expedient, but because his arrival alters the face of affairs. It is the presence of a new element.

Every gardener can change his flowers & leaves into fruit and so is the Genius that today can upheave & balance & toss every object in nature for his metaphor, capable in his next manifestation of playing such a game with his hands instead of his brain. An instinctive suspicion that this may befal, seems to have crept into the mind of men. What would happen to us who live on the surface if this fellow in some new transmigration should have acquired power to do what he now delights to say? He must be watched.

"War," said Archidamus, "cannot be kept at a set diet"

Plutarch, *Cleomenes*

For me, what I may call the autumnal style of Montaigne keeps all its old attraction.

Your reading you may use in conversation, but your writing should stop with your own thought.

The whole history of Sparta seems to be a picture or text of selfreliance.

Waldo's diplomacy in giving account of Ellen's loud cries declares that she put her foot into his sand house & *got pushed.*

—

Lotos eaters

I suppose there is no more abandoned Epicure or opium eater than I. I taste every hour of these autumn days. Every light from the sky, every shadow on the earth ministers to my pleasure. I love this gas. I grudge to move or to labor or to change my book or to will, lest I should disturb the sweet dream.

Our people are easily pleased; but I wonder to see how rare is any deviation from the routine. In Portsmouth a man who had been educated at college put on a grey coat & worked on his own farm. He also chose to wear boots and no stockings under them. These facts proved the topic of inexhaustible conversation in the streets of the town & if he passed by he was looked after & whispered about as if he had been Black Hawk or Colonel Crockett. If Mr & Mrs Wigglesworth go to walk with their family in the mornings they are the speculation of Boston.

The moment is all. The boys like to have their swing of peaches once in the season & it suffices them; or of plums, or cherries; we like to be rested; we like to be thoroughly tired by labor; I sit on a stone & look at the pond & feel that having basked in a nature so vast & splendid I can afford to decease & yet the antecedent generations have not quite lost their labor. "In the midst of the battle Pericles smiled on me," &c.

We animate as much as we can, and we see no more than we animate. I find a few passages in my biography noticeable. But it is the present state of mind which selects those anecdotes and the selection characterises the state of mind. All the passages will in turn be brought out.

—

September 9.

Rightly says Elizabeth, that, we do not like to hear our authors censured, for we love them by sympathy as well as for cause, and do not wish to have a reason put in the mouth of their enemies. It is excellent criticism & I will write it into my piece.

11 September. The Poet; the Maker;
It is much to write sentences; it is more to add method, & write out the spirit of your life symmetrically. Of all the persons who read good books & converse about them, the greater part are content to say I was pleased; or I was displeased; it made me active or inactive, and rarely does one eliminate & express the peculiar quality of that life which the book awoke in him. So rare is a general reflection. But to arrange many general reflections in their natural order so that I shall have one homogeneous piece, a Lycidas, an Allegro, a Penseroso, a Hamlet, a Macbeth, a Midsummer's Night's Dream, this continuity is for the great. The wonderful men are wonderful hereby. The observations that Pythagoras made respecting sound & music are not in themselves unusually acute; but he goes on: adds fact to fact, makes two steps, three, or even four; and every additional step counts a thousand years to his fame.

—

But I sympathize with all the sad angels who on this planet of ours are striking work and crying, O for something worthy to do! What they do, is done only because they are overpowered by the humanities that speak on all sides, & they consent to the drudgeries of writing epics or Hamlets or building cities or making fortunes.

Life Osman

We are all of us very near to sublimity. As one step freed Wordsworth's Recluse on the mountains from the blinding mist & brought him to the view of "Glory beyond all glory ever seen" so near are we all to a vision of which Homer & Shakspeare are only hints & types and yet cannot we take that one step. It does not seem worth our while to toil for anything so pitiful as skill to do one of the little feats we magnify so much, when presently the dream will scatter & we shall burst into universal power. The reason of all idleness & of all crime is the same. Whilst we are waiting we beguile the time, one with jokes, one with sleep, one with eating, one with crimes.

*

It is pedantry to give such importance to property. Whoso does shows how much he desires it. Can I not play the game with these counters as well as with those; with land & money as well as with brown bread & serge? A good wrestler does not need the costume of the ring, and it is only indifferent writers who are so hard to be suited with a pen.

—

Jones Very told George P. B. that "he valued his poems not because they were his, but because they were not."

"The Transcendentalists do not err in excess but in defect, if I understand the case. They do not hold wild dreams for realities; the vision is deeper, broader, more spiritual than they have seen. They do not believe with too strong faith; their faith is too dim of sight, too feeble of grasp, too wanting in certainty."
Thomas T. Stone's letter to M.M.E. June, 1841.

Sept. 21. Dr Ripley died this morning. The fall of this oak of ninety years makes some sensation in the forest old & doomed as it was. He has identified himself with the forms at least of the old church of the New England Puritans; his nature was eminently loyal, not in the least adventurous or democratical & his whole being leaned backward on the departed so that he seemed one of the rearguard of this great camp & army which have filled the world with fame & with him passes out of sight almost the last banner & guide's flag of a mighty epoch. For these men however in our last days they have declined into ritualists, solemnized the heyday of their strength by the planting & the liberating of America.

Great, grim, earnest men I belong by natural affinity to other thoughts & schools than yours but my affection hovers respectfully about your retiring footprints, your unpainted churches, street platforms & sad offices, the iron-gray deacon & the wearisome prayer rich with the diction of ages. Well the new is only the seed of the old. What is this abolition & non-resistance & temperance but the continuation of Puritanism tho' it operate inevitably the destruction of the church in which it grew, as the new is always making the old superfluous.

Dr R. was a gentleman, no dandy: courtly, hospitable, manly, public spirited: his nature social, his house open to all men. Mr R. H., I remember, said "No horse from the eastern country would go by his gate." His brow serene & open for he had no studies, no occupations which company could interrupt. To see his friends unloosed his tongue & talents: they were his study. His talk was chiefly narrative: a man of anecdote he told his stories admirably well. Indeed all his speech was form & pertinence itself. There was no architect of sentences who built them so well. In private discourse or in debate of a more public kind the structure of his speech was perfect, so neat, so natural, so terse, no superfluous clause, his words fell like stones & commonly tho' quite unconscious of it his speech was a satire on the loose, voluminous, draggletail periods of other speakers. He sat down when he had done. A foresight he had when he opened his mouth of all that he would say & he marched straight to the conclusion. E.B.E. used to say that "a man who could tell a story so well was company for kings & John Quincy Adams." His knowledge was an external experience, an Indian wisdom, the observation of such facts as country life for nearly a hundred years could supply. He sympathized with the cow, the horse, the sheep, & the dog whose habits he had watched so long & so friendly. For those who do not separate poetry blend it with things. His eye was always on the horizon & he knew the weather like a sea captain. All the plain facts of humanity,—birth, marriage, sickness, death, the common temptations, the common ambitions, —he knew them all & sympathized so well that as long as the fact was quite low & external he was very good company & counsel, but he never divined, never speculated, & you might as well ask his hill to understand or sympathize with an extraordinary state of mind, an enthusiasm or an Idea as ask him. What he did not, he affected not to do. There was no nonsense about him. He was always sincere, & true to his mark & his mark was never remote. But his conversation was always strictly personal & apt to the party & the occasion. An eminent skill he had in saying difficult & unspeakable things, saying to a man or woman that which all his other friends abstained from saying, uncovering the bandages from the sore place & applying the surgeon's knife with a truly surgical skill. Was a man a sot or too long a bachelor, or suspected of some secret crime or had he quarreled with his wife or collared his father or was there any cloud or suspicious circumstance in his behavior the doctor leaped on the quarry like hunter on his game. He thought himself entitled to an explanation & whatever relief to one or both parties plain speech could effect that was procured. Right manly he was & the manly thing he could always say. When Put. Meriam that graduate of the State Prison had the effrontery to call within the last year on the Doctor as an old acquaintance, in the midst of general conversation Mr Frost came in & the Doctor presently said, "Mr Meriam, here is my brother & colleague Mr Frost, has come to take tea with me. I regret very much the causes which you know very well, that make it impossible for me to ask you to stay & take bread with us." For the man had for years been setting at defiance every thing which the Doctor esteemed social & sacred. Another man might easily have taken another view of his duty but with the doctor's views it was a matter of religion to say thus much. I liked very well his speech to Charles M. at the funeral of his father. Mr M. was supposed to be in bad habits when his father died. "Sir, I condole with you; Madam I condole with you; Sir, I knew your great grandfather. When I came to this town, your great grandfather was a substantial farmer in this very place & an excellent citizen. Your grandfather followed him & was a virtuous man. Now your father has gone to his grave full of labors & virtues. There is none of that large family left, but you, and it rests with you to bear up the good name & usefulness of your ancestors. If you fail—Ichabod—the glory is departed.—&c. &c."

He was the more competent to these searching discourses from his long family knowledge. He knew everybody's grandfather. This day has perished more history, more local & personal anecdote for this village & vicinity than in any ten men who have died in it before. He was the patriarch of all the tribe and his manners had a natural dignity that comported with his office. The same skill of speech made him incomparable in his parochial visits and in his exhortations & prayers with the sick & mourners. He gave himself up to his feeling & said the best things in the world much like Protogenes throwing the brush at the dog's mouth he had been painting. Many & many a felicity he had in his prayer now forever lost which eclipsed all the rules of all the rhetoricians. He did not know when he was good in prayer or sermon, for he had no literature & no art. But he believed & therefore spoke. He was sincere in his attachment to forms & he was the genuine fruit of a ritual church. The incarnation of the platform of the Puritan Church. A modern Israelite, a believer in the Genius or Jehovah of the Jews to the very letter. His prayers for rain & against the lightning, "that it may not lick up our spirits," and for good weather & against "these violent sudden changes" and against sickness & insanity & the like, all will remember. I remember his pleading almost reproachful looks at the sky when the thundergust was coming up to spoil his hay—"We are in the Lord's hand," he said & seemed to say "You know me: this field is mine, Dr Ripley's thine own servant." He was a punctual fulfiller of all duties. What order! what prudence! no waste, & no stint. Always open handed; just & generous. My little boy a week ago carried him a peach in a calabash but the calabash brought home two pears. I carried him melons in a basket but the basket came home with apples. He subscribed to all charities; he was the most public spirited citizen in this town; he gave the land for the monument. He knew the value of a dollar as well as another man. Yet he always sold cheaper than any other man. If the fire bell rang he was on horseback in a minute & away with his buckets & bag.

> Wo that the linden & the vine should bloom
> And a just man be gathered to the tomb.

But out of his own ground he was not good for aught. To talk with the insane he was as mad as they; to speculate with the thoughtful & the haters of forms he was lost & foolish. He was credulous & the dupe of Colonizationist or Antipapist or any charlatan of iron combs or tractors or phrenology or magnetism who went by. Credulous & opinionative, a great brow beater of the poor old fathers who still survived from the Nineteenth of April in order to make them testify to his history as he had written it. A man of no enthusiasm, no sentiment. His horror at the doctrine of non-resistance was amusing, for he actually believed that once abrogate the laws, promiscuous union of the sexes would instantly take place!

He was a man very easy to read, for his whole life & conversation was consistent & transparent: all his opinions & actions might be certainly predicted by any one who had good opportunities of seeing him. In college, F King told me from Governor Gore who was the Doctor's classmate, he was called "Holy Ripley," perhaps in derision, perhaps in sadness. And now in his old age when all the antique Hebraism & customs are going to pieces it is fit he too should depart, most fit that in the fall of laws a loyal man should die.

Shall I not say in general, of him, that, given his constitution, his life was harmonious & perfect.

His body is a handsome & noble spectacle. My mother was moved just now to call it "the beauty of the dead." He looks like a sachem fallen in the forest, or rather like "a warrior taking his rest with his martial cloak around him". I carried Waldo to see him & he testified neither repulsion nor surprise, but only the quietest curiosity. He was ninety years old the last May, yet this face has the tension & resolution of vigorous manhood. He has been a very temperate man.

A man is but a little thing in the midst of these great objects of nature, the mountains, the clouds, and the cope of the horizon & the globes of heaven, yet a man by moral quality may abolish all thoughts of magnitude & in his manners equal the majesty of the world.

—

Oct. 30. On this wonderful day when Heaven & earth seem to glow with magnificence & all the wealth of all the elements is put under contribution to make the world fine as if Nature would indulge her offspring it seemed ungrateful to hide in the house. Are there not dull days enough in the year for you to write & read in that you should waste this glittering season when Florida & Cuba seem to have left their seats & come to visit us with all their shining Hours and almost we expect to see the jasmine & the cactus burst from the ground instead of these last gentians & asters which have loitered to attend this latter glory of the year. All insects are out, all birds come forth, the very cattle that lie on the ground seem to have great thoughts & Egypt & India look from their eyes.

Love is a word of many degrees. To behold the beauty of another character which inspires a new interest in our own; to behold the beauty lodged in a human being with such vivacity of apprehension that I am instantaneously forced home to inquire if I am not deformity itself; to behold the expression of a love which assures itself, which assures itself to me against every possible casualty except my own unworthiness.

When I passed a plate of sponge-cake to Dr Ripley, & asked him to take a piece, he said "No, unless you will give me a ram-rod to get it down."

> "Though by constitution so sensitive to cold that no enthusiasm for nature will enable me to support the slightest chill" *George Sand.*

Plato condemned the temperance whose root is intemperance, & the valor which grew from cowardice. "The true coin for which all else ought to be changeable, is, a right understanding of what is good" Ritter Vol.2, p 412

"How dare I go to a person who will look at me only as a psychological fact?" said the threadwoman of G. R. and said well. But alas that this awe which the writers inspire, should prove at last to be so ill founded! they ought to inspire most reverence when seen and when they can thunder so loud at a distance not cheep so small in the chamber. "Ah! if they knew John as well as I!" said Mrs Maffit. Good Paul whose letter was so mighty & whose bodily presence mean & contemptible, has too many imitators.

So little action amidst such audacious & sincere profession that we begin to doubt if this great Reform be not a war of posts, a paper blockade in which each party is to manifest the utmost resources of his spirit & belief and no crisis occur; but the world take that course which the demonstration of the truth shall indicate.

The Age
Shelley is wholly unaffecting to me. I was born a little too

soon: but his power is so manifest over a large class of the best persons, that he is not to be overlooked.

There are tests enough of character if we really dare to apply them. Are you setting your expectation of happiness on any circumstance or event not within your control?

—

The new vegetable is always made out of the materials of the decomposed vegetable and the triumph of thought today is over the ruin of some old triumph of thought. I saw a man who religiously burned his Bible & other books: and yet the publication of the Bible & Milton & the rest was the same act, namely the burning of the then books of the world, which had also once been a cremation of more.

—

10 November. Genius is very well but it is enveloped & undermined by Wonder. The last fact is still Astonishment, mute, bottomless, boundless, endless Wonder. When we meet an intelligent soul all that we wish to ask him,—phrase it how we will,—is, 'Brother have you wondered? Have you seen the Fact?' To come out from a forest in which we have always lived, unexpectedly on the Ocean, startles us, for it is a symbol of this. To learn as the boy does, that this earth with its wide & mottled map, its towered cities, & what it calls its antiquities & history, is a bit of bullet now glimmering & now darkling through a small cubic space on the edge of the Immeasurable unimaginable pit of Emptiness, is a symbol of this.

November 11. "I can, like the unhappy Charles I, not see an action until it is done."

—

M.M.E. has the misfortune of spinning with a greater velocity than any of the other tops. She tears into the chaise, or out of it; she tears into the house, or out of it; she tears into the conversation, into the thought, into the character of the person,—disdaining all the graduation by which her fellows time their steps; and though she could do very well in a planet where others moved with the like velocity, she is offended here by the irritating phlegm of all others & disgusts all others by her impatience. She can keep step with no human being.

—

As to the *Miracle* too of Poetry. There is truly but one miracle, the perpetual fact of Being & Becoming, the ceaseless Saliency, the transit from the Vast to the particular, which miracle, one & the same, has for its most universal name, the word *God*. Take one or two or three steps where you will, from any fact in nature or art, & you come out full on this fact; as you may penetrate the forest in any direction & go straight on, you will come to the SEA. But all the particulars of the poet's merit, his sweetest rhythms, the subtlest thoughts, the richest images, if you could pass into his consciousness, or rather, if you could exalt his consciousness would class themselves in the common chemistry of thought & obey the laws of the cheapest mental combinations.

Not to be appreciated by one we dearly love,—Yes that would be inconvenient & must at last reduce the flame.

In every moment and action & passion, you must be a man, must be a whole Olympus of gods. I surprised you, o Waldo E! yesterday eve hurrying up one page & down another of a little book of some Menzel, panting & straining after the sense of some mob better or worse of German authors. I thought you had known better. Adhere here, sit fast, lie low,

—

Anti-Transcendentalists.

Yet we must not blame those who make the outcry against these refiners. It comes from one of two causes; either an instinctive fear that this philosophy threatens property & sensual comfort; or, a distrust of the sincerity & virtue of persons who preach an impracticable elevation of life.

If from the first, it is a good sign, an eulogy of the innovators which should encourage them. And let them not be too anxious to show how their new world is to realize itself to men but know that as the Lord liveth, it shall be well with them who obey a spiritual law.

If from the second,—why perhaps the world is in the right, and the reformer is not sound. There is an instinct about this too. It is in vain that you gild gold & whiten snow in your preaching if when I see you, I do not look through your pure eye into a society of angels & angelic thoughts within. If you make on me the impression of a turbid dreamer withdrawing your thoughts from my gaze, I shall not trust you. It is worth remarking that it is a touch of eloquence which refreshes us all when amid an overrefined society the savage speaks out: We feel it as an evidence of truth & innocence; for example when the Amistad captive says, "I am cold the weather in this country is become too cold for me I wish to go to my land:" or when the child says "I am hungry; or I am sleepy." We are more touched than by all the arts of rhetoric.

A mere fiction this of no property to the youth. Every man has access to all he can use. Better as now than if it lay before him unfenced, untilled.

No man can write anything who does not think that what he writes is for the time the history of the world, or do anything well who does not suppose his work to be of greatest importance. My work may be of none but I must not think it of none or I shall not do it with impunity. Whoso does what he thinks mean, is mean.

How finely we are told in the Hebrew story that the anger of the Lord was kindled against David because he had made a census of the people. Philosophy also takes an inventory of her possessions; and an inventory is of pride; it is the negative state. But Poetry is always affirmative, & Prayer is affirmative.

How much of life is affirmative? How many dare show their whole hand? For the most part we hide, & parry as we can the inquisition of each other.

I am for preserving all those religious writings which were in their origin poetic, ecstatic expressions which the first user of did not know what he said but they were spoken through him & from above, not from his level, things which seemed a happy casualty but which were no more random than the human race are a random formation. "It is necessary," says Iamblichus, "that ancient prayers like sacred asyla should be preserved invariably the same neither taking anything from them nor adding anything to them which is elsewhere derived."

This is the reason doubtless why Homer declares that Jove loved the Ethiopians. And Iamblichus in answer to the query "Why of significant names we prefer such as are Barbaric to our own?" says, among other reasons; "Barbarous names have much emphasis, great conciseness, & less ambiguity, variety, & multitude"; and then afterwards; "But the Barbarians are stable in their manners & firmly continue to employ the same words. Hence they are dear to the gods, & proffer words which are grateful to them." And the ancients spoke of the Egyptians & Chaldaeans as "sacred nations".

Now the words "God," "Grace," "Prayer," "Heaven", "Hell", are these Barbarous & Sacred words, to which we must still return, whenever we would speak an ecstatic & universal sense. There are objections to them, no doubt, for academical use, but when the professor's gown is taken off, Man will come back to them.

The granite comes to the surface & towers into the highest mountains & if we could dig down we should find it below all the superficial strata. And so in all the details of our domestic or civil life there is hid an elemental Reality which ever & anon comes to the surface & forms the grand men who are the leaders & examples rather than the companions of the race. It is curiously concealed all the time under a thousand formations & surfaces, under fertile soils & grasses & flowers, under large towns & cities & well manured arable fields but it makes the foundation of these, & is always indicating its presence by slight & sure signs. So is it, so is it with the Law. I read it in glad & in weeping eyes; I read it in the pride & in the humility of people; it is recognized in every bargain & in every complaisance, in every criticism, & in all praise: it is voted for at elections, it wins the cause with juries: it rides the stormy eloquence of the senate sole victor. Histories are written of it, Holidays decreed to it, Statues, tombs, Churches, built in its honor, yet it is always rejected when it comes barely to view in our immediate neighborhood. It seems as if it was not permitted in good society to see it near or name it but by indirection.

The question of Property wants seers. All the persons are on one side, the staunchest Whig & the poorest philosopher are all on the Property side, all abettors of the present abuse, all either owners or enviers: no man is on the other side, no man can give us any insight into the remedy, no man deserves to be heard against Property; only Love, only an Idea is on the right side against Property as we hold it.

Good scholar, what are you for but for hospitality to every new thought of your time? Have you property, have you leisure, have you accomplishments & the eye of command, you shall be the Maecenas of every new thought, every untried project that proceeds from good will & honest seeking. The newspapers of course will defame what is noble and what are you for but to withstand the newspapers & all the other tongues of today; you do not hold of today but of an age, as the rapt & truly great man holds of all ages or of Eternity. If you defer to the newspaper, where is the scholar?

Hints, fragments, scintillations of men enough & more than enough but men valiant & who can execute the project they learned of no man but which was born with them there are none. Perfect & execute yourself an Orson if Orson; a Valentine if Valentine. Let us see at least a good Orson, & know the best & worst of that.

Edith

22 November 1841. There came into the house a young maiden, but she seemed to be more than a thousand years old. She came into the house naked & helpless but she had for her defence more than the strength of millions. She brought into the day the manners of the Night.

from
Journal H
1841

Acquiescence, patience have a large part to play. The plenty of the poorest place is too great,—the harvest cannot be gathered. The thought that I think excludes me from all other thoughts. Culture is to cherish a great susceptibility, to turn the man into eyes, but as the eye can see only that which is eye-form or of its own state, we tumble on our walls in every part of the universe, & must take such luck as we find, & be thankful. Let us deserve to see. Too feeble & faint fall the impressions of nature on the sense. Let us not dull them by intemperance & sleep. Too partially we utter them again: the symbols in which I had hoped to convey a universal sense are rejected as partial. What remains but to acquiesce in the faith that by not lying, nor being angry, we shall at last acquire the voice & language of a man?

Sun & moon are the tablets on which the name & fame of the good are inscribed.

Nature is a silent man.

It would be well if at our schools some course of lessons in Idealism were given by way of showing each good Whig the gunpowder train which lies under the ground on which he stands so firmly. Let him know that he speaks to ghosts & phantasms, let him distinguish between a true man & a ghost.

"We do not wake up every morning at four to write what all the world thinks," said the good German.

—

The whole game at which the philosopher busies himself every day, year in, year out, is to find the upper & the under side of every block in his way. Nothing so large & nothing so thin but it has two sides, and when he has seen the outside he turns it over to see the other face. We never tire of this game, because ever a slight shudder of astonishment pervades us at the exhibition of the other side of the button,—at the contrast of the two sides. The head & the tail are called in the language of philosophy *Finite & Infinite*, Visible & Spiritual, Relative & Absolute, Apparent & Eternal, & many more fine names.

The virtue of books is to be readable.

—

I was astonished one morning by tidings that genius had appeared in a youth who sat near me at table. He had left his work, he had gone rambling none knew whither, he had written hundreds of lines, but could not tell whether that which was in him was therein told, he could tell nothing but that all was changed, man, beast, heaven, earth, & sea. How gladly we listened! how credulous! Society seemed to be compromised. We sit in the aurora of a sunrise which is to put out all the stars. Boston already goes for nothing. Rome—what's Rome? Plutarch & Shakspeare are in the yellow leaf, & Homer no more shall be heard of. It is strange how fast *Experience & Idea*, the wonderful twins, the Castor & Pollux of our firmament change places. One rises & the other instantaneously sets. Today & for a hundred days experience has been in the ascendant, and Idea has lurked about the life merely to enhance sensation, the firework-maker, master of the revels & hired poet of the powers that be: but in a moment a revolution! the dream displaces the working day & working world, and they are now the dream & this the reality. All the old landmarks are swept away in a flood, and geography & history, the laws & manners, aim & method of society are as fugitive as the colors which chase each other when we close our eyes. All Experience has become mere language now. Idea drags it now a chained poet to adorn & sing his triumph.

—

It is an inestimable advantage to slip up into life in the shade with no thousand-eyed Athens to watch & blazon every new thought, every blushing emotion of young Genius. Yet some natures are too good to be spoiled by praise. And to such it is very irritating, when annoyed by one of these trumpets, to receive the warnings of solemn but inferior friends on the danger of the head's being turned by this flourish. I remember Edward Taylor's indignation at the kind admonitions of Dr P. The right answer is, 'My friend, a man can neither be praised nor insulted.'

On rolls the old world and these fugitive colors of political opinion like dove's neck lustres chase each other over the wide encampments of mankind, whig, tory; pro- & anti-slavery; Catholic, Protestant; the clamor lasts for some time, but the persons who make it, change; the mob remains, the persons who compose it change every moment. The world hears what both parties say & swear, accepts both statements, & takes the line of conduct recommended by neither, but a diagonal line of advance which partakes of both courses.

—

The Poet. The Idealist at least should be free of envy; for every poet is only a ray of his wit, & every beauty is his own beauty reflected. He is ever a guest in his own house & his house is the biggest possible.

Exaggeration is a law of nature. As we have not given a peck of apples or potatoes, until we have heaped the measure, so nature sends no creature, no man into the world without adding a small excess of his proper quality. She gives a bias to every bowl. They say we must assume on any theory of cosmogony a projection given to the globes of the system. So always a slight generosity in nature, a drop too much. The air would rot without lightning. And without this violence of direction which men & women have, without bigots, no excitement, no efficiency. Aim above the mark to hit the mark. Every act hath some falsehood of exaggeration in it, every sentence. For the infinite diffuseness refuses to be epigrammatized, the world to be shut in a word. The thought being spoken in a sentence becomes by mere detachment falsely emphatic.

G. W. Tyler patronizes Providence.

The Whig party in the Universe concedes that the radical enunciates the primal law but makes no allowance for friction and this omission makes their whole doctrine impertinent. The Whig assumes sickness, and his social frame is a hospital. His total legislation is for the present distress,—a universe in slippers & flannels, with bib & pap-spoon, swallowing pills &

herb-tea, whig preaching, whig poetry, whig philosophy, whig marriages. No rough truth telling Miltons, Rousseaus.

Exaggeration in nature, said I? And must we suppose some where in the Universe a slight treachery, a slight derision at us 'light troops,'—we tickled trout, we nose-led bullocks? Only so long as we put God outside of nature but when we have transferred our sympathy from the effect to the cause, then we escape the satire & over see our own absurdity.

Art. I think that Milton wrote his verse to his own ear, well knowing that England did not hold & might not for a century another ear that could hear their rhythm. That is the magnanimity of a poet—that he writes for the gods,—as those Egyptian obelisks which Goethe saw raised from the ground at Rome, were carved with the utmost finish on the upper surface which faced the heaven & which man was never to see. Blue Heron, loon, & sheldrake come to Fairhaven Pond, raccoon & otter to Walden.

Napoleon hated Lafayette & the ideologists; the merchant will not allow a book in the countinghouse, suspects every taste & tendency but that for goods, has no conversation, no thought but cotton, qualities of cotton, and its advance or fall a penny or a farthing. What a cramping of the form in wooden cap, wooden belt, & wooden shoes, is this, and how should not the negro be more a man than one of these victims? the negro, who, if low & imperfect in organization, is yet no wooden sink, but a wild cedar swamp rich with all vegetation of grass & moss & confervae & ferns & flags, with rains & sunshine, mists & moonlight, birds & insects filling its wilderness with life & promise. Queenie (who has a gift to curse & swear,) will every now & then in spite of all manners & christianity rip out on Saints, reformers, & Divine Providence with the most edifying zeal. In answer to the good Burrill Curtis who asks whether trade will not check the free course of love she insists "it shall be said that there is no love to restrain the course of, & never was, that poor God did all he could, but selfishness fairly carried the day."

It is plain that none should be rich but those who understand it. Cushings & Perkinses ought to be rich who incline to subscribe to college & railroad, to endow Atheneums, & open public gardens, & buy & exhibit pictures, liberalities which very good & industrious men who have earned their Money a penny or a shilling at a time would never think of. Yet what are rich men for? It is a most unnecessarily large & cumbrous apparatus for any body who has not a genius for it & to produce no other result than the most simple contrivance of an acre & a cabin. That also will give shelter & sustenance, and the capitalist has no more morning, night, thought, love, character, than the Spartan with his broth & bare feet; and if he sell cotton too much, he has less. Young Fuller thought his masters spent five months of every year in reading newspapers.

—

S.A.R. is a bright foreigner: she signalizes herself among the figures of this masquerade. I do not hope when I see her to gain any thing, any thought; she is choked, too, by the multitude of all her riches, Greek & German, Biot & Bichat, chemistry & philosophy. All this is bright obstruction. But capable she is of high & calm intelligence & of putting all the facts, all life aloof; as we sometimes have done. But when she does not, & only has a tumultuous time, it is time well wasted. I think her worth throwing time away upon.

I talked with C. A. Greene. He said he had wished to write me, *but had not done it, & supposed he need not because I must have known at that time that he wished me to come to him.* Then of divining & of the Swedenborgians who divine. I slighted his parish geography which would find that souls meet in particular confines of time & space, and begged him to cease thinking of that skin & flesh, (bright & pure though they be,) of the soul. Was it not enough that souls should meet in a law, in a thought,—obey the same love, demonstrate the same idea? These alone are the true nuptials of minds. Eupatorium white & red. I see only two or three persons & allow them all their room; they spread themselves at large to the horizon. If I looked at many as you do, or compared these habitually with others, these would look less. Yet are they not entitled to this magnificence? Is it not their own? And is not munificence the only insight?

We cannot rectify marriage because it would introduce such carnage into our social relations, and it seems, the most rabid radical is a good Whig in relation to the theory of Marriage. Yet perhaps we can see how the facts stand in heaven. Woman hides her form from the eyes of men in our world: they cannot, she rightly thinks, be trusted. In a right state the love of one, which each man carried in his heart, should protect all women from his eyes as by an impenetrable veil of indifferency. The love of one should make him indifferent to all others, or rather their protector & saintly friend, as if for her sake. But now there is in the eyes of all men a certain evil light, a vague desire which attaches them to the forms of many women, whilst their affections fasten on some one. Their natural eye is not fixed into coincidence with their spiritual eye. Therefore it will not do to abrogate the laws which make Marriage a relation for life, fit or unfit. Plainly marriage should be a temporary relation, it should have its natural birth, climax, & decay, without violence of any kind,—violence to bind, or violence to rend. When each of two souls had exhausted the other of that good which each held for the other, they should part in the same peace in which they met, not parting from each other, but drawn to new society. The new love is the balm to prevent a wound from forming where the old love was detached. But now we could not trust even saints & sages with a boundless liberty. For the romance of new love is so delicious, that their unfixed fancies would betray them, and they would allow themselves to confound a whim with an instinct, the pleasure of the fancy with the dictates of the character. *Spiraea tomentosa.*

CRITICISM

Into one of the chambers of hell came a man with his head under his arm, then several men carrying their heads under their arms. Well I suppose a man will come to that in his time also to put up his brain & his heart neatly in a box to carry, and put his irritabilities aloof from him as a fact, out of which the interpretation of the dream was also to be extorted. But why do I write another line, since my best friends assure me that in every line I repeat myself? Yet the God must be obeyed even to ridicule. The criticism of the public is, as I have often noted, much in advance of its invention. The ear is not to be cheated. A continuous effect cannot be produced by discontinuous thought and when the eye cannot detect the juncture of the skilful mosaic, the Spirit is apprised of disunion simply by the failure to affect the Spirit. This other thing I will also concede, —that the man Fingal is rather too swiftly plastic, or, shall I say, works more in the spirit of a cabinet maker, than of an architect. The thought which strikes him as great & Dantesque, & opens an abyss, he instantly presents to another transformed into a chamber or a neat parlor, and degrades ideas.

1841.

I have seen scores of people who can silence me, but I seek one who shall take me off my feet, and make me forget or overcome those sudden frigidities & imbecilities to which I am prone to fall. I told H.T. that his freedom is in the form, but he does not disclose new matter. I am very familiar with all his thoughts,—they are my own quite originally drest. But if the question be, what new ideas has he thrown into circulation, he has not yet told what that is which he was created to say. I said to him what I often feel, I only know three persons who seem to me fully to see this law of reciprocity or compensation,—himself, Alcott, & myself: and 'tis odd that we should all be neighbors, for in the wide land or the wide earth I do not know another who seems to have it as deeply & originally as these three Gothamites.

But now of poetry I would say, that when I go out into the fields in a still sultry day, in a still sultry humor, I do perceive that the finest rhythms & cadences of poetry are yet unfound, and that in that purer state which glimmers before us, rhythms of a faery & dreamlike music shall enchant us, compared with which the finest measures of English poetry are psalm-tunes. I think now that the very finest & sweetest closes & falls are not in our metres, but in the measures of eloquence, which have greater variety & richness than verse. And further, that the difference between poetry & stock-poetry is this,—that in poetry the sense dictates the rhythm, & in stock poetry, the rhythm is given, & the sense is adapted to it. Now, alas, we know something too much about our poetry,—we are not part & parcel of it: it does not descend like a foreign conqueror from an unexpected quarter of the horizon upon us, carry us away with our flocks & herds into a strange & appalling captivity, to make us, at a later period, adopted children of the Great King, &, in the end, to disclose to us that he was our real parent, & this realm & palace is really our native country.

Yet I please myself with thinking that there may yet be somewhere such elation of heart, such continuity of thought, that a man shall see the little sun & moon whisk about, making day & night, making month & month, without heed, in the grandeur of his absorption. Now we know not only when it is day, & when night,—but we hear the dinner-bell ring with the most laudable punctuality. I am not such a fool but that I taste the joy which comes from a new & prodigious person, from Dante, from Rabelais, from Piranesi, flinging wide to me the doors of new modes of existence, and even if I should intimate by a premature nod my too economical perception of the old thrum that the basis of this joy is at last the instinct that I am only let into my own estate, that the poet & his book & his story are only fictions & semblances in which my thought is pleased to dress itself, I do not the less yield myself to the keen delight of difference & newness. I think that the importance of fine scenery is usually greatly exaggerated, for the astonishing part of every landscape is the meeting of the sky & the earth, and that is seen from a hen coop as well as from the top of Mount Jura. The stars at night stoop down over the brownest homeliest wold with all that spiritual magnificence which they have in Italy or in the marble desart of Egypt. The rolled up clouds & the colors of morn & even transfigure an alder bush. The difference between landscape & landscape is small: the difference between beholder & beholder is vast.

O the maple, mountain maple, O the Norway pine
The walnut grove, the cedar swamp with ladders of the vine.

The cool disengaged air of these objects makes them enviable to us chafed & irritable creatures with red faces, and we think we shall be as grand as they if we camp out & eat roots. But let us aspire to be man instead of stooping to be musquash, and the oak & elm shall from their hills draw near to our dwelling to serve & shade us, though we sit in chairs of ebony & ivory, on carpets of silk. A man in black came in while I spoke & my countenance fell. Then I said, surely I see that the Swedenborgian finds a sweetness in his church and is enveloped by it in a love & society that haunts him by night & by day but if the

Unitarian is invited to go out & preach to Unitarians at Peoria Illinois I see no question so fit or inevitable as that he should ask whether they will pay the expense of his journey and maintain him well. It is not to be denied that there is this wide difference between my faith & other faith, that mine is some brief affecting experience which surprised me on the highway or in the market place—in some place at some time whether in the body or out of the body, I cannot tell, God knoweth,—& made me aware that I had played the fool with fools all this time, but that there was for me & for all,—law, and ineffable sweetness of childlike carriage—and I should never be fool more; well, in the space of an hour probably I was let down from this height, I was at my old tricks, the selfish member of a selfish society. My life is superficial, takes no root in the world, I ask when shall I die & be relieved of the responsibility of having an universe which I do not use? We wish to exchange this flash-of-lightning faith for continuous day-light, this fever glow for a benign climate.

Well, all that is clearly due today is not to lie. When we pass, as we presently shall pass, into some new infinitude out of this Siberia of negations, it will please us to reflect that though we had few virtues or consolations we bore with our indigence, nor once strove to repair it with a hypocrisy or false heat of any kind. Then it may be that our truth shall be rewarded with a tropic summer of faith.

—

I value Shakspeare, yes, as a Metaphysician, and admire the unspoken logic which upholds the structure of Iago, Macbeth, Antony, & the rest. Is it the real poverty at the bottom of all this seeming affluence, the headlong speed with which in London, Paris, & Cochin China, each seeing soul comes straight through all the thin masquerade on the old fact, is it the disgust at this indigence of nature which makes these raging livers like Napoleon, Timour, Byron, Trelawney, & J Q Adams drive their steed so hard, in the fury of living to forget the *soupe maigre* of life? They would know the worst & tread the floors of hell. Is it true that every now & then comes along some sad sharpeyed man who sees how paltry a game is played & refuses to play, but blabs the Maelzel secret? How then? Is the murder out? O no the wary Nature sends a new troop of fairer forms, of lordlier youths, with a little more excess of direction to hold them fast to their several aim, makes them (that is) a little wrong-headed in that direction in which they are rightest,—and on goes the game again with new whirl for a generation or two more.

It is a bad fact that our editors fancy they have a right to call on Daniel Webster to resign his office, or, much more, resign his opinion & accept theirs. That is the madness of party. I account it a good sign indicative of public virtue in the Whigs that there are so many opinions among them, & that they are not organized & drilled.

—

If life is sad, & do not content us, if the heavens are brass, & rain no sweet thoughts on us, & especially we have nothing to say to shipwrecked & self-tormenting & young-old-people, let us hold our tongues. The martyrs were sawn asunder or hung alive on meat hooks. Cannot we screw our courage to patience & truth; and if to my soul the day does not seem dark, nor the cause lost, why should I use such ruinous courtesy as to concede that God has failed, because the plain colors or the storm-suit of grey clouds in which the day is drest, do not please the rash fancy of my companions? Patience and truth, patience with our own frosts & negations, and few words must serve.

Let us not use convulsion and a fantastic theism & philosophy in default of the saliency of health. Let us not be frisky. If our sleeps are long, if our flights are short, if we are not plumed & painted like orioles & birds of paradise, but like sparrows & plebeian birds, if our taste & training are earthen, let that fact be humbly & happily borne with. The wise God beholds that also with complacency. Wine & honey are good, but so are rice & meal.

Perhaps all that is not performance is preparation, or performance that shall be. I hope the words Humility, gratitude, patience, & hope, have not lost their meaning. Must Life necessarily be an explosion of fire-works? is every Action or book or lecture a clap-trap?

—

Elizabeth H. consecrates. I have no friend whom I more wish to be immortal than she, an influence I cannot spare, but must always have at hand for recourse. When Margaret mentioned "an expression of unbroken purity," I said, "That is hers." M. replied "Yes, but she knows." I answer,—Know or know not, the impression she makes is that her part is taken, she has joined herself irrevocably to the sanctities,—to the Muses, & the Gods. Others suggest often that they still balance, their genius draws them to happiness: they contemplate experiment: they have not abdicated the power of election. Opium & honey, the dagger & madness, they like should still lie there in the background, as shadows & possibilities. But E.'s mind is made up, & she has soared into another firmament, & these exist not for her. Bonaparte did not like ideologists: Elizabeth is no poet, but her holiness is substantive & must be felt, like the heat of a stove, or gravity of a stone: and Bonaparte would respect her.

—

I would have my book read as I have read my favorite books not with explosion & astonishment, a marvel and a rocket, but a friendly & agreeable influence stealing like the scent of a flower or the sight of a new landscape on a traveller. I neither wish to be hated & defied by such as I startle, nor to be kissed and hugged by the young whose thoughts I stimulate.

Partridgeberry, white Alder or Prinos.

The sum of life ought to be valuable when the fractions & particles are so sweet. A man cannot resist the sweet excitements of opium or brandy. Well then, the universe must be worth somewhat.

The *Daguerrotype* is good for its authenticity. No man quarrels with his shadow, nor will he with his miniature when the sun was the painter. Here is no interference and the distortions are not the blunders of an artist, but only those of motion, imperfect light, & the like.

—

The view taken of Transcendentalism in State Street is that it threatens to invalidate contracts.

Men shall not, like poultry, eat all day.

*

Plutarch's heroes are my friends & relatives.

A difference between you & me is that I like to hear of my faults and you do not like to hear of yours.

Character is sacrificed to talent.

Ah if there were not always a new fact! if I could put any dependence in your word of love! but now whilst it still rings in my ear & sweetens the springs of life we are both changed, wiser, sadder, I dare not ask you if you love me still.

As we drive it, the artist is in some degree sacrificed. Michel Angelo to paint Sistine frescoes must lose for a time the power to read without holding the book over his head, and Dr Herschel to keep his eyes for nocturnal observation must shield them from daylight.

The gallipots of Socrates,—what means that stiff adherence to mean objects & such as were offensive to his exquisite companions but the conviction of this great Identity which makes all objects indifferent? Thomas H. Benton's speeches and the Protocols of Vienna & St Petersburg are as much in the circuit of today's Universe, have got to be accounted for, as are the most vital & beautiful appearance;—and the theory of Heaven & earth can be equally established on the lowest & the highest fact. The permissive as much characterizes God as the beloved.

As I looked at the Madonnas & Magdalens in the Atheneum I saw that for the most part the painter seemed to draw from *models*, & from such beauties therefore as models are likely to be, flesh & color & emotion, but from lordly intellectual spiritual beauties, "the great seraphic lords & cherubim" of the sex, no sign but in Raphael's. Yet two or three Greek women clear, serene, & organically noble as any forms which remain to us on vase or temple adorn my group & picture of life. And we demand that character shall have nothing muddy or turbid, but shall be transparent,—sublime as God pleases, but not eccentric. 12 October. I would that I could, I know afar off that I cannot give the lights & shades, the hopes & outlooks that come to me in these strange, cold-warm, attractive-repelling conversations with Margaret, whom I always admire, most revere when I nearest see, and sometimes love, yet whom I freeze, & who freezes me to silence, when we seem to promise to come nearest. Yet perhaps my old motto holds true here also

"And the more falls I get, move faster on."

Oct. 16. I saw in Boston Fanny Elsller in the ballet of Nathalie. She must show, I suppose, the whole compass of her instrument and add to her softest graces of motion or "the wisdom of her feet,"—the feats of the rope dancer & tumbler: and perhaps on the whole the beauty of the exhibition is enhanced by this that is strong & strange, as when she stands erect on the extremities of her toes, or on one toe, or "performs the impossible" in attitude, but the chief beauty is in the extreme grace of her movement, the variety & nature of her attitude, the winning fun & spirit of all her little coquetries, the beautiful erectness of her body & the freedom & determination which she can so easily assume, and what struck me much the air of perfect sympathy with the house and that mixture of deference and conscious superiority which puts her in perfect spirits & equality to her part. When she courtesies, her sweet & slow & prolonged Salam which descends & still descends whilst the curtain falls, until she seems to have invented new depths of grace & condescension, she earns well the profusion of bouquets of flowers which are hurled on to the stage.

As to the morals, as it is called, of this exhibition, that lies wholly with the spectator. The basis of this exhibition like that of every human talent is moral, is the sport & triumph of health or the virtue of organization. Her charm for the house is that she dances for them or they dance in her not being (fault of some defect in their forms & educations) able to dance themselves. We must be expressed. Hence all the cheer & exhilaration which the spectacle imparts and the intimate property which each beholder feels in the dancer, & the joy with which he hears good anecdotes of her spirit & her benevolence. They know that such surpassing grace must rest on some occult foundations of inward harmony.

But over & above her genius for dancing are the incidental vices of this individual, her own false taste or her meretricious arts to please the groundlings & which must displease the judicious. The immorality the immoral will see, the very immoral will see that only, the pure will not heed it, for it is not obtrusive, perhaps will not see it at all. I should not think of danger to young women stepping with their father or brother out of happy & guarded parlors into this theatre to return in a few hours to the same; but I can easily suppose that it is not the safest resort for college boys who have left Metaphysics, Conic Sections, or Tacitus to see these tripping satin slippers and they may not forget this graceful silvery swimmer when they have retreated again to their baccalaureate cells.

It is a great satisfaction to see the best in each kind, and as a good student of the world, I desire to let pass nothing that is excellent in its own kind unseen, unheard.

In town I also heard some admirable music. It seemed, as I groped for the meaning, as if I were hearing a history of the adventures of fairy knights,—some Wace, or Monstrelet, or Froissart, was telling, in a language which I very imperfectly understood, the most minute & laughable particulars of the tournaments & loves & quarrels & religion & tears & fate of airy adventurers, small as moths, fine as light, swifter than shadows,—and these anecdotes were illustrated with all sorts of mimicry & scene painting, all fun & humor & grief, and, now & then, the very persons described broke in & answered, & danced, & fought, & sung for themselves.

I saw Webster in the street,—but he was changed since I saw him last,—black as a thunder cloud, & care worn: the anxiety that withers this generation among the young & thinking class had crept up also into the great lawyer's chair, & too plainly, too plainly he was one of us. I did not wonder that he depressed his eyes when he saw me, and would not meet my face. The canker worms have crawled to the topmost bough of the wild elm & swing down from that. No wonder the elm is a little uneasy.

—

I rode to town with some insane people: the worst of such company is that they always bite you, and then you run mad also.

The aim of aristocracy is to secure the ends of good sense & beauty without vulgarity or deformity of any kind, but they use a very operose method.

What an apparatus of means to secure a little conversation.

This great palace of brick, these servants, this kitchen, these stables, horses, & equipage; this bankstock & mortgages, trade to all the world, country-house, & cottage by the water side—all for a little conversation, high, clear & spiritual! Could it not be had as well by beggars on the highway? No; all these things came from successive efforts of these beggars to remove one & another interference or friction of the wheels. But unhappily in addressing themselves to this task of obviating obstructions, they have lost their way, they have overdone it, they have become servants of these fine clothes, fine dinners, & fine houses.

It would give me no pleasure to sit in your house, it would give me none to be caressed by you so long as this infernal infantry hinder me from that dear & spiritual conversation that I desire. There will come a time when these obstructions, arising from I know not what cause, will pass away; if it is a poorness of spirit in me, I shall be warmed with the wine of God, & shall walk with a firmer step; if it is some unreasonable demand in you, experience will have reduced your terms to the level of practicability. The tone, the tone is all. Let our eyes not look away, but meet: let our thoughts not look east & west for subjects, but for a moment let us dwell in one home, & all topics are indifferent, & speech, & silence.

I see that the lights of the common day as they fall on every face & figure of animal or plant are more excellent & speaking than any of those lights which painters like better, twilight, deep shade, moonlight or torchlight; yet what avails my cold knowledge that they are better if I find them unaffecting.

Ann Priest attends the children to school rather as childherd than as guide as the farmers send a cowherd with the cattle not to drive them but to keep them in certain bounds.

In writing, the casting moment is of greatest importance, just as it avails not in Daguerre portraits that you have the very man before you, if his expression has escaped.

Every body, old men, young women, boys, play the doctor with me & prescribe for me. They always did so.

*

Expressions. The Retreat of the Ten Thousand was not suspected in its time to be inimitable. Yet there stands that fact a high water mark in military history.

Oct. 24. Life in Boston: A play in two acts, Youth & Age. Toys, dancing school, *Sets*, parties, picture galleries, sleighrides, Nahant, Saratoga Springs, lectures, concerts, *sets* through them all, solitude & poetry, friendship, ennui, desolation, decline, meanness, plausibility, old age, death.

Those persons who constitute the natural aristocracy i.e. sacred persons are not found in the actual aristocracy or only on its edge as the chemical energy of the spectrum is found to be greatest just outside of the spectrum. S A R

Society is fussy & frisky. Garrison is fussy & Greene & Chase are frisky.

In the republic must always happen what happened here that the steamboats & stages & hotels vote one way & the nation votes the other; and it seems to every meeting of readers & writers as if it were intolerable that Broad Street paddies & barroom politicians, the sots & loafers & all manner of ragged & unclean & foul mouthed persons without a dollar in their pocket should control the property of the country & make the lawgiver & the law. But is that anymore than their share whilst you hold property selfishly? They are opposed to you: yes, but first you are opposed to them: they to be sure malevolently, menacingly, with songs & rowdies & mobs: you cunningly, plausibly, & well bred; you cheat & they strike: you sleep & eat at their expense, they vote & threaten & sometimes throw stones, at yours.

Goethe said that when you had found one bone in one skeleton of an animal take the skeleton of any other animal & you should be sure to find that bone in the same place or near it. I suppose that expresses a universal truth & that whatever human trait has been shown in any times is shown in our times. If you know anything that was in Ctesiphon or Rome, I can find its counterpart in Boston. Was there religion in Jerusalem there is at least criticism in Massachusetts—criticism which appeals to a high, the highest standard.

Always will you give me results? Will you never, my friend, invite me to be present with you at your invocation of truth & to enjoy with you its proceeding into your mind? Then, one question more:

Were you ever Daguerrotyped, O immortal man? And did you look with all vigor at the lens of the camera or rather by the direction of the operator at the brass peg a little below it to give the picture the full benefit of your expanded & flashing eye? and in your zeal not to blur the image, did you keep every finger in its place with such energy that your hands became clenched as for fight or despair, & in your resolution to keep your face still, did you feel every muscle becoming every moment more rigid: the brows contracted into a Tartarean frown, and the eyes fixed as they are fixed in a fit, in madness, or in death; and when at last you are relieved of your dismal duties, did you find the curtain drawn perfectly, and the coat perfectly, & the hands true, clenched for combat, and the shape of the face & head? but unhappily the total expression escaped from the face and you held the portrait of a mask instead of a man. Could you not by grasping it very tight hold the stream of a river or of a small brook & prevent it from flowing?

The young people are very ungrateful, they will not thank a man for his second Discourse or book for they charge him with want of variety if he says so much as 'God' or 'Truth' twice. But the Garrisons & fanatics,—forgive me, if when I come near to them & sit in the same stage coach, I seem to see nothing but management, tactics, boys' play & *philisterei*. Unreal, spectral, masks.

I told Garrison that I thought he must be a very young man or his time hang very heavy on his hands who can afford to think much & talk much about the foibles of his neighbors, or '*denounce*' and play 'the son of thunder' as he called it. I am one who believe all times to be pretty much alike and yet I sympathize so keenly with this. We want to be expressed, yet you take from us War, that great opportunity which allowed the accumulations of electricity to stream off from both poles, the positive & the negative.—Well, now you take from us our cup of alcohol as before you took our cup of wrath. We had become canting moths of peace, our helm was a skillet, & now we must become temperance watersops. You take away, but what do you give me? Mr Jefts has been preached into tipping up his barrel of rum into the brook, but day after tomorrow when he wakes up cold & poor, will he feel that he has somewhat for somewhat? No, this is mere thieving hypocrisy & poaching. If I could lift him by happy violence into a religious beatitude, or into a Socratic trance & imparadise him in ideas, or into the pursuit of human beauty a divine lover, then should I have greatly more than indemnified him for what I have taken. I should not take, he would put away, or rather ascend out of this litter & sty, in which he had rolled, to go up clothed & in his right mind into the assembly & conversation of men. I fight in my fashion but you, o paddies & roarers, must not fight in yours. I drink my tea & coffee, but as for you & your cups, here is the pledge & the Temperance Society. I walk on Sundays & read Aristophanes & Rabelais in church hours; but for you, go to Church. Good vent or bad we must have for our nature, somewhere we must let out all the length of all the reins. Make love a crime & we shall have lust. If you cannot contrive to raise us up to the love of science & make brute matter our antagonist which we shall have joy in handling, mastering, penetrating, condensing to adamant, dissolving to light, then we must brawl, carouse, gamble, or go to bull-fights. If we can get no full demonstration of our heart & mind we feel wronged & incarcerated: the philosophers & divines we shall hate most, as the upper turnkeys. We wish to take the gas which allows us to break through your wearisome proprieties, to plant the foot, to set the teeth, to fling abroad the arms, & dance & sing. The great Condé withdrew in the fury of the battle from the line, rolled himself on the grass to cool & refresh himself, then flew again to his post in the action.

I like these exacting children—they are now a class of some extent—who prolong their privilege of childhood in this wise—of doing nothing but making immense demands on all the gladiators. There is no compliment, no smooth speech with them, they pay you only this one compliment of insatiable expectation; they aspire, they severely exact, and if they only hold fast to this watch tower, & persist in demanding unto the end, & without end, then are they terrible friends whereof poet & priest cannot choose but stand in awe, and what if these eat clouds & drink wind.

There is no school so poor or meagre, no withered & starveling Unitarian Divinity School, or Diffusion Society, but if a new strong man could be born into it, would immediately redeem & replace it. Good & true was Mr Austin's saying that an eloquent man could be settled in Brattle St. of what sect soever. And yet though we pine for great men, we do not use them when they come. Here is a Damascus blade of a man such as you may search through nature in vain to parallel, laid up on the shelf in our village to rust & ruin. It seems as if they were never quite available for that very idea which they represent. H. is a person of extraordinary health & vigor, of unerring perception, & equal expression; and yet he is impracticable, and does not flow through his pen or (in any of our legitimate aqueducts) through his tongue. A stands for Spirit itself & yet when he writes, he babbles. When he acts, the ladies find something very unsightly which he can very well explain to himself and which I like well enough but they set their faces like a flint against him, and that makes him feel uncomfortable, then is he less himself, is belligerent, unhappy, & thoughtless.

—

Very trivial seem the contests of the abolitionist, his objects trifling whilst he aims merely at the circumstance of the slave. Give the slave the least elevation of religious sentiment, & he is no slave, you are the slave; he not only in his humility feels his superiority, feels all that deplored condition of his to be a fading trifle, but he makes you instantly feel it too. He is the master. The exaggeration our young people here make of his wrongs, characterises themselves. What are no trifles to them, they naturally think are no trifles to Pompey. But there is no saint yet engaged in that cause.

Nobody can oppress me but myself. Once more, the degradation of that black race, though now lost in the starless spaces of the past, did not come without sin. The condition is inevitable to the men they are, & nobody can redeem them but themselves. An infusion from God of new thought & grace can retrieve their loss, but nothing less. The exertions of the abolitionist are nugatory except for themselves. As far as they can emancipate the North from Slavery, well.

Mrs B. inquires whether Transcendentalism does not mean Sloth, for the moment people are classed under that name they sit down & do nothing. I think that the virtue of some persons is now to sit & wait,—though all the saints should wonder. "She had as lief hear that they were dead as that they were Transcendentalists they are paralysed & never do anything for humanity" said Mrs B.

Each of our *causes*, as we call them, Orthodoxy, Unitarianism, Education, Abolition, is rapidly converted into a little shop where the article is made up in portable & convenient forms & retailed in small quantities to suit purchasers.

The best persons hold themselves aloof, they feel the disproportion between their faculties & the work offered them, & they prefer to go into the country & gaze at the skies & the waters & perish of ennui, to the degradation of such charities or such ambitions as Boston can propose to them.

You wish railroads through my house & garden. I do not like to have the mountains skip like rams & the little hills like lambs.

—

"What are you doing Zek?" said Judge Webster to his eldest boy.

"Nothing"

"What are you doing, Daniel?"

"Helping Zek."

A tolerably correct account of most of our activity today.

It seems to me sometimes that we get our education ended a little too quick in this country. As soon as we have learned to read & write & cipher, we are dismissed from school & we set up for ourselves. We are writers & leaders of opinion & we write away without check of any kind, play whatsoever mad prank, indulge whatever spleen or oddity or obstinacy comes into our dear head and even feed our complacency thereon and thus fine wits come to nothing as good horses spoil themselves by running away & straining themselves. I cannot help seeing that Dr Channing would have been a much greater writer had he found a strict tribunal of writers, a graduated intellectual empire established in the land & knew that bad logic would not pass & that the most severe exaction was to be made on all who enter these lists. Now if a man can write a paragraph for a newspaper, next year he writes what he calls a history and reckons himself a classic incontinently. Nor will his contemporaries in Critical Journal or Review question his claims. It is very easy to reach the degree of culture that prevails around us, very hard to pass it and Dr C. had he found Wordsworth, Southey, Coleridge, & Lamb, around him would as easily have been severe with himself & risen a degree higher as he has stood where he is. I mean of course a genuine intellectual tribunal not a literary junto of Edinburg Wits or dull conventions of Quarterly or Gentleman's Reviews. Somebody offers to teach me mathematics. I would fain learn. The man is right. I wish that the writers of this country would begin where they now end their culture.

It is easy to see in the youth who was here the other day the shortcoming which results from his position. In a small town he easily fills all measures & so lies on his oars with the fame of the villages. He does not see any body who calls him to account or who in all respects overtops him & so he has contented himself with easy exertions. No Douglas cast of the bar, no pale Cassius reminds him of inferiority. The Americans are too easily pleased.

—

Every young person writes a journal into which when the hours of prayer & penitence arrive he puts his soul. The pages which he has written in the rapt moods are to him burning & fragrant. He reads them on his knees by midnight & by the morning star he wets them

—

October 21. And why not draw for these times a portrait gallery? The genius of this day does not seem to incline to a deed but rather to a beholding. The hot agitators have a certain cheap & ridiculous air; they even look smaller than the others, these idle gazers. Well if we cannot stoop to action let us then make the greatest approximation to an act the spirit of the hour permits & paint the painters. A camera! A camera! cries the century, that is the only toy. Come let us paint the agitator and the dilettante and the member of Congress and the college professor, the Unitarian minister, the editor of the newspaper, the fair contemplative girl, the aspirant for fashion & opportunities, the woman of the world who has tried & knows better,—let us examine how well she knows. Good fun it would be for a master who with delicate finger in the most decisive yet in the most parliamentary & unquestionable manner should indicate all the lions by traits not to be mistaken yet so that none should dare wag his finger whilst the shadow of each well known form flitted for a moment across the wall. So should we have at last if it were done well a series of sketches which would report to the next ages the color & quality of ours.

Yet is it not ridiculous this that we do in this languid idle trick that we have gradually fallen into of writing & writing without end. After a day of humiliation & stripes if I can write it down I am straightway relieved & can sleep well. After a day of joy the beating heart is calmed again by the diary. If grace is given me by all angels & I pray, if then I can catch one ejaculation of humility or hope & set it down in syllables, devotion is at an end.

—

When the Erl King was sung, my gentle neighbor, Mrs —— said, "I suppose every one thinks of their own totties." We are impatient of our Eves & Maries at home, if they will never be pleased with fit expression, but think only of the subject or story, and yet if it were not so, if some day they should wake up artists, if teat & navel should turn connoisseurs, we should be in worse plight, cursed by the granting of our prayer.

Immanuel Kant said Detestable is the company of literary men.

INHUMANITY

You come into this company meanly. How so?
We have come for the love of seeing each other & of conversing together. You have come to give us things which are written already in your note-books, and when you have told them, you are spent. The best of our talk is invented here, and we go hence greater than we came by so much life as we have

awakened in each other; but you, when your quiver is emptied, must sit dumb & careful the rest of the evening. Every thing you say makes you poorer, and every thing we say makes us richer: you go home when the company breaks up forlorn: we go home (without a thought on ourselves,) full of happiness to pleasant dreams.

To be sure there is a class of discreet citizenlike secret-keeping men, good providers for their households whom you know where to find; but do not measure by their law this wild influence which I found, to be sure, in space & time, but knew at once it could not be there imprisoned; a nature that lay enormous, indefinite, hastening every moment out of all limitation and to be treated like oxygen & hydrogen, of a diffusive, universal, irrevocable elasticity. He could keep no secret, he could keep no property, he could keep no law but his own.

Margaret is "a being of unsettled rank in the Universe". So proud & presumptuous yet so meek; so worldly and artificial & with keenest sense & taste for all pleasures of luxurious society, yet living more than any other for long periods in a trance of religious sentiment; a person who according to her own account of herself, expects everything for herself from the Universe.

Oct. 23. Milton describes religion in his time as leaving the tradesman when he goes into his shop to meet him again when he comes out. Well, it is true until now. Religion was not invited to eat or drink or to go to bed with us or to make or to divide an estate, but was a holiday friend called in on state occasions. In so pure a church as the Swedenborgian I cannot help feeling the neglect which leaves holiness out of trade. These omissions damn the church as the corrupt compromise made with the slaveholder, not much noticed at first, every day appears a more flagrant mischief to the American Constitution. But the purists now look into all these matters. The more intelligent are growing uneasy on the subject of marriage. They wish to see the character represented also in that covenant; there shall be nothing brutal in it, but it shall honor the man & the woman as much as his most diffusive & universal action. So it casts its eye on trade & day labor. And so it goes up & down paving the earth with eyes & destroying privacy, & making thorough lights. Is all this for nothing? Do you suppose that the reforms which are now preparing will be as superficial as those we know?

—

We forget in taking up a cotemporary book that we see the house that is building & not the house that is built. A glance at my own MSS. might teach me that all my poems are unfinished, heaps of sketches but no masterpiece, yet when I open a printed volume of poems, I look imperatively for art.

—

There is a perfect chain—see it or see it not—of reforms emerging from the surrounding darkness, a complete choir of reformers each cherishing some part of the general idea, each suggesting some other, and all must be seen in order to do justice to any one. Meantime there comes now & then a bolder spirit, I should rather say, a more surrendered soul, more informed & led by God which is much in advance of the rest, quite beyond their sympathy, mayhap passes for mad, but this predicts what shall soon be the general fulness, as when we stand by the sea-shore whilst the tide is coming in a wave comes up the beach far higher than any foregoing one, and recedes, & for a long time none comes up to that mark,—but after some time, the whole sea is there & beyond it.

I think Society has the highest interest in seeing that this movement called the Transcendental is no boys' play or girls' play but has an interest very near & dear to them. That it has a necessary place in history is a Fact not to be overlooked, not possibly to be prevented, and however discredited to the heedless & to the moderate & conservative persons by the foibles or inadequacy of those who partake the movement yet is it the pledge & the herald of all that is dear to the human heart, grand & inspiring to human faith.

I think the genius of this age more philosophical than any other has been, righter in its aims, truer, with less fear, less fable, less mixture of any sort.

—

We read either for antagonism or for confirmation. It matters not which way the book works on us, whether to contradict & enrage, or to edify & inspire. "Bubb Dodington" is of the first class, which I read today. A good indignation brings out all one's powers.

28 October. Good not to let the conscience sleep, but to keep it irritated by the presence & reiterated action of reforms & ideas.

Ellen. H. asks "whether Reform is not always in bad taste?" Oh no, the poet, the saint are not only elegant but elegance. It is only the half poet, the half saint, who disgust. Thus now the saint in us proposes, but the sinner in us executes so lamely. But who can be misled who trusts to a thought? That profound deep whereunto it leads is the Heaven of Heavens. On that pillow softer than darkness he that falls can never be bruised.

I told C. & M. that Aunt M. was no easy flute but a quite national & clanlike instrument, a bagpipe, for instance, from which none but a native Highlandman could draw music.

I sometimes fancy that the bitterness & prosaic side of our condition only obtrude in our conversation or attempts to paint our portrait to another.

Silent & alone I have no such sad unredeemed side.

—

Treacherous, short memoried, suicidally selfish, all illogical world! It subsists by reinforcement from the country: that which it vaunts against the country is what the country gave it but yesterday: the city died long ago, rotted, vanished; could it have staid in mass it would have exploded—such hot putrefaction. It is only country which came to town day before yesterday that is city & court today, the plague being as yet internal and it lifts its head against villages!

Calculation if that would only go far enough would go for enthusiasm too. We only ask arithmetic to go on not to stop & bolt, and the conclusions of the broker & of the poet shall be one. We are not Manichaeans, not believers in two hostile principles but we think evil arises from disproportion, interruption, mistake of means for end. Is Transcendentalism so bad? And is there a Christian, or a civilian, a lawyer, a naturalist or physician so bold as not to rely at last on Transcendental truths? He dares not say it—the blind man.

We can well enough discuss this topic with any one because we believe we are all too deeply implicated for any man to give himself airs & talk down to the rest. That virtue, that heaven which we see is of that grandeur as quite to abolish the little differences of human virtue & puts them all easily to the account of condition. We are purists & prudes. My dear little abolitionist, do not puff & swell so; I am afraid our virtue is a little geographical and that there are sins nearer home that will one day be found of the self-same dye as this scarlet crime of the Virginians. I am not mortified by our vice: that is obduracy, it colors & palters, it curses & swears, and I can see to the end of it; but I own our virtue makes me ashamed, so sour & narrow, so thin & blind, virtue so vice-like. I hoped it had been better. The world leaves no track in Space and the greatest action of man no mark in the vast Idea.

Whoever can speak can sing, is the modern doctrine of music masters.

"Donde hai tu pigliato tante coglionerie?"

And where did you pick up all this heap of fripperies, Messer Lodovico Ariosto? said the duke to the poet. "Here in your court, your Highness" he replied. I own that all my universal pictures are nothing but very private sketches; that I live in a small village, and am obliged to guess at the composition of society from very few & very obscure specimens, and to tell Revolutions of France by anecdotes, &c. &c. yet I supposed myself borne out in my confidence that each individual stands for a class by my own experience. Few as I have seen I could do with fewer and I shrink from seeing thousands when in fifteen or twenty I have already many duplicates. The small red lion

I have sympathy with war & sin, with pleasure & insanity, with sleep & death.

—

There is this advantage also about the new pictures that whereas in painted miniatures it will not do to hold them near the eye, for then I see the paint & the illusion is at an end, these are like all nature's works, incapable of being seen too near.

The strangeness of the discovery is that Daguerre should have known that a picture was there when he could not see any. When the plate is taken from the camera it appears just as when it was put there—spotless silver; it is then laid over steaming mercury & the picture comes out.

—

False valuations are not in nature. A pound of water in the ocean tempest or in the land flood has no more momentum than in a midsummer pond. All things do exactly according to their property, attempt nothing they cannot do, except man only. He has pretension. He wishes to do & essays to do things beyond his force. "Mr Fox said he must have the Treasury: he had served up to it, & would have it." Xenophon & his Ten Thousand were quite equal to what they attempted & did it. Many have attempted it since, & not been equal to it. We are equal to something if it is only silence, waiting, & dying. Let us do that. The piece must have shades too. When the musicians are learning their first scores every one wishes to scream & country orchestras usually have a reasonable volume of voice. Afterwards they learn to be still & to sing underparts. Perhaps we may trust the Composer of our great Music to give us voice when our aid is needed, and to apply the bellows to other stops when we should mar the harmony. Character will one day suffice for the government of the world, when each aims at no connexions or conversation or offices which he has not served up to; offers at nothing in which his faculties will not play him true; attempts nothing he cannot as easily do as forbear. It is fit to break when the bond is unfit, & say, 'I do not maintain myself in your presence, you do not maintain yourself in mine.' We are both able for our own ends undoubtedly, but do not fit.

Do what you can & the world will feel you: speak what you must, & only that, and the echoes will ring with music.

Daguerre

'Tis certain that the Daguerrotype is the true Republican style of painting. The Artist stands aside & lets you paint yourself. If you make an ill head, not he but yourself are responsible and so people who go Daguerrotyping have a pretty solemn time. They come home confessing & lamenting their sins. A Daguerrotype Institute is as good as a national Fast.

—

Nov. 18. Queenie's dream of the statue so beautiful that the blooming child who was in the room looked pale & sallow beside it, and of the speech of the statue which was not quite speech either, but something better, which seemed at last identical with the thing itself spoken of. It described to the fair girl who sat by, & whose face became flushed with her earnest attention,—Life & being;—and then, by a few slight movements of the head & body, it gave the most forcible picture of decay & death & corruption, & then became all radiant again with the signs of resurrection.

I thought it a just description of that Eloquence to which we are all entitled—are we not? which shall be no idle tale, but the suffering of the Action, and the action it describes. That shall make intent & privileged hearers.

from

Journal J

1841–1842

When J. V. was in Concord, he said to me, "I always felt when I heard you speak or read your writings that you saw the truth better than others, yet I felt that your Spirit was not quite right. It was as if a vein of colder air blew across me." He seemed to expect from me a full acknowledgment of his mission and a participation of the same. Seeing this, I asked him if he did not see that my thoughts & my position were constitutional, that it would be false & impossible for me to say his things or try to occupy his ground as for him to usurp mine? After some frank & full explanation he conceded this. When I met him afterwards one evening at my Lecture in Boston, I invited him to go home to Mr Adams's with me & sleep which he did. He slept in the chamber adjoining mine. Early the next day in the grey dawn he came into my room and talked whilst I dressed. He said "When I was at Concord I tried to say you were also right; but the Spirit said, you were not right. It is just as if I should say It is not morning but the Morning says It is the Morning."

"Use what language you will," he said, "you can never say anything but what you are."

All writing is by the grace of God. People do not deserve to have good writing, they are so pleased with bad. In these sentences that you show me I can find no beauty, for I see death in every clause & every word. There is a fossil or a mummy character which pervades this book. The best sepulchres, the vastest catacombs, Thebes, & Cairo pyramids are sepulchres to me. I like gardens and nurseries. Give me initiative, spermatic, prophesying man-making words.

*

Education with the mothers is an affair of shoes & stockings, apron & bonnet.

I am probably all the better spectator that I am so indifferent an actor. Some who heard or read my reports misjudged me as being a good actor in the scene which I could so well describe. But when they came to talk with me, even those who fancied they strictly sympathized with me, found I was dumb for them as well as for others. In this, both I & they must be passive & acquiescent, and take our fortune. And now that I have said it I shall not suffer again from this misadventure.

Two persons lately, children of the most wise God, have admonished me by their silent being. It seemed as if each answered to my heart's inquiry, Whence is your power?

"From my nonconformity. I never listened to your people's law, or to what they call their gospel, & wasted my time. I was content with the simple rural poverty of my own. Hence this sweetness. My work never reminds you of that, is pure of that."

It is never worthwhile to worry people with your contritions. We shed our follies & absurdities as fast as the rosebugs drop off in July & leave the apple tree which they so threatened. Nothing dies so fast as a fault & the memory of a fault. I am awkward, sour, saturnine, lumpish, pedantic, & thoroughly disagreeable & oppressive to the people around me. Yet if I am born to write a few good sentences or verses, these shall endure & my disgraces utterly perish out of memory.

—

The rude reformer rose from his bed of moss & dry leaves, gnawed his roots & drank water, & went to Boston. There he met fair maidens who smiled kindly on him, then gentle mothers with their babes at their breasts who told them how much love they bore them & how they were perplexed in their daily walk. What! he said and this on rich embroidered carpets with fine marbles & costly woods & rare books & pictures all about you.

Look at our pictures & books they said & hear how we

spent last evening. They are stories of godly children & holy families & the hope of other worlds, and last eve our husband & brother were here & discoursed sadly on what we could save & give. Then came in the men & they said, What cheer brother! and gave him gifts. Then he went home. swiftly with other thoughts than he came saying This way of life is wrong yet these Assyrians whom I prayed God to destroy are Lovers, are Lovers; what can I do?

—

Those who defend the establishment are always less than it. Those who speak from a thought must always be greater than any actual fact. I see behind the Whig no mighty matter, nothing but a very trite fact of his land titles & certificates of stock. But through the eyes of the theorist stares at me a formidable gigantic Spirit who will not down if I bid him, who has much more to say & do than he has yet told, & who can do great things with the same facility as little.

We can seldom hear the acknowledgments of any person who would thank us for a benefit without some shame & humiliation for we feel that it was not direct but incidental. We can seldom strike a direct stroke but must be content with an oblique one. I mean we seldom have the satisfaction of giving a direct benefit which is directly received.

In the feudal table the humblest retainer sat in the company of his lord & so had some indemnity for his thraldom in the education he derived from the spectacle of the wit, the grace, & the valor of his superiors.

Mr Frost thought that there would not be many of these recusants who declared against the state &c. I told him he was like the good man of Noah's neighbors who said "Go to thunder with your old ark! I don't think there'll be much of a shower."

—

Dec. 18. The reason offered why the legislature should not give money to Harvard College to build their Library, was that Harvard had so much already. But that is the very reason why it should have more: that certainly is its strongest claim at this moment. If I have a valuable antique in my possession, I should not give it to a stage driver, but to some collector who had already a cabinet. Better yet, to a state- or national-cabinet, for then it would be sure to be seen by the greatest number of those whom it concerned.

We believe in the existence of matter not because we can touch it or conceive of it but because it agrees with ourselves & the Universe does not jest with us but is in earnest.

A man founding a reputation for benevolence on his expenditure! a great blunder.

I have no pleasure in thinking of a benevolence that is only measured by its works, for that which requires always a new volition and a new & conspicuous action, can only make so many actions in a year & soon exhausts itself. But that benevolence which radiates all the time like odor from an aromatic body, so that if its estate is exhausted, if its house is burned, if its granary is emptied, it is still the same magnificent influence still cheers, enriches, endows—poor or rich—so that the man though he sleep seems to sweeten the air, and his house, because it is his, to adorn the landscape & strengthen the laws, —that benevolence is the presence of the author of good. People always know who is benevolent by quite other means than the amount of our subscriptions to relief societies. They will say of that man though he gives nothing, 'he has a heart;' and of this other who gives much, 'he has none.'

All the value which attaches to Swedenborg, Paracelsus, Cardan, Schelling, Oken, Kepler or any other who introduces questionable facts into his cosmogony such as angels, devils, magic, & so on is only the certificate this gives us of departure from routine & that here we have a new Witness.

As the limestone in our quarries is found to consist of infinite masses of the remains of animalcules, so language is made up of images or poetic tropes which now in their familiar secondary use have quite ceased to remind us of their poetic origin, as *howl* from *owl*, *ravenous* from *raven*, *rotation* from *wheel*, and so on to infinity.

All that Fashion seems to demand in its circles is composure, self truth. A circle of men perfectly well-bred would be a company of sensible persons in which every man's native manners & character appeared.

How much one person sways us, we have so few. The presence or absence of Milton will very sensibly affect the result of human history: the presence or absence of Jesus, how greatly! Well, tomorrow a new man may be born, not indebted like Milton to the Old, & more entirely dedicated than he to the New, yet clothed like him with beauty.

As we take our stand on Necessity or on Ethics, shall we go for the Conservative or the Reformer? If we read the world historically, we shall then say,—of all the ages the present hour & circumstance is the cumulative result: this is the best throw of the dice of Nature that has yet been: this is the best that is yet possible. If we see it from the side of Will or the moral sentiment, we shall accuse the past & the present, and require the impossible perfect. The view of Necessity is always good tempered, permits wit & pleasantry. The view of Liberty is sour & dogmatical. Both may be equally free of personal consideration. Wo unto me if I preach not the gospel.

I like the spontaneous persons of both classes; and those in the Conservative side have as much truth & progressive force as those on the Liberal. For who has a right

What a plague is this perplexity. We are so sharpsighted—that we are miserable & E. H. says can neither read Homer nor not read him.

Do not be so grand with your one objection. Do you think there is only one? If I should go out of church whenever I hear a false sentiment, I could never stay there five minutes. But why come out? the street is as false as the church, & when I get to my house or to my manners or my speech, I have not got away from the falsehood.

*

"According to Boehmen the world was nothing else than the relievo the print of a seal of an invisible world concealed in his own bosom." See Penhoen vol. 1 p 123

His world was a bible in relief and Swedenborg's "Relations" will hold because human mind cannot if it would write anything but human mind.

I add to what was said at bottom of last page, that when in our discontent with the pedantry of scholars, we prefer farmers, & when, suspecting their conservatism, we hearken after the hard words of drovers & Irishmen, this is only subjective or relative criticism, this is alkali to our acid, or shade to our too much sunshine; but abide with these and you will presently find they are the same men you left. A coat has cheated you.

When we see an Abolitionist or a special Reformer, we feel like asking him What right have you Sir to your one virtue? Is virtue piecemeal? This is like a costly scarf or a jewel on the rags of a beggar.

"Kepler's science was a strange alliance of that sublime science of antiquity which proceeded by inspiration with that modern science which measures compares analyses" *Penhoen.*

—

Reading Herrick I feel how rich is nature & his art of poetry. I see that here is work & beauty enough to justify a man for quitting all else & sitting down with the Muses. Did not Caesar say to the Egyptian priest Come I will quit army, Empire, & all if you will show me the fountains of the Nile. Well all topics are indifferent: you may reach the centre by boring a shaft from any point on the surface, with equal ease. And yet in this instance of poetry the provocation is not that the Law is there but the means are alluring.

—

28 January 1842
Yesterday night at 15 minutes after eight my little Waldo ended his life.

30 Jan What he looked upon is better, what he looked not upon is insignificant. The morning of Friday I woke at 3

oclock, & every cock in every barnyard was shrilling with the most unnecessary noise. The sun went up the morning sky with all his light, but the landscape was dishonored by this loss. For this boy in whose remembrance I have both slept & awaked so oft, decorated for me the morning star, & the evening cloud,   how much more all the particulars of daily economy; for he had touched with his lively curiosity every trivial fact & circumstance in the household the hard coal & the soft coal which I put into my stove; the wood of which he brought his little quota for grandmothers fire, the hammer, the pincers, & file, he was so eager to use; the microscope, the magnet, the little globe, & every trinket & instrument in the study; the loads of gravel on the meadow the nests in the hen-house and many & many a little visit to the doghouse and to the barn,—For every thing he had his own name & way of thinking   his own pronunciation & manner. And every word came mended from that tongue.   A boy of early wisdom, of a grave & even majestic deportment, of a perfect gentleness

Every tramper that ever tramped is abroad but the little feet are still
He gave up his little innocent breath like a bird

Dear Waldo

He dictated a letter to his cousin Willie on Monday night to thank him for the Magic Lantern which he had sent him, and said I wish you would tell Cousin Willie that I have so many presents that I do not need that he should send me any more unless he wishes to very much.

The boy had his full swing in this world Never I think did a child enjoy more   he had been thoroughly respected by his parents & those around him & not interfered with; and he had been the most fortunate in respect to the influences near him for his Aunt Elizabeth had adopted him from his infancy & treated him ever with that plain & wise love which belongs to her   and, as she boasted, had never given him sugar plums. So he was won to her & always signalized her arrival as a visit to him & left playmates playthings & all to go to her. Then Mary Russell had been his friend & teacher for two summers with true love & wisdom. Then Henry Thoreau had been one of the family for the last year, & charmed Waldo by the variety of toys whistles boats popguns & all kinds of instruments which he could make & mend; & possessed his love & respect by the gentle firmness with which he always treated him. Margaret Fuller & Caroline Sturgis had also marked the boy & caressed & conversed with him whenever they were here. Meantime every day his Grandmother gave him his reading lesson & had by patience taught him to read & spell; by patience & by love for she loved him dearly.

Sorrow makes us all children again destroys all differences of intellect The wisest knows nothing

It seems as if I ought to call upon the winds to describe my boy, my fast receding boy, a child of so large & generous a nature that I cannot paint him by specialties, as I might another.

"Are there any other countries?" Yes "I wish you to name the other countries" so I went on to name London, Paris, Amsterdam, Cairo, &c But HDT well said in allusion to his large way of speech that "his questions did not admit of an answer; they were the same which you would ask yourself"

He named the parts of the toy house he was always building by fancy names which had a good sound as "the Interspeglium" & "the Coridaga" which names he told Margaret "the children could not understand."

If I go down to the bottom of the garden it seems as if some one had fallen into the brook.

Every place is handsome or tolerable where he has been. Once he sat in the pew.

His house he proposed to build in summer of burs & in winter of snow

"My music," he said, "makes the thunder dance;" for it thundered when he was blowing his willow whistle.

Mamma, may I have this bell which I have been making, to stand by the side of my bed.

Yes it may stand there.

But Mamma I am afraid it will alarm you. It may sound in the middle of the night and it will be heard over the whole town, it will be louder than ten thousand hawks it will be heard across the water, and in all the countries. It will be heard all over the world.

It will sound like some great glass thing which falls down & breaks all to pieces.

Waldo asked If the strings of the harp open when he touches them?

—

I have seen the poor boy when he came to a tuft of violets in the wood, kneel down on the ground, smell of them, kiss them, & depart without plucking them.

For marriage find somebody that was born near the time when you were born.

Wisdom with his solar eye. His look was classification.

Is it not droll to see Plato visiting Hipparchus & he inquiring whether he had brought him some Bird? or Cineas the Entomologist & he inquiring if he had brought him a wasp or a spider?

As if one needed eyes in order to see. Look at yonder tree which the Sun has drawn out of the ground by its continual love & striving towards him and which now spreads a hundred arms, a thousand boughs in gratitude basking in his presence. Does that not see? It sees all over, with every leaf & every blossom.

I am not a man to read books, but one receiving that which books are written to report, said the Poet.

Sirocco of a stove. My thoughts run about vainly seeking to arrive at those distant persons. Then I see Facts or objects which serve me as horses. Each of my thoughts seizes one of these and being mounted rides directly to men.

—

Bores are good too. They may help you to a good indignation, if not to a sympathy; to a "mania better than temperance" as Proclus would say. Long Beard & Short Beard who came hither the other day with intent as it seemed to make Artesian Wells of us, taught me something.

Ben Jonson is rude & Tennyson is fine but Ben's beauty is worth more than Tennyson's. He has a right to it. It is a natural manly grace: a robust man behind it. Health on the cheek & not hectic & not rouge. Ben's flowers are no show flower-stand, but a cart, a tough ox-cart coming from the fields loaded with potatoes & apples, with grapes & plums, with nuts & berries, & the sweetbriars, fern, & pond lilies which the children have gathered scattered on the top.

My life is optical not practical. I go out to walk for exercise & not to answer a necessity. I speculate on virtue, not burn with love. Is not this as if one should quiz Michael & Gabriel through an opera glass? I would go because I am sent. If I am not at the Convention, my presence wherever I chance to be should be as efficient as would be my presence there. I am the same & I exert the same quality of power in all places. It would be easy, would it not, to give your own color & character to any meeting if your spirit & insight was better than that of the speakers. Wait till the noisy man has done & then speak & leave him out; he will feel that he is left out. What takes place in every parlor will surely take place there, that the less will yield to the greater & feel that his contribution is unnecessary.

—

6 May. There is something grand in the relation of two men between whom a perfect good understanding subsists.

Here is a proposition for the formation of a good neighborhood. Hedge shall live at Concord, & Mr Hawthorn: George Bradford shall come then; & Mrs Ripley afterward. Who knows but Margaret Fuller & Charles Newcomb would presently be added? These if added to our present kings & queens, would make a rare, an unrivalled company. If these all had their hearth & home here, we might have a solid social satisfaction, instead of the disgust & depression of visitation. We might find that each of us was more completely isolated & sacred than before. You may come—no matter how near in place, so that you have metes & bounds, instead of the confounding & chaos of visiting.

15 May. The instruction at Church seemed very infantile. Calvinism seems complexional merely: as Gam. Bradford said, "The Calvinists have the liver complaint: the Unitarians have not." In general, I recognize in stage coach & elsewhere the Constitutional Calvinist, the inconvertible. And in all companies we find those who are self accusing, who live in their memories & charge themselves with the seven deadly sins daily, like my queen without guile; and the other class, who cumber themselves never with contrition, but appeal from their experience always hopefully to their faith.

Our poetry reminds me of the catbird who sings so affectedly & vaingloriously to me near Walden. Very sweet & musical! very various! fine execution! but so conscious, & such a *performer! not a note is his own* except at last, *miow, miow.*

—

Talent makes comfort. I propose to set an Athenaeum on foot in the Village: but to what end? We know very well what is its utmost, to make namely such agreeable & adorned men as we ourselves, but not to open doors into heaven, as genius does in every deed of genius. This goes rather to fix & to content with fixedness; the comfort of talent. London is the kingdom of talent. Every paper & book & journal come from that tree. Civilization is Talent's version of human life.

A highly endowed man with good intellect & good conscience is a Man-woman & does not so much need the complement of Woman to his being, as another. Hence his relations to the sex are somewhat dislocated & unsatisfactory. He asks in Woman, sometimes the Woman, sometimes the Man.

As when I have walked long in one direction, & then, if I turn round, discover that a large fair star has long risen & shined on me, I feel a kind of wonder that I should be so long in such a presence without knowing it, so feel I when a fine genius which has been born & growing to full age in my neighborhood, now first turns its full deep light on my eyes.

Wilhelm Meister gave the hint of a cultivated society which I found nowhere else. It was founded on power to do what was necessary each person finding it an indispensable qualification of membership that he could do something useful, as in mechanics or agriculture or other indispensable art; then a probity, a justice was to be its element, symbolized by the insisting that each property should be cleared of privilege, & should pay its full tax to the state; then a perception of beauty was the equally indispensable element of the association, by which each was so dignified and all were so dignified; then each was to obey his genius to the length of abandonment. They watched each candidate vigilantly without his knowing that he was observed & when he had given proof that he was a faithful Man, then all doors, all houses, all relations were open to him; high behaviour fraternized with high behaviour without question of heraldry, and the only power recognized is the force of character.

—

Shut your eyes and hear a military band play on the field at night and you shall have Kings & queens & all regal behaviour & beautiful society, all chivalry walking visibly before you. Hear the echoes of a horn in the mountains & you shall have no mortal hunting but a hunting of Apollo, Diana, & all gods. When I was younger I believe my fancies of what was fine society outwent as far all reality. To the poor young poet thus fabulous is its beauty; he is loyal; he respects inequalities of condition; respects the rich; they are rich for the sake of his imagination; how poor his fancies would be, if they were not rich. That they have some high fenced grove, which they call a park; that they live in larger & better garnished saloons than he has yet frequented, & go in coaches, keeping only the society of the elegant, to watering places, to cities, & the springs, are facts which are groundwork to him of romances to which all their actual possessions & enjoyments are shanties & paddocks. There is something well known to me which without the Muse I cannot express, which enhances all the gifts of wealth & fine society & cultivated beauty and seems to be in fine autumn days a radiation out of the air & clouds, & forests that skirt the road, a certain haughty favor as if from patrician genii to patricians, a kind of aristocracy in Nature, "the prince of the power of the air."

Dr Bradford said it was a misfortune to be born when children were nothing & live until men were nothing.

A beauty of character which could make ugliness of no account.

Wisdom flies from us at an unintelligent question.

June 16. Literary criticism how beautiful to me: and I am shocked lately to detect such omnipresent egotism in my things. My prayer is that I may be never deprived of a fact but be always so rich in objects of study as never to feel this impoverishment of remembering myself.

That the Intellect grows by moral obedience, seems to me the Judgment Day. Let that fact once obtain credence, and all wrongs are righted; sorrow & pity are no more, nor fear nor hatred; but a justice as shining & palpable as the best we know of kings & caliphs & ordeals, & what we call "poetical justice", that is, thorough justice, justice to the eye and justice to the mind—takes place.

—

The same depth which dew gives to the morning meadow, the fireflies give to the evening meadow. Fire though a spark on the chimney back is always a deep.

"It is impossible not to believe in the children of the gods, though they should speak without probable & necessary arguments." Plato in Timaeus. p. 472 I read the Timaeus in these days but am never sufficiently in a sacred & holiday health for the task. The man must be equal to the book. A man does not know how fine a morning he wants until he goes to read Plato & Proclus.

E. H. says that Shelley is like shining sand, it always looks attractive & valuable but try never so many times you cannot get anything good. And yet the mica-glitter will still remain after all.

I admire the unerring instinct with which like an arrow to its mark the newborn fine genius always flies to the geniuses. Here is this young stripling darting upon Shakspeare, Dante, Spenser, Coleridge, & can see nothing intervening.

Charles King Newcomb took us all captive. He had grown so fast that I told him I should not show him the many things I had bribed him with. Why teaze him with multitude? Multitude is for children. I should let him alone. His criticism in his "Book-Journal" was captivating and in its devotion to the author, whether Æschylus, Dante, Shakspeare, Austin, or Scott as feeling that he had a stake in that book, 'who touches that, touches me'—; and in the total solitude of the critic, the Patmos of thought from which he writes in total unconsciousness of any eyes that shall ever read this writing, he reminds me of Aunt Mary. Charles is a Religious Intellect. Let it be his praise that when I carried his MS story to the woods, & read it in the armchair of the upturned root of a pinetree I felt for the first time since Waldo's death some efficient faith again in the repairs of the Universe, some independency of natural relations whilst spiritual affinities can be so perfect & compensating.

Robert Bartlett defined the Church as "the organic medium of life from the Lord to the Divine Humanity." He & Weiss gave an amusing account of the truckman who came with the square-cap-mob to the College Yard & bullied for an hour.—It was the richest swearing, the most aesthetic, fertilizing,—and they took notes.

June 26. Nelly waked & fretted at night & put all sleep of her seniors to rout. Seniors grew very cross, but Nell conquered soon by the pathos & eloquence of childhood & its words of fate. Thus after wishing it would be morning, she broke out into sublimity; "Mother, it must be morning." Presently, after, in her sleep, she rolled out of bed; I heard the little feet running round on the floor, and then, "O dear! where's my bed?" She slept again, and then woke; "Mother I am afraid; I wish I could sleep in the bed be side of you. I am afraid I shall tumble into the waters—It is all water." What else could papa do? He jumped out of bed & laid himself down by the little mischief, & soothed her the best he might.

I think that language should aim to describe the fact, & not merely suggest it. If you, with these sketchers & dilettanti, give me some luscious indeterminate compound word, it is like a daub of colour to hide the defects of your drawing. Sharper sight would see & indicate the true line. The poet both draws well & colors at the same time.

When C says, "If I were a Transcendentalist I should not seal my letters," what does he truly say but that he sees he ought not to seal his letters?

"When I shall be deserted," said the scholar. And he told his thoughts & read his favorite pieces to many visitors & when he saw the club moss or when he saw the night heaven and when he saw his dead mistress, he knew that this though fair & sorrowful was good for his song; and it seemed then as if what had been a sphere of polished steel became a surface, or a convex mirror. Then he defended copyright until the Muse left him & Apollo said he may die. Yet before this befel, he had been a lover of things which he did not know how to praise nor suspected they were loved by others. Again the scholar will come to scorn this putting his gods at vendue. The loosestrife waved over him its pagoda of yellow bells.

—

In June about the time when Alcott sailed for England, Manlius C Clarke a lawyer came to E. P Peabody & told her that he was going to sell 750 copies of Alcott's Conversations on the Gospels in sheets for the sum of 50.00 to trunkmakers for waste paper. There are 900 pounds and they are sold at 5 cents a pound.

I hear with pleasure that a young girl in the midst of rich decorous Unitarian friends in Boston is well nigh persuaded to join the Roman Catholic Church. Her friends who are also my friends, lamented to me the growth of this inclination. But I told them that I think she is to be greatly congratulated on the event.

She has lived in great poverty of events. In form & years a woman, she is still a child, having had no experiences, and although of a fine liberal susceptible expanding nature, has never yet found any worthy object of attention; has not been in love, nor been called out by any taste except lately by music, and sadly wants adequate objects. In this church perhaps she shall find what she needs, in a power to call out the slumbering religious sentiment. It is unfortunate that the guide who has led her into this path is a young girl of a lively forcible but quite external character who teaches her the historical argument for the Catholic faith. I told A. that I hoped she would not be misled by attaching any importance to that. If the offices of the Church attract her, if its beautiful forms & humane spirit draw her, if St Augustine & St Bernard, Jesu & Madonna, Cathedral, Music & Masses, then go, for thy dear heart's sake, but do not go out of this icehouse of Unitarianism all external, into an icehouse again of externals. At all events I charged her to pay no regard to dissenters but to suck that orange thoroughly.

In Boston I saw the new second volume of Tennyson's Poems. It had many merits but the question might remain whether it has *the* merit. One would say it was the poetry of an exquisite; that it was prettiness carried out to the infinite, but with no one great heroic stroke; a too rigorous exclusion of all mere natural influences.

In reading aloud, you soon become sensible of a monotony of elegance. It wants a little north west wind, or a northeast storm; it is a lady's bower-garden-spot; or a lord's conservatory, aviary, apiary, & musky green-house. And yet, tried by one of my tests, it was not found wholly wanting—I mean, that it was liberating; it slipped or caused to slide a little "this mortal coil." The poem of "Locksley", & "the talking oak", I bear cheerful witness both gave me to feel a momentary sense of freedom & power.

In town I also talked with Sampson Reed, of Swedenborg & the rest. "It is not so in your experience, but is so in the other world."—"Other world?" I reply, "there is no other world; here or nowhere is the whole fact; all the Universe over, there is but one thing,—this old double, Creator-creature, mind-matter, right-wrong." He would have devils, objective devils. I replied, That pure malignity exists, is an absurd proposition. Goodness & Being are one. Your proposition is not to be entertained by a rational agent: it is atheism; it is the last profanation. In regard to Swedenborg, I commended him as a grand poet: Reed wished that if I admired the poetry, I should feel it as a fact. I told him All my concern is with the subjective truth of Jesus's or Swedenborg's or Homer's remark, not at all with the object. To care too much for the object were low & gossipping. He may & must speak to his circumstance and the way of events & of belief around him; he may speak of angels or jews or gods or Lutherans or Gypsies, or whatsoever figures come next to his hand; I can readily enough translate his rhetoric into mine.

Plutarch quotes from Euripides the lines;

"Being & goodness in the Gods are one;
He who imputes ill to them makes them none."
Euripides apud Plutarch

Bartlett at Cambridge said "there seemed little use in trying to convince any body of the other persuasion, for these differences seem so organic."

Every consciousness repeats mine and is a sliding scale from Deity to Dust. Sometimes the man conspires with the Universe & sometimes he is at the other extreme & abides there a criminal confessing sin. The moment he begins to speak I apprehend his whole relations & fix him at his point in the scale.

—

Montaigne vol 3 p 12 "The wise Dandamy, hearing the lives of Socrates, Pythagoras, Dilogenes read, judged them to be great men every way, excepting that they were too much subjected to the reverence of the laws, which, to second & authorize, true virtue must abate very much of its original vigour; and many vicious actions are introduced not only by their permission but advice."

M. F. wrote to E. H. from New Bedford 19 June 1842 after the death of Maria Randall "You must have been happy too that you had lived long enough to do all you did for them. You filled just the place to which Goethe wished to train his Meister. What you knew & were, bore full upon the case, and there was no other person for whom your office of helping, raising, & interpreting seemed so much appointed. You helped to make bad not only better, but good. When we do this, we have not paid too dear for our schooling."

—

Three Classes.

I had occasion to say the other day to E. H. that I like best the strong & worthy persons like her father who support the social order without hesitation or misgiving. I like these: they never incommode us by exciting grief, pity, or perturbation of any sort.

But my conscience, my unhappy conscience respects that hapless class who see the faults & stains of our social order and who pray & strive incessantly to right the wrong, this annoying class of men & women commonly find the work altogether beyond their faculty & though their honesty is commendable, their results are for this present distressing. But there is a third class who are born into a new heaven & earth with organs for the new element and who from that Better behold this bad world in which the million gropes & suffers. By their life & happiness in the new, I am assured of the doom of the Old, & these therefore I love & worship.

—

Education

It should be remembered that Captain Chandler formerly of the Farm-School told me, "he did not wish any good boys. The worse boys were, the better scholars & men they would make."

It is sad to outgrow our preachers, our friends, & our books and find them no longer potent. Proclus & Plato last me still, yet I do not read them in a manner to honor the writer, but rather as I should read a dictionary for diversion & a mechanical help to the fancy & the Imagination. I read for the lustres as if one should use a fine picture in a chromatic experiment merely for its rich colours. It is not Proclus but a piece of Nature & Fate that I explore.

I read these English Tracts with interest. Goodwyn Barmby is another Ebenr Elliott but more practical. Revolution is no longer formidable when the Radicals are amiable. If Jack Cade loves poetry, & goes for "Love Marriage" with Milton & Shelley, for Community, Phalanxes, Dietetics, & so forth, I no longer smell fagots. Strange it is that Carlyle should skip this remarkable class of Dissenters & Radicals so near him, Lane, Owen, Wright, Fry, &c &c.

It probably arises from that necessity of isolation which genius so often feels. He must stand on his glass tripod if he would keep his electricity. Keep them off then, my brave Carlyle, thou worshipper of Beauty, & publisher of beauty to the world. Every sentence of thine is joyful proclamation that Beauty the Creator, Venus Creatrix, yet exists; the sentences are written for no utility, to no moral but for the joy of writing.

Yes Carlyle represents very well the literary man; makes good the place of & function of Erasmus & Johnson, of Dryden & Swift, to our generation. He is thoroughly a gentleman and deserves well of the whole fraternity of scholars, for sustaining the dignity of his profession of author in England. Yet I always feel his limitation, & praise him as one who plays his part well according to his light, as I praise the Clays & Websters. For Carlyle is worldly, and speaks not out of the celestial region of Milton & Angelo.

15 July. There are two in every man, a sane and an insane. The sane thinks; the insane speaks. Our thought is as great as the horizon & this whole cope overhead; our speech petty, sneaking; so that we seem mocked by our own organs. The day will come when speech shall be adequate, commensurate with thought. When I consider this antagonism, this god & this trifler, so strictly tied together, I understand what the the-

ologists whom Proclus quotes (In Tim. vol 1, p 469) mean by saying, "The God who is the Demiurgus of the corporeal nature, is lame in both feet, as constituting the Universe without legs or feet. They say too, that the Gods laugh at him with inextinguishable laughter, and [but this is more mystical] by their laughing incessantly attend with providential care to mundane natures."

It is not strange that my child springs away from me & I cannot command a little girl, when I also habitually spring away from myself and being wise in my brain have a foolish tongue & more foolish feet & hands.

Do not wonder at the fair landscape but at the necessity of Beauty under which the universe is. All is & must be pictorial. Eyes make eyemarks, and now & then somebody discovers & makes ado about some special picture.

16 July. Chaucer is such a poet as I have described Saadi, possessing that advantage of being the most cultivated man of the times. So he speaks always sovereignly & cheerfully. For the most part, the poet-nature, being very susceptible, is over-acted on by others. The most affecting experience, that of the religious sentiment, goes to teach the Immensity of every moment, the indifferency of magnitudes. The present moment is all; that the Soul is God;—a great ineffable lesson whose particulars are innumerable.

Yet experience shows that great as is this lesson, great & greatest, yet this discipline also has its limits. One must not seek to dwell always in contemplation of the Spirit. So should the man decline into an indolent & unskilful person & stop short of his possible enlargement, into a gloomy person; under churches are tombs, but Intellect is cheerful.

As bookbinders separate each sheet or each set of sheets in a large pile, by interposing a small block or pasteboard, so it seemed as if some Genius had laid a ray of light underneath every thought & fact in nature to this man's eye so that all things separated themselves according to their laws before him & he never confounded the similar with the same.

*

21 July. I looked into Pope's Odyssey yesterday. It is as correct & elegant after our canon of today, as if it were newly written. The modernness of all good books seems to give me an existence as wide as man. What is well done I feel as if I did. What is ill done I reck not of.
Profound meaning of "Goodwill makes insight." It is as when one finds his way to the sea by embarking on a river; or finds a passage for the mind through a lump of matter by following the path of electricity or magnetism or heat or light through it; Anyhow, knows the nature by sharing the nature; is at once victim & victor.

I would not have the babe shrink from me as the poor mesmeric from the sick man when she called "meat" but let the rivers of water, air, & light pour thro' me.

All our days are so unprofitable whilst they pass that 'tis wonderful where or when we ever got any thing of this which we call wisdom, poetry, or virtue. We never got it on any dated calendar day. There must have been some heavenly days intercalated somewhere like those which Hermes won with dice, of the Moon, that Osiris might be born.

Very often there seems so little affinity between the man & his works that it seems as if the wind wrote the book & not he.

Put Dittany in your greenhouse, asphodel, nepenthe, moly, poppy, rue, selfheal

—

2 August. Zanoni. We must not rail if we read the book. Of all the ministers to luxury these novelwrights are the best. It is a trick, a juggle. We are cheated into laughter or wonder by feats which only oddly combine acts that we do every day. There is no new element, no power, no furtherance. It is only confectionary, not the raising of new corn; and being such, there is no limit to its extension and multiplication. Mr Babbage will presently invent a Novel-Writing-Machine. The old machinery cannot be disguised however gaily vamped. Money & killing and the Wandering Jew, these are the mainsprings still; new names but no new qualities in the dramatis personae, Italics & Capitals are the stale substitutes for natural epigram & the revelations of loving speech. Therefore the vain endeavor to keep

any bit of this fairy gold which has rolled like a brook through our hands. A thousand thoughts awoke; great rainbows seemed to span the sky, & morning among the mountains; but as we close the book, we end the remembrance, nothing survives, not a ray,

The power to excite which the page for moments possessed it derived from you. You read it as you read words in a dictionary or hear a sonorous name of some foreigner and invest the stranger with some eminent gifts. But because there was not wisdom in the book nothing fixes itself, all floats, hovers, & is dissipated forever.

The young men are the readers & victims of Vivian Grey. Byron ruled for a time but Vivian rules longer. They would quiz their father & mother, lover & friend. They discuss sun & moon, liberty & fate, love & death, and ask you to eat baked fish. They never sleep, go nowhere, stay nowhere, eat nothing, & know nobody: but are up to anything, Festus-like, Faust-like, Jove-like, and could write an Iliad any rainy morning, if Fame were not such a bore. Men & women, the greatest or fairest, are stupid things, but a rifle and a mild pleasant gunpowder, a spaniel and a cigar are themes for kings. One would say of Vivian G. that it was written by a person of lively talent who had rare opportunities of society & access to the best anecdotes of Europe. Beckendorf is a sketch after nature & whoever was the model was a strong head, a strong humorist, who deserved his empire for a day over these college boys.

Bulwer evidently is the dissolute Alcibiades who has been the pupil once of Socrates and now & then recites a lesson which his master taught him. But the worst of Bulwer is that he has no style of his own; he is always a collector and neither contributes flash, nor low life, nor learning, nor poetry, nor religion, nor description from his own stores.

—

Life

A ship is a romantic object but as soon as one embarks, the romance instantly quits that vessel & hangs on all other ships, on every sail in the horizon; but the old curse makes your deck a few dull planks,—no more.

Some play at Chess, some at cards, some at the stock exchange. I prefer to play at Cause & Effect.

Bettine is more real, more witty than Geo Sand or Mme de Stael, as profound & greatly more readable.

Gold represents labor and rightly opens all doors, but labor is higher & opens secreter doors, opens man, & finds new place in the kingdom of intelligence.

We read Zanoni with pleasure because magic is natural; a man, a perfect man, would need no other instruments than his eyes & his hands; whoever looked at him would obey his will, being certified by the glance of his eye that his aims were universal, not selfish, and he would be obeyed as naturally as the rain & the sunshine are. For the same reason the child delights in the Arabian Nights. Nature is there described as the servant of man, which he feels to be true. But Zanoni pains us and the author gets no respect from us because he speedily shows us that his view is partial; that this power which he gives to his hero is a toy and not flowing from its legitimate fountains in the mind, is a power for London, a divine power converted into a highwayman's pistol to rob & kill with.

A mean obscure weed by the doorstep trodden by every foot that entered the house was the plantain, yet when the master's foot was wounded & lame they went out at night with a lamp to seek its leaves and it brought refreshment & healing. Temperance is the poor plantain, a mean virtue in its daily details but what an interest, compound on compound interest it yields at last.

But in Zanoni is at least the merit of not being dull: Bulwer's books are readable, although, I own, I skip much. The story is rapid & interesting: he has really seen London society & does not give us ignorant caricatures though he caricatures sometimes from want of skill.

Our Concord Athenaeum ought to be celebrated in the

town's newspaper. What shall we say but that it is good for us to club our newspapers & journals, that it will liberalize the village to make readers here, that it will give us a good & handsome hospitality to our guests; and that we shall value small subscriptions more than large ones, for they always look sincere & affectionate.

11 August. Yes they are all children & when we speak of actual parties that must be borne in mind.

Queenie says that according to Edmund it was a piece of weak indulgence in the good God to make plums & peaches.

20 Aug.

Last night a walk to the river with Margaret and saw the moon broken in the water interrogating, interrogating. Thence followed the history of the surrounding minds. M. said she felt herself amidst Tendencies: did not regret life, nor accuse the imperfections of her own or their performance whilst these strong native Tendencies so appeared, and in the children of all of us will be ripened. I told her that I could not discern the least difference between the first experience & the latest in my own case, I had never been otherwise than indolent, never strained a muscle, and only saw a difference in the Circumstance, not in the man; at first a circle of boys—my brothers at home, with aunt & cousins, or the school room; all agreed that my verses were obscure, nonsense; and now a larger public say the same thing, "obscure nonsense", and yet both conceded that the boy had wit. A little more excitement now but the fact identical both in my consciousness & in my relations. M. would beat with the beating heart of nature; I feel that underneath the greatest life, though it were Jove's or Jehovah's, must lie an astonishment that embosoms both action & thought.

In talking with W. E. C. on Greek mythology as it was believed at Athens, I could not help feeling how fast the key to such possibilities is lost, the key to the faith of men perishes with the faith. A thousand years hence it will seem less monstrous that those acute Greeks believed in the fables of Mercury & Pan, than that these learned & practical nations of modern Europe & America, these physicians, metaphysicians, mathematicians, critics, & merchants, believed this Jewish apologue of the poor Jewish boy, & how they contrived to attach that accidental history to the religious idea, and this famous dogma of the Triune God &c, &c.; nothing more facile so long as the detachment is not made;—nothing so wild & incredible the moment after that shall happen.

from

Journal K

1842

Friday Evening, 4 Feb. 1842.

I have read that Sheridan made a good deal of *experimental writing* with a view to take what might fall, if any wit should transpire in all the waste pages. I in my dark hours may scratch the page if perchance any hour of recent life may project a hand from the darkness & inscribe a record. Twice today it has seemed to me that Truth is our only armor in all passages of life & death. Wit is cheap & anger is cheap, but nothing is gained by them. But if you cannot argue or explain your self to the other party, cleave to the truth against me, against thee, and you gain a station from which you can never be dislodged. The other party will forget the words that you spoke, but the part which you took pleads for you forever. I will speak the Truth also in my secret heart, or, *think the truth* against what is called God. Born & bred as we are in traditions, we easily find ourselves denying what seems to us sacred. I must resist the tradition however subtile & encroaching, & say, 'Truth against the Universe.' Truth has its holidays which seem to come but once in a century, when she absolves her children with triumph to all souls. The being that can share a thought & feeling so sublime as the confidence in Truth, is no mushroom. Be this then our *evidence of the Immortality*, as we call it.

—

What opium is instilled into all that is called pain in the world! It shows formidable as we approach it, but there is at last no rough friction to be endured but the most slippery sliding surfaces. We fall soft on a thought. People wail & some people gnash their teeth, but it is not half so bad with them as they say. We court suffering in the hope that here at least we shall find reality, sharp angular peaks & edges of truth. But it is scene painting, a counterfeit, a goblin. Nothing now is left us but Death. We look to that with a certain grim satisfaction, saying, There, at least, is reality. That will not dodge me; if aught can act & react with energy on the Soul, this will.

21 February. Home again from Providence to the deserted house. Dear friends find I, but the wonderful Boy is gone. What a looking for miracles have I! As his walking into the room where we are, would not surprise Ellen, so it would seem to me the most natural of all things.

—

20 March.

> "There is no ceremony of anointing performed by the other animals upon the lion. To be head of the beasts is the natural right of him who subdues the Kingdom by his prowess" Veeshnoo Sarma

The Dial is to be sustained or ended & I must settle the question, it seems, of its life or death. I wish it to live but do not wish to be its life. Neither do I like to put it in the hands of the Humanity & Reform Men, because they trample on letters & poetry; nor in the hands of the Scholars, for they are dead & dry. I do not like the Plain Speaker so well as the Edinburg Review. The spirit of the last may be conventional & artificial, but that of the first is coarse, sour, indigent, dwells in a cellar kitchen & goes to make suicides.

In N.Y. Thomas Delf modestly inquired as if the question lay hard on his conscience whether there could not be in every number of the Dial at least one article which should be a statement of principles, good for doctrine, good for edification, so that there should be somewhat solid & distinct for the eye of the constant reader to rest upon, and an advancing evolution of truth. A very reasonable question.

Life goes headlong. Each of us is always to be found hurrying headlong in the chase of some fact, hunted by some fear or command behind us. Suddenly we meet a friend. We pause. Our hurry & empressement look ridiculous. Now pause, now possession is required, and the power to swell the moment from the resources of our own heart until it supersedes sun & moon & solar system in its expanding immensity. The moment is all, in all noble relations. When I read the "Lord of the Isles" last week at Staten Island, and when I meet my friend, I have the same feeling of shame at having allowed myself to be a mere huntsman & follower. Why art thou disquieted, o Soul?

In New York lately, as in cities generally, one seems to lose all substance, & become surface in a world of surfaces. Every thing is external, and I remember my hat & coat, and all my other surfaces, & nothing else. If suddenly a reasonable question is addressed to me, what refreshment & relief! I visited twice & parted with a most polite lady without giving her reason to believe that she had met any other in me than a worshipper of surfaces, like all Broadway. It stings me yet.

"What are brothers for?" said Charles G. Loring when somebody praised a man who helped his brother. William Emerson is a faithful brother.

The least differences in intellect are immeasureable. This beloved and now departed Boy, this Image in every part beautiful, how he expands in his dimensions in this fond Memory to the dimensions of Nature!

I cannot get into a sufficiently private place, I cannot get enough alone to write a letter to one whom I love.

A man at peace would go through men & nature commanding all things by his eye alone. The reason why men do not obey me, is, because they see the mud at the bottom of my eye.

That Spirit which alone suffices to quiet hearts & which seems to come forth to such from every dry knoll of sere grass, from every pine stump & half-embedded stone on which the dull March sun shines will come forth only to the poor & hungry & such as are of simple taste. If thou fillest thy brain with Boston & New York, with fashion & covetousness, and wilt stimulate thy jaded senses with wine & French coffee thou shalt find no radiance of Wisdom in the lonely waste by the pinewoods.

Ellen asks her Grandmother "whether God can't stay alone with the angels a little while & let Waldo come down?"

And Amy Goodwin too thinks that "if God has to send any angel for anything to this world, he had better send Waldo."

The chrysalis which he brought in with care & tenderness & gave to his Mother to keep is still alive and he most beautiful of the children of men is not here.
I comprehend nothing of this fact but its bitterness. Explanation I have none, consolation none that rises out of the fact itself; only diversion; only oblivion of this & pursuit of new objects.

Ellen says, I believe God has a feeding-tire for Waldo up in heaven.

And today (23 March) Nelly thinks "the snow is on the ground & the trees so white as a tablecloth & so white as parched corn."

In every court the judge is on trial as well as the culprit.

The scholar is a man of no more account in the street than another man; as the sound of a flute is not louder than the noise of a saw.

But as the tone of the flute is heard at a greater distance than any noise, so the fame of the scholar reaches farther than the credit of the banker.

Osric was always great in the present time. He had hoarded nothing from the past, neither in his trunks, neither in his memory. He had no designs on the future, neither for what he should do to men, nor for what men should do for him.

Tecumseh: a Poem. A wellread clerical person with a skilful ear and with Scott & Campbell in full possession of his memory has written this poem in the feeling that the delight he has experienced from Scott's effective lists of names might be reproduced in America from the enumeration of the sweet or sonorous Indian names. The costume as is usual in all such essays crowds the man out of nature. The most Indian thing about the Indian is surely not his moccasins or his calumet, his wampum or his stone hatchet, but traits of character & sagacity, skill, or passion which would be intelligible to all men and which Scipio or Sidney or Col Worth or Lord Clive would be as likely to exhibit as Osceola & Black Hawk. As Johnson remarked that there was a middle style in English above vulgarity & below pedantry which never became obsolete & in which the plays of Shakspeare were written, so is there in human language a middle style proper to all nations & spoken by Indians & by Frenchmen so they be men of personal force.

—

Brisbane in N.Y. pushed his Fourierism with all the force of memory, talent, honest faith, & impudence. It was the sublime of mechanics, for the system was the perfection of Arrangement & Contrivance. The force of Arrangement could no farther go. The merit of the plan was that it was a System; that it had not the partiality & hint & fragment character of most patent schemes but was coherent & comprehensive of facts to a wonderful degree. It was not daunted by distance or magnitude or remoteness of any sort but strode about nature with a giant's step & skipped no fact but made its fine Ptolemaic system of cycle & epicycle, of phalanx & phalanstery with the most laudable assiduity. Mechanics were pushed so far as fairly to meet Spiritualism. One could not but be struck with strange coincidences betwixt Fourier & Swedenborg. The Desert of Sahara, the Campagna di Roma, the Frozen Polar Circles which by their pestilential or hot or cold airs poison the temperate regions, accuse man. "Attractive Industry" would speedily subdue by adventurous, scientific, & persistent tillage these fatal tracts, would give health to the globe & cause the earth to yield healthy "imponderable fluids" to the solar system as now it yields noxious fluids. The hyaena, the jackal, the gnat, the bug, the flea, were all beneficent parts of the system. The good Fourier knew what those creatures should have been had not the mould slipped through the bad state of the atmosphere, produced no doubt by these same vicious imponderable fluids. All these shall be redressed by human culture & the useful goat & dog & innocent poetical moth, or the wood tick to consume decomposing wood shall take their place. It takes 1680 men to make one man complete in all the faculties, i.e. to be sure you have got a good joiner, a good cook, a poet, a judge, an umbrella maker, a mayor & aldermen, and so on. You ought to make your community consist of 2000 persons to prevent accidents of omission and take up 6000 acres of land. Now fancy the earth planted with some fifty or a hundred of these communities side by side, what tillage, what refectories, what dormitories, what reading rooms, what concerts, what lectures, what architecture, what gardens! what baths! What is not in one will be in another, and many will be within easy distance. Then know you & all that Constantinople is the natural Capital of the globe. There then in the Golden Horn will be the Arch Phalanx established, there will the Omniarch reside. Aladdin & his Magician, the beautiful Scherzarade, can alone in these prosaic times before the sight describe the material splendors collected there. Mr Brisbane does not doubt that in the Reign of Attractive Industry all men will speak in blank verse.

What shall we say then? This only, that Fourier has skipped no fact but one, namely, Life. He treats man as a fine Thing, something that may be put up & down, polished, moulded, roasted, made into solid or fluid or gas at the will of the owner or perhaps as a vegetable from which though now a poor crab, a very good peach can by manure & exposure be in time produced; but skips the faculty of Life which laughs at Circumstance & can make or supplant a thousand phalanxes & New Harmonys with one pulsation.

The value of this system is this, it is a statement of the order which in a logical mind the faculties always assume, externized or carried outward into a picture of the world. The mistake is that this particular statement which is beautiful as the unconscious result of one mind is to be carried by force of preaching & votes into rigid execution. Could not the conceiver of this have also believed that a similar model lay in every mind & that the will of the mind might be trusted as well as his particular committee & office, No 30 Warren street. Nay that it would be far better to say that as soon as Nature or persuasion has made us lovers & servants of the Soul, straightway every man becomes the centre of a holy & beneficent republic like that of Plato & of Christ. The world becomes Fourierized or Christianized or humanized before such a man and all things are vehicles of his life, plastic to his will.

Mr Brisbane seems as one who should laboriously arrange a heap of shavings of steel *by hand* in the direction of their magnetic poles instead of thrusting a needle into the heap, and instantaneously they are magnets.

Yet in a day of small, sour, & fierce schemes one is admonished

& cheered by a scheme of such bold & generous air & proportion; there is an intellectual courage & strength in it which is superior & which is so much truth & destined to be fact.

Here prepares now the good A B A to go to England after so long & strict acquaintance as I have had with him for seven years. I saw him for the first time in Boston in 1835. What shall we say of him to the wise Englishman?

He is a man of ideas, a man of faith. Expect contempt for all usages which are simply such. His social nature & his taste for beauty & magnificence will betray him into tolerance & indulgence, even, to men & to magnificence, but a statute or a practice he is condemned to measure by its essential wisdom or folly.

He delights in speculation, in nothing so much and is very well endowed & weaponed for that work with a copious, accurate, & elegant vocabulary; I may say poetic; so that I know no man who speaks such good English as he, and is so inventive withal. He speaks truth truly; or the expression is adequate. Yet he knows only this one language. He hardly needs an antagonist, —he needs only an intelligent ear. Where he is greeted by loving & intelligent persons his discourse soars to a wonderful height, so regular, so lucid, so playful, so new & disdainful of all boundaries of tradition & experience, that the hearers seem no longer to have bodies or material gravity, but almost they can mount into the air at pleasure, or leap at one bound out of this poor solar system. I say this of his speech exclusively, for when he attempts to write, he loses, in my judgment, all his power, & I derive more pain than pleasure from the perusal. The Boston Post expressed the feeling of most readers in its rude joke when it said of his Orphic Sayings that they "resembled a train of 15 railroad cars with one passenger." He has moreover the greatest possession both of mind & of temper in his discourse, so that the mastery & moderation & foresight, & yet felicity, with which he unfolds his thought, are not to be surpassed. This is of importance to such a broacher of novelties as he is, & to one baited, as he is very apt to be, by the sticklers for old books or old institutions. He takes such delight in the exercise of this faculty, that he will willingly talk the whole of a day, and most part of the night, & then again tomorrow, for days successively, and if I, who am impatient of much speaking, draw him out to walk in the woods or fields, he will stop at the first fence & very soon propose either to sit down or to return. He seems to think society exists for this function, & that all literature is good or bad as it approaches colloquy, which is its perfection. Poems & histories may be good, but only as adumbrations of this; and the only true manner of writing the literature of a nation would be to convene the best heads in the community, set them talking, & then introduce stenographers to record what they say. He so swiftly & naturally plants himself on the moral sentiment in any conversation that no man will ever get any advantage of him unless he be a saint as Jones Very was. Every one else Alcott will put in the wrong.

It must be conceded that it is speculation which he loves & not action. Therefore he dissatisfies everybody & disgusts many. When the conversation is ended, all is over. He lives tomorrow as he lived today for further discourse, not to begin, as he seemed pledged to do, a New Celestial life. The ladies fancied that he loved cake; very likely; most people do. Yet in the last two years he has changed his way of living which was perhaps a little easy & selfindulgent for such a Zeno, so far as to become ascetically temperate. He has no vocation to labor, and, although he strenuously preached it for a time, & made some efforts to practise it, he soon found he had no genius for it, and that it was a cruel waste of his time. It depressed his spirits even to tears.

He is very noble in his carriage to all men, of a serene & lofty aspect & deportment in the street & in the house, of simple but graceful & majestic manners, having a great sense of his own worth, so that not willingly will he give his hand to a merchant, though he be never so rich,—yet with a strong love of men, and an insatiable curiosity concerning all who are distinguished either by their intellect or by their character. He is the most generous & hospitable of men, so that he has been as munificent in his long poverty, as Mr Perkins in his wealth, or I should say much more munificent. And for his hospitality, every thing in the form of man that entered his door as a suppliant would be made master of all the house contained. Moreover every man who converses with him is presently made sensible that although this person has no faculty or patience for our trivial hodiernal labors, yet if there were a great courage, a great sacrifice, a self immolation to be made, this & no other is the man for a crisis,—and with such grandeur, yet such temperance in his mien.

(Such a man with no talent for household uses, none for action, and whose taste is for precisely that which is most rare & unattainable, could not be popular,—he could never be a doll, nor a beau, nor a bestower of money or presents, nor even a model of good daily life to propose to virtuous young persons. His greatness consists in his attitude merely; of course he found very few to relish or appreciate him; and very many to dispraise him.) Somebody called him a "Moral Sam Patch."

Another circumstance marks this extreme love of speculation. He carries all his opinions & all his condition & manner of life in his hand, &, whilst you talk with him, it is plain he has put out no roots, but is an air-plant, which can readily & without any ill consequence be transported to any place. He is quite ready at any moment to abandon his present residence & employment, his country, nay, his wife & children, on very short notice, to put any new dream into practice which has bubbled up in the effervescence of discourse. If it is so with his way of living, much more so is it with his opinions. He never remembers. He never affirms anything today because he has affirmed it before. You are rather astonished, having left him in the morning with one set of opinions, to find him in the evening totally escaped from all recollection of them, as confident of a new line of conduct, & heedless of his old advocacy. *Sauve qui peut.*

Another effect of this speculation is that he is preternaturally acute & ingenious to the extent sometimes of a little jesuitry in his action. He contemns the facts so far that his poetic representations have the effect of a falsehood, & those who are deceived by them ascribe the falsehood to him: and sometimes he plays with actions unimportant to him in a manner not justifiable to any observers but those who are competent to do justice to his real magnanimity & conscience.

Like all virtuous persons he is destitute of the appearance of virtue, and so shocks all persons of decorum by the imprudence of his behaviour & the enormity of his expressions. When I told him the story of F. E. he said he should like to have been one of the party.

This man entertained in his spirit all vast & magnificent problems. None came to him so much recommended as the most universal. He delighted in the fable of Prometheus; in all the dim gigantic pictures of the most ancient mythology; in the Indian & Egyptian traditions; in the history of magic, of palmistry, of temperaments, of astrology, of whatever showed any impatience of custom & limits, any impulse to dare the solution of the total problem of man's nature, finding in every such experiment an implied pledge & prophecy of worlds of Science & Power yet unknown to us. He seemed often to realize the pictures of the old Alchemists; for he stood brooding on the edge of the discovery of the Absolute from month to month, ever & anon affirming that it was within his reach, & nowise discomfited by uniform short comings.

The other tendency of his mind was to realize a reform in the Life of Man.

This was the steadily returning, the monotonous topic of years of conversation. This drew him to a constant intercourse with the projectors & saints of all shades who preached or practised any part or particle of reform, & to a continual coldness, quarrel, & non-intercourse with the scholars & men of refinement who are usually found in the ranks of Conservatism. Very soon the Reformers whom he had joined would disappoint him; they were pitiful persons, &, in their coarseness & ignorance, he began to pine again for literary society. In these oscillations from the Scholars to the Reformers, & back again, he spent his days.

His vice, an intellectual vice, grew out of this constitution, & was that to which almost all spiritualists have been liable,—a certain brooding on the private thought which produces monotony in the conversation, & egotism in the character. Steadily subjective himself, the variety of facts which seem necessary to the health of most minds, yielded him no variety of meaning, & he quickly quitted the play on objects, to come to *the Subject*, which was always the same, viz. *Alcott in reference to the World of Today*.

From a stray leaf I copy this: Alcott sees the law of man truer & farther than any one ever did. Unhappily, his conversation never loses sight of his own personality. He never quotes; he never refers; his only illustration is his own biography. His topic yesterday is Alcott on the 17 October; today, Alcott on the 18 October; tomorrow, on the 19th. So will it be always. The poet rapt into future times or into deeps of nature admired for themselves, lost in their law, cheers us with a lively charm; but this noble genius discredits genius to me. I do not want any more such persons to exist. Part of this egotism in him is a certain comparing eye which seems to sour his view of persons prosperously placed, & to make his conversation often accusing & minatory. He is not selfsufficing & serene.

What for the visions of the Night? Our life is so safe & regular that we hardly know the emotion of terror. Neither public nor private violence, neither natural catastrophes, as earthquake, volcano, or deluge; nor the expectation of supernatural agents in the form of ghosts or of purgatory & devils & hellfire, disturb the sleepy circulations of our blood in these calm, well spoken days. And yet dreams acquaint us with what the day omits. Eat a hearty supper, tuck up your bed tightly, put an additional bedspread over your three blankets, & lie on your back, & you may, in the course of an hour or two, have this neglected part of your education in some measure supplied. Let me consider: I found myself in a garret disturbed by the noise of some one sawing wood. On walking towards the sound, I saw lying in a crib an insane person whom I very well knew, and the noise instantly stopped: there was no saw, a mere stirring among several trumpery matters, fur-muffs, & empty baskets that lay on the floor. As I tried to approach, the Muffs swelled themselves a little as with wind, & whirled off into a corner of the garret, as if alive, and a kind of animation appeared in all the objects in that corner. Seeing this, and instantly aware that here was Witchcraft, that here was a devilish Will which signified itself plainly enough in the stir & the sound of the wind, I was unable to move;—my limbs were frozen with fear; I was bold & would go forward, but my limbs I could not move; I mowed the defiance I could not articulate & woke with the ugly sound I made. After I woke and recalled the impressions, my brain tingled with repeated vibrations of terror,—and yet was the sensation pleasing, as it was a sort of rehearsal of a Tragedy.

We see each other under social excitement, we hear from each his best thought & go away thinking that great moment his habitude.

What room for Fourier phalanxes, for large & remote schemes of happiness when I may be in any moment surprized by contentment?

Strange that we should be thus caricatured & satirized continually by our bodies! Thus, short legs which constrain a man to short mincing steps are a perpetual insult & contumely to him.

Here was Edward Palmer, with somewhat ridiculous yet much nobility, always combined in his person & conversation truth, honesty, love, independence, yet this listening to men, & this credulity in days & conventions & Brisbane projects. His look has somewhat too priestly & ecclesiastic in its cut. He looks like an Universalist minister. But though his intellect is something low & limitary, prosaic, and a good roadster, yet he has great depth of character, and grows on your eye. Pathetic it was to hear of his little circle of six young men who met one evening long ago in a little chamber in Boston, & talked over his project of *No-Money* until all saw that it was true, & had new faith in the Omnipotence of love. In Alabama & Georgia, he seems to have stopped in every printing-house, & the only signs of hope & comfort he found were Newspapers, like Brisbane's "Future," which he found in these dusky Universities. When shall we see a man whose image blends with nature, so that when he is gone, he shall not seem a little ridiculous, that same small man!

I am most of the time a very young child who does not pretend to oversee nature & dictate its law. I play with it like other infants as my toy. I see sun & moon & river without asking their causes. I am pleased by the mysterious music of falling water or the rippling & washing against the shores without knowing why. Yet child as I am I know that I may in any moment wake up to the sense of authority & deity herein. A seer, a prophet passing by will bring me to it; poetry will; nay I shall think it in the austere woods & they will tremble & turn to dreams.

Edmund Hosmer

Edmund Hosmer is a noble creature so manly, so sweet tempered, so faithful, so disdainful of all appearances, who always looks respectable & excellent to you in his old shabby cap & blue frock bedaubed with the slime of the marsh & makes you respect & honor him through all. A man to deal with who always needs to be watched lest he should cheat himself; with his admiration of that great swarthy gipsy looking wife, harried by the care of her poor household & ten children. Edmund says, the first time he saw her, he did not observe that she was much different from other women, but now he thinks her the handsomest woman he ever saw! And so you come to think also, when you see this big Meg in her house at her work, or hear her artless stories of her sufferings and her works & opinions & tastes.

We talked of G. R. & his project. I cannot help feeling a profound compassion for G. R. & S. R. who by their position are or must be inevitably, one would say, transformed into charlatans, by the endeavor continually to meet the expectation & admiration of all this eager crowd of men & women seeking they know not what who flock to them. Unless he have a Cossack roughness of clearing himself of that which does not belong to him, charlatan he must be. Theresa in the story says "I can do anything but make a show." I say, "I could do any thing but meet an expectation."

Friendship, fine people; yes; Association & grand phalanx of the best of the human race; the best, banded for some transcendant project; o yes; Excellent; but remember, that nothing & no society can ever be so large as one man. He in his friendship, he in his natural momentary associations enriches, enlarges, doubles himself; but the first hour in which he mortgages himself to two or ten or twenty he dwarfs himself below the stature of one.

—

Nov. 25. Yesterday I read Dickens's American Notes. It answers its end very well, which plainly was to make a readable book, nothing more. Truth is not his object for a single instant, but merely to make good points in a lively sequence, and he succeeds very well. As an account of America it is not to be considered for a moment: it is too short, & too narrow, too superficial, & too ignorant, too slight, & too fabulous, and the man totally unequal to the work. A very lively rattle on that nuisance a sea voyage is the first chapter. And a pretty fair example of the historical truth of the whole book. We can hear throughout every page the dialogue between the author & his publisher, "Mr Dickens the book must be entertaining,—that is the essential point. Truth! damn truth. I tell you it must be entertaining." As a picture of American manners nothing can be falser. No such conversations ever occur in this country in real life, as he relates. He has picked up & noted with eagerness each odd local phrase that he met with and, when he had a story to relate, has joined these together, so that the result is the broadest caricature; and the scene might as truly have been laid in Wales or in England as in the States. Monstrous exaggeration is an easy secret of romance. But Americans who, like some of us Massachusetts people, are not fond of spitting, will go from Maine to N. Orleans, & meet no more annoyance than we should in Britain or France. So with "yes," so with "fixings," so with soap & towels; & all the other trivialities which this trifler detected in travelling over half the world. The book makes but a poor apology for its author who certainly appears in no dignified or enviable position. He is a gourmand & a great lover of wines & brandies, & for his entertainment has a cockney taste for certain charities. He sentimentalizes on every prison & orphan asylum, until dinner time. But science, art, Nature, & charity itself all fade before us at the great hour of Dinner.

—

I began to write of Poetry & was driven at once to think of Swedenborg as the person who of all men in the recent ages stands eminently for the translator of Nature into thought. I do not know a man in history to whom things stood so uniformly for words. Before him the Metamorphosis continually plays. And if there be in Heaven Museums of Psychology, the most scientific angel could scarcely find a better example than the brain of Swedenborg of the tendency to interpret the moral by the material.

There was this perception in him which makes the poet or perceiver an object of awe & terror, namely; that the same man or society of men may wear one aspect to themselves & those in like state with them, & a very different aspect to higher intelligences. Certain priests whom he describes as conversing very learnedly together, appeared to the children who were at some distance like dead horses: & many the like misappearances. And instantly the mind inquires if these fishes that swim under the bridge, these pigs that grunt in the pen, these dogs that bark in the yard by night are verily fixed unchangeable fishes, swine, & dogs or only so appear to me; & perchance to themselves appear upright men? and whether I appear as man to all eyes. So thought the Brahmin & Pythagoras, & many a poet has doubted or has seen it. But the man who sees through the flowing vest the firm nature & can declare it will draw us with love & terror.

Swedenborg never indicates any emotion,—a cold passionless man.

What we admire is the majestic & beautiful Necessity which necessitated him to see these Heavens & Hells of his. The Heaven which overpowered his & every human mind in proportion to the apprehensiveness of each, is more excellent than his picture; the Hell which is its negation, is more formidable than he had skill to draw.

Very dangerous study will Swedenborg be to any but a mind of great elasticity. Like Napoleon as a military leader, a master of such extraordinary extent of nature & not to be acted on by any other that he must needs be a god to the young & enthusiastic.

*

6 April.

Having once learned that in some one thing although externally small, greatness might be contained, so that in doing that, it was all one as if I had builded a world; I was thereby taught, that everything in nature should represent total nature; & that whatsoever thing did not represent to me the sea & sky, day & night, was something forbidden or wrong.

The revolutions that impend over society are not now from ambition & rapacity, from impatience of one or another form of government, but from new modes of thinking which shall recompose society after a new order, which shall destroy the value of many kinds of property.

Heroes

"Heaven's exiles straying from the orb of light."
Empedocles.

> "Pericles the father of these youths has beautifully & well instructed them in those things which are taught by masters; but in those things in which he is wise he has neither instructed them himself, nor has he sent them to another to be instructed; but they feeding, as it were, without restraint, wander about, to see if they can casually meet with virtue." *Plato* in Protagoras

Swedenborg's interlocutors all speak Swedenborgese Sir Isaac Newton, Sir Hans Sloane, King George II, and all? Only when Cicero comes by, the good Baron sticks a little at saying he talked with Cicero, but with a human modesty remarks, "One whom it was given me to believe was Cicero;" and when the *soi disant* Roman opens his mouth all Rome, all Eloquence has oozed out of him, it is plain Swedenborg like the rest. (See Heaven & Hell Sect. 322) The Universe in his poem suffers under a magnetic sleep, & only reflects the mind of the magnetizer.

You should never ask me what I can do. If you do not find my gift without asking, I have none for you. Would you ask a woman wherein her loveliness consists? Those to whom she is lovely will not discover it so. Such questions are but curiosity & gossip. Beside I cannot tell you what my gift is unless you can find it without my description.

—

The history of Christ is the best document of the power of Character which we have. A youth who owed nothing to fortune & who was "hanged at Tyburn,"—by the pure quality of his nature has shed this epic splendor around the facts of his death which has transfigured every particular into a grand universal symbol for the eyes of all mankind ever since.

He did well. This great Defeat is hitherto the highest fact we have. But he that shall come shall do better. The mind requires a far higher exhibition of character, one which shall make itself good to the senses as well as to the soul; a success to the senses as well as to the soul. This was a great Defeat. We demand Victory. More character will convert judge & jury, soldier & king; will rule human & animal & mineral nature; will command irresistibly and blend with the course of Universal Nature.

In short there ought to be no such thing as Fate. As long as we use this word, it is a sign of our impotence & that we are not yet ourselves. There is now a sublime revelation in each of us which makes us so strangely aware & certain of our riches that although I have never since I was born for so much as one moment expressed the truth, and although I have never heard the expression of it from any other, I know that the whole is here,—the wealth of the Universe is for me. Every thing is explicable & practicable for me. And yet whilst I adore this ineffable life which is at my heart, it will not condescend to gossip with me, it will not announce to me any particulars of science, it will not enter into the details of my biography, & say to me why I have a son & daughters born to me, or why my son dies in his sixth year of joy. Herein then I have this latent omniscience coexistent with omnigorance. Moreover, whilst this Deity glows at the heart, & by his unlimited presentiments gives me all power, I know that tomorrow will be as this day, I am a dwarf, & I remain a dwarf. That is to say, I believe in Fate. As long as I am weak, I shall talk of Fate; whenever the God fills me with his fulness, I shall see the disappearance of Fate.

I am *Defeated* all the time; yet to Victory I am born.

—

The Poet should not only be able to use nature as his hieroglyphic, but he should have a still higher power, namely, an adequate message to communicate; a vision fit for such a faculty. Therefore, when we speak of Poet in the great sense, we seem to be driven to such examples as Ezekiel & St John & Menu with their moral Burdens; and all those we commonly call poets become rhymesters & poetasters by their side.
He will be a critic who can show us from within the relation between Shakspeare & Swedenborg.

All our works which we do not understand are symbolical. If I appear to myself to carry rails into the shed under my barn, if I appear to myself to dig parsnips with a dung fork, there is reason no doubt in these special appearances as much as in the study of metaphysics or mythology, in which I do see meaning.

We are greatly more poetic than we know; poets in our drudgery, poets in our eyes, & ears, & skin.

The school boys went on with their game of baseball without regard to the passenger, & the ball struck him smartly in the back. He was angry. Little cared the boys. If you had learned how to play when you was at school, they said, you would have known better than to be hit. If you did not learn then, you had better stop short where you are, & learn now. Hit him again, Dick!

Sunday Eve. I say that he will render the greatest service to criticism which has been known for ages who shall draw the line of relation that subsists between Shakspeare & Swedenborg. For here stands ever the human mind in the old perplexity demanding intellect, demanding moral sentiment; impatient equally of either without the other, & yet no man yields them both. That great Reconciler has not yet appeared. When we are weary of the saints as we so quickly are, Shakspeare is our City of Refuge. And yet the Instincts of man presently teach him that the problem of Essence is the one which must take precedence of all others; the great questions of Whence? & What? and that solution of these must be in a life & not in a book; that the finest drama or poem is only a proximate or oblique reply, but the Pythagoras & Menu & Jesus work directly on this problem.

Partiality of any kind we hate.

Always there is this Woman as well as this Man in the mind; Affection as well as Intellect.

You might know beforehand that your friends will not succeed since you have never been able to find the Institution in the Institutor. All their action will be tentative merely. It is a piece of Boston gone out into the fields and will be Boston still & no new fact and cannot inspire enthusiasm. Had there been something latent in the man, a terrible undemonstrated fact agitating & embarrassing his demeanor we had watched for its Advent.

—

We shun to record the circumstance which we best know for example, the clergyman his "Unitarian Association," his "Christian Register," his "Exchanges," & his pecuniary and social and amiable or odious relations to his parish; and, in like manner, each of us so much of his hodiernal economy as occupies most of his time & thoughts; but if we consider how fast the wheel of nature revolves, we shall know that very soon this will be irrevocably gone, intrusive and unpleasing as it now appears. Gladly we would learn from Shakspeare, gladly from Chaucer, from Plato, those daily facts. At a distance it will appear to ourselves also, what was the significance of these employments & meannesses as symbolical. By great living now, we might dignify the moment & either decline these trivialities, or make them illustrious. At a distance, we shall see the character lifting the condition, & giving its quality to all the parts. In the perspective of ages & orbs your daily employment will surely appear the fit fable of which you are the moral.

From the mountain we see the mountain.

As soon as my guests are gone, they show like dreams.

Mr. Clapp of Dorchester to whom I described the Fourier project thought it must not only succeed but that agricultural association must presently fix the price of bread, & drive single farmers into association in self defence, as the great commercial & manufacturing companies had done.

Last night I read many pages in *Chester Dewey's Report of Herbaceous Plants in Massachusetts.* With what delight we always come to these images! the mere names of reeds & grasses, of the milk weeds, of the mint tribe & the gentians, of mallows & trefoils, are a lively pleasure. The odorous waving of these children of beauty soothes & heals us. The names are poems often. *Erigeron* because it grows old early, is thus named *The Old man of the Spring.* The Pyrola umbellata is called *Chimaphila, Lover of Winter* because of its bright green leaves in the snow; called also Princes' Pine. The Plantain, (splantago major) which follows man wherever he builds a hut, is called by the Indians "White man's foot." And it is always affecting to see Lidian or one of her girls stepping outside the door with a lamp at night to gather a few plantain leaves to dress some slight wound or inflamed hand or foot. What acres of Houstonia whiten & ripple before the eye with innumerable pretty florets at the mention of May. My beloved Liatris in the end of August & September acquires some added interest from being an approved remedy for the bite of serpents, & so called "Rattlesnake's Master."

The naming of the localities comforts us: "ponds," "shady woods," "sandy woods," "wet pastures," &c. I begin to see the sun & moon & to share the life of nature as under the spell of the sweetest pastoral poet.

Fire weed, a *Hieraxcium* which springs up abundantly on newly cleared land. The aromatic fields of dry *Gnaphalium*; the 'sweet flags' live in my Memory this April day. But this dull country professor insults some of my favourites as the well beloved *Lespedeza*, for instance. The beautiful *Epigaea*, pride of Plymouth woods, he utterly omits.

He who loves a flower though he knows nothing of its botany or medicine is nearer to it than one of these catalogue makers. Yet flowers so strictly belong to youth that we soon come to feel that their beautiful generations concern not us. We have had our day; now let the children have theirs. The flowers jilt us, and we are but old bachelors in our ridiculous tenderness.

These are our Poetry. What I pray thee O Emanuel Swedenborg have I to do with jasper, sardonyx, beryl, & chalcedony? What with tabernacles, arks, ephahs & ephods, what with lepers & emeroids, what with midnight bridal processions, with chariots of fire? with dragons crowned & horned, or Behemoth or Unicorn?

Good for orientals, these are nought to me. The more learning you bring to explain them the more glaring the impertinence. My learning is in my birth & habits, in the delight of my eyes, and not another man's. Of all the absurdities of men this of some foreigner proposing to take away my poetry & substitute his own & amuse me with pelican & stork instead of robin & thrush; palm trees & shittim wood instead of sugar maple & sassafras—seems the most needless & insulting. One would think that God made fig trees & dates, grapes & olives but the devil made Baldwin apples & pound pears, cherries & whortleberries, Indian corn & Irish potatoes. I tell you, I love the peeping of a Hyla in a pond in April, or the evening cry of a whip-poor-will, better than all the bellowing of the Bulls of Bashan or all the turtles of whole Palestina. The County of Berkshire is worth all Moab, Gog, & Kadesh, put together.

When Swedenborg described the roads leading up from the "world of spirits" into heaven as not visible at first to any spirit, but after some time visible to such as are pure, he figuratively reports a familiar truth in relation to the history of thought. The gates of thought how slow & late they discover themselves! Yet when they appear, we see that they were always there, always open.

13 April. Read last night Mr Colman's Fourth Report of the Agriculture of Massachusetts. The account he gives of the fat cattle raised on Connecticutt River & sold at Brighton is pathetic almost. The sale sometimes will not pay the note the farmer gave for the money with which he bought his stock in the fall. The Miseries of Brighton would make a new chapter in Porphyry on Abstinence from Animal Food. The Maple Sugar business is far more agreeable to read of. One tree may

be tapped for eighty or 90 years & not injured. One man can tap 300 in a day. I read with less pleasure that a principal crop of Franklin County is broom-corn.

The babe is not disconcerted. I delight in her eyes: they receive good humoredly everything that appears before them, but give way to nothing. Scrap as she is she is never displaced, as older children are.

I like a meeting of gentlemen; for they also bring each one a certain cumulative result. From every company they have visited, from every business they have transacted, they have brought away some thing which they wear as a certain complexion or permanent coat and their manners are a certificate, a trophy of their culture. What we want when you come to see us is country culture. We have town culture enough & to spare. Show us your own, inimitable & charming to us, o country man!

At New York I saw Mrs Black, a devout woman bred in the Presbyterian Church, but who had left it & come out into the light, as she said "in a moment of time." She was spiritual and serene. The contemplation of the presence & perfection of the Moral Law contented her. She had read Mme Guion & Jacob Behmen, & now, lately, the Book of Esdras, the author of which she said was of an impatient spirit, but yet wise. She quoted Scripture a good deal, but in the poetic & original way of Jones Very. I was greatly contented with her, at my first interview; but at the second I asked her "Had she no temptations?" No. Had she no wish to serve some creature who could only be served by her involving herself in affairs? No.

For herself she satisfied me pretty well, but I soon felt that she had no answers to give to the Inquirers whom I usually meet. She only said, They must be willing to be fools. 'Yes,' I said, 'but they already are fools & have been so a long time, & now they begin to whimper, How long, O Lord!' Goodness is not good enough, unless it has insight, universal insights, results that are of universal application.

Men whom we see are whipped through the world; they are harried, anxious. They seem all the hacks of some invisible riders. How seldom do we behold tranquillity, living peace. We have never yet seen a man. We do not know the majestic manners which belong to him, which appease & exalt the beholder. As soon as we behold that fact we shall lose at once this insanity of going abroad, or working with numbers, to accomplish something. We shall see that the most private is the most public energy. We shall see that quality atones for quantity, that creative action on one outvalues feeble exhibition & philanthropic declamation to crowds; and that grandeur of character acts in the dark, & succours them who never saw it. I ought to be obeyed. The reason I am not is because I am not real. Let me be a lover, & no man can resist me.

I will pay you homage as long as you do not know it: the moment you know it, I will pay it no longer.

"Every intellect," says Proclus, "is an *im*partible essence." Very likely & very unimportant; but that every intellect is an impart*a*ble essence, or, is communicable in the same proportion with its amount or depth,—is a theme for the song of angels.

Quotation

It is a great advantage to come first in time. He that comes second must needs quote him that came first. You say that Square never quotes: You say something absurd. Let him speak a word, only to say, 'chair,' 'table,' 'fire,' 'bread,'—What are these but quotations from some ancient savage?

I am not united, I am not friendly to myself, I bite & tear myself. I am ashamed of myself. When will the day dawn of peace & reconcilement when self-united & friendly I shall display one heart & energy to the world?

I have sometimes fancied my friend's wisdom rather corrective than initiative, an excellent element in conversation to counteract the common exaggerations & preserve the sanity, but chiefly valuable so & not for its adventure & exploration or for its satisfying peace.

*

Swedenborg's types all mean the same thing: horses, ships, garments, leaven, sea, islands,—all mean either *love* or *wisdom* or the reverse.

19 April.

My daily life is miscellaneous enough but when I read Plato or Proclus, or, without Plato, when I ascend to thought, I do not at once arrive at satisfactions, as when I drink being thirsty, or go to the fire being cold; no; I am only apprized at first of my vicinity to a new & most bright region of life. By persisting to read or to think, this region gives farther sign of itself, as it were, in flashes of light, in momentary revealings of its profound tranquillity & beauty,—as if the clouds that covered it, parted at intervals, & showed the approaching traveller the inland mountains with the tranquil eternal meadows spread at their base, whereon flocks graze & shepherds pipe & dance. But that characterizes every insight that is vouchsafed me from this realm of thought that it is felt as initial, that it promises a sequel. Two things: 1. I do not make it, I arrive there & behold what was there already. I make? O God, No! I clap my hands in infantine joy & happy astonishment before the first dread opening to me of this August Magnificence, old with the love & homage of innumerable Ages, young with the life of life, the sunbright Mecca of the Desart of Infinite Power.

2. It affirms continuance. It gives the first assurance I have had of permanence not by indicating continuance but increase. Love, Desire are born in my breast—and all signs of enlargement. Instantly the world in which I had lived so long becomes an apparition & I am brave with the celestial blood that beats in my heart whilst I worship the new beauty, & I am ready to die out of Nature and be born more fully into the new America I have found in the West.

Lidian says, It is with her as it is with little Ellen when she is put out into the entry.

Life

Where do we find ourselves? In a series, of which we do not know the extremes, & believe that it has none. We wake & find ourselves on a stair; there are stairs below us up which we seem to have come; there are stairs above us many a one, they go up to heaven.

"Since neither now nor yesterday began
These thoughts which have been ever, nor yet can
A man be found who their first entrance knew"

22 April. This P.M. I found Edmund Hosmer in his field after traversing his orchard where two of his boys were grafting trees; Mr H. was ploughing and Andrew driving the oxen. I could not help feeling the highest respect as I approached this brave labourer. Here is the Napoleon, the Alexander of the soil, conquering & to conquer, after how many & many a hard fought summer's day & winter's day, not like Napoleon of sixty battles only but of 6000, & out of every one he has come victor, & here he stands with Atlantic strength & cheer, invincible still. I am ashamed of these slight & useless limbs of mine before this strong soldier. What good this man has or has had he has earned. No rich father left him any inheritance of land or money; he borrowed the money with which he bought his farm & has supported his large family of ten children, given them a good education, and improved his land in every way year by year, & is a man, every inch of him. Innocency & Justice have written their name on his brow. Toil has not broken his spirit. His laugh rings with the sweetness & hilarity of a child. He told me he had been reading Mr Colman's Agric. Report. But he did not speak of it with much respect. He noticed Mr C's advice to the farmers to sell their cattle in the fall & also their hay & buy in the spring. Hosmer said the farmer always knows what his interest dictates in these cases & does accordingly. "Down below where manure is cheap & hay dear, they will sell their oxen but for me to sell my cattle & my produce in the fall would be to sell my farm, for I should have no manure to renew a crop in the spring." But chiefly the Model farms & Model farmers seemed to nettle Mr H. "Why one would think who reads this Report," he said, "that Mr Phinney & Capt. Moore were the supporters of the Commonwealth. And yet Mr Phinney would starve in two years on any one of fifty poor farms in this neighborhood on each of which

now a farmer gets a good living—Mr P. with all his knowledge & present skill."

Mr P. has a salary of 2000 dollars a year, which he spends on his farm. Otherwise he had been ruined long ago. And Capt. Moore never got rich by his skill in making land produce, but by his skill in *making men produce.* He gets his labor for nothing. And Mr H. went on to relate anecdotes of various ways in which men get rich. He could not point at any example of a man who had honestly got rich by farming alone.

What does the Agric. Surveyor know of all this? he said. What can he know. The true men of skill, the poor farmers who by the sweat of their face & without inheritance & without offence to their conscience have raised a family, & made a good farm although their buildings are shabby, these make no figure in the Report, yet these were the true subject of it.

So true it is I thought as he talked that Necessity farms it, that Necessity finds out when to go to Brighton & when to feed in stall better than Mr Colman.

—

We look wishfully to emergences to eventful revolutionary times from the desart of our ennui and think how easy to have taken our part when the drum was rolling & the house was burning over our heads. But is not peace greater than war and has it not greater wars & victories? Is there no progress? To wish for war is atheism.

—

This business of reform is dangerous, because it is always partial. It is handsomer to remain in the Establishment, better than it, & conduct that in the best manner than to launch on some particular improvement without supporting it by a total regeneration. This Copyright business for example: Plainly it is no work for a poet to be defending his property so cunningly. If he can show well that it is stealing to print his book, plainly he was no man to write a book, for the whole use of his book, is to affirm spiritual law over material & forensic law.

Dr James Jackson said it always took some time to learn the *scale* of patients & nurses: what they meant by "*violent pain*," "feeling that they should die," &c. &c. Almost all persons delight in the superlative and for this reason seize on an exaggeration as on sugar in all their actual observations of each character. It proceeds from the want of skill to detect quality that they hope to move your admiration by quantity: for they feel that here in this or that person is somewhat remarkable.

A reading man or a child self-entertained is the serpent with its tail in the mouth. Let Saadi sit alone.

Yet the surfaces threaten to carry it in nature. The fox & musquash, the hawk & snipe & bittern when nearly seen are found to have no more root than man, to be just such superficial tenants in the globe. Then this new molecular philosophy goes to show that there are astronomical interspaces betwixt atom & atom; that the world is all outside; it has no inside.

E. H says, when we spoke of the beauty of morning & the beauty of evening,—"I go a beggar to the sunset, but in the morning I am equal to nature."

Atom from atom yawns as far
As moon from earth, as star from star

from

Journal N

1842

The young people, like Brownson, Channing, Greene, E. P. P., & possibly Bancroft think that the vice of the age is to exaggerate individualism, & they adopt the word *l'humanité* from Le Roux, and go for "*the race*." Hence the Phalanx, owenism, Simonism, the Communities. The same spirit in theology has produced the Puseyism which endeavours to rear "the Church" as a balance and overpoise to the Conscience.

Clubhouse.
London, New York, Boston, are phalanxes ready made where you shall find concerts, books, balls, medical lectures, prayers, or Punch & Judy according to your fancy on any night or day.

It is indifferent whether you show a new object to the child, or a new relation in an old object. You may give him another toy, or you may show him that the iron block among his blocks is a magnet. The avaricious man seeks to add to the number of his toys, the scientific man to find new relations.

You never can hurt us by new ideas. God speed you, gentlemen reformers.

Bancroft & Bryant are historical democrats who are interested in dead or organized but not in organizing liberty. Bancroft would not know George Fox whom he has so well eulogized, if he should meet him in the street. It is like Lyell's science, who did not know by sight, when G. B Emerson showed him them, the shells he has described in his Geology.

I think four walls one of the best of our institutions. A man comes to me, & oppresses me by his presence: he looks very large & unanswerable: I cannot dispose of him whilst he stays; he quits the room, & passes not only out of the house but, as it were, out of the horizon; he is a mere phantasm or ghost, I think of him no more. I recover my sanity, the Universe dawns on me again.

W.H.C. thinks that not in solitude but in love, in the actual society of beloved persons have been his highest intuitions. To me it sounds like shallow verbs & nouns; for in closest society a man is by thought rapt into remotest isolation.

We ought to have a pure joy now & then,—oftener than we do, and feel ourselves traversed.

No man can be criticised but by a greater than he. Do not then read the reviews. Wordsworth dismisses a whole regiment of poets from their vocation.

The world is waking up to the idea of Union and already we have Communities, Phalanxes and Aesthetic Families, & Pestalozzian institutions. It is & will be magic. Men will live & communicate & ride & plough & reap & govern as by lightning and galvanic & etherial power; as now by respiration & expiration exactly together they lift a heavy man from the ground by the little finger only, & without a sense of weight. But this Union is to be reached by a reverse of the methods they use. It is spiritual and must not be actualized. The Union is only perfect when all the Uniters are absolutely isolated. Each man being the Universe, if he attempt to join himself to others, he instantly is jostled, crowded, cramped, halved, quartered, or on all sides diminished of his proportion. And the stricter the union the less & more pitiful he is. But let him go alone, & recognizing the Perfect in every moment with entire obedience, he will go up & down doing the works of a true *member*, and, to the astonishment of all, the whole work will be done with concert, though no man spoke; government will be adamantine without any governor.

—

This old Bible if you pitch it out of the window with a fork, comes bounce back again.

Several steps: a man's greatness is to advance on a line. Simple recipiency is the virtue of Space not of Man. To him belongs progress. He builds himself on himself. Angelo, Dante, Milton, Swedenborg, Pythagoras, Paracelsus were men of great robustness; they built; not only with energy, but symmetry, & their work could be called Architecture. Napoleon lately was an architect; but we now have short memories & short aims, & short flights, and after ten years are where we were. Fourier was an architect.

We are very impatient of our infirmities, especially of our incompetence to reply to sophistries and the selfdeceived: but we must be patient. We have our native method of reply to each, & if we never usurp another, our own will appear, and will reach the sophist & selfdeceiver at last.

11 Nov. The selfish man suffers more from his selfishness than he from whom that selfishness withholds some important benefit. That which he wishes most of all is to be lifted to some higher platform so that he may see beyond his present fear the trans-alpine good, so that his fear, his coldness, his custom may be broken up like fragments of ice melted & carried away in the great stream of goodwill. I also wish to be a benefactor, I wish more to be a benefactor, a servant, than you wish to be served by me; and surely the greatest good fortune that could befal me, is precisely that, to be so moved by you that I should say, Take me and all mine, & use me & mine freely to your ends! for I could not say that otherwise than because a great enlargement had come to my heart & mind which made me superior to all my fortunes. Here we are paralyzed with fear, we hold on to our little properties, house & land, office & money, as things, detached dead things for profit only, for the bread that they have in our experience yielded us, although we know & confess that our being does not flow through them. We desire to be made great: we desire to be touched with that fire that shall command all this ice to stream; that I shall be a benefit thoroughly, thoroughly.

If therefore we make objections to your project o friend! o friend of the slave, or friend of the poor, or of the race, understand well that it is because we wish to drive you to drive us; we would compel you to explain yourself and elevate us. We are haunted with a belief that you have a secret which it would highliest advantage me to learn, and I would drive you to impart it to me though it should bring me to prison & the gallows.

11 Nov. Today I have the feeling to a degree not experienced by me before, that discussions like that of yesterday and many the like in which I have participated, invade & injure me. I often have felt emptiness and restlessness & a sort of hatred of the human race after such prating by me & my fellows, but, never so seriously as now, that absence from them is better for me than the taking an active part in them.

You may associate on what grounds you like, for economy, or for good neighborhood, for a school, or for whatever reason, only do not say that the Divine Spirit enjoins it. The Spirit detaches you from all associations, & makes you to your own astonishment secretly a member of the Universal Association but it descends to no specialties, draws up no Articles of a Society, but leaves you just as you were for that matter, to be guided by your particular convenience & circumstance whether to join with others, or whether to go alone.

It seems to be true that our New England population was settled by the most religious & ideal of the Puritans of England. It is natural enough that we should be more ideal than old England.

Books.

It is taking a liberty with a man to offer to lend him a book as if he also had not access to that truth to which the bookmaker had access. Each of the books, if I read, invades me, displaces me; the law of it is that it should be first, that I should give way to it, I who have no right to give way and, if I would be tranquil & divine again, I must dismiss the book.

And yet I expect a great man to be a good reader or in proportion to the spontaneous power should be the assimilating power.

Every book serves us at last only by adding some one word to our vocabulary, or perhaps two or three. And perhaps that word shall not be in the volume or shall only be the author's name. And yet there are books of no vulgar origin but the work & the proof of faculties so comprehensive, so nearly equal to the universe which they paint, that although one shuts them also with meaner ones, yet he says with a sigh the while, this were to be read in long thousands of years by some stream in Paradise. Swedenborg, Behmen, Plato, Proclus, Rabelais, & Greaves.

Do not gloze & prate & mystify. Here is our dear grand Alcott says you shall dig in my field for a day & I will give you a dollar when it is done, & it shall not be a business transaction! It makes me sick. Whilst money is the measure *really* adopted by us all as the most convenient measure of all material values let us not affectedly disuse the name, & mystify ourselves & others; let us not "say no, & take it." We may very well & honestly have theoretical & practical objections to it; if they are fatal to the use of money & barter, let us disuse them; if they are less grave than the inconvenience of abolishing traffic, let us not pretend to have done with it, whilst we eat & drink & wear & breathe it.

You must either lay to more strength or you must sharpen the edge of your knife. But wit always will be a substitute for drudgery, not for labor but for drudgery or excess of labor. For wit selects the right point wherein my stroke shall be bestowed, & so saves all the supernumerary strokes. A dim sighted man strikes with his hammer all about the nail: a good eye will hit the nail upon the head. You call on twenty men to help you: I go to the only man that can help me. You send information to several persons; I send it to the newspaper, & it goes at once to twenty thousand.

Do not be too timid & squeamish about your actions. All life is an experiment. The more experiments you make, the better. What if they are a little coarse, & you may get your coat soiled or torn? What if you do fail, & get fairly rolled in the dirt once or twice? Up again, you shall nevermore be so afraid of a tumble. This matter of the lectures, for instance. The engagement drives your thoughts & studies to a head, & enables you to do somewhat not otherwise practicable; that is the action. Then there is the reaction; for when you bring your discourse to your auditory, it shows differently. You have more power than you had thought of, or less. The thing fits, or does not fit; is good or detestable.

It is a peculiar feature of New England that young farmers & mechanics who work all summer on the soil, or in a shop, take a school in the winter months. Mr Fay the pumpmaker in this town goes to Marlborough this winter for that purpose; Young, Wheeler, & Wood do the same thing.

Edmund Hosmer was willing to sell his farm five years ago for $3800 & go to the west. He found & still finds that the Irish, of which there are 200 in this town, are underselling him in labor, and he does not see how he & his boys can do those things which only he is willing to do; for, go to market he will not, nor shall his boys with his consent do any of those things for which high wages are paid, as, for example, take any shop, or the office of foreman or agent in any corporation wherein there seems to be a premium paid for faculty, as if it were paid for the faculty of cheating. He does not see how he & his children are to prosper here, & the only way for them is to run, the Caucasian before the Irishman.

I call the terror of starving, skepticism, & say that I do not believe that I can be put in any condition in which I cannot honestly maintain myself, & honestly be rich, that is, not be poor. It is in vain that you put to me any case of misfortune or calamity—the extremest, the Manchester weaver, the Carolina Slave; I doubt not that in the history of the individual is always an account of his condition, & he knows himself to be party to his present estate. Put me in his condition, & I should see its outlets & reliefs, though now I see them not. The main & capital remedy of the religious sentiment and all the abundance of its counsels for his special distresses, it were atheism to doubt. But do not require of me sitting out here to say what he within there ought to do. I can never meddle with other people's facts, I have enough of my own. But this one thing I know, that, if I do not clear myself, I am in fault, & that my condition is matched point for point with every other man's. I can only dispose of my own facts.

Last night H. T. read me verses which pleased if not by beauty of particular lines, yet by the honest truth, and by the length of flight & strength of wing; for, most of our poets are only writers of lines or of epigrams. These of H.T. at least have rude strength, & we do not come to the bottom of the mine. Their fault is, that the gold does not yet flow pure, but is drossy & crude. The thyme & marjoram are not yet made into honey; the assimilation is imperfect.—It seems as if poetry was all written before time was, before the world was; and whenever we are so finely organized that we can penetrate into that pure region where the Air is Music, we hear these primal aboriginal warblings, & attempt to write them, but lose every now & then a word or syllable or whole verse, & substitute ignorantly something of our own, & so miswrite the poem, which becomes stupid & unaffecting by our blunders. The men of purer fire write down the catches much more faithfully & so we have the Comus and Penseroso, Hamlet & Lear. But it is a great pleasure, to have poetry of the second degree also, & mass here as in other instances is some compensation for superior quality for I find myself stimulated & rejoiced like one who should see a cargo of sea-shells discharged on the wharf, whole boxes & crates of conchs, cypraeas, cones, neritas, cardiums, murexes, though there should be no pearl oyster nor one shell of great rarity & value among them.

Time is the little grey man who takes out of his breast pocket first a pocket book, then a Dollond Telescope, then a Turkey carpet, then four saddled & bridled nags and a sumptuous canvass tent. We are accustomed to chemistry & it does not surprise us. But chemistry is but a name for changes & developments as wonderful as those of this Breast pocket. I was a little chubby boy trundling a hoop in Chauncey Place and spouting poetry from Scott & Campbell at the Latin School. But Time the little grey man has taken out of his vest pocket a great aukward house (in a corner of which I sit & write of him) some acres of land, several fullgrown & several very young persons, & seated them close beside me; then he has taken that chubbiness & that hoop quite away (to be sure he has left the declamation & the poetry) and here left a long lean person threatening soon to be a little grey man, like himself.

Religion has failed! Yes, the religion of another man has failed to save me. But it has saved him. We speak of the past with pity & reprobation, but through the enormities, evils & temptations of the past, saints & heroes slipped into heaven. There is no spot in Europe but has been a battle field, there is no religion, no church, no sect, no year of history, but has served men to rise by, to scale the walls of heaven, & enter into the banquets of Angels. Our fathers are saved. The same, precisely the same conflicts have always stood as now, with slight shiftings of scene & costume.

September, 1842.
There is reality however in our relations to our friend, is there not? Yes, and I hail the grander lights & hints that proceed from these, as the worthiest fruits of our being, thus far.
But do not these show that the existence you so loved is not closed? I have no presentiment of that.
Alas, my friend, you have no generosity; you cannot give yourself away. I see the law of all your friendships. It is a bargain. You tell your things, your friend tells his things, and as soon as the inventory is complete, you take your hats.

Do you see that kitten chasing so prettily her own tail. If you could see with her eyes you would see her surrounded with hundreds of figures performing complex dramas, with tragic & comic issues, long conversations, many characters, many ups & downs of fate, & meantime it is only puss & her own tail. How long before our masquerade will cease its noise of tambourines & laughter & shouting and we shall suddenly find it was all a solitary performance.

A subject & an object: it takes always so much to make the galvanic circuit complete; but magnitude is of no moment.

What matters it whether it is Kepler & his sphere, Napoleon & Spain, Columbus & America, or a child with a doll or pussy with her tail.

How slowly how slowly we learn that witchcraft & ghost-craft, palmistry, & magic and all the other so called superstitions, which, with so much police, boastful skepticism & scientific committees, we had finally dismissed to the moon as nonsense, are really no nonsense at all, but subtle & valid influences, always starting up, mowing, muttering in our path, & shading our day. The things are real, only they have shed their skin which with much insult we have gibbetted & buried. One person fastens an eye on us and the very graves of the memory render up their dead, the secrets that make us wretched either to keep or to betray, must be betrayed; and another person fastens an eye on us, and we cannot speak a syllable, & the very bones of the body seem to lose their cartilages.

We must not inquire too curiously into the absolute value of literature. Enough that it amuses and exercises us. At last, it leaves us where we were. It names things but not adds things. It is with Literature as it is with the Faculty of Medicine. The poor man catches the disease & dies, nobody knows how; the rich man takes the same disease & dies also but has the honor & the satisfaction of having the disease named by his physician & a council of physicians. It is a great matter to have a thing named. The Boy & the W.

Chemistry, Entomology, Conic Sections, Medicine, each science, each province of science will come to satisfy all demands; the whole of poetry, of mythology, of ethics, of demonology will be expressed by it; a new rhetoric, new methods of philosophy, perhaps new political parties will celebrate the culmination of each one.

Just to fill the hour, that is happiness, that is perfection; just fill my hour, ye gods! so that I shall not say, 'Behold I have done this; but behold also, an hour of my life is gone;' but rather, I have lived an hour, no regrets, no comparisons.

*

It pains me never that I can not give you an accurate answer to the question, What is God? What is the operation we call Providence? & the like. There lies the answer: there it exists, present, omnipresent to you, to me. Every time we converse, I seek to translate that fact into speech; hit or miss, you have it. Every one is an approximate answer, & every successive one, no doubt, a better approximation, but it is of small consequence that we do not get it into verbs & nouns whilst it lies there & will lie there for contemplation forever.

What obstinate propensity to solitude is this. I fancied that I needed society & that it would help me much if fine persons were near, whom I could see when I would, but now that C. & H. are here, and A. is returning, I look with a sort of terror at my gate.

I woke up and found the dear old world, wife, babe, & mother, Concord & Boston, the dear old spiritual world, and even the dear old Devil not far off.

Ed. Hosmer says, that A. M. relates that when he came to Concord, he resolved to be honest, and he kept his resolution for one week; but he found that he should never get his living so, & he gave it up. Also Ed. H. said of the voters one day at town meeting, I have no doubt that the greatest part of these men mean to vote right.

—

That were a right problem for a dramatist to solve; *given* a bandit, the strongest temptation & opportunity for violence or plunder,—how to bring off the man of wit by his wit only, exercised not mediately but directly through speech. It is a problem perfectly easy to solve in action whenever the right Caesar comes. He does not exert courage but wit. The Corsair has caught a Captain.

—

Goethe received four, Fichte five, & Richter seven louis d'ors a sheet for their best works. louis = $4.00

I have a kind of promise to write one of these days a verse or two to the praise of my native city which in common days we often rail at, yet which has great merits to us wards. That, too, like every city, has certain virtues, as a museum of the arts. The parlors of private collectors; the Athenaeum Gallery; & the College; become the city of the City. Then a city has this praise, that as the bell or band of music is heard outside beyond the din of carts, so the beautiful in architecture or in political & social institutions endures: all else comes to nought. So that the antiquities & permanent things in each city are good & fine.

—

Milnes brought Carlyle to the railway, & showed him the departing train. Carlyle looked at it & then said, "These are our poems, Milnes." Milnes ought to have answered, Aye, & our histories, Carlyle. But it is worth noticing how fast the poet can dispose of these formidable facts. One sees the Factory village & the Railway, & thinks of Wordsworth & what will be his dismay. Wordsworth has the sense to see that this also falls in, un bête de plus, with the known multitude of mechanical facts and that all Mechanics have not gained a grain's weight from the addition. The spiritual Fact remains alike Unalterable by many or by few particulars, as no mountain is of any appreciable height, to break the curve of the sphere.

Men are great in their own despite. They achieve a certain greatness, but it was while they were toiling to achieve another conventional one. The boy at college apologizes for not learning the tutor's task, & tries to learn it, but stronger nature gives him Otway & Massinger to read, or betrays him into a stroll to Mount Auburn in study-hours. The poor boy instead of thanking the gods and slighting the Mathematical tutor, ducks before the functionary, & poisons his own fine pleasures by a perpetual penitence. Well at least let that one never brag of the choice he made; as he might have well done, if he had known what he did when he was doing it.

Alcott when he went to England wished to carry with him miniatures of Elizabeth Peabody, of Margaret Fuller, & of me. —I remember once that A. thought that the head would soon put off from it the trunk, which would perish, whilst the brain would unfold a new & higher organization.

Of the antique sculpture of gods Richter said "The repose of perfection not of weariness looks from their eyes & rests upon their lips"

There is no crime to intellect. All stealing is comparative. If you come to absolutes, pray who does not steal?

Richter said "In the great world I despise the men & their joyless joys, but I esteem the women; in them alone can one investigate the spirit of the times."

"Happy," he says, "shall he be, if one falls to his lot, upon whose opened eyes & heart, the flowery earth & beaming heavens strike not in infinitesimals, but in large & towering masses; for whom the great whole is something more than a nursery or a ball room."

A song is no song unless the circumstance is free & fine. If the singer sings from a sense of duty or from seeing no way of escape, I had rather have none. And now when you sing, it seems extorted & the pleasure I derive from it is from association with the same song before. And so I think that in my house where there are no ears, no fine person should be so much wronged as to be asked to sing.

When the poet comes into the wood, he first looks cautiously around like a maiden who undresses herself to step into a woodland bath—to see if any witness be near. Satisfied that he is quite alone, his form dilates, & he liberally suffers the sweet intoxication to which every fern & moss & fungus contribute, to enter & exalt his senses.

White Lies. It shall be the law of this society that no member shall be reckoned a liar who is a sportsman and indicates the wrong place when asked where he shot his partridge; or who is an angler, & misremembers where he took his trout; or who is an engineer, and misdirects his inquiring friends as to the best mill-privilege; or who is a merchant, & forgets in what stock he proposes to invest; or who is an author, and being asked if he wrote an anonymous book, replies in the negative. GHOST. (*under the floor*) It shall not be the law.

There was an influence on the young people from Everett's genius which was almost comparable to that of Pericles in Athens. That man had an inspiration that did not go beyond his head, but which made him the genius of elegance. He had a radiant beauty of person, of a classic style, a heavy large eye, marble lids which gave the impression of mass which the slightness of his form needed, sculptured lips, a voice of such rich tones, such precise & perfect utterance that although slightly nasal it was the most mellow & beautiful & correct of all the instruments of the time. The word that he spoke in the manner in which he spoke it became current & classical in New England.

He had in common with all his family a great talent for collecting facts & for bringing those he had to bear with ingenious felicity on the topic of the moment. Let him rise to speak on what occasion soever a fact had always just transpired which composed with some other fact well known to the audience the most pregnant & happy coincidence which made one remember that it is always 100 years from something. It was remarked of him that for a man who ventured to say so many things he was seldom convicted of a blunder. He had a good deal of special learning, and all his learning was available for purposes of exhibition. It was all new learning that wonderfully took & stimulated the young men. It was so coldly & weightily communicated from so commanding a platform as if in the consciousness & consideration of all history & all learning adorned with so many simple & austere beauties of expression and enriched with so many excellent digressions & significant quotations that though nothing could be conceived beforehand less attractive or indeed less fit for green boys from Connecticutt, New Hampshire, & Massachusetts, with their unripe Latin & Greek reading, than exegetical discourses in the style of Hug & Wolf & Ruhnken on the Orphic & Ante-Homeric remains, yet this learning instantly took the highest place to our imagination in our unoccupied American Parnassus. All his auditors felt the extreme beauty & dignity of the manner & even the coarsest were contented to go punctually to listen for the manner, when they had found out that the subject matter was not for them. He had nothing in common with vulgarity & infirmity but speaking, walking, sitting, was as much aloof & uncommon as a star. In the lecture-room he abstained from all ornament & pleased himself with the play of detailing erudition in a style of perfect simplicity. In the pulpit he made amends to himself & his auditor for the self denial of the Professor's Chair, & with an infantine simplicity still of manner, he gave the reins to his most florid & quaint & affluent Fancy. Then was exhibited all the richness of a Rhetoric which we have never seen rivalled in this country. Wonderful how memorable were words made which were only pleasing pictures & covered no new or valid thoughts. He abounded in sentences, in wit, in satire, in splendid allusion, in quotation, impossible to forget, in daring imagery, in parable and even in a sort of defying experiment of his own wit & skill in giving an oracular weight to Hebrew or Rabbinical words—as Selah; Ichabod; Tekel Mene Upharsin, & the like: feats which no man could better accomplish, such was his self command & the security of his manner. All his speech was music, & with such variety & invention that the ear was never tired. Especially beautiful were his poetic quotations. He quoted Milton; more rarely Byron; & sometimes a verse from Watts and with such sweet & perfect modulation that he seemed to give as much beauty as he borrowed and whatever he has quoted will seldom be remembered by any who heard him without inseparable association with his voice & genius. This eminently beautiful person was followed like an Apollo from church to church wherever the fame that he would preach led, by all the most cultivated & intelligent youths with grateful admiration. His appearance in any pulpit lighted up all countenances with delight. The smallest anecdote of his behaviour or conversation was eagerly caught & repeated and every young scholar could repeat brilliant sentences from his sermons with mimicry good or bad of his voice. This influence went much farther, for he who was heard with such throbbing hearts & sparkling eyes in the lighted & crowded churches did not let go his hearer when the church was dismissed, but the bright image of that eloquent form followed the boy home to his bed chamber & not a sentence was written in a theme, not a declamation attempted in the college chapel but showed the omnipresence of his genius to youthful heads. He thus raised the standard of taste in writing & speaking in New England.

Meantime all this was a pure triumph of Rhetoric. This man had neither intellectual nor moral principles to teach. He had no thoughts. It was early asked when Massachusetts was full of his fame what truths he had thrown into circulation? and how he had enriched the general mind? and agreed that only in graces of manner, only in a new perception of Grecian beauty had he opened our eyes.

It was early observed that he had no warm personal friends. Yet his genius made every youth his defender & boys filled their mouths with arguments to prove that the orator had a heart. There was that finish about this person which is about women, and which distinguishes every piece of genius from the works of talent, that these last are more or less matured in every degree of completeness according to the time bestowed on them but works of genius in their first & slightest form are still wholes. In every sermon or lecture or public harangue or printed page, there was nothing left for the compassion & indulgence of his hearer or reader, no marks of late hours & anxious unfinished study, but the goddess of grace had breathed on the work a last fragrancy & glitter.

—Everett's fame had the effect of giving a new lustre to the university which it greatly needed. Students flocked thither from the South & the West, from the remote points of Georgia, Tennessee, Alabama & Louisiana.

Well this bright morning had a short continuance. Mr Everett was soon attracted by the vulgar prizes of politics & quit coldly the splendid career which opened before him (& which not circumstances but his own genius had made)—for the road to Washington where it is said he has had the usual fortune of flattery & mortification, but is wholly lost to any real & manly usefulness.

Everett had as lief his MS. was
in your pocket, he read so well.

In every conversation even the highest there is a certain trick, one may say, which may be soon learned by an acute person & then that particular style be continued indefinitely. This is true of Very's, Alcott's, Lane's, and all such specialists or mystics; more true of these than of other classes.

S.G.W. said that men died to break up their styles: but Nature had no objection to Goethe's living, for he did not form one.

Sept. 27 was a fine day, and Hawthorn & I set forth on a walk. We went first to the Factory where Mr Demond makes Domett cloths, but his mills were standing still, his houses empty. Nothing so small but comes to honour & has its shining moment somewhere; & so was it here with our little Assabet or North Branch; it was falling over the rocks into silver, & above was expanded into this tranquil lake. After looking about us a few moments we took the road to Stow. The day was full of sunshine and it was a luxury to walk in the midst of all this warm & coloured light. The days of September are so rich that it seems natural to walk to the end of one's strength, & then fall prostrate saturated with the fine floods, & cry *Nunc dimittis me.* Fringed gentians, a thornbush with red fruit, wild apple trees whose fruit hung like berries, and grapevines were the decorations of the path. We scarcely encountered man or boy in our road nor saw any in the fields. This depopulation lasted all day. But the outlines of the landscape were so gentle that it seemed as if we were in a very cultivated country, and elegant persons must be living just over yonder hills. Three or four times, or oftener, we saw the entrance to their lordly park. But nothing in the farms or in the houses made this good. And it is to be considered that when any large brain is born in these towns it is sent, at sixteen or twenty years, to Boston or New York, and the country is tilled only by the inferior class of the people, by the second crop or *rowan* of the men. Hence all these shiftless poverty-struck pig-farms. In Europe where society has an aristocratic structure, the land is full of men of the best stock, & the best culture, whose interest & pride it is to remain half of the year at least on their estates & to fill these with every convenience & ornament. Of course these make model-farms & model-architecture, and are a constant education to the eye & hand of the surrounding population. Our walk had no incidents. It needed none, for we were in excellent spirits, had much conversation, for we were both old collectors who had never had opportunity before to show each other our cabinets, so that we could have filled with matter much longer days. We agreed that it needed a little dash of humor or extravagance in the traveller to give occasion to incident in his journey. Here we sober men easily pleased kept on the outside of the land & did not by so much as a request for a cup of milk creep into any farmhouse. If want of pence in our pocket or some vagary in our brain drove us into these "huts where poor men lie" to crave dinner or night's lodging, it would be so easy to break into some mesh of domestic romance, learn so much pathetic private history, perchance see the first blush mantle on the cheek of the young girl when the mail stage came or did not come, or even get entangled ourselves in some thread of gold or grey. Then again the opportunities which the taverns once offered the traveller of witnessing & even sharing in the joke & the politics of the teamster & farmers on the road, are now no more. The Temperance Society emptied the barroom; it is a cold place. H. tried to smoke a cigar, but I observed he was soon out on the piazza. After noon we reached Stow, and dined, then continued our journey towards Harvard, making our day's walk, according to our best computation, about 20 miles. The last mile, however, we rode in a wagon, having been challenged by a friendly fatherly gentleman, who knew my name, & my father's name & history, & who insisted on doing the honours of his town to us, & of us to his townsmen; for he fairly installed us at the tavern, introduced us to the Doctor, & to General ——, & bespoke the landlord's best attention to our wants. We get the view of the Nashua River valley from the top of Oak-Hill, as we enter Harvard village. Next morning, we begun our walk at 6 1/2 o'clock for the Shaker Village distant 3 1/2 miles. Whilst the good Sisters were getting ready our breakfast, we had a conversation with Seth Blanchard & Cloutman of the Brethren, who gave an honest account by yea & by nay of their faith & practice. They were not stupid like some whom I have seen of their society, & not worldly like others. The conversation on both parts was frank enough; with the downright I will be downright, thought I, and Seth showed some humour. I doubt not we should have had our own way with them to a good extent, (not quite after the manner of Hayraddin Magraber with the Monks of Liege,) if we could have staid twenty four hours: although my powers of persuasion were crippled by a disgraceful barking cold, & Hawthorn inclined to play Jove more than Mercurius. After breakfast Cloutman showed us the farm, vineyard, orchard, barn, herb room, pressing room &c. The vineyard contained two noble arcades of grapes, both White & Isabella, full of fruit; the orchard fine varieties of pears, & peaches & apples.

They have 1500 acres here, a tract of wood-land and in Ashburnham, and a sheep pasture somewhere else, enough to supply the wants of the 200 souls in this family. They are in many ways an interesting Society, but at present have an additional importance as an experiment of Socialism which so falls in with the temper of the times. What improvement is made is made for ever, this capitalist is old & never dies, his subsistence was long ago secured, & he has gone on now for long scores of years in adding easily, compound interests to his stock. Moreover, this settlement is of great value in the heart of the country as a model farm, in the absence of that rural nobility we talked of yesterday. Here are improvements invented or adopted from the other Shaker Communities which the neighboring farmers see & copy. From the Shaker Village we came to Littleton, & thence to Acton, still in the same redundance of splendour. It was like a day of July, and from Acton we sauntered leisurely homeward to finish the nineteen miles of our second day before four in the afternoon.

—

Landor, though like other poets he has not been happy in love, has written admirable sentences on the passion.

Perhaps, said Hawthorn, their disappointment taught them to write these things.

Well, it is probable. One of Landor's sentences was worth a divorce; "Those to whom love is a secondary thing, love more than those to whom it is a primary."

This thought appeared in all the Shakers said about the admission of members to their society, that people came, and proved themselves; they soon showed what they were, and remained or departed, as the Spirit made manifest, alike *to themselves* & to the Society. No man should join them for a living:

and no man should be turned off because he was poor or bedridden, but only for not being of them.

Cloutman told us their hospitality was costly, for they entertain without price all the friends of any member who visit them.

We talked of Scott. There is some greatness in defying posterity & writing for the hour, & so being a harper. Dickens at the Philadelphia dinner was willing to out-America America, & daub Irving as he himself had been daubed. In C's talk we must make allowance for his petulances. Piety like chivalry has no stationary exemplar but is evanescent & receding like rainbows. You cannot find any specimen of a religious man now in your society; you hear the fame of one; you go far & find him; & he begins, "I had a friend in my youth" &c. Yet it seems as if nothing would make such good picture in National Sketches as genuine Connecticutt, if you could lay your hand on it. At night the frogs were loud but the eagle was silent in his cliff. Cobmeal, & Katydids, or, as the miller called them, "scrapers" at Acton.

If in this last book of Wordsworth there be dulness, it is yet the dulness of a great & cultivated mind.

We have our culture like Allston from Europe & are Europeans. Perhaps we must be content with this & thank God for Europe for a while yet, and there shall be no great Yankee, until, in the unfolding of our population & power, England kicks the beam, & English authors write to America; which must happen ere long.

I have not yet begun to regret much the omission to see any particular part of nature or art, but perhaps as we live longer we begin to compare more narrowly the chances of life with the things to be seen in it, & count the Niagaras we have not visited. For me, not only Niagara but the prairie and the Ohio & the Missisippi rivers are still only names. And yet better see nothing beyond your village than to go coldly & hardly to work to see the Meccas of the mind. It were indeed an enlargement, a duplication of life, if in fit company & with good reason, I can go to Italy but Florence is not Florence if the visit is forced.

—

Queenie says that Edie spends half her time in looking innocent, & the other half in looking dignified. Nelly asleep in her bed had the air & attitude of one who rides a horse of Night.

Ed Hosmer thinks there is a great deal of unnecessary labor spent to feed the animals—especially the pig & horse. Many a farmer is but a horse's horse or a pig's pig. At the Shaker's house in Harvard I found a spirit level on the windowseat a very good emblem for the society; but, unfortunately, neither the table, nor the shelf, nor the windowseat were plumb. Death, said the good editor of Dittany, has been busy among our subscribers.

—

Oct. 1842.

The merit of a poem or tragedy is a matter of experience. An intelligent youth can find little wonderful in the Greeks or Romans. These tragedies, these poems are cold & tame. Nature & all the events passing in the street are more to him, he says, than the stark unchangeable crisis of the Iliad or the Antigone; and as for thoughts, his own thoughts are better and are more numerous. So says one, so say all. Presently, each of them tries his hand at expressing his thought;—but there is a certain stiffness, or a certain extravagance in it. All try, and all fail, each from some peculiar & different defect. The whole age of authors tries; many ages try; and in millions & millions of experiments these confessedly tame & stark poems of the Ancient are still the best. It seems to be certain that they will go on discontenting yet excelling the intelligent youths of the generations to come.

But always they will find their admirers not in the creative & enthusiastic few, who will always feel their ideal inferiority, but in the elegant cultivated & conservative class.

You praise Homer, & disesteem the art that makes the tragedy. To me it seems higher,—the unpopular and austere muse that casts human life into a high tragedy, Prometheus, Œdipus, Hamlet (mid way between the Epic & the Ode) than the art of the epic poet which condescends more to common humanity, & approaches the ballad. Man is nine parts fool for one part wise, and therefore Homer & Chaucer more read than Antigone, Hamlet or Comus.

—

A man cannot free himself by any selfdenying ordinances, neither by water nor potatoes, nor by violent passivities, by refusing to swear, refusing to pay taxes, by going to jail, or by taking another man's crop or squatting on his land— By none of these ways can he free himself; no nor by paying his debts with money; only by obedience to his own genius; only by the freest activity in the way constitutional to him, does an angel seem to arise & lead him by the hand out of all wards of the prison.

—

I think Dr Channing was intellectual by dint of his fine moral sentiment, and not primarily. He too was one of those who spoke so well that he could not afford to print, for the voice & the eye could not be printed, & all his discourses must read poorly to those who heard them. His paper on Milton contained the true doctrine of Inspiration; "Milton observes higher laws than he transgresses."

When the friend has newly died, the survivor has not yet grief, but the expectation of grief. He has not long enough been deprived of his society to feel yet the want of it. He is surprized and is now under a certain intellectual excitement, being occupied & in a manner amused by the novelty of the event & is exploring his changed condition. This defends him from sorrow. It is not until the funeral procession has departed from his doors, and the mourners have all returned to their ordinary pursuits, & forgotten the deceased, that the grief of the friend begins. In the midst of his work, in the midst of his leisure, in his thoughts which are now uncommunicated, in his successes which are now in vain, in his hopes which now are quickly checked & run low, he sees with bitterness how poor he is. As it is with the mourner so is it with the man of virtue in respect to the practice of virtue. The evil practice of the country & the time is exposed by some preacher of righteousness and after some time the land is filled with the noise of the reform. Men congratulate themselves on the great evil they have escaped and on the signal progress of society. But it is not until after this tumult is over, & all have, one after another, come in to the new practice, & the reaction has occurred, and great numbers are disgusted & have gone back again, not until then, does the true reformer, the noble man, begin to find his virtue & advantage. Through the clamor he has said nothing,—he embraced the right which was shown, at once & forever. Now society is back again where it was before, but he has added this beauty to his life.

—

Everything good, we say, is on the highway. A virtuoso hunts up with great pains a landscape of Guercino, a crayon sketch of Salvator, but the Transfiguration, The Last Judgment, the Communion, are on the walls of the Vatican where every footman may see them without price. You have got for 500 pounds an autograph receipt of Shakspeare; but for nothing a schoolboy can read Hamlet, and if he has eyes can detect secrets yet unpublished & of highest concernment therein. I think I will never read any but the commonest of all books; the Bible, Shakspeare, Milton, Dante, Homer.

—

Dr Channing is currently said to have become odious to the men of wealth & influence in Boston. But that is not true. And the instances are given that he was insulted by an orator at a public meeting at Faneuil Hall: but that was by some person surcharged with venom, and the Doctor happened to be the nearest person when the secretion was discharged. And I heard that a Boston minister had ceased from all intercourse with him for years. The Doctor probably never knew of his existence, or if he had known, had forgotten it. He was not a man to provoke any such warmth of feeling as *odium*, and there was always an air of good society about him that would secure him the good observances of the proudest circles.

Somebody cried to him out of the walnut woods, "Ho, ho, be sure not to get imposed upon, Ho! Ho!" And Arthur rubbed his eyes, looked round him, & bethought him that he would not again. But at night be found the whole journey was a blunder, and he was a dupe. The next morning when he woke, he heard his old neighbor calling to the cattle in the yard under his window, & when Arthur looked out, the man said, "Ho, ho, be sure you don't get imposed upon. Ho! Ho!" Forewarned, forearmed, thought Arthur once more.

—

My farm only holds the world together. I, oh, I am only here to see. Droll privilege of spectatorship that we all feel; I have an unquestioning presumption on hearing that a good man is coming by, that this man is true, consistent & his conscience greatly more faithful & effective than mine. And unluckily he has the same feeling respecting me & others, that not he but I and they are the responsible persons.

What bone you have found in any one skeleton, in any other skeleton though of a different species you shall find the same in the same place or near it. Well; you shall find the same trait in each. Napoleon was the farmer who wished for all the land that joined his own.

But why should a great man be at last, to a degree, a melancholy object?

—

Animal vocabulary

raven	ravenous
owl	howl
snake	sneak
worm	worm out
ram	ram-rod
dog	dog
ape	ape
cow	cowed
badger	badger

Cheerfulness is so much the order of nature that the superabundant glee of a child lying on its back & not yet strong enough to get up or to sit up, yet cooing, warbling, laughing, screaming with joy is an image of independence which makes power no part of independence. Queenie looks at Edie kicking up both feet into the air, & thinks that Edie says "The world was made on purpose to carry round the little baby; and the world goes round the sun only to bring titty-time and creeping-on-the-floor-time to the Baby."

Ogden respected nothing in T. so much as this tenacious trick of asking at breakfast & on change, at work or at bedtime, between glasses of wine or drops taken for fever,—questions touching God & duty, & the salvation of the soul. The Devil take you & your soul, said Ogden, but on second thought nothing seemed to him that he had met with in Marseilles more respectable than this determined curiosity & thoughtfulness in a being in so many ways inferior, in one so superior.

And really & truly,—so ought a sermon to end,—we cannot spare any the coarsest muniment of virtue, and the purest sense of justice that lives in any human breast needs a law founded on force as index & remembrancer.

M described E as hobgoblin nature and full of indirections. But he is a good vagabond & knows how to take a walk. The gipsy talent is inestimable in the country, and so rare. In a woman it would be bewitching. M. F. has not a particle, and C. S. only the possibility. And yet this is a relative talent, & to each there doubtless exists a gipsy-maker. I told Hawthorn yesterday that I think every young man at some time inclines to make the experiment of a dare-God & daredevil originality like that of Rabelais. He would jump on the top of the nearest fence & crow. He makes the experiment, but it proves like the flight of pig-lead into the air which cannot cope with the poorest hen. Irresistible custom brings him plump down, and he finds himself instead of odes, writing gazettes & leases. Yet there is imitation & model or suggestion to the very archangels if we knew their history, and if we knew Rabelais's reading we should see the rill of the Rabelais river. Yet his hold of his place in Parnassus is as firm as Homer's. A jester, but his is the jest of the world, & not of Touchstone or Clown or Harlequin. His wit is universal, not accidental, and the anecdotes of the time which made the first butt of the satire & which are lost, are of no importance, as the wit transcends any particular mark, & pierces to permanent relations & interests. His joke will fit any town or community of men.

The style at once decides the high quality of the man. It flows like the river Amazon, so rich, so plentiful, so transparent, & with such long reaches, that longanimity or longsightedness which belongs to the Platos. No sand without lime, no short, chippy, indigent epigrammatist or proverbialist with docked sentences but an exhaustless affluence.

Rabelais born 1483 died 1553

It is only a young man who supposes there is anything new in Wall Street. The merchant who figures there so much to his own satisfaction & to the admiration or fear or hatred of younger or weaker competitors, is a very old business. You shall find him, his way that is of thinking concerning the world & men & property & eating & drinking & marriage & education & religion & government,—the whole concatenation of his opinions, the very shade of their colour, the same laughter, the same knowingness, the same unbelief, & the same ability & taste, in Rabelais & Aristophanes. Panurge was good Wall Street. Pyrrhonism & Transcendentalism are just as old; and I am persuaded that by & by we shall find them in the chemical elements, that excess of oxygen makes the sinner & of hydrogen the saint.

'My evening visitors,' said that excellent Professor Fortinbras, 'if they cannot see the clock, should find the time in my face. As soon as it is nine, I begin to curse them with internal execrations that are minute-guns. And yet,' he added, 'the devil take half-hospitalities, this self protecting civility whose invitations to dinner are determined exclusions from the heart of the inviter, as if he said, I invite you to eat, because I will not converse with you. If he dared only say it, that exclusion would be hospitality of angels, an admission to the thought of his heart.'

M Rotch inclined to speak of the spirit negatively & instead of calling it 'a light,' 'an oracle,' 'a leading,' she said; "when she would do that she should not, she found an obstruction."

—

In these Indian summers, of which we have eight or ten every year, you can almost see the Indians under the trees in the wood. These are the reconciling days which come to graduate the autumn into winter, & to comfort us after the first attacks of the cold. Soothsayers, prediction as well as memory, they look over December & January into the crepuscular lights of March & April.

This feeling I have respecting Homer & Greek, that in this great empty continent of ours stretching enormous almost from pole to pole with thousands of long rivers and thousands of ranges of mountains, the rare scholar who under a farmhouse roof reads Homer & the Tragedies adorns the land. He begins to fill it with wit, to counterbalance the enormous disproportion of unquickened earth. He who first reads Homer in America is its Cadmus & Numa, and a subtle but unlimited benefactor.

Rabelais is not to be skipped in literary history as he is source of so much proverb, story, & joke which are derived from him into all modern books in all languages. He is the Joe Miller of modern literature.

—

We indicate the low ground of Marriage, by using the word Courtship. Religion, heroism teach us never to court, but to obey our affinities. Go to your own place & you shall there find lover & friend.

It is no small thing to know of a man that he does not accept the conventional opinions & practices. That non-conformity will remain a perpetual remembrancer & goad, & every inquirer will have to dispose of him in the first place.

—

Bartlett & the sad saints seem to make the mistake of conversing of sin and contemplating it in their thought always from the point of view of the conscience & not of the intellect; a confusion of thought. Sin seen from the thought is a *diminution*, a *less*; seen from the conscience or will, it is *pravity* or *bad*. The Intellect sees it to be darkness, shade, the absence of light and no essence. The Conscience must esteem it as essence—essential evil. This it is not,—has an objective existence merely, but no subjective.

26 October. Boston is not quite a mean place since in walking yesterday in the street I met George Bancroft, Horatio Greenough, Sampson Reed, Sam Ward, Theodore Parker, George Bradford, & had a little talk with each of them.

I doubt if I have recorded what pleased me so well when J. Very related it, years ago, that at the M'Lean Asylum the patients severally thanked him when he came away, & told him that he had been of great service to them.

—

The strangers have brought with them a complete library of the mystical writers, and the first feeling I have in looking at them is, I am too old for so many books. These are for younger men and what fuel, what food for an open youth is here. Then comes the suggestion of our old plan of the University—but these men though excellent are none of them gifted for leaders. They are admirable instruments for a master's hand, if some instituting Pythagoras, some marshalling Mirabeau, some royal Alfred were here; he could not have better professors than Alcott & Lane & Wright. But they are too desultory, ignorant, imperfect, and whimsical to be trusted for any progress. Excellent springs, worthless regulators.

A. is a singular person, a natural Levite, a priest forever after the order of Melchizedek whom all good persons would readily combine, one would say, to maintain as a priest by voluntary contribution to live in his own cottage, literary, spiritual, and choosing his own methods of teaching & action. But for a founder of a family or institution, I would as soon exert myself to collect money for a madman.

E. is a man full of shallow goodnesses; he has a two inch enthusiasm which is very well-bred & becoming.

Read Cornelius Agrippa this morning on the Vanity of Arts & Sciences. (Born began to be known 1530.) Another specimen of that scribaciousness which distinguishes the immense readers of his time. Robert Burton is the head of the class. They had read infinitely & now must disburthen themselves. So they take any loose general topic like Melancholy or Praise of Science or Praise of Folly, & write & quote without method or end. One must have a great deal of time who can read them. They do not pay you. Now & then out of that affluence of their learning comes a fine sentence from Theophrastus or Boethius and perhaps six or seven in the entire volume, but no high method, no high inspiring state. One cannot afford to read for a few sentences. He will learn more by praying. They are good to read as a dictionary is, for suggestion, and I use them much for that. Plato or Shakspeare are not suggestive; their method is so high & fine, that they take too much possession of us.

—

Yes, there is a wolfish hunger for knowledge, as Paracelsus says, and the scholar is farthest from a priest; he looks to fame not truth. In G.P.B.'s sad talk last Monday on our walk there seemed no thing to live for. All the dancers are out,—out of step, out of the figure.

Today I think the common people very right, and literary justice to be certain. These London Newspapers are sure to be just to each new book. Books full of matter they accept; for the matter is like the atmosphere or bread, & — small thanks to the author of the book. But other books, of thought, of poetry, of taste, in which the author mainly appears, they readily damn, if they are not admirable; and if they are not admirable such books are damnable. But the people—no thanks to them—are always nearly right, have a low sort of right, that of common sense & instinct; & the man of talent & transcendant ingenuity, is wrong.

The Ways to Say

═══

"Waste not thy gifts
 In profitless waiting for the gods' descent"

Would God translate me to his throne, believe
That I should only listen to his words
To further my own aims. p 106

*

Paracelsus is written for a natural-history of a Scholar who following his ambition through great successes at last finds himself arrived at being a quack. He is too proud for this, very impatient of quackery, & tells his friend that he cannot afford to spare the luxury of being sincere to one friend, so unbosoms himself to him and in all scorn & bitterness depicts the quackery & the barrenness of his results and the despair into which he seems sinking. And here the poet leaves him, a disease without a remedy. The laws of disease are beautiful as the laws of health say the physicians & the poet is of that mind & so contents himself with painting with great accuracy & eloquence the symptoms. But the poem is withering, the wolfish hunger for knowledge for its own sake.

Our friends Lane & Wright have brought with them a thousand volumes, making, no doubt, one of the best mystical libraries in the world, and twelve manuscript volumes of J. P. Greaves, and his head in a plaster cast; and with these possessions they think that they have brought England with them; that the England they have left behind is a congregation of nothings, spiritless & therefore not to be taxed or starved or whipped into revolution.

—

Oh if they could take a second step, & a third! The reformer is so confident, that all are erect whilst he puts the finger on your special abuse, & tells you your great want in America. I tell him, yea, but not in America only, but in the Universe ever since it was known, just this defect has appeared.—But when he has anatomized the evil, he will be called out of the room, or have got something else in his head. Remedied it never will be. But C. L. gives a very good account of his conversation with Brownson, who would drive him to an argument. He took his paper & pencil out of his pocket, & asked Brownson to give him the names of the profoundest men in America. Brownson stopped, & gave him one, and then another, & then his own for third. Brownson never will stop & listen, neither in conversation but what is more, not in solitude.

Men of aim must always rule the aimless. And yet there will always be singing-birds.

Union Many voices call for it, Fourier, Owen, Alcott, Channing. And its effect will be magical. That is it which shall renovate institutions & destroy drudgery. But not in the way these men think, in none of their ways. But only in a method that combines union with isolation; silent union, actual separateness; ideal union, actual independence.

If a man will kick a fact out of the window, when he comes back he finds it again in the chimney corner.

from

Journal Z [A]

1842–1843

I should willingly give you an account of one of these conversations. For example we had one yesterday afternoon. I begged A. to paint out his project and he proceeded to say that there should be found a farm of a hundred acres in excellent condition with good buildings, a good orchard & grounds which admitted of being laid out with great beauty; and this should be purchased & given to them, in the first place. I replied, You ask too much. This is not solving the problem; there are hundreds of innocent young persons, whom, if you will thus stablish & endow & protect, will find it no hard matter to keep their innocency. And to see their tranquil household, after all this has been done for them, will in nowise instruct or strengthen me. But he will instruct & strengthen me, who, there where he is, unaided, in the midst of poverty, toil, & traffic, extricates himself from the corruptions of the same & builds on his land a house of peace & benefit, good customs, & free thoughts. But, replied A. how is this to be done, how can I do it who have a wife & family to maintain?

I answered that he was not the person to do it, or he would not ask the question. When he that shall come is born, he will not only see the thing to be done, but invent the life, invent the ways & means of doing it.

The way you would show me, does not commend itself to me as the way of greatness. The Spirit does not stipulate for land & exemption from taxes, but in great straits & want, or even on no land, no where to lay its head, it manages without asking for land, to occupy & enjoy all land, for it is the law by which land exists; it classifies & distributes the whole creation anew. If you ask for application to particulars of this *Way of the Spirit*, I shall say that the cooperation you look for is such cooperation as colleges & all secular institutions look for, money. But the true cooperation comes in another manner. A man quite unexpectedly shows me that which I & all souls looked for, and I cry, 'That is it; take me & mine; I count it my chief good to do in my way that very thing.'—That is real cooperation, unlimited, uncalculating, infinite cooperation.

The Spirit is not half so slow or mediate, or needful of conditions or organs, as you suppose. A few persons in the course of my life have at certain moments appeared to me not measured men of 5 feet, five or ten inches, but large, enormous, indefinite, but these were not great proprietors, nor heads of communities, nor men in office, or in any action which affected large numbers of men, but, on the contrary, nothing could be more private, they were in some want, or affliction, or other relation which called out the emanation of the spirit, which dignified & transfigured them to my eye.

And the good Spirit will burn & blaze in the cinders of your condition, in the drudgeries of your endeavor—in the very process of extricating us from the evils of want & of a bad society.

This fatal fault in the logic of our friends still appears: Their whole doctrine is spiritual, but they always end with saying, Give us much land & money. If I should give them anything, it would be facility & not beneficence. Unless one should say after the maxims of the world: Let them drink their own error to saturation, and this will be the best hellebore.

I know the spirit,—*by its victorious tone.*

An immense force has that man whose part is taken, and who does not wait for society in any part of his conduct of life. Now it is plain of our three adventurers, that this gives them the most of their importance with us, and the deductions to be made from each are the hesitations at the plunge, the reserves which they still make and the reliances & expectations they still cherish on the arm of flesh, the aid of others.

*

A Reformer must be born; he can never be made such by reasons. All reform like all form, is by the grace of God, & not otherwise.

—

You ask, O Theanor, said Amphitryon that I should go forth from this palace with my wife & my children and that you & your family may enter & possess it. The same request in substance has been often made to me before by numbers of persons. Now I also think that I & my wife ought to go forth from this house, & work all day in the fields, & lie at night under some thicket, but I am waiting where I am, only until some god shall point out to me which among all these applicants, yourself or some other, is the rightful claimant.

Transcendentalism is the Saturnalia of faith. It is faith run mad. Nature is transcendental primarily necessarily exists & works & proceeds yet takes no thought for the morrow. Man feels the dignity of the life that exults around him in chemistry & tree & animal & in his own body, heaves the heart & the lungs, & forms the limbs, & makes himself a spectacle to him yet is baulked when he tries to fling himself into this enchanted circle where all is done without degradation.

—

The other night at the Lyceum young R. spoke so well and rose so naturally into eloquence, and over all his manner of speech was spread such an air of innocence that it seemed as if eloquence were so easy that no man should ever again be forgiven for dulness.

Nature tends to a Fact; she will be expressed. Then scholars are her victims of expression.

You who see the artist, the orator, the poet too near, & find them victims of *partiality*, very hollow & haggard, and pronounce them failures, not heroes but quacks, naturally conclude that these arts of theirs are not for man, but are disease. Yet Nature will not bear you out. Irresistible Nature made them such, gave them the first impulse, & makes legions more of such every day: and up to a certain point, you do not blame them. Thus you see without dislike a boy reading in a book, looking at a painting or a cast. Yet these millions who read and behold are only incipient writers & sculptors. Add a little more of that very vitality which now reads & sees, & they will seize the pen & chisel. And if one remembers how innocently he began to be an artist, he sees that Nature joined with his Enemy.

Very hard it is to keep the middle point. It is a very narrow line.

W. said that there was a great deal of deferring and a great deal of wondering & quotation, but of calm affirming very little. Cannot a man only communicate that which he knows? But Nature hates calm system-makers, her methods are saltatory, impulsive. Man lives by pulses, all his organic movements are such, and all chemical & etherial, even seem to be undulatory or alternate. And so with the mind, it antagonizes ever, & gets on so. Our experience would teach us that we thrive by casualties. Our capital experiences have been casual.

—

Ellery said "his verses were proper love poems;" and they were really genuine fruits of a fine, light, gentle, happy intercourse with his friends. C.'s eyes are a compliment to the human race; that steady look from year to year, makes Phidian sculpture & Poussin landscape still real & contemporary, & a poet might well dedicate himself to the fine task of expressing their genius in verse.

I study you as long as you do not study or even know yourself. Where you have gone before me in any inquiry into your merits, I have no care to follow. Self-Praise is the sweetest of all sugars, but it is very bad for the teeth, it destroys beauty. And thus Nature persists to withhold from us the greatest pleasure, the enjoyment of ourselves.

—

There is a comparative innocence in this country & a correspondent health. We do not often see bald boys & grayhaired girls, children victims of gout & apoplexy; the street is not full of nearsighted & deaf people; nor do we see those horrid mutilations & disgusting forms of disease as leprosy & undescribed varieties of plague which European streets exhibit,

stumps of men. Alcott remarked in England that he saw a great deal of hereditary disease & not the innocent New Hampshire complexions which abound here.
How often in Rome & Naples one sees a fragment of a man sitting all day on a stone in some public crossing place to beg with a plate with his head covered, and only some sign of dreadful meaning peeping under his cowl as if day was not to see nor mankind his rottenness.

—

The fine & finest young people despise life, but E. H. & I agree that it is a great excess of politeness in us to look scornful or to cry for company, we to whom a day is a sound & solid good. I am grown by sympathy a little craving & sentimental but leave me alone & I should relish every hour & what it brought me, *the potluck of the day*, as heartily as old Montaigne in his saddle.

Naming, yes that is the office of the newspapers of the world, these famous editors from Moses, Homer, Confucius, & so on, down to Goethe & Kant: they name what the people have already done, & the thankful people say, 'Doctor, 'tis a great comfort to know the disease whereof I die.'

Nature.

Feb. 7. 1843. Nature asked Whether troop & baggage be two things; whether the world is all troop or all baggage, or whether there be any troop that shall not one day be baggage? Easy she thinks it to show you the Universal Soul; we have all sucked that orange; but would you please to mention what is an Individual.

She apologized for trifling with you in your non-age, & adding a little sugar to your milk that you might draw the teat, & a little glory afterward to important lessons, but declared she would never tell you another fib, if you had quite settled it that Buddhism was better than hands & feet, & would keep that conviction in the presence of two persons. As for *far* & *too far*, she wondered what it meant. She admires people who read, & people who look at pictures, but if they read until they write, or look at pictures until they draw them, she curses them up & down. She has the oddest tastes & behaviour. An onion which is all coat she dotes on; and among birds she admires the godwit, but when I hinted that a blue weed grew about my house called *self-heal*, she said, A coxcomb named it; but she teaches cobwebs to resist the tempest, & when a babe's cries drove away a lion, she almost devoured the darling with kisses. She says her office of Dragoman is vacant, though she has been much pestered with applications, & if you have a talent of asking questions, she will play with you all your life; but if you can answer questions, she will propose one, which, if you answer, she will die first. She hates authors, but likes Montaigne.

Webster is very dear to the Yankees because he is a person of very commanding understanding with every talent for its adequate expression. The American, foreigners say, always reasons, and he is the most American of the Americans. They have no abandonment, but dearly love logic, as all their churches have so long witnessed. His external advantages are very rare & admirable; his noble & majestic frame, his breadth & projection of brows, his coalblack hair, his great cinderous eyes, his perfect self possession, and the rich & well modulated thunder of his voice (to which I used to listen sometimes, abstracting myself from his sense merely for the luxury of such noble explosions of sound,) distinguish him above all other men. In a million you would single him out. In England, he made the same impression by his personal advantages as at home, & was called the Great Western. In speech he has a great good sense, —is always pertinent to time & place, and has an eye to the simple facts of nature,—to the place where he is, to the hour of the day, to the Sun in heaven, to his neighborhood, to the sea or to the mountains,—but very sparingly notices these things, & clings closely to the business part of his speech with great gravity & faithfulness. "I do not inflame," he said on one occasion, "I do not exaggerate, I avoid all incendiary allusion." He trusts to his simple strength of statement, in which he excels all men,—for the attention of his assembly. His statement is lucid throughout, & of equal strength. He has great fairness & deserves all his success in debate, for he always carries a point from his adversary by really taking superior ground, as in the Hayne debate. There are no puerilities, no tricks, no academical play in any of his speeches,—they are all majestic men of business. Every one is a first-rate Yankee.

He has had a faithful apprenticeship to his position for he was born in New Hampshire a farmer's son & his youth spent in those hardships & privations which add such edge to every simple pleasure & every liberalizing opportunity. The Almanac does not come unnoticed but is read & committed to heart by the farmer's boys. And when it was announced to him by his father that he would send him to college he could not speak. The struggles. Brothers & sisters in poor men's houses in N. E. are dear to each other & the bringing up of a family involves many sacrifices each for the other.

The faults that shade his character are not such as to hurt his popularity. He is very expensive, and always in debt; but this rather recommends him, as he is known to be generous, & his countrymen make for him the apology of Themistocles that to keep treasure undiminished is the virtue of a chest & not of a man. Then there is in him a large share of good nature & a sort of bonhommie. It is sometimes complained of him that he is a man of pleasure & all his chosen friends are easy epicures & debauchees. But this is after Talleyrand's taste, who said of his foolish wife that he found nonsense very refreshing: so Webster, after he has been pumping his brains in the Courts & the Senate, is no doubt heartily glad to get among cronies & gossips where he can stretch himself at his ease & drink his mulled wine. They also quote as his *three rules* of living; 1. never to pay any debt that can by any possibility be avoided.

2. Never to do anything today that can be put off till tomorrow;

3 Never to do anything himself which he can get any body else to do for him.

All is forgiven to a man of such surpassing intellect, & such prodigious powers of business which have been so long exerted. Then there is no malice in the man, but broad good humor & much enjoyment of the hour; so that Stetson said of him "It is true that he sometimes commits crimes, but without any guilt."

*

A great man is always entitled to the most liberal interpretation and the few anecdotes by which his opponents have most deeply stabbed at his reputation admit of explanation. I can not but think however that his speech at Richmond was made to bear a meaning by his southern backers which he did not intend & I have never forgiven him that he did not say Not so fast, good friends, I did not mean what you say.
He has missed the opportunity of making himself the darling of the American world in all coming time by abstaining from putting himself at the head of the Antislavery interest by standing for New England and for man against the bullying & barbarism of the South.

I should say of him that he was not at all magnetic, but the purest intellect that was ever applied to business. He is Intellect applied to affairs. He is the greatest of lawyers; but a very indifferent statesman for carrying his points. He carries points with the bench, but not with the caucus. No following has he, no troop of friends but those whose intellect he fires. No sweaty mob will carry him on their shoulders. And yet all New England to the remotest farm house, or lumberers' camp in the woods of Maine, delights to tell & hear of anecdotes of his forensic eloquence. What he said at Salem, at the Knapp trial, & how in Boston he looked a witness out of court.—Once, he set his great eyes on him, and searched him through & through. Then as the cause went on, & this prisoner's perjury was not yet called for, he looked round on him as if to see if he was safe & ready for the inquisition he was preparing to inflict on him. The witness felt for his hat, & edged towards the door: a third time he looked on him, & the witness could sit no longer, but seized his opportunity, fled out of court, and could no where be found, such was the terror of those eyes.

—

Queenie makes herself merry with the Reformers who make unleavened bread and are foes to the death to fermentation. Queenie says God made yeast as well as wheat, & loves fermentation just as dearly as he loves vegetation, that the fermentation developes the saccharine element in the grain, & makes it more palatable & more digestible. But that they wish the "pure wheat" & will die but it shall not ferment. Stop dear nature these incessant advances, let me scotch these ever rolling wheels.

Earth Spirit, living, a black river like that swarthy stream which rushes through the human body, is thy nature, demoniacal, warm, fruitful, sad, nocturnal.

—

No 107, Barnum's Hotel, Baltimore.
7 January, 1843—4 hours, 20′ p.m. Here today from Philadelphia. The railroad which was but a toy-coach the other day is now a dowdy lumbering country wagon. Yet it is not prosaic, as people say, but highly poetic, this strong shuttle which shoots across the forest, swamp, rivers, & arms of the sea, binding city to city.—The Americans take to the little contrivance as if it were the cradle in which they were born.

At Phila.
Philosophy shakes hands at last with the simplest methodist & teaches one fact with him, namely, that it is the grace of God,—all grace,—no inch of space left for the impertinence of human will. Every thing is good which a man does naturally, & nothing else. And sitting in railroad cars, happy is he who is moved to talk, & knows nothing about it; & happy he who is moved to sit still, & knows not that he sits still: but I hate him with a perfect hatred who thinks of himself. Let a man hate eddies, hate the sides of the river, but keep the middle of the stream. The hero did nothing apart & odd, but travelled on the highway & went to the same tavern as the whole people, & was very heartily & naturally there, no dainty protected person. I feel very sensibly when I travel, & see many people, that the net amount of man & man does not much vary. Each man is incomparably superior to you in some faculty. All his want of your skill has added to his fitness for that other work which he can do.

—

The Christmas tree with 150 candles on it. A poor little boy had heard how beautiful it was & longed to see one. He did not wish their tree, but wished to see it; & at a large lighted house he plucked up courage & rang the doorbell. But he was very weak & the bell did not easily ring or the children & family were too much occupied with their happy tree to hear, so that nobody came. Presently he knelt down & prayed God that he might see a Christmas tree and he saw a star & presently an angel came down to him & said, "Do you wish, dear boy, to see a Christmas tree? I will show you one." So he laid his hand on the star, & brought it near, & then went & brought a great many stars, & set a tree in the ground & filled the branches with stars. The next day's paper contained the following advertisement. "Found, on the doorstep of a large brick house in —— Square, the dead body of a small boy, very much emaciated & dressed in rags. His death occasioned by starvation."

—

All audiences are just.

I am greatly pleased with the merchants. In railcar & hotel it is common to meet only the successful class, & so we have favorable specimens: but these discover more manly power of all kinds than scholars; behave a great deal better, converse better, and have independent & sufficient manners.

Dreamlike travelling on the railroad. The towns through which I pass between Phila. & New York, make no distinct impression. They are like pictures on a wall. The more, that you can read all the way in the car a French novel.

Feb. 8. As we go along the street, the eyes of all the passengers either ask, ask, continually of all they meet, or else, assert, assert to all. Only rarely do we meet a face which has the balance of expression, neither asking leave to be, nor rudely egoistic, but equally receptive & affirmative. W.A.T. says, that when a man is looked at, he instantly assumes a new expression, and strangers whom he meets every day in the street, grow angry at being regarded.

—

Strict conversation with a friend is the magazine out of which all good writing is drawn.

God delights to isolate us every day & hide from us the past & the future. Quite politely he draws down before us an impenetrable screen of purest sky & another behind us of purest sky. 'Please not to remember,' he says, '& please not to expect.' All great conversation, manners, & action come from a spontaneity which forgets usages and makes the moment great.

People forget that it is the eye which makes the horizon, & the rounding *mind's eye* which makes this or that man a hero or saint or representative of humanity. Jesus this "Providential Man," is a good man on whom several people have agreed that these optical laws shall take effect, we will look at him in the centre of the horizon, & ascribe to him the properties that will attach to any man so seen.

Skepticisms are not gratuitous, but are all limitations of the affirmative statement, and the new philosophy must take them in & make affirmations outside of them just as much as it must include the oldest beliefs.

H. J. apologizes for his unfavorable picture of Mrs B. and I must forget it. I reply that I have no sponge to wipe out the words, and they must lie there written. But I will go see Mrs B. and perhaps she will have the sponge. But I fear such words are of fate.

I know well if you look at any book the human mind will look indigent but when you have enjoyed high conversation, or seen fine works of art, or had any other stimulation which has gone to raise & liberate you, do you not then feel that a new statement is already possible, the elements already exist in many minds around you, & the statement may be made which shall far transcend any written record we yet have. The new statement must comprehend the skepticisms as well as the faiths, and must recognize the lives of men & women, of boys & girls, as no statement yet has done.

Name a friend once too often & we feel that a wrong is done to the friend & to ourselves. Yet you name the good Jesus until I hate the sound of him.

*

All that you say is just as true without the tedious use of that symbol as with it. Let us have a little algebra instead of this trite rhetoric, universal signs instead of these village symbols, and we shall both be gainers.

—

A man going out of Constantinople met the Plague coming in, who said he was sent thither for 20 000 souls. Forty thousand persons were swept off, and when the traveller came back, he met the Plague coming out of the city. "Why did you kill Forty thousand?" he asked. "I only killed twenty," replied the Pest; "Fear killed the rest."

Mr Adams chose wisely & according to his constitution, when on leaving the Presidency he went into Congress. He is no literary old gentleman, but a bruiser, & loves the melée. When they talk about his age & venerableness & nearness to the grave, he knows better, he is like one of those old Cardinals who as quick as he is chosen pope, throws away his crutches & his crookedness, and is as straight as a boy. He is an old roué who cannot live on slops, but must have sulphuric acid in his tea.

There is no line that does not return; I suppose the mathematicians will tell us that what are called straight lines are lines with long curves, but that there is no straight line in nature. If, as you say, we are destroying number by affirming the strict infinite, why then I concede that number also is swallowable, & that one of these days we shall eat it like custard.

—

The world has since the beginning an incurable trick of taking care of itself or every hilltop in America would have counsel to offer. We sit & think how richly ornamented the wide champaign & yonder woodlands to the foot of those blue mountains shall be & meanwhile here are ready & willing thousands strong & teachable who have no land to till. If Government in our present clumsy fashion must go on,—could it not assume the charge of providing each citizen, on his coming of age, with a pair of acres, to enable him to get his bread honestly? Perhaps one day it will be done by the state's assuming to distribute the estates of the dead. In the U. S. almost every State owns so much public land, that it would be practicable to give what they have, & devise a system by which the state should continue to possess a fund of this sort.

—

"It did not seem to me right, but it was not mine to condemn you. Or the time was past when I should have blamed you. All work for me. I & my day. Some persons use my language, but are foreign to me, & others who use a language foreign to me, are very near me. Events are the clothes of the Spirit. Why should we try to steal & strip them. And we know God so, as we know each other by our garments. You flee fast, but the pursuers flee after you as fast." So said to me Mrs Black, in Mulberry Street, N. York.

At the Five Points, I heard a woman swearing very liberally, as she talked with her companions; but when I looked at her face, I saw that she was no worse than other women; that she used the dialect of her class, as all others do, & are neither better nor worse for it; but under this bad costume was the same repose, the same probity as in Broadway. Nor was she misinterpreted by her mates. There is a virtue of vice as well as of virtue.

from
Journal R
1843

I find it easier to read Goethe than Mundt, and it must always be easier to understand a sensible than a weak man in a foreign tongue, because things themselves translate for the one & not for the other. Yet very pleasant is the progress which we make in a new language, the medium through which we explore the thoughts ever growing rarer until at last we become unconscious of its presence in its transparency.

In the growth of the embryo Sir Everard Home, I think, noticed that the evolution was not from one central point, but coactive from three or more points. Life has no memory. That which proceeds in succession might be remembered, but that which is coexistent, or ejaculated from a deeper cause as yet far from becoming conscious, knows not its own tendency. So is it with us, now skeptical, or without unity, because immersed in forms, and effects, all seeming to be of equal yet hostile value; and now religious, whilst in the reception of spiritual law. Bear with these distractions, with this coetaneous growth of the parts; they will one day be *members*, & obey one will.

Ellery's verses should be called poetry for poets. They touch the fine pulses of thought & will be the cause of more poetry & of verses more finished & better turned than themselves: but I cannot blame the North Americans & Knickerbockers if they should not suspect his genius. When the rudder is invented for the balloon, railroads will be superseded. And when Ellery's muse finds an aim, whether some passion, or some fast faith, any kind of string on which all these wild & sometimes brilliant beads can be strung, we shall have a poet. Now he *fantasies* merely as *dilettanti* in music. He breaks faith continually with the intellect. The sonnet has merits, fine lines, gleams of deep thought; well worth sounding, worth studying, if only

I could confide that he had any steady meaning before him, that he kept faith with himself; but I fear that he changed his purpose with every verse; was led up & down, to this or that, with the exigences of the rhyme, and only wanted to write & rhyme some what, careless how or what, & stopped when he came to the end of the paper. He breaks faith with the reader, wants integrity.

Yet for poets it will be a better book than whole volumes of Bryant & Campbell. Miss Peabody has beautiful colours to sell, but her shop has no attraction for house builders & merchants: Mr Allston and Mr Cheney will probably find the way to it.

A man of genius is priveleged only as far as he is a genius. His dulness is as insupportable as any other dulness. Only success will justify a departure and a license.

But Ellery has freaks which are entitled to no more charity than the dulness & madness of others which he despises.
He uses a license continually which would be just in oral improvisation, but is not pardonable in written verses. He fantasies on his piano.

E. H. said, that he was a wood-elf which one of the maids in a story fell in love with; & then grew uneasy, desiring that he might be baptised. M. said, he reminded one of a great genius with a little wretched boy trotting beside him.

—

The one thing which I should wish to know of any new great man of whom I should hear, would be, how he got his living? For that is the smallness of the present race, that they get their living by vicious methods, & have not wisdom enough to use pure means.

The fish lives well enough in the deeps but unhappily must come to the top for air, then is he harpooned or ensnared. The bird lives safely enough in the air but unhappily must descend to the ground for food, then the cat & the snake are stronger than he.

Jock could not eat rice, because it came west, nor molasses because it came north, nor put on leathern shoes, because of the methods by which leather was procured, nor indeed wear a woolen coat. But Dick gave him a gold eagle that he might buy wheat & rye, maple sugar & an oaken chest, and said, This gold piece, unhappy Jock! is molasses, & rice, & horse hide & sheepskin.

SHANG MUNG.

"I fully understand language, (or doctrines), & nourish well my vast flowing vigour," said Mencius.

"I beg to ask what you call vast flowing vigour," said Kung Sun Chow.

Mencius replied, "The explanation is difficult. This vigour is supremely great, and in the highest degree unbending; nourish it correctly, & do it no injury, & it will fill up the vacancy between heaven & earth. This vigour accords with & assists justice and reason, & leaves no hunger (or deficiency). It is produced by an accumulation of righteous deeds, & not by a few accidental acts. If our actions do not give pleasure to our hearts, they leave an aching void."

Criticism

There are limits to criticism. When a Work is produced by men as the Shakspearian drama, the Gothic Cathedral, the Egyptian cyclopean architecture, the ladder is drawn up and its history is not to be searched out. It can only be understood by the idea that produced it, & we cannot by any struggles come into that. So the Gothic Cathedral & the Shakspeare perfection is as wild & unaccountable as a geranium or a rabbit or an ornithorhynchus. It is done, & we must go to work & do something else, that undone something which is now hinting & working & impatient here in & around us.

The Eleusinian Mysteries, the Egyptian architecture, the Greek sculpture show one thing plain & clear, that there always were seeing knowing men in the planet, who heard from the ages & spoke to the ages. The world is full of masonic ties, of guilds & secret or public legions of honor. That of Scholars is one; that of Gentlemen fraternizing with the upper class of every country & every culture, whether English, Russian, Chinese, Malay, Polynesian, or Esquimaux, is another and the World itself is directly degraded into a means & convenience before an end so delicious and lofty as this of nobility, or the greatest superiority of vigour & moral & intellectual worthiness. Goethe's Fraternity in Wilhelm Meister is a fable of the world.

Visiting. We outgrow our books, our preachers, & at last our society, o frightful! & when we go to the house of a stranger we only find the old air, the old daylight, which we left at home; for the man who was wont to give his quality to the surrounding nature is negative & insignificant.

The coldness continually increasing & superficialness continually thinning of our Unitarian faith justified Dr Beecher's remark on Henry Ware's book called Formation of the Christian Character, that "it was the best counterfeit he had met with."

Drawing, M R said from Mr Cheney, was only a good eye for distances; and the descriptive talent in the poet seems to depend on a certain lake-like passiveness to receive the picture of the whole landscape in its native proportions, uninjured, & then with sweet heedfulness, the caution of love, to transfer it to the tablet of language.

Health

Health is the most objective of subjects. The Veeshnoo Sarma said, "It is the same to him who wears a shoe as if the whole earth were covered with leather." So I spread my health over the whole world & make it strong, happy, & serviceable. To the sick man, the world is a medicine chest.

Poet.

Poets do not appear to advantage abroad, for, sympathetic persons, in their instinctive effort to possess themselves of the natures of others, lose their own, & exhibit suppliant manners, whilst men of less susceptibility stand erect around him like castles.

Poet Man-Woman

It is true that when a man writes poetry, he appears to assume the high feminine part of his nature. We clothe the poet therefore in robes & garlands, which are proper to woman. The Muse is feminine. But action is male. And a king is dressed almost in feminine attire.

The philosophers at Fruitlands have such an image of virtue before their eyes, that the poetry of man & nature they never see; the poetry that is in man's life, the poorest pastoral clownish life; the light that shines on a man's hat, in a child's spoon, the sparkle on every wave & on every mote of dust, they see not.

Lectures.

> "Aristo said, that neither a bath nor a lecture did signify any thing unless they scoured & made men clean."
>
> 3 P 339

Pride is a great convenience; so much handsomer & cheaper than vanity, but proud people are intolerably selfish, & the vain are gentle & giving.

Translations.

I thank the translators & it is never my practice to read any Latin, Greek, German, Italian, scarcely any French book, in the original which I can procure in an English translation. I like to be beholden to the great metropolitan English speech, the sea which receives tributaries from every region under heaven, the Rome of nations, and I should think it in me as much folly to read all my books in originals when I have them rendered for me in my mother's speech by men who have given years to that labor, as I should to swim across Charles River when ever I wished to go to Charlestown.

August 17th Webster at Concord.

Mr Webster loses nothing by comparison with brilliant men in the legal profession: he is as much before them as before the ordinary lawyer. At least I thought he appeared among these best lawyers of the Suffolk bar, like a schoolmaster among his boys. His wonderful organization, the perfection of his elocution, and all that thereto belongs, voice, accent, intonation, attitude, manner, are such as one cannot hope to see again in a century; then he is so thoroughly simple & wise in his rhetoric. Understanding language, & the use of the positive degree, all his words tell, and his rhetoric is perfect, so homely, so fit, so strong. Then he manages his matter so well, he hugs his fact so close, & will not let it go, & never indulges in a weak flourish, though he knows perfectly well how to make such exordiums & episodes & perorations as may give perspective to his harangue, without in the least embarrassing his plan or confounding his transitions. What is small, he shows as small, & makes the great, great. In speech he sometimes roars. And his words are like blows of an axe. His force of personal attack is terrible, he lays out his strength so directly in honest blows, and all his powers of voice, arm, eye, & whole man are so heartily united & bestowed on the adversary that he cannot fail to be felt.

His "Christian religion" is always weak, being merely popular. And so most of his religion. Thus he spoke of the value of character: it was simply mercantile: it was to defend a man in criminal prosecutions, & the like; and bear him up against the inspection of all *but* the Almighty &c ! and in describing Wyman's character, he said, he wanted that sternness of Christian principle which teaches to "avoid even the appearance of evil." And one feels every moment that he goes for the actual world, & never one moment for the ideal. He is the triumph of the understanding and is undermined & supplanted by the Reason for which yet he is so good a witness, being all the time fed therefrom & his whole nature & faculty presupposing that, that I felt as if the children of Reason might gladly see his success as a homage to their law, & regard him as a poor rude soldier hired for sixpence a day to fight their battles.* Perhaps it was this, perhaps it was a mark of having outlived some of my once finest pleasures that I found no appetite to return to the Court in the afternoon & hear the conclusion of his argument. The green fields on my way home were too fresh & fair, & forbade me to go again.
His splendid wrath, when his eyes become fires, is good to see, so intellectual it is, and the wrath of the fact and cause he espouses, & not at all personal to himself.

E.R.H. said, nothing amused him more than to see Mr Webster adjourn the Court every day, which he did by rising, &

*I looked at him sometimes with the same feeling with which I see one of these strong paddies on the railroad.

taking his hat & looking the Judge coolly in the face; who then bade the Crier adjourn the Court.

Choate Webster

R. C. is a favorite with the bar and a nervous fluent speaker with a little too much fire for the occasion, yet with a certain temperance in his fury & a perfect self-command: but he uses the superlative degree, and speaks of affairs altogether too rhetorically. This property of $300 000, the property of a Bank, he spoke of as "vast," and quite academically. And there was no perspective in his speech. The transitions were too slight & sudden. But the cast-iron tones of the man of men, the perfect machine that he is for arguing a case, dwarfed instantly Choate and all the rest of the learned Counsellors.

Webster behaves admirably well in society. These village parties must be dishwater to him, yet he shows himself just good-natured, just nonchalant enough, & has his own way without offending any one or losing any ground. He told us that he never read by candle light.

—

Swedenborg taught that the whole was made up of similars, the liver of little livers, the heart of little hearts, & so on, and Webster seems to be composed of little Websters, such power & admirable intellect is expressed from every feature of his person, & from every attitude & act. He quite fills our little town, & I doubt if I shall get settled down to writing, until he is well gone from the county. He is a natural Emperor of men: they remark in him the kingly talent of remembering persons accurately, & knowing at once to whom he has been introduced, & to whom not.

Webster

He has lately bought his father's farm in Franklin, (formerly Salisbury) N.H. as Waller the poet wished to buy his birthplace Winchmore-Hill, saying to his cousin Hampden "A stag when he is hunted & near spent, always returns home."

E. H. says that she talked with him as one likes to go behind the Niagara Falls, so she tried to look into these famed caverns

of eyes, & see how deep they were, and the whole man was magnificent.
Mr Choate told her, that he should not sleep for a week when a cause like this was pending, but that when they met in Boston on Saturday p.m. to talk over the matter, the rest of them were wide awake, but Mr Webster went fast asleep amidst the consultation.

E. H. said that in Mr W's case, modesty ceased to be a virtue: She was glad to see one man who carried himself erect & grandly, whilst all the rest ducked & were ashamed of themselves.

—

It seems to me the Quixotism of criticism to quarrel with Webster because he has not this or that fine evangelical property. He is no saint, but the wild olive wood, ungrafted yet by grace, but according to his lights a very true & admirable man. His expansiveness seems to be necessary to him. Were he too prudent a Yankee it would be a sad deduction from his magnificence. I only wish he would never truckle, I do not care how much he spends.
Webster's force is part of nature & the world, like any given amount of azote or electricity. He works with that closeness of adhesion to the matter in hand which a joiner or a blacksmith uses, & the same quiet but sure feeling of right to his place that the oak or the rock have to theirs. Other men seem dilettanti, but he is a piece of the world. After all his great talents have been told, there remains that perfect propriety, which belongs to every world-genius, which animates all the details of action & speech with the character of the whole so that his beauties of detail are endless. Great is life. ABW also.

—

Webster

Webster's power like that of all great masters is not in some excellent details, but is total. He has a great & everywhere equal propriety. He has the propriety, the power of countenance & the gravity of a Sachem. But he is so much a piece of nature & to be admired like an oak or an elephant, that I have set his Concord visit in the same line of events with the Herr Driesbach & his caravan which came hither the foregoing week. Then was shown the power of cats. The tiger & the leopard whose body is like a wave in its perpetual flexility.

I cannot consent to compare him with his competitors but when the Clay men & Van Buren men and the Calhoun men have had all their way & all their political objections have been conceded, & they have settled their little man whichever it be on the top of the martin box of state; then & not before will we begin to state the claims of this world's-man, this strong paddy of the times & laws & state, to his place in history.

—

Queenie's epitaph: "Do not wake me."

—

It is a pathetic thing to meet a friend prepared to love you, to whom yet, from some inaptitude, you cannot communicate yourself with that grace & power which only love will allow. You wish to repay his goodness by showing him the dear relations that subsist between you & your chosen friends but you feel that he cannot conceive of you whom he knows so slow & cold, under these sweet & gentle aspects.

Confide in your power whether it be to be a wet nurse or a woodsawyer, lion-taming Von Amburgh, or Stewart maker of steam candy, keep your shop, magnify your office. Fear smears our work & ignorance gilds our neighbor's, but the sure years punish our faint heartedness.

Captain Rich one day told me of a pilot who in letting go the cable that made fast his vessel to the wharf, had meant to let her swing round in a certain direction to come into the channel; but after she was loose, had changed his plan, & brought her into her course by a different method; and it happened, that a smaller vessel, deceived by his first demonstrations, lay in his way & was run into & injured. The pilot was broken, or lost his "branch" (I think they call it,) for this fault. The story is very instructive to artists. One of these spiritual chatterboxes broke in & ended all.

—

March 23. Two brave chanticleers go up & down stripping the plumes from all the fine birds, showing that all are not in the best health. It makes much unhappiness on all sides; much crowing it occasions on the part of the two cockerels who so shrewdly discover & dismantle all the young beaux of the aviary. But alas the two valiant cocks who strip, are no better than those who are stripped, only they have sharper beak & talons. In plain prose, I grieved so much to hear the most intellectual youth I have met, C. N., so disparaged, & our good & most deserving scholar T. P. threatened as a morsel to be swallowed when he shall come tomorrow, & all this by my brave friends who are only brave, not helpful, not rejoicing, not humble, not loving, not creative,—that I said, Cursed is preaching,—the better it is, the worse. A preacher is a bully: I who have preached so much,—by the help of God will never preach more.

We want the fortification of an acknowledgment of the good in us. The girl is the least part of herself; God is in the girl. That is the reason why fools can be so beloved by sages, that, under all the corsets & infirmities, is life, & the revelation of Reason & of Conscience.

Manners

To live with, good taste seems more necessary than freedom from vice. One could easier live with a person who did not respect the truth, or chastity, than with a filthy person.

Margaret.

A pure & purifying mind, selfpurifying also, full of faith in men, & inspiring it. Unable to find any companion great enough to receive the rich effusions of her thought, so that her riches are still unknown & seem unknowable. It is a great joy to find that we have underrated our friend, that he or she is far more excellent than we had thought. All natures seem poor beside one so rich, which pours a stream of amber over all objects clean & unclean that lie in its path, and makes that comely & presentable which was mean in itself. We are taught by her plenty how lifeless & outward we were, what poor Laplanders burrowing under the snows of prudence & pedantry. Beside her friendship, other friendships seem trade, and by the firmness with which she treads her upward path, all mortals are convinced that another road exists than that which their feet know. The wonderful generosity of her sentiments pours a contempt on books & writing at the very time when one asks how shall this fiery picture be kept in its glow & variety for other eyes. She excels other intellectual persons in this, that her sentiments are more blended with her life; so the expression of them has greater steadiness & greater clearness. I have never known any example of such steady progress from stage to stage of thought & of character. An inspirer of courage, the secret friend of all nobleness, the patient waiter for the realization of character, forgiver of injuries, gracefully waiving aside folly, & elevating lowness,—in her presence all were apprised of their fettered estate & longed for liberation, of ugliness & longed for their beauty; of meanness, & panted for grandeur.

Her growth is visible. All the persons whom we know, have reached their height, or else their growth is so nearly at the same rate with ours, that it is imperceptible, but this child inspires always more faith in her. She rose before me at times into heroical & godlike regions, and I could remember no superior women, but thought of Ceres, Minerva, Proserpine, and the august ideal forms of the Foreworld. She said that no man gave such invitation to her mind as to tempt her to a full expression; that she felt a power to enrich her thought with such wealth & variety of embellishment as would no doubt be tedious to such as she conversed with. And there is no form that does seem to wait her beck,—dramatic, lyric, epic, passionate, pictorial, humourous.

She has great sincerity, force, & fluency as a writer, yet her powers of speech throw her writing into the shade. What method, what exquisite judgment, as well as energy, in the selection of her words, what character & wisdom they convey! You cannot predict her opinion. She sympathizes so fast with all forms of life, that she talks never narrowly or hostilely nor betrays, like all the rest, under a thin garb of new words, the old droning castiron opinions or notions of many years standing. What richness of experience, what newness of dress, and fast as Olympus to her principle. And a silver eloquence, which inmost Polymnia taught. Meantime, all the pathos of sentiment and riches of literature & of invention and this march of character threatening to arrive presently at the shores & plunge into the sea of Buddhism & mystic trances, consists with a boundless fun & drollery, with light satire, & the most entertaining conversation in America.

Her experience contains, I know, golden moments, which, if they could be fitly narrated, would stand equally beside any histories of magnanimity which the world contains; and whilst Dante's 'Nuova Vita' is almost unique in the literature of sentiment, I have called the imperfect record she gave me of two of her days, 'Nuovissima Vita.'

I confess that Plato seems to me greatly more literary than strong—weak inasmuch as he is literary. Shakspeare is not literary, but the strong earth itself. Veracity is that which we want in poets that they shall say how it was with them & not what might be said.

A working King is one of the best symbols. Alfred & Ulysses are such. And we see them now & then in society;—oftener off the throne, of course, than on it. This is the right country for them.

A chamber of flame in which the martyr passes, is more magnificent than any royal apartment: and this martyr palace may be built up on any waste place instantly.

A scholar is a diamond-merchant.

Persons are fine things, but they cost so much! for *thee* I must pay *me*.

Fine constellation of people; rare force of character & wealth of truth; they ought to cluster & shine & illuminate the nation & the nations. A. said reasonable words about the Dial, that it ought to be waited for by all the newspapers & journals. The Abolitionists ought to get their leading from it, & not be able to shun it as they do. It should lead. Here the sceptre is offered us, & we refuse it from poorness of spirit.

When I see what fine people we have, I think it a sort of King Réné period: there is no doing, but rare & shrilling prophecy from bands of competing minstrels & the age shall not sneak out, but affirm all the beauty & truth in its heart.

"Dial has not piety."

The same persons should not constitute a standing Committee on Reform. A man may say 'I am the chief of sinners,' but once. He is already damned, if having come once to the insight of that condition, he remains there to say it again. But the Committee on Reform should be made of new persons every day: of those just arrived at the power of comparing the state of society with their own daily expanding spirit. Fatal to discuss reform weekly! The poorest poet or young beginner in the fine arts hesitates to speak of the design he wishes to execute, lest it die in your cold fingers. And this art of life has the same pudency & will not be exposed.

It is a great joy to get away from persons, & live under the dominion of the Multiplication Table.

Life

Form always stands in dread of power. What the devil will he do next?

—

The conversation turned upon the state & duties of Woman. As always, it was historically considered, & had a certain falseness so. For to me today, Woman is not a degraded person with duties forgotten, but a docile daughter of God with her face heavenward endeavouring to hear the divine word & to convey it to me.

Nuova Vita
Nuovissima Vita

I read again the verses of M. with the new commentary of beautiful anecdotes she had given, freshly in my mind. Of course, the poems grew golden, the twig blossomed in my hands: but a poem should not need its relation to life to explain it; it should be a new life, not still half engaged in the soil like the new created lions in Eden.

—

E. H says, "I love H., but do not like him." Young men like H. T. owe us a new world & they have not acquitted the debt: for the most part, such die young, & so dodge the fulfilment. One of our girls (M.A.W.) said, that H. never went through the kitchen without colouring.

—

MONTAIGNE

In Roxbury, in 1825, I read Cotton's translation of Montaigne. It seemed to me as if I had written the book myself in some former life, so sincerely it spoke my thought & experience. No book before or since was ever so much to me as that. How I delighted afterwards in reading Cotton's dedication to Halifax, and the reply of Halifax which seemed no words of course, but genuine suffrages. Afterwards I went to Paris in 1833 & to the Pere le Chaise & stumbled on the tomb of , who, said the stone, formed himself to Virtue on the Essays of Montaigne. Afterwards, John Sterling wrote a loving criticism on Montaigne in the Westminster Review, with a journal of his own pilgrimage to Montaigne's estate & chateau,—and soon after Carlyle writes me word that this same lover of Montaigne is a lover of me. Now, I have been introducing to his genius, two of my friends, James & Tappan, who both warm to him as their brother. So true is S.G.W.'s saying that "all whom he knew, met."

—

The Brook farm Community is an expression in plain prose & actuality of the theory of impulse. It contains several bold & consistent philosophers both men & women who carry out the theory; Odiously enough, inasmuch as this centripetence of theirs is balanced by no centrifugence; this wish to obey impulse, is guarded by no old old Intellect—or that which knows metes & bounds. The young people who have been faithful to this their testimony, have lived a great deal in a short time, but have come forth with shattered constitutions. It is an intellectual Sans-culottism. Happily C.K.N. & G.P.B. have been there & their presence could not but be felt as sanitary & retentive. C.K.N., I hear, was greatly respected & his conduct even in trifles observed & imitated. The quiet, retreating, demoniacal youth. N. H. said that Burton felt the presence of C.K.N. all the time.

I read in S.G.W.'s Chinese book the other day, of bards, many sentences purporting that bards love wine. Tea & coffee are my wine. And I have finer & lighter wines than these. But some nectar an intellectual man will naturally use. For he will soon learn the secret that beside the energy of his conscious intellect, his intellect is capable of new energy by abandonment to the nature of things, that beside his privacy of power as an individual man he has a great public power on which he can draw by only letting himself go; by unlocking at all risks his human doors & suffering the inundation of the etherial tides to roll & circulate through him; then he is caught up into the life of the Universe, his speech is thunder, his thought is law, & his words as universally intelligible as the plants & animals. All persons avail themselves of such means as they can to add this extraordinary power to their normal powers. One finds it in music, one in war, one in great pictures or sculpture; one in travelling; one in conversation; in politics, in mobs, in fires, in theatres, in love, in science; in animal intoxication. I take many stimulants & often make an art of my inebriation. I read Proclus for my opium, it excites my imagination to let sail before me the pleasing & grand figures of gods & daemons & demoniacal men. I hear of rumors rife among the most ancient gods, of azonic gods who are itinerants; of daemons with fulgid eyes, of the unenvying & exuberant will of the gods; the aquatic gods, the plain of truth, the meadow, the nutriment of the gods, the paternal port, & all the rest of the Plutonic rhetoric quoted as household words. By all these & so many "rare & brave words" I am filled with hilarity & spring, my heart dances, my sight is quickened, I behold shining relations between all beings, and am impelled to write and almost to sing. I think one would grow handsome who read Proclus much & well.

But of this inebriation I spoke of, it is an old knowledge that Intellect by its relation to what is prior to Intellect is a god. This is inspiration.

They speak of the gods with such pictorial distinctness often that one would think they had actually been present, Swedenborg-like, at the Olympic feasts. e.g. "this is that which emits the intelligible light, that, when it appeared, astonished the intellectual gods & made them admire their father, as Orpheus says."

—

Much poor talk concerning woman which at least had the effect of revealing the true sex of several of the party who usually go disguised in the form of the other sex. Thus Mrs B is a man. The finest people marry the two sexes in their own person. Hermaphrodite is then the symbol of the finished soul. It was agreed that in every act should appear the married pair: the two elements should mix in every act.

To me it sounded hoarsely the attempt to prescribe didactically to woman her duties. Man can never tell woman what her duties are: he will certainly end in describing a man in female attire, as Harriet Martineau a masculine woman solved her problem of woman. No. Woman only can tell the heights of feminine nature, & the only way in which man can help her, is by observing woman reverentially & whenever she speaks from herself & catches him in inspired moments up to a heaven of honor & religion, to hold her to that point by reverential recognition of the divinity that speaks through her.

I can never think of woman without gratitude for the bright revelations of her best nature which have been made to me unworthy. The angel who walked with me in younger days, shamed my ambition & prudence by her generous love in our first interview. I described my prospects; She said, I do not wish to hear of your prospects.

April 10. The slowly retreating snow blocks the roads & woodpaths & shuts me in the house. But yesterday the warm southwind drew me to the top of the hill like the dove from the ark to see if these white waters were abated, & there was place for the foot. The grass springs up already between the holes in the snow, and I walked along the knolls & edges of the hill wherever the winter bank was melted but I thrust my cane into the bank two feet perpendicular. I greeted the well known pinegrove which I could not reach; the pine tops seemed to cast a friendly gold-green smile of acquaintance toward me, for it was in my heart that I had not yet quite got home from my late journey, until I had revisited & rejoined these vegetable daemons. The air was kind & clear, the sky southward was full of comets, so white & fanshaped & ethereal lay the clouds as if the late visit of this foreign wonder had set the fashion for the humbler meteors. And all around me the new come sparrows, robins, bluebirds & blackbirds were announcing their arrival with great spirit.

—

Daniel Webster is a great man with a small ambition. Nature has built him & holds him forth as a sample of the heroic mould to this puny generation. He was virtual president of the United States from the hour of the Speech on Foot's Resolutions in the U. S. Senate in 182 ; being regarded as the Expounder of the Constitution & the Defender of Law. But this did not suffice; he wished to be an Officer, also; wished to add a title to his name, & be a President. That ruined him. He should have learned from the Chinese that "It has never been the case that when a man in a place where no mulberry trees yet grew, could cause the aged to wear silks, & where there were no breeders of fowls or hogs or sheep could cause the aged to eat flesh & the young did not suffer hunger or cold,—he did not become Emperor."

—

April 17th. How sincere & confidential we can be, saying all that lies in the mind, & yet go away feeling that we have spun a rope of sand, that all is yet unsaid, from the incapacity of the parties to know each other *although they use the same words.* My companion assumes to know my mood & habit of thought, and so we go on from explanation to explanation, until all is said which words can, & we leave matters just as they were at first, because of that vicious assumption. Is it that every man believes every other to be a fatal partialist, & himself an universalist? I fear this is the history of our conversation at the cottage yesterday, when we all behaved well & frankly as we could. I endeavoured to show my good men that I loved every thing by turns & nothing long; that I loved the Centre, but doated on the superficies, that I loved Man, but men seemed to me mice & rats, that I revered saints but woke up glad that the dear old Devil kept his state in Boston, that I was glad of men of every gift & nobility, but would not live in their arms. Now could they but once understand that I loved to know that they existed & heartily wished them Godspeed, yet out of my poverty of life & thought, had no word or welcome for them when they came to see me and could well consent to their living in another town for any claim that I felt on them—it would be great satisfaction. Not this, but something like this, I said, and then, as the discourse, as so often, touched character, I added, that they were both intellectual, they assumed to be substantial & central, to be the thing they said, but were not, but only intellectual, or the scholars, the learned, of the Spirit or Central Life. If they were that, if the centres of their life were coincident with the Centre of Life, I should bow the knee, I should accept without gainsaying all that they said, as if I had said it: just as our saint (though morbid) Jones Very had affected us with what was best in him, but that I felt in them the slight dislocation of these Centres which allowed them to stand aside & speak of these facts *knowingly.* Therefore I was at liberty to look at them not as the commanding fact but as one of the whole circle of facts. They did not like pictures, marbles, woodlands, & poetry; I liked all these & Lane & Alcott too, as one figure more in the various landscape.

And now, I said, will you not please to pound me a little, before I go, just by way of squaring the account, that I may not remember that I alone was saucy. Alcott contented himself with quarreling with the injury done to greater qualities in my company, by the tyranny of my taste;—which certainly was very soft pounding. And so I parted from the divine lotos-eaters.

—

Carlyle esteems all living men mice & rats, but that is one of the conditions of his genius. Take away that feeling, & you would possibly make him dumb.

Beauty fluxional

Beauty, all agree, is the medium state, the balance of expression, which means among other things, *just ready to flow*, or be metamorphosed into all other forms. Any fixedness, any heaping or concentration on one feature, a long nose, a sharp chin, a hump back, is the reverse of *flowing*.

—

Art

Orestes supplicates Apollo whilst the Furies sleep on the threshold in Flaxman's drawing. The face of the God expresses a shade of regret & compassion for the sufferer, but is filled with the calm conviction of disparity & irreconcileableness of the two spheres. He is born into other politics, into the eternal & beautiful; the man at his feet asks for his interest in turmoils of the earth, into which his nature cannot enter. And the Eumenides there lying express pictorially this disparity. The god is surcharged with his divine destiny.

—

2 May. Yesterday I read an old file of Aunt Mary's letters, & felt how she still gains by all comparison with later friends. Never any gave higher counsels, as E. H. most truly said, nor played with all the household incidents with more wit & humour. My life and its early events never look trivial in her letters, but full of eyes, & acquire deepest expression.

The kitchen which yields fire & water to the whole house, will be the most frequented room.

In America out of doors all seems a market; in-doors, an air tight stove of conventionalism. Every body who comes into the house savors of these precious habits, the men, of the market; the women, of the custom. In every woman's conversation & total influence mild or acid lurks the *conventional devil.* They look at your carpet, they look at your cap, at your saltcellar, at your cook & waiting maid, conventionally,—to see how close they square with the customary cut in Boston & Salem & New Bedford. But M.M.E and E. H. do not bring into a house with them a platoon of conventional devils.

7 May. Yesterday G.P.B. walked & talked of the community, and cleared up some of the mists which gossip had made; and expressed the conviction shared by himself & his friends there, that plain dealing was the best defence of manners & morals between the sexes. I suppose that the danger arises whenever bodily familiarity grows up without a spiritual intimacy. The reason why there is purity in marriage, is, that the parties are universally near & helpful, & not only near bodily. If their wisdoms come near & meet, there is no danger of passion. Therefore the remedy of impurity is to come nearer.—

G. also described the faith of his friend S. S. that there was no need of trying to dodge a cross, if you fled it now, it would meet you elsewhere.

—

At Brook-Farm this peculiarity, that there is no head. In every family, a paterfamilias; in every factory, a foreman; in a shop, a master; in a boat, a boatswain; but in Brook Farm, no authority, but each master & mistress of their own actions—happy hapless Sansculottes.

Yesterday English visitors, and I waited all day when they should go.

If we could establish the rule that each man was a guest in his own house, and when we had shown our visitors the passages of the house, the way to fire, to bread, & water, & thus made them as much at home as the inhabitant, did then leave them to the accidents of intercourse, & went about our ordinary business, a guest would no longer be formidable.

At Brook-Farm again, I understand that the authority of G. & S. R. is felt unconsciously by all: and this is ground of regret to individuals, who see that this patriarchal power is thrown into the conservative scale. But G. & S. R are the only ones who have identified themselves with the community. They have married it & they are it. The others are experimenters who will stay by this if it thrives, being always ready to retire, but these have burned their ships, and are entitled to the moral consideration which this position gives. The young people agree that they have had more rapid experiences than elsewhere befel them, have lived faster.

—

Ellery has reticency, Carlyle has not. How many things this book of Carlyle gives us to think. It is a brave grappling with the problem of the times, no luxurious holding aloof as is the custom of men of letters who are usually bachelors & not husbands in the state, but Literature here has thrown off his gown & descended into the open lists. *The gods are come among us in the likeness of men.* An honest Iliad of English woes. Who is he that can trust himself in the fray? Only such as cannot be familiarized, but nearest seen & touched is not seen & touched, but remains inviolate, inaccessible, because a higher interest, the politics of a higher sphere bring Him here & environ him, as the Ambassador carries his country with him. Love protects him from profanation. What a book this in its relation to English privileged estates! How shall Queen Victoria read this? How the Primate & Bishops of England? how the lords? how the Colleges? how the rich? & how the poor? Here is a book as full of treason as an egg is full of meat, and every lord & lordship & high form & ceremony of English conservatism tossed like a foot-ball into the air & kept in the air with merciless rebounds & kicks & yet not a word in the book is punishable by statute. The wit has eluded all official zeal, and yet these dire jokes, these cunning thrusts, this flaming sword of cherubim waved high in air illuminates the whole horizon & shows to the eyes of the Universe every wound it inflicts. Worst of all for the party attacked, it bereaves them beforehand of all sympathy, by anticipating the plea of poetic & humane conservatism and impressing the reader with the conviction that Carlyle himself has the truest love for everything old & excellent & a genuine respect for the basis of truth in those whom he exposes. *Gulliver among the Lilliputians.*

This book comes so near to life & men, that one can hardly help looking ahead a little & inquiring whether this strong brain will always be shut up in a scholar's library, whether the most intelligent Englishman will nourish no ambition to do that which he describes, & when the hour comes that these volleys of pungent counsels shall have got thoroughly sunk into the ear & heart of the population & the population is Carlyle's, whether our vigorous Samson will not have a ruler's part to play. Yet nobody, neither law-sergeant nor newspaper yet cries "Cromwell."

—

Literature = eavesdropping

—

My farm only holds the world together.

Our life is trivial & we shun to record it.

A trick of nature, a good deal of buz & somewhere a result slipped magically in. Nothing great came to us calculated. Every ship beautiful but that we sail in. Every roof lifted is full of tragedy & moaning women; & the men ask, What is the news? as if the old were so bad. And yet I never see a quite unmusical character. Beautiful results are everywhere lodged.

All intercourse is random & remote, yet what fiery & consoling friendships we have, the Ideal journeying alway with us, the heaven without rent or seam. We never know while the days pass which day is valuable. The surface is vexation but the serene lies underneath.

Nature lives by making fools of us all, adds a drop of nectar to every man's cup.

—

May 19. A youth of the name of Ball, a native as he told me of Concord, came to me yesterday who towered away in such declamatory talk that at first I thought it rhodomontade & we should soon have done with each other. But he turned out to be a prodigious reader, and writer too, (for he spoke of whole volumes of prose & poetry barreled away) and discovered great sagacity & insight in his criticisms,—a great impatience of our strait New England ways, and a wish to go to the Ganges, or at the least to live in Greece & Italy. There was little precision in his thinking, great discontent with metaphysics and he seemed of a musical, rather than a mathematical structure. With a little more repose of thought, he would be a great companion. He thought very humbly of most of his contemporaries & Napoleon he thought good to turn periods with, but that he could see through him; but Lord Bacon he could not pardon for not seeing Shakspeare, for said he, "as many Lord Bacons as could stand in Concord could find ample room in Shakspeare's brain," and Pope's mean thought & splendid rhetoric he thought "resembled rats' nests in kings' closets, made up in a crown & purple robe & regalia." He knows Greek well & reads Italian, German, & Spanish. He spent five hours with me & carried off a pile of books. He had never known but one person of extraordinary promise, a youth at Dartmouth of the name of Hobart.

—

Nothing is dead. Men & things feign themselves dead and endure mock funerals & mournful obituaries and there they are looking out of the window hale & hearty in some new strange disguise. Plato is not dead. I know well the eyes through which he still looks; Jesus is not dead, he is very well alive; nor Rabelais, nor Montaigne, nor Swift, nor Scaliger, nor Calvin, nor Becket; I have seen them all, & they have seen me, & I could easily tell the names under which they now pass.

O aye, he takes my cat for a griffin.

The Sky is the daily bread of the eyes. What scutlpture in these hard clouds; what expression of immense amplitude in this dotted & rippled rack, here firm & continental, there vanishing into plumes & auroral gleams. No crowding; boundless, cheerful, & strong.

Men representative

The gods are jealous and their finest gifts of men, they deface with some shrewd fault that we may hate the vessel which holds the nectar. And hence men have in all ages suffered the heralds of heaven to starve and struggle with evils of all kinds; for the gods will not have their heralds amiable; lest men should love the cup & not the nectar.

Every man is an impossibility until he is born. Every thing impossible until we see a success. Do it, & we quote the old Unities or scholastic rules or examples of genius, Moses or Christ to you no longer.

My friends are leaving the town and I am sad at heart that they cannot have that love & service from me to which they seem by their aims & the complexion of their minds & by their unpopularity to have rich claims. Especially C. L. I seem to myself to have treated with the worst inhospitality inasmuch as I have never received that man to me not for so much as one moment. A pure superior mystical intellectual & gentle soul, free & youthful too in character, & treating me ever with marked forbearance, he so formidable,—a fighter in the ring, —yet he has come & has staid so long in my neighborhood an alien: for his nature & influence do not invite mine, but always freeze me. It sometimes seems to me strange that English & New Englanders should be so little capable of blending. Their methods & temperaments so differ from ours. They strike twelve, the first time. Our people have more than meets the ear. This man seems to me born a warrior, the most expert swordsman we have ever seen; good when the trumpet sounds, metallic in his nature, not vegetable enough. No eye for Nature, and his hands as far from his head as Alcott's own.—We are not willing to trust the Universe to give the hospitality of the Omnipresent to the good, but we too must assume to do the honours with offices, money, & clatter of plates.

—

20 May. Walked with Ellery. In the landscape felt the magic of colour; the world is all opal & those ethereal tints the mountains wear have the finest effects of magic on us. Mountains are great poets, and one glance at this fine cliff scene undoes a great deal of prose, & reinstates us wronged men in our rights. All life, all society, begins to get illuminated & transparent, & we generalize boldly & well. Space is felt as a great thing. There is some pinch & narrowness to us, & we laugh & leap to see the world, & what amplitudes it has of meadow, stream, upland, forest, & sea, which yet are but lanes & crevices to the great Space in which the world swims like a cockboat in the sea. A little canoe with three figures put out from a creek into the river & sailed down stream to the Bridge & we rejoiced in the Blessed Water inviolable, magical, whose nature is Beauty, which instantly began to play its sweet games, all circles & dimples & lovely gleaming motions,—always Ganges, the Sacred River, & which cannot be desecrated or made to forget itself. But there below are these farms yet are the farmers unpoetic. The life of labor does not make men, but drudges. Pleasant it is, as the habits of all poets may testify, to think of great proprietors, to reckon this grove we walk in a park of the noble, but a continent cut up into ten acre farms is not desireable to the imagination. The Farmer is an enchanted laborer & after toiling his brains out sacrificing thought, religion, taste, love, hope, courage at the shrine of toil, turns out a bankrupt as well as the merchant. It is time to have the thing looked into & with a transpiercing criticism settled whether life is worth having on such terms. If not, let us eat less food & less, & clear ourselves of such a fool's universe. I will not stay, for one, longer than I am contented. Ellery thinks that very few men carry the world in their thoughts. But the actual of it is thus, that every man of mediocre health stands there for the support of fourteen or fifteen sick; & though it were easy to get his

own bread with little labour, yet the other fourteen damn him to toil. See this great shovelhanded Irish race who precede everywhere the civilization of America, & grade the road for the rest!

I suppose that if society were transparent, the noble would everywhere be gladly received & accredited as such, & would not be asked for his day's work but would be felt as benefit in that he was noble. That were his duty & stint to keep himself clean & elevating, the leaven of the nation.

Ellery said, "the village (of Concord) did not look so very bad from our point;—the three churches looked like geese swimming about in a pond."

All the physicians I have ever seen call themselves believers, but are materialists; they believe only in the existence of matter, & not in matter as an appearance, but as substance, & do not contemplate a cause. Their idea of sprit is a chemical agent.

—

Edward Everett did long ago for Boston what Carlyle is doing now for England & Europe, rhetoricising the conspicuous objects.

—

I enjoy all the hours of life. Few persons have such susceptibility to pleasures; as a countryman will say "I was at sea a month & never missed a meal" so I eat my dinner & sow my turnips yet do I never, I think, fear death. It seems to me so often a relief, a rendering up of responsibility, a quittance of so many vexatious trifles,

A soft lovely child always truer & better, unhurt amidst the noxious influences of wealth & ultra whiggism, & can resist everything unless it were the vitriolic acid of marriage.

How poetic this wondrous web of property! J. P. sitting in his parlour talking of philanthropy has his pocket full of papers, representing dead labour done long ago not by him nor by his ancestor but by hands which his ancestor had skill to set at work & get the certificates of. And now these signs of the work of hands long ago mouldered in the grave, are honoured by all men & for them J P can get what vast amounts of

work done by new young hands—canals, railways, houses, gardens, coaches, pastures, sheep, oxen, & corn.
One great wrong must soon appear—this right to burden the unborn with state loans.

—

It is very odd that nature should be so unscrupulous. She is no saint; no abolitionist, nor abstemious person, she comes eating & drinking & sinning. Her darlings the great, the strong, the beautiful, though children of a law are not children of our law, do not come out of the Sunday School nor weigh their food nor always keep the ten Commandments.

Luther said, "he preached coarsely. That giveth content to all. Hebrew, Greek, & Latin I spare until we learned ones come together, & then we make it so curled & finical that God himself wondereth at us."

—

——Life
If any of us knew what we were doing, or whither we were going!—

We are all dying of miscellany.

As I looked at the landscape Government seemed to be asked for.

I think we are not quite yet fit for Flying Machines and therefore there will be none. When Edie comes trotting into my study I put the inkstand & watch on the high shelf, until she be a little older; and the God has put the sun & moon in plain sight & use but laid them on the high shelf where these roystering boys may not in some mad Saturday afternoon pull them down or burn their own fingers. So I think the air will not be granted until our beards are grown a little. The sea & iron road are safer toys for such young fingers at present. We are not ripe to be birds.

The political effects of the Rail Road will shortly be studied. It will require an expansion of the old police of Europe. When a railroad train shoots through Europe every day from Brussels to Vienna, from Vienna to Constantinople, it cannot stop every twenty or thirty miles at a German Custom house for examination of property & passports.

—

The mountains in the horison acquaint us with more exalted relations to our friends than any we sustain.

Carlyle must write thus or nohow, like a drunken man who can run, but cannot walk. What a *man's book*, is that! no prudences, no compromises, but a thorough independence. A masterly criticism on the times. Fault perhaps the excess of importance given to the circumstance of today. The poet is here for this, to dwarf & destroy all merely temporary circumstance, & to glorify the perpetual circumstance of men. E.g. dwarf British Debt & raise Nature & social life.

But everything must be done well once; even bulletins & almanacs must have one excellent & immortal bulletin & almanac.—So let Carlyle's be the immortal Newspaper—

—

June 10. Strange difference between the quality of an act & its consequences in what we call crimes. Murder in the murderer is no such ruinous thought, it does not unsettle him or fright him from his sphere, it is a quite contemplable act, but in its sequel it turns out to be a horrible jangle & confounding of all relations. Much more is this true of all the crimes that spring from love. They often seem very right & fair from the actor's point of view, but when acted, are found destructive of society. Strange that the act should look so differently on the inside & on the outside.

Hawthorne & I talked of the number of superior young men we have seen. H. said, that he had seen several from whom he had expected much, but they had not distinguished themselves; and he had inferred that he must not expect popular success from such; he had in nowise lost his confidence in their power.

I am often refreshed by seeing marks of excellence and of excellence which makes no impression on people at large who reckon it a bar-room wit, and swaggering intellect, not presentable, and of no great value.—Then I take comfort that these gifts are so cheap, and it would seem that all men are great, only some are adjusted to the delicate mean of this world & can swim in it wherever put.

—

18 June. Yesterday at Bunker Hill, a prodigious concourse of people but a village green could not be more peaceful, orderly, sober, & even affectionate. Webster gave us his plain statement like good bread, yet the oration was feeble compared with his other efforts, and even seemed poor & Polonius like with its indigent conservatisms. When there is no antagonism as in these holiday speeches, & no religion, things sound not heroically. It is a poor oration that finds Washington for its highest mark. The audience give one much to observe, they are so light headed & light timbered, every man thinking more of his inconveniences than of the objects of the occasion, & the hurrahs are so slight & easily procured. Webster is very good—America himself. Wonderful multitudes; on the top of a house I saw a company protecting themselves from the sun by an old large map of the United States. A charitable lumber merchant near the Bridge had chalked up over his counting room door "500 seats for ladies, free" and there the five hundred sat in white tiers. The ground within the square at the monument was arranged to hold 80 000 persons.

22 June. It was evident that there was the monument & here was Webster, and he knew well that a little more or less of rhetoric signified nothing: he was only to say plain & equal things, grand things if he had them, and if he had them not, only to abstain from saying unfit things, & the whole occasion was answered by his presence. It was a place for behaviour much more than speech, & Mr Webster behaved well or walked through his part with entire success. He was there as the representative of the American continent, there in his Adamitic capacity, and that is the basis of the satisfaction the people have in hearing him that he alone of all men does not disappoint the eye & ear but is a fit figure in the landscape.

It was a memorable scene enough for the broad good nature of the people. A vast multitude friendly & intelligent as cousins.

I do not know what I saw more beautiful than George Bradford's conscience. We stood outside the chain, coveting a place in the great vacant space before us, from which the sentinels excluded us. George went farther to a corner, & got within the guard, & came near me again to show me how I might enter. I begged him to hasten far into the square, or he would be ordered out by some sentinel, but he presently came back again & went up to the sentinel to ask him whether he had any objections to his passing in.

—

I was at Brook Farm, and had a cheerful time. Some confidences were granted me; & grief softened the somewhat hard nature of S R. so that I had never seen her to such advantage. Fine weather, cheerful uplands, & every person you meet is a character & in free costume. Charles N. I saw, & was relieved to meet again on something of the old footing, after hearing of so much illness & sensitiveness. But C. is not a person to be seen on a holiday or in holiday places, but one should live in solitude & obscurity, with him for the only person in the county to speak to. Also George B. let me a little into the spiritual history & relations that go forward, but one has this feeling in hearing of their spiritualism, Ah! had they never heard of it first! and did not know it was spiritualism!

Sais.

The scholars are the true hierarchy only that now they are displaced by hypocrites, that is, sciolists. For is not that the one want of man to meet a brother who being fuller of God than he, can hold him steady to a truth until he has made it his own. O with what joy I begin to read a poem which I confide in as an inspiration. And now my chains are really to be broken, my destiny shall have a vacation. I am to mount above these clouds & thick opaque airs in which I live,—opaque though they seem transparent,—& from the free heaven of truth, I shall see my relation to the world. That will reconcile me to life; that will rebuild the world, life, & the universe for me, to see these trifles so discordant & insignificant combined into a tendency, & to know what I am doing. Life will no more be a fuss: now I shall see men & women, & know the signs by which they may be discerned from fools & Satans. I shall not forget the lesson; Never fear it. This day shall be better to me than my birthday: then I became an animal, now I am invited into the Eternal. Such is the hope; and the fruition should be conformable. But this winged man who will carry me to the heaven of clear vision, whirls me into the clouds, & then leaps & frisks about with me from cloud to cloud, still affirming that he is bound heavenward, and I, long time deceived, as being myself a novice, am slow in finding out that he does not know the way into the heavens, & is no true pilot & is merely intent like a child that I should admire his bird-like skill to rise a little way from the ground; but the piercing & ocular air of heaven that man shall never behold. I tumble down again soon to my old nooks, & lead the life of exaggerations as before, and have lost my faith in the possibility of any guide who can lead me thither where I would be.

—

How strongly I have felt of pictures, that, when you have once seen one, bid goodbye to it,—you shall never see it again. I have had real instruction from pictures, which I have since seen without emotion or remark. This deduction is therefore to be made from the opinion which even the most intelligent express of a new book or new thing: their opinion surely gives me tidings of their mood, & some very general guess at the new thing, but is nowise to be trusted as the permanent relation between that intellect & that thing. "Mamma," says the child, "why don't I like the story as well as when you told it me the other day?"—Alas, child, it is even so with mamma, with grandmamma, & the oldest cherubim of knowledge: But will it answer thy question to say, Because thou wert born to a whole, & this story is a particular? The reason of the pain this discovery causes us, (& we make it in respect to works of art & of intellect very late,) is the dim augury of tragedy which moans from it in regard to persons;—to friendship & love.

Eat or be eaten.

We used to read in our textbooks of natural philosophy an illustration of the porosity of bodies, from a barrel of cannon balls, whose interstices were filled with grapeshot, whose interstices again were filled with small shot, and theirs again with powder. It is an emblem of nature whose problem seems to have been to see how she could crowd in the most life into the world & for every class of eaters which she inserted, she adds another class of eaters to prey on them, & tucked in musquitoes among the last like an accommodating stage-coachman, who, when twelve insides are jammed down solid, puts in a child at the window, & guesses there will be room for that.

—

July 8. The sun & the evening sky do not look calmer than Alcott & his family at Fruitlands. They seemed to have arrived at the fact, to have got rid of the show, & so to be serene. Their manners & behaviour in the house & in the field were those of superiour men, of men at rest. What had they to conceal? What had they to exhibit? And it seemed so high an attainment that I thought, as often before, so now more because they had a fit home, or the picture was fitly framed, that these men ought to be maintained in their place by the country for its culture. Young men & young maidens, old men & women should visit them & be inspired. I think there is as much merit in beautiful manners as in hard work. I will not prejudge them successful. They look well in July. We will see them in December. I know they are better for themselves, than as partners. One can easily see that they have yet to settle several things. Their saying that things are clear & they sane, does not make them so. If they will in very deed be lovers & not selfish; if they will serve the town of Harvard, & make their neighbors feel them as benefactors, wherever they touch them; they are as safe as the sun.

—

Only the Eminent Experiences.

All that can be thought, can be written.

'Tis high time we should have a bible that should be no provincial record, but should open the history of the planet, and bind all tendencies and dwarf all the Epics & philosophies we have. It will have no Books of Ruth & Esther, no Song of Solomon, nor excellent, sophistical Pauls.

As if any taste or imagination could supply fidelity. The old duty is the old God.

Readiness is youthfulness; to hold the old world in our hand, awaiting our new errand, & to be rebuked by a child, by a sot, by a philistine, & thankfully take a new course. The moral sentiment is well called the newness. For it is never other than a surprise. And the oldest angels are its boys whom it doth whip & scourge, though its scars give the gladness of the martyr flame.

I have got in my barn a carpenter's bench & two planes, a shave, a saw, chisel, a vice, & a square. These planes seem to me great institutions, whose inventor no man knoweth, yet what a stroke of genius was each of these tools! When you have them, you must watch a workman for a month, or a year, or seven years, as our boys do, to know all his tricks with them. Great is Tubal Cain. A good pen is a finer stronger instrument and a language, an algebra, a calculus, music, or poetic metre, more wondrous tools yet, for this polygon or pantagon that is called man. Thanks too to Pythagoras for the multiplication table.

To lay down the heavy burden
Of herself as woman would

5 August. Home from Plymouth where I spent a fine day in an excursion to Half Way Pond dining at the house of Mrs Raymond, Mary & Lucia Russell made the party for us and Abraham Jackson, & Helen Russell accompanied us. Mrs R. was a genuine Yankee and so fluent in her provincial English that Walter Scott or Dickens could not desire a better sample of local life. Mr Faunce, Mr Swift, & Mr Stetson, her ministers at Ponds (meaning Monument P.) baptism by immarsion & by sprinkling, Mr Whitfield's "sarmons," the "Univarsallers," the schools, & the Reformation in the church at Ponds & elsewhere, and the drowning of her son Allen in a vessel loaded with pavingstones which sunk in a tempest near Boston Light, and the marriage of her son's widow, were the principal events of her life, & the topics of her conversation. She lives alone in this pleasing tranquil scene at the head of a pond, and never is uneasy except in a tempest in the night.

I cannot well say what I found at Plymouth, beyond the uneasiness of seeing people. Every person of worth, man or woman whom I see, gives me a pain as if I injured them, because of my incapacity to do them justice in the intercourse that passes between us. Two or more persons together deoxygenate the air, apathize & paralyze me, I twist like the poor eel in the exhausted receiver, and my conviction of their sense & virtue only makes matters worse for me by accusing my injustice. I am made for chronic relations not for moments, and am wretched with fine people who are only there for an hour. It is a town of great local & social advantages, Plymouth; lying on the sea with this fine broken inland country pine-covered & scooped into beds of two hundred lakes. Their proverb is that there is a pond in P. for every day of the year. Billington Sea is the best of all, & yet this superb chain of lakes which we pass in returning from Half Way Pond might content one a hundred years. The botany of the region is rare. The Epigaea named Mayflower at P. is now found elsewhere. The beautiful & fragrant Sabbatia, the Empetrum, the sundew, the Rhinanthus or yellow-rattle, and other plants are almost peculiar to this spot. Great linden trees lift their green domes above the town as seen from the Sea, and the graveyard hill shows the monuments of the Pilgrims & their children as far out to sea as we could see anything of the town. The virtues of the Russells are as eminent & fragrant here at this moment, as ever were the glories of that name in England: and Lucia is a flower of the sweetest & softest beauty which real life ever exhibited. These people know so well how to live, and have such perfect adjustment in their tastes and their power to gratify them, that the ideal life is necessarily thrown into the shade, and I have never seen a strong conservatism appear so amiable & wise. We saw their well built houses which an equal & generous economy warmed & animated; and their good neighborhood was never surpassed: the use of the door bell & knocker seem unknown. And the fine children who played in the yards & piazzas appeared to come of a more amiable & gentle stock. I went also over the new house of Mr A. J. and afterwards went with L. to his comptinghouse, & took a lesson in arithmetic, as he showed us our inventory & our bad debts. What L. told of her youth struck us all as still true, that "she liked the apples very well, but never knew where the orchard was."

from

U

1843–1844

I wish to speak with all respect of persons, but sometimes it needs much heedfulness to preserve the due decorum, they melt so fast into each other, that they are like grass, or trees, and it needs an effort to treat them as individuals. A metaphysician, a saint, a poet of God has nothing to do with them; he sees them as a rack of clouds or as a fleet of ripples which the wind drives over the surface of water: but the uninspired man in household matters finds persons a conveniency.

—

August 25.

The railroad whose building I inspected this P.M. brings a multitude of picturesque traits into our pastoral scenery. This bold mole carried out into a broad meadow silent & almost unvisited since the planting of the town, the presence of forty or fifty sturdy labourers, the energy with which they strained at their tasks, & the vigour of the superintendent of the gang, the character of the work itself which reminded one of miners & of negro drivers, the near shanties in and around which their wives & daughters & infants were seen, the villages of shanties at the water's edge & in the most sequestered nooks of the town and the number of laborers men & women whom now one encounters singly in the forest paths, the blowing of rocks, explosions all day, & now & then a painful accident, as lately, and the indefinite promise of what the new channel of trade may do & undo for the town hereafter,—are all noticeable. In the process of roadbuilding, to sink the hill & fill the hollow, they make use all the way of little railroads, which reminded me of Swedenborg's doctrine that the lungs are made up of lunglets, the liver of little livers, & so on.

—

I think we are as often deceived by being over wise & imputing too much character to individuals of whom we have heard, as by underestimating them. This young C., after he has turned the heads of so many, and been heard of so far, turns out to be the very youth he seemed when years ago I saw him.

Fourier carries a whole French revolution in his head, & much more. This is arithmetic with a vengeance. His ciphering goes where ciphering never went before, stars & atmospheres, & animals, & men, & women, & classes of every character. It is very entertaining, the most entertaining of French romances and will suggest vast & numerous possibilities of reform to the coldest & least sanguine.

To Genius everything is permitted.

In the points of good breeding, what I most require & insist upon is deference. I like that every chair should be a throne & hold a king. And what I most dislike is a low sympathy of each with his neighbor's palate & belly at table, anticipating without words what he wishes to eat & drink. If you wish bread, ask me for bread, & if you wish anchovies or lobster, ask me for them, & do not hold out your plate as if I knew already. I respect cats, they seem to have so much else in their heads besides their mess. Yet every natural function can be dignified by deliberation & privacy. I prefer a tendency to stateliness to an excess of fellowship. In all things I would have the island of a man inviolate. No degree of affection is to invade this religion. Lovers should guard their strangeness. As soon as they surrender that, they are no more lovers.

The charge which a lady in much trust made to me against her companions was that people on whom beforehand all persons would put the utmost reliance were not responsible. They saw the necessity that the work must be done, & did it not; and it of course fell to be done by herself and the few principals. I replied, that, in my experience good people were as bad as rogues, that the conscience of the conscientious ran in veins, & the most punctilious in some particulars, were latitudinarian in others. And, in Mr Tuttle's opinion, "Mankind is a damned rascal."

*

Society always values inoffensive people susceptible of conventional polish. The clergyman who would live in Boston must have taste.

H. D. T. sends me a paper with the old fault of unlimited contradiction. The trick of his rhetoric is soon learned. It consists in substituting for the obvious word & thought its diametrical antagonist. He praises wild mountains & winter forests for their domestic air; snow & ice for their warmth; villagers & wood choppers for their urbanity; and the wilderness for resembling Rome & Paris. With the constant inclination to dispraise cities & civilization, he yet can find no way to honour woods & woodmen except by paralleling them with towns & townsmen. WEC declares the piece is excellent: but it makes me nervous & wretched to read it, with all its merits.

The thinker looks for God in the direction of the consciousness, the churchman out of it. If you ask the former for his definition of God, he would answer, "my possibility;" for his definition of man, "my actuality."

—

The farmer whom I visited this P.M. works very hard & very skilfully to get a good estate, & gets it. But by his skill & diligence & that of thousands more his competitors, the wheat & milk by which I live are made so cheap that they are within reach of my scanty monies, and I am not yet forced to go to work & produce them for myself. Tuttle told me that he had once carried 41 cwt of hay to Boston & received 61.50 for the load.
But it is no part of T.'s design to keep down the price of hay or wheat or milk.

If our friends at Fruitlands should lose their confidence in themselves,——

—

The founders of Brook Farm ought to have this praise, that they have made what all people try to make, an agreeable place to live in. All comers & the most fastidious find it the pleasantest of residences.

If you look at these railroad labourers & hear their stories, their fortunes appear as little controuled as those of the forest leaves. One is whirled off to Albany, one to Ohio, one digs on the levee at New Orleans & one at Walden Pond; others on the wharves in Boston, or the woods in Maine, and they have too little foresight & too little money to leave them any more election of whither to go or what to do than the poor leaf which is blown into this dike or that brook to perish. "To work from dark to dark for fifty cents the day," as the poor woman in the shanty told us, is but pitiful wages for a married man.

The uniform terms of admission to the advantages of civilized society, are,—You shall have all as a member, nothing as a man.

—

Ellery's Poetry shows the Art, though the poems are imperfect, as the first Daguerres are grim things yet show that a great engine has been invented.

—

Never strike a king unless you are sure you shall kill him.

—

I would live in a house which I did not build, & whose history I do not know; in a large house occupying small room; having always more than I show.

September 3, 1843. *Representive*

We pursue ideas, not persons, the man momentarily stands for the thought, but will not bear the least examination. And a society of men will cursorily represent well enough a certain culture & state of thought, as e.g. a beauty of manners, but it is only in their congregation: detach them, & there is no gentleman, no lady in the group.

My friend came hither and satisfied me in many ways, and, as usual, dissatisfied me with myself. She increased my knowledge of life, and her sketches of manners & persons are always valuable, she sees so clearly & steadily through the veils. But best of all is the admonition that comes to me from a demand of beauty so naturally made wheresoever her eye rests, that our ways of life, our indolences, our indulgences, our want of heroic action are shamed. Yet I cordially greet the reproof. When that which is so fair & noble passes I seem enlarged; all my thoughts are spacious; the chambers of the brain & the lobes of the heart are bigger. How am I cheered always by traits of that "vis superba formae" which inspires art & genius but not passion: there is that in beauty which cannot be caressed, but which demands the utmost wealth of nature in the beholder properly to meet it.

We cannot quite pull down & degrade our life & divest it of poetry. The day-labourer is popularly reckoned as standing at the foot of the social scale: yet talk with him, he is saturated with the beautiful laws of the world. His measures are the hours, the morning & the night, the solstice and the geometry, the astronomy, and all the lovely accidents of nature play through his mind continual music. Property keeps the accounts of the world, and always reveals a moral cause. The property will be found where the labor, where the wisdom, where the virtue have been, in nations, in classes, and, (a life taken together & the compensations considered) in the individual also. How wise looks the world when in detail the laws & usages of nations are examined, & the completeness of all the provisions is considered. Nothing is left out. If you go into the markets & the customhouses, the insurance & notary offices, offices of sealers of weights & measures, of inspection of provisions, it will appear as if one man had made it all; wherever you go, a wit like your own has been before you & has realized his thought.

Any form of government would content me in which the rulers were gentlemen, but it is in vain that I have tried to persuade myself that Mr Calhoun or Mr Clay or Mr Webster were such; they are underlings, & take the law from the dirtiest fellows. In England it usually appears as if the power were confided to persons of superior sentiment, but they have not treated Russia as they ought in the affair of Poland. It is time these fellows should hear the truth from other quarters than the antislavery papers and Whig papers & Investigators & all other committed organs. We have allowed them to take a certain place in private society as if they were at the head of their countrymen: they must be told that they have dishonoured themselves & it can be allowed no longer; they are not now to be admitted to the society of scholars.

A man should carry nature in his head, should know the hour of the day & the time of the year by the sun & the stars, should know the solstice & the equinox, the quarter of the moon, & the daily tides. The Egyptian pyramids, I have heard, were square to the points of the compass, & the custom of different nations has been to lay the dead with the feet to the east. It testifies a higher civilization than the want of regard to it.

The relation of parents & children is usually reversed. The children become at last the parents of their parents.

I am in the habit of surrendering myself to my companion, so that it may easily happen that my companion finds himself some what tasked to meet the occasion. But the capital defect of my nature for society, (as it is of so many others) is the want of animal spirits. They seem to me a thing incredible, as if God should raise the dead. I hear of what others perform by their aid, with fear. It is as much out of my possibility as the prowess of Coeur de Lion or an Irishman's day's work on the railroad. Animal spirits seem the power of the Present, and their feats equal to the Pyramids of Karnac. Before them what a base mendicant is Memory with his leathern badge. I cannot suddenly form my relation to my friend, or rather can very slowly arrive at its satisfaction. I make new friendships on the old; we shall meet on higher & higher platforms until our first intercourse shall seem like an acquaintance of tops, marbles, & ball-time. I am an architect & ask a thousand years for my probation. Meantime I am very sensible to the deep flattery of omens.

Has the South European more animal spirits than we, that he is so joyous a companion? I well remember my stay at the *Hotel Giaccheri*, in Palermo, where I listened with pleasure to the novelty of the melo-dramatic conversation of a dozen citizens of the world. They mimicked in telling a story the voice & manner of the persons they described. They crowed like cocks, they hissed, cackled, barked, & screamed, and were it only by the physical strength they exerted in telling the story, kept the table in sympathetic life.

A visit to the railroad yesterday, in Lincoln, showed me the labourers—how grand they are; all their postures, their air, & their very dress. They are men, manlike employed, and the art of the sculptor is to take these forms & set on them a cultivated face & head. But cultivation never except in war makes such forms & carriage as these.

"Germans who love their country with understanding must know," says Borne, "that it is not so much the Leipsic Battle as the Leipsic Fair Catalogue which raises us above the French."

I think it will soon become the pride of this country to make gardens & adorn country houses. That is the fine art which especially fits us. Sculpture, painting, music, architecture do not thrive with us, but they seem as good as dead, & such life as they show, is a sort of second childhood. But land we have in greater extent than ever did any people of the same power, and the new modes of travelling are making it easy to cultivate very distant tracts & yet remain in strict intercourse with the great centres of trade & population. And the whole force of all the arts goes to facilitate the decoration of lands & dwellings. A garden has this advantage, that it makes it indifferent where you live. If the landscape around you is pleasing, the garden shows it: if tame, it excludes it. A little grove which any farmer can find or cause to grow, will in a few years so fill the eye & mind of the inhabitant, as to make cataracts & chains of mountains quite unnecessary, and he is so contented with his alleys, his brook, his woodland, his orchard, his baths, & his piazza, that Niagara and the Notch of the White Hills and Nantasket Beach are superfluities. The other day came C. S. with eyes full of Naushon & Nahant & Niagara, dreaming by day & night of canoes, & lightning, & deer-parks, & silver waves, & could hardly disguise her disdain for our poor cold low life in Concord, like rabbits in a warren. Yet the interiors of our woodland, which recommend the place to us, she did not see. And the capital advantage which we possess here, that the whole town is permeable, that I can go through it like a park, distinguishes it above towns built on three or four New Hampshire hills, having each one side at 45 degrees & the other side perpendicular. Then as the Indians dwell where they can find good water, so my wife values her house because of the pump in the kitchen above all palaces. The great sun equalizes all places,—the sun & the stars. The grand features of nature are so identical that whether in a mountain or a waterfall or whether in a flat meadow, the presence of the great agents makes the presence or absence of the inferior features insignificant. With the sun, with morning & evening, we are nearer to Niagara than 500 miles: Niagara is in every glance at the heavens & earth. Mr Perkins, W E C says, built a house such as you need never go out of: bath, well, woodhouse, barn, conservatory, offices, it had all under cover.

—

A poet in his holidays, or vacations rather, should write Criticism.

It is in vain to tell me that you are sufficient to yourself but have not anything to impart. I know & am assured that whoever is sufficient to himself will, if only by existing, suffice me also.

Autob.

Let others grumble that they see no fairies nor muses, I rejoice that my eyes see the erect eternal world, always the same & erect, without blur or halo.

—

'Tis a great convenience to be educated for a time in a countingroom or attorney's business; then you may safely be a scholar the rest of your life & will find the use of that partial thickening of the skin every day as you will of your shoes or your hat. What mountains of nonsense will you have cleared your brain of forever!

I reckon the inaction & whining of the literary class debility of course, & when I admit the existence of this grief, it is only as I hear with their ears & see with their eyes.

We want, we say, some steep antagonism to draw an articulate sound or a great act from this incapable giant whose long arms hang so listless.

Pruning: so many of our best youth must die of consumption, so many of despair, & so many be dunces or insane before the one shoot which they all promised to be can force its way upward to a thrifty tree.

I fell today upon the sentence which I have often searched in Montaigne, in vain, to find. It is this. "I will say a prodigious thing, but I will say it however. I find myself in many things more curbed & retained by my manners than my opinion, & my concupiscence less debauched than my reason."

Essay on Cruelty. Vol. II p 152

—

Sept. 26. This morning Charles Lane left us after a two days' visit. He was dressed in linen altogether, with the exception of his shoes, which were lined with linen, & he wore no stockings. He was full of methods of an improved life: valued himself chiefly just now on getting rid of the animals; thinks there is no economy in using them on a farm. He said, that they could carry on their Family at Fruitlands in many respects better, no doubt, if they wished to play it well. He said that the clergy for the most part opposed the Temperance Reform, and conspicuously this simplicity in diet, because they were alarmed, as soon as such nonconformity appeared, by the conviction that the next question people would ask, would be, "Of what use are the clergy?" In the college he found an arithmetic class, Latin, German, Hebrew classes, but no Creative Class. He had this confidence, namely, that Qui facit per alium facit per se: that it was of no use to put off upon a second or third person the act of serving or of killing cattle, as in cities, for example, it would be sure to come back on the offending party in some shape, as in the brutality of the person or persons you have brutalized.

—

The poet should walk in the fields drawn on by new scenes supplied each with vivid pictures & thoughts until insensibly the recollection of his home was crowded out of his mind & all memory obliterated & he was led in triumph by nature.

When he spoke of the stars, he should be innocent of what he said; for it seemed that the stars, as they rolled over him, mirrored themselves in his mind as in a deep well, & it was their image & not his thought that you saw.

It is of no importance to real wisdom how many propositions you add on the same platform, but only what new platforms. I knew somewhat concerning the American Revolution, the action at Bunker hill, the battle of Monmouth, of Yorktown, &c. Now today I learn new particulars of Gen. Greene, of Gen Lee, of Rochambeau. But now that I think of that event with a changed mind and see what a compliment to England is all this self glorification, and betrays a servile mind in us who think it so overgreat an action, makes the courage & the wit of the admirers suspected, who ought to look at such things as things of course.

Let us shame the fathers by the virtue of the sons, & not belittle us by brag.

A great deal of laughing & minute criticism but it helps not, but the austere impracticable unavailable man who is a firebrand in society, whom society cannot let pass in silence, but must either worship or hate, and to whom all people feel drawn, both the leaders and the obscure & eccentric, he puts the entire America & entire Europe into doubt & destroys the Skepticism which says, "Man is a poltroon, let us eat & drink, 'tis the best we can do,"—by intimating the untried & unknown.

We ought to thank the nonconformist for every thing good he does. Who has a right to ask him why he compounds with this or that wrong?

Certainly the objection to Reform is the Common sense of Mankind, which seems to have settled several things; as traffic, and the use of the animals for labor & food. But it will not do to offer this by way of argument, as *that* is precisely the ground of dispute.

Read Montaigne's Journey into Italy, which is an important part of his biography. I like him so well that I value even his register of his disease—Is it that the valetudinarian gives the assurance that he is not ashamed of himself? Then what a treasure, to enlarge my knowledge of his friend by his narrative of the last days & the death of Etienne de la Boetie. In Boston when I heard lately Chandler Robbins preach so well the funeral sermon of Henry Ware, I thought of Montaigne, who would also have felt how much this surface called Unitarianism admits of being opened & deepened, and that this was as good & defensible a post of life to occupy as any other. It was a true cathedral music & brought chancels & choirs, surplices, ephods, & arks & hierarchies into presence. Certainly Montaigne is the antagonist of the fanatic reformer. Under the oldest mouldiest conventions he would prosper just as well as in the newest world. His is the common sense which though no science is fairly worth the seven. In his "Journey," I am much struck with the picture of manners. His arrival in each place is an event of some importance, the arrival of a gentleman of France. Wherever he goes, he calls upon whatever Prince or gentleman of note, as a duty to himself & to civilization. When he leaves any house in which he has lodged a few weeks, he causes his arms to be painted & hung up as a perpetual sign to the house, as was the custom of gentlemen. He looks as he enters each town to see whether the lilies of France appear on the houses & public squares. The wines he drunk appear in every page. His house, Ellery says, looks like a powder mill.

A newspaper lately called Daniel Webster "a steam engine in breeches" and the people are apt to speak of him as "Daniel," and it is a sort of proverb in New England of a vast knowledge —"if I knew as much as D. W." Os oculosque Jovi par.

Henry Ware with his benevolence & frigid manners reminded men how often of a volcano covered with snow. But there was no deep enthusiasm. I think his best eulogy was Dr Beecher's remark on his "Formation of Xn Character," that "it was the best counterfeit he had met with." All his talent was available & he was a good example of the proverb no doubt a

hundred times applied to him of "a free steed driven to death." He ought to have been dead ten years ago, but hard work had kept him alive. In the post mortem examination his lungs were found healed over & sound & his disorder was in the brain. A very slight & puny frame he had, & the impression of size was derived from his head. Then he was dressed with heroical plainness. I think him well entitled to the dangerous style of Professor of Pulpit eloquence, none but W E Channing so well & he had ten times the business valour of Channing. This was a soldier that flung himself into all risks at all hours, not a solemn martyr kept to be burned once & make the flames proud.
In calm hours & friendly company, his face expanded into broad simple sunshine; and I thought le bon Henri a pumpkin-sweeting.

Plato paints & quibbles & by & by a sentence that moves the sea & land.

G.B.E. read me a criticism on Spenser, who makes twenty trees of different kinds grow in one grove, wherein the critic says it was an imaginary grove. G.B.E., however, doubts not it was after nature, for he knows a piece of natural woodland near Boston, wherein twentyfour different trees grow together in a small grove.

—

Nature seems a little wicked & to delight in mystifying us. Every thing changes in ourselves & our relations, and for twenty or thirty years I shall find some old cider barrel or well known rusty nail or hook or rag of dish clout unchanged.

—

In this country where land is so cheap & the disposition of the people so pacific every thing invites to the arts of domestic architecture & gardening. In this country we have no garden such as the Boboli Garden in Florence or the Villa Borghese in Rome. Such works make the land dear to the citizen & inflame patriotism. A noble garden makes the face of the country where you live, of no account; low or high, noble or mean, you have made a beautiful abode worthy of man. It is the fine art which is left for us now that sculpture & painting & religious

& civil architecture have become effete & have a second childhood.

In this climate what a joy to build! The south side of the house should be almost all window for the advantage of the winter sun. The house should be built so as that one should never need to go out of doors, & the grounds should be so richly laid out that one should never need to take a journey to see better orchards, mills, woods, & waters. Marble baths, a turret for a library like Montaigne, or a cave for a summer study, like (See Aubrey)

—

In Saadi's Gulistan, I find many traits which comport with the portrait I drew. He replied to Nizari;—"It was rumoured abroad that I was penitent & had forsaken wine but this was a gross calumny for what have I to do with repentance?" Like Montaigne, he learns manners from the unmannerly and he says "there is a tradition of the prophet that poverty has a gloomy aspect in this world & in the next!" There is a spice of Gibbon in him when he describes a schoolmaster so ugly & crabbed that the sight of him would derange the ecstasies of the orthodox.

Like Homer and Dante & Chaucer, Saadi possessed a great advantage over poets of cultivated times in being the representative of learning & thought to his countrymen. These old poets felt that all wit was their wit, they used their memory as readily as their invention, & were at once the librarian as well as the poet, historiographer as well as priest of the muses.

—

In Montaigne, man & thinker are inseparable: you cannot insert the blade of a pen knife betwixt the man & his book.

Young people admire talents or particular excellences. But as we grow older, we only value total powers & effects, as, the impression, the spirit, the quality or genius of the man.

Ellery says, Wordsworth writes like a man who takes snuff.

"Was this a coloured person you speak of?" said M.M.E. to my story of the mystic.

Criticism may go to great fineness. Tennyson is a master of metre but it is as an artist who has learned admirable mechanical secrets. He has no woodnotes. Great are the dangers of education—skepticism. Tennyson a cosmetic poet. No man but is so much a skeptic as not to feel a grateful surprise now & then at finding himself safe & sound & things as he thought them.

Would you have property, stick where you are: then shingle: put dollars to dollars, & let them beget sons & daughters.

I will say it again today,—I am very much struck in literature by the appearance that one person wrote all the books. As if the Editor of the Journal planted his body of reporters in different parts of the field of action & relieved some by others from time to time, but there is such equality & identity in the story that it is plainly the production of one all-seeing, all-hearing person.

A man on whom words made no impression

The noble river Jumna
"Her bed is India;—there she lies—a pearl."

Immense benefit of Party I feel today in seeing how it reveals faults of character in such an idol as Webster which the intellectual force in the persons, if in equilibrium, & not hurled to its aphelion by hatred, could not have seen. What benefit, since the world is so stupid, that there should be *two stupidities!* It is the same brute advantage, so essential to astronomy, in having the diameter of the earth's orbit for a base of its triangle. The great men dull their palm by entertainment of those they dare not refuse. And lose the tact of greeting the wise with sincerity, but give that odious brassiness to those who would forgive coldness, silence, dislike,—everything but simulation & duping.

—

In Goethe, is that sincerity which makes the value of literature and is that one voice or one writer who wrote all the good

books. In Helena, Faust is sincere & represents actual cultivated strong natured Man; the book would be farrago without the sincerity of Faust. I think the second Part of Faust the grandest enterprise of literature that has been attempted since the Paradise Lost. It is a philosophy of history set in poetry. It is the work of a man who found himself the master of histories, mythologies, philosophies, sciences, & national literatures, in the encyclopaediacal manner in which modern erudition, aided by the wonderful mechanical aids of modern time such as international intercourse of the whole earth's population, researches into Indian & Etruscan & all Cyclopaean arts; geology; astronomy; &c and every one of these deep kingdoms assuming a certain aerial & poetic character from the circumstance of the multitude. One looks at a king with devotion, but if one should chance to be at a congress of kings the eye would take liberties with the peculiarities of each.
It labours with the *fault*, if you please, at all events, with the fact, that these are not wild miraculous songs but profoundly thought and elaborated designs to which the poet has confided the results of his life & eighty years of observation. But this reflective & critical wisdom only makes the poem more truly the result & flower of this time. It dates itself. Still he is a poet, possesses the highest poetic talent of all his contemporaries, & *under* this genius of microscopes (his eyes are microscopes) strikes the harp with a man's strength, variety, & grace,

But the wonder of the book is its superior intelligence. It enlarges the known powers of the human mind, as was said of Michael's Sistine Chapel. What a strong menstruum was this man's wit! how the ages past & the present century & their religions & politics & modes of thinking lie there dissolved into archetypes & Ideas. What new mythologies sail through his head! They said that Alexander got as far as Chaos. Goethe got, only the other day as far, & one step farther he hazarded, & brought himself back.

—

I thought yesterday as I read letters of MME that I would attempt the arrangement of them. With a little selection & compiling and a little narrative thinly veiled of the youth of Ellen & Charles & if brought far enough with letters from C. and later letters from my sweet saint, there should be a picture of a

New England youth & education so connected with the story of religious opinion in N. England, as to be a warm & bright life picture.

Autobiography.

My great grandfather was Rev. Joseph Emerson of Malden, son of Emerson, Esq. of Newbury(port). I used often to hear that when William, son of Joseph, was yet a boy walking before his father to church, on a Sunday, his father checked him, "William, you walk as if the earth was not good enough for you." "I did not know it, sir," he replied with the utmost humility. This is one of the household anecdotes in which I have found a relationship. 'Tis curious but the same remark was made to me, by Mrs Lucy Brown, when I walked one day under her windows here in Concord.

—

We come down with freethinking into the dear institutions & at once make carnage amongst them. We are innocent of any such fell purpose as the sequel seems to impute to us. We were only smoking a cigar, but it turns out to be a powder mill that we are promenading.

If one could have any security against moods! If the profoundest prophet could be holden to his words & the hearer who is ready to sell all and join the crusade, could have any certificate that tomorrow his prophet shall not unsay his testimony! But the Truth sits veiled there on the Bench & never interposes an adamantine Syllable: and the most sincere & revolutionary doctrine, put as if the ark of God were carried forward some furlongs and planted there for the succour of the world, shall in a few weeks be coldly set aside by the same speaker as morbid: "I thought I was right, but I was not," and the same immeasureable credulity demanded for new audacities.

The best yet, or T T's last.

My divine Thomas Taylor in his translation of Cratylus (p 30 (note)) calls Christianity "a certain most irrational & gigantic impiety," αλογιστος και γιγαντικη ανοσιουργια.

People came, it seems, to my lectures with expectation that I was to realize the Republic I described, & ceased to come when they found this reality no nearer. They mistook me. I am & always was a painter. I paint still with might & main, & choose the best subjects I can. Many have I seen come & go with false hopes & fears, and dubiously affected by my pictures. But I paint on. I count this distinct vocation, which never leaves me in doubt what to do but in all times, places, & fortunes, gives me an open future, to be the great felicity of my lot. Dr C.T.J. too, was born to his chemistry & his minerals.

Yet what to say to the sighing realist as he passes & comes to the vivid painter with a profound assurance of sympathy saying, "he surely must be charmed to scale with me the silver mountains whose dim enchantments he has so affectionately sketched." The painter does not like the realist: sees his faults: doubts his means & methods: in what experiments they make, both are baffled: no joy. The painter is early warned that he is jeopardising his genius in these premature actualisations.

Very painful is the discovery we are always making that we can only give to each other a rare & partial sympathy: for, as much time as we have spent in looking over into our neighbor's field & chatting with him is lost to our own, & must be made up by haste & renewed solitude.

—

A. came, the magnificent dreamer, brooding as ever on the renewal or reedification of the social fabric after ideal law, heedless that he had been uniformly rejected by every class to whom he has addressed himself and just as sanguine & vast as ever;—the most cogent example of the drop too much which nature adds of each man's peculiarity. To himself he seems the only realist, & whilst I & other men wish to deck the dulness of the months with here & there a fine action or hope, he would weave the whole a new texture of truth & beauty. Now he spoke of marriage & the fury that would assail him who should lay his hand on that institution, for reform: and spoke of the secret doctrines of Fourier. I replied, as usual,—that, I thought no man could be trusted with it; the formation of new alliances is so delicious to the imagination, that St Paul & St

John would be riotous; and that we cannot spare the coarsest muniment of virtue.——Very pathetic it is to see this wandering emperor from year to year making his round of visits from house to house of such as do not exclude him, seeking a companion, tired of pupils.

The stealing is not to be determined by the law of the land, as, whether this property is mine or another's, but by the spirit in which it is taken. The rich man steals his own dividends.

Let us not europize—neither by travel, neither by reading. Luckily for us, now that steam has narrowed the Atlantic to a strait, the nervous rocky West is intruding a new & continental element into our national mind, & we shall have an American genius. We early men at least have a vast advantage: We are up at 4 o'clock in the morning, & have the whole market: We Enniuses & venerable Bedes of the empty American Parnassus. "Wish not a man from England."

The Shakers do not exclude any body yet have no difficulty in excluding. Disinclination excludes without bolts. The Shakers —but the Shaken.

—

November 5. To Genius everything is permitted, & not only that, but it enters into all other men's labours. A tyrannical privilege to convert every man's wisdom or skill as it would seem to its own use or to show for the first time what all these fine & complex preparations were for. See how many libraries one master absorbs. Who hereafter will go gleaning in those contemporary & anterior books, from each of which he has taken the only grain of truth it had, & has given it tenfold value by placing it? The railroad was built for him; for him history laboriously registered; for him arms & arts & politics & commerce waited, like so many servants, until the heir of the manor arrived, which he quite easily administers.

Genius is a poor man & has no house but see this proud landlord who has built the great house & furnished it so delicately opens it all to him & beseeches him respectfully to make it honourable by entering there & eating bread.

—

The Reformers wrote very ill. They made it a rule not to bolt their flour & unfortunately neglected also to sift their thoughts. But Hesiod's great discovery Πλεον ημισυ παντος is truest in writing, where half is a great deal more than the whole. Give us only the eminent experiences.

Alcott & Lane want feet; they are always feeling of their shoulders to find if their wings are sprouting; but next best to wings are cowhide boots, which society is always advising them to put on.

Married women uniformly decided against the communities. It was to them like the brassy & lackered life in hotels. The common school was well enough, but the common nursery they had grave objections to. Eggs might be hatched in ovens, but the hen on her own account greatly preferred the old way. A hen without chickens was but half a hen.

I sometimes think the health of the sick is the best health: they value it & husband it. Rude health is wasted.

Ellery says that Hawthorn agrees with him about Washington that he is the extreme of well dressed mediocrity.

9 November. I have written much in prose & verse on the Poet but neither arrive at nor tend to any conclusion. This morning I think that the right conclusion of the Essay is a man, the poet that shall be born, the new religion, the Reconciler, for whom all things tediously wait.

12 November. The "Community" of socialism is only the continuation of the same movement which made the joint stock companies for manufactures, mining, insurance, banking, & the rest. It has turned out cheaper to make calico by companies, & it is proposed to bake bread & to roast mutton by companies, & it will be tried & done. It is inevitable.

It is wiser to live in the country & have poverty instead of pauperism. Yet citizens or cockneys are a natural formation also, a secondary formation, and their relation to the town is organic—but there are all shades of it and we dwellers in the country are only half countrymen. As I run along the yard from my woodpile I chance to see the sun as he rises or as he hangs in beauty over a cloud & am apprised how far off from that beauty I live, how careful & little I am. He calls me to solitude.

The Italians have a good phrase to express the injury of translations; *traduttore traditore.*

—

25 Dec. At the performing of Handel's Messiah I heard some delicious strains & understood a very little of all that was told me. My ear received but a little thereof. But as the master overpowered the littleness & incapableness of the performers, & made them conductors of his electricity, so it was easy to see what efforts nature was making through so many hoarse, wooden, & imperfect persons to produce beautiful voices, fluid & soulguided men & women. The genius of nature could well be discerned. By right & might we should become participant of her invention, & not wait for morning & evening to know their peace, but prepossess it. I walked in the bright paths of sound, and liked it best when the long continuance of a chorus had made the ear insensible to the music, made it as if there was none, then I was quite solitary & at ease in the melodious uproar. Once or twice in the solos, when well sung, I could play tricks, as I like to do, with my eyes, darken the whole house & brighten & transfigure the central singer, and enjoy the enchantment.

This wonderful piece of music carries us back into the rich historical past. It is full of the Roman Church & its hierarchy & its architecture. Then further it rests on & requires so deep a faith in Christianity that it seems bereft of half & more than half its power when sung today in this unbelieving city.

We love morals until they come to us with mountainous melancholy & grim overcharged rebuke: then we so gladly prefer intellect, the light mocker. Dear sir, you treat these fantastical fellow men too seriously, you seem to believe that they exist.

*

The solid earth exhales a certain permanent average gas which we call the atmosphere; & the spiritual solid sphere of Mankind emits the volatile sphere of literature, of which books are single & inferior effects.

31 December. The year ends, and how much the years teach which the days never know! The individuals who compose our company converse, & meet, & part, & variously combine, and somewhat comes of it all, but the individual is always mistaken. He designed many things, drew in others, quarrelled with some or all, blundered much, & something is done; all are a little advanced; but the individual is always mistaken.

—

At the Convention of Socialists in Boston last week, Alcott was present & was solicited to speak, but had no disposition, he said, to do so. Although none of the representatives of the "Communities" present would probably admit it, yet in truth he is more the cause of their movements than any other man. He feels a certain parental relation to them without approving either of their establishments. His presence could not be indifferent to any speaker, & has not been nothing to any of them in the past years.

—

We rail at trade, but the historian of the world will see that it was the principle of liberty, that it settled America, & destroyed feudalism, and made peace & keeps peace, that it will abolish slavery.

Belief & Unbelief

Kant, it seems, searched the Metaphysics of the Selfreverence which is the favourite position of modern ethics, & demonstrated to the Consciousness that itself alone exists.

The two parties in life are the believers & unbelievers, variously named. The believer is poet, saint, democrat, theocrat, free-trade, no-church, no capital punishment, idealist,
The unbeliever supports the church, education, the fine arts, &c as *amusements*,
Horace Mann urges the Education of the State as a defence; to

keep the fingers of the poor from our throats. I see it plainly that a man has not much to say when he speaks for an hour.

But the unbelief is very profound: who can escape it? I am nominally a believer: yet I hold on to property: I eat my bread with unbelief. I approve every wild action of the experimenters. I say what they say concerning celibacy or money or community of goods and my only apology for not doing their work is preoccupation of mind. I have a work of my own which I know I can do with some success. It would leave that undone if I should undertake with them and I do not see in myself any vigour equal to such an enterprise. My Genius loudly calls me to stay where I am, even with the degradation of owning bankstock and seeing poor men suffer whilst the Universal Genius apprises me of this disgrace & beckons me to the martyr's & redeemer's office.

This is belief too, this debility of practice, this staying by our work. For the obedience to a man's genius is the *particular* of Faith: by & by, shall come the *Universal* of Faith.

I take the law on the subject of Education to read thus, *the Intellect sees by moral obedience.*

—

For the matter of marriage, it is falsified to the common sense as all other doctrines are, by emphasis or detachment, but it is honest & intelligible to say, (Shaker or Hermit) I am clear that in the state of prayer I neither marry, nor vote, nor buy, nor sell: I have experiences that are above all civil or nuptial or commercial relations: and I wish to vow myself to those. If you ask how the world is to get on, &c. &c. I have no answer. I do not care for such cattle of consequences. It is not my question, it is your own; answer it who will: I am contented with this new & splendid revelation of the One, and will not dispute.

A man should not go where he cannot carry his whole sphere or society with him,—not bodily, the whole circle of his friends, but atmospherically; I mean he should preserve in a new company the same attitude of mind and reality of relation which his daily associates call out, else he is shorn of his best beams, and will be an orphan & a mourner in the merriest club. "If you could see Vich ian Vohr with his tail on!" But Vich ian Vohr must always carry his belongings in some fashion; if not added as honour, then severed & made a disgrace. What is mine & not appropriated by me is noxious to me.

—

30 January 1844
I wrote to M F that I had no experiences nor progress to reconcile me to the calamity whose anniversary returned the second time last Saturday. The senses have a right to their method as well as the mind; there should be harmony in facts as well as in truths. Yet these ugly breaks happen there, which the continuity of theory does not compensate. The amends are of a different kind from the mischief.

—

It is impossible to write a sentence with malice prepense. I sit hours in vain over the correction of a bad paragraph in a proof—And nothing is easier than to write well with the favouring gales.

The greatness of the centuries is made out of the paltriness of the days & hours. See with what motives & by what means the railroad gets built, and Texas annexed or rejected,

I am sorry to say that the Numas & Pythagorases have usually a spice of charlatanism & that abolition Societies & Communities are dangerous fixtures. The manliness of man is a frail & exquisite fruit which does not keep its perfection twenty four hours. Its sweet fragrance cannot be bottled or barreled or exported. Carlyle is an eloquent writer but his recommendations of emigration & education appear very inadequate. Noble as it seems to work for the race, & hammer out constitutions for phalanxes, it can only be justly done by mediocre thinkers, or men of practical, not theoretic faculty. As soon as a scholar attempts it, I suspect him. Good physicians have least faith in medicine. Good priests the least faith in church-forms.

That bread which we ask of Nature is that she should entrance us, but amidst her beautiful or her grandest pictures, I cannot escape the *second thought.* I walked this P.M. in the woods, but there too the snow banks were sprinkled with tobacco juice. We have the wish to forget night & day, father & mother, food & ambition, but we never lose our dualism. Blessed wonderful Nature nevertheless! without depth but with immeasureable lateral spaces. If we look before us, if we compute our path, it is very short. Nature has only the thickness of a shingle or a slate; we come straight to the extremes: but sidewise & at unawares the present moment opens into other moods & moments, rich, prolific, leading onward without end. Impossible to bring her, the goddess, to parle: coquettes with us, hides herself in coolness & generalities; pointed & personal is she never.

—

"And fools rush in where angels fear to tread."

So say I of Brook Farm. Let it live. Its merit is that it is a new life. Why should we have only two or three ways of life & not thousands & millions? This is a new one so fresh & expansive that they are all homesick when they go away. The shy sentiments are there expressed. The *correspondence* of that place would be a historiette of the spirit of this age. They might see that in the arrangements of B. F. as out of them it is the person not the communist that avails.

Of Succession.

It is not enough to say that we are bundles of moods, for we always rank our mental states. The graduation is exquisite. We are not a bundle but a house.

Ellery Channing is quite assured that he has a natural music of expression, which is wanting in all the so called poets of the day. He is very good natured, & will allow them any merit you choose to claim; but this he always feels to be true. It is infinitely easy to him, as easy as it is for running water to warble, but at the same time impossible to any to whom it is not natural.

Every act of man has the ground tone and the high treble. Nothing but is dual, or goes through the gamut.

The Highest should alternate the two states of the contemplation of the fact in pure intellect, and the total conversion of intellect into energy: angelic insight alternating with bestial activity: sage & tiger.

When I address a large assembly, as last Wednesday, I am always apprised what an opportunity is there: not for reading to them as I do, lively miscellanies, but for painting in fire my thought, & being agitated to agitate. One must dedicate himself to it and think with his audience in his mind, so as to keep the perspective & symmetry of the oration, and enter into all the easily forgotten secrets of a great nocturnal assembly & their relation to the speaker. But it would be fine music & in the present well rewarded; that is, he should have his audience at his devotion and all other fames would hush before his. Now eloquence is merely fabulous. When we talk of it, we draw on our fancy. It is one of many things which I should like to do, but it requires a seven years' wooing.

Now when at any time I take part in a public debate, I wish on my return home to be shampooed & in all other ways aired & purified.

Precisely what the painter or the sculptor or the epic rhapsodist feels, I feel in the presence of this house, which stands to me for the human race, the desire, namely, to express myself fully, symmetrically, gigantically to them, not dwarfishly & fragmentarily. H.D.T., with whom I talked of this last night, does not or will not perceive how natural is this, and only hears the word Art in a sinister sense. But I speak of instincts. I did not make the desires or know anything about them: I went to the public assembly, put myself in the conditions, & instantly feel this new craving,—I hear the voice, I see the beckoning of this Ghost. To me it is vegetation, the pullulation & universal budding of the plant man. Art is the path of the creator to his work. The path or methods are ideal and eternal, though few men ever see them: not the artist himself for years, or for a lifetime, unless he come into the conditions. Then he is apprised with wonder what herds of daemons hem him in. He can no more rest: he says, 'By God, it is in me & must go forth of me.' I go to this place and am galvanized, and the torpid eyes of my sensibility are opened. I hear myself speak as a stranger —Most of the things I say are conventional; but I say something which is original & beautiful. That charms me. I would say nothing else but such things. In our way of talking, we say, that is mine, that is yours; but this poet knows well that it is not his, that it is as strange & beautiful to him as to you; he would fain hear the like eloquence at length.

Once having tasted this immortal ichor, we cannot have enough of it. Our appetite is immense. And, as "an admirable power flourishes in intelligibles," according to Plotinus, "which perpetually fabricates," it is of the last importance that these things get spoken. What a little of all we know, is said! What drops of all the sea of our science are baled up! And by what accident it is that these are spoken, whilst so many thoughts sleep in nature!

Hence the oestrum of speech: hence these throbs & heart beatings at the door of the assembly to the end, namely, that the thought may be ejaculated as Logos or Word.

Some men have the perception of difference predominant, and are conversant with surfaces & trifles, with coats & coaches, & faces, & cities; these are the men of talent. Hence Paris city & the western European, and New York & New England. And other men abide by the perception of Identity; these are the Orientals, the philosophers, the men of faith & divinity, the men of genius. These men, whose contempt of *soi disant* conservatism cannot be concealed, which is such a conserving as the Quaker's, who keeps in his garments the cut of Queen Ann's time but has let slip the fire & the love of the first Friends, are the real loyalists.

—

The question of the annexation of Texas is one of those which look very differently to the centuries and to the years. It is very certain that the strong British race which have now overrun so much of this continent, must also overrun that tract, & Mexico & Oregon also, and it will in the course of ages be of small import by what particular occasions & methods it was done. It is a secular question. It is quite necessary & true to our New England character that we should consider the question in its local & temporary bearings, and resist the annexation with tooth & nail.

It is a measure which goes not by right nor by wisdom but by feeling.

It would be a pity to dissolve the union & so diminish immensely every man's personal importance. We are just beginning to feel our oats.

What a pity that a farmer should not live three hundred years.

We fancy that men are individuals; but every pumpkin in the field goes through every point of pumpkin history. The rabid democrat, as soon as he is senator & rich man, has ripened beyond the possibility of sincere radicalism and unless he can resist the sun he must be conservative the rest of his life. Lord Eldon said in his old age, that "if he were to begin life again he would be damned but he would begin as Agitator."

Most of the world lives by humbug, & so will I, is the popular conclusion.

—

I cannot often enough say that a man is only a relative & representative nature, that each is a hint of a truth, but is far enough from being himself that truth which yet he quite newly & inevitably suggests to us. If I seek it in him I shall not find it. We have such exorbitant integrating eyes that the smallest arc of a curve being shown us we instantly complete the curve, & when the curtain is lifted from the diagram which we saw, we are vexed to find that no more was drawn than just that fragment of an arc which we first beheld. We are greatly too liberal in our construction of each other's faculty & promise. Exactly what they have already done they shall do again, but that which we inferred from their nature & inception, they shall not do. That is in nature but not in them. That is in us.

Ah if any man could conduct into me the pure stream of that which he pretends to be. Long afterwards, I find that quality elsewhere which he promised me. Intoxicating is to me the genius of Plotinus or of Swedenborg yet how few particulars of it can I glean from their books. My debt to them is for a few thoughts. They cannot feed that appetite they have created. I should know it well enough if they gave me that which I seek of them.

—

Otherness

H.D.T. said, he knew but one secret which was to do one thing at a time, and though he has his evenings for study, if he was in the day inventing machines for sawing his plumbago, he invents wheels all the evening & night also; and if this week he has some good reading & thoughts before him, his brain runs on that all day, whilst pencils pass through his hands. I find in me an opposite facility or perversity, that I never seem well to do a particular work, until another is due. I cannot write the poem though you give me a week, but if I promise to read a lecture day after tomorrow, at once the poem comes into my head & now the rhymes will flow. And let the proofs of the Dial be crowding on me from the printer, and I am full of faculty how to make the Lecture.

—

Railroads make the country transparent.

Somebody said of me after the lecture at Amory Hall within hearing of A. W., "The secret of his popularity is, that he has a *damn* for everybody."

I tell the Shakers that the perfect unit can alone make a perfect member.

12 March. On Sunday evening, 10th inst. at the close of the fifteenth year since my ordination as minister in the Second Church, I made an address to the people on the occasion of closing the old house, now a hundred & twenty three years old, and the oldest church in Boston. Yesterday they begun to pull it down.

Love shows me the opulence of nature by disclosing to me a world in my friend hidden from all others, & I infer an equal depth of good in every other direction.

*

Bohemian.

Intellect is a piratical schooner cruising in all latitudes for its own pot.

It is not the intention of Nature that we should live by general views. We fetch fire & water, run about among the shops & get our boots mended, day by day, and are the victims of these details, and once in a fortnight we arrive perhaps at a general remark. If we were not thus infatuated, if we saw the real from hour to hour, we could not preserve a due regard to the sensible world but should surely be burned or frozen.

—

It is curious that intellectual men should be most attractive to women. But women are magnetic; intellectual men are unmagnetic: therefore as soon as they meet, communication is found difficult or impossible. Various devices are tried in the villages to *wont* them, such as candy parties, nut-crackings, picnics, sleighrides, charades, but with slender success.

Quotation is good only when the writer goes my way & better mounted than I, and "gives me a cast," as we say; but if I like the gay equipage so well as to go out of my road, I had better have gone a-foot.

It was a good saying, Age gives good advice when it is no longer able to give a bad example. By acting rashly we buy the power of talking wisely. People who know how to act are never preachers.

I have always found our American day short. The constitution of a Teutonic scholar with his twelve, thirteen, or fourteen hours a day, is fabulous to me. I become nervous & peaked with a few days editing the Dial, & watching the stagecoach to send proofs to printers. If I try to get many hours in a day, I shall not have any.

We work hard in the garden and do it badly & often twice or thrice over, but "we get our journey out of the curses," as Mr H's Brighton drover said of his pigs.

Allston is adamas ex veteri rupe; chip of the old block; boulder of the European ledge; a spur of those Appennines on which Titian, Raphael, Paul Veronese, & Michel Angelo sat—cropping out here in this remote America unlike anything around it, & not reaching its natural elevation. What a just piece of history it is that he should have left this great picture of Belshazzar *in two proportions!* The times are out of joint, & so is his masterpiece.

Allston & Irving & Dana are all European.

There is a genius of a nation as of individuals which is not to be found in the numerical men but characterises the society. England, strong, practical, punctual, well-spoken England, I should not find, if I should go to the island to seek it; in parliament or in the play house or at dinner tables, I should see a great number of rich, ignorant, or book-read, conventional, proud men, many of them old women, and not the Englishman who made the good speeches, combined the accurate engines, & did the bold persistent deeds.

But in America I grieve to miss the strong black blood of the English race: ours is a pale diluted stream. What a company of brilliant young persons I have seen with so much expectation! the sort is very good, but none is good enough of his sort. Every one an imperfect specimen, respectable not valid. Irving thin, & Channing thin, & Bryant & Dana, Prescott & Bancroft. There is Webster, but he cannot do what he would; he cannot do Webster. Then the youth, as I said, are all promising failures. No writing is here, no redundant strength, but declamation, straining, correctness, & all other symptoms of debility.

The orientals behave well, but who cannot behave well who has nothing else to do? The poor Yankees who are doing the work, are all wrinkled & vexed.

The Shaker told me they did not read history not because they had not inclination for there were some who "took up a sound cross in not reading." Milton's "Paradise Lost," he knew, was among Charles Lane's books, but he had never read it. Most of them did not know it was there; he knew. There would be an objection to reading it. They read the Bible & their own publications. They write their own poetry. "All their hymns & songs of every description are manufactured in the society."

—

The Peace Society speaks civilly of Trade, in its attacks on War. Well, let Trade make hay whilst the sun shines; but know very well that when the war is disposed of, Trade is the next object of incessant attack and has only the privilege of being last devoured.

Very sad indeed it was to see this halfgod driven to the wall, reproaching men, & hesitating whether he should not reproach the gods. The world was not, on trial, a possible element for him to live in. A lover of law had tried whether law could be kept in this world, & all things answered, NO. He had entertained the thought of leaving it, & going where freedom & an element could be found. And if he should be found tomorrow at the roadside, it would be the act of the world. We pleaded guilty to perceiving the inconvenience & inequality of property & he said "I will not be a convict." Very tedious & prosing & egotistical & narrow he is, but a profound insight, a Power, a majestical man, looking easily along the centuries to explore *his contemporaries* with a painful sense of being an orphan & a hermit here. I feel his statement to be partial & to have fatal omissions, but I think I shall never attempt to set him right any more. It is not for me to answer him: though I feel the limitations & exaggeration of his picture, and the wearisome personalities. His statement proves too much: it is a *reductio ad absurdum*. But I was quite ashamed to have just revised & printed last week the old paper denying the existence of tragedy, when this modern Prometheus was in the heat of his quarrel with the gods.

Alcott has been writing poetry, he says, all winter. I fear there is nothing for me in it. His overpowering personality destroys all poetic faculty.

*

It is strange that he has not the confidence of one woman. He would be greater if he were goodhumoured but such as he is he "enlarges the known powers of man," as was said of M. Angelo.

A man sends to me for money that he may pursue his studies in theology; he wants fifty or sixty dollars, & says he wants it the "last of this week or fore part of next."—

—

I have read a proverb somewhere "—the cards beat all the players at last," which is as good a text as Eripitur persona, manet res, for my piece on the Genius of Life.

An example of the prevailing genius over all wilfulness is the veracity of language which cannot be debauched. Proverbs, words, & grammar inflections are wiser than the wisest man.

Character brings to whatever it does a great superfluity of strength which plays a gay accompaniment, the air with variations. Hear D W argue a jury cause. He imports all the experience of the senate & the state & the man of the world into the county court.

C. inquired why I would not go to B? But the great inconvenience is sufficient answer. If I could freely & manly go to the mountains, or to the prairie, or to the sea, I would not hesitate for inconvenience: but to cart all my pots & kettles, kegs, & clothespins, & all that belongs thereunto, over the mountains seems not worth while. I should not be nearer to sun or star.

The Genius is friendly to the noble and in the dark brings them friends from far. I had fancied my friend was unmatchable and now a stone is cut out from the mountain without hands, of miraculous virtues.

"My dear sir," said my friend to her suitor, "I cannot realize you."

Sunday, April 14, 3 P.M. After more than a week of finest weather, the mercury stands now at 82° in the shade.

May 8. This morn the air smells of vanilla & oranges.

Let us guard our strangeness, & if our relations lose something of tenderness let them gain in nobility.

Let us sit apart as the gods talking from peak to peak all round Olympus.

Our people are slow to learn the wisdom of sending character instead of talent to Congress. Again & again they have sent a man of great acuteness, a fine scholar, a fine forensic orator, and some master of the brawls has crunched him up in his hand like a bit of paper. At last they sent a man with a back and he defied the whole southern delegation when they attempted to smother him & has conquered them. Mr Adams is a man of great powers, but chiefly he is a sincere man & not a man of the moment and of a single measure. And besides the success or failure of the measure there remains to him the respect of all men for his earnestness. When Mr Webster argues the case there is the success or the failure, and the admiration of the unerring talent & intellectual nature, but no respect for an affection to a principle. Could Mr Webster have given himself to the cause of Abolition of Slavery in Congress, he would have been the darling of this continent, of all the youth, all the genius, all the virtue in America. Had an angel whispered in his young ear, Never mind the newspapers, Fling yourself on this principle of freedom, Show the legality of freedom; though they frown & bluster they are already half convinced & at last you shall have their votes; the tears of the love & joy & pride of the world would have been his.

from

V

1844–1845

Tom Appleton Beckford

Beckford's Italy & Spain is the book of a Sybarite of the Talleyrand, Brummel, Vivian Grey school written in 1787–9, and much of the humor consists in the contrast between the volume of this Johnson-&-Gibbon sentence and the ball-room petulance it expresses. He delights in classic antiquity; in sunsets as associated with that mythology; in music; in picturesque nature. He is only a dilettante, and before the humblest original worker would feel the rebuke of a solid domestic being as of a creator of that classic world, which he only gazes at, but lays no stone of it. He would affect contempt, but his confidence would be the great foolish multitude, and that steads him not; for when a man has once met his master, that is a secret which he cannot keep. Yet the travellers why should we blame any more than the thousands who stay at home to do less, or worse?

He loves twilight, & sleep.

Many of his criticisms are excellent. He says of the Duomo at Florence that the architect seems to have turned his church inside out, such is the ornate exterior & so simple is the interior. He says of Paul Veronese's Cana in Galilee, that the people at the table seem to be decent persons accustomed to miracles.

In sleeping figures he likes sculpture best.

Ole Bull a dignifying civilizing influence. Yet he was there for exhibition, not for music; for the wonders of his execution, not as St. Cecilia incarnated, who would be there to carry a point, & degrading all her instruments into meekest means. Yet he played as a man who found a violin in his hand, & so was bent to make much of that; but if he had found a chisel or a sword or a spyglass or a troop of boys, would have made much of them. It was a beautiful spectacle. I have not seen an artist with manners so pleasing. What a sleep as of Egypt on his lips in the midst of his rapturous music!

We are impressed by a Burke or a Schiller who believes in embodying in practice ideas; because literary men, for the most part, who are cognisant of ideas, have a settled despair as to the realization of ideas in their own times.

In Boston, I trod the street a little proudly, that I could walk from Allston's *Belshazzar's Feast* to the sculpture Gallery, & sit before Michel Angelo's "Day & Night," & the Antiques; then into the Library; then to Ole Bull.

—

The effect of these calamitous pictures of Pauperism which obtrude every where, even in the comic literature, in Punch & Judy, in Hood & Dickens suggests an admonition not so much to charity as to economy, that we may be selfcontained & ready, when the calamity comes nearer, to do our part.

Fourier is a French mind, destitute of course of the moral element. Brisbane, his American disciple, is also a French mind. The important query is *what will women say to the Theory?* Certainly not Brisbane but Channing must propose it to them. These are military minds, and their conversation is always insulting; for they have no other end than to make a tool of their companion.

I think Genius alone finishes.

Classifying words outvalue many arguments; upstart, cockney, granny, pedant, prig, precisian, rowdy, niggers,

Goethe with his extraordinary breadth of experience & culture, the security with which, like a great continental gentleman, he looks impartially over all literatures of the mountains, the provinces, & the sea, and avails himself of the best in all, contrasts with the rigour of the English, & superciliousness & flippancy of the French. His perfect taste, the austere felicities of his style.
It is delightful to find our own thought in so great a man.

—

H.'s conversation consisted of a continual coining of the present moment into a sentence & offering it to me. I compared it to a boy who from the universal snow lying on the earth gathers up a little in his hand, rolls it into a ball, & flings it at me.

In January 1845 arose the question again in our village Lyceum whether we should accept the offer of the Ladies who proposed to contribute to the Course a Lecture on Slavery by Wendell Phillipps. I pressed the acceptance on the part of the Curators of this proffer, on two grounds; 1. because the Lyceum was poor, & should add to the length & variety of their Entertainment by all innocent means, especially when a discourse from one of the best speakers in the Commonwealth was volunteered; 2. because I thought in the present state of this country the particular subject of Slavery had a commanding right to be heard in all places in New England in season & sometimes out of season, that, as in Europe the partition of Poland was an outrage so flagrant that all European men must be willing once in every month or two to be plagued with hearing over again the horrid story; so this iniquity of Slavery in this country was a ghost that would not down at the bidding of Boston merchants, or the best democratic drill-officers; but the people must consent to be plagued with it from time to time until something was done, & we had appeased the negro blood so.

The proposition was later made to have a Lyceum supplied by enthusiasts only.

We want a Lyceum just as much as a shoe-shop. It must be boundless in its hospitality.

Aristo compared lectures to baths.

—

H.D.T. said that the other world was all his art; that his pencils would draw no other; that his jackknife would cut nothing else. He does not use it as a means.

Henry is a good substantial childe, not encumbered with himself. He has no troublesome memory, no wake, but lives extempore, & brings today a new proposition as radical &

revolutionary as that of yesterday, but different. The only man of leisure in the town. He is a good Abbot Samson: & carries counsel in his breast. If I cannot show his performance much more manifest than that of the other grand promisers, at least I can see that with his practical faculty, he has declined all the kingdoms of this world. Satan has no bribe for him.

In America we are such rowdies in church & state, and the very boys are so soon ripe, that I think no philosophical skepticism will make much sensation. Spinosa pronounced that there was but one substance;—yea, verily; but that boy yonder told me yesterday he thought the pinelog was God, & that God was in the jakes. What can Spinoza tell the boy?

Even Dickens is doubtless of much use to this country, though in so humble a way as to circulate into all towns & into the lowest classes the lesson which is pasted in the waterclosets of public houses,—*Do not spit, & please close the covers.*

In America, fusion.

What a mistake is the universal usage of statesmen here to make long papers, as the Presidents' & Governors' messages, Addresses of Conventions, &c. What care our rowdy people for a constitutional argument? Cannot you give a short reason?

Poetry has never dived. It hovers opaline about the brighter surfaces, but rarely ventures into the real world. How pungent are the words that once in an age or two record those experiences.

Fourier has the immense merits of originality & hope. Whilst society is distracted with disputes concerning the negro race, he comes to prescribe the methods of removing this mask & caricature of humanity, by bringing out the true & real form from underneath.

In America, we drag a pine-log to a mill, turn a crank, & it comes out at the other end chairs & tables.

*

Whenever Heaven sends a great man into the world, it whispers the secret to one or two confidants.

In the woods with their ever festal look I am ever reminded of that parable which commends the merchant who, seeing a pearl of great price, sold all to buy that: so I could not find it in my heart to chide the Yankee who should ruin himself to buy a patch of heavy-timbered oak-land. I admire the taste which makes the avenue to a house, were the house ever so small, through a wood, as it disposes the mind of guest & host alike to the deference due to each. Hail vegetable gods!

I observe two classes very easily among those capable of thought & spiritual life, namely, those who are very intelligent of this matter, & can rise easily into it on the call of conversation, & can write strongly of it, & secondly those who think nothing else & live on that level & are conscious of no effort or even variety in experience.

—

It is strange that Jesus is esteemed by mankind the bringer of the doctrine of immortality. He is never once weak or sentimental: he never preaches the personal immortality; whilst Plato & Cicero had both allowed themselves to overstep the stern limits of the Spirit & gratify the people with that picture.

The Lyceum gives opportunity for Mr Hudson & other writers to read their impatient thoughts; but it also immediately constitutes a mark at which young men write: a mark or rather a market. The Lyceum should refuse all such pieces as were written *to* it.

—

Woman. It is the worst of her condition that its advantages are permissive. Society lives on the system of money and woman comes at money & money's worth through compliment. I should not dare to be woman. Plainly they are created for that better system which supersedes money. But today,—— In our civilization her position is often pathetic. What is she not expected to do & suffer for some invitation to strawberries & cream. Mercifully their eyes are holden that they cannot see.

*

Pythagoras was right who used music as a medicine. I lament my want of ear, but never quite despair of becoming sensible to this discipline. We cannot spare any stimulant or any purgative, we lapse so quickly into flesh & sleep. We must use all the exalters that will bring us into an expansive & productive state, or to the top of our condition. But to hear music, as one would take an ice-cream or a bath, & to forget it the next day, gives me a humble picture.

—

Jan. 30. In Boston to hear the debates of the Texan Convention with the hope that I might catch some sparks of the Typhonic rage. But I was unlucky in my visits to the house & heard only smooth whig speeches on moderation, &c. to fill time. The poor mad people did not come.

The Unitarian the milk & water era, the day of triviality & verbiage. Once "the rose of Sharon perfumed our graves," as Behmen said; but now, if a man dies, it is like a grave dug in the snow, it is a ghastly fact abhorrent to nature, & we never mention it. Death is as natural as life, and should be sweet & graceful.

—

In general, I am pained by observing the indigence of nature in this American Commonwealth. Ellen H. said she sympathized with the Transcendental movement, but she sympathized even more with the objectors. I replied that when I saw how little kernel there was to that comet which had shed terror from its flaming hair on the nations, how few & what cinders of genius, I was rather struck with surprize at the largeness of the effect, & drew a favorable inference as to the intellectual & spiritual tendencies of our people. For there had not yet appeared one man among us of a great talent. If two or three persons should come with a high spiritual aim & with great powers the world would fall in to their hands like a ripe peach.

The objection of Men of the world to the socalled Transcendentalists, is not a hostility to their truth, but that they unfit their children for business in their state-street sense & do not qualify them for any complete life of a better kind.

Go & hear a great orator to see how presentable truth & right are, & how presentable are common facts. As we read the newspapers, and as we see the effrontery with which money & power carry their ends, and ride over honesty & good-meaning, morals & religion seem to become mere shrieking & impotence. We will not speak for them, because to speak for them seems so weak & hopeless. But a true orator will instantly show you that all the states & kingdoms in the world, all the senators, lawyers, & rich men are caterpillars' webs & caterpillars, when seen in the light of this same despised & imbecile truth. Grand grand truth! the orator himself becomes a shadow & a fool before this light which lightens through him. It shines backward & forward; diminishes, annihilates everybody, and the prophet so gladly, so sublimely feels his personality lost in this gaining triumphing godhead.

"He'd harpit a fish out of saut water,
Or water from a stone,
Or milk out of a maiden's breast
That bairn had never none."

"O I did get the rose water
Whair ye wull neir get nane,
For I did get that very rose-water
Into my mither's wame."

Every man has his own courage, and is betrayed because he seeks in himself the courage of other persons, which is not there.

All reading is a kind of quotation.

Whoever can write something good himself, is thenceforward by law of the Muses' Parliament entitled to steal at discretion.

The gradual submerging of the eastern shore of America, and so of all the continents, & the correspondent rise of the western shore; the continual formation of new edge to the teeth of mastodons, &c.; the new races rise all predivided into parties ready armed & angry to fight for they know not what: Yet easy it is to see that they all share to the rankest Philistines, the same idea; that the drygoods-men & brokers are idealists; and only in quantity differ,—only differ in the degree of intensity. The idea rides & rules like the sun. Therefore, thou philosopher, rely on thy truth; bear down on it with all thy weight; add the weight of thy town, thy country, & the whole world: triumphantly, thou shalt see, it will bear it all like a scrap of down.

I think the best argument of the conservative is this bad one; that he is convinced that the angry democrat who wishes him to divide his park & chateau with him, will, on entering into the possession, instantly become conservative, & hold the property & spend it as selfishly as himself. For a better man, I might dare to renounce my estate; for a worse man, or for as bad a man as I, why should I? All the history of man with unbroken sequence of examples establishes this inference. Yet is it very low & degrading ground to stand upon. We must never reason from history, but plant ourselves on the ideal.

—

Men are edificant or otherwise. Samuel Hoar is to all men's eyes conservative & constructive: his presence supposes a well ordered society, agriculture, trade, large institutions & empire. If these things did not exist, they would begin to exist through his steady will & endeavours. Therefore he cheers & comforts men, who feel all this in him very readily. The reformer, the rebel, who comes by, says all manner of unanswerable things against the existing republic, but discovers to my groping Daemon no plan of house or empire of his own. Therefore though Samuel Hoar's town & state are a very cheap & modest commonwealth men very rightly go for him & flout the reformer.

June 15. A second visit to the Shakers with Mr Hecker. Their family worship was a painful spectacle. I could remember nothing but the Spedale dei Pazzi at Palermo; this shaking of their hands like the paws of dogs before them as they shuffled in this dunce-dance seemed the last deliration. If there was anything of heart & life in this it did not appear to me: and as Swedenborg said that the angels never look at the back of the head so I felt that I saw nothing else. My fellow men could hardly appear to less advantage before me than in this senseless jumping. The music seemed to me dragged down nearly to the same bottom. And when you come to talk with them on their topic, which they are very ready to do, you find such exaggeration of the virtue of celibacy, that you might think you had come into a hospital-ward of invalids afflicted with priapism. Yet the women were well dressed and appeared with dignity as honoured persons. And I judge the whole society to be cleanly & industrious but stupid people. And these poor countrymen with their nasty religion fancy themselves *the Church* of the world and are as arrogant as the poor negroes on the Gambia river.

—

Fourier said, Man exists to gratify his twelve passions: and he proposes to remove the barriers which false philosophy & religion & prudence have built against indulgence. Some of the old heroic legislators proposed to open public brothels as safety-valves to defend virtuous women from the occasional extravagances of desire in violent persons & to yield a resort of less danger to young men in the fury of passion. And in Amsterdam & other cities, the governments have authorized the stews. Well, Swedenborg too wandered through the Universe and found not only heavenly societies but horrid cavernous regions where imps & dragons delighted themselves in all bestialities and he said these too enjoyed their condition & recreations, as well as the cherubim theirs. Fourier too has a sacred Legion and an order called sacred, of Chastity, Virgins & bachelors; a lower order of husband & wife; a lower of free companions & harlots. In having that higher order he gives all up. For the vulgar world not yet emancipated from prejudice replies to his invitation, Well, I will select only that part from your system, and leave the sty to those who like it. I have observed that indulgence always effeminates. I have organs also & delight in pleasure, but I have experience also that this pleasure is the bait of a trap.

—

If I made laws for Shakers or a School, I should gazette every Saturday all the words they were wont to use in reporting religious experience as 'Spiritual life,' 'God,' 'soul,' 'cross,' &c. and if they could not find new ones next week they might remain silent.

Be an opener of doors for such as come after thee and do not try to make the Universe a blind alley.

—

Novels make us skeptical by giving such prominence to wealth & social position, but I think them to be fine occasional stimulants, and, though with some shame, I am brought into an intellectual state. But great is the poverty of their inventions. The perpetual motive & means of accelerating or retarding interest is the dull device of persuading a lover that his mistress is betrothed to another. D'Israeli is well worth reading; quite a good student of his English world, and a very clever expounder of its wisdom & craft: never quite a master. Novels make us great gentlemen whilst we read them. How generous, how energetic should we be in the crisis described, but unhappy is the wife, or brother, or stranger who interrupts us, whilst we read: nothing but frowns & tart replies from the reading gentleman for them. Our novel reading is a passion for results, we admire parks & the love of beauties, & the homage of parliaments.

—

People seem to me often sheathed in their tough organization. I know those who are the charge each of their several Daemon, and in whom the Daemon at intervals appears at the gates of their eyes. They have intervals, God knows, of weakness & folly like other people. Of these I take no heed: I wait the reappearings of the Genius, which are sure and beautiful.

The abolitionists with their holy cause; the Friends of the Poor; the ministers at large; the Prison Discipline Agents; the Soup Societies, the whole class of professed Philanthropists,—it is strange & horrible to say—are an altogether odious set of people, whom one would be sure to shun as the worst of bores & canters. Religion must be a crab, not a cultivated tree.

—

Do not lead me to question whether what we call science, is help or hurt. Yet unluckily in my experience of the scientific, it is a screen between you & the man having the science. He has his string of anecdotes and rules as a physician, which he must show you, & you must endure, before you can come at the colour & quality of the man. Phrenology too, I hate. C. adapts his conversation to the form of the head of the man he talks with! Alas! I dreamed that the value of life lay in its inscrutable possibilities: that I never know in addressing myself to a new individual what may befall me. I carry ever the keys of my castle in my hand ready to throw them at the feet of my lord whenever & in whatever disguise in this great carnival, I may encounter him. But the assurance that he is in the neighborhood, hidden among these vagabonds, consoles me. And shall I preclude my fortune & my future by setting up for graduate & doctor & kindly adapting my conversation to the shape of heads? When I come to that, you shall buy me for a cent.

Presently the railroads will not stop at Boston but will tunnel the city to communicate with each other. The same mob which has beat down the Bastille will soon be ready to storm the Thuilleries.

Henry described Hugh as saving every slip & stone & seed, & planting it. He picks up a peach stone & puts it in his pocket to plant. That is his vocation in the world, to be a planter of plants. Not less is a writer to heed his vocation of reporting. Whatever he beholds or experiences, he is to daguerrotype. It is all nonsense that they say that some things rebuke literature, & are undescribable; he knows better, & would report God himself or attempt it. Nothing so sudden, nothing so broad, nothing so subtle, nothing so dear, but it comes therefore commended to his pen, & he will write. In his eyes a man is the faculty of reporting, & the universe is the possibility of being reported.

In every profound conversation he saw plainly that all he had yet written was exoteric, was not the law, but gossip on the eternal politics; but true to his art he instantly endeavoured to record the conversation that so by some means he might yet save some one word of the heavenly language.

The vice of Swedenborg's mind is its theologic determination. Nothing with him has the liberality of universal wisdom but every sentence respects the Bible or some church. But a rose, a sunbeam, the human face do not remind us of deacons.

—

In common with all boys, I held a river to be good, but the name of it in a grammar hateful.

Ah! how different is it to render account to ourselves of ourselves & to render account to the public of ourselves.

> "Tis the most difficult of tasks to keep
> Heights which the soul is competent to gain"

Granted; sadly granted, but the necessity by which Deity rushes into distribution, into variety & particles, is not less divine than the unity from which all begins. Forever the Demiurgus speaks to the junior gods as in the old tradition of the Timaeus, "Gods of gods that mortal natures may subsist & that the Universe may be truly all, convert (or distribute) yourselves according to your nature to the fabrication of animals" &c &c.

The use of geology has been to wont the mind to a new chronology. The little dame school measures by which we had gauged everything, we have learned to disuse, & break up our European & Mosaic & Ptolemaic schemes for the grand style of nature & fact. We knew nothing rightly for want of perspective. Now we are learning the secularity of nature; & geology furnishes us with a metre or clock, a coarse kitchen clock, it is true, compared with the vaster measures which astronomy has to make us acquainted with! Now first we learn what weary patient periods must round themselves ere the rock is formed, then ere the rock is broken, & the first lichen race has disintegrated the thinnest external plate into soil, & opened the door for the remote Flora, Fauna, Pomona, & Ceres, to come in.

How far off yet is the trilobite: how far the quadruped: how inconceivably remote is man. All duly arrive, & then race after race. It is a long way from granite to a woodpecker, farther yet to Plato & the preaching of the immortality of the soul. Yet all must come, as surely as the first atom has two sides. The progress of physics & of metaphysics is parallel; at first it is lowest instinctive life loathsome to the succeeding tribes like the generation of sour paste. It is animalcules, earwigs, & caterpillars writhing, wriggling, devouring, & devoured. As the races advance & rise order & rank appear, & the aurora of reason & of love. Who cares how madly the early savages fight, who sides with one or another: their rage is organic and has its animal sweetness. The world goes pregnant with Europe & with better than Europe.

Nothing interests us of these or ought to. We do not wish a world of bugs or of birds. Neither afterwards do we respect one of Scythians, or Caraibs, or Feejees. As little interests us the crimes of the recent races, the grand style of nature & her periods is what they show us, but they are not for permanence, her foot will not rest. Onward & onward that evergoing progression. That breathless haste what god can tell us whither? Who cares for the crimes of the past, for oppressing whites or oppressed blacks, any more than for bad dreams? These fangs & eaters & food are all in the harmony of nature: & there too is the germ forever protected, unfolding gigantic leaf after leaf, a newer flower, a richer fruit in every period. Yet its next is not to be guessed. It will only save what is worth saving & it saves not by compassion but by power. It saves men through themselves. It appoints no police to guard the lion but his teeth & claws, no fort or city for the bird but his wings, no rescue for flies & mites but their spawning numbers, which no ravages can overcome. It deals with men after the same manner. If they are rude & foolish down they must go. When at last in a race a new principle appears, an idea, that conserves it. Ideas only save races. If the black man is feeble & not important to the existing races, not on a par with the best race, the black man must serve & be sold & exterminated. But if the black man carries in his bosom an indispensable element of a new & coming civilization, for the sake of that element no wrong nor strength nor circumstance can hurt him, he will survive & play his part. So now it seems to me that the arrival of such men as Toussaint if he is pure blood, or of Douglas if he is pure blood, outweighs all the English & American humanity. The Anti-slavery of the whole world is but dust in the balance, a poor squeamishness & nervousness; the might & the right is here. Here is the Anti-Slave. Here is Man; & if you have man, black or white is an insignificance. Why at night all men are black. The intellect, that is miraculous, who has it has the talisman, his skin & bones are transparent, he is a statue of the living God, him I must love & serve & perpetually seek & desire & dream on: and who has it not is superfluous. But a compassion for that which is not & cannot be useful & lovely, is degrading & maudlin, this towing along as by ropes that which cannot go itself. Let us not be our own dupes; all the songs & newspapers & subscriptions of money & vituperation of those who do not agree with us will avail nothing against eternal fact. I say to you, you must save yourself, black or white, man or woman. Other help is none. I esteem the occasion of this jubilee to be that proud discovery that the black race can begin to contend with the white; that in the great anthem of the world which we call history, a piece of many parts & vast compass, after playing a long time a very low & subdued accompaniment they perceive the time arrived when they can strike in with force & effect & take a master's part in the music. The civilization of the world has arrived at that pitch that their moral quality is becoming indispensable, & the genius of this race is to be honoured for itself. For this they have been preserved in sandy desarts, in rice swamps, in kitchens & shoe-shops so long. Now let them emerge clothed & in their own form. I esteem this jubilee & the fifty years' movement which has preceded it to be the announcement of that fact & our antislavery societies, boastful as we are, only the shadow & witness to that fact. The negro has saved himself, and the white man very patronisingly says, I have saved you. If the negro is a fool all the white men in the world cannot save him though they should die.

The light of the public square must at last test the merit of every statue.

*

All our literature is a quotation, our life a custom or imitation, and our body is borrowed like a beggar's dinner from a hundred charities.

But I am struck in George Sand with the instant understanding between the great; and in I Promessi Sposi with the humiliation of Fra Cristoforo; & in Faustina with the silent acquiescence of Andlau in the new choice of Faustina; for truth is the best thing in novels also.

Does not he do more to abolish Slavery who works all day steadily in his garden, than he who goes to the abolition meeting & makes a speech? The antislavery agency like so many of our employments is a suicidal business. Whilst I talk, some poor farmer drudges & slaves for me. It requires a just costume then, the office of agent or speaker, he should sit very low & speak very meekly like one compelled to do a degrading thing. Do not then, I pray you, talk of the work & the fight, as if it were any thing more than a pleasant oxygenation of your lungs. It is easy & pleasant to ride about the country amidst the peaceful farms of New England & New York &, sure every where of a strict sympathy from the intelligent & good, argue for liberty, & browbeat & chastise the dull clergyman or lawyer that ventures to limit or qualify our statement. This is not work. It needs to be done but it does not consume heart & brain, does not shut out culture, does not imprison you as the farm & the shoeshop & the forge. There is really no danger & no extraordinary energy demanded; it supplies what it wants. I think if the witnesses of the truth would do their work symmetrically, they must stop all this boast & frolic & vituperation, & in lowliness free the slave by love in the heart. Let the diet be low, & a daily feast of commemoration of their brother in bonds. Let them eat his corn cake dry, as he does. Let them wear negro-cloths. Let them leave long discourses to the defender of slavery, and show the power of true words which are always few. Let them do their own work. He who does his own work frees a slave. He who does not his own work, is a slaveholder. Whilst we sit here talking & smiling, some person is out there in field & shop & kitchen doing what we need, without talk or smiles. Therefore, let us, if we assume the dangerous pretension of being abolitionists, & make that our calling in the world, let us do it symmetrically. The world asks, do the abolitionists eat sugar? do they wear cotton? do they smoke tobacco? Are they their own servants? Have they managed to put that dubious institution of servile labour on an agreeable & thoroughly intelligible & transparent foundation? It is not possible that these purists accept the accommodations of hotels, or even of private families, on the existing profane arrangements? If they do, of course, not conscience, but mere prudence & propriety will seal their mouths on the inconsistences of churchmen. Two tables in every house! Abolitionists at one & *servants* at the other! It is a calumny that you utter. There never was, I am persuaded, an asceticism so austere as theirs, from the peculiar emphasis of their testimony. The planter does not want slaves: give him money: give him a machine that will provide him with as much money as the slaves yield, & he will thankfully let them go: he does not love whips, or usurping overseers, or sulky swarthy giants creeping round his house & barns by night with lucifer matches in their hands & knives in their pockets. No; only he wants his luxury, & he will pay even this price for it. It is not possible then that the abolitionist will begin the assault on his luxury, by any other means than the abating of his own. A silent fight without war-cry or triumphant brag, then, is the new abolition of New England sifting the thronging ranks of the champions, the speakers, the poets, the editors, the subscribers, the givers, & reducing the armies to a handful of just men & women. Alas! alas! my brothers, there is never an abolitionist in New England.

—

I understand very well in cities how the Southerner finds sympathy. The heat drives every summer the planter to the north. He comes from West & South & Southwest to the Astor & the Tremont Houses. The Boston merchant bargains for his cotton at his counting house, then calls on him at the hotel, & politely sympathizes with all his modes of thinking. 'He never sided with those violent men,—poor Garrison, poor Phillips are on the coals': well, all that is very intelligible, but the planter does not come to Concord. Rum comes to Concord but not the slave driver & we are comparatively safe from his infusions. I hardly understand how he persuades so many dignified persons,—who were never meant for tools,—to become his tools.

Intense selfishness which we all share. Planter will not hesitate to eat his negro, because he can. We eat him in milder fashion by pelting the negro's friend. We cannot lash him with a whip, because we dare not. We lash him with our tongues. I like the southerner the best; he deals roundly, & does not cant. The northerner is surrounded with churches & Sunday schools & is hypocritical. How gladly, how gladly, if he dared, he would seal the lips of these poor men & poor women who speak for him. I see a few persons in the church, who, I fancy, will soon look about them with some surprise to see what company they are keeping.
I do not wonder at feeble men being strong advocates for slavery. They have no feeling of worthiness which assures them of their own safety. In a new state of things they are by no means sure it would go well with them. They cannot work or facilitate work or cheer or decorate labour. No, they live by certain privileges which the actual order of the community yields them. Take those and you take all. I do not wonder that such would fain raise a mob for fear is very cruel.

—

The conscience of the white & the improvement of the black cooperated, & the Emancipation became inevitable. It is a great deed with great sequel & cannot now be put back. The same movement goes forward with advantage; the conscience is more tender & the black more respectable. Meantime the belly is also represented & the ignorant & sensual feel the danger & resist, so it goes slower. But it gains & the haters of Garrison have lived to rejoice in that grand world-movement which every age or two casts out so masterly an agent of good. I cannot speak of that gentleman without respect. I found him the other day in his dingy office

I have no doubt there was as much intense selfishness, as much cowardice, as much paltering then as now; many held back & called the redeemers of their race fanatics & methodists; there were many who with the utmost dignity & sweetness gave such peppercorn reasons. There were church carpets then too. And many an old aunt in man's clothes that would nail up her pew to keep Clarkson out.

The moral sense is always supported by the permanent interest of the parties. Else I know not how in our world any good thing would get done. England had an interest in abolishing slavery & pushed it.

—

Our politics very superficial. The poor in despair of Bread cry out for Bread & become unruly. They are met by bayonets. Kings & presidents know not what to do. There are no dragons or monsters described in mythology so dreadful as the real monster that is at this hour eating Europe & laying his curse on this country,—pauperism.

Buonaparte was sensible to the music of bells. Hearing the bell of a parish church, he would pause & his voice faltered as he said, "Ah! that reminds me of the first years I spent at Brienne, I was then happy."

Bonaparte by force of intellect is raised out of all comparison with the strong men around him. His marshals, though able men, are as horses & oxen. He alone is a fine tragic figure related to the daemons, & to all time. Add as much force of intellect again to repair the immense defects of his *morale*, and he would have been in harmony with the ideal world.

—

Time is the great assistant of criticism. We see the gallery, & the marble imposes on us. We cannot tell if it be good or not. But long after the truly noble forms reappear to the imagination & the inferior are forgotten.

I wish that Webster & Everett & also the young political aspirants of Massachusetts should hear Wendell Phillips speak, were it only for the capital lesson in eloquence they might learn of him. This, namely, that the first & the second & the third part of the art is to keep your feet always firm on a fact. They talk about the Whig party. There is no such thing in nature. They talk about the Constitution. It is a scorned piece of paper. He feels after a fact & finds it in the money-making, in the commerce of New England, and in the devotion of the Slave states to their interest, which enforces them to the crimes which they avow or disavow, but do & will do. He keeps no terms with sham churches or shamming legislatures, and must & will grope till he feels the stones. Then his other & better part, his subsoil, is the *morale*, which he solidly shows. Eloquence, poetry, friendship, philosophy, politics, in short all power must & will have the real or they cannot exist.

The ground of Hope is in the infinity of the world, which infinity reappears in every particle. I know, against all appearances, that there is a remedy to every wrong, and that every wall is a gate.

—

A man of Napoleon's stamp almost ceases to have a private speech & opinion. He is so largely receptive & is so posited that he comes to be an office for all the light, intelligence, wit, & power of the age & country. He makes the code,—the system of weights & measures. All distinguished engineers, savans, statists, report to him; so likewise do all good heads in every kind. He catches not only the best measures & adopts them, sets his stamp on them, but also every happy & memorable expression (as illustrated by Mirabeau & Dumont). Every line of Napoleon's therefore deserves reading as it is the writing of France, & not of one individual. Napoleon was truly France.

He was nicknamed *Cent mille hommes.*

—

Alcott does not do justice to the merits of labour: The whole human race spend their lives in hard work from simple & necessary motives, and feel the approbation of their conscience; and meet with this talker at their gate, who, as far as they see, does not labour himself, & takes up this grating tone of authority & accusation against them. His unpopularity is not at all wonderful. There must be not a few fine words, but very many hard strokes every day, to get what even an ascetic wants.

Putnam pleased the Boston people by railing at Goethe in his ΦBK oration because Goethe was not a New England Calvinist. If our lovers of greatness & goodness after a local type & standard could expand their scope a little they would see that a worshipper of truth and a most subtle perceiver of truth like Goethe with his impatience of all falsehood & scorn of hypocrisy was a far more useful man & incomparably more helpful ally to religion than ten thousand lukewarm churchmembers who keep all the traditions and leave a tithe of their estates to establish them. But this clergyman should have known that the movement which in America created these Unitarian dissenters of which he is one, begun in the mind of this great man he traduces; that he is precisely the individual in whom the new ideas appeared & opened to their greatest extent & with universal application, which more recently the active scholars in the different departments of Science, of State, & of the Church have carried in parcels & thimblefuls to their petty occasions. Napoleon I join with him as being both representatives of the impatience & reaction of nature against the morgue of conventions, two stern realists. They want a third peer who shall stand for sentiment as they for truth & power.

S.A.R is a person externally very successful, (respectably married & well provided for,) with most happy family around her by whom she is loved & revered, & surrounded too by old & tried friends who dearly cherish her. She has quick senses and quick perceptions and ready sympathies which put her into just relations with all persons, and a tender sense of propriety which recommends her to persons of all conditions.
Her bias is intellectual. It is not her delicacy of moral sentiment that sways her, but the absence of all motive to vice in one whose passion is for the beauty of laws. She would pardon any vice in another which did not obscure his intellect or deform him as a companion. She knows perfectly well what is right & wrong, but it is not from conscience that she acts, but from sense of propriety in the absence too of all motives to vice. She has not a profound mind, but her faculties are very muscular, and she is endowed with a certain restless & impatient temperament, which drives her to the pursuit of knowl-

edge not so much for the value of the knowledge but for some rope to twist, some grist to her mill. For this reason it is almost indifferent to her what she studies, languages, chemistry, botany, metaphysics, with equal zeal, & equal success, grasping ever all the details with great precision & tenacity, yet keeping them details & means, to a general end which yet is not the most general & grand.
I should say that her love of ends is less than her impartial delight in all means; delight in the exercise of her faculties, and not her love of truth, is her passion. She has a wonderful catholicity, not at all agreeable to precisians, in her creed & in her morality. She sympathizes with De Stael, & with Goethe, as living in this world, & frankly regrets that such beings should die as had more fitness to live in this world than any others in her experience. In like manner, whilst she would rapidly appreciate all the objections which speculative men would offer to the actual society among us, she would deprecate any declaration or step which pledged one of her friends to any hostility to society, fearing much more the personal inconvenience to one she loved, than gratified by his opportunity of spiritual enlargement.

This delight in detail, this pleasure in the work, & not in a result, appears in her conversation, wherein she does not rest for the tardy suggestions of nature & occasion, but eagerly recalls her books, her studies, her newest persons, and recites them with heat & enjoyment to her companion.

extreme gentleness

excels in what is called using philosophy against the hurts of life. She follows nature in many particulars of life where others obtrude their own will & theory. She leaves a dunce to be a dunce, & rather observes & humours than guides a scholar. She is necessitarian in her opinions, & believes that a loom which turns out huckabuck can never be talked into making damask. This makes her very despondent in seeing faults of character in others, as she deems them incurable. She however has much faith in the maturation & mellowing of characters, which often supplies some early defect.

She will by no means content an absolutist by her reliance on principles. She has too much respect to facts. She delights in French science for its precision & experiment and its freedom from English convention.

Very little taste in the fine arts, not at all disposed to hazard a judgment on a picture, or a statue, or a building, and only a secondary taste in music, & even in poetry,—admiring what those whom she loves & trusts admire, & so capable of pleasure, that she can easily be pleased by what she is assured by those she trusts is pleasing. If they say 'tis good, 'tis good; if they say 'tis bad, 'tis bad.

She is feminine in her character, though she talks with men. She has no disposition to preach, or to vote, or to lead society. She is superior to any appetites or arts. She wishes to please & to live well with a few, but in the frankest, most universal & humane mode: but in her unskilfulness & inattention to trifles, likes very well to be treated as a child & to have her toilette made for her by her young people, too confident in her own legitimate powers of engaging the best, to take any inferior methods.

An innate purity & nobility which releases her once for all from any solicitudes for decorum, or dress, or other appearances. She knows her own worth, & that she cannot be soiled by a plain dress, or by the hardest household drudgery.

She is a pelican mother, and though one might not say of her what was said of the Princess Vaudemont, "ask any beggar the way to her house; they all know it;" yet of her house & her husband's, it is certain that every beggar & every guest who has once visited it, will never forget it. It is very certain that every young man of parts remembers it as the temple of learning & ideas.

After all, we have not described her, for she is obviously inspired by a great bright fortunate daemon.

*

She is of that truth of character that she torments herself with any injustice real or imagined she may have done to another.

—

The critic knows very well that Nature will outwit the wisest writer, though it were Plato or Spinoza, and his book will fall into this dead limbo we call literature; else the writer were God too, & his work another nature.

February 26. A thaw for more than a week & three days of heavenly weather bringing all mythology on their breezy dawns. Down falls the water from the steeps; up shoots the northern-light after sunset from the horizon. But nature seems a dissipated hussey. She seduces us from all work, listen to her rustling leaves,—to the invitations which each blue peak, and rolling river, & fork of woodland road offers, & we should never wield the shovel or the trowel.
March 15. How gladly, after three months sliding on snow, our feet find the ground again!

Venus or Beauty, author of sport & jest, cheerer & rejoicer of men by the illuminations of beauty, was worshipped as the mother of all things. What right have you scholars & thinkers to pretend to plans of philanthropy, who freeze & dispirit me by that selfish murderous hang-dog face?

Proclus. I not only do not think he has his equal among contemporary writers, but I do not know men sufficiently athletic to read him. There is the same difference between the writings of these Platonists & Scotch metaphysics as between the sculptures of Phidias & the statues of Tam o'Shanter & My Uncle Toby. They abound in personification. Every abstract idea, every element, every agent in nature or in thought, is strongly presented as a god, in this most poetic philosophy, so that the universe is filled with august & exciting images. It is imaginative & not anatomical. It is stimulating.

—

The history of Buonaparte is the commanding romance of modern times because every reader studies in it his own history. He is a good average man because he was a citizen like his reader who arrived by very intelligible merits at such a free position that he could indulge & did indulge all those tastes which the reader possesses but is obliged to conceal and deny. Good society, good books, fast travelling, personal weight, the execution of his ideas, the standing in the attitude of a benefactor to all persons, the refined enjoyment of pictures, statues, music, palaces, & conventional honours, precisely what is agreeable to the heart of every man in the 19th Century this powerful man possessed.

—

I believe our political parties have nothing fantastic or accidental in their origin, but express very rudely some lasting relation. We cannot quarrel with the parties with more reason than with the east wind, or the winter; for, on the whole, no option is made, but the men stand for the defence of those interests in which they find themselves. Our quarrel with them is when they quit this deep natural ground at the bidding of some leader, &, altogether from personal considerations, throw themselves into the defence & maintenance of points nowise belonging to their system. A party is perpetually corrupted by personality, and, whilst we absolve the party from all wilfulness or dishonesty, we cannot extend the same charity to the leaders. They reap the rewards of the fidelity & zeal of the masses they direct, and no party was ever without adroit & unscrupulous guides who turned their docility & ardour to a private account.

Bonaparte delighted in tasting his good fortune. Raguideau, who had dissuaded Mme Beauharnois from "marrying a soldier with nothing but his cloak & his sword," was sent for on the day of the Coronation of the Emperor, and asked "Well, have I nothing but my cloak & my sword?"

When Bourrienne stated the difficulty of getting acknowledged by the old reigning families of Europe, Bonaparte said, "If it comes to that I will dethrone them all, & then I shall be the oldest sovereign among them."

"Courage," said he to Caulincourt, "may defend a crown, but infamy never."

"Gentlemen" said he in 1814, "You may say what you please but in the situation in which I stand my only nobility is the rabble of the faubourgs, & I know of no rabble but the nobility whom I have created." *Bourrienne*

I neither think our democratic institutions dangerous to the citizen, nor on the other hand do I think them better than those which preceded them. They are not better but only fitter for us. We may be wise in asserting the advantage in modern times of the democratic form, but to other states of society in which religion consecrated the monarchical, that & not this was expedient. The democracy is better for us, because the religious sentiment of the present time accords better with it. We are in our whole education & way of thinking & acting, democrats, & are nowise qualified to judge of monarchy, which to our fathers living & thinking in the monarchical idea was just as exclusively right.

As a pendant to the Corsican anecdote, and to the story, in Aubrey, of —— who covered himself with dead bodies to keep himself warm on a battle field, I read in Bentley magazine of a soldier at Borodino who crept into the carcass of a horse to sleep. At Nantucket, I saw a ship master who had eaten a man and at New Bedford one who had been in the mouth of a whale.

> "Before he fought a battle Bonaparte thought little about what he should do in case of success, but a great deal about what he should do in case of a reverse of fortune."
>
> Bourrienne Vol 2 p 27

He risked everything & spared nothing.
What he had determined to do he did thoroughly: on any point he poured hosts: he rained grape & cannon shot.
He promised the troops in his proclamation at Austerlitz that he would not expose his person, the reverse of the ordinary declaration of generals & sovereigns in their proclamations.

*

The idol of common men because he had in transcendant degrees the qualities & powers of common men. This terrific ciphering, this just expectation from gold & iron, from earth & water, from wheels & ships, from troops & cabinets, that each should do after its kind & not the folly of expecting that from them which in ordinary experience they do not. Herein resembling Luther a little.
He was moreover entitled to his crowns. He won his victories in his head before he won them on the field. He was not lucky only.
But this ciphering is specially French. Fourier is another arithmetician. Laplace, Lagrange, Berthollet walking metres & destitute of worth. These cannot say to men of talents, I am that which these express, as Character always seems to say.

Yet man always feels that Napoleon fights for him; these are honest victories: this strong steam-engine does our work.

—

A despair has crept over the Whig party in this country. They the active, enterprizing, intelligent, well meaning, & wealthy part of the people, the real bone & strength of the American people, find themselves paralysed & defeated everywhere by the hordes of ignorant & deceivable natives & the armies of foreign voters who fill Pennsylvania, N. Y., & New Orleans, and by those unscrupulous editors & orators who have assumed to lead these masses. The creators of wealth and conscientious, rational, & responsible persons, those whose names are given in as fit for jurors, for referees, for offices of trust, those whose opinion is public opinion, find themselves degraded into observers, & violently turned out of all share in the action & counsels of the nation.

How many degrees of power! That which we exert, political, social, intellectual, moral, is most superficial. We talk & work half asleep. Between us & our last energy lie terrific social & then sublime solitary exertions. Let our community rise en masse, the undrilled original militia; or let the private man put off the citizen, & awake the hero; then is one a match for a nation.

*

The position of Massachusetts seems to me to better for Mr Hoar's visit to S. Carolina, in this point, that one illusion is dispelled. Massachusetts was dishonoured before; but she was credulous in the protection of the Constitution & either did not believe or affected not to believe that she was dishonoured. Now all doubt on that subject is removed, & every Carolina boy will not fail to tell every Massachusetts boy, whenever they meet, how the fact stands. The Boston merchants would willingly salve the matter over, but they cannot hereafter receive Southern gentlemen at their tables, without a consciousness of shame. I do not like very well to hear a man say he has been in Carolina. I know too well what men she suffers in her towns. He is no freeman.

In every government there are wild lawless provinces where the constituted authorities are forced to content themselves with such obedience as they can get. Turkey has its Algiers & Morocco, Naples its Calabria, Rome its Fondi, London its Alsatia, & Bristol County its Slab Bridge, where the life of a man is not worth insuring. South Carolina must be set down in that infamous category, and we must go there in disguise & with pistols in our pockets leaving our pocketbooks at home, making our wills before we go.

Literature is resorted to as consolation, not as decalogue; then is literature defamed & disgraced.

Lord Edward Fitzgerald, after travelling amongst barbarous nations, said "I have seen human nature in all its forms; it is everywhere the same, but the wilder it is, the more virtuous."

—

I talked yesterday with the Shaker Elders Joseph Myrick & Grove Blanchard and stated my chief objection to their community as a place of education, that there was too much interference. In heaven, a squadron of angels would be a Squadron of Gods, with profoundest mutual deference; so should men live.

It is true that a community cannot be truly seen from the outside. If deep sympathy exists, what seems interference, is not, being justified by the heart of the suffering party. And in

Lane's representation of their society, they appear well. He thinks them open to the greatest improvement & enlargement on every side, even of science, learning, & elegance: only not suddenly. In that case, one can well enjoy their future, and leave them as an order of American monks & nuns, and willingly release from nuptial vows a class of Virgins & Children of light, who would dedicate themselves to austerity & religion, labor, & love.

Lane thought that they looked on their speech, their dress, & even their worship as not sacred, nor even the best, but as open to revisal, & though not rashly alterable, yet modifications were likely to be received. Elder Grove had said, that their mode of worship was once spontaneous; now it was only preserved as a condition for exciting the spirit.
I told him they seemed peasants, with a squalid contentment.

—

The aim of writers is to tame the Holy Ghost, & produce it as a show to the city. But the sole terms on which the Infinite will come to cities, is the surrender of cities to its Will. And yet Nature seems sometimes to coquette with great poets, and, in its willingness to be expressed, suffers them to be knowing men of the world, yet does not withdraw its inspirations.

The Daemons lurk & are dumb: they hate the newspapers.

—

The state is our neighbors; our neighbors are the state. It is a folly to treat the state as if it were some individual arbitrarily willing thus and so. It is the same company of poor devils we know so well, of William & Edward & John & Henry, doing as they are obliged to do, & trying hard to do conveniently what must & will be done. They do not impose a tax. God & the nature of things imposes the tax, requires that the land shall bear its burden, of road, & of social order, & defence; & I confess I lose all respect for this tedious denouncing of the state by idlers who rot in indolence, selfishness, & envy in the chimney corner.

—

Alas! our penetration increases as we grow older, and we are no longer deceived by great words when unrealized or unembodied. Say rather we detect littleness in expressions &

thoughts that once we should have taken & cited as proofs of strength.

—

We do not live an equal life but one of contrasts & patchwork; now a little joy, then a sorrow, now a sin, then a generous or brave action. We must always be little whilst we have these alternations. Character is regular & homogeneous. Our world, it is true, is like us: it has many weathers, here a shade & there a rainbow; here gravel, & there a diamond; polar ice, then temperate zone, then torrid; now a genius, then a good many mediocre people.

H.D.T. said that the Fourierists had a sense of duty which led them to devote themselves to their second best.

—

I am far from wishing that Mass should retaliate. If we could bring down the N. Eng culture to the Carolina level, if we were cartwhip gentlemen, it might be possible to retaliate very effectively, and to the apprehensions of Southerners. Shut up Mr Calhoun and Mr Rhett when they come to Boston as hostages for the mulattoes & negroes they have kidnapped from the caboose & the cabin of our ships. But the N. Eng. culture is not so low. Ours is not a brutal people, but intellectual & mild. Our land is not a jail; we keep open house; we have taken out the bolt & taken off the latch & taken the doors off the hinges. Does S.C. warn us out & turn us out, and then come hither to visit us? She shall find no bar. We are not afraid of visiters. We do not ring curfews nor give passes nor keep armed patroles; from Berkshire to the sea our roads are open; from N.H. to Connecticutt the land is without a guard; we have no secrets, no fears. For her flying slave & for his degraded master here is rest & plenty and wisdom & virtue which he cannot find at home.

We don't expect a sovereign state to treat us like a footpad. But S.C. does so treat us.

The doctrine of S.C. proves too much.

*

But new times have come & new policy subtler & nobler & more strong than any before. It is the inevitable effect of culture—it cannot be otherwise—to dissolve the animal ties of brute strength, to insulate, to make a country of men, not one strong officer but a thousand strong men, ten thousand. In all S.C. there is but one opinion, but one man: Mr Calhoun. Its citizens are but little Calhouns. In Massachusetts there are many opinions, many men. It is coming I hope to a pass when there shall not be an Atlas and a Post, the Daily Advertiser & the Courier, but these voices shall lose their importance in a crowd of equal & superior men.

And such shall their influence be. Every one a new & finished man whom the rogue shall have no increased skill to meet by his dealing with his predecessor but here is a new accuser with new character & all the majesty of wisdom & virtue.

—

Let us not pretend an union where union is not. Let us not cowardly say that all is right where all is damnable. Let us not treat with fawning hospitalities & deceive others by harbouring as a gentleman a felon & a manstealer but let us put all persons on their guard & say this dog will bite. Come not into his company, he will kidnap & burk you.

—

"I am convinced I shall have as much pleasure in reading your work as I have had in receiving it," wrote Talleyrand to every author.

Where does the Princess of Vaudemont live? "Rue St Lazare but really I have forgotten the number. You have only to ask the first beggar you meet;—they all know her house," replied Talleyrand.

The use of all books is suggestional or critical and who reads Swedenborg will be struck with its spirit of true science. It shames literature by hugging things so closely. One would say there never was a book before. The others were pert, were false inasmuch as they were detachments & declarations of independence, false by being fragmentary, as nature or things never are; whilst Swedenborg is systematic & respective of the world in every sentence & in every word. This is no writer of sentences, weak because they are bon mots, & not parts of natural discourse; mere childish expressions of surprise or pleasure in nature, or, worse, owing their brief notoriety to their petulance or aversion from the order of nature, being some curiosity or oddity, designedly not in harmony with nature, & so framed as to excite surprise & attention, as jugglers do by concealing the means. In Swedenborg all the means are evenly given without any trick or defect. This admirable writing is pure from all pertness or egotism.

That Plato is philosophy, & philosophy Plato, is the stigma of mankind. Vain are the laurels of Rome, vain the pride of England in her Newton, Milton, & Shakspeare, whilst neither Saxon nor Roman have availed to add any idea to the categories of Plato.

—

The annexation of Texas looks like one of those events which retard or retrograde the civilization of ages. But the World Spirit is a good swimmer, and storms & waves cannot easily drown him. He snaps his finger at laws.

"As we grow old," said A., "the beauty steals inward."

New Hampshire is treacherous to the honor, honesty, & interest of New England: is & has been. I do not look at the Massachusetts democrats in the same light. Theirs is a sort of fancy politics. I have a better opinion than to believe they would vote as they do, if the question depended on them. But as the proverb goes, "You may well walk if you hold the bridle of your horse in your hand," so I interpret the caprice of & tactics of our compatriots in this Commonwealth on the subject of Texas. They know that the great & governing sentiment of the State is anti-slavery & anti-Texas, and whilst it is so, they can safely indulge a little flirting with the great Mother Democracy at Tammany Hall or at Washington which has made Texas the passport to its grace.

The constitutional argument is ever trivial for the *animus* of the framers is not a fixed fact but a Proteus. The Constitution was an arrangement, not an organic somewhat, and in

S. Carolina means one thing, in Massachusetts another. In such a case, nothing avails but morals & might:—'You hurt me, and I will blow your brains out, but I will put an end to this.' I do not see why the two states cannot immediately settle the dispute by a treaty. Let them appoint commissioners to meet at Philadelphia, & fix a rule of conduct to which both states will agree.

from

W

1845

The English nation is full of manly clever men, well-bred, who write these pungent off-hand paragraphs in the literary & political journals expressing clearly & courageously their opinion on any person or performance, & so far very satisfactory to read. In all this wide America littered with newspapers, there is not a solitary writer of this sort, so common in England. They do this, & they write poetry, as they box: by education. The Praeds & Freres & Milneses & Hoods & Cannings & Macaulays seem to me to make poems as they make speeches in Parliament or at the hustings or as they shoot and ride. It is a *coup de force.* All this is convenient & civilized: But I had rather take very uncultured, inornate, irregular, very bad poetry with the chance of now & then an urgent fiery line like threads of gold in a mass of ore.

We in America have the comfort of the wretched, that out of this zone of clever mediocrity, England is as indigent as America in great writers.

Ah we busybodies! Cannot we be a little abstemious? We talk too much, & act too much, & think too much. Cannot we cease doing, & gravitate only to our ends? Cannot we let the morning be?

The only use which the country people can imagine of a scholar, the only compliment they can think of to pay him, is, to ask him to deliver a Temperance Lecture, or to be a member of the School Committee.

A few foolish & cunning managers ride the conscience of this great country with their Texas or Tariff or Democracy or other mumbo jumbo, & all give in & are verily persuaded that that is great,—all else is trifling. And why? Because there is really no great life; not one demonstration in all the broad land of that which is the heart & the soul of every rational American Man: the mountains walking, the light incarnated, reason & virtue clothed in flesh,—he does not see.

Friends have nothing to give each other; nothing to withhold; nothing to ask for, or that can be refused: such liberty would infer imperfect affinity. All that behoves them is clearness, or, not to miscall relations. Truth forevermore & love after that.

—

I have found a subject, *On the use of great men*; which might serve a Schleiermacher for monologues to his friends. But, in the first place, there should be a chapter *on the distribution of the hand into fingers*, or on the great value of these individuals as counterweights, checks on each other. What a satisfaction, a fortress, a citadel I find in a new individual who is undoubtedly of this class. How much now Schelling avails, and how much every day Plato! What storms of nonsense they silently avert.

It is but a few years ago that Swedenborgism was exhibited to our people in a pamphlet of garbled extracts from Swedenborg's writings as a red rag of whoredom. Dr Ripley lived & died in the belief that it was a horrible libertinism. Now Fourier is represented in the same light by the Swedenborgians, who get their revenge so.

It is easy to see what must be the fate of this fine system in any very serious & comprehensive enterprise to set it on foot in this country. As soon as our people got wind of the doctrine of sexual relations of this master, it would fall at once into the hands of the rowdies, who would flock in troops & gangs to so fair a game. "Who would see fun must be on hand!" And like the dreams of poetic people on the first outbreak of the old French Revolution they must disappear in a slime of mire & blood.

Fourier is of the opinion of St Evremond's philosopher, Bernier, who confided to St E. a secret, that, "abstinence from pleasure appeared to him a great sin."

No, it is not the part & merit of a man to make his stove with his own hands, or cook & bake his own dinner: Another can do it better & cheaper; but it is his essential virtue to carry out into action his own dearest ends, to dare to do what he believes & loves. If he thinks a sonnet the flower & result of the world, let him sacrifice all to the sonnet; if he loves the society of one or of several friends, more than life, let him so arrange his living & make everything yield to the procuring him that chief good. Now, we spend our money for that which is not bread, for paint & floor-cloths, for newspapers, & male and female servants that yield us the very smallest fraction of direct advantage. The friction of this social machine is grown enormous, & absorbs almost all the power applied.

—

Art requires a living soul. The dunces believe, that, as it must, at any one moment, work in one direction, an automaton will do as well, or nearly; & they beseech the Artist to say, "In what direction?" "In every direction," he replies, "in any direction, or in no direction, but it must be alive."

—

Fourier, in his talk about women, seems one of those salacious old men who are full of the most ridiculous superstitions on this matter. In their head, it is the universal rutting season. Any body who has lived with women will know how false & prurient this is; how serious nature always is; how chaste is their organization, & how lawful a class of people women are.

The Native American party resembles a dog which barks at all strangers.

Bonap represents the Business Men's Party against the Morgue.
But the Morgue is only the Bu M Party gone to seed.

The lesson he teaches is that which vigour always teaches, that, there is always room for it. He would not take No for an answer. When he was born there could be nothing new in war. And he found impediments that would have stopped anybody else, but he saw what gibbering quaking ghosts they were, &

he put his hand through them. If you listen to your commissary, he said, an army would never move.

Bonaparte is a confutation of heaps of cowardly doubts. When he appeared it was the belief of all military men in Europe that "there could be nothing new in war." As it is always the belief of society that the world is used up. But Genius always sees room for one man more.

Practical Man
There is always room for a man of force, and not only so, but he makes room for many. There is always room for a man of force, if it were only as Buonaparte replied to Bourrienne when he showed the difficulty of getting acknowledged by the old reigning families of Europe, "If it comes to that, I will dethrone them all, & then I shall be the oldest sovereign among them." For really society is at any time only a troop of thinkers, and the best heads among them take the best seats. It is with the prizes of power & place as it is with estates. A feeble man can only see the farms that are fenced & tilled; the houses that are built. At the end of the town, he is at the end of the world. The strong man sees not only the actual but the possible houses & farms. His eye makes estates & villages, as fast as the sun breeds clouds.
There is always room for a man of force as I think even swindlers & impostors show. A man of more talent than Cagliostro or Monroe Edwards would take the wind out of the sails of kings & governors, cotton-lords & Rothschilds and make asses of the heads of Society. For, as these are the slaves of appearance also, & not of truth, they have not an intrinsic defence to make, but only stand on opinion. But the lover of truth is invulnerable.
Yet a bully cannot lead the age.

—

I have now arrived at a perfect selfishness on the most enforced consideration. For I am constrained by many lapses & failures to proportion my attempts to my means. Now I receive daily just so much vital energy as suffices to put on my clothes, to take a few turns in my garden & in my study with a book or a pen in my hand. If I attempt anything beyond this, if I so much as stretch out my hand to help my neighbor in his field, the stingy Genius leaves me faint & sprawling; and I must pay for this vivacity by a prostration for two or three days following. These are costly experiments to try, I cannot afford two or three days when I count how many days it requires to finish one of my tasks; so I grow circumspect & disobliging beyond the example of all the misers. My kings & exemplars are St Hunks & St Elwes—.

—

I stood methought in a city of beheaded men, where the decapitated trunks continued to walk. Purposeless, confounded, and to seek, were all the parties. Is it the odours of a city, so mnemonical in their properties, which degrade & jade the mind of a countryman? I have in Boston a disease of skepticism, hunger, & miscellany.

What argument, what eloquence can avail against the power of that one word *niggers*? The man of the world annihilates the whole combined force of all the antislavery societies of the world by pronouncing it.

I have charged the Abolitionist sometimes with stopping short of the essential act of abstaining from all products of slave-labour. The apology for their use is not comfort & self indulgence, but, I doubt not, the same feeling which I & others insist on, that we will not be headlong & abandoned to this one mania.

—

In reading books as in seeing men, one may well keep, if he can, his first thoughts; for they will soon be written over by the details of argument & sentiment in the book, and yet they are a juster judgment of the book than a digest of the particular merits can yield. As W. T said of the first impression of a face, that after your friend has come & gone many times & now is long absent that first seen face comes back to the memory & not the more intimate knowledge of recent days.

Is it not good that the muse should not govern; that men of thought & of virtue should be at leisure, and ridiculously vacant, & to seek,—rambling ingloriously in woods & by seashores;—that things should be left to themselves, as now in America all goes to a merry prosperous tune,—good & bad is done, government is not felt, & the governers have an idle time of it?

Society at all times has the same want, namely, of one sane man with adequate powers of expression to hold up each new object of monomania in its right relations. The ambitious & the mercenary bring their last new mumbo-jumbo, whether it be Tariff or Texas or Mesmerism or Phrenology or Antimasonry or Trade in Eastern lands or Puseyism, and by detaching this one object from its relations easily succeed in making it seen insanely: and a great multitude go suddenly mad on the subject; and they are not to be reproved or cured by the opposite multitude, who are kept from this particular insanity only by an equal frenzy on another crotchet. But let one man have so comprehensive an eye that he can replace this isolated wonder in its natural neighborhood & relations, it loses instantly all illusion, and the returning reason of the community thanks the reason of the monitor.

The eager Shaker charged Adam with the capital sin of generation, and all his posterity with the same, compromising the existence of Mother Ann, and of the accuser himself with sincere absurdity. And most of our criticism is of the same web.

I had rather stand charged in your eyes with the melancholy & weakness of Skepticism, than with the meanness of an untruth. I will not lie for the truth.

All the arguments are against literature yet one verse of a poem will blow them & me away.

Ballads show the indifferency of subjects, times, styles, & manners.

I woke this morn with a dream which perchance was true that I was living in the morning of history amidst barbarians, that right & truth had yet no voice, no letters, no law, every one did what he would & grasped what he could.

—

Strange superfluity of nature, that so little account is made of multitudes of men. The masses, from the dawn of history down, are food for powder. The idea dignifies a few leaders in whom is sentiment, opinion, love, self devotion, and they make war & death sacred, but the wretches whom they hire and kill, remain the wretches whom they hire & kill.

We have received the opinion, let us hope unjustly, that the men who surround us value a long life, and do not esteem life simply as a means of expressing the sentiment. But Beauty belongs to the sentiment & is always departing from those who depart out of that. The hero rises out of all comparison with contemporaries & with ages of men, because he scorns old age & lands & money & power, and will brave all mankind just as readily as a single enemy at the call of that private & perfect Right & Beauty in which he lives.

"Man is a torch borne in the wind"

Is there only one courage & one warfare? I cannot manage sword & rifle, can I not therefore be brave? I thought there were as many courages as men, and as many weapons as men. Is a man only the breech of a gun or a hasp to a bowie knife? I think the reason why men fail in fighting giants, is because they wear Saul's armour instead of their own. The shepherd boy very sensibly fought with a sling & a pebble. I decline henceforward (ah would God it were so!) foreign methods & foreign courages. I will do that which I can do: I will fight by my strength, not by my weakness.

"Not dead but living are ye to account those who are slain in the way of God."

Mahomet.

—

The poet and the citizen perfectly agree in conversation on the wise life. The poet counsels his own son as if he were a merchant. The poet with poets betrays no amiable weakness; they all chime in, and are as inexorable as bankers on the subject of real life. They have no toleration for literature: it is all dilettantism and disgusts. Not Napoleon hated ideologists worse than they. Art is only a fine word for appearance in default of matter. And they sit white over their stoves and talk themselves hoarse on the mischief of books and the effeminacy of bookmakers.

But at a single strain of a flute out of a window, at the dashing among the stones of a brook from the hills, or at the suggestion of a word from an imaginative person all this grave conclusion is blown out of memory, the sun shines & the worlds roll to music, and the poet replaces all this cowardly self-denial & God-denial of the literary class, with the one blazing assurance that to one poetic success the world will surrender on its knees. Instantly he casts in his lot with the pearl-diver or the diamond merchant & joyfully will lose days & months & estates & credit also in the profound hope that one restoring, all-rewarding, immense success will arrive at length which will give him at one bound the throne of the universe. And rightly; for if his wild prayers are granted, if he is to succeed, his achievement is the piercing of the brass heavens of Boston & Christendom and letting in one beam of the pure Eternity which instantly burns up this whole universe of shadows & chimaeras in which we dwell. Every poet knows the unspeakable hope & represents its audacity by throwing it out of all probability in his conversation.

Mrs R. "hated to hear of the opposition of clergymen & others to the Fast Day, for she thought our people had so few festivals and this was now well established," and the penitential form of the proclamation gives it a certain zest which the other holidays want.

—

Frivolous reasons have allowance with all men & with poets also, but no man says, I was reading Plato & therefore could not come; I had new rhymes jingling in my brain, and would not risk losing them.

Today is carnival in Heaven, the angels almost assume flesh, and repeatedly have been visible. The imagination of the gods is excited, & rushes on every side into forms. Yesterday not a bird peeped, scarcely a leaf was left, the world was thin & barren, peaking & pining. Today it is inconceivably populous, creation swarms.

One would think from the talk of men that riches & poverty were a great matter whilst they are really a thin costume & our life, the life of all of us, is identical. For we transcend circumstance continually and taste the real quality of existence; as, in our employments which only differ in the manipulation but express the same laws; or in our thoughts, which wear no coats & taste no ice creams. We see God face to face every hour & know the savour of nature.

The muse demands real sacrifices. I must lose an important advantage by neglect. I must suffer the well of my house to be dug in the wrong place. I must sacrifice a tree.

A man shall not be a pond. As the water came in, so it shall go out. I think the charm of rhetoric is still that; the hint or advertisement it gives us of our constitution; the pilgrim, the palmer, shell on shoulder, marching fraternity,—we are bound on a long tramp. Before God, why sit ye here?

One man all ligament & another all explosion.

—

You say that we talk of slavery & patriotism but will not do any thing. Why, but because we have not sufficient insight? In this new matter of association, are men to blame that they will not leave their homesteads & try the hazardous experiment of a new colony in the woods of the west or in Brook Farm or Skeneateles, perilling the means of living of their families? They wish well to your Enterprise but it looks to them by no means wise & secure. They want sight, certainty, thorough knowledge.

They are perfectly right in refusing their contribution & their personal aid to your project. Better certainly that you should lack their aid, than that they should do a foolish thing. Then let us have insight before all things.

—

Is there a book that will not leave us where it found us?
"The Republic," perhaps?

Yes, if there were one to read it with.
What we want, then, is a class.
A class of two.

Society is a great boarding house in which people of all characters & habits meet for their dinner & eat harmoniously together; but, the meal once over, they separate to the most unlike & opposite employments.

On the superlative. The low expression is strong & agreeable. In the fine scenery on the Hudson river one boy said to another "Come up here, it looks pretty out of doors." In crossing Mount Holly in Vermont one of the country girls on the top of the coach said to another "We shall soon come to that rocky spot," which turned out to be a wild place. They do not call particular summits as Killington Peak, Camel's Rump, Mansfield Mt. &c. mountains, but only "*them ere rises*" & reserve the word mountain for the *range* as when they cross the mountain at Mt Holly or Woodstock or ——

I avoid the Stygian anniversaries at Cambridge, those hurrahs among the ghosts, those yellow, bald, toothless meetings in memory of red cheeks, black hair, and departed health. Most forcible Feeble made the only oration that fits the occasion that contains all these obituary eloquences. Bluebirds celebrate theirs.

Animal Spirits. On common grounds as at a feast common people entirely meet or even blend. Each new comer is only the animal spirit of the other extended. Instead of carrying the water in a hundred buckets we have a hose, and every hose fits every hydrant.

1845
Saturday, 7 June. I went with C. S. to see Charles K. N. We found him rapt as ever in his great Gothic cathedral of fancies; pained now, it seems, by the doubt whether he should retire to more absolute inward priesthood, or accept the frequent & to him dear solicitations of domestic & varied life. His idea of

love, which he names so often, is, I think, only the wish to be cherished. He is too full of his prophecy, once to think of friendship. Saints in a convent who all recognize each other, & still retire,—that is his image. A purer service to the intellect was never offered than his,—warm, fragrant, religious,—& I feel, when with him, the pertinency of that Platonistic word, "all-various." Beautiful & dear, God & all his hosts shall keep him.

What shall I say of the friend with whom I have spent so many hours of the past month? Very dear & pleasing memories, though the future, it now seems, may be changed. Of all the persons I know, this child, called romantic & insane & exaggerating, is the most real. And it is strange that she should not have that which she wants, somewhat to do.

> "If we look at the shadow of a bare head upon a white wall we shall see very distinctly the shadow of a flying smoke issuing from the head & mounting upwards." Winslow
>
> ap A.K. p 415 Vol II

—

The Farm once more! The unanimous voice of thoughtful men is for the life of labor & the farm. All experience is against it, it being found, 1. that a small portion of the people suffice for the raising of bread for the whole. 2. that men are born with the most positive peculiarities of power as for music, for geometry, for chemistry, for care of animals, &c, &c, 3. that hard labor on the farm untunes the mind, unfits for the intellectual exercises which are the delight of the best men. I suppose that all that is done in ploughing & sowing & reaping & storing is repeated in finer sort in the life of men who never touch the plough handles. The essence of those manipulations is subtle & reappears in countinghouses & council boards, in games of cards & chess, in conversations, correspondences, & in poets' rhymes.

The obvious objection to the indulgence of particular talent & refusing to be man of all work is the rapid tendency to farther subdivision & attenuation, until there shall be no manly man.

The good of doing with one's own hands is the honouring

of the symbol. My own cooking, my own cobbling, fence-building, digging of a well, building of a house, twisting of a rope, forging of a hoe & shovel,—is poetic.

—

Against low assailants we have also low defenders. As I came home by the brook, I saw the carcass of a snake which the mud-turtles were eating at both ends.

Poetry aids itself both with music & with eloquence, neither of which are essential to it. Say rather that music is proper to it, but that within the high organic music proper to it are inferior harmonies & melodies, which it avails itself of at pleasure. Thus in W.E.C.'s piece called "Death," the line

> "I come, I come, think not I turn away"

is a turn of eloquence. And Byron, when he writes,

> "For who the fool that doth not know
> How bloom & beauty come & go
> And how disease & pain & sorrow
> May chance today, may chance tomorrow
> Unto the merriest of us all."

enhances the pleasure of the poem by this bit of plaintive music. In like manner,

> "Out upon time who will leave no more
> Of the things to come than the things before
> Out upon time who forever will leave
> But enough of the past for the future to grieve
> Relics of things that have passed away
> Fragments of stone reared by creatures of clay."

—

There are days when the angels of the great are near us; when there is no frown on their brow, no condescension even, when they take us by the hand, and we share their thought.

Intoxication with brandy is a remedy sometimes applied in cases of lockjaw to relax excessively the tense muscles.

We require that the man should give us tokens that he has not given up the holy ghost, that he knows where to plant his foot again. On that condition, we will indulge him with any length of repose, any quantity of wine or folly. Otherwise, he has the very secret of ugliness, namely, of being uninteresting to us. You shall have the love of a goddess, if you are yet alive: but the husband of yonder beautiful dame does not continue to deserve her: He is not here, & his merit is not here to lead her home; but, in its place, a rope of custom & cowardice.

> "There is not anything in this world to be compared with wisdom for purity." Bhagvat Geeta

All conversation, as all literature, appears to me the pleasure of rhetoric, or, I may say, of metonomy. "To make the great little, & the little great," Isocrates said, "was the orator's part." Well that is what poetry & thinking do. I am a reader & writer, please myself with the parallelism & the relation of thoughts, see how they classify themselves on the more fundamental & the resultant & then again the new & newer result. I go out one day & see the mason & carpenters busy in building a house, and I discover with joy the parallelism between their work & my construction, and come home glad to know that I too am a housebuilder. The next day I go abroad & meet hunters, and, as I return, accidentally discover the strict relation between my pursuit of truths & theirs of forest game. Yet how have I gained in either comparison or see the seed, the plant, & the tree.

Bhagvat Geeta

> "Children only & not the learned speak of the speculative & the practical doctrines as two. They are but one for both obtain the selfsame end, & the place which is gained by the followers of the one is gained by the followers of the other. That man seeth who seeth that the speculative doctrines & the practical are one." Bhagvat Geeta. p. 57

—

June 23,

It was a pleasure yesterday to hear Father Taylor preach all day in our country church. Men are always interested in a man, and the whole various extremes of our little village society were for once brought together. Black & white, poet & grocer, contractor & lumberman, methodist & preacher joined with the regular congregation in rare union.

The speaker instantly shows the reason in the breadth of his truly social nature. He is mighty nature's child, another Robert Burns trusting heartily to her power as he has never been deceived by it and arriving unexpectedly every moment at new & happiest deliverances. How joyfully & manly he spreads himself abroad. It is a perfect Punch & Judy affair, his preaching. The preaching quite accidental & ludicrously copied & caricatured from the old style, as he found it in some Connecticutt tubs. As well as he can he mimics & exaggerates the parade of method & logic of text & argument but after much threatening to exterminate all gainsayers by his syllogisms he seldom remembers any of the divisions of his plan after the first, and the slips & gulfs of his logic would involve him in irreparable ridicule if it were not for the inexhaustible wit by which he dazzles & conciliates & carries away captive the dullest & the keenest hunter. He is perfectly sure in his generous humanity. He rolls the world into a ball & tosses it from hand to hand. He says touching things, plain things, grand things, cogent things, which all men must perforce hear. He says them with hand & head & body & voice; the accompaniment is total & ever varied. "I am half a hundred years old, & I have never seen an unfortunate day. There are none"——"I have been in all the four quarters of the world, and I never saw any men I could not love."

"We have sweet conferences & prayer meetings. We meet every day. There are not days enough in the year for us."

Everything is accidental to him: his place, his education, his church, his seamen, his whole system of religion a mere confused rigmarole of refuse & leavings of former generations—all has a grinning absurdity, *except* the sentiment of the man. He is incapable of thought; he cannot analyse or discriminate; he is a singing dancing drunkard of his wit—Only he is sure of the sentiment. That is his mother's milk, that he feels in his bones, heaves in his lungs, throbs in his heart, walks in his feet, and gladly he yields himself to the sweet magnetism & sheds it abroad on the people rejoicing in his power. Hence he is an example,—I, at this moment say—the single example, we have of an inspiration; for a wisdom not his own, not to be appropriated by him, which he cannot recall or ever apply, sails to him on the gale of this sympathetic communication with his auditory. There is his closet, there his college, there his confessional, he discloses secrets there, & receives informations there, which his conversation with thousands of men (and he knows every body in the world almost,) and his voyages to Egypt & journeys in Germany & in Syria never taught him. Indeed I think that all his talk with men and all his much visiting & planning for the practical in his "Mariners' House," &c &c, is all very fantastic, all stuff; I think his guardians & overseers & treasurers will find it so. Not the smallest dependence is to be put on his statement of facts. Arithmetic is only one of the nimble troop of dancers he keeps—. No; this free happy expression of himself & of the deeps of human nature, of the happier sunny facts of life, of things connected & lying amassed & grouped in healthy nature, that is his power and his teacher. He is so confident, that his security breathes in all his manners, & gestures, in his tones, & the expressions of his face, & he lies all open to men a man, & disarms criticism & malignity by perfect frankness. We open our arms too & with half closed eyes enjoy this rare sunshine. A wondrous beauty swims all the time over the picture gallery & touches points with an ineffable lustre.

Obviously he is of the class of superior men and every one associates him necessarily with Webster, and, if Fox & Burke were alive, with Fox & Burke.

What affluence! There never was such activity of fancy. How wilful & despotic is his rhetoric—"No not *the blaze of Diogenes's lamp* added to the noonday sun would suffice to find it," he said. Every thing dances & disappears, changes & becomes its contrary in his sculpturing hands. How he played with the word "*lost*" yesterday, "the parent who had lost his child." "Lost!" Lost became found in the twinkling of an eye. So will it always be.

His whole work is a sort of day's sailing out upon the sea not to any voyage, but to take an observation of the sun, & come back again. Again & again & again, we have the whole wide horizon,—how rare & great a pleasure! That is the Iliad, that is picture, that is art, that is music. His whole genius is in minstrelsy. He calls it religion, methodism, Christianity, & other names, it is minstrelsy, he is a minstrel; all the rest is costume. For himself, it is easy to see that though apparently of a moderate temperament he would like the old cocks of the barroom a thousand times better than their temperate monitors.

—

Men go through the world each musing on a great fable dramatically pictured & rehearsed before him. If you speak to the man, he turns his eyes from his own scene, & slower or faster endeavors to comprehend what you say. When you have done speaking, he returns to his private music. Men generally attempt early in life to make their brothers first, afterwards their wives, acquainted with what is going forward in their private theatre, but they soon desist from the attempt on finding that they also have some farce or perhaps some ear- & heart-rending tragedy forward on their secret boards on which they are intent, and all parties acquiesce at last in a private box with the whole play performed before himself *solus*.

Even for those whom I really love I have not animal spirits.

What an eloquence Taylor suggests! Ah could he guide those grand sea-horses of his with which he caracoles on the waves of the sunny ocean. But no, he is drawn up & down the ocean currents by the strong sea monsters,—only on that condition, that he shall not guide. How many orators sit mute there below! They come to get justice done to that ear & intuition which no Chatham & no Demosthenes has begun to satisfy.

Oliver Houghton, Kimball, John Garrison, Belknap, Britten, Weir, & the Methodist preachers, W E Channing, Thoreau,

H. Mann, Samuel Hoar, the Curtises, Mrs Barlow, Minot Pratt, Edmund Hosmer, were of Taylor's auditory. Nobody but Webster ever assembles the same extremes.

A traveller wants universal presence of mind, a sublime lassitude, or his opportunities avail him nothing.

The scholar is very unfurnished who has only literary weapons. He must be spiritual man. He must be ready for bad weather, poverty, insult, weariness, reputation of failure, & many other vexations. He ought to have as many talents as he can. Memory, practical talent, good manners, temper, lion-courage are all good things. But these are superficial, and if he has none of them he can still do, if he has the main mast, if he is anything. But he must have the resource of resources, be planted on Being. He must ride at anchor and vanquish every enemy whom his small arms cannot reach, by the grand resistance of submission, of ceasing from himself, of ceasing to do. He is to know that he is here not to work but to be worked upon, and is to eat insult, drink insult, be clothed & shod in insult, until he has thoroughly learned that this bitter bread and shameful dress is also wholesome & warm, is in short absolutely indifferent, is of the same chemistry as praise & fat living, that they also, *they also* are disgrace & shabbiness to him who has them. I think that much may be said to discourage & dissuade the young scholar from his career. Freely be that said. Dissuade all you can from the lists. Sift the wheat. Blow away the light spirits. But let those who come, be those who cannot but come, and who see that there is no choice here, no advantage & no disadvantage compared with other careers. For the great Necessity comes bursting in, and distributes sun & shade according to the laws of life, & not of street-laws. Yes, he has his dark days, he has weakness, he has waitings, he has bad company, he is pelted by a storm of petty cares, untuning cares, untuning company, that is the sting of them; they are like some foul beasts of prey, who spoil much more than they devour. Well let him meet them; he has not consented to the frivolity nor to the dispersion. The practical aim is forever higher than the literary aim. I shall not submit to degradation but will bear these crosses with what grace I can and I know that with every self truth come mysterious offsets for all that is lost in some pearl of great price which is gained. Self truth, then instrumentality.

—

I am sorry we do not receive the higher gifts justly & greatly. The reception should be equal. But the thoughts which wander through our mind we do not absorb & make flesh of, but we report them as thoughts, we retail them as stimulating news to our lovers & to all Athenians.

At a dreadful loss, we play this game; for the secret God will not impart himself to us for teatable talk; he frowns on moths & puppets, passes by us & seeks out a solitary & religious heart.

—

See how many cities of refuge we have. Skepticism & again skepticism? Well, let abyss open under abyss, they are all contained & bottomed at last, & I have only to endure. I am here to be worked upon.

We expose our skepticism out of probity. We meet, then, on the ground of probity, & not of skepticism.

I am shamed in reflecting on the little new skill the years bring me, at the power trifles have over me, at the importance of my dinner, & my dress, & my house, more than at the slenderness of my acquisitions.

For we do acquire some patience, some temper, some power of referring the particular to the general. We acquire perspective so as to rank our experiences & know what is eminent. Else the term *An old one* would have no meaning.

—

I know that the slaveholding is not the only manstealing and that white men are defrauded & oppressed as well as black but this stealing is not so gross & is not so legalized & made hopeless.

Aug. 25.

I heard last night with some sensibility that the question of slavery has never been presented to the south with a kind & thoroughly scientific treatment, as a question of pure political economy in the largest sense.

A practical question, you say, is, what are common people made for? You snub them, and all your plans of life & all your poetry & philosophy only contemplate the superior class. — This is a verbal question, never practical. Common people, uncommon people, all sorts of people, dispose of themselves very fast, and never wait for the sentences of philosophers. The truth seems to be, there are no common people, no populace, but only juniors & seniors; the mob is made up of kings that shall be; the lords have all in their time taken place in the mob. The appearance in any assembly is of a rapid self-distribution into cliques & sets, and the best are accused of a fierce exclusiveness. Perhaps it is truer & more charitable to say, they separate as children do from old people, as oil does from water, without any love or hatred in the matter. Each seeking his own like, and any interference with the affinities would produce constraint & stupidity enough. All conversation is a relative power, not an absolute quality; like magnetism, which does not act on wood or gold or silver but only on iron. You know he can talk eloquently; you have heard him. I too know that he can be struck with dumbness & be unable to articulate a reasonable syllable for hours & days.
Each of these persons you implicate, has, no doubt, made the experiment more than once to speak in unfit company, & been baffled. A good heart made him willing to serve everybody. A sacred voice checked him & forbade him to leave his place. Go back into thy solitude, it said, Why shouldest thou be frivolous? Assort, assort your party or invite none. Put Oliver Houghton & Mr Hoar; Ellery Channing & Aunt Betsey; Ellen Emerson & Gazetteer Worcester into pairs and you will make them all wretched. It is an extempore Auburn or Sing Sing built in a parlour. Leave them, to seek their own mates and they will find them as fast as the flies & the birds do.

The games & amusements of men vary with their work. The soldier's son plays with sword & plume & toy-cannon, the boy nowadays with a mimic locomotive & steamboat; & the girls' dolls dance the Polka: the boys have toy-printing presses. As they grow older, the young men's diversions & fancies borrow their color from the despotic Genius of the time, and now, instead of fitting their straps & promenading the fashionable streets, they go to farms, & taking a pruning knife in hand, they affect to learn the country-work. Instead of managing balls, or aspiring to the command of a military corps, they now are found in the committees & rostrums of the Abolition agitators and write melodious prose & verse for this & kindred societies. For abolition & for socialism. You will not exaggerate the depth of this benevolence; it is facility & fashion in great part. You will not expect more justice or magnanimity in his private dealings of an abolitionist or of a socialist than of a politician or soldier of the old school.

Do you think we should be practical? I grieve that we have not yet begun to be poetical. It is after long devotion to austere thought that the soul finds itself only on the threshold, and that truth has steeps inaccessible to any new & profane foot; long noviciate, long purgation, maceration, vigils, enthusiasm, she requires. Human life seems very short to the student. Its practical importance in your sense vanishes like a cloud. They have all eaten lotos alike.—

Over & above all the particular & enumerable list of talents & merits of any distinguished person is their superiority, not to be described, but which brought into notice all those talents & merits. One face of it is a certain eminent propriety, which is taste & reason & symmetry and makes all homogeneous. Homer & Milton & Shakspeare all have this atmosphere or garment of fitness to clothe themselves withal and we sometimes call it their "humanity." In Webster our great lawyer it is a propriety again.

Plato is no Athenian. An Englishman says how English! a German, how Teutonic! an Italian, how Roman & how Greek! It transcends sectional lines, the great humane Plato. But we read impatiently, still wishing the chapter or the dialogue at its close. [A trans-national book again is the Bhagvad Geeta] The reader in Plato is soon satisfied that to read is the least part. The whole world may read the Republic & be no wiser than before. It is a chief structure of human wit, like Karnac or the mediaeval cathedrals or Cuma, is as broad as man & requires all the variety of human faculty to know it. One man or one generation may easily be baffled in the endeavor to account for it. When we say, It is a fine collection of fables or when we praise his style or his common sense or his logic or his arithmetic we speak as boys. And much of our impatient criticism about the dialectic, I suspect, is no better. The criticism is like our impatience of the length of miles when we are in a hurry. The great-eyed Plato proportioned the lights & shades after the Genius of our life.

As they say that every one seemed related to Helen the universal beauty so Plato seems to us an American genius.

I lent him my book: it was as if he had lent me a book of logarithms, the wisdom of Plato was still safe & uncommunicated.

B A told me that when he saw Cruikshank's drawings, he thought him a fancy caricaturist, but when he went to London he saw that he drew from nature without any exaggeration.

—

I was in the Courthouse a little while to see the sad game. But as often happens the judge & jury, the government & the counsel for the prisoner were on trial as much as he. The prisoner's counsel were the strongest & cunningest lawyers in the Commonwealth; they drove the attorney for the state from corner to corner taking his reasons from under him & reducing him to silence, but not to submission. When hard pushed, he revenged himself in his turn on the Judge by requiring the Court to define what a Trust was. The Court thus hard pushed tried words, and said every thing it could think of to fill the time; supposed cases, & described duties of cashiers, presidents, & miscellaneous officers that are or might be; but all this flood not serving the cuttle fish to get away in, the horrible shark of district attorney being still there grimly awaiting with his "The Court must define," the poor Court pleaded its "inferiority." The superior Court must establish the law for this, —and it read away piteously the decisions of the Supreme Court, but to those who had no pity. The Judge was at last forced to rule something, & the lawyers saved their rogue under the fog of a definition. The parts were so well cast & discriminated that it was an interesting game to watch. The

Government was well enough represented. It was stupid, but had a strong will & possession, and stood on that to the last. The Judge was no man, had no counsel in his breast, yet his position remained real, & he was there merely as a child might have been to represent a great Reality, the Justice of States, which we could well enough see there beetling over his head, and which his trifling talking nowise affected, & did not impede, since he was innocent & well meaning. There are judges on all platforms, & this of Child-judge, where the position is all, is something.

Three or four stubborn necessary words are the pith & fate of the business; all the rest is expatiating & qualifying: three or four real choices, acts of will of somebody, the rest is circumstance, satellite, & flourish.

There was Webster the great cannon loaded to the lips: he told Cheney that if he should close by addressing the jury, he should blow the roof off. As it was, he did nothing but pound. Choate put in the nail & drove it; Webster came after & pounded. The natural grandeur of his face & manners always satisfies; easily great; there is no strut in his voice or behaviour as in the others. Yet he is all wasted; he seems like a great actor who is not supported on the boards, & Webster like the actor ought to go to London. Ah if God had given to this Demosthenes a heart to lead New England! what a life & death & glory for him. Now he is a fine symbol & mantel ornament—costly enough to those who must keep it; for the great head aches, & the great trunk must be curiously fed & comforted. G. B. said, the Judge looked like a schoolmaster puzzled by a hard sum who reads the context with emphasis. The *amicus curiae* doctrine is the right of revolution. Always a loophole.

Hahnemann's hypothesis is that seven eighths of the chronic maladies affecting the human frame are forms of psora, & that *all* such maladies are referable in some sense to three types of skin disease.

See Wilkinson's Introd to Swedenborg's
Animal Kingdom p. xxxv.

—

In reading the old mythology how easily we detect the men & women we know, clothed there in colossal masks & stilted on high buskins to go for gods & goddesses.

Old Dr Henry Ware said one day,—(I think to Mussey,)—that old as he was in preaching, he never prepared to go on Sunday into the pulpit of the College Chapel without a slight peristaltic motion.

—

The old dramatists wrote the better for the great quantity of their writing and knew not when they wrote well. The playhouse was low enough to have entire interests for them; they were proprietors; it was low & popular; and not literary. That the scholars scorned it, was its saving essence. Shakspeare & his comrades, Shakspear evidently thought the mass of old plays or of stage plays *corpus vile*, in which any experiment might be freely tried. Had the prestige which hedges about a modern tragedy or other worthless literary work existed, nothing could have been done. The coarse but warm blood of the living England circulated in the play as in street ballads, & gave body to his airy & majestic fancy. For the poet peremptorily needs a basis which he cannot supply; a tough chaos-deep soil, or main, or continent, on which his art may work, as the sculptor a block of stone, and this basis the popular mind supplies: otherwise all his flowers & elegances are transcendental & mere nuisance.

—

See how the translation of Plutarch gets its wonderful excellence as does the Eng. Bible by being translation on translation: there never was a time when there was none: and all the truly idiomatic & nationally generic phrases are kept, & all the others successively picked out & thrown away.

Something like the same process had gone on long before with the originals of these books. The world takes liberties with world-books; Vedas, Aesop's fables, Homer, Arabian Nights, are not the work of single men. The time thinks for us; the parliament thinks for us; the market thinks for us; the mason, the carpenter, the merchant, the farmer, the dandy, all think for us. Every book supplies us with one good word,—every law, every trade, every folly; and the generic catholic genius who is not afraid or ashamed to owe his originality to the originality of all, [and who perhaps is looked down upon as feeble and a treasuring word-catching student,] stands with the next age as the true recorder & embodiment of his own.

—

But dispose, dispose of these things. You are not the candidate for so gross a discipline. Your preoccupied mind has happily made you no slaveholder, no sot, no drone, but given you by privilege of beauty the possession of those things you desire.

You are here to chant the hymn of Destiny, to be worked upon, here for miracle, here for resignation, here for intellect, love, & being; here to know the awful secret of genius, here to become not readers of poetry but Dante, Milton, Shakspeare, Homer, Swedenborg, in the fountain through that: here to foresee India & Persia & Judaea & Europe in the old paternal mind.

If I could reach to initiate you, if I could prevail to communicate the incommunicable mysteries, you should see the breadth of your realm; that even as you ascend inward your radiation is immense; that you receive the keys of history & of nature.

You assimilate the remote, & rise on the same stairs to science & to piety.

from
Y
1845–1846

Identity, identity. If a wise man should appear in our village, he would create in all the inhabitants a new consciousness of wealth by opening their eyes to the sparkle of half concealed treasures that lie in everybody's door-yard; he would establish a sense of immoveable equality, as every body would discern the checks & reciprocities of condition, and the rich would see their mistakes & poverty, whilst the poor would behold their own resources.

Father Taylor valuable as a psychologic curiosity. A man with no proprium or peculium, but all social. Leave him alone & there is no man: there is no substance, but a relation. His power is a certain mania or low inspiration that repeats for us the tripod & possession of the ancients. I think every hearer feels that something like it were possible to himself if he could consent: he has sold his mind for his soul (soul in the low semi-animal sense, soul including animal spirits). Art could not compass this fluency & felicity. His sovereign security results from a certain renunciation & abandonment. He runs for luck, & by readiness to say everything, good & bad, says the best things. Then a new will & understanding organize themselves in this new sphere of no-will & no-understanding, and as fishermen use a certain discretion within their luck, to find a good fishing-ground, or the berry women to gather quantities of whortleberries, so he knows his topics, & his unwritten briefs, and where the profusion of words & images will likeliest recur. With all his volleys of epithets & imagery, he will ever & anon hit the white. He called God in a profusion of other things "a charming spirit"; he spoke of "Men who sin with invention, sin with genius, sin with all the power they can draw,"———

But you feel this inspiration. It clothes him like an atmosphere, & he marches into untried depths with the security of a grenadier. He will weep, and grieve, & pray, & chide, in a tempest of passionate speech, & never break the perfect propriety with a single false note; and when all is done, you still ask, or I do, "What's Hecuba to him?"

September

We sidle towards the problem. If we could speak the direct solving word, it would solve us too; we should die, or be liberated as the gas in the great gas of the atmosphere.

Call it by whatever name, we all believe in personal magnetism, of which mesmerism is a lowest example. But the magnetisers are few. The best head in the company affects all the rest. We believe that if the angels should descend, we should associate with them easily, & never shame them by a breach of celestial propriety.

—

I think the Platonists may be read for sentences, though the reader fail to grasp the argument of the paragraph or the chapter. He may yet obtain gleams & glimpses of a more excellent illumination from their genius outvaluing the most distinct information he owes to other books. The grandeur of the impression the stars & heavenly bodies make on us is surely more valuable than our exact perception of a tub or a table on the ground.

—

I will tell you my dream of last night: I was in the East Indian Heaven & watched the proceeding

Metempsychosis

For this Indian doctrine of transmigration, it seems easy of reception where the mind is not preoccupied. Not more wonderful than other methods which are in use. And so readily suggested not only by the manners of insects, but by the manners of men. Here is a gentleman who abused his privileges when in the flesh as a gentleman, & curtailed therefore his amount of vital force. We cannot kill him, for souls will not die. His punishment self-imposed, is, that he take such a form as his diminished vital force can maintain. Now it takes to make a good dog, say, half a grain; to make a peacock, a quarter grain; to make a great general, a pennyweight; a philosopher, two; a poet, ten; & a good & wise man a thousand pounds. Now our ill behaved man on emerging from his rotten body & a candidate for a new birth has not capital enough to maintain himself as man, & with his diminished means nothing is left for it, but that he should take a turn through nature this time as monkey. That costs very little, & by careful governance in the monkey form, he shall have saved something & be ready at his return, to begin the world again more decently, say, as dog. There he saves again, &, at the end of that period, may drop his tail, & come out Hottentot. Good Hottentot, he will rise, and one of these ages will be a Massachusetts man. What other account is to be given of these superfluous triflers who whisk through nature, whom we are sure we have seen before, and who answer no purpose to the eye while they are above the horizon? They are passing through their grub state, or are expiating their ill economy of long ago.

"Travelling the path of life through thousands of births"

It requires for the reading & final disposition of Plato, all sorts of readers, Frenchmen, Germans, Italians, English, & Americans. If it were left to apprehensive, gentle, imaginative, Plato-like persons, no justice would be done to his essence & totality, through the excess or violence of affection that would be spent on his excellence of reason & imagination. But Frenchmen have no reverence, they seize the book like merchants, it is a piece of goods, and is treated without ceremony after the manner of commerce; and though its diviner merits are lost by their profanation, the coarser, namely, the texture & coherence of the whole, & its larger plan, its French availableness, its fitness to French taste, by comprehending that. Too much seeing is as fatal to just seeing, as blindness is. People speak easily of *Cudworth*, but I know no book so difficult to read as Cudworth proper. For, as it is a magazine of quotations, of extraordinary ethical sentences, the shining summits of ancient philosophy, and as Cudworth himself is a dull writer, the eye of the reader rests habitually on these wonderful revelations, & refuses to be withdrawn; so, that, after handling the book for years, the method & the propositions of Cudworth still remain a profound secret. Cudworth is sometimes read without the Platonism; which would be like reading Theobald's Shakspeare leaving out only what Shakspeare wrote.

I think the best reader of Plato the least able to receive the totality at first, just as a botanist will get the totality of a field of flowers better than a poet.

—

Plato & the great intellects have no biography. If he had wife, children, we hear nothing of them; he ground them all into paint. As a good chimney burns up all its own smoke, so a good philosopher consumes all his own events in his extraordinary intellectual performances.

Webster says, The curse of this country is eloquent men.

In the convention yesterday it was easy to see the drunkenness of eloquence. As I sat & listened, I seemed to be attending at a medical experiment where a series of patients were taking nitrous oxide gas. Each patient, on receiving it in turn, exhibited similar symptoms; redness in the face, volubility, violent gesticulation, the oddest attitudes, occasional stamping, a loss of perception of the passage of time, a selfish enjoyment of the sensation, & loss of perception of the suffering of the audience. Plato says that the punishment which the wise suffer who refuse to take part in the government, is to live under the government of worse men. That is the penalty of abstaining to speak in a public meeting, that you shall sit & hear wretched & currish speakers. I have a bad time of it on these occasions, for I feel responsible for every one of the speakers, & shudder with cold at the thinness of the morning audience, & with fear lest all will fail at every bad speech. Mere ability & mellowness is then inestimable. Stephen C. Phillips was a great comfort to me, for he is a good housewarmer with his obvious honesty & good meaning & his hurra- & universal-scream sort of eloquence which inundates the assembly with a flood of animal spirits & makes all safe & secure so that any & every sort of good speaking becomes at once practicable. His animal eloquence is as good as a stove in a cold house.

An orator is a thief of belief.

Garrison is a masculine speaker; he lacks the feminine element which we find in men of genius. He has great body to his discourse, so that he can well afford occasional flourishes & eloquence. He is a man in his place. He brings his whole history with him, wherever he goes, & there is no falsehood or patchwork, but sincerity & unity.

—

Kosmos

The wonderful Humboldt, with his extended centre & expanded wings, marches like an army, gathering all things as he goes. How he reaches from science to science, from law to law, tucking away moons & asteroids & solar systems, in the clauses & parentheses of his encyclopaediacal paragraphs!

Gibbon has a strength rare with such finish. He built a pyramid, & then enamelled it.

—

A great man is he who answers questions which I have not skill to put.

One man all his lifetime answers a question which none of his contemporaries put: he is therefore isolated.

Our quarrel with religion, philosophy, & literature is that they answer some other question. After much reading, I am not furthered. I want a hammer, you bring me a bucket.

Phedo p 202. Ah, if Cebes & Simmias had now said, Yes the Reminiscence is well enow but if my future is related to my Present only as my present to my past, that is no immortality for Cebes & Simmias. It does for the Universe. That suffers no detriment; but I have not sufficient property in it to interest me a moment in such a sky high concern. I wish to be certified that these dear Johns & Henries, Anns and Maries shall keep the traits that are most their own & make them dear.

—

Defining

How unskilful definers we are may be seen in the poverty of our speech respecting those traits which our feelings discriminate instantaneously. We say the man has talent, he has character, he has force, or he has none: and then we are at an end. But these words discriminate not well enough: the man is still not described:—we gaze again, & say, there is a great deal of something about him.

"For we should dare to affirm the truth," says Plato, "especially when speaking concerning the truth." Phaedrus p 323

The Universe is traversed with paths or bridges or stepping stones across all the gulfs of space in every direction. To every soul that is created is its path, invisible to all but to that soul. Each soul therefore walking in its own path walks firmly & to the astonishment of all other souls, who see not its path. Yet it goes as softly & effeminately & playfully on its way, as if instead of being a line narrow as the edge of a sword over terrific pits right & left, it were a wide prairie.

Parallelism

We know in one mood that which we are ignorant of in another mood, like mesmerised patients who are clairvoyant at night & in the day know nothing of that which they told.

A man who did not need to economize his strength, but could toil at his desk week after week almost without sleep or exercise—

The scholar is led on by the sweet opium of reading to pallor & squalor, to anxiety & timorousness, to a life as dry & thin as his paper, to coldness & hardness & inefficiency.

—

We are cast into a situation contemptible & of marked insignificance, of persons nowise parties to that which is done, something is always done or doing but over our heads & under our feet we are made to feel that we are strangers & loafers.

Compensation.

The law by which the centrifugence is increased by the increase of centripetence consoles us in the wildest outbreaks of the Spirit.

—

The greatest man underlies the human nature. The longest wave quickly is lost in the sea. No individualism can make any head against the swallowing universality. Plato would willingly have a Platonism, a known & accurate expression for the world, and it should be adequate:—it shall be—the world passed through the mind of Plato—nothing less; every atom shall have the Platonic tinge. Every atom, every relation, every quality you knew before, you shall know again, & find here, but now, ordered; not nature, but art, & you shall feel that Alexander indeed overran with some men & horses some countries of the planet,—but countries, & things of which countries are composed,—elements,—planet itself, & laws of planet, & of men, thoughts, truths, all actual & possible things, have passed through this man as bread into his body & become no longer bread but body; so all this mammoth mouthful has become Plato.
Well this is the ambition of Individualism: but the mouthful proves too great. Boa Constrictor has good will to eat it, but he is foiled. He falls abroad in the attempt and, biting, gets strangled, & the bitten world holds him fast by his own teeth. There he perishes, & the Unconquered Nature goes on & forgets him. Alas, alas, Plato turns out to be philosophical exercitations. He argues now on this side, now on that. The acutest searcher, the lovingest disciple could never tell what Platonism was; indeed admirable texts can be quoted on both sides of every great question, from him.

The sea shore; sea seen from shore, shore seen from sea, must explain the charm of Plato. Art expresses The One, or The Same, by the Different. Thought seeks to know Unity in unity; Poetry, to show it by Variety, i.e. always by an object or symbol. Plato keeps the two vases, one of aether & one of pigment, always at his side, & invariably uses both. Things added to things, as, statistics, geography, civil history, are mere inventories or lists. Things used as language or symbols, are inexhaustibly attractive. Plato is a master of the game, & turns incessantly the obverse & the reverse of the medal. He prefixes to the science of the naturalists the dogma

"Let us declare the cause which led the Supreme Ordainer

to produce & compose the Universe. He was good, & he who is good, has no kind of envy: Exempt from envy, he wished that all things should be as much as possible like himself. Whosoever taught by wise men shall admit this as the prime cause of the origin & foundation of the world, will be in the truth" *Timaeus.*

"All things are for its sake, & it is the cause of every thing beautiful." This dogma animates the whole philosophy.

The eloquent man is he who is no beautiful speaker, but who is inwardly & desperately drunk with a certain belief; it agitates & tears him, & almost bereaves him of the power of articulation. Then it rushes from him as in short abrupt screams, in torrents of meaning. The possession by the subject of his mind is so entire, that it ensures an order of expression which is the order of Nature itself, and so the order of greatest force & inimitable by any art. And the main distinction between him & other well graced orators is the conviction communicated to the hearer by every word, that his mind is contemplating a whole, and inflamed with the contemplation of the whole, & that the words & sentences uttered by him, however admirable, fall from him as unregarded parts of that terrible whole, which he sees, & means that you shall see.

The hearer, occupied with the excellence of the single thoughts & images, is astonished to see the inspired man still impatient of the tardiness of words & parts, pressing forward to new parts, and in his prodigality ever announcing new & greater wealth to come. Add to this concentration, a certain regnant calmness which (in all the tumult) never utters one premature syllable, but keeps the secret of its means & method, (never gossips, nor lets the hearer sidewise into any gossiping information of arts & studies) and the orator stands before the people as a daemoniacal power to whose miracles they have no key.

It is vanity that gossips; anything to secure your attention to itself. Earnestness, with its eye nailed to the argument, has no wish to give you anecdotes about itself & its talents.

Memory

This prolific past never ceases to work. With every new fact a ray of information shoots up from the long buried years. Who can judge the new book? He who has seen many books before. Who the new assertion? He who has heard a thousand like ones. Who the new man? He who has seen men.

—

Conversation.

A convertible proverb, *It is Greek to him.*

Those eastern story tellers whose oily tongues turn day into night, & night to day, who lap their hearers in a sweet drunkenness of fancy so that they forget the taste of meat. Coleridge too, who could dissipate the solar system to a thin transparency.

Are not Lectures a kind of Peter Parley's story of Uncle Plato, and of a puppetshow of Eleusinian Mysteries?

Knowledge

The railroad companies write on their tickets "good for this trip only" but in all action or speech which is good, there is a benefit beyond that contemplated by the doer. In seeing it, I seem to have learned a new tactics, applicable to all action.

World full of tools or machines, every one a contrivance to exclude some one error or inconvenience & make a practical thinker. Thus in making coffee many errors are likely to intervene & spoil the beverage. The biggin thinks for us, is a practical thinker, and excludes this & that other imprudence. It hinders the riling, it determines the quantity.

What a stroke of genius is each carpenter's tool.

It would be so easy to draw two pictures of the literary man, as of one possessed & led by muses, or, as of one ridden by some dragon, or dire distemper. A mechanic is driven by his work all day, but it ends at night; it has an end. But the scholar's work has none. That which he has learned is that there is much more to be learned. He feels only his incompetence. A thousand years, tenfold, a hundredfold his faculties, would not suffice: the demands of the task are such, that it becomes omnipresent; he studies in his sleep, in his walking, in his meals, in his pleasures. He is but a fly or a worm to this mountain. He becomes anxious: if one knock at his door, he scowls: if one intimate the purpose of visiting him, he looks grave.

—

Abu Said Abulkhair the mystic, & Abu Ali Seena the philosopher, on leaving each other said; the one, "All that he sees, I know," and the other, "All that he knows, I see."

"There are two that I cannot support, the fool in his devotions, & the intelligent in his impieties" Koran

Bias.

"If ye hear that a mountain has changed its place, believe it: but if ye hear that a man has changed his disposition, believe it not."

"He shall assuredly return to that for which he was created." *Koran*

Idiodynamics

"Men have their metal like the metal of gold & silver: those of you who were the worthy ones in the state of ignorance, will be the worthy ones in the state of faith as soon as they embrace it." Koran

—

Whoso teaches me a letter renders me his slave. *Ali.*

His very flight is presence in disguise.

Men resemble their contemporaries even more than their progenitors.

—

Vishnu Purana

At the moment of the birth of the Budhu Gautama, the hellfire suffered a momentary extinguishment; the brutes banished their dread, the salt water of the Ocean became fresh, the sea was adorned with flowers, the flowers were blown on the surface of land & sea; every tree was bent down with flowers; these covered the earth & emerged through stones.

Brahma descended from the highest heaven which decayeth not & with the light of his own body illumined the dark abyss which now constitutes this world & walking in the heavens joyed in the possession of his glory.

One Brahma & then another from time to time descended & dwelt in the heavens & from the selfinherent virtue of the said Brahmas this world below became sweet as the honey of the honeybee.

One of the Brahmas beholding the earth said to himself What thing is this? & with one of his fingers having touched the earth put it to the tip of his tongue & perceived the same to be deliciously sweet: from which time all the Brahmas ate of the sweet earth for the space of 60 000 years. In the meantime, having coveted in their hearts the enjoyment of this world, they began to say one to another, this part is mine; that is thine; & so fixing boundaries divided the earth between them. On this account, the earth lost its sweetness.

then grew a mushroom
then a creeping plant
then a tree
then a grain rice
then rice grain

Then later, because of the sons of the Brahmas having used substantial food, the light which once shone in their bodies was extinguished.

—

W E C. said A. is made of earth & fire. He wants water & air. How fast all that magnetism would lick up water. He discharges himself in volleys. Can you not hear him snap when you are near him?

"I never find anything which I look for"

He cannot drive a nail.

—

Plato well guarded from those to whom he does not belong by a river of sleep.

> "During passion, anger, fury, great trials of strength, wrestling, fighting, &c a large amount of blood is collected in the arteries, the maintenance of bodily strength requiring it & but little is sent into the veins. This

condition is constant with intrepid persons,—with those who are animated with what we term heroic valour." Swedenborg: Animal Kingdom. Vol. II. p. 205

Budha or he who knows.

Intellect puts an interval: if we converse with low things, with crimes, with mischances, we are not compromised, the interval saves us. But if we converse with high things, with heroic actions, with heroic persons, with virtues, the interval becomes a gulf, & we cannot enter into the highest good.

Icy light.

It is the chief deduction, almost the sole deduction from the merit of Plato (that which is no doubt incidental to this regnancy of the intellect in his work,) that his writings have not the vital authority which the screams of prophets & the sermons of unlettered Arabs & Jews possess. There is an interval, & to the cohesion, contact is necessary. Intellect is the king of non-committal.

—

In Spenser (Book III Canto XI p 181) is the Castle of Busyrane on whose gate is writ Be bold, on the second gate, Be bold, be bold, and the inner iron door, Be not too bold.

Skepticism.

There are many skepticisms. The Universe is like an infinite series of planes, each of which is a false bottom, and when we think our feet are planted now at last on the Adamant, the slide is drawn out from under us.

Value of the Skeptic is the resistance to premature conclusions. If he prematurely conclude, his conclusion will be shattered, & he will become malignant. But he must limit himself with the anticipation of law in the mutations,—flowing law.

The scholar blunders along on his own path for a time, assured by the surprise & joy of those to whom he first communicates his results; then new solitudes, new marches; but after a time on looking up, he finds the sympathy gone or changed, he fancies himself accused by all the bystanders; the faces of his friends are shaded by grief; and yet no tongue ever speaks of the cause. There is some indictment out against him, on which he is arraigned in many counts, & he cannot learn the charge. A prodigious power we have of begetting false expectations. These are the mistakes of others' subjectiveness. The true scholar will not heed them: Jump into another bush, & scratch your eyes in again. He passes on to acquit himself of their charges by developments as surprising as was his first word, by indirections & wonderful *alibis* which dissipate the whole crimination.

No wonder a writer is rare.—It requires one inspiration or transmutation of nature into thought to yield him the truth; another inspiration to write it.

One service which this age has rendered to men, is, to make the life & wisdom of every past man accessible & available to all. Mahomet is no longer accursed; Voltaire is no longer the scarecrow: Plato is no longer a pagan. Even Rabelais is citable.

Economy.

Nobody need stir hand or foot, the custom of the country will do it all. I know not how to build or to plant, how to buy wood, nor what to do with the house lot or the field or the wood lot when bought. Never fear: it is all settled how it shall be, long beforehand, in the custom of the country; whether to sand or whether to clay it, when to plough, & how to dress, & whether to grass or to corn: And you can not help or hinder it.

Croisements.

Symbols. The seashore, and the taste of two metals in contact, and our enlarged powers in the presence or rather at the approach & at the departure of a friend, and the mixture of lie in truth, and the experience of poetic creativeness which is not found in staying at home, nor yet in travelling, but in transitions from one to the other, which must therefore be adroitly managed to present as much transitional surface as possible. "A ride near the sea, a sail near the shore;" said the ancient. So Montaigne travelled with his books, but did not read in them.

La nature aime les croisements, says Fourier.

The poem must be *tenax propositi*, the fable or myth must hold, or it is worth no man's while to read it. If a pilot swings his vessel from the wharf with one intention, &, after letting go, changes his intention, & a vessel deceived by his first demonstrations is run afoul of & injured, the pilot loses his branch. Certainly we must hold the poet to as strict a law.

Winter apples.

The worst day is good for something. All that is not love, is knowledge, and all that is not good today, is a store laid up for the wants of distant days.

I am touched with nothing so much as with words like these; —"Yes, that is an example of a destiny springing from the character." And again—"I see your destiny hovering before you, but it always escapes you."

The faerie kingdom stands to men & women not as the Angelic hierarchy above our heads, & with the same direction as we, but feet to feet. And, in Faerieland, all things are reversed. Thus the faeries are small, and they that are more powerful among them are smaller than the commonalty, their energy increasing with their parvitude. And the Faerie-king's chief title of honor is, *The smallest of the small.*

Fate is found in the bill of the bird which determines tyrannically its limits.

The President of the Temperance Society would think it poetic justice, if on every unlicensed tavern the word *Rum* should appear scrawled in vast letters every morning, and on trial it should be found that no rasp or whitewash or paint would obliterate them, but on the first refusal of the landlord to sell liquor, the letters should fade away, & become invisible, and on any attempt of the landlord to renew the sale of poison, R U M should instantly appear in scarlet letters all over the house. But this substantially happens to good eyes.

Spartans, who wrote to be read, & spoke to be understood; whose laws were not written; the whole business of whose legislation was the bringing up of youth, whose ceilings were wrought with no tool but the axe, & the doors only with the saw. Leotychidas at Corinth asked "Whether trees grew square in that country?" Who planted the human seed in a beauty-bearing soil; whose king offered a sacrifice to the Muses, before a battle, whose aristocracy consisted in the enjoyment of leisure, being forbidden to exercise any mechanic trade; a little statue to the god of laughter in each eating hall; terrific pre-fourierites; bees; "if successful, for the public; if unsuccessful, for ourselves." Alas for the poor Helots with the Cryptia or ambuscade,—the price with which this grandeur was bought. The death of lawgivers should have its use, said Lycurgus & in exile & by his own act lay down in the red cloth & with the olive leaves of the dead. Other nations asked of them no other aid than a Spartan General. So Gylippus by the Sicilians, Brasidas by Chalcidians, Lysander, Agesilaus, by the people of Asia.

—

Native Americans.

I hate the narrowness of the Native American party. It is the dog in the manger. It is precisely opposite to all the dictates of love & magnanimity: & therefore, of course, opposite to true wisdom. It is the result of science that the highest simplicity of structure is produced, not by few elements, but by the highest complexity. Man is the most composite of all creatures, the wheel-insect, *volvox globator*, is at the beginning. Well, as in the old burning of the Temple at Corinth, by the melting & intermixture of silver & gold & other metals, a new compound more precious than any, called the Corinthian Brass, was formed so in this Continent,—asylum of all nations, the energy of Irish, Germans, Swedes, Poles, & Cossacks, & all the European tribes,—of the Africans, & of the Polynesians, will construct a new race, a new religion, a new State, a new literature, which will be as vigorous as the new Europe which came out of the smelting pot of the Dark Ages, or that which earlier emerged from the Pelasgic & Etruscan barbarism.

La Nature aime les croisements.

—

Whilst Dhruva sat entranced apart
Passed Vishnu into Dhruva's heart

> "Whilst Dhruva's mind was absorbed in meditation, the mighty Hari identical with all beings & all natures, took possession of his heart. Vishnu being thus present in his mind, the earth the supporter of elemental life could not sustain the weight of the ascetic. As he stood upon his left foot, one hemisphere bent beneath him, & when he stood upon his right, the other half of the earth sunk down."

See in this short passage the depravation effected by simply passing a bold trope into popular use as literal fact. A poet describes the powers of contemplation; a fanatic seizes the words, & goes to standing first on one leg, then on the other, a week at a time, to propitiate god. &

One dissenter countervails a thousand assenters. Swedenborg's theology does well as long as it is repeated to & by those who are wont to accept something positive, & find this as likely to be true as their own. But when I hear it, I say, All this is nothing to me. The more coherent & elaborate your system, the less I like it. I say with the Spartan "Why do you speak so much to the purpose concerning that which is nothing to the purpose?" The intricacy & ingenuity of your insanity makes you only the harder to be undeceived. This is the excess of form. The fallacy seems to be in the equivocal use of the term *The Word*. In the high & sacred sense of that term used by a strong Oriental rhetoric for the energy of the Supreme Cause (in act,) all that is predicated of it, is true: it is equivalent to Reason.
But this being granted, theologians shift the word from this grand sense to signify a written sentence of St Matthew or St John, and instantly assume for this wretched written sentence all that was granted to be true of the Divine Reason.

—

Every man who would do any thing well must come to it from a higher ground, and a philosopher must be much more than a philosopher. Plato is a poet.

—

There were Swedenborgs in those days, Missouriums, Mastodons of literature, not to be measured by a whole population of modern scholars.

Every genius is defended from approach by great quantities of unavailableness. Good only for himself. What property! says the hungry mind as it sees it afar, and swims toward it as a fish to its food.

—

Lycurgus, Pythagoras, Plato, all poets, all women believe in the plasticity or Education of man, but the whig world is very incredulous.

Oct. 27.

In this finest of all Indian summer days it seems sad that each of us can only spend it once. We sigh for the thousand heads & thousand bodies of the Indian gods, that we might celebrate its immense beauty in many ways & places, & absorb all its good.

Trace these colossal conceptions of Buddhism & of Vedantism home, and they are always the necessary or structural action of the human mind. Buddhism read literally is the tenet of Fate; Worship & Morals, or the tenet of freedom, are the unalterable originals in all the wide variety of geography, language, & intelligence of the human tribes. The buyer thinks he has a new article; but if he goes to the factory, there is the selfsame old loom as before, the same mordaunts & colours, the same blocks even; but by a little splicing & varying the parts of old patterns, what passes for new is produced.

Fate

The Indian system is full of fate, the Greek not. The Greek uses the word indeed, but in his mind the Fates are three respectable old women who spin & shear a symbolic thread, so narrow, so limitary is the sphere allowed them, & it is with music. We are only at a more beautiful opera or at private theatricals. But in India, it is the dread reality, it is the cropping out in our planted gardens of the core of the world: it is the abysmal Force untameable & immense. They who wrestle with Hari, see their doom in his eye before the fight begins.

Skeptic
In the V. Purana it is a vice "a man by selfish desires devoted to his family."

As for King Swedenborg I object to his cardinal position in Morals that evils should be shunned as sins. I hate preaching. I shun evils as evils. Does he not know—Charles Lamb did,—that every poetic mind is a pagan, and to this day prefers Olympian Jove, Apollo, & the Muses & the Fates, to all the barbarous indigestion of Calvin & the Middle Ages?

Great King is King Swedenborg. I will not deny him his matchless length & breadth. Such a world of mathematics, metallurgy, astronomy, anatomy, ecclesiastic history, theology, demonology, ouranology, love, fear, terror, form, law, all to come out of that quiet sleepy old gentleman with the gold headed cane, lodging at Mr Shearsmith's!

He is a theoretic or speculative man whom no practical man in the Universe could scorn. Plato is a gownsman; the robe, though of purple, & almost skywoven, is yet an academic robe, & would hinder the rapid action, if need were, with its voluminous folds. But Swedenborg is awful to Caesar. Lycurgus himself would bow.—

—

We are very clumsy writers of history. We tell the chronicle of parentage, birth, birthplace, schooling, companions, acquisition of property, marriage, publication of books, celebrity, & death, and when we have come to an end of this external history, the reader is no whit instructed, no ray of relation appears between all this lumber & the goddess-born, and it really appears as if, had we dipped at random into the modern Plutarch or Universal Biography, & read any other life there, it would have fitted to the poems quite as well. It is the very essence of

Poetry to spring like the rainbow daughter of Wonder from the invisible: to abolish the Past, & refuse all history. Dyce & Collier, Malone & Warburton have exhausted their life in vain. The builders of the Theatres, proprietors of the Covent Garden & Haymarket & Drury Lane, of Park & Tremont, have wrought in vain. Garrick, Kean, Kemble, & Macready dedicate in various ways their lives to this Genius, him they adorn or would fain help adorn, elucidate, obey, & express. The Genius knows not of them. The moment we come at last to hear one golden word, it leaps out immortal from all this wretched mortality and sweetly torments us with invitations to its own inaccessible homes. I remember I came to the city once to hear Macready's Hamlet and all I now remember of that master was that in which the master had no part, simply the magical expression,

Revisit'st now the glimpses of the Moon

What can any biography biographize the wonderful world into which the Midsummer Night's dream admits me? Did Shakspeare confide to any Notary or Parish Recorder, sacristan or surrogate in Stratford upon Avon, the genesis of that delicate creation? The forest of Arden, the air of Scone Castle, the moonlight of Portia's villa; where is the third cousin or grandnephew, the prompter's book or private letter that has heard one word of those transcendant secrets? Shakspeare is the only biographer of Shakspeare. And ah, what can Shakspeare tell in any way but to the Shakspeare in us? He cannot any more stoop from off his tripod & give us anecdotes of his inspirations. Read now the laborious results of years of Dyce & Collier—read, one sentence at a time.
And now

my delicate Ariel

or

mandragora

or

bleak virtue's bones

or

Shackle accident & bolt up change

In fine it is very certain that the genius draws up the ladder after him when the creative age goes up to heaven, & gives way to a new, who see the works & ask vainly for a history. Your criticism is profane. Shakspeare by Shakspeare. Poet in his interlunatim is a critic.

—

The Indian teaching through its cloud of legends has yet a simple & grand religion like a queenly countenance seen through a rich veil. It teaches to speak the truth, love others as yourself, & to despise trifles. The East is grand,—& makes Europe appear the land of trifles. Identity, identity! friend & foe are of one stuff, and the stuff is such & so much that the variations of surface are unimportant. All is for the soul, & the soul is Vishnu; & animals & stars are transient paintings; & light is whitewash; & durations are deceptive; and form is imprisonment and heaven itself a decoy. That which the soul seeks is resolution into Being above form, out of Tartarus & out of Heaven; liberation from existence is its name. Cheerful & noble is the genius of this cosmogony. Hari is always gentle & serene,—he translates to heaven the hunter who has accidentally shot him in his human form; he pursues his sports with boors & milkmaids at the cow-pens; all his games are benevolent, and he enters into flesh to relieve the burdens of the world.

Wisdom consists in keeping the soul liquid, or, in resisting the tendency to too rapid petrifaction.

Contemporaries.

We learn of our contemporaries what they know with little effort and almost through the pores of the skin. We catch it by sympathy, or as a wife arrives at the intellectual & moral elevations of her husband.

—

The fault of Alcott's community is that it has only room for one.

Majorities, the argument of fools, the strength of the weak. One should recall what Laertius records as Socrates' opinion of the common people, "that, it was as a man should except against one piece of bad money, & accept a great sum of the same."

—

Nov. 5, 1845.

Yesterday evening, saw Robert Owen at Mr Alcott's. His four elements are Production, Distribution, Formation of Character, and Local & General governing. His *Three Errors*, on which society has always been based, & is now, are, 1. That we form ourselves. 2. That we form our opinions. 3. That we form our feelings. The Three Truths which he wishes should replace these, are, 1. That we proceed from a creating power; 2. That our opinions come from conviction; 3 That our feelings come from our instincts.

The five Evils which proceed from our Three Errors & which make the misery of life are

1 Religious perplexities
2 Disappointment in affections
3 Pecuniary difficulties
4 Intemperance
5 Anxiety for offspring.

He also requires a Transitional state. *Fourier* he saw in his old age. Fourier learned of him all the truth he had, & the rest of his system was imagination, & the imagination of a banker.

You are very external with your evils, Mr Owen: let me give you some real mischiefs:

Living for show
Losing the whole in the particular
Indigence of vital power

I am afraid these will appear in a phalanstery or in a tub.

We were agreed, that Mr Owen was right in imputing despotism to circumstances & that the priest & poet are right in attributing responsibility to men. Owen was a better man than he knew, & his love of men made us forget his "Three Errors."

His charitable construction of men, classes, & their actions was invariable. He was always a better Christian in his controversy with Christians, and he interpreted with great generosity the acts of the Holy Alliance & Prince Metternich. "Ah," he said, "you may depend on it, there are as tender hearts, and as much good will to serve men, in palaces, as in cottages."

—

The Owen & Fourier plans bring no *a priori* convictions. They are come at merely by counting & arithmetic. All the fine aperçus are for individualism. The Spartan broth, the hermit's cell, the lonely farmer's life are poetic; the Phalanstery, the "self supporting Village" (Owen) are culinary & mean.

—

Reality bursting through all these men, through Plato, through Swedenborg, through Shakspeare.

Skepticism & gulfs of Skepticism; strangest of all that of the Saints. They come to the mount, & in the largest & most blissful communication to them, somewhat is left unsaid, which begets in them doubt & horrible doubt. 'So then,' say they, before they have yet risen from their knees, 'even this, even this does not satisfy: we must still feel that this our homage & beatitude is partial & deformed. We must fly for relief & sanity to that other suspected & reviled part of nature, the kingdom of the understanding, the gymnastics of talent, the play of fancy.'

Ah Lycurgus, old slyboots!

—

Locke said, "God, when he makes the prophet, does not unmake the man." Swedenborg's history confirms & points the remark. A poor little narrow pragmatical Lutheran for whom the heavens are opened, so that he sees with eyes & in the richest symbolic forms the awful truth of things, and utters again in his endless books the indisputable secrets of moral nature, remains with all these grandeurs resting upon him, through it all, & after all, a poor little narrow pragmatical Lutheran. His judgments are those of a Swedish polemic, and his vast enlargements seem purchased by adamantine limitations. He reminds me again & again of our Jones Very, who had an illumination that enabled him to excel every body in wit & to see farthest in every company & quite easily to bring the proudest to confession: & yet he could never get out of his

Hebraistic phraseology & mythology, &, when all was over, still remained in the thin porridge or cold tea of Unitarianism.

Influences

We are candidates, we know we are, for influences more subtle & more high than those of talent & ambition. We want a leader, we want a friend whom we have not seen. In the company, & fired by the example of a god, these faculties that dream & toss in their sleep, would wake. Where is the Genius that shall marshal us the way that we were going? There is a vast residue, an open account ever.

The great inspire us: how they beckon, how they animate, and show their legitimate power in nothing more than in their power to misguide us. For, the perverted great derange & deject us, & perplex ages with their fame. Alexander, Napoleon, Mahomet. Then the evil genius of France at & before the Revolution, a learned fiend.

—

It is the largest part of a man that is not inventoried. He has many enumerable parts: he is social, professional, political, sectarian, literary, & of this or that set & corporation. But after the most exhausting census has been made, there remains as much more which no tongue can tell. And this remainder is that which interests. This is that which the preacher & the poet & the musician speak to. This is that which the strong genius works upon; the region of destiny, of aspiration, of the unknown. Ah they have a secret persuasion that as little as they pass for in the world, they are immensely rich in expectancy & power. Nobody has ever yet dispossessed this adhesive self to arrive at any glimpse or guess of the awful Life that lurks under it.

For the best part, I repeat, of every mind is not that which he knows, but that which hovers in gleams, suggestions, tantalizing unpossessed before him. His firm recorded knowledge soon loses all interest for him. But this dancing chorus of thoughts & hopes is the quarry of his future, is his possibility, & teaches him that his man's life is of a ridiculous brevity & meanness, but that it is his first age & trial only of his young wings, but that vast revolutions, migrations, & gyres on gyres in the celestial societies invite him.

Inward miracles. Deliverances

That which so mightily annoyed & hampered us ceases utterly & at unawares. We wist not how or whence the redemption came. What so rankled at heart, & kept the eyes open all night, & which, we said, will never down; lo! we have utterly forgot it; cannot by any effort of memory realize it again, & give it importance. The crises in our history come so. Thus they steal in on us, a new life which enters, God knows how, through the solidest blocks of our old thoughts & mental habits, makes them transparent & pervious to its subtle essence; sweetens & enlightens all, & at last dissolves them in its new radiance.

The miracles of the spirit are greater than those of the history.

Men also representative.

Swedenb. & Behmen saw that things were representative. They did not sufficiently see that men were. But we cannot, as we say, be in two places at once. My doing my office entitles me to the benefit of your doing yours. This is the secret after which the Communists are coarsely & externally striving. Work in thy place with might & health, & thy secretion to the spiritual body is made, I in mine will do the like. Thus imperceptibly & most happily, genially & triumphantly doing that we delight in, behold we are communists, brothers, members one of another.

—

Shakspeare's fault that the world appears so empty. He has educated you with his painted world, & this real one seems a huckster's shop.

The transmigration must take effect; it is of no use to stand balancing there, first on one foot, then on the other. In he must, in to the new element, &, loth though he be, he must leave this body which now clings to him, & cast it off like a coat. It is of no use to try to stay where he is, & speak or project poetry. No, his life must pass out of him,—the gentleman, & be converted into it,—the poetry, or there is no poem.

"None any work can frame
Unless himself become the same."

It is sad to see people reading again their old books, merely because they don't know what new books they want.

It does not content me if the coat only fits Montaigne; I go out into the street, & try it on the world.

—

He is a lord & he is a goosy gander; and he is a lord in virtue of being a gander; & a gander again in virtue of being a lord. Let the saint say, I am a scamp, & I will trust his sanctity; but let him not try to come it over me by affecting to saint it all the time. If he harp on that string too much, & never loosen it, there is no music. I suspect the string is rotten. For I, who know the inevitable alternations,—if I see no relaxing of the sanctity, suspect at once that he has dishonest relaxations,—that the whole is rotten.

—

But that which he sought was the meaning of the world. It is strange that now that I come to this matter I am at a loss for any book in which the symbolical force of things is opened. Plato knew somewhat of it as is evident by his twice bisected line. Bacon said Truth & nature differed only as seal & print. Behmen implies it in all his writing. So do all poets but only playfully. But one would say that as soon as such a race as this is had once discovered or only so much as had a hint that the thing was so, that every material object subsists here not by itself nor finally to a material end but all as a picture language to tell another story of beings & duties, all other science would be put by & a science so grand & of such magnificent presage, would absorb all competition & research.
But whether it is, that God does not wish this lesson to be learned intellectually, as if we ought not to discover that the materials we use are only means, lest we should throw them away, & no longer eat, & work, & beget children, it is certain that all men occupy themselves with the symbols as if they were the things signified.

How is it, I say in my bed, that the people manage to live along, so aimless as they are? After their ends (& they so petty) are gained, it seems as if the lime in their bones alone held them together, & not any worthy purpose. And how do I manage it? A house, a bargain, a debt, some friends, some book, some names & deeds of heroes, or of geniuses, these are the toys I play with, these intercept between me & heaven, or these are they that devastate the soul.

—

Alcott says, that to Goethe he should say, Thou sawest God, & didst not die.

Into the district school he goes,—clowns & clowns; a clown in the chair, & his clowns around him.

When one sees good men in any society or rule, he does not value the rule, but the good man, & feels him to be disadvantaged just so far as the rule works on him. Thus Myrick or Blanchard among the Shakers, Shakerism gains nothing by them, with the wise.
The Shakers also live for show, with buildings ostentatiously neat. They have good accommodation for strangers, but the stranger should be accommodated as ourselves & not better.

As I listened to the fine music, I considered the musicians, & thought that music seems to fall accidentally & superficially on most of its artists. They are not essentially musical.

What confidence can I have in a fine behaviour & way of life that requires riches to bear it out? Shall I never see a greatness of carriage & thought combined with a power that actually earns its bread, & teaches others to earn theirs?

Uses of great men.

The people make much ado of quitting this sect & entering that & publish to the world a manifesto of reasons. Great man, —good when he stands strong on his legs, good when he is handsome, eloquent, & loaded with advantages. Better he seemed to me yesterday, when he had the power to eclipse himself & all heroes by letting in the Divine element into our minds, he himself a splendid nobody hiding himself, not like the cuttle fish in ink, but like God in deluges of light.

—

We see the law gleaming through like the sense of a half-translated ode of Hafiz.
The poet who plays with it with the most boldness best justifies himself. He is most profound & most devout.
Light thickens
Thought has its material side
Spirit is not all spirit but will be fluid, gas, solid already.

Nature seems to us like a chamber lined with mirrors, & look where we will in botany, mechanics, chemistry, astronomy, the image of man comes throbbing back to us.

—

They who believe, & through their belief, delight in the preacher or poet, are not ignorant that he may fall away; that he has a salary, and, that if he should come to an estate, he might serve them with his eloquence less sedulously. They know that, but they also know that what they love & adore exists independently of its ministers; and they will hearken to him heedfully, as long as he speaks for it, & to another when their preacher speaks for it no longer. They who put down chestnut posts know well enough that stone posts would last longer, but they have considered that these will last twenty years, & when they are rotten it will be cheaper to buy new ones than to set granite once for all.

from

O

1846–1847

Nature may be cooked into all shapes, & not recognized. Mountains & oceans we think we understand;—yes, so long as they are contented to be such, and are safe with the geologist; but when they are melted in Promethean alembics, & come out men; & then, melted again, come out words, without any abatement but with an exaltation of power—!

To know the virtue of the soil, we do not taste the loam, but we eat the berries & apples; and to mend the bad world, we do not impeach Polk & Webster, but we supersede them by the Muse,

—

The life which we seek is expansion: the actual life even of the genius or the saint is obstruction.

What a contest between personality & universality! The man listens to stoic, epicurean, or Christian, & acknowledges his mistakes. But he was right; and a little afterward comes a new infusion of his own, and he is triumphantly right again in his own way against the prejudices of the universe.

What a dancing jacko'lanthorn is this estimate of our contemporaries. Some times I seem to move in a constellation. I think my birth has fallen in the thick of the Milky Way: and again I fancy the American Blight & English narrowness & German defectiveness & French surface have bereaved the time of all worth.

That unlimited

In your music, in your speech, in your writing, I am amused by your talents; but in the presence of one capable of serving & expressing an idea, the finest talents become an impertinence.

In nature every creature has a tail. The brain has not yet availed to drop that respectable appendage. How odious is hunger! Well enough in the animal, well in the citizen, but in the illstarred intellectualist a calamity: he can neither eat nor not eat. If he could eat an oak forest or half a mountain; I should like that; a good Kurouglou; supper for thirteen; but hunger for any dinner he is likely to get, degrades him. If we cannot have a good rider, at least let us have a good horse: now, 'tis a haggard rider of a haggard horse.

In Germany there still seems some hidden dreamer from whom this strange genial poetic comprehensive philosophy comes, & from which the English & French get mere rumours & fragments, which are yet the best philosophy we know. One while we thought that this fontal German was Schelling, then Fichte, Novalis, then Oken, then it hovered about Schleiermacher, & settled for a time on Hegel. But on producing authenticated books from each of these masters, we find them clever men, but nothing like so great & deep a poet sage as we looked for. And now we are still to seek for the lurking Behmen of modern Germany.
Hegel's philosopheme blazoned by Cousin, that an idea always conquers, &, in all history, victory has ever fallen on the right side, (a doctrine which Carlyle has, as usual, found a fine idiom for, that Right & might go together;) was a specimen of this Teutonism. Something of it there is in Schelling; more in his quoted Maader; something in Goethe, who is catholic & poetic. Swedenborg had much; Novalis had good sentences; Kant, nothing of it. Kepler was "an unitarian of the united world." Si non errasset, fecerat ille minus.

—

Eloquence wants anthracite coal. Coldness is the most fatal quality. Phaedrus-horses, one winged, one not; there must be both. Burke had the high principles (in Chatham never a generalization). Burke dragged them down to facts which he never loses sight of: he had mania, & yet also gives Mosaic accounts. You must speak always from higher ground. Webster does.

But give us the rare merits of impassivity, of marble texture, against which the mob of souls dashing is broken like crockery falling on stone: the endurance which can afford to fail in the popular sense, because it never fails in its own; it knows what it wants & advances today, & tomorrow, & every day, to that which belongs to it:

—

What satisfactions in detecting now & then a long relation far over bounds of space & time in two parts of consciousness! Well, but we drop one thing when we grasp another. The least acceleration in our intellectual processes, and an increased tenacity, would constitute a true paradise.

Alcott thinks that the happiness of old age consists in transforming the Furies into the Muses.

Nov. 23. Burke a little too Latin in Debi Sing but what gradation! such opulence as permits selection. Webster too always has senatorial propriety. I wish to see accomplished translators of the world into language. I wish the leisures of the spirit. I please me with I know not what accounts of Oriental taletellers who transport & ravish the hearer & make him forget the hours of the day & the taste of meat.
But our careful Americans blurt & spit forth news without grace or gradation, parenthetically between the mouthfuls of their hasty dining.

Swedenborg, how strange, that he should have persuaded men & drawn a church after him, this enchanter with his mob of dreams! It recalls De Foe and Drelincourt & Mrs. Veal, the circumstantiality of his pictures, the combination of verity & of moonshine, dreams in the costume of science.

The effect of his religion will be denied by his disciples, but inevitable, that he leads them away from Calvinism, & under the guise of allegiance to Christianity, supplants both Calvin & Christ. When they awake, they have irrecoverably lost the others, & Swedenborg is not to be found.

Like a man with diseased eyes he carries *muscae volitantes* wherever he looks. He is a Prospero who travels with what a train! All the kinds that went by pairs into Noah's ark surround this Æsop, and furnish an appropriate mask for every conceit of his brain. The most fanciful of men, he passes for the most precise & mathematical.

I grow old, I accept conditions;—thus far—no farther;—to learn that we are not the first born, but the latest born; that we have no wings; that the sins of our predecessors are on us like a mountain of obstruction.

Every person is right, or to make him right needs only more personality.

—

Women waddle; men also do not make a straight but a zig zag path; their essence is bifold, & undulates or alternates. I see not how a man can walk in a straight line, who has ever seen a looking glass. He acts, & instantly his act is reflected to him by the opinion of men. He cannot keep his eyes off of these dancing images; and that is the death of glory, the death of duty in him. Safer, o far safer, is the reflection of his form that he finds in Zoology, in Botany, in Chemistry. Anthropomorphize them,—'tis all well & poetical.

I cannot hope to make any thorough lights into the caverns of the human consciousness. That were worth the ambition of angels! no! but only to make special, provincial, local lights? Yes, but we obey the impulse to affirm & affirm & neither you nor I know the value of what we say.

Henry Thoreau objected to my "Shakspeare," that the eulogy impoverished the race. Shakspeare ought to be praised, as the sun is, so that all shall be rejoiced.

—

What a discovery I made one day that the more I spent the more I grew, that it was as easy to occupy a large place & do much work as an obscure place & do little; and that in the winter in which I communicated all my results to classes, I was full of new thoughts.

Queenie came it over Henry last night when he taxed the new astronomers with the poverty of their discoveries & showings —not strange enough. Queenie wished to see with eyes some of those strange things which the telescope reveals, the satellites of Saturn, &c. H. said that stranger things might be seen with the naked eye. "Yes," said Queenie "but I wish to see some of those things that are not quite so strange."

The one good in life is concentration, the one evil is dissipation, and it makes no difference whether our dissipations are coarse or fine, whether they be property & its cares, friends, & a social turn of mind, or politics, or practicks, or music, or pleasure.

Everything is good which takes away one plaything & delusion more, & drives us home to do one poor indigent spartan thing. The book I read of lately, taught, that there are two brains in every man, as two eyes, two ears, &c. & that culture consisted in compelling the two to the entertainment of one thought.

Friends, pictures, books, lower duties, talents, flatteries, hopes, all are distractions which cause formidable oscillations in our giddy balloon, & seem to make a good poise & a straight course impossible.

—

We frigidly talk of reform, until the walls mock us with contempt. It is that of which a man should never speak, but if he have cherished it in his bosom, he should steal to it in the dark as an Indian to his bride. Or, a monk should go privily to another monk, & say, Lo we two are of one opinion; a new light has shined in our hearts. Let us dare to obey it.

—

Imagination

There are two powers of the imagination, one, that of knowing the symbolic character of things & treating them as representative; & (the other, Elizabeth Hoar thinks, is) practically the tenaciousness of an image, cleaving unto it & letting it not go, and, by the treatment, demonstrating that this figment of thought is as palpable & objective to the poet, as is the ground on which he stands, or the walls of houses about him. And this power appears in Dante & Shakspeare.

I should say that the imagination exists by sharing the ethereal currents. The poet is able to glance from heaven to earth, from earth to heaven, because he contemplates the central identity and sees it undulate & stream this way & that, with divine flowings through remotest things &, following it, can detect essential resemblances in things never before named together. The poet can class things so audaciously because he is sensible of the celestial flowing from which nothing is exempt: his own body also is a fleeing apparition, his personality as fugitive as any type, as fugitive as the trope he employs. As one said, in certain hours we can almost pass our hand through our own bodies. I think the use or value of poetry to be the suggestion it affords of the flux or fugaciousness of the poet.

The caste of India, how shocking to your feelings, my dear democrat! uproot it with ax, stubhoe, & gunpowder, leave not a trembling fibre or radicle alive. And yet how could it not be,—close transcript or shadow as it is of the decagraded or centigrade man? Each man is a scale of how many levels or platforms! What a manifold many-chambered aristocracy is systematised or unexpanded in his structure,—king, senate, consistory, judiciary, Army, chorus of poets, tradesman, husbandman, mob,—room is found for them all in the brain & scope of each human form, & when we meet our neighbor, we inquire of his air & action which of all these rules the passing hour.

—

The "Community" in its technical sense should exist, or our vulgar community should be elevated & socialized: There ought to be in every town a permanent proprietor which should hold library, picture & sculpture gallery, museum, &c. There are so many books that are merely books of reference that no man cares to buy, yet each should have access to; so much more with the elegances, nobilities, & festivities of pictures, prints, statues, music, it is much that I should have them sometimes. How often I think could I only have music on my own terms! Could I live in a great city, & know where I could go, whenever I wished the ablution & inundation of musical waves, that were a medicine & a purification. I do not wish to own pictures & statues. I do not wish the bore of keeping & framing & exhibiting. Yet I have to buy them, because no one is here to own them for me, no duke, no noble, no municipal or collegiate gallery. It does not help that my friend buys, if not permanent here. The best use by far of these comes when they are collected in one fit stately place, & their influence can be had occasionally as a strain of music, & to be the fitting decoration of public halls.

Tennyson & Browning, though full of talent, remind one of the catbird's knowing music.
Without their talent there is a certain dandy poetry, a certain dapper deftness & flourish.

tea tray style

Hymns There are a great many excellent hymns in use in our Unitarian Churches. The best collection in the English language is no doubt Dr Greenwood's; excellent in what he retained, in what he discovered & brought into use again from Cowper, Wesley, & the Moravians, &c & in what he sunk, as I had hoped, forever. But already the scribaciousness of our ministers has produced a number of pretended new collections; the Plymouth, the Cheshire, &c. All that is good in these they take from Greenwood. I will venture to say you cannot find one good piece in either of them that is not in his. But they have restored or added a great deal of trash. Their collections will pass away & his judicious book will come into lasting use.

Have you seen Webster? Calhoun? Have you heard Everett, Garrison, Theodore Parker? Do you know Alcott? Then you may as well die. All conversation is at an end, when we have discharged ourselves of the five or six personalities that make up, domestic & imported, our American existence. Nor do we expect anybody to be other than a faint copy of Napoleon, Byron, Goethe, Webster, Astor, Channing, or Abbott Lawrence.

Every word of Webster has passed through the fire of the intellect. The statement is always erect & disengaged.

The non-resistants go about & persuade good men not to vote, & so paralyse the virtue that is in the conservative party. And thus the patriotic vote in the country is swamped in the legion of paddies. But though the non-voting is right in the non-resistants, it is a patch & a pedantry in their converts, not in their system, not a just expression of their state of mind.

I did not write when I should how strongly I felt in one hour that the moral was the only

31 July, 1846. Webster knows what is done in the shop & remembers & uses it in the Senate. He saw it in the shop with an eye supertabernal & supersenatorial or it would not have steaded. He is a ship that finds the thing where it is cheap, & carries it where it is dear. Knowledge is of some use in the best company. But the grasp is the main thing. Most men's minds do not grasp any thing. All slips through their fingers, like the paltry brass grooves that in most country houses are used to raise & drop the curtain, but are made to sell, & will not hold any curtain but cobweb. I have heard that ideot children are known from the birth by the circumstance that their hands do not close round any thing. Webster naturally & always grasps, & therefore retains some thing from every company & circumstance. One of these tenacities, it is no matter where it goes. It gets an education in a shanty, in an alehouse, over a cigar, or in a fishingboat, as good as it could find in Germany or in Sais: for the world is unexpectedly rich, & everywhere tells the same things. The grasp is much, but not quite all; the juggle of commerce never loses its power to astonish & delight us, namely, the unlooked for juxtaposition of things. Take the peaches from under the tree, & carry them out of sight of the tree, & their value is centupled.
Sex; the Sex of things, whose attractions work under all mutations.

—

Byron is no poet: what did he know of the world & its Law, & Lawgiver? What moment had he of that Mania which moulds history & man, & tough circumstance,—like wax? He had declamation; he had music, juvenile & superficial music. Even this is very rare. And we delight in it so much that Byron has obtained great fame by this fluency & music. It is delicious. All the "Hebrew Melodies" are examples.

*

"Warriors & Chiefs! should the shaft or the sword."

How neat, how clever, how roundly it rolls off the tongue,—but what poetry is here? It is the sublime of Schoolboy verse. How many volumes of such jingle must we go through before we can be filled, sustained, taught, renewed?

The office of poetry I supposed was Tyrtaean,—consoling, indemnifying; and of the Uranian, deifying or imparadising.

Homer did what he could,—& Callimachus, Pindar, & the Greek tragedians: Horace & Persius; Dante was faithful, & Milton, Shakspeare & Herbert.

But now shall I find my heavenly bread in Tennyson? or in Milnes? in Lowell? or in Longfellow?

Yet Wordsworth was mindful of the office.

—

1 May. I was at Cambridge yesterday to see Everett inaugurated. His political brothers came as if to bring him to the convent door, & to grace with a sort of bitter courtesy his taking of the cowl. It is like the marriage of a girl: not until the wedding & the departure with her husband, does it appear that she has actually & finally changed homes & connexions & social caste. Webster I could so willingly have spared on this occasion. Everett was entitled to the entire field; & Webster came, who is his evil genius, & has done him incalculable harm by Everett's too much admiration of his iron nature;—warped him from his true bias all these twenty years, & sent him cloud-hunting at Washington & London, to the ruin of all solid scholarship, & fatal diversion from the pursuit of his right prizes. It is in vain that Everett makes all these allusions to his public employments; he would fain deceive me & himself; he has never done any thing therein, but has been, with whatever praises & titles & votes, a mere dangler & ornamental person. It is in vain for sugar to try to be salt. Well, this Webster must needs come into the house just at the moment when Everett was rising to make his Inaugural Speech. Of course, the whole genial current of feeling flowing towards him was arrested, & the old Titanic Earth-son was alone seen. The house shook with new & prolonged applause, & Everett sat down, to give free course to the sentiment. He saved himself by immediately saying, "I wish it were in my power to use the authority vested

in me & to say, '*Expectatur oratio in lingua vernacula,*' from my illustrious friend who has just taken his seat."

Everett's grace & propriety were admirable through the day. Nature finished this man. He seems beautifully built, perfectly sound & whole, & eye, voice, hand exactly obey his thought. His quotations are a little trite, but saved by the beautiful modulation & falls of the recitation.

The satisfaction of men in this appointment is complete. Boston is contented because he is so creditable, safe, & prudent, and the scholars because he is a scholar, & understands the business. Old Quincy with all his worth & a sort of violent service he did the College, was a lubber & a grenadier among our clerks.

Quincy made an excellent speech, so stupid good, now running his head against a post, now making a capital point; he has motherwit, & great fund of honour & faithful serving. And the faults of his speech increased my respect for his character.

The Latin allusions flew all day; "Sol occubuit, nulla nox sequitur," said Webster. "Uno avulso, non deficit aureus alter," said Winthrop.

It is so old a fault that we have now acquiesced in it, that the complexion of these Cambridge feasts is not literary, but some what bronzed by the colours of Washington & Boston. The aspect is political, the speakers are political, & Cambridge plays a very pale & permitted part in its own halls. A man of letters— who was purely that,—would not feel attracted, & would be as much out of place there as at the Brokers' Board. Holmes's poem was a bright sparkle, but Frothingham, Prescott, Longfellow, old Dana, Ward, Parker, Hedge, Clark, Judd the author of "Margaret," & whoever else is a lover of letters, were absent or silent; & Everett himself, richly entitled on grounds of scholarship to the chair, used his scholarship only complimentarily.

The close of Everett's Inaugural Discourse was chilling & melancholy. With a coolness indicating absolute skepticism & despair, he deliberately gave himself over to the corpse-cold Unitarianism & Immortality of Brattle street & Boston.

Everett's genius is Persian. The poetry of his sermons in his youth, his delight in Destiny, the elements, the colours & forms of things; & the mixture he made of physical & metaphysical, strongly recalls the genius of Hafiz.

—

Daguerrotype gives the sculpture of the face, but omits the expression, the painter aims at the expression & comes far short of Daguerre in the form & organism. But we must have sea and shore, the flowing & the fixed, in every work of art. On the sitter the effect of the Daguerrotypist is asinizing.

—

An artist took a sketch of the Senate of the U.S. at the moment of Henry Clay's resignation and to finish it procured Daguerre heads of all the members. Well such a picture as those grim fixtures would make does the piecemeal writer draw when he combines his sketches into one.

Nature is always gainer, & reckons surely on our sympathy. The Russians eat up the Poles. What then? when the last Polander is gone, the Russians are men, are ourselves, & the Pole is forgotten in our identification with Russian parties. A philosopher is no philosopher unless he takes lively part with the thief who picks his pocket and with the bully that insults or strikes him.

—

American idea, Emancipation, appears in our freedom of intellection, in our reforms, & in our bad politics; has, of course, its sinister side, which is most felt by the drilled & scholastic. But, if followed, leads to heavenly places. The embarrassment of Boston-bred men is the confusion of European & American culture. European & American are each ridiculous & offensive out of his sphere. There is a Columbia of thought & art which is the last & endless sequel of Columbus's adventure.

—

Webster. When he comes into the house astronomy & geology are suggested, the force of atoms. Here is the working nature. A spark also he has of the benignant fire that enables him to make an economy of his coals for the laboratory & for the altar which had otherwise been only a kitchen fire.

—

The more it is considered, the more it will appear that Eloquence is an universal organ, valued because it costs the total integrity of a man to produce it. The valour of the orator is not less indispensable than that of the general.

—

Art acquaints us with the wonderful translations of the same thought into the several languages of drawing, of sculpture, of music, of poetry, of architecture, still further into scenery, into animals, that express it or harmonize with it, and lastly into human form & character.

Bring any club or company of intelligent men together again, after ten years, & if the presence of some penetrating & calming genius could dispose them all to recollection & frankness, what a confession of insanities would come up! How costly then would the "Causes" appear, Abolition, Temperance, Socialism, Non Resistance, Grahamism, Romanism, &c. What roots of bitterness, what dragons of wrath! How dangerous & mischievous would every man's 'talents' appear! It would seem as if each had been seized upon in early youth by some delusion as a bird of prey which had whisked him about, taken him out of his path, out of society, away from fortune, from the truth, from the poets & God,—some zeal, some bias, some bee in the bonnet, & only when he was now grey & nerveless, was it relaxing its claws, & he awaking to a sense of his situation.

—

When summer opens, I see how fast it matures, & fear it will be short; but after the heats of July & August, I am reconciled, like one who has had his swing, to the cool of autumn. So will it be with the coming of death.

A good invention was the Individual or Differential. Here are all the members of my body:—How they use & rely on each other, trust each other beyond all the fables of friendship, & yet without love of each other! Well, so live two young brothers or sisters, & have no good of their intimacy & use, because they know it not. Love never forgets the Differential.

"I will get you to mow this piece of grass for me," says the prudent mechanic, "for I can earn more in the shop:" And the poet replies in the same wisdom on a higher plane, to those who beg him to come in to the aid of the disturbed institutions: I can best help them by going on with the creation of my own. I am a sad bungler at laws, being afflicted with a certain inconsecutiveness of thought, impertinent association, & extreme skepticism; but I recover my eyesight & spirits, in solitude.

And the way to taste the soil is not to eat earth, but wheat & blackberries, and my way to help the govt is to write sonnets.

I can reason down or at least deny every thing except this perpetual belly. Feed he must, & will, and I cannot make him respectable.

—

Men quarrel with your rhetoric. Society chokes with a trope, like a child with the croup. They much prefer Mr Prose, & Mr Hoarse-as-Crows, to the dangerous conversation of Gabriel and the archangel Michael perverting all rules, & bounding continually from earth to heaven.

Walking one day in the fields I met a man.

We shall one day talk with the central man, and see again in the varying play of his features all the features which have characterised our darlings, & stamped themselves in fire on the heart: then, as the discourse rises out of the domestic & personal, & his countenance waxes grave & great, we shall fancy that we talk with Socrates, & behold his countenance: then the discourse changes, & the man, and we see the face & hear the tones of Shakspeare,—the body & the soul of Shakspeare living & speaking with us, only that Shakspeare seems below us. A change again, and the countenance of our companion is youthful & beardless, he talks of form & colour & the riches of design; it is the face of the painter Raffaelle that confronts us with the visage of a girl, & the easy audacity of a creator. In a moment it was Michel Angelo; then Dante; afterwards it was the Saint Jesus, and the immensities of moral truth & power embosomed us. And so it appears that these great secular personalities were only expressions of his face chasing each other like the rack of clouds. Then all will subside, & I find myself alone. I dreamed & did not know my dreams.

*

Thine & Mine.

Be the condition what it may, you must support it, & by resources native or constitutional to you. Why then should I envy you, how brilliant soever your lot? I cannot support mine & yours. And if you really have yours, you cannot have mine; and I, if I really have mine, can well afford to spare yours, which I could not maintain. If you have not the spirit for your place, your place torments you, & nature is so avenged.

—

Alcott & Edward Taylor resemble each other in the incredibility of their statement of facts. One is the fool of his idea, the other of his fancy. When Alcott wrote from England that he was bringing home Wright & Lane I wrote him a letter, which I required him to show them, saying, that they might safely trust his theories, but that they should put no trust whatever in his statement of facts. When they all arrived here, he & his victims,—I asked them if he showed them that letter; they answered that he did: So I was clear.

—

Poetaster.

No man deserves a patron until first he has been his own. What do you bring us slipshod verses for? no occasional delicacy of expression or music of rhythm can atone for stupidities. Here are lame verses, false rhymes, absurd images, which you indulge yourself in, which is as if a handsome person should come into a company with foul hands or face. Read Collins. Collins would have cut his hand off before he would have left from a weak selfesteem a shabby line in his ode.

—

The Indians and the old monks chose their dwellingplace for beauty of scenery. The Indians have a right to exist in this world: they are, (like Monadnoc & the Ocean,) a part of it, & fit the other parts, as Monadnoc & the sea, which they understand & live with so well, as a rider his horse. The teamster, the farmer, are jocund & hearty, & stand on their legs: but the women are demure and subdued, as Shaker Women, &, if you see them out of doors, look, as H.T. said, "as if they were going for the Doctor." Has our Christianity saddled & bridled us?

"As I rode thro' sawder's wood,
A possum passed me by,—
He curled his tail, & served the Lord,
But how he grinned at I."

These are the wretched verses which Carlyle seemed to like to repeat.

There never was an eloquence: it is a fabulous power, as I have said, concerning which men are credulous, because there is in them all a tantalizing picture, which they would fain verify on some personal history of Chatham or Demosthenes. Whoso assays to speak in a public assembly is conscious instantly of this lambent flame enlarging, elongating, contracting to a point, a Zodiacal light, a Jacko'lanthorn, evanescent, refusing to be an instrument. Ah! could he confine that lambent fire! once manage to catch & confine that wild fire,—confine & direct it in a blowpipe, he would melt or explode the planet. There is no despotism like this clutching with one strong hand the master nerve which carries all the pulsations from the brain to the heart of humanity.

Bust of Demosthenes, a face of ropes; all cord & tendon.

—

Criticism

The next generation will thank Dickens for showing so many mischiefs which parliaments & Christianities had not been strong enough to remove. Punch too has done great service. And Fourier & other earnest teachers whose direct teaching is rejected, render an oblique service of searching criticism on Marriage, Church, Courts, Fourier, St Simon, Bentham, Louis Blanc, Owen, Leroux, and the Chartist leader, all crazy men & so they pound on one string till the whole world knows *that.*

—

That none but a writer should write, & that he should not dig.

Tell children what you say about writing & laboring with the hands. I know better. Can you distil rum by minding it at odd times? or analyse soils? or carry on the Suffolk Bank? or the Greenwich observatory? or sail a ship through the Narrows by

minding the helm when you happen to think of it? or serve a glass-house, or a steam-engine, or a telegraph, or a rail-road express? or accomplish anything good or anything powerful in this manner? Nothing whatever. And the greatest of all arts, the subtlest, & of most miraculous effect, you fancy is to be practised with a pen in one hand & a crowbar or a peat-knife in the other. All power is of geometrical increase.
And to this painting the education is the costliest, & mankind cannot afford to throw away on ditching or wood-sawing the man on whom choicest influences have been concentrated, its Baruch or scribe. Just as much & just such exercise as this costly creature needs, he may have; & he may breathe himself with a spade, or a rapier, as he likes, not as you like: & I should rather say, bad as I think the rapier, that it were as much to his purpose as the other implement. Both are bad, are only rare & medicinal resorts. The writer must live & die by his writing. Good for that, & good for nothing else. A war; an earthquake, the revival of letters, the new dispensation by Jesus, or by Angels, Heaven, Hell, power, science, the Neant,—exist only to him as colours for his brush. That you think he can write at odd minutes only shows what your knowledge of writing is. American writing can be written at odd minutes,—Unitarian writing, Charlatan writing, Congress speeches, Railroad novels.

Hawthorn invites his readers too much into his study, opens the process before them. As if the confectioner should say to his customers Now let us make the cake.

Truth indeed; we talk as if we had it, or sometimes said it, or know any thing about it: truth, that terrific reagent. That gun has a kick that will knock down the most nimble artillerist, and therefore is never fired. The ideal is as far ahead of the videttes & the van, as it is of the rear.

Morals. We have never heard that music, it is that which is sung to the Fates by Sirens or by their mystic whirling wheel. That is what all speech aims to say, & all action to evolve. Literature, epics, tragedies, histories, are only apology, interlude, make-shift, in the absence of that. It is the basis of all the elements we know, and is as readily reached from one as from another point. Anacreon, Hafiz, Horace, Herrick, come out on it from drinking songs, as easily as Newton from stars, & Jeremy Taylor from a Funeral Sermon. In the Delphin Juvenals, & other poets, they print the moral sentences in Roman capitals, and Pope asterisked Shakspeare, and, in early Greece, they carved the sentences of the seven Wise Masters on stones by the roadside, & the Christians inscribed the Churchwalls with the Commandments & Lord's Prayer.

—

The reason why I pound so tediously on that string of the exemption of the writer from all secular works is our conviction that his work needs a frolic health to execute. He must be at the top of his condition. In that prosperity he is sometimes caught up into a perception of means & materials, of feats & fine arts, of faery machineries & funds of poetic power, which were utterly unknown to him hitherto, & of which, if his organs are sufficiently subtle, he can avail himself, can transfer to mortal canvas, or reduce into iambic or trochaic, into lyric or heroic rhyme. These successes are not less admirable & astonishing to the poet, than they are to his audience. He has seen something which all the mathematics & the best industry could never bring him unto. And like our rich Raffaelle or Michel Angelo, it only shows how near man is to creating. Now at this small elevation above his usual sphere, he has come into new circulations, the marrow of the world is in his bones, the opulence of forms begins to pour into his intellect, & he is permitted to dip his brush into the old paint pot with which birds, flowers, the human cheek, the living rock, the ocean, the broad landscape, & the eternal sky were painted.

—

All life, say the naturalists, is a superficial phenomenon. The animals crawl on or fly over the rind of the planet & the fishes & whales swim only at the surface of the water. You might skim the whole Mammalia with a kitchen dipper. In the deep sea, & under the crust, all is still, nothing stirs. Human life & thought is not less external. Nobody is profoundly good or bad. Were they profound, they would satisfy. History is superficial.

If a carpenter were a carpenter to the bone, or a painter or a blacksmith had a native predilection for his craft, they were objects of admiration; but now if they take off their coat, they take off the carpenter or smith, & must remember every morning what it was they did yesterday, in order to know what they shall do today.

Neither is Samuel Hoar, Samuel Hoar to the bone, but our politics, opinions, & way of living are deciduous. Our manifoldness is betrayed.

—

"St Peter a unitarian," 'Isaac Newton a unitarian,' that is neither here nor there, but if you will find the maple & elm, granite, slate, & lime, to be of your party & opinion, that were something. That moral nature abhors slavery, & New England sides with moral nature against South Carolina & animal nature.

Born with a public nature, millions of eyes seemed to rest on him. He could not live without attempting something worthy & memorable.

The skeptics have got hold of Park street Church & will not let the body of the Martyr Torrey come into it, for fear the crowd will spoil their carpets.
The skeptics have got into the Abolition society, & make believe to be enraged.

—

If I were a member of the Massachusetts legislature, I should propose to exempt all coloured citizens from taxation because of the inability of the government to protect them by passport out of its territory. It does not give the value for which they pay the tax.

Also I should recommend that the executive wear no sword, and the office of general be abolished & the whole militia disbanded; for if these persons do not know that they pretend to be & to do somewhat which they are not & do not, Hoar of Concord, Walker of the branded hand, Torrey the Martyr, knew that the sword of Massachusetts is a sword of lath, or a turkey feather. It gives me no pleasure to see the governor attended by military men in plumes; I am amazed that they do not feel the ridicule of their position.

—

Oliver Wellington describes to me Semanthe Crawford of Oakham, who thought & felt in such strict sympathy with a friend in the spiritual world, that her thought ultimated itself in a preternatural writing on her arm, and again into writing on a paper which seemed to float in at the open window, & alighted on her lap.

—

In the city of Makebelieve is a great ostentation bolstered up on a great many small ostentations. I think we escape something by living in the villages. In Concord here, there is some milk of life, we are not so raving-distracted with wind & dyspepsia. The mania takes a milder form. People go a fishing & know the taste of their meat. They cut their own whippletree in the woodlot, they know something practically of the sun & the east wind, of the underpinning & the roofing of the house, of the pan & the mixture of the soils.

In the city of Makebelieve all the marble edifices were veneered & all the columns were drums.

Scholar's expenditure.

A Scholar is a literary foundation. All his expense is for Plato, Fabricius, Selden, Bently. Do not ask him to help young grocers to stock their shops with his savings. That is also to be done, but not by such as he. How could such a book have come down as the Poem of Sextus, but for the sacred savings of scholars & their fantastic appropriation of them? We must not make believe with our money, but spend heartily, and we must buy *up* & not *down*.

—

23 May. In Carlyle's head (photograph), which came last night, how much appears! How unattainable this truth to any painter! Here have I the inevitable traits, which the sun forgets not to copy, & which I thirst to see, but which no painter remembers to give me. Here have I the exact sculpture, the form of the head, the rooting of the hair, thickness of the lip, the man that God made. & all the Lawrences & Dorsays will now serve me well as illustration. I have the form & organism, & can better spare the expression & color. What would I not give for a head of Shakspeare by the same artist? of Plato? of Demosthenes? Here I have the jutting brow, and the excellent

shape of the head. And here the organism of the eye full of England, the valid eye, in which I see the strong executive talent which has made his thought available to the nations, whilst others as intellectual as he, are pale & powerless. The photograph comes dated 25 April, 1846, and he writes I am fifty years old.

—

I value the varieties & the extremes of literature for their certification of that which is real & central.

Thus Romaic, Scaldic, Ceylonese, Hindu, Lenapé

Superstition

The metre of poetic genius is the power to fuse the circumstance of today; not to use Walter Scott's superstitions, but to convert those of Concord & 1846 into universal symbols. Thus, it is boyish in Swedenborg to cumber himself with the dead scoriae & exuviae of the Hebrew & Canaanitish antiquity when the questions that were then alive & fraught with good & evil to men have vanished before the questions of property, of politics, of democratic life, which now prompt young men.

How beautiful the manners of wild animals, the bird that trims herself by the stream, the habits of antelope & buffalo. Well, the charm of genius is the same. We wish man on the higher plane to exhibit also the wildness or nature of that higher plane but the biography of genius so thirsted for is not yet written.

I should say of the memorable moments of my life that I was in them & not they in me. I found myself by happy fortune in an illuminated portion or meteorous zone, & passed out of it again,—so aloof was it from any will of mine. Law of that! To know the law of that, & to live in it! o thought too wild! o hope too fond!

—

We are slain by indirections. Give us the question of slavery, —yea or nay; Texas, yea or nay; War, yea or nay; we should all vote right. But we accept the devil himself in an indirection. What taxes will we not pay in coffee, sugar, &c but spare us a direct tax.

—

To the fir tree by my study-window come
  the groundsparrow
    oriole
    cedar-bird
    common crossbill
    yellow bird
    goldfinch
    cat-bird
    parti-coloured warbler
    robin

—

Cotten thread holds the union together, unites John C. Calhoun & Abbott Lawrence. Patriotism for holidays & summer evenings with music & rockets, but cotten thread is the union.

Eloquence

We go to the bar, the senate, the shop, the study, as peaceful professions. But you cannot escape the demand for courage, no, not in the shrine of Peace itself. Certainly, there is no orator who is not a hero. His attitude in the rostrum requires that he shall counterbalance his auditory. He is challenger & must answer all comers. The orator must always stand with forward foot in the very attitude of advancing. His speech must be just ahead of the whole human race, or it is prattle. His speech is not to be distinguished from action. It is the salt & electricity of action. It is action, as the General's word of command or chart of battle is action.

"The path of the gods is steep & craggy" said Porphyry,

I must feel that the speaker compromises himself to his auditory, comes for something; it is a cry on the perilous edge of fight, or let him be silent. Pillsbury, whom I heard last night, is that very gift from New Hampshire which we have long expected, a tough oak stick of a man not to be silenced or insulted or intimidated by a mob, because he is more mob than they; he mobs the mob. John Knox is come at last, on whom neither money nor politeness nor hard words nor rotten eggs nor kicks & brickbats make the slightest impression. He is fit to meet the barroom wits & bullies; he is a wit & a bully himself & something more, he is a graduate of the plough & the cedarswamp & the snowbank and has nothing new to learn of labor, or poverty, or the rough of farming. His hard head too had gone through in boyhood all the drill of Calvinism with text & mortification so that he stands in the New England Assembly a purer bit of New England than any, & flings his sarcasms right & left, sparing no name, or person, or party, or presence. The "Concord Freeman" of the last week he held in his hand, (the Editor was in the audience,) and read the paragraph on Mexican War from it, & then gave his own version of that fact.

What question could be more pertinent than his to the Church: "What is the Church for? if, whenever there is any moral evil to be grappled with, as Intemperance, or Slavery, or War, there needs to be originated an entirely new instrumentality?"

Every man in the presence of the orator is to feel that he has not only got the documents in his pocket to answer to all his cavils & to prove all his positions, but he has the eternal reason in his head; and that this man does not need any society or Governor or Army for he has latent but really present in himself in a higher form navy & artillery, judge & jury, farmer, mechanic, mob, & executioner. Danger is not so dangerous as he.

Mr Ruggles of Fall River, whom I once heard in a conversation at the Lyceum, appeared to me a formidable debater. He had a strong personality which made nothing of his antagonists. They were baubles for his amusement. His light, scoffing, &, as it were, final dealing with them, seeming to weigh them & find them nothings, was exquisitely provoking.

—

Life is a selection, no more. The work of the gardener is simply to destroy this weed, or that shrub, or that tree, & leave this other to grow. The library is gradually made inestimable by taking out from the superabounding mass of books all but the best. The palace is a selection of materials; its architecture, a selection of the best effects. Things collect very fast of themselves; the difference between house & house is the wise omissions.

—

I look for poetry above rhyme, poetry which the inspirer makes & applauds. The orator & the poet must be cunning Daedaluses & yet made of milk like the mob.

My friend said that the orator must have a dash of the devil in him to suit an audience: at least his rhetoric must be satanic.

There is also something excellent in every audience, capacity of virtue; it is expectant & greatly expectant. They are ready to be beatified also. They know so much more than the orators. And are so just. There is a tablet there for every line he can inscribe. Archangels listen in lowly forms. Archangels in satinette & gambroon.

So fleeting as it is, yet what is so excellent of present Power as the riding this wild horse of the People?

I suppose we shall never find in actual history the orator: he is a fabulous personage. We know very well what eloquence is, but no man was ever continuously eloquent. And our examples are private, felicities of colloquial energy. Webster never says any thing great to a popular assembly. At the bar & in the Senate he is good.

—

Every reform is only a mask under cover of which a more terrible reform, which dares not yet name itself, advances. Slavery & Antislavery is the question of property & no property, rent & anti-rent; and Antislavery dare not yet say that every man must do his own work, or, at least, receive no interest for money. Yet that is at last the upshot.

—

The United States will conquer Mexico, but it will be as the man swallows the arsenic, which brings him down in turn. Mexico will poison us.

The Southerner is cool & insolent. "We drive you to the wall, & will again." Yes, gentlemen, but do you know why Massachusetts & New York are so tame? it is because we own you, and are very tender of our mortgages, which cover all your property.

*

The stout Fremont, in his Report of his Expedition to Oregon & California, is continually remarking on "the group," on "the picture," &c. "which we make." Our secondary feeling, our passion for seeming, must be highly inflamed, if the terrors of famine & thirst for the camp, & for the cattle, terrors from the Arapahoes & Utahs, anxieties from want of true information as to the country & the trail, & the excitement from hunting, & from the new & vast features of unknown country, could not repress this eternal vanity of *how we must look!*

I play with the miscellany of facts & take those superficial views which we call Skepticism, but I know or might know, at the same time, that they will presently appear to me in their orderly order, which makes Skepticism impossible. How can a man of any inwardness not feel the inwardness also of the Universe? If he is capable of Science & of moral sentiment, the masses of nature instantly undulate & flow. The world, the galaxy is a scrap before the metaphysical power.

—

The Poet should instal himself & shove all usurpers from their chairs by electrifying mankind with the right tone, long wished for, never heard. The true centre thus appearing, all false centres are suddenly superseded, and grass grows in the Capitol. Now & then we hear rarely a true tone, a single strain of the right ode; but the Poet does not know his place, he defers* to these old conventions, and though sometimes the rogue knows well enough that every word of his is treason to all the kings & conventions of the world, yet he says "It is only I," "Nobody minds what I say," and avails himself of the popular prejudice concerning his insignificance, as a screen from the police.

We had conversation today concerning the poet & his problem. He is there to see the type & truly interpret it; O mountain, what would your highness say? thou grand expressor of the present tense; of permanence; yet is there also a

*He defers. We defer. That is the mischief. We are outvoted, the Nays have it, and we let the Nays have it. We who should say, 'What is the majority but the strength of weakness, the reason of fools?' suffer a majority to be somewhat in our own eyes.

taunt at the mutables from old Sitfast. If the poet could only forget himself in his theme, be the tongue of the mountain, his egotism would subside and that firm line which he had drawn would remain like the names of discoverers of planets, written in the sky in letters which could never be obliterated.

A man is entitled to pure air and to the air of good conversation in his bringing up, & not, as we or so many of us, to the poor-smell, & musty chambers, cats & paddies.

I told A.B.A. that he resembled a steam-engine which should stand outside one of our new depots, & see hundreds of paddies with pick & shovel making small impression, and should say, Let me come in, I will give you all leisure.

A man is caught up and takes a breath or two of the Eternal, but instantly descends, & puts his eternity to commercial uses. There is no other, no example of any who did not so.

But a pretty kettle of fish we have here, men of this vast ambition, who wish an ethics commensurate with nature, who sit expectant to be challenged to great performances, and are left without any distinct aim; there are openings only in the heavens before them, but no star which they approach; they have an invincible persuasion that the Right is to come to them in the social form, but they are aghast & desolate to know that they have no superiors in society. Society treats their conscience as it does men of genius; the only compliment it knows how to pay a man of genius, is to wait on him & to ask him to deliver a Temperance Address. So it proffers to these holy angels wishing to save the world, some bead or button of Communism, an Antislavery Cause, Prison Discipline, or Magdalen Refuge, or some other absorbent to suck his vitals into some one or other bitter partiality, & anyhow to deprive him of that essential condition which he prays for, adequateness.

H.D.T. seems to think that society suffers for want of war, or some good excitant. But how partial that is! the masses suffer for want of work as barbarous as they are. What is the difference? Now the tiger has got a joint of fresh meat to tear & eat: Before, he had only bones to grind & gnaw. But this concerns only the tigers, & leaves the men where they were.

He points to the respectability of earnestness on every platform. Yes, but what avails it, if it be fatal to earnestness to know much? The snails believe, the geniuses are constitutionally skeptical. I lament that wit is a light mocker, that knowledge is the knowing that we cannot know, that genius is criticism. I lament to have life cheap; that a great understanding should play with the world as he tosses his walking-stick & catches it again. I wish the years & months to be long, the days centuries, loaded, fragrant: now we reckon them basely, as bank days, by some debt that we are to pay or that is to be paid us.

—

The Yankee means to make moonlight work if he can; & he himself, after he has spent all the business hours in Wall street, takes his dinner at a French boardinghouse that his soup & cutlet may not be quite unprofitable, but he shall learn the language between the mouthfuls.

I rode in the stage coach with a pedler; "Mind the half cent," said my companion. "A man can about pay his shop rent by minding the half cent."

Symbol

In the dance, some dance, & others stand still awaiting their turn when the music & the figure comes to them. In the dance of God there is not one of the chorus but can & will begin to spin, monumental as he now looks, when ever the music & the figure reach his place & capacity.

—

Criticism. Literature

We are a little civil, it must be owned, to Homer & Æschylus, to Shakspeare & Dante, and give them the benefit of the largest interpretation. We must be a little strict also, & faithfully ask whether, if I sit at home & do not go to Hamlet, Hamlet will come to me; whether I shall find my tragedy written in his, and my wants & pains & disgraces described to the life.

—

Criticism is in its infancy. The anatomy of Genius it has not unfolded. Milton in the egg, it has not found. Milton is a good apple on that tree of England. It would be impossible by any chemistry we know to compound that apple other wise: it required all the tree; & out of thousands of apples good & bad, this specimen apple is at last procured. That is, we have a well-knit, hairy, industrious Saxon race, Londoners intent on their trade, steeped in their politics, wars of the roses, voyages, & trade to the Low Countries, to Spain, to Lepanto, to Virginia, & Guiana, all bright with use & strong with success. Out of this valid stock choose the validest boy, & in the flower of this strength open to him, the whole Dorian & Attic beauty and the proceeding ripeness of the same in Italy. Give him the very best of this Classic beverage. He shall travel to Florence & Rome in his early manhood: he shall see the country & the works of Dante, Angelo & Raffaelle. Well, on the man to whose unpalled taste this delicious fountain is opened, add the fury & concentration of the Hebraic Genius, through the hereditary & already culminated Puritanism—and you have Milton, a creation impossible before or again; and all whose graces & whose majesties involve this wonderful combination;—quite in the course of things once, but not iterated. The drill of the regiment, the violence of the pirate & smuggler, the cunning & thrift of the haberdasher's counter, the generosity of the Norman earl, are all essential to the result.

Mixture

The whole art of nature is in these juxtapositions of diverse qualities to make a lucky combination, as green & gold, dry oakleaves & snow enhance each other, & make a delicious mixture to the eye.

Mixture

Everything that makes a new sort of man is good; for though he is only a chemic dose in this generation, in the next, or next but one, he becomes a poet, & then the new metal becomes inestimable.

Mixture (Chemical Combination)

People do not value raw material. The Laws of Menu,—Bhagavat, Behmen, Swedenborg, Alcott, Channing, & what not, I may have to myself: nobody to quarrel with me for these masses or particles. But when I have mixed these simples with a little Boston water, it makes what they call poetry & eloquence, & will sell, it seems, in New York & London.

O Bacchus, make them drunk, drive them mad, this multitude of vagabonds, hungry for eloquence, hungry for poetry, starving for symbols, perishing for want of electricity to vitalize this too much pasture; &, in the long delay, indemnifying themselves with the false wine of alcohol, of politics, or of money. Pour for them, o Bacchus, the wine of wine. Give them, at last, Poetry.

Test, opportunity.

Do they stand immoveable there,—the sots, & laugh at your socalled poetry? They may well laugh; it does not touch them yet. Try a deeper strain. There is no makebelieve about these fellows; they are good tests for your skill; therefore, a louder yet, & yet a louder strain. There is not one of them, but will spin fast enough when the music reaches him, but he is very deaf, try a sharper string. Angels in satinette & calico,—angels in hunting knives, & rifles,—swearing angels, roarers with liquor;—O poet, you have much to learn.

Styles

There is the Periclean & there is the slambang style.

O Carlyle, the merit of glass is not to be seen but to be seen through but every crystal & lamina of the Carlyle glass is visible.

Let the poet work in the aim to eliminate beauty; that is verily his work; in that block of stone, in that rough verse, to free the noble conception, until it shall be as truly God's work as is the globe of the earth, or the cup of the lily.

Metre of the Poet again, is his science of love. Does he know that lore? Never was poet who was not tremulous with love-lore.

—

These rabble at Washington are really better than the snivelling opposition. They have a sort of genius of a bold & manly

cast, though Satanic. They see, against the unanimous expression of the people, how much a little well directed effrontery can achieve, how much crime the people will bear, & they proceed from step to step & it seems they have calculated but too justly upon your Excellency, O Governor Briggs. Mr Webster told them how much the war cost, that was his protest, but voted the war, & sends his son to it. They calculated rightly on Mr Webster. My friend Mr Thoreau has gone to jail rather than pay his tax. On him they could not calculate. The abolitionists denounce the war & give much time to it, but they pay the tax.
It seems now settled that the world is no longer a subject for reform: it is too old for that, & is to have custard & calves' jelly. We are no longer to apply drastic or alterative pills, nor attempt remedies at all, but if we have any new game, or some fireworks or ice-cream,—if Jenny Lind come hither, or Fanny Elssler return, it is all the case admits.
Boston is represented by Mr Winthrop whose ready adhesion to Southern policy outspeeds even the swift sequaciousness of his constituents.

The State is a poor good beast who means the best: it means friendly. A poor cow who does well by you,—do not grudge it its hay. It cannot eat bread as you can, let it have without grudge a little grass for its four stomachs. It will not stint to yield you milk from its teat. You who are a man walking cleanly on two feet will not pick a quarrel with a poor cow. Take this handful of clover & welcome. But if you go to hook me when I walk in the fields, then, poor cow, I will cut your throat.

Sparta & Christianity are two social things.

Don't run amuck against the world. Have a good case to try the question on. It is the part of a fanatic to fight out a revolution on the shape of a hat or surplice, on paedo-baptism or altar-rails or fish on Friday. As long as the state means you well, do not refuse your pistareen. You have a tottering cause: ninety parts of the pistareen it will spend for what you think also good: ten parts for mischief. You can not fight heartily for a fraction. But wait until you have a good difference to join issue upon. Thus Socrates was told he should not teach. "Please God, but I will." And he could die well for that. And Jesus had a cause. You will get one by & by. But now I have no sympathy.

The abolitionists ought to resist & go to prison in multitudes on their known & described disagreements from the state. They know where the shoe pinches; have told it a thousand times; are hot headed partialists. I should heartily applaud them; it is in their system.
Good beastie help itself by reform & resistance as well as by law. But not so for you generalizers. You are not citizens. You are not as they to fight for your title to be churchmembers or citizens, patriots. Reserve yourself for your own work.

A B A thought he could find as good a ground for quarrel in the state tax as Socrates did in the Edict of the Judges. Then I say, Be Consistent, & never more put an apple or a kernel of corn into your mouth. Would you feed the devil? Say boldly "There is a sword sharp enough to cut sheer between flesh & spirit, & I will use it, & not any longer belong to this double faced equivocating mixed Jesuitical universe."

The Abolitionists should resist, because they are literalists; they know exactly what they object to, & there is a government possible which will content them. Remove a few specified grievances, & this present commonwealth will suit them. They are the new Puritans, & as easily satisfied. But you, nothing will content. No government short of a monarchy consisting of one king & one subject, will appease you. Your objection then to the state of Massachusetts is deceptive. Your true quarrel is with the state of Man.

In the particular it is worth considering that refusing payment of the state tax does not reach the evil so nearly as many other methods within your reach. The state tax does not pay the Mexican War. Your coat, your sugar, your Latin & French

& German book, your watch does. Yet these you do not stick at buying.

But really a scholar has too humble an opinion of the population, of their possibilities, of their future, to be entitled to go to war with them as with equals.
This prison is one step to suicide.

He knows that nothing they can do will ever please him. Why should he poorly pound on some one string of discord, when all is jangle?

—

College Class of 1821

We have the less time to spend, for these many years since we met, & I must not detain you. We were here before, mere lambs & rams, & we have come back solemn Abrahams; and on account of Mrs A. & the young *A's*, we had some ado to get here now; we that so ran & skipped . . . Scots like to come of "kenned folk," and there is an eminent use in having one's training in the public eye. But it is curious to see how identical we are. We can remember ourselves, about as good & bad as today, 25, 30, 40 years & more. In college, I had unpreparedness for all my tasks. I have the same unpreparedness at this moment. Who is he that does not remember the roots of all the habits of his chum & his set in Dr Popkin's recitation room or in Commons Hall? We have had clients, pupils, patients, parishes. We have had hay to make, horses to buy, cargoes to manage, estates to settle, railroads to superintend, banks to direct, cities to preside over, states to govern, colleges to rule; but if we have done these things well, as I doubt not, it was because we could carry ourselves goodhumouredly as boys. With a fair degree of speed, I think there is still more bottom in the company; and what pleases me best in the history of the class, is its good position & promise at this moment. Its strength is not exhausted: our day has not been short; but we are not yet thinking of going to bed, & being tucked up for the long night. I see an open future before us; and I offer the sentiment The next twentyfive years shall be, God willing, as large a gain on the last as these were on the first score.

—

All the notable Americans, except Webster, as I have said before, are female minds; Channing, Irving, Everett, Greenough, Allston, &c.

Ah the careful American faces

To the youth the hair of woman is a meteor.

I think that he only is rightly immortal to whom all things are immortal; he who witnesses personally the creation of the world; he who enunciates profoundly the names of Pan, of Jove, of Pallas, of Bacchus, of Proteus, of Baal, of Ahriman, of Hari, of Satan, of Hell, of Nemesis, of the Furies, of Odin, & of Hertha;—knowing well the need he has of these, and a far richer vocabulary; knowing well how imperfect & insufficient to his needs language is; requiring music, requiring dancing, as languages; a dance, for example, that shall sensibly express our astronomy, our solar system, & seasons, in its course.—

Greatness Man of the World

A man of the world I wish to see, not such men as are called of the world who more properly are men of a pistareen, men of a quart pot, men of a wine-glass; whose report reaches about as far as the pop of a champagne cork, & who are dumb as soon as they stray beyond that genial circle.

But I wish catholic men who read ciphers which they see for the first time; who know the beauty of a quince-orchard; of a heron; of a wood pigeon; of a lonesome pasture. Men who see the dance in men's lives, as well as in a ballroom; & can feel & convey the sense which is only collectively or totally expressed by a population: men who are charmed by the beautiful Nemesis, as well as by the dire Nemesis; and wish to be its poets & dare trust their inspirations for their welcomes. Our poets have not the poetic magnanimity, but a miniminity rather; &, when they would go abroad, instead of inspecting their inward poem, they count their dollar bills.

The saints dare more, but I hate lampsmoke; I wish them to know the beautiful equality & rotation of merits, destroying their saintly egotism or prigism; let them worship the apple-trees, the thistles, & their beautiful lovers the humblebees, humming birds, & yellow butterflies, as they pass, & as I say, know the Beautiful Nemesis.

All men are of a size, and true art is only possible on the conviction that every talent, trait, & property has also its apotheosis some where. Fair play! We are willing that Christianity should have its glories, & Greece its own, & India, & England; but we are inly persuaded that Heaven reserves an equal universe of good for each of us, & until we have produced our short ray unto the concave sphere of the heavens & beheld our talent also in its last nobility & exaltation we shall be malcontents.

Poets do not need to consider, how fruitful the topic is, for with their superfluity of eyes every topic is opulent.
Spenser seems to delight in his art for his own skill's sake. In the Muiopotmos see the security & ostentation with which he draws out & refines his description of a butterfly's back & wings, of a spider's thread & spinning, of the Butterfly's Cruise among the flowers, "bathing his tender feet in the dew which yet on them does lie,"——it is all like the working of an exquisite loom which strongly & unweariedly yields fine webs, for exhibition, & defiance of all spinners.

—

Sunday, 20 Sept. Suffices Ellery Channing a mood for a poem. 'There, I have sketched more or less in that color & style. You have a sample of it. What more would you get, if I should work on forever?' He has no proposition to affirm or support. He scorns it. He has, first of all Americans, a natural flow and can say what he will. I say to him, if I could write as well as you, I would write a great deal better.

"As for beauty, I need not look beyond an oar's length for my fill of it."—I do not know whether he used the expression with design or no, but my eye rested on the charming play of light on the water which he was striking with his paddle. I fancied, I had never seen such colour, such transparency, such eddies: it was the hue of rhine wines; it was jasper & verdantique, topaz & chalcedony; it was gold & green & chesnut & hazel in bewitching succession & relief without cloud or confusion.

Rhyme

I know something more of rhyme, as all conversation with it strengthens the argument for it. I observe that it is the right material; as we do not enclose the face of watches in oaken but in crystal cases, so rhyme is the transparency that allows almost the pure architecture of thought to become visible to the reader. The genius of the sentence appears. There is great difference in mode & form. This artist presents like an enraptured boy a succession of rainbow bubbles, opaline, airborne, spherical as the world, and instead of a few drops of soul, soap suds.

—

1846
Bangor, October 6, 7, 8
Three hundred townships good for timber & for nothing else. Palmer mills that I saw building,—the whole property was reckoned worth 60,000. before the freshet, but would not have been relinquished for that sum.
Pines a thousand years old. Every year they must go farther for them: they recede, like beavers & Indians, before the white man.

Those Bangor men buy townships merely for the logs that can be cut on them, and add township to township. Some day a mine, a slate quarry, good marble, or soapstone, or lime is found in them, or a new railroad is projected, the timber land becomes unexpectedly what is called a settling township, and the lumber merchant suddenly finds himself the lord of villages, towns, & cities, & his family established as great proprietors.

My friend W. E. at Bangor told me that he thought "Judge Story might be a great man, O yes, a man of a good deal of talent & learning & fame," but he did not think so highly of him as a Judge, as many did; "that he had two failings as a Judge; first, in pint of judgment; & second, in pint of integrity;—you take my id*e*a."

—

New England

I think again of the true history of New England, & wish to see the just view taken with such grand sight as to omit all or almost all the chronologies & personalities which ordinarily constitute the tale. Now let us have only the aboriginal features, a god stepping from peak to peak nor planting his foot but on a mountain. Calvinism & Christianity being now ended, shall be ended. Their powerful contribution to the history shall be acknowledged. England shall be dealt with as truly. English conventions & the English public shall not have so much politeness from us. Neither shall the forms of our government & that wearisome constitutional argument mislead us, as it has Whig parties and good-boy statesmen. But we will see what men here really wish & try to obtain, often against their professions. What New England gravitates toward.

All the materialities should be freely received to refresh the picture; the ice, the lumber, leather, iron, & stone, and the cotton manufacture; and we should not spare to trace these facts to their grand home in the geology, and show the man the contemporary of pine, chestnut, & oak, granite, ice, waterfalls, & therefore a worker in them; & how his commerce brought him hides from Valparaiso & lead from Missouri.

The negative merit of the piece would be its resolute rejection of the faded or regnant superstitions, as of the Christian mythology, of the agricultural, commercial, & social delusions which pass current in men's mouths, but have long lost all reality.

—

Alcott, among many fine things he said of my volume of Poems, said, the sentiment was moral and the expression seemed the reverse.

I suppose if verses of mine should be compared with those of one of my friends, the moral tendency would be found impressed on all mine as an original polarity, that all my light is polarized.

Our system is one of poverty. 'Tis presumed that there is but one Homer, one Shakspeare, one Jesus, one Newton, not that all are or shall be inspired. If every man wrote poems, there were no readers. But should we truly suffer social detriment, if the wit of all were exalted? No, surely, but rapid & magical methods of disposing of its food the Intellect knows & would employ.

1847, Jan. 10. Read Alfieri's Life: Who died the year I was born, was a dear lover of Plutarch & Montaigne, a passionate lover of beauty & of study. His rare opportunities & the determination to use them, make him a valuable representative. His temperament however isolated him, & he travels in a narrow track with high walls on either side. Yet he is most fortunate in his friendships, & at last in his love. The noble is seeking the same good as the republican, namely one or two companions of intelligence, probity, & grace, to wear out life with, & rebut the disparagement he reads in the sea & the sky. Gori, Caluso, & the Countess of Albany were sea & sky to him. One has many thoughts, in reading this book, of the uses of Aristocracy & Europe to the native scholar.

The systems of blood & culture which we call France, Spain, Piedmont, &c must not be set down as nothing. There is a strong, characterised, resultant man, result of race, climate, mountain, sea, occupation, & institutions who is the Frenchman & appears well enough & acutely interesting to any one who has the opportunity of conversing with many of the best individuals of that nation; not recognized in any one man but well enough exhibited in the most distinguished French circles. In like manner there is a Spaniard, an Englishman, a Roman & the rest. This is plainer when we remember how fast Nature adopts art, & whatever form of life calculation leads us into for one or two generations Nature presently adopts into the blood, & creates men organized for that accidental & artificial way of working. To be a noble is to have a ticket of admission to the flower of each of these races with their peculiarities exalted by nature & custom to the best degree. Also to be noble & rich, is to see the sea & take possession of it by sea voyaging, to see the mountains, the Nile, Niagara, the desart, Rome, Paris, Constantinople, to see galleries, libraries, arsenals, navies, manufactories.

The stoic sect, which are never far off, need not tell me that the man is all these & they are superfluous. No, grant the man divine, he wants also a divine fact; and no man, let him be never so thoughtful, ever went to the sea shore, from an inland home, without a surprise, & a feeling that here was new invitation for somewhat that hitherto slept.

It appears too from this book that there are no large cities. Boston is a little town, & if any man buys a loaf of bread, every other knows where he had it; but so is Rome, & Italy, & England, each a little province, in which gossip & the surveillance of a petty public opinion is equally tyrannical.

Machiavelli

I have tried to read Machiavelli's Histories but find it not easy. The Florentine factions are as tiresome as the history of the Philadelphia Fire Companies, & the mobs of the Liberties of Southwark and Moyamensing. The biography of Dante, of Raffaelle, of Michel Angelo, to whom no word is spared, (excepting a line twice to Dante) would be worth all this noise of Signories & Gonfalonieri.

H.D.T. wants to go to Oregon, not to London. Yes surely; but what seeks he but the most energetic nature? & seeking that, he will find Oregon indifferently in all places; for it snows & blows & melts & adheres & repels all the world over.

Superlative

In Athens the Pelasgicon, a strip of land under the western wall of the citadel,—a curse had been pronounced on any who should tenant it and the oracle declared it "Better untrodden."

On they came to the Dorian mood
Of flutes & soft recorders.

I live amidst dresses:—if I could live amidst persons—

from
AB
1847

—What is the oldest thing? a dimple or whirlpool in water. That is Genesis, Exodus, & all.

—

Vice of men is setting up for themselves too early. I can't go into the quarrel or into the tavern, &c. because I am old; or into the abolition meeting at Faneuil Hall & attempt to speak, it won't do for me to fail!
But I look at wise men, & see that I am very young. I look over those stars yonder & into the myriads of the aspirant & ardent souls, & I see I am a stranger & a youth, & have yet my spurs to win. Too ridiculous are these airs of age.
Ancora imparo. I carry my satchel still.

—

All conversation is a series of intoxications; the talkers recover themselves at intervals, see how pleasant the gas was, inhale it again, and disport themselves gladly. If they kept cool, there would be no joy.

'Tis merry in hall
When beards wag all

—

Affirmative
Set down nothing but what will help somebody.

Saadi's five classes of men that may travel, are, the rich merchant; the learned; the beautiful; the singer; and the mechanic; because these are everywhere sure of good reception.

The rich, he says, is everywhere expected, & at home; whilst the poor man is an alien in his own house,—not being able even there to command the comforts of life.

*

And see this terrible Atlantic stretching its stormy chaos from pole to pole terrible by its storms, by its cold, by its ice-bergs, by its Gulf stream the desert in which no caravan loiters, but all hurry as thro' the valley of the Shadow of Death as unpassable to the poor Indian through all ages as the finer ocean that separates him from the moon; let him stand on the shore & idly entreat the birds or the wind to transport him across the roaring waste. Yet see, a man arrives at the margin with 120 dollars in his pocket, and the rude sea grows civil, and is bridged at once for the long three thousand miles to England, with a carpeted floor & a painted & enamelled walls & roof, with books & gay company & feasting & music & wine.

—

Mesmerism

I thought again of the avarice with which my man looks at the Insurance Office & would so fain be admitted to hear the gossip that goes forward there. For an hour to be invisible there & hear the best informed men retail their information he would pay great prices. But every company dissolves at his approach. He so eager—& they so coy. A covey of birds do not rise more promptly from the ground when he comes near, than merchants, brokers, lawyers, disperse before him. He went into the tavern, he looked into the window of the grocery shop with the same covetous ears. They were so communicative,—they laughed aloud,—they whispered, they proclaimed their sentiment:—he opened the door—& the conversation received about that time a check,—& one after another went home. Boys & girls who had so much to say provoked scarcely less curiosity, & were equally inaccessible to the unmagnetic man.

—

March 3.

At Lincoln, last night, read a lecture in the schoolhouse. The architect had a brighter thought than ordinary there. He had felicitously placed the door at the right of the desk, so that when the orator is just making a point and just ready to drive the last nail, the door opens at his side & Mr Hagar & Deacon Sanborn & Captain Peck come in, & amiably divide with him the attention of the company. Luckily the sleighbells, as they drove up to the door, were a premonitory symptom, & I was able to rein in my genius a little, whilst these late arrivers were bundling out & stamping their feet before they usurped the attention of the house.

—

Alcott wishes to call together the Club of Notables again. But the old objection recurs: Better let your tongue lie still till it forgets its office, than undertake for God before he calls you. Thence comes Charlatanism, Unitarianism. "If the other train do not arrive," said Mr Superintendent of the Single-track Rail Road, "do not move until your wheels rust off." And many a life was saved by his tyrannical caution.

We lie for the right.

On the Beauties of Concealment.

I have a question to propose to the company. Whether it is worth any man's while to relax any private rule. If he has drank water, why should he not drink wine? If he finds it best to add mortgages & securities to the good strength of love; to pray and also keep his powder dry; prayer, but also manure.

What is the harm of a little indulgence, so it be decent—that is—secret?

Why nothing; an imbecility is the only consequence. And that does not signify, does it? To remain a boy, an old boy at 50 years. He covered up all his particular frauds, but they made his face sharp. He concealed as well as he could all his effeminate & cowardly habits, but they made him cowering, & threw him on the Whig side, & he looked irritable & shy, & on his guard in public.

—

On the Power of Insanities, or the blinding of men by their talents. The New York men dwell in delusions: the poor countryman having no system of carpets, carriages, dinners, wine, & dancing, in his head to confuse him, is able to look straight at you without refraction or prismatic glories; and he sees whether you look straight also, or whether your head is addled by all this mixture of wines.

Concord had certain roads & waste places which were much valued for their beauty but which were difficult to find. There was one which whoso entered could not forget,—but he had more than common luck if he ever found it again, let him search for it with his best diligence. Run boy from the swamp beside the lake to the big hemlock where a chestnut has been chopped down at twelve feet high from the ground then leave the high wood road & take the ox path to the right;—pass one right hand turn, & take the second, & run down a valley with long prairie hay covering it close; an old felled pine-tree lies along the valley, follow it down till the birds do not retreat before you; then till the faint daymoon rides nearer; then till the valley is a ravine with the hills of Nobscot seen at the bottom of it across the Bay

I value morals because it gives me something to do today. It enhances all my property. The foreign has lost its charm. The beauty of my youth has come back. I woke up one morning & find the ice in my pond promised to be a revenue. It was as if somebody had proposed to buy the air that blew over my field. Well, it should have taught me that my richest revenues were in fasting & abstaining, in enduring & waiting, in bearing insult & rendering good service. Can you go to Boston in the cars tomorrow & come back at night safe & not degraded?

Purpose, tendency I have learned to value & nothing else. Have you made the life of man clearer of any snag or sawyer? Is Marriage righted? this despicable conservatism defied? Is your love, your freedom, the love & the freedom of all souls? & not a screened corner of self indulgence? Are you clear with your expenditure? Do you pay for the Church? for the state, and its wars, & slaves?

They who are in Boston up to their breasts or up to their chins, it does not signify that with their heads still aloft over the stream they cry aloud that it is dirty, & that they prefer the land.

The basis of reformers & poets is mercantile. What signifies then a little Latin or jingle?

—

What shall I say of a costly skill in Eloquence we have not seen? a Master who should play on an assembly as a Musician on a Piano: who seeing the temper of the people furious, should soften & compose them; seeing them dull, should know how to inflame them; seeing them reckless & animalized, should call out the imagination & the Intellect; and so should bring them at will into that key which he desired. Show him his audience, he carries their hearts in his mouth, & they shall carry & execute that verdict he pronounces.

—

Scholar

We must have society, provocation, a whip for the top. A Scholar is a candle which the love & desire of men will light. Let it not lie in a dark box. But here am I with so much all ready to be revealed to me as to others if only I could be set aglow. I have wished for a professorship. Much as I hate the church, I have wished the pulpit that I might have the stimulus of a stated task. N. P. Rogers spoke more truly than he knew, perchance, when he recommended an Abolition-Campaign to me. I doubt not, a course of mobs would do me much good. A snowflake will go through a pine board, if projected with force enough. I have almost come to depend on conversation for my prolific hours. I who converse with so few & those of no adventure, connexion, or wide information.—A man must be connected. He must be clothed with society, or we shall feel a certain bareness & poverty, as of a displaced, disfurnished person.—He is to be drest in arts, picture-galleries, sculpture, architecture, institutions, as well as in body garments. Pericles, Plato, Caesar, Shakspeare, will not appoint us an interview in a hovel. — — My friends would yield more to a new companion. In this emergency, one advises Europe, & especially England. If I followed my own advices,—if I were master of a liberty to do so—I should sooner go toward Canada. I should withdraw myself for a time from all domestic & accustomed relations & command an absolute leisure with books—for a time.

I think I have material enough to serve my countrymen with thought & music, if only it were not scraps. But men do not want handfuls of gold dust, but ingots.

The name of Washington City in the newspapers is every day of blacker shade. All the news from that quarter being of a sadder type, more malignant. It seems to be settled that no act of honor or benevolence or justice is to be expected from the

American Government, but only this, that they will be as wicked as they dare. No man now can have any sort of success in politics without a streak of infamy crossing his name.

Things have another order in these men's eyes. Heavy is hollow & good is evil. A western man in Congress the other day spoke of the opponents of the Texan & Mexican plunder as "Every light character in the house," & our good friend in State street speaks of "the solid portion of the community" meaning, of course, the sharpers. I feel, meantime, that those who succeed in life, in civilized society, are beasts of prey. It has always been so. The Demostheneses, the Phocions, the Aristideses, the Washingtons even, must bear that deduction that they were not pure souls, or they would not have been fishers & gunners. They had large infusions of virtue, & hence their calamities & the mischievous dignity they have lent to the rogues that belong in those piratical employments.

—

We are necessary partialists; such halves; men of war are birds of prey; & success is an infamy. Yet we that are in the Academy, are impatient of that, & of each other, & see no spheral men.

We live in Lilliput. The Americans are free willers, fussy, self asserting, buzzing all round creation. But the Asiatics believe it is writ on the iron leaf & will not turn on their heel to save them from famine, plague, or sword. That is great, gives a great air to the people.

We live in Lilliput. Men are unfit to live, from their obvious inequality to their own necessities, or they suffer from politics or from sickness, & they would gladly know that they were to be dismissed from the duties of life.

Now let these people know that when they die they are not dismissed. They shall not wish for death out of pusillanimity: but the weight of the Universe is pressed down on the shoulders of each slave to hold him to his task: the only path of escape is Virtue. Cause & Effect are the gamesters who win and it will beget a resignation to Fate that even the Americans will be exalted.

—

The question recurs whether we should descend into the ring. My own very small experience instructs me that the people are to be taken in very small doses. Vestry meetings & primary assemblies do not edify me. And I caution philosophers & scholars to use lenses & media.

Articulateness, finished extremities, complete development, is Man.
A snake is Man's spine, make the head a new spine only for a new evolution and open every vertebra into ribs and each extremity as shoulder or thigh into a new spine for new evolution of extremities & we have Man.

Club Café Procope

Theology, Medicine, Law, Politics, Trade have their meetings & assembly rooms. Literature has none. See how magnificently the Merchants meet in State street. Every Bank & Insurance office is a Palace, & Literature has not a poor café, not a corner even of Mrs Haven's shop in which to celebrate its unions. By a little alliance with some of the rising parties of the time, as the Socialists, & the Abolitionists, and the Artists, we might accumulate a sufficient patronage to establish a good room in Boston. As Ellery Channing says there is not a chair in all Boston where I can sit down.

Alcott said, The rest of the man will follow his head. His head is not his contemporary, but his ancestor & predecessor. Let him be a Cause.

Here, said the foreigner, your astronomy is an espionage. I dare not go out of doors & see the moon or stars, but they seem to ask me how many lines or pages are finished since I saw them last. Not so as I told you was it in Mull.

Forever where the trees grow biggest
Huntsmen find the easiest way

I hate vulnerable people.

To the lonely his loneliness yield.

Ancients & Moderns

The ancients brought the fire, the moderns collect coal.

It becomes those who want animal spirits to take the low tone; never to take the initiative. Such are chameleons, &, in the presence of the wise, they are transparent & serene; in the presence of the worldly, they are turbid & weak.

Superlative

Let others grumble that they see no faeries nor muses, I rejoice that my eyes see the real world always stable & erect, without blur or halo.

—

Police

Nature has taken good care of us. She knew what rowdies & tigers she was making & she created a police first in the Conscience, then in the preaching propensity, which she gave indifferently to the worst and to the decent; & lastly in the terror of gossip with which she cowed the boldest heart. God has delegated himself to a thousand deputies.

The virtue of Democrats is to rail against England, the Lowell companies, & Mr Webster's pension.

Scholar

Centrality Centrality. "Your reading is irrelevant." Yes, for you, but not for me. It makes no difference what I read. If it is irrelevant, I read it deeper. I read it until it is pertinent to me & mine, to nature & to the hour that now passes. A good scholar will find Aristophanes & Hafiz & Rabelais full of American history.

I believe in Omnipresence & find footsteps in Grammar rules, in oyster shops, in church liturgies, in mathematics, and in solitudes & in galaxies. I am shamed out of my declamations against churches by the wonderful beauty of the English liturgy, an anthology of the piety of ages & nations.

*

Courage

I have written in different places of the courage pertinent to Scholars. The Greeks seem to have had a fine audacity as in Aristophanes. I remember the saying of Brumoy (?) that the Greeks believed that the gods understood fun as well or better than men, & therefore the comic writers did not hesitate to joke the gods also pretty hardly.

Courage

Here is a man who loves fight. "Stranger, will you liquor?" "No." "Then perhaps you will fight." Our Kentuckian cannot see a man of good figure but he thinks he should like to break his back over an iron banister, or give him a fall that would finish him. But the other man cannot see the sun or stars without the wish to wrestle with them, & here is Descartes, Kepler, Newton, Swedenborg, Laplace, Schelling, who wish to wrestle with the problem of Genesis & occupy themselves with constructing Cosmogonies. Nature is saturated with deity, the particle is saturated with the elixir of the Universe. Little men just born, Copernicise. They cannot radiate as suns or revolve as planets, and so they do it in effigy, by building the orrery in their brain.

A man complained that in his way home to dinner he had every day to pass through that long field of his neighbor's. I advised him to buy it, & it would never seem long again.

—

Mesmerism

We want society on our own terms. Each man has facts that I want, &, though I talk with him, I cannot get at them for want of the clue. He does not know what to do with his facts; I know. If I could draw them from him, it must be with his keys, arrangements & reserves. Here is all Boston,—all railroads, all manufactures, & trade, in the head of this well-informed merchant at my side: What would not I give for a peep at his rows & rows of facts! Here is Agassiz with his theory of anatomy & nature: I am in his chamber & I do not know what question to put. Here is Charles T. Jackson whom I have known so long, who knows so much, & I have never been able to get anything truly valuable from him. Here is all Fourier in Brisbane's head; all languages in Kraitsir's; all Swedenborg in Reed's; all the Revolution in old Adams's head; all modern Europe & America in J.Q.A.'s, and I cannot appropriate any fragment of all their experience. I would fain see their picture-books as they exist. Now if I could cast a spell on this man at my side & see his pictures without his intervention or organs, and, having learned that lesson, turn the spell on another, lift up the cover of another hive & see the cells & suck the honey, & then another, & so without limit,—they were not the poorer, & I were rich indeed. So I think this mesmerism, whereof the fable adheres so pertinaciously to all minds, will one day realize itself. It is for this news, these facts, that I go to Boston, and visit A. & B. & C. Boston were ten times Boston if I could learn what I go thither for.

The ring of Gyges prefigures this—society on our own terms.

But Osman answered & said, I do not know whether I have the curiosity you describe. I do not want the particulars which the merchant values, or the lawyer, or the artist, but only the inevitable result which he communicates to me in his manner & conduct & in the tone & purpose of his discourse.

Speech is to conceal

Then again said Guy, If he could inspect these experiences, what would it signify? He can, if he wishes, as things are. He can devote himself to brokerage & stocks until he sympathizes practically with the merchant. Then he will have that clue he wants. He can study Humboldt until he can talk with Humboldt. He can read Bettine until he can predict her speech. If he could arrive at their pictures by the short cut you imagine, he must still be imprisoned in their minds by his dedication to their experience, & lose so much career of his own, or so much sympathy with still higher souls than theirs.

—

Scholar's courage should be as terrible as the Cid's.

Scholar's courage should grow out of his conversation with spiritual nature, not out of temperament & brawn, like Johnson's knocking down Osborne.
Fine audacity of the Greeks;
No weakness, Danton. No imbecilities of men, of cigars & wine! Let the scholar measure his valour by his power to cope with intellectual giants. Others can count votes, & calculate stocks. Can he weigh Plato? judge of the probabilities of Laplace's hypothesis? give me a considered opinion on the modern cosmogonies; & know Newton & Humboldt; criticize Swedenborg; dispose of Fourier?

Courage of insight, courage of the chart, courage of having done it before.

I see the same courage in Æschylus's poetry as in Nelson's fight.

Courage

Can the scholar disentangle the thread of truth through all the confused appearances of the Free Trade facts?—

Every man has his own courage, & is betrayed because he seeks in himself the courage of other persons.

When I read Proclus, I am astonished at the vigor & breadth of his performance. Here is no epileptic modern muse with short breath & short flight, but Atlantic strength everywhere equal to itself, & dares great attempts because of the life with which it is filled.

—

Transit

Some men cannot possibly make the metonomy or transit so far as to illustrate their experience by any circumstance but the historical one that befel them. If they would describe an insult, my life on it, it is the very insult they suffered; if they speak of an accident or a wound to which human life is liable, & he the speaker was once hurt by a pitchfork or a peat-knife, he is sure to speak of a wound by pitchfork or a peat-knife.

It is like Dr Chauncy's torpidity in prayer who at Thursday Lecture prayed that the death of the little boy who was just drowned in Frog Pond might be made salutary to all.

—

La Nature aime les Croisements

We seem to approach an analysis of Burke's wonderful powers by observing the employment of his early years. To a man quite ignorant of mechanic arts, a penknife, a thimble, a pin, seems to be made with inexplicable ingenuity. But, on visiting the shop where it is made, & seeing the successive parts of the work, in how simple a manner it is put together, the fabric loses part of its value, the composition is so easy. Something like this disappointment is felt by those who trace that complex product eloquence to its elements. We listen with joy to Burke explaining to the House of Commons on the rise of an unexpected debate all the intricacy of the Revenue Laws or the constitution of a commission or reviewing the details of legislation for years.—In the midst of accurate details, he surprises us with some deep philosophic remark which besides its own splendour astonishes by contrast with the habits of so practical a man of business.

But when we explore his youth & find him for years the author of the Annual Register & in the service of that work spent his days in the gallery of the House of C. & that in those same years he also wrote a philosophical Treatise on Taste & the Sources of the Sublime & Beautiful, we cease to wonder at the minuteness of his official knowledge or of the loftiness of his speculation.

—

Journal

'Tis purposed to establish a new Quarterly Journal. Well, 'tis always a favorable time, & now is.

The essential ground of a new book is that there be a new spirit; that the authors really have a new idea, a higher life, see the direction of a more comprehensive tendency than others are aware of and this with that fulness or steadiness of perception as to falter never in affirming it, but take the victorious tone, as did the Edinburgh Review, the London Times, & the Boston Chronotype.

—

An autobiography should be a book of answers from one individual to the main questions of the time. Shall he be a scholar? the infirmities & ridiculousness of the scholar being clearly seen. Shall he fight? Shall he seek to be rich? Shall he go for the ascetic or the conventional life? he being aware of the double consciousness.—Shall he value mathematics? Read Dante? or not? Aristophanes? Plato? Cosmogonies, & scholar's courage. What shall he say of Poetry? What of Astronomy? What of Religion?

Then let us hear his conclusions respecting government & politics. Does he pay taxes and record his title deeds? Does Goethe's Autobiography answer these questions? So of love, of marriage, so of playing providence. It should be a true Conversation's Lexicon for earnest men. Saadi's Gulistan is not far from this. It should confirm the reader in his best sentiment. It should go for imagination & taste. It should aspire & worship.

Every man prefers something, calling it Art or Music or something else, perhaps a misnomer.

It should contemplate a just metaphysics and should do justice to the coordinate powers of man. Imagination, Understanding, Will, Sensation, Science.

Novels, Poetry, Mythology must be well allowed for an imaginative being. You do us great wrong, Henry T., in railing at the novel reading. The novel is that allowance & frolic their imagination gets. Everything else pins it down. And I see traces of Byron & D'Israeli & Walter Scott & George Sand in the deportment of these stately young clerks in the streets & hotels. Their education is neglected but the ballroom & the circulating library, the fishing excursion & Trenton Falls make such amends as they can.

Autobiography

In this circle of topics will come *Education* & what we have to say of guns as liberalizers & dancers, & chess, & dancing & dress & languages. For if the man is not a profound man, a quarry, but is rather legged & winged & intended for locomotion he must be furnished with all that breeding which gives currency as sedulously as with that which gives worth.

Travelling is as fit for some men as it is pernicious for others.

Nature has given us in a shell the architecture applied to locomotion.

—

My first distribution of mankind is into the class of benefactors & malefactors. The second class is by far the largest as is obvious by this that a person seldom falls sick without inspiring the hope in the bystanders that he will die. Valuable lives are few. 'Tis a case for a gun.

—

Longevity

The fable of the Wandering Jew is agreeable to men because they want more time & land to execute their thoughts in:—but a higher poetic use must be made of that fable. Take me as I am with my experience & transfer me to a new planet, & let me digest for its inhabitants what I could of the wisdom of this. After I have found my depth there, & assimilated what I could of the new experience, transfer me to a new scene. In each transfer I shall have acquired a new mastery of the old thoughts in which I was too much immersed, by seeing them at a distance.

Our system is artificial. We are born into government, trade, & cities. We drive wooden piles & lay stonework on them & build an eternal city on punk.

Take hay & egg shells, & lay granite on that, then build up.

—

Why have the minority no influence? If Lycurgus were in the cars Boutwell would not dare that morning to offer resolutions of homage to Zachary Taylor.

Is it not better not to mix or meddle at all, than to do so ineffectually? Better mind your lamp & pen as man of letters, interfering not with politics, but knowing & naming them justly, than to inculpate yourself in the federal crime without power to redress the state, & to debilitate yourself by the miscellany & distraction for your proper task.

Our people have no proper expectations in regard to literary men: They expect a practical reformer.

Gustavus was justly censured for not distinguishing between a carabine & a general.

Whip

A whip for our top! A cold sluggish blood thinks it has not quite facts enough to the purpose in hand and must decline its turn in the conversation. But they who speak have no more;—have less; the best success of the day is without any new facts.

Heat, heat, is all. Heat puts you in rapport with magazines & worlds of facts.

My stories did not make them laugh, my facts did not quite fit the case, my arguments did not hit the white. Is it so? then warm yourself, old fellow, with hot mincepie and half a pint of port wine, & they will fit like a glove, & hit like a bullet.

—

Look at literary New England, one would think it was a national fast. All are sick with debility and want of object; so that the literary population wears a starved, puny, & piteous aspect.

Transcendentalism says, The Man is all. The world can be reeled off any stick indifferently. Franklin says, The tools; riches, old age, land, health; the tools. But experience says, The Man and the tools. We must have the best of both.

A master *and* tools,—is the lesson I read in every shop and farm and library. There must be both. The populace of science & of the streets insist on the value of tools.—Who could not do it that had them?—The man of genius insists on the commanding genius who is not nice in pencils, who can do every thing with nothing:—but the wise man sees that we cannot spare any advantages, and that the tools are effigies & statues of men also; their wit, their genius perpetuated; and he that uses them becomes a great society of men as wise as himself.

What a tool is money in a skilful hand. What a nuisance in a fool's.

from

CD

1847

Henry Truman Safford born at Royalton, Vt Jan 6, 1836. In 1846 was examined for 3 hours by Rev H W Adams of Concord N.H. & Rev C N Smith of Randolph Vt. and at last was bidden:

> "Multiply in your head 365 365 365 365 365 365 by 365 365 365 365 365 365!" eighteen figures by eighteen. "He flew round the room like a top pulled his pantaloons over the top of his boots, bit his hand rolled his eyes in their sockets sometimes smiling & talking & then seeming to be in agony until in not more than one minute, he said, 133,491,850,208,566,925,016,658,299,941,583,225. The boy's father Rev C. N. Smith & myself had each a pencil & slate to take down the answer, & he gave it us in periods of three figures each as fast as it was possible for us to write them. And what was still more wonderful he began to multiply at the left hand & to bring out the answer from left to right giving first 123, 491 &c. Here confounded above measure I gave up the examination. The boy looked pale & said he was tired. He said, it was the largest sum he ever did."

May 24. The days come & go like muffled & veiled figures sent from a distant friendly party, but they say nothing, & if we do not use the gifts they bring, they carry them as silently away.

Safford

"He has found a new rule to calculate eclipses. He told me it would shorten the work nearly one third. When finding this rule for two or three days, he seemed to be in a sort of trance. One morning very early he came rushing down stairs, not stopping to dress him, poured on to his slate a stream of figures, & soon cried out in the wildness of his joy, 'O, father, I have got it! I have got it! it comes, it comes.'"

Mr Knowall the American has no concentration: he sees the artists of fame, the Raffaelles & Cellinis with despair. He is up to Nature & the First Cause in his consciousness; but that wondrous power to collect & swing his whole vital energy into the act, and leave the product there for the despair of posterity, he cannot approach.

Safford

"In the spring of 1845 Henry began to be much engaged with the idea of calculating an almanac—Every old almanac in the house was treasured up in his little chest,—and sun's declination rising & setting, moon southings, risings & settings, seemed to occupy all his thoughts.

"His almanac was put to press in the autumn of 1845, & was cast when Henry was 9 years & six months old. 'the most accurate of any of the common almanacs of N. England'"

Eighteen or twenty centuries of European & Asiatic men have been trained to check their actions by regard for a Judgment Day. Now it begins to look to the knowing ones as if life were more correctly an affair for Punch.

Safford

"His infant mind drinks in knowledge as the sponge does water. Chemistry botany philosophy geography & history are his sport."

H. W. Adams

——Trumannus Henricus Safford graduated at Harvard College, 1854.

On the seashore at Nantucket I saw the play of the Atlantic with the coast. Here was wealth: every wave reached a quarter of a mile along shore as it broke. There are no rich men, I said to compare with these. Every wave is a fortune. One thinks of Etzlers and great projectors who will yet turn this immense waste strength to account and save the limbs of human slaves. Ah what freedom & grace & beauty with all this might. The wind blew back the foam from the top of each billow as it rolled in, like the hair of a woman in the wind. The freedom makes the observer feel as a slave. Our expression is so slender, thin, & cramp; can we not learn here a generous eloquence? This was the lesson our starving poverty wanted. This was the disciplinary Pythagorean music which should be medicine.

Then the seeing so excellent a spectacle is a certificate that all imaginable good shall yet be realized. We should not have dared to believe that this existed: Well what does not the actual beholding of a hero or of a finished woman certify?

> "Il faudrait pour bien faire que tout le monde fût millionnaire."
>
> Scribe
> Le Mariage d'Argent

Nation of Nantucket makes its own war & peace. Place of winds bleak shelterless & when it blows a large part of the island is suspended in the air & comes into your face & eyes as if it was glad to see you. The moon comes here as if it was at home, but there is no shade. A strong national feeling. Very sensitive to every thing that dishonours the island because it hurts the value of stock till the company are poorer.

50 persons own 5/7 of all the property in the island. Calashes. At the fire they pilfered freely as if after a man was burnt out his things belonged to the fire & every body might have them.

Before the Athenaeum is a huge jawbone of a sperm whale & at the corners of streets I noticed (Chester street) the posts were of the same material. They say here that a northeaster never dies in debt to a southwester but pays all back with interest.

Capt Isaac Hussey who goes out soon in the "Planter" had his boat stove in by a whale; he instantly swum to the whale & planted his lance in his side & killed him before he got into another boat. The same man being dragged under water by the coil of his line got his knife out of his pocket & cut the line & released himself. Capt Brayton was also dragged down but the whale stopped after a short distance & he came up.

I saw Captain Pollard.

The captains remember the quarter deck in their houses.

Fifty five months are some voyages.

9500 people 80 ships
New Bedford 300 ships

I saw Capt Isaac Hussey in the steamboat & asked him about that penknife. He said no he felt in his pocket for his knife but had none there; then he managed to let down his trowsers & get the line off from his leg & rose. At last he saw light overhead & instantly felt safe. When he broke water his men were a quarter of a mile off looking out for him. They soon discovered him & picked him up.

Capt Brooks told me that the last whale he killed was 72 feet long, 52 feet in girth & he got 200 bbls of oil from him.

The young man sacrificed by lot in the boats of the ship Essex was named Coffin, nephew of Capt Pollard & a schoolmate of Edw. Gardner.

"Grass widows" they call the wives of these people absent from home 4 or 5 years.

Walter Folger has made a reflecting telescope and a clock which is now in his house & which measures hours, days, years, & *centuries.* In Wm Mitchell's observatory I saw a nebula in Casseopeia the double star at the Pole, the double star Zeta Ursi.

At Nantucket every blade of grass describes a circle on the sand.

Community

At Brook Farm one man ploughed all day, & one looked out of the window all day & drew his picture, and both received the same wages.

—

Loose the knot of the heart, says Hafiz. At the Opera I think I see the fine gates open which are at all times closed, and that tomorrow I shall find free & varied expression. But tomorrow

I am mute as yesterday. Expression is all we want: Not knowledge, but vent: we know enough; but have not leaves & lungs enough for a healthy perspiration & growth. Hafiz has: Hafiz's good things, like those of all good poets, are the cheap blessings of water, air, & fire. The observations, analogies, & felicities which arise so profusely in writing a letter to a friend. An air of sterility, poor, thin, arid, reluctant vegetation belongs to the wise & the unwise whom I know. If they have fine traits, admirable properties, they have a palsied side. But an utterance whole, generous, sustained, equal, graduated-at-will, such as Montaigne, such as Beaumont & Fletcher so easily & habitually attain, I miss in myself most of all, but also in my contemporaries. A palace style of manners & conversation, to which every morrow is a new day, which exists extempore and is equal to the needs of life, at once tender & bold, & with great arteries like Cleopatra & Corinne, would be satisfying, and we should be willing to die when our time came, having had our swing & gratification. But my fine souls are cautious & canny, & wish to unite Corinth with Connecticutt. I see no easy help for it. Our virtues too are in conspiracy against grandeur, and are narrowing.

Benvenuto Cellini.—He had concentration and the right rage.

—

Thus the name of Sappho inspires; the expressive person; not that Casella or Corinne or Simonides has better thoughts than we, but that what we all have, shall not be pent & smouldered & noxious in the possessor, but shall pass over into new forms.

"Keep the body open," is the hygeian precept, and the reaction of free circulations on growth & life.—The fact that the river makes its own shores,—is true for the artist.

Large utterance! The pears are suffering from *frozen sap-blight*, the sap being checked in its fullest flow, & not being able to form leaves & fruit, which is the perspiration & utterance of the tree, becomes thick, unctuous & poisonous to the tree.

The jockey looks at the chest of the horse, the physician looks at the breast of the babe, to see if there is room enough for the free play of the lungs.—

Arteries, perspiration. Shakspeare sweats like a haymaker,—all pores.

—

What beauty in the mythology of Arabia; the Anka or Simorg, the Kaf mountain, the fountain Chiser, the tree of Paradise, Tuba; the mirror of Jamschid, the seal of Solomon, the treasure of Karun, the horse of Solomon— that is, the East Wind, his bird language, Kaf the mountain ridge which begirt the world.

Well is it less in Greece or much more in the fine picture gallery which has become an alphabet of the world's poetry & conversation?

Is it less in India with its colossal & profuse growth, like a giant jungle in which elephants & tigers pass?
the adventures of Hari, the Metamorphosis, the Fate,

or less in the Danish & Scaldic—Thor, Freya, Loki, Asgard, Igdrasil & Balder, where Sea, Fire, Old Age, and Thought are the mead, the Eater, the wrestler & the runner? Valhalla thatched with shields for shingles.

Zal son of Sam was born with white hair; was exposed on Kaf; was taken by the Simorg, & cherished for several years by that respectable griffin: taught the language of the country, & some accomplishments, as there were no schools—Sam came, & the Simorg gave him up, & gave him a feather of his own wing, bidding him put it in the fire when his aid should be wanted.
It was burned when Rudebeh his wife was about to bring forth Rustem. Rustem looked a year old when newborn, & required milk of ten nurses.

Afrasiyab was as strong as an elephant, his shadow extended miles, his heart bounteous as the ocean, & his hands like the clouds when rain falls to gladden the thirsty Earth. The crocodile has in the rolling stream no safety.

Yet he was but an insect in the grasp of Rustem who seized him by the girdle & dragged him from his horse. Rustem was so moved with anger at the arrogance of the K of Mazenderan that every hair on his body started up like a spear. The gripe of his hand cracked the sinews of an enemy.

—

Every thing teaches transition, transference, metamorphosis: therein is human power, in transference, not in creation; & therein is human destiny, not in longevity but in removal. We dive & reappear in new places.

—

My only secret was that all men were my masters. I never saw one who was not my superior, & I would so gladly have been his apprentice if his craft had been communicable.

Alas for America as I must so often say, the ungirt, the diffuse, the profuse, procumbent, one wide ground juniper, out of which no cedar, no oak will rear up a mast to the clouds! it all runs to leaves, to suckers, to tendrils, to miscellany. The air is loaded with poppy, with imbecility, with dispersion, & sloth.

Eager, solicitous, hungry, rabid, busy-body America attempting many things, vain, ambitious to feel thy own existence, & convince others of thy talent, by attempting & hastily accomplishing much; yes, catch thy breath & correct thyself and failing here, prosper out there; speed & fever are never greatness; but reliance & serenity & waiting & perseverance, heed of the work & negligence of the effect.

—

America is formless, has no terrible & no beautiful condensation. Genius always anthropomorphist, runs every idea into a fable, constructs, finishes, as the plastic Italian cannot build a post or a pumphandle but it terminates in a human head.

—

In history the great moment is when the savage is just ceasing to be a savage with all his Pelasgic strength directed on his opening sense of beauty; you have Pericles & Phidias, not yet having passed over into the Parisian civility. Every thing good in nature & the world is in that moment of transition, the foam hangs but a moment on the wave; the sun himself does not pause on the meridian; literature becomes criticism, nervousness, & a gnawing when the first musical triumphant strain has waked the echoes.

—

Worship of the Dollar.

I may well ask when men wanted their bard & prophet as now? They have a Quixote gallery of old romances & mythologies, Norse, Greek, Persian, Jewish, & Indian, but nothing that will fit them, and they go without music or symbol to their day labor.

Channing proposed that there should be a magnified Dollar, say as big as a barrel head, made of silver or gold, in each village & Col. Shattuck or other priest appointed to take care of it & not let it be stolen; then we should be provided with a local deity, & could bring it baked beans or other offerings & rites, as pleased us.

But what have we to do with elucidating Shakspeare & reading that which ends with the reading? Let life be a stately self-respecting march, & not a mendicant tricked out in foreign patchwork.

Literature should be the counterpart of nature & equally rich. I find her not in our books. I know nature, & figure her to myself as exuberant, tranquil, magnificent in her fertility,—coherent, so that every thing is an omen of every other. She is not proud of the sea or of the stars, of space or time; for all her kinds share the attributes of the selectest extremes. But in literature her geniality is gone—her teats are cut off, as the Amazons of old.

Rocking stones

It is said that when manners are licentious, a revolution is always near: the virtue of woman being the main girth or bandage of society; because a man will not lay up an estate for children any longer than whilst he believes them to be his own. I think, however, that it is very difficult to debauch society. This chastity which people think so lightly lost, is not so. 'Tis like the eye which people fancy is the most delicate organ, but the oculist tells you it is a very tough & robust organ, & will bear any injury; so the poise of virtue is admirably secured. Unchastity with women is an acute disease, not a habit; the party soon gets through it. Men are always being instructed more & more in the chastity of women.

"In March many weathers" said the proverb; and in life, many. If any thing were but true two days. But now we go forth austere & dedicated, believing in the iron links of Destiny irreversible & will not turn on our heel to save life, and we become strong with the same magnetism.

Well if it could last.

But tomorrow we are spiritualists, beleive in power of the will. We are the angel Gabriel & the Archangel Michael, the ring on our finger is the seal of Solomon, our sword or spade or pencil or pen is to open the secret caverns of the Universe. Who but we? and where is the bondman of the Parcae? Well, next day, we whistle & are speculative, & have a profusion of common sense, and think that the army is, after all, the gate to fame & poetry & "all that"; and that one story is good till another is told; and also that English scholars have been eaters & drinkers.

We go by Captain M.'s farm, and say, Selfishness plants best, & prunes best; Selfishness makes the best citizen & the best state. The good & the true make us puke. Resistance is good, and obedience is good, but who under Heaven knows how to mix the two? Our approval of one or another is all retrospective. No man ever said "I will do well" & then did well. Instinct, yes; but that is to be born not won.

Then we look over into George Minott's field & resolve to plough & hoe by old Cause & Effect henceforward. Life is a puzzle & a whirl & the cards beat the best players.

—

Song to his horse. "I shall kiss all over thy dear little head, my darling Kyrat. If a man were to buy thee at the price of his soul he would have thee at a low price. I give him every evening 40 measures of barley. I have furnished his curry comb with two little bells that he may not find his time too tedious in the stable. Trappings of velvet upon thy back will be cheap to me. Thy silver shoes with their nails of gold are cheap to me."

Socrates (in Gorgias) "I myself heard Pericles when he gave us his advice concerning the middle wall."

"For I know how to procure one witness of what I say, namely, him with whom I discourse, but I bid farewell to the multitude."

Socrates was celebrated for his exact domestic economy which Boeckh thinks consisted in keeping his family at work. "His income, according to Xenophon from his property might amount to 24 drachmas, together with some additional contributions of his friends, his necessary expenses were exceedingly small, & no one could live as he did. He lived in the strictest sense upon bread & water, except when he was entertained by his friends; and may have been much rejoiced at barley being sold at the low price of a quarter obolus the choenix. He wore no undergarment & his upper garment was slight, the same for summer & winter. He generally went barefooted, & his dress shoes which he sometimes wore, probably lasted him his whole life. A walk before his house served him for opson for meals, in short no slave lived so poorly as he did"

—

Criticism should not be querulous & wasting, all knife & root puller, but guiding, instructive, inspiring, a south wind, not an east wind.

Contrarious temperament with chills, Muff, & buffalo when the mercury reaches 90 degrees, and a fan at Zero and parasol. On going to bed wants strong coffee as a soporific and when we must write at night sup on baked beans, lettuce, and poppy-juice. He dislikes to hear nightingales hallooing all night but finds something soft & lulling in the voice of a pig.

"This religious coat," says Hafiz to his mistress, "puts me into no small confusion; make thou me a monk with thy irresistible glances." Unlike his commentator, I should read— Not the dervish, not the monk, but I, in spite of all my love of pleasure, have at heart the true spirit which makes the ascetic & the saint: and not their mummeries, certainly, but, what is strange to say, thy glances only can impart to me the fire & virtue needful to such selfdenial.

—

The problem of the poet is to do the impossible in this wise, namely to unite the wildest freedom with the hardest precision; he is to give the pleasure of colour, and is not less the most powerful of sculptors. Music seems to you sufficient, or the subtile & delicate scent of lavender; but Dante was free imagination, all wings, yet he wrote like Euclid.

In the garden a most important treatment is a good neglect. It must be a capital care that will make tomato or apple or pear thrive like a lucky neglect. Put a good fence round it & then let it alone a good deal. Fence it well, & let it alone well.

In George Sand's books, of course, the deduction is to be made of the cockney civilization. There is genius, yes, but also the fifteen thousand francs. The genius draws Porpora; the franc draws the underground plot of Zdenko and the caves of castles & the law of Vehm. One must not look for music & emancipation in a book, unless of one of those stalwart harpers who go by only once in 500 years.

—

In an evil hour I pulled down my fence & added Warren's piece to mine. No land is bad, but land is worse. If a man own land, the land owns him. Now let him leave home, if he dare. Every tree and graft, every hill of melons, every row of corn, every hedge-shrub, all he has done and all he means to do, stand in his way like duns when he so much as turns his back on his house. Then the devotion to these vines & trees & cornhills I find narrowing & poisonous. I delight in long free walks. These free my brain & serve my body. Long marches would be no hardship to me. My frame is fit for them. I think I compose easily so. But these stoopings & scrapings & fingerings in a few square yards of garden are dispiriting, drivelling, and I seem to have eaten lotus, to be robbed of all energy, & I have a sort of catalepsy, or unwillingness to move, & have grown peevish & poorspirited.

The garden is like those machineries which we read of every month in the newspapers which catch a man's coatskirt or his hand & draw in his arm, his leg, & his whole body to irresistible death.

Everything hastens to its Judgment Day. The merriest poem, the sweetest music rushes to its critic. From Calvinism we shall not get away. See how sedulously we plant a pair of eyes in every window to overlook our own goings & comings. And I know my Parcae through all the old hats, pea jackets, and blue farmer's frocks which they wear on every road I walk in.

The parents wished the girl to stay from home; the girl insisted on living at home. The girl was right, though the parents were poor. Work grows like grass everywhere; and labor is capital. Wherever created, it is exchangeable for every coin of the globe.

Garrison accepts in his speech, all the logic & routine of tradition, and condescends to prove his heresy by text & sectarian machinery with a whole new calendar of saints. What a loss of juice & animal spirits & elemental force!

I cannot live as you do. It is only by a most exact husbandry of my resources that I am any body.

—

Montaigne took much pains to be made a citizen of Rome. I should greatly prefer to have the freedom presented me of a peach-orchard or of some old plantations of apples & pears that I know than of any city.

June 22

An orientalist recommended to me who was a Hercules among the bugs and curculios, a Persian experiment of setting a lamp under the plum tree in a whitewashed tub with a little water in it, by night. But the curculio showed no taste for so elegant a death. A few flies & harmless beetles perished, & one genuine Yankee spider instantly wove his threads across the tub, thinking that there was likely to be a crowd & he might as well set up his booth & win something for himself. At night in the garden all bugdom & flydom is abroad.—

This year is like Africa or New Holland, all surprising forms & masks of creeping, flying, & loathsomeness.

—

Mythology

We do not understand in old biblical history the idol business; but we have a plenty of sub-gods ourselves. Who is not an idolater? I remember being at a loss to know why those Israelites should have such a passion for the idols.

Art's office is to furnish us with an ideal circumstance so that our flour barrel & milk pan, bureau & wash stand shall begin to be symbols.

A says Why is an arbour ornamental & intellect is not surely so regarded? I reply, Because an arbour remains an arbour; but the man of intellect is willofthewisp & fantastical—a bird, a bat. It should have reverence enow if it remained itself.

The solitude. All intellectual men are believers in an aristocracy, that is, a hierarchy. But I think them honest; because it is the prerogative of genius to melt every many ranked society into one company, merging distinction in their sincere curiosity & admiration.

The solitude. Dreadful to sit on the dais, happy to sit near the salt. Happy who is never seen except rightly seen! Happy whose dress no man ever could remember to describe.

Ah—who has society! people to talk to? people who stimulate? Boston has 120 000 and I cannot now find one: and elsewhere in the world I dare not tell you how poor I am, how few they are.

—

The mysterious laws of Poetry, the natural history of a poem are not known, no practical rules, no working-plan was ever given. It is miraculous at all points. The slate given, a little more or a good deal more or less performance seems indifferent. There is much difference in the stops, but the running time need be but little encreased to add great results.

As we say, one master could so easily be conceived as writing all the books of the world. They are all alike.

—

Tools. The ship Skidbladnir made by dwarves & given to Freyr was so great that all the asa with their wargear might find room on board; and as soon as the sail is set, she has a fair wind whither she shall go, & when the voyage is over, Freyr can fold her together like a cloth & keep her in his bag.

We make dahlias to order, & horses & swine. Owen & Fourier say we shall make men yet of the right sort.

He likes the garden because it minds him so well.

My young friend believed his calling to be musical, yet without jewsharp, catgut, or rosin. Yes, but there must be demonstration. Look over the fence yonder into Captain Abel's land. There's a musician for you, who knows how to make men dance for him in all weathers, & all sorts of men, paddies, felons, farmers, carpenters, painters, yes, and trees, & grapes & ice & stone, hot days, cold days. Beat that, Menetrier de Meudon! if you can! Knows how to make men saw, dig, mow, & lay stone wall, and how to make trees bear fruit God never gave them, and grapes from France & Spain yield pounds of clusters at his door. He saves every drop of sap as if it were his own blood. His trees are full of brandy. You would think he watered them with wine. See his cows, see his swine, see his horses and he, the musician that plays the jig which they all must dance, biped & quadruped & centipede, is the plainest, stupidest looking harlequin in a coat of no colours. But his are the woods & the waters, the hills & meadows.

With a stroke of his instrument he danced a thousand tons of gravel from yonder blowing sandheap on to the bog meadow beneath us where now the English grass is waving over countless acres. With another he terraced the sand hill, and covered it with peaches & grapes; with another he sends his lowing cattle every spring up to Peterboro to the mountain pastures.

—

An American in this ardent climate gets up early some morning & buys a river; & advertises for 12 or 1500 Irishmen; digs a new channel for it, brings it to his mills, and has a head of 24 feet of water: then, to give him an appetite for his breakfast, he raises a house; then carves out within doors a quarter township into streets & building lots, tavern, school, & methodist meeting house—sends up an engineer into New Hampshire, to see where his water comes from &, after advising with him sends a trusty man of business to buy of all the farmers such mill privileges as will serve him among their waste hill & pasture lots and comes home with great glee announcing that he is now owner of the great Lake Winnipiseosce, as reservoir for his Lowell mills at Midsummer.

Nantucket Bangor Lawrence

They are an ardent race and are as fully possessed with that hatred of labor, which is the principle of progress in the human race, as any other people. They must & will have the enjoyment without the sweat. So they buy slaves where the women will permit it; where they will not, they make the wind, the tide, the waterfall, the steam, the cloud, the lightning, do the work, by every art & device their cunningest brain can achieve.

The one event which never loses its romance is the alighting of superior persons at my gate.

—

Among the seven ages of human life the period of indexes should not be forgotten.

Gardens, trees in clumps, a bath in the brook, the pond paved with coloured pebbles, an arboretum, fireworks over water.

—

10 July

Ellery Channing has written a lively book on Rome which certifies that he has been there. He has the reputation of being a man of genius and this is some guarantee of it. He has approached sometimes the lightness & pungency of his talk, but not often. He has used his own eyes and many things are brought to notice here that had not been reported, as the fountains, the gardens, lively charcoal sketches of the cafe, the trattoria, and the bacon dealer's shop, the vettura & postillion, the agriculture in the Campagna. It was a lucky thought to introduce Montaigne in Rome, and the tribute to Raffaelle over his tomb in the Pantheon, & to Michel Angelo, are warm & discerning. A very catholic spirit.

—

Conversation that would really interest me would be those old conundrums which at Symposia the seven or seventy Wise Masters were wont to crack—What is intellect? What is time? What are the runners and what the goals?

But now there is no possibility of treating them well. Conversation on intellect & scholars becomes pathology. What a society it needs! I think you could not find a club at once acute & liberal enough in the world. Bring the best wits together and they are so impatient of each other, so worldly, or so babyish, there is so much more than their wit, so many follies & gluttonies & partialities, so much age & sleep & care that you have no academy. The questions that I incessantly ask myself as, What is our mythology? (which were a sort of test object for the power of our lenses) never come into my mind when I meet with clergymen; & what Academy has propounded this for a prize?

But of what use to bring the men together, when they will torment & tyrannize over each other, & play the merchant & the statesman. Conversation in society is always on a platform so low as to exclude the Saint & the Poet after they have made a few trials. Ah we must have some gift of transcending time also, as we do space, & collecting our club from a wider brotherhood. Crier, call Pythagoras, Plato, Socrates, Aristotle, Proclus, Plotinus, Spinoza, Confucius & Menu, Kepler, Friar Bacon

Gardening, A. thought today, was a good refuge for reformers, Abolitionists, &c. that they might acquire that realism which we so approve in merchants and in Napoleon. Yes; gardening and architecture would certainly be affirmative wholly, & so remedy this "unlimited contradicting" & chiding which is "a flat affair."

Insufficient Forces

We have experience, reading, relatedness enough, o yes, & every other weapon, if only we had constitution enough. But, as the doctor said in my boyhood,—"You have no *stamina*."

—

July 25

Of Alcott it is plain to see that he never loses sight of the order of things & thoughts before him. The thought he would record is something, but the place, the page, the book, in which it is to be written are something also, not less than the proposition, so that usually in the attention to the marshalling, the thing marshalled dwindles & disappears.

One thing more. I used to tell him, that he had no senses. And it is true that they are with him merely vehicular, and do not constitute a pleasure & a temptation of themselves. We had a good proof of it this morning. He wanted to know "why the boys waded into the water after pond lilies?"—Why, because they will sell in town for a cent apiece & every man & child likes to carry one to church for a cologne bottle. "What," said he, "have they a perfume? I did not know it."

—

W.E.C. describes the effect of sulphuric ether as a whole railroad train driving all the time thro' his brain: he is fast arriving at the jumping off place: that which he has been searching for in all his life, he is now just on the edge of finding: but, over all this power, on the tip-top, is perched still a residuum of the old state, the old limitation, & he learns that it can in no wise be got rid of; so that sulphuric ether "shows him the ring of necessity." Brandy, opium, nitrous oxide gas, sulphuric ether, hell-fire itself, cannot get rid of this limp band, O Asa!

July 18, 1847. Thor, too, I think—or Skrymir was it?—must have taken ether, when he mistook the fierce strokes of Thor's hammer for the dropping of acorns, or of leaves from the trees.

Books

O day of days, when we can read! The reader and the book. Either without the other is naught.

Thursday 15 July. Alcott, Thoreau & I went to the "island" in the Walden wood-lot, & cut down & brought home 20 hemlocks for posts of the arbour. And these have been growing when I was sleeping, fenced, bought, & owned by other men, and now in this new want of mine for an ornament to my grounds, their care and the long contribution of the great agents, sun & earth, rain & frost, supply this rich botanic wonder of our isle.

—

The Divine Man

Alexander the Great emitted from his skin a sweet odour, and Henry More believed the same thing of himself, and who does not remember the southwind days when he was a boy, when his own hand had a strawberry scent.

from

GH

1847–1848

Selfhelp

In the Edda, the wolf Fenris made a very sensible remark to the gods who coaxed him to suffer them to put their limp band upon his feet. If you can not break it, they said, we shall see that you are too feeble to excite alarm, & shall set you at liberty without delay.

"I am very much afraid," replied Fenris, "that if you once tie me so fast that I cannot work my deliverance myself, you will be in no haste to unloose me."

Our chapter on the superlative should be inscribed to the God Brage, "celebrated for his wisdom, eloquence, & majestic air."

—

There came here, the other day, a pleasing child, whose face & form were moulded into serenity & grace. We ought to have sat with her serene & thankfully with no eager demand. But she was made to run over all the list of South Shore acquaintance. How is Mrs H's cholera-morbus, & the Captain's rheumatism? When will Miss B. buy her carpets, and are there plums this year in P? When I got into the P. coach in old times a passenger would ask me, "How's fish?"

—

The highest value of natural history & mainly of these new & secular results like the inferences from geology, & the discovery of parallax, & the resolution of Nebulae, is its translation into an universal cipher applicable to Man viewed as Intellect also. All the languages should be studied abreast, says Kraitsir. Learn the laws of music, said Fourier, & I can tell you any secret in any part of the universe, in anatomy, for instance, or in astronomy. Kepler thought as much before.

Ah that is what interests me. When I read in a true History what befals in that kingdom where a thousand years is one day,

I see that it is true through all the sciences, in the laws of thought as well as of chemistry. No Marsaillaise is sung in that high region.

—

I read the fabulous magnificence of these Karuns & Jamschids & Kai Kans & Feriduns of Persia, all gold and talismans; then I walk by the newsboys with telegraph despatches; by the Post Office; & Redding's shop with English steamer's journals; & pass the Maine Depot; & take my own seat in the Fitchburg cars; & see every man dropped at his estate, as we pass it; & see what tens of thousands of powerful & armed men, science-armed society-armed men sit at large in this ample land of ours obscure from their numbers & the extent of territory, and muse on the power which each of these can lay hold of at pleasure. These men who wear no star nor gold laced hat, you cannot tell if they be poor or rich. And I think how far these chains of intercourse & travel go, what levers, what pumps, what searchings are applied to nature for the benefit of the youngest of these exorbitant republicans, and I say, What a negrofine royalty is that of Jamschid & Solomon; what a real sovereignty of nature does the Bostonian possess!

Caoutchouc, steam, ether, telegraph, what bells they can ring! Every man who has a hundred dollars to dispose of, a hundred dollars a year over his bread, is rich beyond the dreams of the Caesars.

Tools

And as all this leaves the man where he was before, the individualism, the importance of a man to himself, the fact that his power of self & social entertainment is all, makes quickly these miracles cheap to him; the greater they are the less they really become.

Value of a servant.

The New Englander is attentive to trifles, values himself on a sort of omniscience, knows when the cars start at every depot; feels every waterpipe & furnace-flue in his house; knows where the rafters are in the wall, how can he be absorbed in his thought? how can he be contemplative? He must have a servant, he must call Tom to ask the prices & hours. What day of the month it is, & when the mail closes. Who is Governor of the state, & where is the police office? But Tom does not come at a call. Nothing is so rare in New England as Tom. Bad for the New Englander. His skin is ocular. He is afflicted with the second thought. Not for an instant can he be great & abandoned to a sentiment. Let the countrymen beware of cities. A city is the paradise of trifles. Your hat & your shoes which you knew not of, stick out, and the current sets so strong that way that the city seems a hotel & a shop, a gigantic clothes-mart & tog-shop, and, if one perchance meet in the street a man of probity & wisdom, an accomplished & domestic soul, we are taken by surprise, and he drives the owls & bats that had infested us, home to their holes again.

—

If a man read a book because it interests him and read in all directions for the same reason, his reading is pure, & interests me, but if he read with ulterior objects, if he read that he may write, we do not impute it to him for righteousness. In the first case he is like one who takes up only so much land as he uses; in the second he buys land to *speculate* with.

—

I have that faith in the necessity of all gifts that to implore writers to be a little more of this or that were like advising gunpowder to explode gently, or snow to temper its whiteness, or oaktrees to be less profuse in leaves & acorns, or poplars to try the vinous habit & creep on walls.
They do as they can, or they must instruct you equally by their failure as by their talent. That is they must teach you that the world is farmed out to many contractors, and each arranges all things on his petty task, sacrifices all for that.

—

H. D. T when you talked of art, blotted a paper with ink, then doubled it over, & safely defied the artist to surpass his effect.

CKN the fathomless skeptic was here 8 August. Thought he defies, he thinks it noxious. It makes us old, harried, anxious. Yes, but it is no more to be declined than hands & feet are. We must accept our functions, as well as our organs. Thought is like the weather, or birth, or death: we must take it as it comes. Then this is work which, like every work, reacts powerfully on the workman. Out of this anxiety flows a celestial serenity.

The useful is the badge of the true. How does Hume or Kant profit us?

As to thought & its diseases, like the weather we must take it as it comes.

There is this vice about men of thought: you cannot quite trust them,—not as much as other men of the same natural probity,—without intellect,—as they have a hankering to play Providence, & make a distinction in favor of themselves from the rules they apply to all the human race.

—

Individualism has never been tried. All history, all poetry deal with it only & because now it was in the minds of men to go alone and now before it was tried, now, when a few began to think of the celestial Enterprise, sounds this tin trumpet of a French Phalanstery and the newsboys throw up their caps & cry, Egotism is exploded; now for Communism! But all that is valuable in the Phalanstery comes of individualism. You may settle it in your hearts that when you get a great man, he will be hard to keep step with. Spoons & skimmers may well enough lie together, but vases & statues must have each its own pedestal.

Laws of the world

The fish in the cave is blind; such is the eternal relation between power & use.

Again, that dream of writing in committee returns, the Beaumont & Fletcherism. The Seckle pear is the best in America. But it is small, & the tree is small. So we bud an apple tree just above the root from this pear, and the bud becomes root, and is assisted at the same time by the more succulent roots of the apple, and a most vigorous seckle pear is the result. Can we not help ourselves as discreetly by the force of two in literature? Certainly it only needs two well-placed & well-tempered for cooperation, to get somewhat far transcending any private enterprise in literature.

*

But it requires great generosity & rare devotion to the aim in the parties & not that mean thievish way of looking at every thought as property.

Thought is the property of him who can entertain it. Thought is the property of him who can adequately place it. A certain awkwardness usually marks our use of borrowed thoughts. They are too conspicuous, not being well placed.

The fable of Zohak of whom Eblis asked as the reward of his services that he might kiss the king's naked shoulder, & from the touch sprang two black serpents, who were fed daily with human victims; it is easy to see how fast a figurative description of luxury becomes a legend. The peasant sees that a pound of meal is a day's food, and costs a penny,—but that the courtier drinks a cup of wine, or eats a fowl, which costs 50 or 100 prices of his day's provisions; nay, which costs the wages of a man for ten days. Of course, ten men must toil all day, that this trifler may dine at ease. When this is much exaggerated, he says, The children of the courtier are corrupted from the mother's womb; if their father ate up ten men, they twenty, & with wrath & contempt beside: Two snakes have sprung from his shoulder who feed on human brains.

—

Value of a trope that the hearer is one.
Certainly, the great law of nature will work here; that the more transit, the more continuity; or, we are immortal by force of transits.
We ask a selfish immortality, Nature replies by steeping us in the sea which girds the seven worlds, & makes us free of them all.

—

Patriotism is balderdash. Our side, our state, our town is boyish enough. But it is true that every foot of soil has its proper quality, that the grape on either side of the same fence has its own flavor, and so every acre on the globe, every group of people, every point of climate has its own moral meaning whereof it is the symbol. For such a patriotism let us stand.

—

Why can we not let the broker, the grocer, the farmer, be themselves, and not addle their brains with sciolism & religion?
But the spiritualist needs a decided bias to the life of contemplation. Else what prices he pays! poor withered Ishmaelite, Jew in his Ghetto, disfranchised, odd one; what succors, what indemnities, what angels from the celestial side must come in to make him square!

What a misfortune is a swedenborg church. It requires for the profitable reading of Swedenborg almost an equal understanding to his own.

For just writing a noble fraternity based on magnanimity. Not with our mean thievish way of regarding thought as property & fearing rivals.

The paving stones in our street are boulders rounded by the attrition of a thousand years.

—

How often I have to remember the art of the surgeon, which, in replacing the broken bone, limits itself to relieving the dislocation, relieving the parts from their false position, putting them free, then they fly into place by the action of their own muscles.

On this art of nature all our arts rely. This is that tree which grows when we are sleeping: Ygdrasil;

—

We wish to get the highest skill of finish, an engraver's educated finger, determination to an aim,—& then—to let in mania, ether, to take off the individual's interference & let him fly as with thunderbolt.

—

Hafiz characterised by a perfect intellectual emancipation which also he provokes in the reader. Nothing stops him. He makes the daregod & daredevil experiment. He is not to be scared by a name, or a religion. He fears nothing. He sees too far; he sees throughout; such is the only man I wish to see and to be. The scholar's courage is as distinct as the soldier's and the statesman's—and a man who has it not cannot write for me.

—

N.L.F. twenty years ago, found me in his parlour, & looking at the form of my head, said, "if you are good, it is no thanks to you."

An aristocracy is as if a few inventors, like Fulton, Stephenson, Daguerre, and Charles Jackson, should be able to keep their secrets or impart them only to a few. How would those few ride & tyrannize over society; all the rhetoric applied now to the gods would be legitimately applied to them.

5 Sept.

Channing wished we had a better word than *Nature*, to express this fine picture which the river gave us in our boat yesterday. *Kind* was the old word, which, however, only filled half the range of our fine latin word. But nothing expresses that power which seems to work for beauty alone, as C. said, whilst man works only for use. The mikania scandens, the steelblue berries of the cornel, the eupatoriums, enriched now & then by a wellplaced Cardinal adorned the fine shrubbery with what C. called judicious, modest colours, suited to the climate, nothing extravagant. &c.

The English are distinguished by general culture. There is & was no such man, one would say, so equally & harmoniously developed; & hence his easy pride when he finds every other countryman inferior to him as a man. But this same culture necessitates a hopeless limitation. He reads Plato only for Greek, and has not the smallest interest in speculation. It requires a partialist for that.

O suppose nature had made man's body as agreeable to man's palate as plums & peaches so that a hungry man could not help biting his son.

"Give us peace in our boarders." wrote MME, & when shown the misspelling, said, "it would do as it was."

—

Horoscope Aristocracy

Not the phrenologist but the philosopher may well say, let me see his brain & I will tell you if he shall be poet, king, founder of cities, rich man, magnetic, of a secure hand, of a scientific memory, a right classifier, a just judge; or whether he shall fail in what he attempts. I see well enough, that when I bring one man into an estate, he sees vague capabilities, what others might, could, would, or should do with it; if I bring another man, he sees what he should do himself: He not only appreciates the water privilege, the land fit for orchard, pasturage, tillage, & so on, the woodlot, the cranberry meadow, but just as easily, he foresees all the means, all the steps of the process, and would lay his hand as readily on one point as on another in that series which conducts the capability to the utmost fruit. The indolent poet sees keenly enough the result; the well built head supplies all the intermediate steps, one as perfect as another, in the series. If we could see the man well, we should foresee his history as accurately as we do now that of a ciderpress or a washstand or a paintbrush, a basket, a pump, a corkscrew or a steelpen when I see these tools in a magazine of arts. They are already on their way respectively to apples, to dressingroom, to paint, to the cellar, to the well, to corks, to an inkstand; and the man's associations & fortunes, his love & hatred, his residence & rank, the books he will buy and the roads he will traverse, are foreordained in the result & in the completeness of the details in his brain.

People think it fortune, that makes one rich & another poor. Is it? Yes, but the fortune was earlier in the balance or adjustment between devotion to the present good & a forecast of the good of tomorrow. G. lives for the moment, praises himself for it, & despises E., that he does not. G., of course, is poor, & E., since he is providing, is provided. The odd circumstance is, that G. thinks it a superiority in himself, this improvidence which ought to be rewarded with E.'s property.

All biography auto-biography

I notice that the biography of each noted individual is really at last communicated by himself. The lively traits of criticism on his works are all confessions made by him from time to time among his friends & remembered & printed.

Present & Future

Do not imagine that I should work for the future, if my services were accepted or acceptable in the present. Immortality, as you call it, is my *pis aller.*

We want poetry; we do not want slops. The children want to eat & to run. Avoid, therefore, dysentery & lameness.

Remarkable trait in the American Character is the union not very infrequent of Yankee cleverness with spiritualism. Thus my Wall street cotton-broker, Thomas Truesdale; and William Green of Boonton, N.J., iron manufacturer; and Rebecca Black, living by slop work from the tailors; and Sampson Reed, druggist; & Hermann, toy seller; and Edward Stabler* druggist in Alexandria—were all prospering people who knew how to trade & how to pray. W. G.'s wagon always met T T & R B at the ferry when they went moved by the spirit to visit him, though he had no notice of their coming.
The Quakers blend the same traits.

When people tell me they do not like poetry, and bring me Shelley or Hemans, to show that it is not likeable, I am entirely of their mind. But this only proves that they do not like slops. But I bring them Homer, and they like that, & the Cid, and that goes well; and I read them Lear & Macbeth, Robin Hood's ballads, or Lady Jane, or Fair Annie, or the Hardyknute, or Chevy Chase, or the Cronach's cried or Bennachie, and they like that well enough. For this poetry instead of being daubs of colour, and mere mouthing, is out of the deep breast of man.

The Americans, Dr Harris the Librarian, tells me, are every day inquiring more after the history of families, and we want the English county histories here for that end.

*the friend of Mary Rotch

The Present
The present moment is a boat in which I embark without fear; boat & pilot at once.

—

One might expect a great immorality from the new arts, such as daguerre, telegraph, & railroad, on the ground that all that frees talent without increasing self-command, is noxious—a Gyges-ring, as young travellers are licentious who are faultless at home, but, as these arts are for all, the morals of society remain unaltered.

A tool is that which is used purely for my benefit, without any regard to its own. But all love is of that nature that it instantly respects the instrument also, &, though it be a ship or a wheel or bootjack, raises it instantly into personality & seeks to give it an interest of its own & to treat it as if it had.

—

Good writing is a kind of skating which carries off the performer where he would not go, & is only right admirable when to all its beauty & speed a subserviency to the will like that of walking is added.

—

At sea Oct. 13.
In mines & bottomry the last debt is paid first. The Irishman at Liverpool wished Capt. Barstow to carry him to N.Y. & his brother would meet him there on the wharf, & pay him. Does he live in N Y? No, not just in N.Y. but a little out of it, in a place called Illinois. Cotton pays a fair freight, when it pays a cent a pound to Liverpool. That on board pays a farthing. Yankees up-country have a mill into which they put a stick of wood & it goes through the hopper & comes out a chair. If a man does not like dust, let him go to sea. The sailor says, that all the sailors are runaway boys. The steersman's rule is, it is of no use to carry any more sail than you can steer steady. I detected in our unanimous zeal & interest in the ship's gains every hour that some of our passengers feared to arrive. Oct. 14. The good ship darts thro' the water all night like a fish, quivering with speed. Sliding thro' space, sliding from horizon to horizon. She has passed Cape Sable; she has reached the Banks; gulls, haglets, ducks swim, dive, & hover around;

no fishermen; she has passed the Banks, left five sail behind her, far on the edge of the west, at sundown, who were far east of us at morn, tho' they say at sea a stern chase is a long race. And still we fly for life. The ship cost $56 000.00. The shortest sea line from Boston to Liverpool is 2850 miles. This the steamer keeps, & saves by keeping her course 150 miles. Captain Caldwell says that he can never go in a shorter line than 3000 & usually much longer than that. The sailor is the practical ropedancer. The ship may weigh with all its freight 1500 tons. Every bound & plunge is taking us out of danger. If sailors were contented, if they had not resolved again & again never to go to sea any more, I should respect them. I can tell you what secrets the sea yielded me.

It occurred in the night watches that the true aristocrat is at the head of his own order, & that disloyalty is to mistake other chivalries for his own. Let him stop at the hotel of *his fashion:* &, whatever he does or does not, let him know & befriend his friends.

—

Oct. 18. In reading last night this old diary of Joseph Emerson of Malden ending in the year 1726, one easily sees the useful egotism of our old puritan clergy. The minister *experienced* life for his flock. He gave prominence to all his economy & history for the benefit of the parish. All his haps are providences. If he keeps school, marries, begets children, if his house burns, if his children have the measles, if he is thrown from his horse, if he buys a negro, & Dinah misbehaves, if he buys or sells his chaise, all his adventures are fumigated with prayer & praise, he preaches next Sunday on the new circumstance and the willing flock are contented with this consecration of one man's adventures for the benefit of them all, inasmuch as that one is on the right level & therefore a fair representative.

His cow & horse & pig did duty next sunday in the pulpit.

Another circumstance appears from all the names in the Diary, that the leading families in New England seem chiefly descended from some clergyman of that time, as, Hancock, Lowell, Sewall, Bulkeley, Chauncy, Forbes, Walter, Parsons,

Greenleaf, Thacher, Oxenbridge, Barnard, Colman, Green, Foxcroft, Tappan.

Religion

The Catholic religion respects masses of men & ages. If it elects, it is yet by millions, as when it divides the heathen & christian. The Protestant, on the contrary, with its hateful "private judgment", brings parishes, families, & at last individual doctrinaires & schismatics, &, verily, at last, private gentlemen into play & notice, which to the gentle musing poet is to the last degree disagreeable. This of course their respective arts & artists must build & paint. The Catholic church is ethnical, & every way superior. It is in harmony with Nature, which loves the race & ruins the individual. The Protestant has his pew, which of course is only the first step to a church for every individual citizen—a church apiece—.

Liverpool, 30 Oct. 1847

Everything in England bespeaks an immense population. The buildings are on a scale of size & wealth out of all proportion to ours. The colossal masonry of the docks & of all the public buildings attests the multitudes of men who are to be accommodated by them, & to pay for them. So the manners of the people, the complete incuriosity & stony neglect each of every other:— each man walks, eats, drinks, shaves, dresses, gesticulates, & in every manner is, acts, & suffers, without the smallest reference to the bystanders, & in his own fashion. It is almost an affront to look a man in the eye before being introduced. In mixed or in select companies, they do not introduce persons to each other so that a presentation is a circumstance as valid as a contract. The Englishman has thus a necessary talent of letting alone all that does not belong to him. They are physiognomically & constitutionally distinct from the Americans. They incline more to be large-bodied men; they are stocky, & especially the women seem to have that defect to their beauty; no tall slender girls of flowing shape, but stunted & stocky. The Englishman speaks with all his body; his elocution is stomachic; the American's is labial. The Englishman is very petulant & precise about his accommodation at inns & on the road; a quiddle about his toast & his chop, & every species of convenience, & loud & pungent in his expressions of impatience at any neglect. The axes of his eyes are united to his body, & only move with the trunk. His introductions are sacraments.

The English *Oh* much cheaper than the American *Indeed*, & quite significant. Universal clipping; Dr Cook Taylor who writes for the Athenaeum, I never doubted was Dr *Coutell.* Scotch cadence, "He told me, he would make sh*ooooe*s, and this is a true ve*racio*us account of the thing."

Carlyle has a hairy strength which made his literary vocation a mere chance, and what seems very contemptible to him. I could think only of an enormous trip hammer with an "Aeolian attachment." He said, he had received £800 from his Cromwell in England. i.e. from the first edition.

Rogers told of Talleyrand's visit with the Duchess of Orleans blazing with beauty, & Paméla, afterwards Lady Fitzgerald, who was more attractive by "the sweet seriousness of sixteen." Talleyrand's answer to Mme de Stael who asked which he would save on a plank in shipwreck, Recamier or herself? "Why, you can swim." One who said that if you could only know one English word in coming to England when this princess of Orleans was coming,—they urged "Yes." "No," said the other, "If I knew but one, it would be *no*; because no sometimes means yes, but yes never means no."
To a lady who wished to witness a great victory, Lord Wellington said, "Ah! Madam, a great victory is the greatest of tragedies except one, a defeat." To an Englishman who said, "They worship the sun in your country"; the Persian Ambassador replied, "So would you, if you ever saw him."

Sidney Smith said, Macaulay had improved, he has flashes of silence.
Of the giraffe, he said, that he would take cold; & think of having two yards of sore throat!

—

Among the local objects are horses & hounds *clothed all over*, and postillions in livery on every span of horses; and mourning coaches covered with nodding plumes; and gigs &

carts with little horses of the Canadian(?) breed, & dogs, & sedan chairs; & men dressed in shawls.

and turn their horses to the left hand when they meet, and in Manchester lately there is an order for foot passengers to turn to the right, & escutcheons on the walls for one year after death.

The English love conventional manners, & do not excuse the want of them. A man not *made up* after their fashion, is like a man not drest, & is not presentable. Their bearing, on being introduced, is cold, even though they wish very much to see you, & mean to make much of you.

Penny postage yields £800 000 revenue over the cost. Postage stamps are a very useful currency in a country where there is no paper money of less amount than £5.

—

All life moves here on machinery, 'tis a various mill. The Englishman never touches the ground. The steamer delivers him to the cab; the cab to the railway train; the train to the cab; the cab to the hotel; & so onward.

Most of the differences between American & English, referrible to dense population here, and will certainly be lost as America fills up.

December 4, 1847. What a misfortune to America that she has not original names on the land but this whitewash of English names. Here every name is history. I was at Rochdale yesterday; I asked, where is the Rock? "That river down there." So at Sheffield, the Sheafe. Prestwick, Greenwich, is the Priest's vicus, the green vicus, so that all means somewhat. And poor America is born into cast-off clothes, and her alphabet is secondary, & not organic.

—

This morning more than ever I believed the world is wise; the world & not the individual. Wordsworth knows very little about his Ode, has as little to do with that, as any reader. If you see the man, you would say, he is not the writer; and would warmly advise him to read that poem. In Plutarch's "*Placita Philosophorum*," I remember some one found the soul in the air circulating, respired & expired by all alike. Yes, Wisdom is in the air, & good health gets it all.

Ellen Tucker's poetry was very sweet, & on the way to all high merits & yet as easy as breathing to her who wrote.

—

In Worcester, 27 or 30 000.

30 December. I went over Worcester Cathedral, part of which has stood 900 years (?). I saw the tomb of King John; of Prince Arthur son of Henry VII, and especially, & with most delight, some old tombs of crusaders with their mailed legs crossed in marble, and the countenances handsome & refined as the English gentleman of today, & with that uncorrupt youth in the face of manhood, which I often see here. From the tower I had the fine picture of the Severn for many a mile & the Malvern Hills.

But the reason why any town in England does not grow, is, that it is a Cathedral town. If Birmingham had been a cathedral town, they say it would have been no larger than Worcester.

—

I trace then the peculiarities of English manners to their working climate; their dense population; the presence of an aristocracy or model class for manners & speech; their diet generous & orderly taken; and their force of constitution. Their manners betray real independence, and they are studiously inoffensive. They are castles compared with our men; the porter, the drayman, above all the coachman & guard,—what substantial, respectable old grandfatherly figures they are, & with the manners & speech appertaining. An American feels like some invalid in their company.

At York. I saw the skull of a Roman centurion.

I saw the tree planted by Geo Fox; I saw the prison, the pews in which the prisoners are locked up; the scales with which they can weigh their own food.

casts of felons' faces & skulls

a boy sentenced seven years for stealing boots

In the minster I heard "God Save the King," of Handel, played by Dr Camidge on the grand organ. It was very great. I

thought I had never heard anything so sublime. The music was made for the minster, & the minster for the music.
In the choir was service of evening prayer read & chanted. It was strange to hear the whole history of the betrothal of Rebekah & Isaac in the morning of the world read with all this circumstantiality in York minster, 13 Jan. 1848, to the decorous English audience just fresh from the Times Newspaper & their wine, and they listening with all the devotion of national pride. That was binding old & new to some purpose. The reverence for the Scriptures is a powerful element of civilization, for thus has the history of the world been preserved, & is preserved. Every day a chapter of Genesis and a leader in the Times.

—

I saw a young man yesterday whose body is in greatest part covered over with a hard scale like that of the armadillo. He was naked, or nearly so, and I had the nearest view of him, though I declined touching him. There are a great many talents in a drop of blood, and a little suppression or retardation would unchain & let out what horns & fangs, what manes & hoofs, what fins & flippers, what feathers & coats of mail which are now subdued and refined into smooth & shapely limbs, into soft white skin, into the simple erect royal form of man.

My Nights repeat my day, & I dream of gas light, heaps of faces, & darkness.

It was at Bridlington (pronounced Burlington) that one of the company asked me, if there were *many* rattlesnakes in the city of New York? and another whether the Americans liked to call their country *New England*?

from

Sea-Notes

Oct. 1847

As we see the human body or one of its limbs undraped, so here Nature shows us a limb of our planet in undress, & we see the nakedness of the sea-line. It is a sublime curve, certainly, yet begets in the spectator an uncomfortable feeling. To nature as to man, he says, Still be drest! still hide a poverty even so grand under the ornamented details of a broken landscape.

—

Lettuce, apple, or melon, in season—so long it is good. So is it with every work of man: epic poem, hymn, architecture, ship, naval skill, commerce, law, & whatever else. When their hour is past do not try to move the hand back on the dial & do them again but try that undone something which is in season now, celery, ice, or cucumbers. As long as the faith is settled, the architecture was, & abbeys were built. Now, vacillating faith, & motley architecture.

from

London

1847–1848

The parish church 600 years old.

Near Leeds & Bradford, I observed the sheep were black, & fancied they were black sheep; no, they were begrimed by the smoke. So all the trees are begrimed. The human expectoration is black here. The hopelessness of keeping clothes white, leads to a rather dowdy style of dress, I was told, among the ladies; and yet they sometimes indemnify themselves; & Leeds in the ballroom, I was assured, is a very different creature from Leeds in Briggate.

Mr Marshall's mill covers two acres of ground. The former owner James Marshall presided in this immense hall at a dinner given to O'Connell; and the Chartists having threatened an attack, Mr M. had a waterpipe under his chair which was supplied by a steam engine, & which he was ready to direct on the mob, if they had ventured to disturb him.

—

In the new Parl. House, great poverty of ornament, the ball & crown repeated tediously all over the grand gate, near the Abbey, & *Vivat Regina*, written incessantly all over the casements of the windows in H of Lords. But Barry built the Reform Club House. The Parliament Houses, up to March 1848, have cost £945000 in thirteen years. Houses of Parliament a magnificent document of Eng. power & of their intention to make it last. The Irish harp & shamrock are carved with the rose & thistle over all the house. The houses cover eight acres, & are built of Bolsover stone. Fault, that there is no single view commanding great lines, only, when it is finished, the speaker of the H. of Commons will be able with a telescope to see the Lord Chancellor in the Lords! But mankind can so rarely build a house covering 8 acres, that 'tis pity to deprive them of the joy of seeing a mass & grand & lofty lines.

*

In H. of Commons, when a man makes his first speech, there is a cry of "New member, New member," & he is sure of attention. Afterwards, he must get it if he can. In a body of 648 members every man is sure to have some who understand his views on whatever topic. Facts they will hear, and any measure proposed they will entertain, but no speculation, & no oratory. A sneer is the habitual expression of that body. Therefore Cobbett's maiden speech, "I have heard a great deal of nonsense, since I have been sitting here," was quite in their vein, & secured their ear.

If a member rise a second time in the same debate, they cry, "Spoke." If they do not like his speech, they cry "Divide."

Stand at the door of the House of Commons, & see the members go in & out, & you will say these men are all men of humanity, of good sense,

—

An English lady, on the Rhine, hearing something said to her party, respecting foreigners, exclaimed, "No, we are not foreigners; 'tis you that are foreigners; we are English."

To use the shopkeepers' word, England has "a good *stand*." It is just in the middle of the world, so that every manufacturer knows that he can sell all he can possibly produce.

The commercial relations of the world are so intimately drawn to London, that it seems as if every dollar in the world contributed to strengthen the English government.

—

I hear it said, that the sense which the manufacturers have of their duties to the operatives, & the exertions they have made in establishing schools & Mechanics' Institutions for them, is recent, & is, in great part, owing to Carlyle. At Huddersfield, I was told that they have over-educated the men in the working class, so as to leave them dissatisfied with their sweethearts & wives; and the good Schwanns & Kehls there, were now busy in educating the women up to them.

Mr Kehl thought that my Lecture on Napoleon was not true for the operatives who heard it at H. but was true only for the commercial classes, and for the Americans, no doubt; that the aim of these operatives was to get 20 shillings a week, and to marry; then, they joined the "Mechanics' Institute," hear lectures, visit the newsroom, & desire no more. I thought it despair.

At Rawdon, I inquired, how much the men earned who were breaking stone in the road; & was told Twenty pence; but they can only have work three days in the week, unless they are married; then they have it four days.

—

De Quincey at Mrs Crowe's, very fine face. He had walked 10 miles in the rain— but was so drest that 10 miles could not spoil him. He had walked home in the rain lately from Mrs C's dinner, he told us, because he could not find money to ride; as of two street girls one had taken his 8 shillings out of his pocket, & the other his umbrella. He can now write one article in every number of the N. Brit. Review. The Quarterlies pay 16 guineas a sheet. Tait vulgarizes him. Hanna is Editor of the N B. De Q. has never seen Landor but grieves over the loss of a finely bound copy of Hellenics sent him by L. He has also lost 5 manuscript books of Wordsworth's Excursion (continued), loses every thing. Such gentleness & simplicity perfect. Takes Dr B into the middle of the street to tell him where his lodgings are. Yet does not owe more than 100 pound. Estimates "Paradise Regained" very highly, thinks the author always knows. Thinks the guest has duties. Turnbull said he would go to hell for Sir William Hamilton. Wilson said, I know but I will not tell De Quincey's age, for it is my own. We were at Oxford together, but not acquainted. Game cocks. In Wales a theatre fracas in which W. was ignominiously mauled made their acquaintance. (Indians live by the leg not by the arm) D. W. the biggest hat in America. DeQ said Wordsworth appropriated what another said so entirely as to be angry if the originator claimed any part of it. "Mine". "Yours!" "Yes." "No it is mine".

—

I find here a wonderful crop of mediocre and super-mediocre poets, they lie 3, 6, or 10 deep, instead of single as in America.

But, as at home, the merchants seem to me a greatly superior class to the clerisy. & they have a right to a great contempt of these.

H. M. said that W. W. in his early housekeeping at the cottage was accustomed to offer his friends bread & plainest fare, but if they wanted anything more, they must pay him for their board. I heard the story with admiration, as evincing English pluck more than any thing I know.

H.M. said in her trance that there was no ultimate atom, only forces; and this, she learned, was the stupendous discovery of Faraday.

P. T. visited H. M. at N with R Cobden and on departing came back to say that R.C. said, that 'twas a sad business this agitation, for his own little boy thought him, when he went home, a gentleman who visited his mother.

—

It is remarkable here that no one inquires who wrote this or that paragraph in The Times. The best-informed men, who might easily know, read & admire without asking.
Was never such arrogancy on the face of the earth as the tone of this paper. Every slip of an Oxonian or Cantabridgian who writes his first leader assumes that *we* subdued the world before we sat down to write this particular Times. But the habit of brag runs through all classes from the Times, Wordsworth, Carlyle, Macaulay, down to the boys at Eton.

"Taking their pleasure sadly, after the manner of their nation," said Froissart.

Carlyle's realism is thorough. He is impatient of a literary trifler & if Guizot is to make Essays after being a tool he thinks it nothing. Actors & actresses all mad monkeys. He saw Rachel in an impossible attitude & learned it was the lead in her dress & he despises her ever since. This English parliament with its babble he denounces. They gather up six millions of money every year to give to the poor, & yet the people starve. He thinks if they would give it to him to provide the poor with labor & with authority to make them work or shoot them & he to be hanged if he did not do it, he could find them in plenty of Indian meal. These idle nobles at Tattersall's there is no work or word of serious purpose in them, and they have this great lying Church, & life is a humbug.

Of course, this French Revolution is the best thing he has ever seen & the teaching this great swindler Louis Philippe that there is a God's justice in the Universe after all, is a great satisfaction.

"No man speaks truth to me".

"Yes, they come to hear me and they read what I write, but not one of them has the smallest intention of doing these things."

He values Peel as having shown more valor as a statesman than any other of these men. Wellington he esteems real & honest; he will not have to do with any falsehood.

Chalmers he valued as a naif honest eloquent man, who, in these very days believed in Christianity, and though he himself, when he heard him, had long discovered that it would not hold water, yet he liked to hear him.

Tennyson dined out every day for months; then Aubrey de Vere, a charitable gentleman, 30 miles from Limerick, on a beautiful estate, came up & carried him off. Tennyson surrendered on terms;—that he should not hear anything of Irish distress; that he should not be obliged to come down to breakfast; & that he should smoke in the house. So poor Tennyson, who had been in the worst way, but had not force enough to choose where to go & so sat still, was now disposed of.

Since the new French Revolution, C has taken in the Times newspaper, the first time he has ever had a daily paper.

"If he should go into Parliament, the thing he should do would be to get those reporters thrust out, and so put an end at once to all manner of mischievous speaking 'to Bunkum,' and windbags. In the Long Parliament, the only great parliament, they sat secret & silent grave as an Oecumenical Council, and I know not what they would have done to any body that had got in there & attempted to tell out of doors what they did."

He finds nothing so depressing to him as the sight of a great mob. He saw one once, three or four miles of human beings & fancied that the earth was some great cheese, and these were mites.
He reads Louis Blanc. He can't get any true light on Cobden's Free Trade. He does not believe with Cobden. Every labourer a monopolist. The navigation laws of this country made its commerce. St John was insulted by the Dutch & came home, & got the law passed that foreign vessels should pay high fees, & it cut the throat of the Dutch & made the Eng. trade.
C. says, that a man deposited £100 in a sealed box in the Dublin Bank & then advertised to all somnambulists, mesmerisers, & others that he whoever could tell him the number of his note should have the money. He let it lie there six months, the newspapers now & then stimulating the attention of the adepts, but none ever could tell him; & he said, now let me never be bothered more with this proven lie.
It is droll to hear this talker talking against talkers, and this writer writing against writing.
If such a person as O Cromwell should come now it would be of no use, he could not get the ear of the House of Commons. You might as well go into Chelsea Graveyard yonder, & say, Shoulder Arms! and expect the old dead churchwardens to arise.

In architecture he thought it would be right now for an architect to consult only what was necessary, & to attempt no kind of ornament, & say, I can build you a coffin for such dead persons as you are, & for such dead purposes as you have, but no ornament.
He prefers Cambridge to Oxford. But Oxford & Cambridge education indurates them, as the Styx hardened Achilles so that now they say we are proof; we have gone thro' all the degrees, & are case hardened against all the veracities of the universe, nor man nor God can penetrate us.

"The idea of a pigheaded soldier who will obey orders, & fire on his own father, at the command of his officer,—is a great comfort to the aristocratic mind," said C.

*

C. called Lady G. a female Brummel, & said, Brummel was a sort of inverse Saint Peter, who could tread the waters of humbug without sinking.

Wicksteed told me of an American who enlarged, to Carlyle, on free institutions, sure of his sympathy; and C. replied, "that he preferred a tranquil large-minded White Russian to any other kind of man": for C., it seems, had lately seen Nicholas. And I repeatedly found that Nicholas was one of his few living heroes. For in the ignominy of Europe when all thrones fell like card houses & no man was found with conscience enough to fire a gun for his crown, but every one "ran away in a coucou through the Barriere de Passy," one man remained who believed he was put there by God Almighty to govern his empire, & by the help of God had resolved to stand there.

Chadwick is the other hero, Chadwick who proposes to provide every house with pure water, sixty gallons to every head, at a penny a week; and Carlyle thinks, that the only religious act which a man nowadays can securely perform, is, to wash himself well.

—

On one occasion Thalberg (?) played on the piano at Windsor, & the Queen accompanied him with her voice. On the news of this getting abroad, all England shuddered from sea to sea. It was never repeated.

—

In London only could such a place as Kew gardens be overlooked. Wealth of shops bursting into the streets. Piles of plate breast high on Ludgate hill. In a London Dock Mr B said he had seen 19 miles of pipes of wine piled up to the ceiling.

Many of the characterizing features of London are new. Such as gas light, the omnibuses, the steam ferries, the penny post, & the building up the West end.

One goes from show to show, dines out, & lives in extremes. Electric sparks 6 ft long, light is polarized, Grisi sings, Rothschild is your banker, Owen & Faraday lecture, Macaulay talks, Soyer cooks.

*

Is then not an economy in coming where thus all the dependence is on the first men of their kind?

I stayed in London till I had become acquainted with all the styles of face in the street & till I had found the suburbs & their straggling houses on each end of the city. Then I took a cab, left my farewell cards, & came home.

Trades of despair

—

9 March. I attended a Chartist meeting in National Hall, Holborn. It was called to hear the report of the Deputation who had returned after carrying congratulations to the French Republic. The Marsaillaise was sung by a party of men & women on the platform, & chorused by the whole assembly: then the "Girondins." The leaders appeared to be grave men, intent on keeping a character for order & moral tone in their proceedings, but the great body of the meeting liked best the sentiment, 'Every man a ballot & every man a musket'.
Much was whispered of the soldiers,—that "they would catch it," i.e. the contagion of chartism & rebellion.

"cet affreux silence que l'on observe en marchant en ligne,—" was said of English troops.

In the Times, advertisement of literary assistance. Thomas Roscoe sold his name to a book. Thomas Delf sells his book to a name of Mr Cunningham bookseller.

The British Museum holds the relics of ancient art, & the relics of ancient nature, in adjacent chambers. It is alike impossible to reanimate either.

The arrangement of the antique remains is surprisingly imperfect & careless, without order, or skilful disposition, or names or numbers. A warehouse of old marbles. People go to the Elgin chamber many times & at last the beauty of the whole comes to them at once like music. The figures sit like gods in heaven.
Coventry Patmore's remark was that to come out of the other

room to this was from a room full of snobs to a room full of gentlemen.

—

"Barbarous names have much emphasis, great conciseness, & less ambiguity, variety, & multitude.
The Barbarians are stable in their manners, & firmly continue to employ the same words. Hence they are dear to the Gods." Jamblichus

St Paul's is, as I remembered it, a very handsome noble architectural exploit, but singularly unaffecting. When I formerly came to it from the Italian cathedrals, I said, "Well, here is New York." It seems the best of show-buildings, a fine British vaunt, but there is no moral interest attached to it.

R M told of Landor that he threw his cook out of the window, & then exclaimed, "Good God! I never thought of those poor violets!" He said that he had talked with the son & told him he must be on his guard against his father's furious fits. "O no," he replied, "I just keep out of the way when the fit comes, & besides I am getting stronger every day & he is getting weaker".
L thinks that our custom of eating in company is very barbarous, & he eats alone with half closed windows because the light interferes with the taste. A tribe in Crim Tartary he has heard of who eat alone, much superior to the English, of course. L walking in London came to the top of a street full of people & foamed at the mouth with indignation.

—

If I stay here long, I shall lose all my patriotism, & think that England has absorbed all excellences.
My friend A. came here & brought away a couple of mystics & their shelf of books from Ham Common, & fancied that nothing was left in England, & I see that Kew Gardens & so many great men & things are obscure.
I look at the immense wealth & the solid power concentrated, & am quite faint: then I look in the street at the little girls running barefoot thro' the rain with broom in hand to beg a half penny of the passenger at the crossing & so many Lascars

& pitifullest trades & think of Saadi who barefooted saw the man who had no legs, & bemoaned himself no more.

At Oxford, in the Bodleian Library Mr Bandinell showed me the manuscript of Plato of the date, AD 896, brought by Dr Clarke from Egypt, and a complete MS of Virgil of the 9th Century also. Also the first Bible, printed at Mentz 1450(?) and a duplicate of the same which had been deficient in about 20 leaves at the end. But in Venice, he bought a room full of books & Mss for 4000 louis d'ors, every scrap & fragment, & had the doors locked & sealed by the Consul, & in examining his purchase he found the deficient pages of his Bible perfect & brought them to Oxford & placed them triumphantly in the Volume but will not have it new bound. The oldest building here is 200 years younger than the frail Mss I just now mentioned. No candle or fire is ever lighted in the Bodleian. A catalogue of the Bodleian is the standard catalogue of every library here, and, if the College has the book, they underscore the name of it. But the theory is, that the Bodleian has all books.
I saw a Clarendon's History interleaved with all appertaining scraps, songs, caricatures, portraits on a like plan with Clark's Sartor at home. One chamber is filled with "topography of England" alone. One with Mr Douce's 20 000 books.

In Merton which is the oldest college, I found books still chained to the shelves.
In New College that is Winchester College I found William of Wykeham's motto, "Manners makyth man" on the gates.
The students throughout the University are locked up every night.
Dr Daubeny told me that no duel had ever occurred at Oxford.

—

T. C. thought the clubs remarkable signs of times. That union was no longer sought, but only the association of men who would not offend one another. There was nothing to do but they could eat better.

He was very serious about the bad times. He had seen it coming, but thought it would not come in his time. But now it is coming, and the only good he sees in it, is the visible appearance of the gods. He thinks it the only question for wise men, &, instead of art, & fine fancies, & poetry, & such things especially as Tennyson plays with, to address themselves to the problem of society; he sees this confusion to be the inevitable end of such falsehood & nonsense as they have been.

T. C. said, There are about 70,000 of these people who make what is called "Society." Of course, they do not need to make any acquaintance with new people like Americans.

It costs £4000 to keep a house of Ld. Ashburton's empty. The aristocracy spend most of their money on houses. They might be little providences on earth & they did nothing.

Plato was very unsatisfactory reading. Very tedious. The use of intellect not to know that it was there, but to do something with it.

—

40 *per cent* of the English people cannot write their names. One half of one *per cent* of the Massachusetts people cannot, & these are probably Britons born.

It is certain that more people speak English correctly, in the United States, than in Britain.

The Government offers free passage to Australia for 25 000 women. In A. are six men to one woman. Miss Coutts has established a school to teach poor girls taken out of the street how to read & write & make a pudding & be a colonist's wife. They do very well so long as they are there but when it comes to embarking for Australia they prefer to go back to the London street, though in these times it would seem as if they must eat the pavement. Such is the absurd love of home of English race, said Dickens.

—

Very evang lady wanted the comy to subscribe to send a missionary to India. The people believed in devils & worshipped devils. Yes said the Uncle I tell you my dear those are no jokes of devils, those in India; they actually eat or cause to be destroyed one per cent of the population. But, niece, they worship devils too in Europe and news were just brought that this is creeping into England, and, instead of one per cent, they say their devil sends to eternal damnation nineteen out of every twenty. The niece who had expected a contribution to her missionary purse, shut her eyes & her mouth.

—

In London, one sees that nature aims at certain types of face in thousands of individual faces. For, you shall see close approaches to every kind of face you know in America.

Coventry Patmore described Tennyson as spending the evening with a dozen friends as nearly his own equals as any that could be collected, but Tennyson would not say one word, but sat with his pipe silent, and, at last, said, 'I am going to Cheltenham; I have had a glut of men.' When he himself proposed one day to read to Tennyson a poem which he had just finished, that Tennyson might tell him of anything which his taste would exclude T replied, "Mr Patmore, you can have no idea how many applications of this sort are made to me."

25 April. Dined with Mr Forster, Carlyle & Dickens, & young Pringle. Forster called Carlyle's passion Musketworship. Disraeli, thought C., betrayed whoredom; & all the house of commons universal incontinence. Chastity was given up in Europe. L. Hunt thought it indifferent. Dickens said 'twas so much the rule that he should be scared if his son were particularly chaste.

—

Among the trades of despair is the searching the filth of the sewers for rings, shillings, teaspoons, &c which have been washed out of the sinks. These sewers are so large that you can go underground great distances. Mr Colman saw a man coming out of the ground with a bunch of candles. "Pray Sir Where did you come from?" "O I've been seven miles," the man replied. They say that Chadwick rode all under London on a little brown pony.

—

Mr B. with his courteous manners & real excellence saw Malibran at the opera in former days. And when the actress was to cross the ruined arch, he rose in his place & assured the actress & the audience, that "the bridge is cracked."

Dr Ashburner tells me, that he suspended a gold ring by a filament of silk & willed it to approach him, & it swung towards him; and this experiment succeeded twice.

Mr Sylvester. Pauperism always accrues in English arrangements. Like sediment from brackish water incrusting the locomotive & choking it. Prisons breed prisons, workhouses workhouses. Army, Government, Church all have their pauperism & the means of remedy directly are found to have theirs.

In Westminster Abbey, I was surprised to find the tombs cut & scrawled with penknives, and even in the coronation chair in which is contained the royal stone of Scone & in which for hundreds of years the Kings & Queens of England have been crowned, Mr Butter & Mr Light, and Mr Abbott have recorded their humble pretensions to be remembered: "I Butter slept in this chair" is explicitly recorded by that gentleman's penknife on the seat.

—

3 May I heard Alboni sing last night in Cenerentola, & the Times today calls it the best of her triumphs. I found only the noble bursts of voice beautiful & the trills & gurgling & other feats not only not interesting, but, as in all other performers, painful; mere surgical or, rather, functional acts.

An Englishman of fashion is like one of those souvenirs bound in gold & vellum, enriched with delicate engravings on thick hot-pressed vellum paper fit for ladies & princes but nothing in it worth reading or remembering.

Mr Sylvester told me that Mr Farie could draw a model of any loom or machine after once seeing it, for Rees' Cyclopedia, and did so in Mr Strutt's mills.

Mr Hallam asked me, at Lord Ashburton's, "whether Swedenborg were all mad, or partly knave?"

He knew nothing of Thomas Taylor, nor did Milman, nor any Englishman.

Tennyson no dandy. Plain, quiet, sluggish sense & strength; refined as all English are. Goodhumoured, totally unaffected, the print of his head in Horne too rounded & handsome; an air of general superiority that is very satisfactory.

He lives with his college set. Spedding, Brookfield, Hallam, Rice, & the rest.

Thought Carlyle wholly mistaken in fancying the Christian religion had lost all vitality. They all feel the caprice & variety of his opinions. It is his brother Tennyson Turner, who wrote the verses which Wordsworth praised.

—

In Paris, the number of beggars does not compare with that in London, or in Manchester even.

I looked in all the shopwindows for toys this afternoon, and they are very many & gay; but the only one of all which I really wish to buy is very cheap, yet I cannot buy it, namely, their speech. I covet that which the vilest of the people possesses.

French poetry is peu de chose and in their character & performance is always prose, prose ornée, but never poesy.

Madame de Tocqueville, who is English, tells me, that the French is so beautiful a language, so neat, concise, & lucid, that she can never bear to speak English. 'Tis a peculiarity of the French that they assimilate all foreign words, & do not suffer them to be pronounced in the foreign manner. *libretto* is livret, *charivari* is sharivari, & so on, so that every blouse in the street speaks like an academician; which is not possible in England. I do not distinguish between the language of a blouse talking philosophy in a group, & that of Cousin.

I understand, from young Murray, that Elihu Burritt coming hither with his 50 languages, was sadly mortified to find that he could not understand but one word in any French sentence.

—

In the Spanish Gallery in the Louvre, it is easy to see that Velasquez & Spagnoletto were painters who understood their business. I fancy them both strong swarthy men who would have made good soldiers or brigands, at a pinch. And, in running along the numberless cartoons of old masters, the eye is satisfied, that the art of expression by drawing & colour has been perfectly attained; that on that side, at least, humanity has obtained a complete transference of its thought into the symbol.

These Spaniards paint with a certain ferocity. Zurbarra who paints monks, & specially one monk with a skull in his hands, which seems the reflection of his own head, is a master so far.

—

It is impossible in a French table d'hote to guess the social rank & the employment of the various guests. The military manners universal in young Frenchmen, their stately bow & salutation through their beards, are, like their beards, a screen, which a foreigner cannot penetrate.

At the Club des Femmes, there was among the men some patronage, but no real courtesy. The lady who presided spoke & behaved with the utmost propriety,—a woman of heart & sense,—but the audience of men were perpetually on the look out for some équivoque, into which, of course, each male speaker would be pretty sure to fall; & then the laugh was loud & general.

Le Club des Clubs was one which consisted of the chiefs of all the Clubs, & to which was accorded a tribune in the Assembly. But they were so dictatorial & indolent that the Chamber at last mustered courage enough to silence them, &, I believe, to turn them out.

The noble buildings of Paris are, the truly palatial Thuilleries; Notre Dame; Le Palais de Justice, & the Chapel la Sainte Chapelle, adjoining it, (built by Louis IX in the 13 Century); the old tower, St Jacques de la Bucherie; l'Hotel de Ville; le Pantheon;
I went to the Pantheon & learned that the tomb of Napoleon was at the Invalides. Rousseau & Voltaire sleep under the Pantheon.

I have seen Rachel in Phedre, in Mithridate, & now last night in Lucrece, (of Ponsard) in which play she took two parts, that of Lucrece & that of Tullia. The best part of her performance is the terror & energy she can throw into passages of defiance or denunciation. Her manners & carriage are throughout pleasing by their highly intellectual cast. And her expression of the character is not lost by your losing some word or look, but is continuous & is sure to be conveyed. She is extremely youthful & innocent in her appearance and when she appeared after the curtain fell to acknowledge the acclamations of the house & the heaps of flowers that were flung to her, her smile had a perfect good nature & a kind of universal intelligence.

May

At the Chamber of the National Assembly, by the kindness of Mr Rush, who lent me his diplomatic ticket. Lamartine made his speech on the question of Poland. He was quite the best and indeed the only good speaker I heard in the house. He has a fine head, and a free & superior style of delivery, manly & cultivated. But he was quite at his ease, no swords or pikes over his head this time, and really little energy in his discourse. He read many extracts from letters sent him from Italy, and when he was tired, the members cried out, Reposez vous, & the President gave an intermission for half an hour.

The whole house of 900 members obviously listened with great respect & gladly to Lamartine, for they want information, and it has been rather parsimoniously given by any whom they could trust. His speech is reckoned wise & moderate. To me it looks as if a wise Frenchman should say to his country, Leave Poland & China & Oregon to themselves. You have more than enough to do, at present, in constructing your own government & dealing with disorder, hunger, & faction in France.—But Lamartine praised the new republic because it had not a moment of Egoism, but had adopted Poland & Italy.

We now dine daily at a table d'hote at No 16 Rue de Notre Dame des Victoires, where 500 French habitués usually dine at 1 franc 60 centimes. Of course it is an excellent place for French grammar. Nouns, verbs, adverbs, & interjections furnished gratuitously.

*

I am told that there are 12 000 students connected with the University, including all the faculties. 'Tis a noble hospitality, & well calculated also, as it brings so great a population of foreigners to spend their money in France.

Do thy goo queek lee en Amérique
te mash eens?

Paris has great merits as a city. Its river is made the greatest pleasure to the eye by the quays & bridges: its fountains are noble & copious, its gardens or parks far more available to the pleasure of the people than those of London. What a convenience to the senses of men is the Palais Royal: the swarming Boulevards, what an animating promenade: the furnished lodgings have a seductive independence: the living is cheap & good; then what a luxury is it to have a cheap wine for the national beverage as uniformly supplied as beer in England. The manners of the people & probably their inferiority as individuals make it as easy to live with them as with so many shopkeepers whose feelings & convenience are nowise to be consulted. Meantime they are very civil & goodtempered, polite & joyous, and will talk in knots & multitudes in the streets all day for the entertainment of the passenger. Then they open their treasures of art & science so freely to the mere passport of the traveller & to all the world on Sunday. The University, the Louvre, the Hotel de Cluny, the Institute, the Gallery of the Luxembourg, Versailles. Then the Churches are always open, Notre Dame; La Sainte Chapelle, built by St Louis, & gorgeous within; St Sulpice; the Madeleine;

Then there is the Pantheon; and there is the Jardin des Plantes worthy of admiration. Everything odd & rare & rich can be bought in Paris; & by no means the least attractive of its shows is the immense bookstalls in the streets: maps, pictures, models, busts, sculptures, & libraries of old books spread abroad on tables or shelves at the side of the road. The manners of the people are full of entertainment so spirited, chatty, & coquettish, as lively as monkeys. And now the whole nation is bearded & in military uniform. I have no doubt also that extremes of vice are found here & that there is a liberty & means of animal indulgence hardly known by name or even by rumour in other towns. But any extremes are here also exceptional

& are visited here by the fatal Nemesis who climbs all walls, dives into all cellars (and I notice that every wall in Paris is stigmatized with an advertisement of La Guerison des Maladies secretes) but also the social decorum seems to have here the same rigours as in England with a little variety in the application.

A special advantage which Paris has is in the freedom from aristocratic pride manifest in the tone of society. It is quite easy for any young man of liberal tastes to enter on a good footing the best houses. It is not easy in England. Then the customs are cheap & inexpensive; whilst it is a proverb almost, that, to live in England at all, you must have great fortune; which sounds to me as certain a prediction of revolution as musket shots in the streets.

So that on the whole I am thankful for Paris, as I am for the discovery of Ether & Chloroform; I like to know, that, if I should need an amputation, there is this balm; and if hard should come to hard, & I should be driven to seek some refuge of solitude & independency, why here is Paris.

The cafés are not to be forgotten, filled with newspapers, blazing with light, sauntering places, oubliettes or Remember-nothings. One in Paris who would keep himself up with events must read every day about twelve newspapers of the 200 that are printed there. Then in the street the affiches on every spot of dead wall, attract all eyes & make the text of all talk for the gazing group. The Government reserve to their own the exclusive use of White Paper. All others are in colours.

After 25 days spent in Paris I took the railroad for Boulogne, stopped at Amiens half an hour, & saw the Cathedral (which has nothing equal to it in Paris in the elaboration of the details of its moulding & sculpture on the exterior, [saw the weeping angel also]). And at Boulogne, (where 6000 English reside for cheapness,) I took the night steamboat for Folkestone. The twentyseven miles of roughest sea between Boulogne & Folkestone made a piteous scene, of course, in the Saloon of the boat, but as that wild strip of sea is from age to age the cheap

Standing army of England & worth a million of troops, no Englishman should grudge his qualms.

—

I went with Edwin Field & Mr Stanfield the painter, & his son, to the house of Mr Windus, Tottenham, to see his collection of Turner's pictures & drawings of which altogether he may have a hundred. This gallery was that in which Ruskin had studied. It is quite necessary to see all these pictures to appreciate the genius of Turner through his extravagances. Two days afterwards, Mr Owen carried me to Turner's own house, to see what is there. Mr Owen said, that, in his earlier pictures, he painted conventionally, painted what he knew was there; finished the coat & hat & buttons; in the later he paints only what the eye really sees, & gets the genius of the city or landscape. He was to paint a whaleship, & he came to Owen to see a (mullet)? and studied this with the utmost accuracy. But Owen could not find it in the picture, though he doubted not it was there.

from
LM
1848

The Battery.
The staple figure in novels is the man of aplomb, who sits among the young aspirants & desperates, quite sure & compact, &, never sharing their affections or debilities, hurls his word like a bullet, when occasion requires; knows his way, & carries his points. They may scream like cats, he is never engaged or heated. This figure charms all readers, yet is never imitated in our houses. Napoleon is the type of this class in modern history; yet we are all drawn in to the charivari, answer, cavil, recriminate, and run on.——

History is the group of the types or representative men of any age at only the distance of convenient vision. We can see the arrangement of masses, & distinguish the forms of the leaders. Mythology is the same group at another remove, now at a pictorial distance; the perspective of history. The forms & faces can no longer be read, but only the direction of the march, & the result; so that the names of the leaders are now mixed with the ends for which they strove. Distance is essential. Therefore we cannot say what is *our* mythology. We can only see that the industrial, mechanical, the parliamentary, commercial, constitute it, with socialism; and Astor, Watt, Fulton, Arkwright, Peel, Russell, Rothschild, Geo Stephenson, Fourier, are our mythologic names.

—

CN remarked as W.E.C. had done, the French trait in H.T. & in his family. Here is the precise voyageur of Canada sublimed, or carried up to the seventh power. In the family the brother & one sister preserved the French character of face.

Sea line.
As we see the human body or one of its limbs undraped, so

here nature shows us a limb of our planet in undress & we see the nakedness of the sea line. 'Tis a sublime curve yet causes an uncomfortable feeling. To nature as to man we say, Still be drest! Still hide a poverty even so grand under the ornamented details of a broken landscape.

Every man has his theory, most of them ridiculous. Mr. Reid is a man who is skilful in the theory of ventilation, only he has the misfortune to believe that the one thing needful is ventilation. I came across another who had discovered the key to all the calamities of England; it was the love of music, which was the ruin of England: and, at last, I was doomed to meet Mr Walker, who told me he stood for the deadman's question, and he had written a book called "Gatherings from Graveyards."

—

Of Immortality the soul, when well employed, is incurious. It is so well that it is sure it will be well. It asks no questions of the Supreme Power. The son of Antiochus asked his father, "When he would join battle?" "Dost thou fear," replied the king, "that thou only in all the army wilt not hear the trumpet?"

Nobody should speak on this matter polemically. But it is the Gai Science and only to be chanted by Troubadours.

In dreams, the ordinary theory is that there is but one person; the mystical theory is that there are two or more.

"It was so dry that you might call it wet."

There's a great affinity between wit & oxygen; with the oxygen in these crowded parlours my wit always departs.

T.C. has great vigour of constitution so that he can dispose of poison very well. He is a perfect sot in the strong waters of vituperation & reminds me of the rich swearing of the truckmen which W. described.

England is the country of the rich. The great Poor Man does not yet appear. Whenever he comes, England will fall like France. It would seem that an organizing talent applied directly to the social problem, to bring, for example, labor to market, to bring want and supply face to face, would not be so rare. A man like Hudson, like Trevylian, like Cobden, should know something about it.

Montaigne
In the British Museum, Mr Watts showed me the autograph of Shakspeare found in Florio's translation of Montaigne, & informed me that when they had procured a duplicate copy of this Montaigne for the use of the library, it was found that an autograph of Ben Jonson was in the new book.

—

Grievous amount of dross about men of wit, they are so heavy, so dull, so oppressive with their bad jokes, & monstrous conceit, & stupefying individualism. Avoid the great man as one who is privileged to be an unprofitable companion.
As a class the merchants are out of all comparison manlier & more sensible, and even the farmers are more real & agreeable. But this is babyish. I hate that a scholar should be an old goody. If excellence as scholars has cost too much & spoiled them for society, let religion, let their homage to truth & beauty keep them in chambers or caves, that they may not by personal presence deface the fair festival which their reason & imagination have dressed.

The most agreeable compliment that could be paid W. was to say that you had not observed him, in a house or in a street where you had met him. All he wished of his tailor was to provide just that sober mean of colour & cut which should never fix the eye for one moment. He went to Vienna, to Smyrna, to London. In all the immense variety of costumes he saw in these places,—a mere carnival or kaleidoscope or Monmouth street of clothes,—to his horror he never could discover any man in the street who wore any thing resembling his own dress.
—Briton requires such a tone of voice as excites no attention in the room.

The French Revolution just now has surprised every body, (themselves included,) who took any thought on the matter. No Guizot, no Thiers, no Barrot, no Times newspaper, no party that could remember & calculate but was baulked &

confounded. Only the simple workmen, porters, shoeblacks, & women, and the few statesmen who, like Lamartine, could afford through riches & energy of nature to let themselves go without resistance whither the explosion was hurling them, found themselves suddenly right & well. One would say as S.W. said of the young collegians who drove a gig down his hill, "if they had known how to drive, they would have broken their necks."

The French are to a proverb so formidable in explosions that every boy sees the folly of Guizot & his master in bearding that lion. It had been plain to them a great while that just by dodging an explosion you might lead the monster quietly into a cage.

This revolution has a feature new to history, that of socialism. The American Revolution was political merely.

It is not a good feature, the rhetoric of French politics. The manifestoes read like Buonaparte's proclamations, inflated. It strikes one, too, the identity of the nation through all these changes. I ask myself, what makes it? it is like the identity of an individual.

The king & his party fell for want of a shot, they had not conscience to shoot, so entirely was the heart & pith of monarchy eaten out.

In Germany, said N., the former revolution collapsed for want of an idea. Now, all goes well, for they know what they want.

The book trade in London is reduced to nothing since the new French Revolution. For the "Times," for fivepence every day gives them as much as they can read.

—

Every man's expense & economy must proceed from his character: a lame man must buy crutches & high heels; a blind man goggles, & so on. So it is very well for Socrates & for Franklin, with their famous tongues, to dress in woolen & serge, & go barefoot, & spend nothing; but for a man without a tongue, a conformity in dress must be bought at any price.

*

The Chartist orator O'Brien insisting on no-property qualification for ballot, urged that every working man does pay a tax, & the capitalist pays only what he has robbed the working man of, & 'tis not fair that he should rob him of his ballot also.

The delegate who had carried congratulations to the French Republic, said, that "they had determined not to wait even till they knew whether it was a boy or a girl."

—

Stephenson executed the idea of the age in iron. Who will do it in the social problem?

We want a moral engineer.

I hear sad stories sometimes as of dukes served by bailiffs with all their plate in pawn, and of great lords living by the showing of their houses, and an old man wheeled in his chair from room to room whilst his chambers are shown to the visiter. And many evils & iniquities, no doubt, arise from law of entail: and yet primogeniture built all these sumptuous Halls & Castles, and if they must fall, I am glad to have come hither before their fall. The D. of Northumberland is not rich enough to live in Northumberland House. Their many houses eat them up. They cannot sell them because they are entailed, & they will not lease them but keep them empty, aired, & the grounds mown & dressed at an expense of £.4000 a year.

It was very plain to me that the men of literary & social note such as Sparks, Newman, B., P., Oxenford, Morell, & many more were so only by a sort of beaver activity & not by any superiority of talent to the masses among which their names resounded. They were dull & mediocre men, or even less.

I travelled, as I said, for a whip for my top. I had noticed that to every person are usually sent six or seven priests, in the course of their (impressible) life, &, to find one of these, he may well cross to Asia, or the Antarctic Zone. It was to be expected that I might find the seventh of mine in England.

—

Rags & curds
The whole marrow

Are not worth the devil
Widemouthed laughing
Haggling & gaping
Gaping & buying
Heaps of beasts
Children & brats
Monkeys & cats

The Athenaeum excludes Guizot, when his name is proposed as an honorary member. They would be proud of his name, but the Englishman is not fickle, he really made up his mind to hate & to despise Guizot, & the altered position of the man, as an exile and a guest in the country, make no difference to him, as they would instantly to an American. The Englishman talks of politics & institutions, but the real thing which he values is his home, & that which belongs to it,—that general culture & high polish which in his experience no man but the Englishman possesses, & which he naturally believes have some essential connexion with his throne & laws. That is what he does not believe resides in America, & therefore his contempt of America is only half-concealed.—This English tenacity in strong contrast with our facility. The facile American sheds his Puritanism when he leaves Cape Cod, runs into all English & French vices with great zest & is neither Unitarian, nor Calvinist, nor Catholic nor stands for any known thought or thing; which is very distasteful to English honour. It is a bad sign that I have met with many Americans who flattered themselves that they pass for English. Levity, levity. I do not wish to be mistaken for an Englishman, more than I wish Monadnock or Nahant or Nantucket to be mistaken for Wales or the Isle of Wight.

—

Concord has a horizon like the sea, has woodlands, and is permeable as a park.

—

Agassiz made lectures on anatomy popular by the aid of an idea: homology, analogy, did that for him, which all the police of Boston could not have done, in holding the crowd together at the Odeon, when Wyman lectured on the same subject.

—

I had rather have a good symbol of my thought, or a good analogy, than the suffrage of Kant or Plato. If you agree with me, or if Locke, or Montesquieu, or Spinoza agree, I may still be wrong: but if the elm tree thinks the same thing,—if running water, if burning coal, if crystals, acids, & alkalis, say what I say, it must be true.

Every soul is sent into nature accompanied by its assessors or witnesses. They are attached to it by similarities which keep them through all changes in the same stratum or plane, & within the same sphere; as the bodies of one solar system never quit their respective distances, but remain, as the foot of an animal follows its head. To his astonishment the man finds that he can never think alone, his thought is always apprehended by equal intellect; that he can never hide his action, but witnesses, & those his intimate acquaintance, look out of the dark of every cave, in an Asiatic desart, in an Arabian Sahara. The rule of the Lowell Corporations was, that no girl should walk in the streets at night, unless with two companions.

Everything connected with our personality fails. We are always baulked of a complete success. No prosperity is promised to that. We have our amends only in the sure success of that to which we belong: and, to secure our disinterestedness, the assurance of private immortality is taken away. That, that is immortal, but we are not, or only through that.

People interest as long as there is some reserve about them. Only that mind draws me which I cannot read.

> "The belief that self consists in that which is not self, & that property consists in that which is not our own, is the double fruit of the tree of Ignorance."

The objection, the loud denial not less proves the reality & conquests of an idea, than the friends & advocates it finds. Thus communism now is eagerly attacked, and all its weak points acutely pointed out by British writers & talkers; which is all so much homage to the Idea, whose first inadequate expressions interest them so deeply, & with which they feel their fate to be mingled. If the French should set out to prove that three was four, would British journalism bestir itself to contradict them? The Geologic Society and the Stock Exchange would have no time to share it.

—

If I should believe the Reviews, and I am always of their opinion, I have never written any thing good. And yet, against all criticism, the books survive until this day.

—

People here expect a revolution. There will be no revolution, none that deserves to be called so. There may be a scramble for money. But as all the people we see want the things we now have, & not better things, it is very certain that they will, under whatever change of forms, keep the old system.
When I see changed men, I shall look for a changed world.

—

A curious example of the rudeness and inaccuracy of thought is the inability to distinguish between the private & the universal consciousness. I never make that blunder when I write, but the critics who read impute their confusion to me.

I know, of course, all the grounds on which any man affirms the immortality of the soul. The barrel of water is equally full in every cellar; the difference is in the distribution of pipes & pumps over the house. The spring is common; the difference in the aqueduct.

In the question of socialism, which now proposes the confiscation of France, one has only this guidance. You shall not so arrange property as to remove the motive to industry. If you refuse rent & interest, you make all men idle & immoral. As to the poor a vast proportion have made themselves so, and in any new arrangement will only prove a burden on the state. And there is a great multitude also whom the existing system bereaves forever of all culture & of all hope.
The masses—ah if you could read the biographies of those who compose them!

The word *pay* is immoral.

Now we will work, because we can have it all to our snug selves; tomorrow we will not, because it goes to the community, & we all stand on a pauper's footing.

The wonder of the science of Intellect is that the substance with which we deal is of that transcendant & active nature, that it intoxicates all who approach it. Gloves on the hands, glass guards over the eyes, wire gauze masks over the face, volatile salts in the nostrils, are no defence against this virus, or rather gravitation.

Every thing is mover or moved, & we are admonished of omnipotence when we say, let us have intellect on our own terms.

—

The most important word the Age has given to the vocabulary, is Blouse.* It has not yet got into the Dictionary, and even in America for a year or two it has been of doubtful sound, whether English blouse, or French blouse. But, at last, the French Revolution has decided forever its euphony. It is not that it was new for the workman to have ideas & speak in clubs, but new in its proportions to find not 500, but 200 000 thinkers & orators in blouse. Guizot thought they were but a handful.

—

Happy is he who looks only into his work to know if it will succeed, never into the times or the public opinion; and who writes from the love of imparting certain thoughts & not from the necessity of sale—who writes always to *the unknown friend*.

Man runs through a greater range of climates than any other animal. And when good, he is good in the open air, & good in the house; in a club, & tète a tète; good with a horse, and good to walk forty miles.

—

22 April. I spent last evening with Coventry Patmore, the poet. He explained to me his theories of architecture. In the gothic it was a copresence of growth & geometry, of liberty & law, which he illustrated excellently by details of ornament as the

*and Humbug

ball-flower, & especially the spandril and the toothed-flower. Then in York Minster he showed the ascension, the suggestion of infinite ascension by ascending parallel lines, the power of the tower, the truncation, & the manner in which the eye was prepared for the truncation. In the Egyptian the fundamental idea is the Base or Basis. A Pyramid is the least possible departure from pure base. The base is immensely superfluous, and their temple, he showed, to be a sort of split base. The pillars ridiculously short. The column of Egyptian architecture is a picture of a supporter crushed out by the superincumbent weight. The Greek, I think, he called competence of support: —the flutes of the Doric column represented the upward principle; the metopes the descending, and there was always ample support, & a little to spare, which was indicated by channeling, that is, weakening the column just at the point where these ascenders & descenders met, that is, where the strain was: and whenever a little weight is added by the projection of the entablature, a row of flowers is added to show the exuberance of strength.

How many faces in the street still remind us of visages in the forest; they have not quite yet escaped from the lower form.

—

An artist spends himself, like the crayon in his hand, till he is all gone.

—

What games sleep plays with us! We wake indignant that we have been so played upon, & should have lent ourselves to such mountains of nonsense. All night I was scarifying with my wrath some conjuring miscreant, but unhappily I had an old age in my toothless gums, I was old as Priam, could not articulate, & the edge of all my taunts & sarcasms, it is to be feared, was quite lost. Yet, spite of my dumb palsy, I defied & roared after him, rattled in my throat, until wifey waked me up. Then I bit my lips. So one day we shall wake up from this longer confusion, & be not less mortified that we had lent ourselves to such rigmarole.

But it is base to forget our resolutions; and the difference between men is, that one is obligable, & one is not.

*

The Americans would sail in a steamboat built of lucifer matches, if it would go faster.

—

Paris, Rue des Petits Augustins, No 15; May 13, 1848.
The one thing odious to me now is joking. What can the brave & strong genius of C. himself avail? What can his praise, what can his blame avail me, when I know that if I fall or if I rise, there still awaits me the inevitable joke? The day's Englishman must have his joke, as duly as his bread. God grant me the noble companions whom I have left at home who value merriment less, & virtues & powers more. If the English people have owed to their House of Commons this damnable derision, I think they have paid an overprice for their liberties & empire. But when I balance the attractions of good & evil, when I consider what facilities, what talents a little vice would furnish, then rise before me not these laughers, but the dear & comely forms of honour & genius & piety in my distant home, and they touch me with chaste palms moist & cold, & say to me, You are ours.

—

Paris

Beefsteak in Paris is omnibus-horses.

Palais Royal: on the floor, magasins of clothes, jewellery, perfumery, hairdressers, &c; on the premiere, Restaurants; on the troisieme, Billiards & cards &c; on the quatrieme, lorettes, so that Mr P declares it the complete & true shop for the human body.

In Paris 117 new newspapers have been set on foot since the revolution.

This revolution distinguished from the old by the social problem agitated in every club. Arithmeticians get up & cipher very shrewdly before the masses to show them what is each man's share. The good God, they say, is full of good sense & the extreme inequality of property had got so far as to drive to revolution, & now it will not finish until God's justice is established, nor until the labourer gets his wages, nor until there is no idler left in the land. The idler is a diseased person & is to be treated by the state as a diseased person.

as economical as ants

*

In coming to the city, & seeing in it no men of information, you remain on the outside.

But all this Paris seems to me a continuation of the theatre, when I come out of the theatre, or of a *limonade gazeuse*, when I come out of the restaurant. This is the famous lotus which the mariners ate & forgot their homes. I pinch myself to remember mine.

I went to hear Michelet lecture on philosophy, but the sublime creed of the Indian Buddhists was not meant for a Frenchman to analyze & crack his joke & make his grimace upon.

But I came out hither to see my contemporaries & I have seen Leverrier today working out algebraic formulas on his blackboard to his class quite heedless of politics & revolutions. I have seen Rachel in Phedre & heard her chant the Marseillaise. I have seen Barbé's role in his *Club de la Revolution*, & Blanqui in his *Club des Droits de l'homme*, and today they are both in the dungeon of Vincennes.

—

That unhappy man, called, of genius, pays dear for his paltry distinction. His head runs up into a spire, and, instead of being a healthy, merry, round, & ruddy man he is some mad dominie. Nature is regardless of the individual, when she has points to carry, she carries them. If she wants a big thumb, she starves all the joints & bones & muscles of the body to gain material, & finishes by making a monster all thumb.

The writers are bold & democratic. The moment revolution comes, are they Chartists & Montagnards? No, but they talk & sit with the rich, & sympathize with them. Should they go with the Chartist? Alas they cannot: These have such gross & bloody chiefs to mislead them, and are so full of hatred & murder, that the scholar recoils;—and joins the rich. That he should not do. He should accept as necessary the position of armed neutrality abhorring the crimes of the Chartist, yet more abhorring the oppression & hopeless selfishness of the rich, &, still *writing the truth*, say, the time will come when these poor enfans perdus of revolution will have instructed their party, if only by their fate, & wiser counsels will prevail, & the music & the dance of liberty will take me in also. Then I shall not have forefeited my right to speak & act for the

Movement party. Shame to the fop of philosophy who suffers a little vulgarity of speech & of character to hide from him the true current of Tendency, & who abandons his true position of being priest & poet of those impious & unpoetic doers of God's work.

The Latin *Yes.*

I remember when I was at the Latin School I wondered how the Romans managed to do their daily talking without any word for Yes. Whether it was verily so, I have forgotten since to inquire. I was reminded of it lately by observing how much the French use the Italian affirmative Si, which perhaps is a part of Etiam, which, I believe, was one of the Roman *quasi*-affirmatives.

Alcott said to me, "You write on the genius of Plato, of Pythagoras, of Jesus, of Swedenborg, why do you not write of me?"

The real difficulty lies here. The Intellect uses & is not to be used. Uses London, uses Paris. I wish all that you can show me, tho' it be the conflagration of Moscow, but I decline taking hold of the rope to draw the engine or to hand buckets. And it were a false courtesy to hold out the smallest offers of service.

Mr Doherty said, the *dogmes* were *malfaisants.* It needed not to inquire whether men made them or God made them. In either case they had every right to take them away. In the natural world, they had tigers, snakes, wolves, & other *dogmes malfaisants*, which they did not hesitate to put away & kill; & so, in the moral world, they had the like, which, like these beasts, had answered their use for a time, but were now out of time, unfit, noxious.

It is doubtful whether London, whether Paris, can answer the questions which now rise in the mind.

There are parties which are powerful in the dark, like the legitimists in France; they can pay & work. But the moment they take an avowed public form, they are denounced.

There is a pudency about friendship as about love, and fine souls never lose sight of friendship; it is behind their science, behind their genius, behind their heroic life, the beatitude to which they exist, yet they never name it. It is for young hot masters who kiss & claw, & curse each other after a fortnight, it is for them to talk of it.

Life is cheap. In this anthill of Paris one can see that multitudes sell their future for one day. What prodigality to turn a little beautiful French Edie into the procession to be consumed in the sun & crowd.

I have been exaggerating the English merits all winter, & disparaging the French. Now I am correcting my judgment of both, & the French have risen very fast.
But I see that both nations promise more than they perform. They do not culminate.

The English mind trifles.

'Tis easy to see that France is much nearer to socialism than England. In the gay & admirable illumination of the Champs Elysées, one could see that it was but a few steps to the Phalanstery.

Do not mind trifles,—was the lesson so strenuously inculcated on my childhood. I did not learn it, and now I see, England has not.

—

My good friend G.Jewsbury declared that one was perpetually forgetting that you had ever done anything, you are so quiet.

I write "Mind & Manners in the XIX Century" and my rede is to make the student independent of the century, to show him that his class offer one immutable front in all times & countries, cannot hear the drums of Paris, cannot read the London journals, they are the Wandering Jew or the Eternal Angel that survives all, & stands in the same fraternal relation to all. The world is always childish, and with each gewgaw of a revolution or new constitution that it finds, thinks it shall never cry any more: but it is always becoming evident that the permanent good is for the soul only & cannot be retained in any society or system. This is like naphtha which must be kept in a close vessel.

In England, every man is a castle. When I get into our first class cars on the Fitchburg Road, & see sweltering men in their shirt sleeves take their seats with some well drest men & women, & see really the very little difference of level that is between them all, and then imagine the astonishment that would strike the polished inmates of English first class carriages, if such masters should enter & sit beside them, I see that it is not fit to tell Englishmen that America is like England. No, this is the Paradise of the third class; here every thing is cheap; here every thing is for the poor. England is the Paradise of the first class; it is essentially aristocratic, and the humbler classes have made up their minds to this, & do contentedly enter into the system. In England, every man you met is some man's son; in America, he may be some man's father.

—

I talked with Forster, Dickens, & Carlyle, on the prostitution in the great towns, & said, that, when I came to Liverpool, I inquired whether it was always as gross in that city as it then appeared to me? for it looked to me as if such manners betokened a fatal rottenness in the state, & especially no boy could grow up safe: but that I had been told, that it was not worse nor better than it had been for years. C & D replied, that chastity in the male sex was as good as gone in our times; and in England was so very rare, that they could name all the exceptions. Carlyle evidently believed that the same thing was true in America. I assured them that it was not so with us: that, for the most part, young men of good standing & good education with us go virgins to their nuptial bed, as truly as their brides. Dickens replied, that incontinence is so much the rule with them that if his own son were particularly chaste, he should be alarmed on his account, as if he could not be in good health.

—

I told Carlyle on the way to Stonehenge that, though I was in the habit of conceding everything in honor of England which Englishmen demanded, though I was dazzled by the wealth & power & success everywhere apparent,—yet I knew very well that the moment I returned to America, I should lapse again into the habitual feeling which the vast physical influences of that continent inevitably inspire of confidence that there & there only is the right home & seat of the English race; & this great England will dwindle again to an island which has done well, but has reached its utmost expansion.

—

I find C. always cunning: he denies the books he reads; denies the friends he has just visited; denies his own acts & purposes;—By God, I do not know them—and immediately the cock crows.

—

But after much experience, we find literature the best thing; and men of thought, if still thinking, the best company. I went to England, &, after allowing myself freely to be dazzled by the various brilliancy of men of talent,—in calm hours I found myself no way helped; my sequins were all yellow leaves, I said I have valued days (& must still) by the number of aperçus I get, and I must estimate my company so. Then I found I had scarcely had a good conversation, a solid dealing, man with man, in England. Only in such passages is a reason for human life given, and every such meeting puts a mortal affront on Kings & Governments by showing them to be of no account.

Of course, these people, these & no others, interest us; these dear & beautiful beings who are absorbed in their own dream. Let us then have that told; let us have a record of friendship among six, or four, or two, if there be only two of those who delight in each other, only because both delight in the Eternal laws; who forgive nothing to each other, who by their joy & homage to these, are made incapable of conceit which destroys almost all the fine wits. Any other affection between men than this geometric one of relation to the same thing, is a mere mush of materialism.

—

Lord Melbourne sent his steward to his tenants in Nottingham & told them that they were to vote for whom they pleased. The tenants asked which candidate his Lordship would prefer. The steward would not tell them. They asked the steward, which he should like? He refused to tell them. Then they put their heads together, & said, they thought my lord's body valet would be sure to know his mind, & so they asked to see him, that they might know how he would vote.

—

The Communities hitherto are only possible by installing the Devil as Steward; the rest of the offices may be well filled with saints. So in the Shaker society, they always send the devil to market. And in painting God, poetry & religion have always drawn the energy from hell.

E.C. said of N., that, if a man stays under water too long, he is sure to be drowned.

George Stephenson died the other day in England, the man who made the locomotive, the father of railroads,—and not an engineer on all our tracks heeded the fact, or perhaps knew his name. There should have been a concert of locomotives, and a dirge performed by the whistles of a thousand engines.

—

It is a curious working of the English state that Carlyle should in all his lifetime have never had an opportunity to cast a vote.

I spoke of friendship, but my friends & I are fishes in their habit. As for taking T.'s arm, I should as soon take the arm of an elm tree.

In England old men are as red as roses.

To see contemporaries—

The merits of America were not presentable—the tristesse of the landscape, the quiet stealing in of nature like a religion, how could that be told?

—

When we read the primitive histories as the Pentateuch, the Edda, the Heimskringla, Vishnu Purana &c we think there were very few men when the actions of each had such importance & are circumstantially told. But when we look wisely & genially at our own life, we find the same eminences, the same sparseness & greatness.

Henry Thoreau is like the woodgod who solicits the wandering poet & draws him into antres vast & desarts idle, & bereaves him of his memory, & leaves him naked, plaiting vines & with twigs in his hand. Very seductive are the first steps from the town to the woods, but the End is want & madness.—

We have many platforms of work: thus I have the Review & Lectures; glad should I be to be free of these & left to my studies. Yes, but I have heard the callings of a higher muse & would leave all for that. In the lower works, we have no lack of prompters. In the highest where we most need admonition each has himself only to friend.

In Kew Gardens you should ask for Moly & Haemony.

In the winter of 1832–3 I sailed in a brigantine from Malta to Syracuse, and the master & whole crew on learning where we (Holbrook, Kettell, & I,) came from, got up out of their chest an old soiled Italian gazetteer, & read the account of *Boston* with eagerness & its 25 000 population, curious to know what far Siam or Pegu their passengers had dropped from.

In my woodlot, the pokeweed & mullein grow up rankly in the ruins of the shanties of the Irish who built the railroad.

I am struck with the unimportance of our American politics. We prosper with such vigour that like thrifty trees which grow in spite of lice, borers, & mice, so we do not suffer from the profligate gang who fatten on us.—Same energy in Greek Demos.

The bears in the Jardin des Plantes fight & I thought to call the keeper thinking the bigger would hurt the young one but I found they were tough & did not hurt each other. So I remembered them when I saw bigger boys bullying less ones in London.

Eddy declares that his horse does not wag his tail, because his tail is a tin tail.

—

Shall we not maintain our poets? Shall we suffer those to die of whom the horizon & the landscape speak to us, day by day? They never mention their owner or their diggers, Irishmen or negroes, any more than ants & worms, but superciliously forget these, & fill me with allusions to men & women who owned no acre, & had no practical faculty, as we say.
Our action is sub-action. 'Tis not in the harmony of things.

To say otherwise is skepticism.

He cannot bring us in October a poor bushel of beans; but is not an accomplished & cultivated man worth something?
The soldier cannot fold away his arms, nor can the scholar. impediunt foris.

I observe among the best women the same putting of life into their deed that we admire in the Seton (was it) who put her arm into the bolt to defend Queen Mary or in the women in the old sieges who cut off their hair to make ropes & ladders for the men.

W.E.C. remarks in Alcott the obstruction of his egoism. Cultivated men always must be had; every body sends for them as for peaches. But what to do with this man, when you have first to kick away the man in order to get at what he knows.

In England I found wine enough; as Dr Johnson said, "for once in his life he had as much wall fruit as he pleased." In France I had the privilege of leaving my papers all lying wide in my room; for nobody could read English.

—

H.D.T. working with A B A. on the summerhouse, said, he was nowhere, doing nothing.

A man who can make hard things easy, is an Educator.

*

Alcott declares that a teacher is one who can assist the child in obeying his own mind, and who can remove all unfavorable circumstances. He believes that from a circle of twenty well-selected children he could draw in their conversation everything that is in Plato, & as much better in form than it is in Plato, as the passages I read him from the Heimskringla, are than Bancroft.

He measures ages by teachers, & reckons history by Pythagoras, Plato, Jesus, & Pestalozzi. In his own school in Boston, when he had made the school-room beautiful, he looked on the work as half-done.
He said, that every great man of antiquity had an eminent philosopher as his teacher.
And this is true for Pericles, Alexander, Alcibiades,

The soul is older than the body.

We are very careful of young peartrees & defend them from their enemies, from fireblight, suckers, grass, slugs, pearworm, but we let our young men, in whose youth & flower all inferior kinds have their flowering & completion, grow up in heaps & by chance, take the rough & tumble, as we say, (which is the skepticism of education) exposed to their borers, caterpillars, cankerworms, bugs, moping, sloth, seduction, wine, fear, hatred,

6 August. Lucrezia Floriani of George Sand is a great step from the novels of one termination which we all read 20 years ago. It is a great step towards real life & manners & motives, and yet how far off the novel still is! This life lies about us dumb, the day, as we know it, has not yet found a tongue. E.H. complains of this romance that the tendency is not high. I say, there are always two things to be done by the novelist first, the aspirations of the mind are to be revered, that is, Faith; &, secondly, the way things actually fall out, that is, Fate. Fate & Faith, these two; and it seems as if justice were done, if the Faith is vindicated in the sentiments of the heroes of the tale, & Fate in the course & issue of the events. George Sand is quite conversant with all the ideas which occupy us here in America.

Why did not the last generation of farmers plant the pears & plums & apples & grapes of whose growth time is the chief element & not leave it all to be done by us? Ask in the market: a good pear will sell for a shilling. That price tells as plain as the human race can speak, that there are great & all but insuperable difficulties in raising these fine fruits in this climate, borer, mouse, curculio, & bug, & caterpillar have settled a democratic majority against these whig fruits and they have become a party of despair & only maintain a local existence in some few protected Bostons & Vermonts.

That reply of the shilling is a quite impersonal parliamentary reply; it is a voice of things, of fates, of the general order of the world. It is the broker's quotation of stocks.

It is as a practical answer, however, subject to this question. Was it not a reply for the last generation, & are there no new elements now which will make a new reply? A broad slattern farming, it has been said, was the true policy of our New England men, & not the trim garden farming of the English. Neither were there many buyers of fruit. Now there are more people, the land is more easily manured, and rich fruits can be raised, fed, protected, & ripened. Now there are fences, also.

To me one good pear tree bearing Bartletts, is a verdict. Why should not my trees know the way towards the sky as well as yours? L did not believe in the new land that he could ever be domesticated until the old fruits of his former home, pears & plums, were once ripened on the new farm.

When I go into a good garden & nursery, I think if it were mine, I should never go out of it.

For copyright, it is to expect almost too much magnanimity to believe that our people having had the best English new books so long at 25 cents a volume, should now consent to deprive themselves of the privilege & pay dollars for them. It is like expecting us Concord people, after riding on the railroad now for two years, at 40 cents, & in one hour to Boston, on now discovering that we have violated some vested right of the old stagecoach company, to consent henceforward to go back & pay them 75 cents & ride 3 hours.

I observe that all the bookish men have a tendency to believe that they are unpopular. Parker gravely informs me by word & by letter that he is precisely the most unpopular of all men in New England. Alcott believes the same thing of himself, and I, no doubt, if they had not anticipated me in claiming this distinction, should have claimed it for myself.

Was it MME who said she would borrow S's mantle, "for you know she is sick & wo'nt be likely to want it again, and so, if you have no objection, I'll keep it."

We are all enriched here in Concord by the railroad results mentioned above. And 'tis a quite unlooked for result of these inventions that the geographical extent of the Union should now not be an objection to the Federal Government. Oregon is near to Washington & every day nearing. We do not now hear the threat of removing the Federal Capital across the Alleganies.

Who is not glad to hear of the fruit-cars, which bring 1600 bushels of peaches into Boston from New York every morning; of the milk-cars which carry $20 000 worth of milk from Concord to Boston in a year.

The old writers, such as Montaigne, Milton, Browne, when they had put down their thoughts, jumped into their book bodily themselves, so that we have all that is left of them in our shelves; there is not a pinch of dust beside. The Norsemen wrote with a crowbar, & we with Gillott pens.

If housekeeping & grocery gets into the people so does yellow paper into the writer.

Constitution, pluck, makes wit, you say; then he will hear the most, who offers a minus instead of a plus face to the stranger.

A pedant cannot have an apple tree; he only has apple trees who knows them, & treats them as apple trees. Else the apple trees have him.

The university clings to us.

September 10. D'Israeli the chiffonier wastes all his talent in the House of Commons, for the want of character. He makes a smart cutting speech, really introduces new & important distinctions, as what he says in this new speech concerning "the sentimental principle of Nationality," which the Government have adopted; & what he says of "using forced occasions & invented opportunities;" instead of availing of events. But he makes at last no impression, because the hearer asks Who are you? What is dear to you? What do you stand for? And the speech & the speaker are silent, & silence is confession. A man who has been a man, has foreground & background. His speech, be it never so good, is subordinate & the least part of him and as this man has no planet under him but only his shoes, the hearer infers that the ground of the present argument may be no wider.

You must put your melons in the sun.

None ever heard of a good marriage from Mesopotamia to Missouri and yet right marriage is as possible tomorrow as sunshine. Sunshine is a very mixed & costly thing as we have it, & quite impossible, yet we get the right article every day. And we are not very much to blame for our bad marriages. We live amid hallucinations & illusions, & this especial trap is laid for us to trip up our feet with & all are tripped up, first or last. But the Mighty Mother who had been so sly with us, feels that she owes us some indemnity, & insinuates into the Pandora-box of marriage, amidst dyspepsia, nervousness, screams, Christianity, "help," poverty, & all kinds of music, some deep & serious benefits & some great joys. We find sometimes a delight in the beauty & the happiness of our children that makes the heart too big for the body. And in these ill assorted connections there is ever some mixture of true marriage. The poorest Paddy & his jade, if well-meaning & welltempered, get some just & agreeable relations of mutual respect & kindly observation & fostering each of other. & they learn something, & would carry themselves wiselier if they were to begin life anew in another sphere. But 'tis strange to see how little society there is,—none. Who attaches himself to his partner's greatness & holds him to his greatness? None. Yet it is as possible to help a man to be himself, as to help him pull a rope or load a hay cart. We are dragons & not angels.

Swedenborg & Behmen are great men because they saw that a spiritual force was greater than any material force. They knew, Swedenborg did, that a text of scripture would make men black in the face, drive them out of the house, pull down houses, towns,

Montaigne right, & his critics Scaliger & Pascal wrong.

Net purses are in vogue & all the young people buy beads; then transfer tables & all make workboxes; then tissue paper; & just now, Journals, & every young woman wishes to edit a Journal.

The Arrowhead. Talent or almost genius seems to be the power of isolating by illumination an object.

It is a good mould that the cunningest statuary wants.

Tennyson's poetry is as legitimate a fruit of the veneering or cabinetmaker style of English culture, as the Dinnertable.

Conduct of Life
Alcott needs the devotion of his friend to him & deserves it, and if I had nine lives, I would dedicate one to him; but they must be nine lives abreast. For now each man has the misfortune to have nine friends, & when he is exhausted by one & that one departs behold the second is coming in at the door.

The doctor can do the fast riding excellently, but not the curing.

Intellect
There go to the conduct of the Understanding 7 volumes of latent heat, to one of patent; seven silences to one word.

*

I was accustomed to characterize Alcott in England, by saying that he was the one man I had met who could read Plato without surprise.

The trilobium, which is the eldest of fossil animals, reappears now in the embryonic changes of crab & lobster. It seems there is a state of melioration, pending which, the development towards man can go on; which usually is arrested.

Modern Times
The immense amount of valuable knowledge now afloat in society enriches the newspapers, so that one cannot snatch an old newspaper to wrap his shoes in, without his eye being caught by some paragraph of precious science out of London or Paris which he hesitates to lose forever. My wife grows nervous when I give her waste paper lest she is burning holy writ, & wishes to read it before she puts it under her pies.

George Sand is a great genius, & yet owes to her birth in France her entire freedom from the cant & snuffle of our dead Christianity.

The Railroad is the only sure topic for conversation in these days.—That is the only one which interests farmers, merchants, boys, women, saints, philosophers, & fools.
And now we have one more rival topic, California gold.

The Railroad is that work of art which agitates & drives mad the whole people; as music, sculpture, & picture have done on their great days respectively.

James Baker does not imagine that he is a rich man, yet he keeps from year to year that lordly park of his by Fairhaven Pond, lying idly & nobly open to all comers, without crop or rent, like some Duke of Sutherland or Lord Breadalbane. With its hedges of Arcady, its sumptuous lawns & slopes, the apple on its trees, the mirror at its foot, and the terraces of Holloway Farm on the opposite bank.

*

1. Emerson in 1850 as seen by Fredrika Bremer, a Swedish writer visiting Concord.

2. Emerson's second wife, Lidian Jackson, with son Edward (1847).

3. Emerson with Edward and his younger daughter Edith (1858).

4. Emerson's elder daughter Ellen, born in 1839.

5. At Emerson's request in May 1846, Thomas Carlyle sent Emerson what he called "that sun-shadow, a Daguerreotype likeness." "Here have I the exact sculpture," Emerson wrote on receiving it, "the man that God made."

6. Emerson returned Carlyle's favor, though neither was pleased with the result: It "seems smiling on me as if in mockery," Carlyle wrote. "Dost know me, friend? I am dead, thou seest, and distant, and forever hidden from thee."

7. Bronson Alcott and Henry David Thoreau built Emerson a garden house, designed by Alcott, in 1847, which Emerson named "Tumbledown Hall."

8. "Bush," the Emerson family home in Concord, photographed in 1875.

9. Henry David Thoreau in 1856.

10. Herbert Wendell Gleason, *Walden from Emerson's Cliff* (c. 1917). Emerson bought 14 acres on the shore of Walden Pond in 1844; Thoreau built a cabin on the land the next year.

11. Margaret Fuller in 1846.

12. Ellery Channing (1818–1901), a poet and a frequent companion during Emerson's later years. In 1853, he placed passages from the journals of Emerson and Thoreau alongside his own writing in a manuscript called "Country Walking."

3. Engaged to Emerson's brother Charles before his death, Elizabeth Hoar (1814–1878) became an intimate part of Emerson's circle. In his journal he alled her "Elizabeth the wise." The child has not been identified.

14. A. Bronson Alcott on the steps of the newly founded Concord School of Philosophy (c. 1879). Emerson attended some of the school's summer meetings.

5. William Torrey Harris and Elizabeth Palmer Peabody outside the Concord chool (c. 1879).

16. In Philadelphia with schoolmates Samuel Bradford and William Henry Furness (1875). The three agreed, Emerson wrote, "not to grow old, at least tc each other."

17. Emerson in his study (1879).

18. Emerson with his family on the steps of their Concord home (1879).

As we walked thither, Ellery proposed that we should have a water colour Exhibition in Boston. I say, Yes, but I should like better to have water-colour tried in the art of writing. Let our troubadours have one of these Spanish slopes of the dry ponds or basins which run from Walden to the river at Fairhaven, in this September dress of colour, under this glowering sky,—the Walden Sierras in September, given as a theme, & they required to daguerrotype that in good words.

Individual
If our wishes were undertakers & sextons, we should soon bury half the population.

A Mr Randall, M.C. who appeared before the Committee of H. of Commons on the subject of the American mode of closing a debate, said, that "the *one-hour* rule worked well, made the debate short & graphic." Nothing worse can be said of a debate than that it is *graphic*. The only place in which I know *graphic* to be well used, is Ben Jonson's "Minerva's graphic thread."

The *London twist*, it is a simple but potent secret in literature & consists in inverting the common sense & experience of mankind on any subject whatever, and affirming the reverse. Thus Mr Rae teaches that the N. A. Indian agriculture was greatly more careful & painstaking than the English. My friend L. perceived no change in our party after they met in Paris except that they had lost ground in speaking French; T. C. thinks the only great brave & suffering man in Europe is Nicholas; the D. of Buckingham wished the dog who bit him a young wife & an estate in the country. Lamartine was an ass & a rogue when I was in London; & here at home, Henry always complains that the woods in winter are sultry. "It was so dry that you might call it wet;" was the old verse. Tennyson is a screech owl, and Saint Paul a slyboots.
Yes we are all made of the sun.

W. Ah you should have gathered the tomatos yesterday, when I sent you.

B. O but I don't know all the places in your garden where to find them.
W. The frost does.

God is a substance & his method is illusion.
Who is to save the present moment?
The Intellect is the head of the Understanding but is the feet of the Moral Power.
God is reality & his method is illusion.
I know what I shall find if A. brings me Mss. I shall have a Salisbury Plain full of bases of pyramids to each of which I am to build an apex.

Life
What the deuce has the lapidary to concern himself with the quarry, or the washing whence his stone comes? Must he too be geologist, & prate of strata?

Memory
It is quite essential to the locomotive, that it should be able to reverse its movement, & run backwards & forwards with equal celerity. Is it less needful to the mind that it should have this retroaction, & command its past act & deed?

Every thing must walk Every theory be bipedized

Every man takes care that his neighbor does not cheat him but a day comes when he begins to care that he do not cheat his neighbor. Then all goes well; he has changed his cart into the chariot of the sun.

The Universities give a disparate mechanical integrity & make it impossible to make a mistake.

Cider is our national drink.
A B A is very dependent on his companion & clothes himself with *his* culture.

I ask him, are you sure you have a boy? Then I will help at his birth.

It is better to hold the negro race an inch under water than an inch over.

Better races should perish if a new principle be taught; all the world may well be bankrupt, if they are driven so into a right Socialism.

Races

You cannot preserve races beyond their term. St Michael pears have died out, and see what geology says to the old strata. Trilobium is no more except in the embryonic forms of crab & lobster.

'Tis important that the eye should be achromatic, but *Swedenborg* sees all amiss with this dull prismatic blur of misplaced gaudiness.

Why do his images give no pleasure?

I go twice a week over Concord with Ellery, &, as we sit on the steep park at Conantum, we still have the same regret as oft before. Is all this beauty to perish? Shall none remake this sun & wind, the skyblue river, the riverblue sky, the yellow meadow spotted with sacks & sheets of cranberry pickers, the red bushes, the irongray house with just the colour of the granite rock, the paths of the thicket, in which the only engineers are the cattle grazing on yonder hill; the wide straggling wild orchard in which nature has deposited every possible flavour in the apples of different trees. Whole zones & climates she has concentrated into apples. We think of the old benefactors who have conquered these fields; of the old man Moore who is just dying in these days, who has absorbed such volumes of sunshine like a huge melon or pumpkin in the sun,—who has owned in every part of Concord a woodlot, until he could not find the boundaries of these, and never saw their interiors. But we say, where is he who is to save the present moment, & cause that this beauty be not lost? Shakspeare saw no better heaven or earth, but had the power & need to sing, & seized the dull ugly England, ugly to this, & made it amiable &

enviable to all reading men, and now we are fooled into likening this to that; whilst, if one of us had the chanting constitution, that land would no more be heard of.

The journal of one of our walks would be literature enough for a cockney,—or for us, if we should be shut up in our houses, —and we make no record of them. The cranberry meadow yonder is that where Darius Hubbard picked one hundred bushels in one season worth 200 dollars, and no labor whatever is bestowed on the crop, not so much as to mow the grass or cut down the bushes. Much more interesting is the woodlot which yields its gentle rent of six per cent without any care or thought when the owner sleeps or travels, & is subject to no enemy but fire. But E. declares that the Railroad has proved too strong for all our farmers & has corrupted them like a war, or the incursion of another race;—has made them all amateurs, given the young men an air their fathers never had; they look as if they might be railroad agents any day. We shall never see Cyrus Hubbard or Ephraim Wheeler or grass & oats or Oats & grass, Old Barrett or Hosmer, in the next generation. These old Saxons have the look of pine trees & apple trees, & might be the sons got between the two; conscientious labourers with a science born with them from out the sap vessels of these savage sires.

This savagery is natural to man, & polished England cannot do without it. That makes the charm of grousehunting and deerstalking to these Lord Breadalbanes walking out their doors one hundred miles on their property, or Dukes of Sutherland getting off at last their town coat & donning their hunting gear, exasperated by saloons & dress boots.

But let us have space enough, let us have wild grapes and rock maple with tubs of sugar, let us have huge straggling orchards, let us have the Ebba Hubbard pear, hemlock, savin, spruce, walnut and oak, cidermills with tons of pumice, peat, cows, horses, paddies, carts & sleds.

We came to a fence which a well directed fan would lay flat. I had much discourse concerning the birth, death, & fate of man. E thought he should make a prayer to the Chance that brought him into the world. I, that when the child had escaped out of the womb, he cries: I thank the bridge that brought me safe over. I would not for ten worlds take the next one's chance.

Will they, one of these days, at Fourierville, make boys & girls to order & pattern? I want, Mr Christmas office, a boy, between No 17 & No 134, half & half of both; or you might add a trace of 113. I want another girl like the one I took yesterday only you can put in a leetle more of the devil.

Intellect detaches, yet the way men of talent make fools of themselves is, by too much detachment.
A man knocks at my door & says, "I am, now for six years, devoted to the sun. I study the sun that I may thence deduce the laws of the universe." I say, I will not dispute against the sun, but beware of taking any one thing out of its connexions, for that way folly lies.

A little too much in the French novel about this *superbe chevelure*. The less is said of that meteor the better. It is of quite unspeakable character, seat of illusion, & comes as near to witchcraft & humbugging, as anything in nature.

October 1, 1848. Yesterday, the last day of September, Ellery & I went to Carlisle by the old road passing Daniel Clark's house into the region of the limekiln & the Estabrook farm & a country made up of vast orchards where the apple grows with a profusion that mocks the pains taken by careful cockneys who come out into the country & plant young trees & watch them dwindle. Here no hedges were wanted; the wide distance from any population is fence enough. Here were varieties of apple not found in Downing, the Tartaric, & the Cow-apple, as E. said.—The ground was strewn with them in red & yellow heaps. They grew for their own pleasure; they almost lost price. Barberries flourished at the roadside, & grapes along the walls. The apples were of the kind which I remember in boyhood each containing a barrel of wine & half a barrel of cider.—Touch-me-if-you-dare

Books are like rainbows to be thankfully received in their first impression & not examined & surveyed by theodolite &

chain, as if they were part of the railroad. Perhaps it would be good in the tuition of an emperor that he should never read the same book twice. I owed,—my friend & I,—owed a magnificent day to the Bhagavat Geeta.—It was the first of books; it was as if an empire spake to us, nothing small or unworthy but large, serene, consistent, the voice of an old intelligence which in another age & climate had pondered & thus disposed of the same questions which exercise us. Let us not now go back & apply a minute criticism to it, but cherish the venerable oracle.

I still feel a little uneasiness about these novels. Why should these sorceries have a monopoly of our delicious emotions?—The novel still weakly uses the cheap resource of property married away instead of earned, and that is the chief conjuring-stick it has; for the instincts of man always attach to property, as he knows what accumulations of spiritual force go to the creation of that, and sobs & heart beats & sudden selfsacrifice very easily result from the dealing with it. But the novel will find the way to our interiors, one day, & will not always be novel of costume merely. These stories are to stories of real life what the figures which represent the fashions of the month in the front page of the Magazine are to portraits & inspired pictures.

from

England and Paris

1847–1848

The trilithons of Stonehenge are the simplest & surest structures. Like Achilles' tomb on plain of Troy they keep the vaunt of Homer through all ages.

showery England
delicious sward
pillory of 2 class

Amesbury 7 July

Stonehenge: Brown dwarves on a vast Wiltshire down

Gray stones on a gray evening, here were they, nettles & butter cups at their feet within the enclosure, larks singing over them & the wind old as they ringing among the conscious stones.

C talked of happiness. I fancied the stones had no philosophy of that kind. It is a quiet temple of Destiny & so constructed with infinite judgment in a place where it must ever be conspicuous from far to tens of thousands of eyes.

They understood the English language these British stones of the two talkers one from America one from Scotland who came up to this old ark of the race.

These at least spoke a language which all men understand and in a long solitude of millenniums still keep these undisturbed uninclosed downs. High green barrows lifted themselves all around on the plain, the old contemporaries & compatriots of the circle.

And a shepherd of Salisbury Plain kept his flock within sight & a shower drove the sad haymakers to protect even now on the fall of night their spread windrows.

In the showery England the grass grows long & dark.

Evidently it were possible to some C Fellowes to arrive stone by stone at the whole history of this structure. It is yet new & recent. Here are we in its early times. A thousand years hence they will thank us for the history we shall now save if we begin it. No tree in sight, no house. Hayricks only & a bagman passed.
The geologist had pecked at every stone.

The combed fields have the softest appearance & seem touched with a pencil & not with a plough.

from
RS

1848–1849

Education and the Universities, Alcott proposes for a theme, and it would be a good Essay. And he would provide every fine soul & only every fine soul, (dropping as democratic nonsense all pretence that every soul is fine) with such culture that it shall not at 30 or 40 years have to say, This which I might do, is made hopeless through my want of weapons.

"More are made good by exercitation than by nature."
Democritus.

Once they thought every thing depended on the election of Ames to prevent the election of Jarvis; & if J. had been elected, the world would not have come to an end.

A boy is the most difficult to manage of all wild beasts.
Laws p 203

Ah if a model person would remain a model person for a day! but no, his virtues only serve to give a currency to his foolish acts & speeches.

It is plain that some men may be spared from politics. The salvation of America & of the human race depends on the next Election, if we believe the newspapers. But so it was last year, & so it was the year before, and our fathers believed the same thing forty years ago. And these elections depend on the general bias & system of the people,—on their religion, interest, appetite, & culture,—and not on the particular information that is circulated in one or another set of handbills. The whole action of the scholar is mediate & to remote ends, and voting is not for him. His poem is good because it is not written to any person or moment, but to life generalised & perspectived.

He does not live by the same calender as the banker, but by the sidereal time of cause & consequence.

All my knowledge of mathematics is the story of Thales who measured the Pyramid by its shadow, & of Pythagoras,

"When the famed lines Pythagoras devised,
For which a hecatomb he sacrificed";

and of the Decimal Notation, the invention of Zero, which seems to me one of the triumphs of human wit; and of the Multiplication Table which ranks with astronomy, & lastly of the Science of Fractions as taught by Warren Colburn, for which I even him with Stephenson and Leverrier among our modern benefactors: and I add the beautiful command of the Delphian oracle to the Athenians that they should double his altar.

"*A child is better unborn than untaught.*" *Certainly he is.* Great cities, enormous populations, if they be paddy populations, are disgusting, like the population of cheese, like hills of ants, or swarms of fleas, the more the worse. But if they contain Merlins & Corneliuses, Friar Bacons, & Crichtons, if roadmakers, mathematicians, astronomers, chemists; good kings like Alfred; poets, like Chaucer, inventors, farmers, & sailors, who know the elements, & can make them work, memories, imaginations, combinings, perseverances, arts, music, architecture, nations of Spartans, of Athenians, of English, aristocratic men, & not maggots; then the more the merrier. Open the gates, let the miracle of generation go on.

—

Behmen & Swedenborg & Fox & Luther do with the old nearly effete Christianity what good housewives do with their pies & bread when they are a little old—put them into the oven, & check the fermentation which is turning them sour & putrid.

A book very much wanted is a "Beauties of Swedenborg," or a judicious collection of sentences and symbols & pictures from his diffuse & wearisomely repetitious pages.

I find a vulgarity in his mind of reading always the popular sects of his time.

C. N. came with his fine perceptions, his excellent instincts, his beautiful learning, his catholic mind, but I grudged him the time I gave him. He has become the spoiled child of culture; the *roué* of Art & letters; *blasé* with too much Plato, Dante, Calderon, & Goethe; tickled with music; pampered by his narrow society; amused by ballets; reading novels "like my bible;" and so jealous of partialism, so fearful of losing the level of life, that he has not written for three years, and now communicates nothing, but lies like a bit of bibulous paper. It was very melancholy to see that what I once esteemed the highest privilege, his conversation, was now sloth & weariness and a consumption of my time. What with the unwillingness to disgust him with questions & with "intellectuality," & the entire absence of any demonstration on his part, there was no frankness, no pleasure; there is nothing now but unmixed pain. Farewell my once beautiful genius! I have learned a sordid respect for uses & values: & must have them. I must send him a peat-knife. Are we to say, a man shall not go out to the shed to bring an armful of wood, lest this violence of action hurt the balance of his mind?

—

If I wrote a novel, my hero should begin a soldier & rise out of that to such degrees of wisdom & virtue as we could paint; for that is the order of nature.

What pity that the insanities of our insane are not complemental or compensating, so that we could house two of them together.

Nature loves a joke, for she made the ape.

Her forces are emulous of mental processes.

Nature uniformly does one thing at a time: if she will have a perfect hand, she makes head & feet pay for it. So now, as she is making railroad & telegraph ages, she starves the *spirituel*, to stuff the *materiel* & *industriel*.

—

The transfer.

I am struck with joy whenever genius makes the transfer from one part of nature to a remote part, & betrays the rhymes & echoes that pole makes with pole.

On kicking up our heels.

We have a ridiculous wisdom like that which a man has of his corns, or of his gouty foot, & has become by experience cunning in setting it down so as not to hurt him, so we of our limitations. We have learned not to strut or talk of our wings, or affect angelic moods, but to keep the known ways, knowing that at the end of these fine streets is the Lunatic Asylum.

The Spirit of Knowledge is serious, honest & trustworthy. We say nothing against astronomy & vegetation, because we are roaring here in our bed with rheumatism, we doubt not there are bounding fawns, & lilies with graceful springing stem; so neither do we doubt or fail to love the eternal law of which we are such shabby practisers. A cripple was our father & an Ethiop was our mother. And we worship the Liberty which we shall not see with our eyes, nor help but with our prayer.

Our philosophy is to *wait.* We have retreated on patience, transferring our oft shattered hope now to larger & eternal good. We meant well, but our uncle was crazy & must be restrained from waking the house. The roof leaked, we were out of wood, our sisters were unmarried & must be maintained; there were taxes to pay, & notes, and, alas, a tomb to build: we were obliged continually to postpone our best action, and that which was life to do, could only be smuggled in to odd moments of the month & year. Then we say Dear God, but the life of man is not by man, it is consentaneous & far-related, it came with the sun & nature, it is crescive & vegetative, and it is with it as with the sun and the grass. I obey the beautiful Necessity. The powers that I want will be supplied, as *I* am supplied, and the philosophy of waiting is sustained by all the oracles of the Universe.

*

God never made such a bungler as I am at any practical work, therefore I keep clear of the garden and the phalanstery.

H. T. sports the doctrines of activity: but I say, What do *we*? We want a sally into the regions of wisdom & do we go out & lay stone wall or dig a well or turnips? No, we leave the children, sit down by a fire, compose our bodies to corpses, shut our hands, shut our eyes, that we may be entranced & see truly. Sir D. Brewster gives exact directions for microscopic observation, thus; "lie down on your back & hold the single lens & object over your eye", &c

Do you think ecstasy is ever communicable?

—

L. asks if I saw the spiritual class? O no, I saw the ox & the ass, but rarely the driver.

Oct.

Alcott is a certain fluid in which men of a certain spirit can easily expand themselves & swim at large, they who elsewhere found themselves confined. He gives them nothing but themselves. Of course, he seems to them the only wise & great man. But when they meet people of another sort, critics & practical, & are asked concerning Alcott's wisdom, they have no books to open, no doctrines to impart, no sentences or sayings to repeat, and they find it quite impossible to communicate to these their good opinion.

Me he has served now these twelve years in that way; he was the reasonable creature to speak to, that I wanted.

There is in California a gold ore in great abundance in which the gold is in combination with such elements that no chemistry has yet been able to separate it without great loss. Alcott is a man of unquestionable genius, yet no doctrine or sentence or word or action of his which is excellent can be detached & quoted.

*

He is like C., who possesses a painter's eye, an appreciation of form & especially of colour, that is admirable, but who, when he bought pigments & brushes & painted a landscape on a barrel head could not draw a tree so that his wife could know it was a tree. So Alcott the philosopher has not an opinion or an apothegm to produce.

I shall write on his tomb, *Here lies Plato's reader.* Read he can with joy & naiveté inimitable, and the more the style rises, the more natural & current it seems to him. And yet his appetite is so various that the last book always seems to him the best. *Here lies the amateur.*

The Age

Among the marks of the age of cities must be reckoned conspicuously the universal adoption of cash-payment. Once it was one of many methods. People bought, but they also borrowed, & received much on various claims of goodwill, on hospitality, in the name of God, in the interest of party, of letters, of charity. Young men made essay of their talents for proof, for glory, for enthusiasm, on any reasonable call, nothing doubting that in one or another way their hazarded bread would return to them after many days. But now in the universal expansion of the city by railroads the stock exchange infects our country fairs, & no service is thought reasonable which does not see a requital in money. Yet where is the service which can by any dodge escape its remuneration? For grandeur, at least, let us once in a while serve God.

—

C. L. said, "'Tis so many years since we met, & you have passed over such stages!"—Ah, my friend, I must think so often of Capt. Franklin's Company in the Arctic regions travelling laboriously for six weeks to the north & then discovering by observation that they were south of their starting point. The ice had floated and so with us.

Conceit

I notice that people who wash much, have a high mind about it, & talk down to those who wash little. Carlyle washes, & he has come to believe that the only religion left us is ablution, and that Chadwick, the man who is to bring water for the million, is the priest of these times. So at home I find the morning bathers are proud & haughty scorners, and I begin to believe that the composition of water must be one part hydrogen, & three parts conceit.

—

October

Edith, who until now has been quite superior to all learning, has been smitten with ambition at Miss Whiting's school and cannot be satisfied with spelling. She spells at night on my knees with fury & will not give over; asks new words like conundrums with nervous restlessness and, as Miss W tells me, "will not spell at school for fear she shall miss."

Poor Edie struggled hard to get the white card called an "approbation" which was given out on Saturdays but one week she lost it by dropping out of a book on her way home her week's card on which her marks were recorded. This she tried hard to get safe home but she had no pocket so she put it in her book as the safest place. When half way home she looked in her book & it was there; but when she arrived at home it was gone. The next week she tried again to keep a clean bill but Henry Frost pointed his jack-knife at her; Edie said, "Don't!" & lost her "approbation" again.

—

The penalty of scholarship is that solitariness which hangs a certain wolfish look on the face at the approach of the best people, if they do not converse in a manner exactly to fit him.

Again must I make cheap what I adore,
And play the mountebank one winter more.

—

The Beatitude of Conversation.

I am afraid books do stand in our way; for the best heads are writers, and when they meet & fall into profound conversation, they never quite lose all respects of their own economy & pour out the divinest wine, but each is a little wary, a little checked, by thought of the rare helps this hour might afford him to some page which he has written. Each is apt to become abstracted & lose the remark of the other through too much attention to his own.

Yet I have no book & no pleasure in life comparable to this. Here I come down to the shore of the Sea & dip my hands in its miraculous waves. Here I am assured of the eternity, & can spare all omens, all prophecies, all religions, for I see & know that which they obscurely announce. I seem rich with earth & air & heaven, but the next morning I have lost my keys. To escape this economy of writers, women would be better friends; but they have the drawback of the perplexities of sex.

—

Another walk this Saturday afternoon with Ellery through the woods to the shore of Flint's Pond. The Witchhazel was in full bloom and from the highland we saw one of the best pictures of the New Hampshire Mountains. But E. said that when you come among them they are low & nothing but cowpastures. I say, let us value the woods; they are full of solicitation. My woodlot has no price. I could not think of selling it for the money I gave for it. It is full of unknown mysterious values. What forms, what colours, what powers, null, it is true, to our ignorance, but opening inestimably to human wit.

The crows filled the landscape with a savage sound; the ground was covered with new fallen leaves which rustled so loud as we tramped through them that we could hear nothing else.

One thing our Concord wants, a Berkshire brook which falls, & now beside the road, & now under it, cheers the traveller for miles with its loud voice. C. asks whether the mullein is in England? I do not remember it. It is so conspicuous in our pastures with its architectural spire (especially where it grows with the pokeweed in the ruined shanties of the Irish in my woods) that it must not be forgotten.

E. was witty on Xantippe & the philosophers old & new, & compared one to a rocket with two or three millstones tied to it, or, to a colt tethered to a barn. Channing celebrates Herrick as the best of English poets, a true Greek in England, a great deal better poet than Milton, who, he says, is too much like Dr Channing. I think that the landscape before us would give Herrick all he needed; he who sung a cherry, Julia's hair, Netherby's pimple, his own hen partlet, and Ben Jonson; we have a wider variety here among the maples;—but the prose & the poetry of that Age was more solid & cordial than ours. I find myself always admiring single twigs & leaves of that tree & for a chance example found in Wood's Athenae Oxon Vol I p 225 a quotation from *Edmund Campion's Hist. of Ireland*, that was a proof of the wit of that age.

The past with me turns to snakes.

How impossible to find Germany! Our young men went to the Rhine to find the genius which had charmed them, and it was not there. They hunted it in Heidelberg, in Gottingen, in Halle, in Berlin, no one knew where it was. From Vienna to the frontier, it was not found, and they very slowly & mournfully learned that in the speaking it had escaped, and as it had charmed them in Boston, they must return & look for it there.

—

Love is necessary to the righting the estate of woman in this world. Otherwise nature itself seems to be in conspiracy against her dignity & welfare; for the cultivated, high thoughted, beauty-loving, saintly woman finds herself unconsciously desired for her sex, and even enhancing the appetite of her savage pursuers by these fine ornaments she has piously laid on herself. She finds with indignation that she is herself a snare, & was made such. I do not wonder at her occasional protest, violent protest against nature, in fleeing to nunneries, & taking black veils. Love rights all this deep wrong, but who ever knew in real life a genuine instance of seasonable love?

What are Kant's views of History? Tell me that, Master Brook.

I find out in an instant if my companion does not want me; I cannot comprehend how my visiter does not perceive that I do not want him. It is his business to find out that. I, of course, must be civil. It is for him to offer to go. I certainly shall not long resist. I must pardon much to English exclusiveness when I see how life is left by the swainishness of our fellows.

Another vice of manners which I do not easily forgive is the dulness of perception which talks to every man alike. As soon as I perceive that my man does not know me, but is making his speech to the man that happens to be here, I wish to gag him.

—

Anthony Wood: Athenae Oxonienses

In the article "George Peele," Wood writes, "This person was living in his middle age in the latter end of Qu. Elizabeth; but when or where he died, I cannot tell; for so it is, & always hath been, that most poets die poor, & consequently obscurely, & a hard matter it is to trace them to their graves."

—

Alcott learned to write on the sand & on the snow, when paper & pens were dear.

His journal must be stablished. He sits here & plots an invasion of Cambridge Library, which, he says, has never been reported. He proposes to Thoreau to go down & spend a fortnight there, & lay it open to the day.

Education

It was a right course which Brisbane indicated when he told me of his visit to Paris, & went, he said, to the first men in name & credit in science. I said, Is there any man here who, for any price, will teach me the principles of music? I found the learnedest in the science & put myself diligently down to learn.—And young Ward tells me he went to Von Waagen to hear private lectures on art.

I cannot tell you how many chatterers I see who exercise on me their airy genius for one real observer & honest reporter like my two or three friends. I should be very short & decisive with my visiters, but that I am not sure that I have private employment, when I shall have got rid of them. If my inspiration were only sure, I should disembarrass myself very fast of my company.

Laissez faire. No bounties. Secure life & property, and you need not give alms.

George Minott thinks the cattle used to live much longer, in old times, than they do with modern farmers.

Dreams

I knew an ingenious honest man who complained to me that

all his dreams were servile, and, that, though he was a gentleman by day, he was a drudge, a miser, and a footman, by night. Civil war in our atoms, mutiny of the sub-daemons not yet subdued.

—

When I am walking in Boston, I think how much better had it been if I had stayed at home, & read such or such a book, written such letters, disposed of such affairs, &c. But if I stay at home, I do not those things.
Why?

Yesterday, 28 October, another walk with Ellery well worth commemoration if that were possible; but no pen could write what we saw: it needs the pencils of all the painters that ever existed, to aid the description. We went to White-Pond, a pretty little Indian basin, lovely now as Walden once was; we could almost see the sachem in his canoe in a shadowy cove. But making the circuit of the lake on the shore, we came at last to see some marvellous reflections of the coloured woods in the water, of such singular beauty & novelty that they held us fast to the spot, almost to the going down of the sun. The water was very slightly rippled, which took the proper character from the pines, birches, & few oaks, which composed the grove; & the submarine wood seemed all made of Lombardy poplar, with such delicious green, stained by gleams of mahogany from the oaks, & streaks of white from the birches, every moment growing more excellent, it was the world seen through a prism, & set Ellery on wonderful Lucretian theories of "law" & "design".

Ellery, as usual, found the place with excellent judgment "where your house should be set," leaving the woodpaths as they were, which no art could make over; and, after leaving the pond, & a certain dismal dell, whither a man might go to shoot owls, or to do selfmurder in, we struck across an orchard to a steep hill of the right New Hampshire slope, newly cleared of wood, & came presently into rudest woodland landscapes, unknown, undescribed, & hitherto *unwalked* by us Saturday afternoon professors. The sun was setting behind terraces of pines disposed in groups unimaginable by Downings, or Loudons, or Capability Browns; but we kept our way & fell into the Duganne trail, as we had already seen the glimpse of his cabin in the edge of the barbarous district we had traversed. Through a clump of apple-trees, over a long ridge (qu. what Dr. Jackson calls such ridges? *osars*,) with fair outsight of the river, & across the Nutmeadow brook, we came out upon the banks of the river just below James Brown's. Ellery proposed that we should send the Horticultural Society our notes, 'Took an apple near the White Pond fork of the Duganne trail,—an apple of the *Beware of this* variety, a true *Seek no further of this*.' We had much talk of books & lands & arts & farmers. We saw the original *tumulus* or first barrow, which the fallen pine tree makes with its upturned roots, & which, after a few years, precisely resembles a man's grave. We talked of the great advantage which he has who can turn a verse, over all the human race. I read in Wood's A. Oxoniensis a score of pages of learned nobodies, of whose once odoriferous reputations not a trace remains in the air, & then I came to the name of some Carew, Herrick, Suckling, Chapman, whose name is as fresh & modern as those of our friends in Boston & London, and all because they could turn a verse. Only write a dozen lines, & rest on your oars forever, you are dear & necessary to the human race & worth all the old trumpery Plutarchs & Platos & Bacons of the world. I quoted Suckling's line, "a bee had stung it newly" to praise it, & E. said, "Yes, every body's poetry is good but your own." He declared that the modern books, Tennyson, Carlyle, Landor, gave him no standard, no measure of thought & life and he fancies that the only writing open for us is the Essay. He arrived at three rules, 1. that no mercy is to be shown to poetry, 2. none to artists, 3. lost. I defended Boston people from his charges of bottomless stupidity, by the wit they have shown in these two things I have read today—Fitchburg Road Report, & Hale & Quincy speeches at the Water celebration.— What an use is their arithmetic turned to! For four millions of dollars, (and in any street you can pick up forty men worth a hundred thousand each) they have in two years finished this splendid & durable toy, a strong aquaduct to last forever, running down Snake-Brook bed, placed under navigable salt water, & arriving in Boston, feeding every chamber & closet as well as the Frog Pond fountain. And then, by their judicious ciphering, the sale of city lands, new made, (& rendered available by the water) for the next few years will pay all these four millions, & give the water free, as it is pure, to all.

E. said, he had once fancied that there were some amateur trades, as politics, but he found there were none; these too were fenced by Whig barricades. Even walking could not be done by amateurs, but by professors only. In walking with Ellery you shall always see what was never before shown to the eye of man. And yet for how many ages of lonely days has that pretty wilderness of White Pond received the sun & clouds into its transparency, & woven each day new webs of birch & pine, shooting into wilder angles & more fantastic crossing of these coarse threads, which, in the water, have such momentary elegance.

—

The rules of the game are paramount, & daunt the genius of the best players. Webster does not lead, but always plays a reverential second part to some ancestors, or Whig party, or Constitution, or other primary, who is much his inferior, if he had but courage & a calling.

Plymouth

Lidian says, that when she was a child, her mother never bought any *crash*, but that kitchen towels & coarse cloths were made from old sails brought home from her father's vessels, & were called *sail*-towels.

Wit in Trade

There is no good story in the books to show how much better is wit, liberal wit, in trade, than pennywisdom, & yet, one would think, we should have many. The school text is Thales, who, foreseeing the plenty of olives that would be that year, before the winter was gone, bought up all the oil casks at Miletus & Chios, which he did with little money, &, when the time came that many were sought for in haste, he, setting what rates on them he pleased, by this means got together much money. It might be as the orchardist who cuts open the fruitbud of the peach in winter & observes the black germ. Our common instances are, private information communicated by men in power of measures in progress which affect markets; accidental discoveries, as of a copper, coal, lead mine, or of a new material likely to be useful; pigeon expresses;

The famous Coffee speculation is a good instance, & I should like better to know the true history of that, & the reasons of its failure, than to have many volumes of Political Economy. The wit that elects the site of new mills & a new city, finds the path & true terminus of a new railroad, perceives well where to buy wild land in the western country, judging well where the confluence of streams, the change of soil, climate, or race, will make thoroughfares & markets,

American Climate
When it is warm, 'tis a sign that it is going to be cold.

How nature to keep her balance true invented a cat. What phantasmagoria in these animals! Why is the snake so frightful, which is the line of beauty, & every resemblance of it pleases? See what disgust & horror of a rat, loathsome in its food, loathsome in its form, & a tail which is villanous, formidable by its ferocity; yet interposed between this horror and the gentler kinds, is the cat, a beautiful horror, or a form of many bad qualities but tempered & thus strangely inserted as an offset, check, & temperament, to that ugly horror. See then the squirrel strangely adorned with his tail, which is his saving grace in human eyes.

I went to see the dwarf of dwarfs, Tom Thumb, 28 inches high and 16 years old.

In the hotels the air is buttered and the whole air is a volatilized beefsteak.

Our poetry is an affectation, but read Chaucer, & the old lays in which Merlin & Arthur are celebrated, & you will find it as simple as the speech of children.

Christianity in all the Romantic Ages signified *european culture*, this grafted or meliorated tree in a crab forest; and to marry a paynim wife or husband, was to marry Beast, & voluntarily to take a step backward towards the negro & baboon.

"Hengist had verament
A daughter both fair & gent;
But she was heathen Sarazine;
And Vortigern, for love fine,
Her took to fere & to wife,
And was cursed in all his life!
For he let Christian wed heathen
And meynt* (?) our blood as flesh & mathen."
(maggots)

So Olaf punished eating horseflesh with death.

—

Channing thinks it the woe of life that natural effects are continually crowded out & artificial arrangements substituted. He remembers when an evening, any evening, grim & wintry like this, was enough for him, the houses were in the air; now it takes a very cold winter night to overcome the common & mean.

And this, no doubt, as we agreed is the poet-state. As long as the evening is sufficient, as long as the youth is in the capability of being imparadised by the sights & sounds of common day, he is poet; but as soon as he begins to use them well, knows how to parse & spell, & turns artist, he ceases to be poet.

C. said, drive a donkey & beat him with a pole with both hands;—that's action. But poetry is, revolution on its own axis.

It is curious & universal that the first symptom of madness is to bite. Insanity makes insanity.

Cockneyism & so much that passes as costly English Culture, is fancy-stock merely; great by our allowance. W.E.C. said that a cockney was a horse-louse curried from a horse.

*mixed

—

Dr Johnson said, he always went into stately shops, and good travellers seek always the best hotels in every town; for though they cost more, they do not cost much more, & there is the good company, the best information, & the scholar knows that the best books contain first & last the best thoughts & facts. Now & then by rarest luck in some foolish grub-street lies the gem we want. But, in the best circles is the best information, as I thought when I found what I wanted in "Wykeham's Life". You can get phosphate from cowdung; but better from bones. oxygen best from *conferva rivularis.*

It is one convenience of culture that it has no enemies. The finished man of the world holds his hatreds also at arm's length, so that he can, whenever is fit occasion, receive his foe with all the world at his house, & associate with him in public or in private affairs, unencumbered by old quarrel. But country people are like dogs or cows that quarrel, & remember their spite. William of Wykeham quarreled with the Duke of Lancaster. All Wykeham's temporalities were sequestered, & he excluded from parliament. William managed to get all back, & the Duke was for the time worsted. It does not hinder that the Duke should be solemnly received at William's College at Oxford on the Visitation.
This fast & loose belongs to the Intellect, belongs to that power of detachment which the Intellect introduces.

—

What difference in the hospitality of minds! Some are actually hostile, & imprison me as in a hole. A blockhead makes a blockhead of me: Whilst for my Oriental friend here, I have always claimed for him, that nothing could be so expansive as his element is. The Atlantic Ocean is a tub compared with the atmosphere in which I float, at once inspiring the air & upborne by it.

My friends begin to value each other, now that A. is to go; & Ellery declares, "that he never saw that man without being cheered," & Henry says, "He is the best natured man he ever met. The rats & mice make their nests in him."

*

The apple is our national fruit, & I like to see that the soil yields it; I judge of the country so. The American sun paints himself in these glowing balls amid the green leaves. Man would be more solitary, less friended, less supported, if the land yielded only the useful maize & potato, & withheld this ornamental & social fruit.

I have planted a Pumpkin Sweeting near my summerhouse,—I believe out of agreeable recollection of that fruit in my childhood at Newton. It grew in Mr Greenough's pasture, and I thought it solid sunshine.

"Ere boyhood with quick glance had ceased to spy
The doubtful apple 'mid the yellow leaves."

There are always a few heads & out of these come the mythology & the machinery of the world. Whence came all these books, laws, inventions, parties, kingdoms? Out of the invisible world, through a few brains: and, if we should pierce to the origin of knowledge, & explore the meaning of memory, we might find it some strange mutilated roll of papyrus, on which only a strange disjointed jumble of universal traditions of heavenly scriptures, of angelic biographies, were long ago written, relics of a foreworld.

Let us have the experiences of Metternich, of Humboldt, of General Taylor, of Trelawney.

In my chapter on Intellect, I should wish to catalogue those high commandments which in all the mental history elevate themselves like towers; as, not until our own day, did Herschel go to the Cape, & publish the catalogue of the stars of the Southern Hemisphere.

Midsummer

'Tis very certain that this almanack of the soul may be written as well as that of Greenwich. We have had our heights of sun & depths of shade, & it would be easy in the soul's year to recall & fix its 21 of June. Moses had his Ten Commandments; but we have ours.

In the first age, they wrote on stone, & what was fit to be written on stone. Lycurgus, his laws; Moses, his Decalogue; but we write novels & newspapers. You would not have Bulwer & D'Israeli publish their novel on stone?

There is a sort of climate in every man's speech running from hot noon, when words flow like steam & perfume,—to cold night, when they are frozen.

Library

A man's library is a sort of harem. I observe they have a great pudency in showing their books to a stranger.

We must accept a great deal as Fate. We accept it with protest, merely adjourning our experiment, and not squander our strength in upheaving mountains. Mountain is conquerable also, to be sure; but, whilst you cannot quarry it, let it be a mountain.

Action & idea are man & woman, both indispensable; why should they rail at & exclude each other?

Yes, we must call the anatomist & physiologist to counsel. The human body is undoubtedly the true symbol, true & highest & most instructive; human body & not sun or galaxy.

Library

Every house should be an athenaeum.

There is no privacy that is not penetrable.

—

Alcott.

It occurred in the conversation yesterday repeatedly, that Alcott wants a certain rigour in playing his game of conversation. He shifts his purpose nimbly, &, when you thought you were speaking to one point, lo! he has changed it. It is the same vice for which my Boston Pilot lost his Branch. Then a good deal of the talk has no design, & it is like the curvetting, prancing, arching of the neck, & pawing, of a play-horse.

The Club *Examiners*

How long shall we sit & wait to be challenged by the Examiners? If the Kings of thought came together & asked for results, we too should have our pregnant formulas to give. That occasion would be the iron girdle we want. We should cast off our long holiday, & quit us like men. As much result would be given & received in intellectual & moral science, as in the Section rooms of the British Association at the annual assembling of the chemists & geologists.

Jack says, he must & will have the law go in hat & boots if he is to believe & obey it; none of your mathematics, astronomy, & abstract law, for him. Bring in your mythology, or don't expect to hold him.

—

Nov. 19.

'Tis the coldest November I have ever known. This morning the mercury is at 26. Yesterday afternoon cold fine ride with Ellery to Sudbury Inn, & mounted the side of Nobscot. Finest picture though wintry air of the russet Massachusetts. The landscape is democratic, not gathered into one city or baronial castle, but equally scattered into these white steeples, round which a town clusters in every place where six roads meet, or where a river branches or falls, or where the pan of soil is a little deeper. The horizon line marked by hills tossing like waves in a storm: firm indigo line. 'Tis a pretty revolution which is effected in the landscape by simply turning your head upside down, or, looking through your legs: an infinite softness & loveliness is added to the picture. It changes the landscape at once from November to June. Or as Ellery declared makes *Campagna* of it at once; so he said, Massachusetts is Italy upside down.

> "When Nature is forsaken by her lord be she ever so good she does not survive."

—

I understand Dr C.T.J. that a piece of ordnance may usually be fired 1000 times before it will burst, & only so many times; that it is the rule in the U.S. service, that one piece of each new kind of fire arm should be burst; and that Jenks's Rifle was fired by a sergeant & man appointed to that service 66000 times, when last heard from, & was not yet burst.

The Doctor described the wonderful mirage of Lake Superior; and the analysed sounds; and the aurora borealis. the air in the woods at 100, the water at 38.
The osars or horsebacks, so familiar in our woods, are made, he says, by the combing of waves?

A robin, says Agassiz, (embryonic), is a gull; a gull is a duck; a duck is a fish; add now what I suppose is omitted, pro causa conciliandi gratiam, that a man is a robin,—and the chain is perfect, a man is a fish.

We all like a good superlative. Mitchell in Nantucket showed me a nebula in Orion with his telescope, and assured me it was a great way off. At the Bank of England they are accustomed to put a million of money into the hand of the visiter. Every body climbs Mont Blanc,—if he can; nor will travellers rest until they have looked off Himalaya. We go under the flood of Niagara at Table Rock. The Flying Childers who ran a mile a minute, must be seen, is to see; and General Thumb, the smallest man that ever grew,—or grew not.

—

Dec. 22, 1848.
Directly on the dreadful calamity of young George Emerson's death, comes to me one of my highest prosperities. I received Clough's poem at the bookstore, whilst pondering the dare or dare not of a visit to Pemberton Square.

'Tis, I think, the most real benefit I have had from my English visit, this genius of Clough. How excellent, yet how slow to show itself! He gave no hint of all this to me, & I learned to esteem him for reticent sense, for solidity, & tenacity, after he had given proof of his apprehensiveness & of his thorough Oxford culture, which was manifest enough. An Oxonian is a kind of nobleman, of course. Then he had that interest in life & realities in the state of woman & the questions so rife in Paris through Communism, and through the old loose & easy conventions of that city for travellers,—he talked so considerately of the Grisette estate, that I found him the best *pièce de resistance*, & tough adherence, that one could desire. But I never surmised that this flowing all-applicable expression belonged to him. Where had he concealed it? And now Tennyson must look to his laurels. And now I have a new friend, & the world has a new poet.

—

1849

The word God is the algebraic × in morals, and the Hebrews with right philosophy made it unspeakable. But the stupid world finding a word, assumes this scientific for a baptismal name, and talks of him as easily as of Captain Gulliver.

—

Whatever is good is effective, generative. An apple reproduces seed, a hybrid or monster does not. If a man is a man, working there by authority, I shall find, that, as the river makes its shores, so he has made grand institutions, weapons, disciples, to work by & live on, harvests, also, to eat, that he may work more. But DIsraeli still stands in his shoes, & has no planet under him. Call you that a man, or natural power? 'Tis a dandy, a frippery.

F. went to Father Taylor's prayer-meeting, & an old salt told his experiences, and how intemperate he had been for many years; "but now, dear brother," said he, "Jesus Christ is my grog shop". Father Taylor, thereupon, recommended to his brethren to be short, & sit down when they had done.

The new electrical light in London puts out the gas. The old yellow oil light is avenged. What gas did for that, is now done for gas, by this new lustre. There is no night longer for London. 'Tis time the Nelson column was finished; its defects were charitably hidden for twelve hours, hitherto; but now, it stares in broad light, without an interval. There is no more night. A good lamp is the best police. I wrote formerly what seemed the experience of some of our rural Socialists, that the purity of the sexes depended on plainspeaking, and that to redress the wronged pudency, it needed—to come nearer. A good lamp is the best police.

—

I saw on Saturday at Ward's the Ludovisi Juno, which is again one of the miracles of old sculpture, & indeed of human art, as unaccountable as Shakspeare's drama. There was never that face or figure in nature, from which it could be modelled. I am sure that the artist drew from a cloud when he moulded these features. Then the Jove's head was a combed mountain.

—

Spirit of the Age

Now that the man was ready, the horse was brought. The timeliness of this invention of the locomotive must be conceded. To us Americans, it seems to have fallen as a political aid. We could not else have held the vast North America together, which now we engage to do. It was strange, too, that when it was time to build a road across to the Pacific—a railroad, a shiproad, a telegraph, & in short a perfect communication in every manner for all nations—'twas strange to see how it is secured. The good World-Soul understands us well. How simple the means. Suddenly the Californian soil is spangled with a little gold dust here & there, in a mill race, in a mountain cleft, an Indian picks up a little, a farmer, & a hunter, & a soldier, each a little; the news flies here & there, to New York, to Maine, to London, and an army of a hundred thousand picked volunteers, the ablest & keenest & boldest that could be collected instantly organize & embark for this desart bringing tools, instruments, books, & framed houses, with them. Such a well appointed Colony as never was planted before arrive with the speed of sail & steam on these remote shores, bringing with them the necessity that their government shall instantly proceed to make the road which they themselves are all intimately engaged to assist.

It was strange too that all over the world about the same moment mineral treasures were uncovered. We heard of gold in various parts of the United States; in Siberia; in Africa on the Tomat river near Cassan & in other parts of Europe. Silver, quicksilver, platina, copper, lead, iron, & coal, all appeared in new quarters about the same time i.e. in the year 1848. Peu de moyens, beaucoup d'effet.

—

March 19
Gravitation is the operator in what we call mechanical division. Gravitation is Nature's Grand Vizier & prime favourite. Much that we call chemical, even electrical action, is really, at last, his deed. Look at the sponge-like foliaceous forms which wet sand & clay take when falling with the water, in spring, on the steep sides of "the deep cut" in the RailRoad. And one will suspect that Gravity, too, can make a leaf. In morals, again, Gravity is the Laissez faire principle, or Destiny, or Optimism, than which nothing is wiser or stronger.

That nature works after the same method as the human Imagination.
That nature makes flowers, as the mind makes images.
that metaphysics might anticipate Jussieu
that organic matter, & mind, go from the same law, & so correspond

Our science is very shiftless & morbidly wise; wise where it is not wanted; blind where we most wish to see. What a pother in the last twenty years about geology! Geologists were crossing all seas & lands, like so many squibs. Well, why did not they find California? They all knew what all men most wanted. Why did not they find the copper mines? There is no Columbus in these sciences with an anticipating mind; but they are like critics & amateurs; when the heel of a trapper's foot has turned up gold or copper or quicksilver, they come & give it a name.

24 March
The Indians were a sort of money, it seems, in Spanish colonies. And the poor Lucayans were treated according to the proverb "the kid was seethed in its mother's milk." Columbus seems to have been the principal introducer of American slavery. See Helps, History of the Conquerors of America & their Bondmen.

Town & Country Club.
At Alcott's last Tuesday (20 March) we had a meeting of thirty men, and discussed the expediency of a Club & Clubroom. Alcott was festal & Olympian, as always, when friends come; his

heart is then too great; his voice falters & chokes in his throat. Every newcomer seems large, sacred, & crowned to him. It was proposed that the Club should rent the room in which we sat, (Alcott's,) & that he should be declared perpetual secretary.

It is much wanted by the country scholars a café or Reading Room in the city, where, for a moderate subscription, they can find a place to sit in, & find their friends, when in town, & to write a letter in, or read a paper. Better still, if you can add certain days of meeting when important questions can be debated, communications read, &c. &c. It was proposed by Hale & others, sometime since, to form in Boston a "Graduates' Club." This would be that. Then the ministers have a "Hook & Ladder," or a "RailRoad Club."

—

The key to the age is this thing, & that thing, & that other, as the young orators describe. I will tell you the key to all ages, Imbecility: imbecility in the vast majority of men at all times & in every man, even heroes, in all but certain eminent moments victims of mere gravitation, custom, fear, & sense. This gives force to the strong, that the others have no habit of selfreliance or original action.

—

In my childhood, some peering eyes of boys discovered that the oranges hung on the boughs of Gov. Gray's orange tree were tied on with a thread.—I fear it is so with the novelist's events. Nature has a magic by which she accurately suits the man to his fortunes by making these the fruit of his own character. Ducks take to water & eagles to the sky, and every man to his liking, Lord Palmerston to foreign affairs, hunters to the forest, gardeners to the hothouse, sailors to the sea.

Some temperaments would spoil any success, men of no grasp, whose example & atmosphere enervates all who work for them.

Thus events grow on the same stem with persons, are subpersons.

But the novelist rashly plucks this event & fortune here & there & applies them with little consideration to his figures simply to tickle the fancy of his readers with a visionary prosperity or to scare them with visionary tragedies.

Men. *1849*

3 May I set out in the Warren lot a couple of pears, seedlings from my Bartlett, which I budded myself. The best had died in the Heater Piece & these two poor old looking young things remained. Let us see if they can thrive.

In Richard of Devizes' Chronicle of Richard I's Crusade, p. 62, (Bohn) is a good specimen of the religious opinions of the 12th Century. Richard taunts God with forsaking him; "O fie! O how unwilling should I be to foresake thee in so forlorn & dreadful a position, were I thy lord & advocate, as thou art mine! In sooth, my standards will in future be despised, not through my fault but through thine; in sooth, not through any cowardice of my warfare, art thou thyself, my King & my God, conquered this day, & not Richard thy vassal."

—

I dismiss my labourer with saying "Well, Malachi, I shall send for you as soon as I cannot do without you." Malachi goes off contented with that assurance, for he knows well that the potatoes will grow & the weeds with them; the melons & squashes must be planted week after next. And however unwilling to pay his high wages I must send for him. I wish that all labour should be as real & valuable as his, & should stand on the same simple & surly market. If it is the best of its kind, it will. I want & must have painter, stable-keeper, locksmith, poet, gentleman, priest, doctor, cook, confectioner, carpet weaver, chairmaker, & so on each in turn in course of the year. If each really knows his craft, he cannot be spared. Political Economy rightly read, would be a consolation, like Christianity.

—

Martial gave me to think of the faculty of writers. He can detach the object with unerring taste, & knows he can: sees that the power perfect in him differs infinitely from the imperfect approaches to the same power in ordinary scribblers. It is chemical mixture & not mechanical, which makes the writer. The others have not intelligence enough to know they are not writers. One thing more. Martial suggests again, as every purely literary book does, the immortality. We see we are wiser than we were: We are older: Can nature afford to lose such improvements? Is Nature a suicide?

Macaulay

The historian of England or France seems to be compelled to treat of England as of an Englishman; the nation has a continuous existence, memory, history in his head, knows his rights.

Who buys Channing's house buys a sunset. It should be sold in a fair day, then the purchaser gets rivers, mountains, villages, in the bargain. I would not, if I owned that place, sell it. I would hold onto it as long as I could see.

Life

We must not think that all the charm is in the employment. Life itself is an ecstasy: life is sweet as nitrous oxide; and the fisherman standing dripping all day over a cold pond, the switchman at the railroad intersection, the labourer in the field, the Irishman in the ditch, the flaneur in the street, all ascribe a certain pleasure to their employment which they themselves give it. It is health & appetite that gives sweetness to sugar, & bread, & meat,

And it is easy to see that as insane persons are rendered indifferent to their dress, diet, & other accommodations, & as we do in dreams with great equanimity the most unusual & surprising things, so a drop more of wine in our cup of life will reconcile us to strange company & work.

I meet in the street people full of life. I am, of course, at ebbtide; they at flood; they seem to have come from the south or from the west or from Europe. I see them pass with envy at this gift which includes all gifts.

from

TU

1849

Clough's Beautiful Poem I read again last night in the sitting room. 'Tis a kind of new & better Carlyle; the Homeric Iteration is one secret; the truly modern question & modern treatment another; and there is abundance of life & experience in it; good passages are, the prayer to the sun & moon & hours to pass slowly over Philip & Elspie. And good youth in it, as E. H. says.

The wisdom of words every day might surprise us. After a man has made great progress, & has come, as he fancies, to heights hitherto unscaled, the common words still fit his thought; nay, he only now finds for the first time how wise they were. "*Macrocosm*," *Reason, Conscience, Substance, Accidence, Nature, Relation, Fortune, Fate, Genius,* Element, Person, 'twill be long before he needs a new coat.

—

When men feel & say, "Those men occupy my place," the revolution is near. So we say. But I never feel that any men occupy my place; but that the reason I do not have what I wish, is, that I want the faculty which entitles. All spiritual or real power makes its own place. Revolutions of violence, then, are scrambles merely.

—

Reason of the aversation from metaphysics is the voice of nature. Nature made the eye to see other things, but not itself. If you have sharp eyes, use them, not brag of them.

—

What a privilege is not that of a beautiful person, who knows that whenever he sits, or moves, or leaves a shadow on the wall, or sits for a portrait to the artist, or to the Daguerrotype, —he confers a favor on the world.

—

The sky looks indignantly on all that is doubtful & obscure in man.

Beauty fluxional. Beauty is the medium state; balance of expression; what is just ready to flow, & be metamorphosed into other forms. Any fixedness, or heaping, or concentration on one feature, a long nose, a sharp chin, a humpback, is the reverse of flowing.

Those who painted angels & nativities and descents from the cross, were also writing biographies & satires, though they knew it not. The history of humanity is no hopping squib, but all its discoveries in science, religion & art, consecutive & correlated.

Narrowness has been thy bane.

He makes me rich, him I call Plutus, who shows me that every man is mine, & every faculty is mine; who does not impoverish me in praising Plato, but, contrariwise, is adding assets to my inventory.

—

25 May 1849. Two gravestones have been planted in my path within the year, Ellen Hooper's and David Scott's. Ellen Hooper connected herself with all the noblest & most loved figures that have cheered & enriched me in my own land (or with all but one: my own Ellen she never knew). And she gave a value by her interest to all my writings.

—

Words

The Collegians have seldom made a better word than *Squirt* for a showy sentence. So I find *tin* for money always comic. *Lubber* is a well marked genus.

In conversation, the game is, to say something new with old words. And you shall observe a man of the people picking his way along, step by step, using every time an old boulder, yet never setting his foot on an old place.

*

"Honey-pie," says Statestreet when there is flattery; "All my eye," when any exaggeration.
Fiddle faddle

Wilkinson, Swedenborg's pupil after 100 years, a philosophic critic with a brain like Bacon. Why not read in England? Are there no mornings in England? Do they read Dickens when they first get up as well as overnight?

Swedenborgian Church an imprisonment in the letter; never a hero stirs out of it.

Ah the Imagination has a flute that sets the atoms of our frame in a dance like planets, and once so flagellated, the whole man reeling drunk to the music, they never quite subside to their old marble.

In Swedenborg, the Spirits have the dumps.

In the Conclave the mendicant orders had their cardinal,—and in man, mouse & midge, chalk & marl must be represented. Every affinity & quality, sour & bitter, slime & reek must come to the day. There is no low & high in real being. Each of these things has its translation into the spiritual & celestial & necessary sphere where it plays a part as indestructible as any other. But it is plain that each of these qualities, chlorine, iodine, & what not becomes pronounced in a man. That is their first ascension. He knows what to do with them. Their quality makes his career. And he can variously publish their virtues because he is made of that thing.

—

I conceive the value of railroads to be this, in education, namely, to unite the advantages of town & country life, neither of which we can spare. A man should live in or near a large town; because, let his own genius be what it may, it will repel quite as much of agreeable & valuable talent as it draws; &, in a city, the total attraction is sure to conquer first or last every repulsion, & drag the most improbable hermit within its walls, some day in the year. In the town, he can find the swimming school, the gymnastic teacher, the chemist, the music, the dancing master, the shooting gallery. Opera, ballet, & panorama, Agassiz, Lyell, Webster, & Lafayette & the Club. In the country, he can find solitude & reading, manly labor, & cheap living, moors for game, hills for geology, & groves for devotion.

A great deal that is not set down in the bill. I pay the Schoolmaster, but 'tis the school-boys that educate my son.

—

The tree needs water & digging about & pruning & protection from its enemies the slug, the louse, the borer, & so on, &, more than all, it needs food; it will die without food, if you want fruit, you must give manure. Well, then, a pretty Case you make out for the Cultivator. Well, it is not gainful, & yet it seems to me much, that I have brought a skilful chemist into my ground & keep him there overnight, all day, all summer, for an art that he possesses of cooking pears; he can take common water & clod, & by means of sunshine, manufacture the handsomest & most delicious Bonne de Jerseys, Bartletts, bergamots, & brown beurrés in an inimitable manner which no confectioner can approach & his method of working is no less beautiful than his result.

In the drought, the peartree roots murmured in the dark, & said, they were sorely put to it for water, & could not go on another day, supplying food to the tree above them. But there is the kind old master who so tendered us, & visits the tree daily, we hear his footsteps every morn. If we could only give him a sign of our condition. Be it so. I will instantly, said the taproot, hang him out a signal on the highest bough of the tree, & we will see if he can understand us. So the taproot ceased working, & the top bough wanting food, drooped & hung its head. The master, you may be sure, was not long in seeing the withering of his favourite, & much alarmed he ran in haste & brought a water-pot & soon after a barrel of water, & abundantly refreshed the roots, which, thus restored, showed their good humour to the very top of the tree.

Who climbs best? the monkey; no, the squirrel goes higher. No; sap climbs better, & will go into the top bough, & to the last vein & edge of the highest leaf on the tree. Yes; but a drop of water climbs higher, for look, there is a cloud above the tree. Well, heat climbs higher than water, & space higher than heat.

Your pears, which you raise, cost you more than mine, which I buy.—Yes, they are costly, but we all have expensive vices; you play at billiards, & I at pear trees.

Riches

Neither will poverty suit every complexion. Socrates & Franklin may well go hungry & in plain clothes, if they like it; but there are people who cannot afford this, but whose poverty of nature needs wealth of food & clothes to make them decent.

I do not drink wine, but would have the name of drinking wine

Carlyle is a man of force, of burly, vivacious, aggressive temperament and unimpressionable. The literary man & the fashionable man, & the political man, each fresh from triumphs in his own sphere comes eagerly to see & unite with this man whose fun they so heartily enjoy, but they are struck with despair at the first onset. His cold, victorious, scoffing, sneering, vituperative declamation strikes them with coldness & hesitation on the instant. The Malleus mediocritatis.

—

20 June.

At our sad fire last night, at the Old Court House & the store on the East side, which burned the Court house, James Conner found a door among the Chattels of one family, &, carrying off that prize, he & Sam Staples protected their backs by means of it from the scorching heat, whilst they directed the engine-pipe against the tenfooter under the elm tree. I had not seen a door perform such good extra service, since its famed feat of the Coverlet.

At New York, June 13 14 15 I read Saint Antony's sermon to the fishes, full of bonhommie in the idea & the expletives, but ludicrously inapt in some of the points, e.g. reminding them how much our Lord loved to eat them; but kindly considered in reminding them how safe they were from rain, wind, dust, & deluges, not afraid of crevasses, &, let us add, of conversation; no talking permitted in that atheneum. He should have reminded them of their few duties,—they have the vacation we men sigh for; suggested a piscine philosophy in view of pike & grampus, that if a soldier of the kingdom of Ci has lost a buckler, a soldier of Ci has found it, & not failed to throw in an effective hint of transmigration & ascent to the inconveniences of pantaloons & Westminster Catechism one of these days.

New England Catholics disgusting. And the spread of Popery futile. As to fearing the Pope, we in America should as soon think of fearing a muskmelon.

—

1 July. I find England again this summer in Macaulay's two volumes, as I found it, last summer, in London. The same country of wealth, of birth, of precedent, of decorum. The story is told with all that ability which one meets so abundantly in England, & in no other country,—full of knowledge of books, & men, & customs, which it is creditable to know. The story is quite full of *bon ton*. It is written with extreme diligence & is very entertaining & valuable from the amount of good information & curious anecdote, & really has claims to be a history of the people of England, as the author has studied to make it. The second volume is far the best, the character of James is so dramatically bad, & the character & conduct of William so excellent. At last, in the success of William, tears almost come to the eyes. The persons & incidents are so fine that it seems strange this period has been neglected so long. One sad reflection arises on all the course of the narrative, of wonder, namely, at the depravity of men in power, & at the shocking tameness with which it is endured. One would think the nation was all tailors, & mince-pie-makers. The writer has a great deal of talent, but no elevation of mind. There is not a novel or striking thought in the book, not a new point of view from which to consider the events, & never one thrill or pulse of moral energy imparted. He is always a fine artificial Englishman, & keeping the highway invariably; well-bred, but for sale. (all dated *Windsor Castle.*) Here is good black blood, English

pluck, but no philosophy.—A deal of pamphlets now well bound.

I cannot get enough alone to write a letter to a friend. I retreat & hide. I left the city, I hid myself in the pastures. When I bought a house, the first thing I did was to plant trees. I could not conceal myself enough. Set a hedge here, set pines there, trees & trees, set evergreens, above all, for they will keep my secret all the year round.

I am afraid A. can as little as any man separate his drivelling from his divining.

Brag

The feeling of Boston & Massachusetts for a few years past has been like that of the shopmen & of a village on the morning of a Cattle Show, or other holiday, which is to bring a crowd of strangers into the town; every body is building booths, or arranging shop windows, or laying tables; everywhere a small pan to gather some rill of the expected silver shower. So feels Boston & Massachusetts on the eve of a prodigious prosperity; & we build, & plant, & lay roads, & set up signposts, to attract our share of the general blessing.
In New York, they characterise our hats & books & beauties as Frogpondish; but we, on the other hand, pity the whole *uncochituated* creation.

The Kentuckian said, his country "was bounded on the east by the rising sun, on the north by the aurora borealis, on the west by the precession of the equinoxes, & on the south by the Day of Judgment."

—

'Tis very certain that the man must yield who has omitted inevitable facts in his view of life. Has he left out marriage & the σπερματος ουσιης συντηρησιν, he has set a date to his fame. We are expecting another.

—

13 July. Yesterday, the day before, & today, another storm of heat, like that three weeks ago. The day is dangerous, the sun

acts like a burningglass, on the naked skin, & the very slugs on the pear leaves seem broiled in their own fat.   Mercury at 94° at 3 p.m.

When a man dies in Concord the neighbors sum his epitaph: "he was a good provider," or a bad.

One of the first works of good sense is to build a good dwellinghouse, yet a good house is rare.

Μελετη το παν. I took my hoe & waterpail & fell upon my sleepy pear trees, broke up the soil, pulled out the weeds & grass, I manured, & mellowed, & watered, pruned, & washed, & staked, & separated the clinging boughs by shingles covered with list: I killed every slug on every leaf. The detestable pear worm, which mimics a twig, I detected & killed. The poor tree tormented by this excessive attention & industry, must do something, & began to grow.

My pears & apples were well favoured as long as I did not go beyond my own hedge: but if I went down to Edmund's farm, his trees were three stories high, & high up in the air hung a harvest of fruit.

"Isn't it too bad, father!" says Eddy, "there's a letter from Ellen for me, & none for Edie."

I find Swedenborg to have no future. It is the best sign of a great nature that it opens heaven for you, &, like the breath of morning mountains, invites you onward. Swedenborg is retrospective only. Nor can we divest him therefore of this charnel house odour. With a force of ten men, he could never yet break the umbilical cord which held him to nature, & he did not rise to the platform of pure genius.

Swedenborg.

'Tis curious that he should be entangled with Calvinism. 'Tis curious that all the great mathematicians, be they never so grand, should be unable to pass the materialism barrier. Newton is rusty with Calvinism. Cuvier is calvinistic. All the science of England & France is, all but Goethe & Oken. & Plato & Kepler only have united geometry to the poetic spirit.

I find what L. read me this morning from "Conjugial Love" to be in a Goody-Two-Shoes taste, the description of gold houses, & Sinbad Sailor fruit trees,—all tinsel & gingerbread. Mr Cushing's Watertown garden would out-paradise this French Eden.

What to do with the stupendous old prig?

Education

In Dante pleases the friendly conversation with Brunetto Latini, Inferno XV, 82.

> —in la mente m'è fitta, ed or m'accuora
> La cara buona imagine paterna
> Di voi, quando nel mondo ad ora ad ora
> M'insegnavate come l'uom s'eterna.

I think if I were professor of Rhetoric,—teacher of the art of writing well, to young men, I should use Dante for my text-book. Come hither, youth, & learn how the brook that flows at the bottom of your garden, or the farmer who ploughs the adjacent field,—your father & mother, your debts & credits, & your web of habits are the very best basis of poetry, & the material which you must work up. Dante knew how to throw the weight of his body into each act, and is, like Byron, Burke, & Carlyle, the Rhetorician. I find him full of the *nobil volgare eloquenza*; that he knows "God damn", & can be rowdy if he please, & he does please. Yet is not Dante reason or illumination & that essence we were looking for, but only a new exhibition of the possibilities of genius. Here is an imagination that rivals in closeness & precision the senses. But we must prize him as we do a rainbow, we can appropriate nothing of him. Could we some day admit into our oyster heads the immense figure which these flagrant points compose when united, the hands of Phidias, the conclusion of Newton, the pantheism of Goethe, the all wise music of Shakspeare, the robust eyes of Swedenborg!

—

In the summersaults, spells & resurrections wrought by the imagination a central power which seems to infuse a certain volatility & intoxication into all nature. Yet is that too only an arm or weapon of an interior energy precursor of the Reason. I think Hindoo books excellent gymnastic for the mind as showing treatment. All European libraries might almost be read without the swing of this gigantic arm of the mind being suspected. But those orientals deal with worlds & pebbles very freely.

Passion is logical; and I note that the vine, symbol of the Bacchus which intoxicates the world, is the most geometrical & tractable of all plants.

	1	Cheap Press
The Times.	2	Natural Science
	3	No prayer

The cheap press & the universal reading, which have come in together, have caused a great many translations to be made from the Greek, the German, the Italian, & the French. Bohn's Library now furnishes me with a new & portable Plato, as it had already done with new Goethes. And John Carlyle translates Dante. To me the command is loud to use the time by reading these books. And I should as soon think of foregoing the railroad & the telegraph, as to neglect these. With these belong the Mediaeval Chronicles,—Richard of Devizes, Asser's Life of Alfred, & the rest in Bohn.

A feature of the times is this, that when I was born, private & family prayer was in the use of all well-bred people, & now it is not known.

Another feature of the Age is the paramount place of Natural History.

—

What presents shall we give?

Camera obscura Writing desk, at 6.00, for sale at E. Stearns's 30 Washington St

a pistol—
a paperknife—

a hand to hold papers. bronze
a framed print

shells at Warren's
Compass
microscope
Silver fruit knives, that shut like penknives
a lamp
a basket
a stereoscope
a pair of steps
a mustardpot
a padlock
a burned or branded bracket

The dime-gifts, as, the needlethreader, the cent ring, the pencil-cutter, the pen-maker,

Aeolian harp

—

Mr H. G. Otis said, "that it was of no use to tie up a woman's property; by kissing or kicking, her husband would get it away from her."

—

The houses in Acton seemed to be filled with fat old people who looked like old tomatos, their faces crumpled into red collops, fatting & rotting at their ease.

—

29 August. A long sad strange dream last night in which I carried E. to Naples & lost her.

We are struck if a more powerful & swifter horse than ordinary goes by. A man is not allowed to be so very clever as to browbeat or outwit all other men. No giants. Nature has made up her mind on this point, & is republican in her politics. If he have a transcendent talent, it draws so lavishly on his forces as to lame him.

Love is the bright foreigner, the foreign self.

—

Parker thinks, that, to know Plato, you must read Plato thoroughly, & his commentators, &, I think, Parker would require a good drill in Greek history too. I have no objection to hear this urged on any but a Platonist. But when erudition is insisted on to Herbert or Henry More, I hear it as if to know the tree you should make me eat all the apples. It is not granted to one man to express himself adequately more than a few times: and I believe fully, in spite of sneers, in interpreting the French Revolution by anecdotes, though not every diner out can do it. To know the flavor of tanzy, must I eat all the tanzy that grows by the Wall? When I asked Mr Thom in Liverpool—who is Gilfillan? & who is MacCandlish? he began at the settlement of the Scotch Kirk in 1300 ? & came down with the history to 1848, that I might understand what was Gilfillan, or what was Edin. Review &c &c. But if a man cannot answer me in ten words, he is not wise.

Plato's vision is not illimitable, but it is not self limited by its own obliquity, or by fogs & walls which its own vices create.

Plato is to mankind what Paris or London is to Europe. Europe concentrates itself into a capital. He has not seen Europe, who has not seen its cities. Plato codifies & catalogues & distributes. In his broad daylight things reappear as they stood in the sunlight, hardly shorn of a ray, yet now portable & reportable.
Before, all things stood enchanted,—not tangible. He comes, & touches them, & henceforth anybody may.

—

4 September, 1849. Dante's imagination is the nearest to hands & feet that we have seen. He clasps the thought as if it were a tree or a stone, & describes it as mathematically. I remember I found Page the painter modelling his figures in clay, (Ruth & Naomi), before he painted them on canvas. Dante, one would say, did the same thing before he wrote the verses.

It is true that Webster has never done any thing up to the promise of his faculties. He is unmistakeably able, & might have ruled America, but he was cowardly, & has spent his life on specialties. When shall we see as rich a vase again! Napoleon, on the other hemisphere, obeyed his instincts with a fine audacity, dared all, went up to his line, & over his line, found himself confronted by Destiny, & yielded at last.

I have many metres of men, one is, their perception of identity. 'Tis a good mark of any genius—a single novel expression of the identity. Thus Lord Brooke's

> "So words should sparks be of those fires they strike"

or Donne's

> "That one would almost say her body thought."

I hold that ecstasy will be found mechanical, if you please to say so, or, nothing but an example on a higher field of the same gentle gravitation by which rivers run.

Experience identifies. Shakspeare seems to you miraculous. But these wonderful juxtapositions, parallelisms, transfers, which his genius effected were all to him mechanical also, & the mode precisely as conceivable & familiar as the index-making of the literary hack is to him. The result of Mr Hack is inconceivable also to the Printer's Devil who waits for it. So that Walter Scott,—I think it was,—who defined Genius as Perseverance. And Newton said, "By always intending my mind."

Rhymes

The iterations or rhymes of nature are already an idea or principle of science, & a guide. The sun & star reflect themselves all over the world in the form of flowers & fruits & in the human head & the doctrine of series which takes up again the few functions & modes & repeats them with new & wondrous result on a higher plane. What rhymes are these which Oken or Agassiz show, in making the head only a new man on the shoulders of the old, the spine doubled over & putting out once more its hands & feet, the upper jaw being the hands, the lower jaw the feet; & the teeth being fingers & toes respectively. This too only leads on the anatomist to the anatomy of the Understanding, which is the material body of the mind, whilst Reason is its soul; and the law of Generation is constant, & repeats on the higher plane of intellect every fact in the animal. The true Economy of man, then, is always to prefer spending on the higher plane; always to invest & invest, with holy avarice, that he may spend in spiritual creation & not in begetting animals.

Then, as I have written before, Astronomy is not yet astronomy, until it is applied to human life; & all our things are to be thus exalted or echoed & reechoed in finer & higher rhymes.

The snake or the span-worm is the horizontal spine. Man is the erect spine. Between these two lines which form a quadrant, all beings find their place. Body of man is a spine with appendages which are new spines. On its top the upper vertebra transforms itself into a new spine bending over like a span-worm & constituting a skull. Within that in a new & higher plane the same thing repeats itself.

I think it as much a disease to be silenced when I do not wish it, as to have the measles when I do not wish it.

How difficult to deal erect with the Days! Each of these events which they bring,—this Concord thieving, the muster, the ripening of plums, the shingling of the barn, all throw dust in your eyes, & distract your attention. He is a strong man who can look them in the eye, see through this superficial juggle, feel their identity & keep his own; know surely that one will be like another to the end of the world, nor permit bridal or funeral, earthquake or church, election or revolution to draw him from his task.

1849

Garden Diary Aug. 15 Apricot plums

September 7 We are so late this year that I picked the first muskmelons today—four;—today the first ripe tomato; and all the Bartlett pears to ripen in the house.

The whole product of my Bartlett at the corner of the garden might count 45 pears.

The gages yield every day a supply, and the two purple plumtrees.

Today, too, we dig seven bushels of excellent chenangoes.

12th. Today Tomatoes for the first time on table.

September is the month of melons
melons last with us till 15th October.
I think the Seckle pears should hang on the tree till 15 September. or 20th

—

True Bramin in the morning meadows wet
Expound the Vedas of the violet
Or hid in vines peeping thro' many a loop
See my plums redden & my beurrés stoop

Representative

It is my belief that every animal in our scale of creatures leans upward on man, & man leans downward on it; that lynx, dog, tapir, lion, lizard, camel, & crocodile, all find their perfection in him; all add a support & some essential contribution to him. He is the grand lion, he the grand lynx, he the grand worm; the fish of fishes, & bird of birds, so that if one of these tribes were struck out of being he would lose some one property of his nature. And I have no doubt that to each of these creatures Man appears as of its own kind; to a lion, man appears the archlion; to a stork, the archstork. He is the masterkey for which you must go back, to open each new door in this thousand gated Thebes.

—

An individual body is the momentary fixation of a portion of the solids or fluids of the universe, which, after performing compulsory duty to this enchanted statue, are released, & again flow in the currents of the world. An individual soul, in like manner, is a fixation or momentary eddy in which certain affections, sciences, & powers of immaterial Force are taken up, & work & minister, in petty circles & localities, & then, being released, return to the Unbounded Soul of the World. The tenacity of retention must be in exact proportion to the rank of the idea which the individual represents. So a fixed idea is the unit of this.

In dreams, last night, a certain instructive race-horse was quite elaborately shown off, which seemed marvellously constructed for violent running, & so mighty to go, that he stood up continually on his hind feet in impatience & triumphant power. But my admiration was checked by some one's remarking behind me, that, "in New York they could not get up the smallest plate for him." Then I noticed, for the first time, that he was a show-horse, & had wasted all the time in this rearing on the hind legs, & had not run forward at all. I hope they did not mean to be personal.

> "And that we may know all things that all men know, speech is given us; also the memory of the past; & perpetual experience: wonders too familiar, & too closely environing us, to allow us to wonder at them."
>
> Swedenborg
> E.A.K. II, 312.

Swedenborg Shakspeare

Some minds are viviparous like Shakspeare & Goethe. Every word is a poem. Others are oviparous, alive though incomplete; and others are like trees which leave seeds & fruits on which the living can feed.

It is strange that Swedenborg is never lyric; never a sweet sound; no muse ever breathed in all that vast architecture. 'Tis a kind of Petra, a city of the dead, a palace of catacombs. I find his exclamations those of a country parson.

—

Aunt Mary never liked to throw away any medicine; but, if she found a drop of laudanum here, & a pill or two there, a little quinine & a little antimony, mixed them up & swallowed them. So when she came to the tea-table—"O, no, she never took tea;"—"Can you get a little shells?" The cocoa came, & Aunty took cocoa, because it was soothing, & put a little tea in it to make her lively, & if there was a little coffee, that was good for getting rid of the taste.

—

Well, now it seems as if this Plato's power of grading or ranking all that offers itself at sight was as good as a duration of a thousand years. The reason why life is short, is, because we are confounded by the dazzle of new things, & by the seeming equality which custom sheds on great & small; & we are obliged to spend a large part of life in corrections which we should save, if our judgment was sure when we first beheld things. Plato is like those Tamers who have charmed down the ferocity of vicious animals, or who by some virulence or ferocity in their own nature have terrified frantic madmen. He looks through things at a glance, & they fly into place. & he walks in life with the security of a god. It seems as if the winds of ages swept through this universal thinking, so wide, so just, yet so minute, that it is impossible that an air of such calmness & long maturity can belong to the hasty, crude, experimental blotting of one lifetime.

Art

I read in Ellery Channing's manuscript,—"He who is not naturally great, may acquire some taste for this style by art."

Some minds are incapable of skepticism; the doubts they profess to entertain are rather a civility or accommodation to the common language of their company & of society. But they have no valves of interruption: the blood of the Universe rolls at all times through their veins without impediment. Others there are to whom the heaven is brass, & perhaps it shuts down for them to the very surface of the earth.

Dr Patten of New York was challenged to continue the verses in the Primer;—In Adam's Fall
We sinned all.

Dr Patten proceeded; In Cain's murder,
We sinned furder.
In Tubal Cain,
We sinned again.

Dr Ashbel Green In Doctor Green,
Our sin is seen.

A was nettled at railroads & telegraphs. He thought with impatience, that if those jobs were once done & ended, the intellect of America could be won to some worthy occupation, as Goldsmith did not like to hear a pretty woman praised.

—

Today, carpets; yesterday, the aunts; the day before, the funeral of poor S; & every day, the remembrance in the library of the rope of work which I must spin;—in this way life is dragged down & confuted. We try to listen to the hymn of gods, & must needs hear this perpetual cock-a-doodle-doo, & ke-tar-kut, right under the library windows. They the gods ought to respect a life, you say, whose objects are their own: But steadily they throw mud & eggs at us, roll us in the dirt, & jump on us.

Solitary Imprisonment is written on his coat & hat, on the lines of his face, & the limbs of his body, on his brow, & on the leaves of laurel on his brow. He wrestles hard with the judge, & does not believe he is in earnest. "Solitary Imprisonment," replies the Judge. Yet with some mitigation. Three times a day his keeper comes to the window, & puts bread & water on the shelf. The keeper's dog he may play with, if he will. Bow-wow-wow, says the dog. People may come from Asia to see him, if they like. He is only permitted to become his own friend.

M.M.E.

When E. H. was at Waterford, & had gone out to walk in the woods with Hannah, Aunt Mary feared they were lost, & found a man in the next house & begged him to go & look for them. The man went & returned, saying, that he could not see them. Go & cry "Elizabeth." The man rather declined this service, as he did not know her. Aunt Mary was highly offended, & exclaimed, "God has given you a voice that you might use it in the service of your fellow creatures. Go instantly, & call 'Elizabeth,' 'till you find them." The man went immediately, & did as he was bid, &, having found them, apologised for calling thus, by telling what Miss Emerson said to him.

For good reading, there must be, of course, a yielding, sometimes entire, but always some yielding to the book. Then the reader is refreshed with a new atmosphere & foreign habits. But many minds are incapable of any surrender; they are like knights of a Border Castle, who

> "Carve at the meal
> In gloves of steel,
> And drink the red wine thro the helmet barred."

&, of course, their dining is very unsatisfactory. How admirable a University is Plato's *Republic*; yet set P. to read it, he would read nothing in it but P.

In the conduct of life, let us not parade our rags, let us not, moved by vanity, confess, & tear our hair, at the corners of streets, or in the sitting room; but, as age & infirmity steal on us, contentedly resign the front seat & the games to these bright children, our better representatives, nor expect compliments or inquiries,—much less, gifts or love—any longer, (which to expect is ridiculous,) and, not at all wondering why our friends do not come to us, much more wondering when they do,—decently withdraw ourselves into modest & solitary resignation & rest.

—

Macaulay again

Macaulay's History is full of low merits: it is like English manufactures of all kinds, neat, convenient, portable, saleable, made on purpose for the Harpers to print a hundred thousand copies of. So far can Birmingham go.

Macaulay is the Banvard of English history, good at drawing a Missisippi Panorama, but 'tis cheap work. No memorable line has he written, no sentence. He is remembered by flippancy on one occasion against Plato & Bacon, but has no affirmative talent: he can write quantities of verses, too, to order, wrote "Lays," or something. No doubt wrote good nonsense verses at Eton, better than Virgil. His chef d'oeuvre was a riddle on the Cod-fish. That was really good.

—

Charles Newcomb came, but we grow incapable of events & influences. He too turns the conversation, if I try a general remark. His MSS, which he brought, were six years old, but full of subtle genius. Intense solitude appears in every sentence. They are soliloquies, & the abridged stenographic wit & eloquence, like that or better than that we are wonted to in M.M.E. He is a Bramin existing to little use, if prayer & beauty are not that. Yet he humiliates the proud & staggers the dogmatist, & subverts all the mounds & fortification lines of accustomed thought, eminently aristocratic beyond any person I remember to have met, because self centred on a deep centre of genius,—easy, cheerful, condescending, condescending to the greatest, & mortifying Plato & Jesus, if it were possible, by his genuine preference of children, & ladies, & the first piece of nature, to all their fame & sanctity. If one's centrality is incomprehensible to us, we can do nothing with him. We may as well affect to snub the sun. One will shine as the other. But though C.'s mind is unfounded, & the walls actually taken out, so that he seems open to nature, yet he does not accumulate his wisdom into any amounts of thought: rarely arrives at a result,—perhaps does not care to, so that I say, it seems as if instead of my bare walls your surrounding is really landscapes & perspectives of temples: yet they avail no more to you than if they were landscape-paper-hangings or fresco pictures of temples.

—

Yet it is very true, as Napoleon said, that you must not fight too often with one enemy, or you will teach him all your art of war. Talk with Alcott, or Very, or Carlyle, or Newcomb, & you quickly come to their talent, new eyes bud in your brow, & you see what they see.

C.K.N

C N had a fine subtlety like this, "that, it is not what the thought is, but how he stands to his thought, that we value in friendship."

> "Spiritual persons have an unactual effect by their dependence on the spiritual nature in them. They are only

as it is & their outward position is from action for their deeper nature."

"A deep & delicate person is apt to shun strangers, because knowing them so readily, they come in suddenly upon him, & are near him as fellow natures, while he does not recognise them as congenial ones, or as of the same sphere. & he sees commonness of life, without the identity of nature underneath: for, it is how men are to their thought, not what thought they have, which makes friendship." *C.K. Newcomb.*

Shakspeare was the farthest bound of subtlety & universality compatible with individuality; the subtilest of authors, and only just within the possibility of authorship. C.K.N. is my best key to him, & he is just beyond authorship.—The impartiality of Shakspeare is like that of the light itself, which is no aristocrat, but shines as mellowly on gipsies as on emperors, on bride & corpse, on city & swamp.

"I believe that there is no true theory of disease that does not at once suggest cure." Wilkinson.

Mrs R. suggests that *cholera* is a signal of new life forming, as always death & life are observed to be convertible in nature. The decomposition of the potato or pear is the composition & flourishing of plants not less necessary to Nature in her inscrutable laboratories.

Bigendians	*Littleendians*
Plato	Alcott
Swedenborg	Very
Shakspere	Newcomb
Montaigne	Channing
Goethe	RWE
Napoleon	Thoreau

—

I supposed the landscape to be full of a race of Daemons who move at a faster rate than men,—so fast as just to escape our organ of sight.

—

The children say, "Don't you know how we used to," &c with alarming quickness.

Michel Angelo paints with more will; Raffaelle, with the obedience of water & flame. Every body would paint like Raffaelle, if the power of painting were added to everybody.

Two or three things I have just now observed of Swedenborg. That his distinction of shunning evils as sins is a pounding or preaching distinction, or snuffle. That his Inferno is mesmeric, and, as in dreams we scratch the ground like dogs, grope, watch, & sneak about the stable yards & leavings of creation, imbeciles, underlings, &, when we wake up, do stand erect on our feet, aiming from year to year to be decent & honest people, so is it here; his Spiritual World bears the same relation to the generosities & joys of truth as bad dreams do to each man's ideal life. His whole book is libellous & mere undigested potato.

Swedenborg

He does not know what evil is, or what good is, who thinks any ground remains to be occupied after saying that evil is to be shunned as evil. One man, you say, dreads erysipelas. Show him, then, that this dread is evil: or one dreads hell; show him that *dread* is evil. He who loves goodness, harbours angels, reverences reverence, & lives with God.

Once more, as I have somewhere written, he who addresses himself to modes or wants that can be dispensed with, goes out of fashion, builds his house off the road. But he who addresses himself to problems that every man must come to solve, builds his house on the road, & every man must come to it. Jesus's problems are mine, & therefore to Jesus & through Jesus must we go, & Swedenborg had the like wisdom. Swedenborg is the poet of the spine.

—

Swedenborg strange, scholastic, didactic, passionless, bloodless, fishy man, who describes classes of souls as a botanist would a carex, or shall I say geologizes hells as a stratum of chalk or hornblende. He goes up & down the world of men a

sort of Rhadamanthus in gold-headed cane & peruke, & with the utmost disengagedness & air of a referee distributes souls. The warm many-weathered passionate peopled world is to him only a grammar of hieroglyphs, or an emblematic free-mason's procession. Jacob Behmen how different! he is tremulous with emotion, & listens awestruck with the gentlest humanity, to the Teacher whose lessons he conveys; & when he explains that "love is greater than God," his heart beats so high that the thumping against his leathern coat is audible across the centuries. This makes the greatest difference in their effect. Behmen is healthily & beautifully wise, notwithstanding the mystical narrowness & incommunicableness. Swedenborg is disagreeably wise, and for all his worlds I would not be he.
His Inferno too affects me as when a delicate young girl falls into lunacy, & instantly falls to cursing & swearing & polluting her lips with profane & obscene speech.

He is so painful that I should break with him forever but that I find him really scientific.

Of all Englishmen, Wilkinson seems fittest by his learned & imaginative style, by breadth & vigour to introduce Swedenborg to his countrymen, & to this century. It is wonderful that his books have not yet startled the sleep of the contemplative power in England.

This reappearance after a century of Swedenborg in his pupil is a more startling fact in psychology than any of his Revelations.

In heaven, when a man wants a horse, a horse wants a man.

Symbolism
What I want to know, is, the meaning of what I do; believing that any of my current Mondays or Tuesdays is bible for me; & believing that hints & telegraphic signals are arriving to me every moment out of the interior eternity, I am tormented with impatience to make them out. We meet people who seem to overlook our game, & read us with a smile, but they do not tell us what they read.

*

This is one kind of Symbolism. A more limited one is Swedenborg's fancy that certain books of Scripture were exact allegories or written in the angelic & ecstatic speech, as other books are not.

Of what corn was his bread made? Of what bread had he eaten?

Swedenborg was apt for cosmology because of that native perception of identity, which made magnitude of no account to him. In the atom of magnetic iron he instantly saw the quality which would generate the spiral motion of suns & planets.

The style of his philosophic works is lustrous with points & shooting spicula of thought & reminds me of one of those frosty winter mornings when the air is sparkling with crystals.

For the skeptic, Yes, we may give ourselves what allowance we will, for, once admitted to the heaven of thought, I see no return to Night, but infinite invitation on the other side. Heaven is within heaven, sky over sky, and we are encompassed with divinities. To what purpose dark ages & barbarous Irish, if I know, as I know, five or six men, without hardly going out of my village, to whom & with whom all is possible; who restore to me Plato, Shakspeare, Montaigne, Hindoo cosmology, yea Buddh himself with their audacious intellectual adventure. We are as elastic as the gas of gunpowder, & small & tame as we walk here with our hands in our pockets, an imaginative book sets free our fancy, and in a moment our head is bathed in the Galaxy, & our feet tread on the hells.
Our Indeterminate Size is the delicious secret which books of imagination reveal to us.
O endless ends, o living child! how can you fail! to you I open the ill kept secret that you are Hari, divine & invincible,—cousin to the four elements & the four hundred gods. You were concealed in an egg for thirty millenniums, then born on the side of a brook, confided to a shepherd who brought you up in a shanty, but your enemies have no longer power. It is time you should show yourself, fate is in your eye. You will yet

be a horse, a lizard, a dragonfly, & a swamp full of alligators, but time & space are cheap to you, Hari; you can afford to be multiplied & divided, to bite & to be bitten, to be a bankrupt tradesman, or an acre of Sand; divided you will reunite, & you thrive by dying; do not care o Hari for the speech of men, do not care for a shabby appearance!

from

AZ

1849–1850

They told Edmund Kean, the boxes applauded: "The boxes! a fig for the boxes! *the Pit rose to me*," he replied.

1849
November 17. Yesterday saw the fields covered with cobwebs in every direction, on which the wake of the setting sun appeared as on water. Walked over hill & dale with Channing, who found wonders of colour & landscape everywhere, but complained of the want of invention. "Why, they had frozen water last year; why should they do it again? Therefore it was so easy to be an artist, because *they* do the same thing always, & therefore he only wants time to make him perfect in the imitation. And I believe, too, that *pounding* is one of the secrets." C. thought the cause of cows was, that they made good walking where they fed. All summer, he gets water *au naturel*, and, in winter, *they* serve it up *artistically* in this crystal johnny-cake; and he had observed the same thing at the confectioners' shops, that he could never get but one thing there, though they had two ways of making it up.

—

The world, the universe, is a gigantic flower,—but the flower is one function or state of the plant, and the world but a stage or state of the Pan. As I have written long ago, the Universe is only in transit, or, we behold it shooting the gulf from the past to the future.

A.B.A. is like a slate-pencil which has a sponge tied to the other end, and, as the point of the pencil draws lines, the sponge follows as fast, & erases them. He talks high & wide, & expresses himself very happily, and forgets all he has said. If a Skilful operator could introduce a lancet & sever the sponge, ABA would be the prince of writers.

J's vanity is like a bad sleeper who again & again loses himself in reveries but reappears to his own dismay & the general injury, & cannot die.

I envied a young man in the cars who when his companion told him they had arrived at Waltham, by Massasoit House, was asleep, & his friend shook him, lifted him up, & called in his ear, in vain, he could not wake him, & the cars went on again to the next station before he could be fully aroused. Then I came home & counted every hour the clock struck all night.

Goethe

Nature told everything once.

Angel song & chorus at opening of Faust is magazine or "*squirt*" poetry.

Goethe as a man who wished to make the most of himself was right in avoiding the horrors.

To describe adequately is the high power & one of the highest enjoyments of man.

She was beautiful & he fell in love with her. The thing has happened to millions, yet how few can tell the story. Try some of them, set them at the painting; each knows it all & can communicate nothing. Then comes Shakspeare, & tells it point for point as it befel, or better; and now we have two things, Love & literature.

—

Many after thoughts, as usual, with my printing, come just a little too late; & my new book seems to lose all value from their omission. Plainly one is the justice that should have been done to the unexpressed greatness of the common farmer & labourer. A hundred times I have felt the superiority of George, & Edmund, & Barrows, & yet I continue the parrot echoes of the names of literary notabilities & mediocrities, which, bring them (if they dared,) into presence of these Concord & Plymouth Norsemen, would be as uncomfortable & ridiculous as mice before cats. I believe, when I hear people celebrating a particular sunset, that every day is the finest day in the year:

For, the same elements, & all elements, are always present, only sometimes, these conspicuous; & sometimes, those; what was, yesterday, foreground, being today background; what was surface, playing now a not less effective part as basis.
So it is rare to have the hero & professor united as in Montaigne. Or, I might say, churl & professor. I value Hyde & Therien because Mr Ticknor would shrivel in their presence, they solid & unexpressed, he expressed into gold leaf. And yet the whole human race agree to value a man precisely in proportion to his power of expression, & to the most expressive man that has existed, namely Shakspeare, they have awarded the highest place.

—

14 December. Every day shows a new thing to veteran walkers. Yesterday reflections of trees in the ice; snowflakes, perfect rowels, on the ice; beautiful groups of icicles all along the eastern shore of Flint's Pond, in which, especially where encrusting the bough of a tree, you have the union of the most flowing with the most fixed. Ellery all the way squandering his jewels as if they were icicles, sometimes not comprehended by me, sometimes not heard. How many days can Methusalem go abroad & see somewhat new? When will he have counted the changes of the kaleidoscope?

FARMERS

When I see one of our young farmers in Sunday clothes, I feel the greatest respect for & joy in them, because I know what powers & utilities are so meekly worn. What I wish to know they know, what I would so gladly do, they can do. The cold gloomy day, the rough rocky pasture, the swamp, are invitations & opportunities to them. And yet there is no arrogance in their bearing, but a perfect gentleness, though they know how to take care of cattle, how to raise & cure & keep their crops. Why a writer should be vain, & a farmer not, though the writer admires the farmer, & the farmer does not admire the writer, does not appear.

Japanning.

The Englishman is finished like a sea-shell. After the spines & convolutions are all formed, or, with the formation, the hard enamel varnishes every part. Pope, Swift, Johnson, Gibbon, Goldsmith, Gray. We get good men sometimes in this country; but Everett & Irving are the only persons I think of who have pretensions to finish, & their enamel will not rival the British. It seems an indemnity to the Briton for his precocious maturity. He has no generous daring in this age; the Platonism died in the Elizabethan; he is shut up in French limits; the practical & the comfortable oppress him with inexorable claims, so that the smallest fraction of power remains disposable for poetry. But Birmingham comes in, & says, 'Never mind; I have some patent lustre that defies criticism'; and Moore made his whole fabric of the "lustre," & Tennyson supplied defects with it. Only Wordsworth bought none.

—

Rich & Poor.

The rich man has 1200 acres of land; the poor man has the universe, and much has he to say of it.—But when he, too, comes to hold 1200 acres, we never hear any more about the Universe.

Like the New England soil, my talent is good only whilst I work it. If I cease to task myself, I have no thoughts. This is a poor sterile Yankeeism. What I admire & love is the generous spontaneous soil which flowers & fruits at all seasons.

Superlative.

People like exaggerated event, & activity,—like to run to a house on fire, to a murder, an execution;—like to tell of a bankruptcy, of a death, of a crime, or of an engagement. They like a rattling town, where a great deal of business is done. The student shuns all this. Mr Pickens "would go to the Church when the *interesting Sundays* were *over*."

They like to be in a state of exaggeration. Of course, manly greatness consists in being so much that the mere wash of the sea, the observed passage of the stars, or the *almost heard* current of Time, is event enough, & the full soul cries, Let not the noise of what you call events disturb me!

—

Eddy reads his fairy tales by the help of his memory, (having heard them read by Ellen) as the ostrich runs by help of his wings.

—

I have entirely omitted to record L.'s exquisite plot for the edification of the expressman. "How much will you do an errand for?" *Expressman.* "Nine pence if it do not take extra time, and I do not need to go in my wagon." *L.* "Excellent! Well, I want you to go to the Thursday Lecture in Chauncy Place: go about 11:30, when the sermon begins, & you need not stay longer than you would wait sometimes for an answer, & do you bring me home the text, & as much as you can remember of the sermon. You will not need your wagon, & I will pay you ninepence."

—

Music Eloquence

Chladni's experiment seems to me central. He strewed sand on glass, & then struck the glass with tuneful accords, & the sand assumed symmetrical figures. With discords the sand was thrown about amorphously. It seems, then, that Orpheus is no fable: You have only to sing, and the rocks will crystallize; sing, and the plant will organize; sing, & the animal will be born.

Cat & mouse, hawk & hen, Austrian emperor & Hungarian serf, eater & eaten, Poverty & genius,—I see but one sad fact

—

The Times newspaper attracts the American in London more & more, until at last he wonders that it does not more pique the curiosity of the English themselves. They all repeat what it says; it is their own understanding & day's ideal daguerrotyped. Yet they know nothing about it. He never sees any person capable of writing these powerful paragraphs: and, though he hears up & down in society now & then some anecdote of a Mr Bailey or Mr Moseley who sent his paper to the Times, & received in return twenty guineas, with a request that he would write again, & so, that he did, in due time, become one of the Staff of the Journal,—yet one never hears among well informed men as Milnes, Carlyle, Helps, Gregg, Forster, any accounts of this potentate at all adequate to the fact.

They may well affect not to know or care who wrote it, at the moment when I observe that all they know or say, they read in it.

—

At Attleborough the jewellers say, art does much, but luck does more; yet they believe that art may yet beat luck. They say sometimes the devil is in the gold, and it will not be malleable. They point in the boiling crucible to a point of light darting about like electricity & as long as that stays there, it will not be malleable. This is specially true of California gold, which cracks when worked up into small bars, & rolled into rings.

—

The two statements or Bipolarity.

My geometry cannot span the extreme points which I see. I affirm melioration,—which nature teaches, in pears, in the domesticated animals, and in her secular geology, & this development of complex races. I affirm also the self-equality of nature; or, that only that is true which is always true; and, that, in California, or in Greece, or in Jewry, or in Arcadia, existed the same amounts of private power, as now, & the same deductions, however differently distributed. But I cannot reconcile these two statements. I affirm the sacredness of the individual, the infinite reliance that may be put on his determination. I see also the benefits of cities, and the plausibility of phalansteries. But I cannot reconcile these oppositions. I affirm the divinity of man; but, as I know well how much is my debt to bread, & coffee, & flannel, & heated room,—I shun to be Tartuffe, & do affirm also with emphasis the value of these fomentations. But I cannot reconcile that absolute with this conditional. My ancient Companion in Charleston, S.C. Mr Martin Luther Hurlbut, used to reply to each statement of mine, "Yes, to a certain extent."—

—

Love is temporary & ends with marriage. Marriage is the perfection which love aimed at, ignorant of what it sought. Marriage is a good known only to the parties. A relation of perfect understanding, aid, contentment, possession of themselves & of the world,—which dwarfs love to green fruit.

—

The English journals snub my new book; as indeed they have all its foregoers. Only now they say, that this has less vigour & originality than the others. Where then was the degree of merit that entitled my books to their notice? They have never admitted the claims of either of them. The fate of my books is like the impression of my face. My acquaintances, as long back as I can remember, have always said, "Seems to me you look a little thinner than when I saw you last."

The Times

At Alcott's conversation each person who opened his lips seemed in snuffing the air to snuff nitrous oxide, & away he went—a spinning dervish,—pleasing himself, annoying the rest. A talent is a nuisance. Each rode his nag with devotion round the walls of the universe; I found no benefit in this jar & jangle. There was much ability & good meaning in the room, but some persons present who should not have been there, & these, like an east wind, checked every growth.

—

There is a curious shame in our faces. The age is convict, confessing, sits on the anxious benches.

We say there is no religion, no poetry, no heroism, no rage; death is unperfumed; age of debility; correctness; levity; of the looking-glass; not to be bruised by the bruisers, not to despond in cities, is a mark of merit.

But I hold that all the elements are ever co-present, that what is once true is always true; that Every day is the finest in the year. What was background once, is foreground now. You say, there is no religion now. 'Tis like saying, in rainy weather, there is no sun; when the rain is one of his superlative effects. Religion consists now in avoidance of forms it once created. All kinds of power usually develope at the same time.

Plainly, the Times make a great many people sick.

—

Samuel Hoar, Esq.

Mr Hoar is & remains an entire stranger all his life long, not only in his village, but in his family. He might bow & touch his hat to his wife & daughter as well as to the President. He does the same thing in politics & at the bar. It is not any new light that he sheds on the case, but his election of a side, & the giving his statuesque dignity to that side, that weighs with juries, or with conventions. For he does this naturally.

—

Superlative

The talent sucks the substance of the man. How often we repeat the disappointment of inferring general ability from conspicuous particular ability. But the accumulation on one point has drained the trunk. Blessed are those who have no talent! The expressors are the gods of the world,—Shakspeare & the rest, but the sane men whom these expressors revere, are the solid balanced undemonstrative citizens who make the reserved guard, the central sense of the world.

'Tis because he is not well mixed, that he needs to do some feat by way of fine or expiation.

I have never met a person superior to his talent; one who had money in his pocket, & did not use it.

Carlyle.

Carlyle is wonderful for his rhetorical skill. This trick of rhyme, burden, or refrain, which he uses so well, he not only employs in each new paragraph, suddenly treating you with the last ritornello, but in each new Essay or Book quoting the Burden or Chorus of the last book.—You know me, & I know you;—or,—Here we are again, come take me up again on your shoulders;—is the import of this. 'Tis curious, the magnificence of his genius, & the poverty of his aims. He draws his weapons from the skies, to fight the cause of some wretched English property or monopoly or prejudice or whim. A transcendental John Bull delighting in the music of Bow-bells, who cannot see across the channel, but has the skill to make divine oratorios in praise of the Strand, Kensington & Kew. I was to have said just now that he contrives in each piece to make out of his theme or lucky expression, a proverb before he has done; and this conclusion of the last is the exordium of the next Chapter.

He is no idealist in opinions. He is a protectionist in Political Economy, aristocrat in politics, epicure in diet, goes for slavery, murder, money, punishment by death, & all the pretty abominations, tempering them with epigrams.

—

It is not the least characteristic sign of the Times, that Alcott should have been able to collect such a good company of the best heads for two Monday Evenings, for the expressed purpose of discussing the Times. What was never done by human beings in another age, was done now; there they met to discuss their own breath, to speculate on their own navels, with eyeglass & solar microscope, and no man wondered at them. But these very men came in the cars by steam-ferry & locomotive to the meeting, & sympathized with engineers & Californians. Mad contradictions flavor all our dishes.

Putnam, Whipple, Dewey, W.H. Channing, & I,—and I know not how many more,—are lecturing this winter on the *Spirit of the Times*! And now Carlyle's first pamphlet is "The Present Age."

Commonsense *Eloquence*

Lord Mansfield's merit is like that of Plato, Montaigne, Sam Johnson, Socrates, & Shakspeare, namely, in his commonsense. Each of those decisions contains a level sentence or two, which hits the mark. His sentences are not finished outwardly, but are inwardly. His sentences are involved, but a solid proposition is set forth; a *true* distinction is drawn.—But Alcott can never finish a sentence, but revolves in spirals, until he is lost in air. And it is true that Johnson earned his fame. His reported conversation is up to his reputation.

—

Ellery C. thinks the merit of Irving's "Life of Goldsmith," is, that he has not had the egotism to put in a single new sentence. It is nothing but an agreeable repetition of Boswell, Johnson, & Company. And so Montaigne is good, because there is nothing that has not already been in books. A good book being a Damascus blade made by the welding of old nails & horseshoes. Every thing has seen service, & been proved by wear & tear in the world for centuries, & yet now the article is brand-new.

So Pope had but one good line, & that he got from Dryden, & therefore Pope is the best & only readable English poet.

*

The Age.

God flung into the world in these last ages two toys, a magnet, & a looking glass; and the children of men have occupied themselves wholly with one or the other, or with both. Swedenborg, Des Cartes, and all the philosophers both natural & moral turned themselves into magnets, & have not ceased to express in every way their sense of polarity;—Schelling, and the existing thinkers, most of all. The most unexpected splendid effects are produced by this principle, as a cone is generated by the revolution of a triangle.
Religions, philosophies, friendships, loves, poetries, literatures, are all hid in the horseshoe magnet. As galvanism, electricity, chemistry, light, heat, and LIFE & Thought, are at last only corollaries of this fruitful phenomenon.
A single example occurs for a thousand. Society disgusts and the poet resolves to go into retirement & indulge this great heart & feed his thought henceforwards with botany & astronomy.—Behold, on the instant, his appetites are exasperated: he wants dinners & concerts, scholars & fine women, theatre & club. And life consists in managing adroitly these antagonisms to intensate each other. Life must have continence & abandonment.

For the lookingglass, the effect was scarcely less. Poor dear Narcissus pines on the fountain side. Col. Fremont, on the Rocky Mountains, says, "*How we look*!" And all cities & all nations think what the English, what the French, what the Americans will say. Next, the trick of *philosophising* is inveterate, & reaches its height; and, last, *Symbolism* is the lookingglass raised to the highest power. I wrote above "what I want to know, is, the meaning of what I do; believing that any of my current Mondays or Tuesdays is Fatebook enough for me; believing that hints & telegraphic signals are arriving to me, every moment, out of the interior eternity, I am tormented with impatience to make them out."

Still one thing more occurred in yesterday's conversation,—old hobnails all, that may yet one day help to make a blade,—That, there are not one or two, but six or seven, nay, nineteen or twenty things, that must be considered & had. You wish & must have a good poise, self-equality, or the fine adjustment to the world that enables you to do something well, some piece of work to your own & the world's satisfaction. Very good: 'Tis a great blessing, to be humbly thankful for. Yes, but can you live with other people? Your work is done alone: But when you come into the street,—do you come entire?— —Yes.— Excellent; Then you have two things. But there are new relations; to Women; to cultivated Society; to the Economist; to the Great, to the leaders & to the ideas of the time. There is living for the day, and living for the whole; and all the merits it is impossible to combine.

Garrison is venerable in his plan, like the tart Luther; but he cannot understand anything you say, and neighs like a horse when you suggest a new consideration, as when I told him, that, the *fate*-element in the negro question he had never considered.

Eloquence

Eloquence is like money, of no use for the most part to those who have it, but inestimable it would be to such as have something to say. A course of mobs was recommended to me by N. P. Rogers to correct my quaintness & transcendentalism. And I might have found it as good for me, as the water cure for paralysed stomachs.

—

Abuse is a pledge that you are felt. If they praise you, you will work no revolution.

Language is a quite wonderful city, which we all help to build. But each word is like a work of nature, determined a thousand years ago, & not alterable. We confer & dispute, & settle the meaning so or so, but it remains what it was in spite of us. The word beats all the speakers & definers of it, & stands to their children what it stood to their fathers.

—

We practise our art in unsuspected ateliers.

As far as I know, the misfortune of New England is,—that the Southerner always beats us in Politics. And for this reason, that it comes at Washington to a game of personalities. The Southerner has personality, has temperament, has manners, persuasion, address & terror. The cold Yankee has wealth, numbers, intellect, material power of all sorts, but has not fire or firmness, & is coaxed & talked & bantered & shamed & scared, till he votes away the dominion of his millions at home. He never comes back quite the same man he went; but has been handled, tampered with. What is the remedy? Plainly I think, that we must borrow a hint from the military art. The Hungarians said, they could have easily beaten the Russians, if in any manner they could have made them run: but the Russian soldier is more afraid of his officers, than of the enemy: if he runs, he will assuredly be shot: if he fights, he has a chance of escape, and therefore he is cut down & butchered, but dares not run. So let our representative know that if he misrepresents his constituency there is no recovery from social damnation at home.

—

Intellect

Lagrange thought Newton fortunate in this, that the law of universal gravitation could be discovered but once, whilst the discoverer of Cape of Good Hope had a rival in the discoverer of Cape Horn, of Arctic Sea & land, in Antarctic Sea & land. And yet in metaphysics there is no terminus, & therefore no final discovery. Hegel, or Oken, or whosoever shall enunciate the law which necessitates gravitation as a phenomenon of a larger law, embracing mind & matter, diminishes Newton.

How many centres we have fondly found, which proved soon to be circumferential points! How many conversations or books seemed epochs, at the moment, which we have now actually forgotten!

Nat. History of Intellect must remember that all that is called genius, inspiration *par excellence*, though it appear to the auditor a miracle, is not that to the Poet or orator, but all these cunning juxtapositions, allusions, transitions, & symbols admit of being followed & explained by a snailish arithmetic after usual laws.

Cause & Effect forever!

—

Jane Eyre

In novels, the most serious questions are really discussed. What made the popularity of Jane Eyre but that a central question was answered in some sort. The question there answered will always be treated according to the habit of the party. A person of great breadth of individualism will answer it as Rochester does, as Cleopatra, as George Sand, as Milton does; magnifying the exception into a rule, dwarfing the world into an exception. A person of less courage, that is of less constitution, will answer it as Jane does, giving importance to Fate, to the conventionalism, to the actual state & doings of men & women.

—

Commonsense

I heard a good speech, & a bad one, yesterday, at the town school; one boy in the name of the school presented the master with an escritoire of rosewood, & some books, & made a long speech to him, in which I remember something about "our posterity" that is, the boys' posterity! Another boy, Tolman, in the name of his schoolmates also, presented a portfolio & a book to the assistant, Miss Buttrick, and said, "he only hoped that she would have as much pleasure in receiving it, as they had in giving it."

Eyes & No eyes.

In Nat. Hist of Intellect Goethe becomes a sample of an eye, for he sees the site of Rome, its unfitness, he sees the difference between Palermo & Naples; he sees rivers, & which way they run. Henry Thoreau, too. An advancing eye, that like the heavens journeys too & sojourns not.

The great man is the impressionable man, most irritable, most delicate, like iodine to light, so he feels the infinitesimal attractions. He obeys the main current, that is all his secret, the main current is so feeble a force as can be felt only by bodies delicately poised. He can orient himself. In the woods, I have one guide, namely, to follow the light,—to go where the woods are thinnest; then at last I am sure to come out. So he cannot be betrayed or misguided, for he knows where the

North is, knows painfully when he is going in the wrong direction.

Memory, Imagination, Reason, are only modes of the same power, as Lampblack & diamond are the same chemical matter in different arrangement.

—

He has the best sense whose sense is not good only for one particular thing, but, as Rose Flammock says of her father's, it is like his yardstick, which will measure dowlas & also cloth of gold. Shakspeare was like a looking glass carried through the street.

For no man wishes to be a scarlet feather. It is odious to be a jester, or a poet.
"I stamp in the mire with wooden shoes," said Madame de Stael, "When they would force me into the clouds."

"Did I not drum well?" said Mr Gray to somebody who taunted him with being a drummer's boy.

His face was so constantly varied by expression, that I could not get a single chance to see his face.

—

Beauty

Did one ever see a beautiful woman, & not wish to look again? Could one ever see enough of a beautiful woman?

Personality

The reason why the highwayman masters the traveller is not his pistol but his personality. If the party attacked had really the superiority in character & in love he could really conquer without arms. But he must be so charged & surcharged with love that he is as good a highwayman as the highwayman. You shall not match the pirate with a goody, but with a pirate (i.e. in natural force) & more determined & absolute by dint of his heart than the other by help of his arms.

Col. Forbes who served in Garibaldi's army, (Englishman) told me of his being stopped by brigands in the night in carriage in

Italy. He got out of the coach & walked up to them. What do you want? no answer. Do you want money? Yes. Their guns were aimed. He walked directly up to them & they drew up their guns. My good fellows you have made a mistake. We are soldiers sent by the government to Sienna. We have no money, not even to pay our fare or dinner. It is all paid by order of the government. I wish you better luck the next time. Get in, get in, (to his companions) & tied in the horses, & off with "addio, a rivederc."

—

Watson Haynes, the sailor, testifies that when he attempted to enlist the Clergy in his crusade against flogging in the navy, they replied, that their business was to preach the gospel, & not to interfere with the regulations of the navy.
And Webster thinks the gospel was to touch the heart, & not to abolish slavery.

Washington Allston, when he painted blue sky, begun as nature does, with a ground of deep black, & painted the light on that. And when he had occasion to paint a gem, he wrought on it as long as a lapidary.

—

I have made no note of these long weary absences at New York & Philadelphia. I am a bad traveller, & the hotels are mortifications to all sense of well being in me. The people who fill them oppress me with their excessive virility, and would soon become intolerable, if it were not for a few friends, who, like women, tempered the acrid mass. Henry James was true comfort,—wise, gentle, polished, with heroic manners, and a serenity like the sun.

The worst symptom I have noticed in our politics lately is the attempt to make a gibe out of Seward's appeal to a higher law than the Constitution, & Webster has taken part in it. I have seen him snubbed as "*Higher-law*-Seward." And now followed by Rufus Choate, in his phrase, "the trashy sentimentalism of our lutestring enthusiasts."

—

Lucretia Mott is the flower of Quakerism. That woman has a unity of sense, virtue, & good-meaning perfectly impressed on her countenance which are a guarantee of victory in all the fights to which her Quaker faith & connection lead her. She told exceedingly well the story of her contest with the mob at Dover & Smyrna in Delaware, she and the wife of Mr   attending him down to the place where the mob were to tar & feather him, & it was perfectly easy to see that she might safely go & would surely defend herself & him. No mob could remain a mob where she went. She brings domesticity & common sense, & that propriety which every man loves, directly into this hurly-burly, & makes every bully ashamed. Her courage is no merit, one almost says, where triumph is so sure.

D. *Webster.*

I think there was never an event half so painful occurred in Boston as the letter with 800 signatures to Webster. The siege of Boston was a day of glory. This was a day of petticoats, a day of imbecilities, the day of the old women La Veille. Many of the names very properly belong there,—they are the names of aged & infirm people, who have outlived everything but their night cap & their tea & toast. But I observe some names of men under forty! I observe that very few lawyers have set their names. They are a prudent race though not very fond of liberty.

D Webster

It seems 'tis now settled that men in Congress have no Opinions; that they may be had for any opinion, any purpose.

—

A bag of old copper coins. What can be more unpromising? And yet, being untied & poured out on the table, the company very soon became interested. Romulus & Remus suckled by the wolf were on one coin; *conservator*, with a warrior, and a goose by his side, on another; then Roman heads in a heroic style, and the sternness of the countenances, & the aquiline nose were remarkable.

The Elephantiasis or conceit, which destroys so many fine wits, as Brownson, Beecher, Mitchell, Jackson, & the rest, sends us back with new thankfulness to the Socratic wisdom, that the Pythian oracle pronounced him the wisest, because he knew that he knew nothing. It is an organic distinction of intellects. "In reality, he is truly wise, who knows that he is not truly wise." Proclus.

—

Thackeray's "Vanity Fair" is pathetic in its name, & in his use of the name; an admission it is from a man of fashion in the London of 1850, that poor old Puritan Bunyan was right in his perception of the London of 1650. And yet now in Thackeray is the added wisdom or skepticism, that, though this be really so, he must yet live in tolerance of, & practically in homage & obedience to these illusions.

And there is in the book an admission, too, which seems somewhat new in literature, akin to Froude's formula in the "Nemesis," that "moral deterioration follows on a diminished exchequer;" and State street thinks it is easy for a rich man to be honourable, but that, in failing circumstances, no man can be relied on to keep his integrity. And I felt in New York, that, from the habit of expense, the absence of religion, the absence of bonds, clanship, fellow-feeling of any kind, when a man or a woman is driven to the wall, there is less hope. It seemed as if Virtue was coming to be *a luxury which few could afford*, or "at a market almost too high for humanity", as Burke said of "all that class of the severe & restrictive virtues."

Is life coming to be a luxury which few could afford, or, as Burke said, "at a market almost too high for humanity?"

For egotism, the continent is not wide enough. Is it coffee, he said, or is it pure intellect, pure of love, that makes this desart where I go? The world is not big enough to hide me.

Betaubende. Men want wine, beer, & tobacco, to dull or stupefy a little the too tender papillae. The body is sore with the too quick & harsh impressions of nature. The edge of all objects must be taken off. Close the eyes partly; they are painfully wide open. Drop them to the floor, & do not see every ugly man that goes by.

*

It is the scholar's misfortune that his virtues are all on paper, & when the time comes to use them, he rubs his eyes & tries to remember what is it that he should do.

—

On Friday, 19 July, Margaret dies on rocks of Fire Island Beach within sight of & within 60 rods of the shore. To the last her country proves inhospitable to her; brave, eloquent, subtle, accomplished, devoted, constant soul! If nature availed in America to give birth to many such as she, freedom & honour & letters & art too were safe in this new world. She bound in the belt of her sympathy & friendship all whom I know & love, Elizabeth, Caroline, Ward, the Channings, Ellen Hooper, Charles K. N., Hedge, & Sarah Clarke. She knew more select people than any other person did & her death will interest more.

Yet her taste in music, painting, poetry, character, would not be on universal, but on idiosyncratic grounds, yet would be genuine. Then even the best people must have families, which they foolishly prefer.

She had a wonderful power of inspiring confidence & drawing out of people their last secret.

The timorous said, What shall we do? how shall she be received, now that she brings a husband & child home? But she had only to open her mouth, & a triumphant success awaited her. She would fast enough have disposed of the circumstances & the bystanders. For she had the impulse, & they wanted it. Here were already mothers waiting tediously for her coming, for the education of their daughters. Mrs Ripley thinks that the marriage with Ossoli was like that of De Stael in her widowhood with the young *De Rocca*, who was enamoured of her. And Mrs Barlow has an unshaken trust that what Margaret did, she could well defend.

Her love of art, like that of many, was only a confession of sympathy with the artist in the mute condemnation which his work gave to the deformity of our daily life; her co-perception with him of the eloquence of Form; her aspiration with him to a life altogether beautiful.

"Her heart, which few knew, was as great as her mind, which all knew"—what Jung Stilling said of Goethe, E.H. says of Margaret; and, that she was the largest woman; & not a woman who wished to be a man.

It is the charm of practical men, that, outside of all their practicality, is a certain poetry & play, as if they led this good war-horse "*Power*" by a bridle & preferred to walk, though they can ride so fiercely. Bonaparte is intellectual, as well as Caesar, so is Chadwick, & even seacaptains & railway-men have a gentleness when off duty.—A good natured admission that there are Illusions, & who shall say he is not their sport?

We distinguish what we call "the cast-iron-men," who cannot so detach themselves, as dragon-ridden, thunder-stricken, & fools of fate, with whatever powers endowed.

I have lost in her my audience. I hurry now to my work admonished that I have few days left. There should be a gathering of her friends & some Beethoven should play the dirge.

She poured a stream of amber over the endless store of private anecdotes, of bosom histories which her wonderful persuasion drew out of all to her. When I heard that a trunk of her correspondence had been found & opened, I felt what a panic would strike all her friends, for it was as if a clever reporter had got underneath a confessional & agreed to report all that transpired there in Wall street.

O yes "Margaret & her Friends" must be written, but not post haste. It is an essential line of American history

> "Yes that is an example of a destiny springing from Character"
>
> "I see your destiny hovering before you but it always escapes you"

Elizabeth Hoar quotes Mrs Barlow as saying, that Margaret never disappointed you. To any one whose confidence she had once drawn out, she was always faithful. She could (& she was alone in this) talk of persons & never gossip, for she had a fine instinct that kept her from any reality & from any effect of treachery. The fact is she had large sympathies.

Dr W.E. Channing said to her, "Miss Fuller, when I consider that you are all that Miss P— wished to be, and that you despise her, and that she loves and honors you, I think her place in Heaven must be very high."

Mrs Barlow has the superiority to say of Margaret, that the death seems to her a fit & good conclusion to the life. Her life was romantic & exceptional: So let her death be; it sets the seal on her marriage, avoids all questions of Society, all of employment, poverty, & old age, and besides was undoubtedly predetermined when the world was created.

Our no
Lidian says, that, in the fly-leaf of Margaret's bible, was written a Hymn of Novalis.—

She had great tenderness & sympathy, as M.M.E. has none. If M.M.E. finds out anything is dear & sacred to you, she instantly flings broken crockery at that.

"Nor custom stale
her infinite variety"

Elizabeth Hoar says of Margaret, Her friends were a necklace of diamonds about her neck. The confidences given her were their best, & she held them to them; that the honor of the Conversations was the high tone of sincerity & culture from so many consenting individuals, & that Margaret was the Keystone of the whole. She was perhaps impatient of complacency in people who thought they had claims, & stated their contrary opinion with an air. For such she had no mercy. But though not agreeable, it was just. And so her enemies were made.

—

A man of 45 does not want to open new accounts of friendship. He has said Kitty kitty long enough.

You look as if you had locked your trunk & lost the key.

A larger dialectic, I said, conveys a sense of power & feeling of terror before unknown, & H. T. said, "that a thought would destroy like the jet of a blowpipe most persons," & yet we apologise for the power, & bow to the persons. I want an electrical machine. Slumbering power we have, but not excited, collected, & discharged. If I should be honest, I should say, my exploring of life presents little or nothing of respectable event or action, or, in myself, of a personality. Too composite to offer a positive unity, but it is a recipiency, a percipiency. And I, & far weaker persons, if it were possible, than I, who pass for nothing but imbeciles, do yet affirm by their percipiency the presence & perfection of Law, as much as all the martyrs.

—

1850

Sept. 1. Yesterday took that secluded Marlboro road with W.E.C. in a wagon. Every rock was painted "Marlboro." & we proposed to take the longest day in the year, & ride to Marlboro,—that flying Italy. We went to Willis's Pond in Sudbury & paddled across it, & took a swim in its water, coloured like sugarbaker's molasses. Nature, E. thought, is less interesting. Yesterday Thoreau told me it was more so, & persons less. I think it must always combine with man. Life is ecstatical, & we radiate joy & honour & gloom on the days & landscapes we converse with.

But I must remember a real or imagined period in my youth, when they who spoke to me of nature, were religious, & made it so, & made it deep: now it is to the young sentimentalists frippery; & a milliner's shop has as much reason & worth.

At Latin School we found the longest word—honorificabilitudinibusque.

I have often observed the priority of music to thought in young writers. And last night remembered what fools a few sounding sentences made of me & my mates at Cambridge, as in Lee's & John Everett's Orations. How long we lived on "Licoo;"—on Moore's "Go where glory waits thee"; & Lalla Rookh; & "When shall the swan his death note singing."

I still remember a sentence in Carter Lee's oration, "And there was a band of heroes, & round their mountain was a wreath of light, & in the midst, on the mountain top, stood Liberty, feeding her eagle."

—

My Method

I write Metaphysics, but my method is purely expectant. It is not even tentative. Much less, am I ingenious in instituting *experimenta concis* to extort the secret, & lay bare the reluctant lurking law. No, I confine my ambition to true reporting, though I only get one new fact in a year.

This, of course, is a corollary of the doctrine of Inspiration. But the Scholar may have the mechanical advantage of posting his observations, & so discovering Neptune by three records in his day book.

—

The artist now should draw men together by praising nature, show them the joy of naturalists in famous Indian glens, —natural botanic gardens—in the profusion of new genera, that they could only relieve themselves by cries of joy; then the joy of the conchologist in his *helix pulcherrima*, whose elegant white pattern becomes invisible in water, visible again when dry. Let him unroll the earth & sky, & show the splendour of colour & of form: then let him, on the top of this delight, add a finer, by disclosing the secrets of intellectual law; tell them a secret that will drive them crazy; & things that require no system to make them pertinent, but make everything else impertinent. I think, give me the Memory to tell of, or the Imagination,—& I could win the ear of reasonable people, & make them think common daylight was worth something. Afterwards let him whisper in their ear the moral laws

> "more fair than heaven's broad pathway paved with
> stars
> Which Dion learned to measure with delight."

—

Jenny Lind need not go to California, California comes to her. Jenny Lind needs no police. Her voice is worth a hundred constables, & instantly silenced the uproar of the mob.

Manners

My prayer to women would be, when the bell rings, when visitors arrive, sit like statues.

I wrote that it is difficult to begin the culture too young. Mrs Barbauld said, they should never remember the time when they knew not the name of God, and a well born boy never did not know the names of the men of genius who are to be his escort & fraternity through life. But the young barbarians I see knew nothing but footballs until they went to Latin School & to College, & at Cambridge first learn the names of the Laureates, & use them, as country editors do, awkwardly & barbarously. George Sand has the same thing in view when she points at the defective education of women. They learn casually & irregularly, & are not systematically drilled from childhood to letters.

The Superlative. In the east, a war is as readily undertaken for an epigram or a distich, as in Europe for a duchy.
The reader of Hafiz would infer that all the food was either candy or wormwood.

I learn from the Indian Agent that the Indian is now as keen a money-catcher as the white man.

For the love of poetry, let it be remembered that my copy of Collins, after much search, was found smuggled away into the oven in the kitchen.

Oct. 24.

A ride yesterday to Marlborough, though projected for years, was no good use of the day. That town has a most rich appearance of rural plenty & comfort; ample farms, good houses, profusion of apples, pumpkins, &c. Yellow apple heaps in every enclosure, whole orchards left ungathered, &, in the Grecian piazzas of houses, pumpkins ripening between the columns. At Gates's, where Dr C. & Mr Jona. Phillips used to resort, they no longer keep a public house, closed it to the public last spring;—at Cutting's, though there were oats for the horse, there was no dinner for men,—so we repaired to the chestnut woods & an old orchard, for ours. Ellery, who is a perpetual holiday, & ought only to be used like an oroflamme or a garland for Maydays & Parliaments of wit & love, was no better today nor half so good as in some walks.

It is wonderful how fast in politics cabbages ripen to pomegranates. Isaac Hill was the foulest of low libellous country newspaper editors, whose whole business was malignant lying, in Concord, New Hampshire, for money. Well, he has got into Congress, & into government-contracts, by his lying & subserviency. And he has been doing the same thing up to this day. But his name has been before the public so long with "Honorable" attached to it, that Webster, who thoroughly knows what a dismal dog he is, now gravely has Hill's letter in commendation of his own course, printed, as if it were Albert Gallatin's. & the Daily Advertiser does not disdain to pick it up & print it.

Practical Naturalist.

Now that the *civil* Engineer is fairly established, I think we must have one day a Naturalist in each village as invariably as a lawyer or doctor. It will be a new subdivision of the medical profession. I want to know what plant this is? Penthorum
What is it good for? in medical botany? in industrial botany? Now the Indian doctor, if there were one, & not the sham of one, would be more consulted than the diplomatic one. What bird is this? What hyla? What caterpillar? Here is a new bug on the trees. Cure the warts on the plum, & on the oak. How to attack the rosebug & the curculio. Show us the poisons. How to treat the cranberry meadow? The universal impulse toward natural science in the last twenty years promises this practical issue. And how beautiful would be the profession. C. T. Jackson, John L. Russell, and Henry Thoreau, & George Bradford,

John Lesley would find their employment. All questions answered for stipulated fees; and, on the other hand, new information paid for, as a newspaper office pays for news. To have a man of Science remove into this town, would be better than the capitalist who is to build a village of houses on Nashawtuck. I would gladly subscribe to his maintenance. He is, of course, to have a microscope & a telescope.

from

Xenien

1850

Margaret was heroic, humane, courteous, made society where she came. She had lived in civility & that element is lost in her to our city.

from

BO

1850–1851

Rambling talk with H. T. last night, in accordance with my proposal to hold a session, the first for a long time, with malice prepense, & take the bull by the horns. We disposed pretty fast of America & England, I maintaining that our people did not get ripened, but, like the peaches & grapes of this season, wanted a fortnight's more sun, & remained green,—whilst, in England, because of the density, perhaps, of cultivated population, more calorie was generated, & more completeness obtained. Layard is good example, both of the efficiency as measured by effect on the Arab, & in its reaction of his enterprise on him; for his enterprise proved a better university to him than Oxford or Sorbonne.

Henry thought, the English, "all train," are mere soldiers, as it were, in the world. And that their business is winding up, whilst our pioneer is unwinding his lines.

I like the English better than our people, just as I like merchants better than scholars; for, though on a lower platform, yet there is no cant, there is great directness, comprehension, health, & success. So with English.

Then came the difference between American & English scholars. H. said, the English were all bred in one way, to one thing, he had read many lives lately, & they were all one life, Southey, Campbell, Leigh Hunt, or whosoever, they went to Eton, they went to College, they went to London, they all knew each other, & never did not feel the ability of each. But here, Channing is obscure, Newcomb is obscure, & so all the Scholars are in a more natural, healthful & independent condition.

My own quarrel with America, of course, was, that the geography is sublime, but the men are not; that the inventions are excellent, but the inventors, one is ashamed of; that the means by which events so grand as the opening of California,

Texas, Oregon, & the junction of the two Oceans, are effected, are paltry, the filthiest selfishness, fraud, & conspiracy. As if what we find in nature, that the animalcule system is of ferocious maggot & hideous mite, who bite & tear, yet make up the fibre & texture of nobler creatures; so all the grand results of history are brought about by these disgraceful tools. I am afraid that the upper painters are not nice in their pencils.

It was agreed, however, that what is called a success in America or in England is none; that their book or man or law had no root in nature,—of course!

But in the face of the facts which appear as soon as a couple of meditative men converse, I demand another sort of biography than any of which we have experience, bold, experimental, varied, availing itself of these unspeakable incomputable advantages which this meditative conversation at once discloses as within reach. Thus a man should do the feats he so admires. Why not suddenly put himself to the learning of tongues, &, like Borrow, master in a few months, the dialects of Europe, Moor & gipsy, flash & patois: then, in another summer, put himself at the centre of Sciences, (which seems & is so easy when he meditates,) & read from simple arithmetic the activities of chemistry, of geology, of astronomy; paint out the beautiful botany, as Goethe wished, by figuring not only all actual, but all possible plants: then work out *apriori* politics,: then set himself, like Walter Raleigh, & Columbus, & Cabot, on the finding & survey of new kingdoms or try, say rather, *and try*, after other months, all the melodies of music & poetry with the boldest adventure. Why only one Humboldt, one Crichton, one Pythagoras, one Napoleon, when every thinker, every mind, in the ascensions of conversation, sees his right to all these departments? We arm ourselves with a pretty artillery of tools now in our social national arrangements, ride four times as fast as our fathers did, travel, grind, weave, forge, plant, till, & excavate by formidable mechanical allies,—but we have yet not armed our selves with metaphysical aids, with languages, sciences, calculi, divination, and a whole system of accomplishments & culture tantamount to these new shoes & gloves & glasses & gimlets with which we have armed our bodies.

Why are we so excellent at the humdrum of our musty

household life, when quite aware of these majestic prerogatives? We do not try the virtue of the amulets we have. Thus we can think so much better, by thinking with a wise man. Yet we come together as a pair of six footers, always as six footers, & never on the ground of the immensities, which we have together authentically & awefully surveyed. Why not once meet & work on the basis of the Immensities, & not of the six feet?

Yes, we have infinite powers, but cannot use them. When shall we attain our majority, & come to our estate? Henry admitted, of course, the solstice.

I complain, too, that grandeurs do not ultimate themselves in grandeurs, but in paltriness. The idea of God ends in a paltry Methodist meetinghouse.

Law-abiding, loyal, &c. O yes, the whole creation is made of hooks & eyes, of bitumen, of stickingplaster, &, whether your community is made in Rome, or in California; of saints, or of rogues & pirates, it coheres in one perfect lump.

—

Days
And you think another day another scream of the eternal wail.

—

Beauty
I saw a boy on the common seize an old tin milkpan that was rusting on a dirtheap & poising it on the top of a stick he held in his hand set it a turning & made it describe the most elegant imaginable curves.

—

Culture

It occurred yesterday more strongly than I can now state it, that we must have an intellectual property in all property, & in all action, or they are naught. I must have children, I must have events, I must have a social state & history,—or my thinking & speaking will have no body & background. But having these, I must also have them not, (so to speak), or carry them as contingent and merely apparent possessions to give them any real value.

—

At Harrisburgh, 2 April, I met W. L. Fisher. The good old Quaker believes in Individualism, still: so do I. Fourierism seemed to him boys' play; and so indeed did money; though he frankly admitted how much time he had spent about it: but a vital power in man, identical with that which makes grass grow, & the sweet breeze blow, & which should abolish slavery, & raise the pauper, that he believes in, against all experience. So we held sweet counsel together. A great curiosity he professed, & there again he met me, to know how the fact lies in the minds of these poor men that were sitting in the front car. If there is a right statement, he felt & said, it ought to satisfy Paddy too. We agreed that the power of Carolina over Massachusetts & the states, was in the personal force; and, therefore, it is a triumph of Individualism.

—

16 November.

Yesterday I read Margaret's letters to C. S., full of probity, full of talent & wit, full of friendship, ardent affections, full of noble aspiration. They are tainted with a female mysticism which to me appears so merely an affair of constitution that it claims no more respect or reliance than the charity or patriotism of a man who has just dined well & *feels good*. When I talked with G. H. I remember the eggs & butter seemed to have got into his eyes. In our noble Margaret her personal feeling colours all her judgments of persons, of books, of pictures, & of the laws of the world. This is easily felt in common women & a large deduction is civilly made on the spot, by whosoever replies to their remark. But when the speaker has such brilliant talent & literature as Margaret, she gives so many fine names to these merely sensuous & subjective objects, that the hearer is long imposed upon, and thinks so precise & glittering nomenclature cannot be of mere *muscae volitantes*, but must be of some real ornithology hitherto unknown to him.

This mere feeling exaggerates a host of trifles, as birthdays, seals, bracelets, ciphers, coincidences & contretemps, into a dazzling mythology; but when one goes to sift it, & find if there be a real meaning, it eludes all search. Whole sheets of warm fluent florid writing are here, in which the eye is caught by "carbuncle," "heliotrope," "dragon," "aloes," "Magna

Dea," "limboes," "stars," & "purgatory," but can connect all this or any part of it with no universal experience.

Yet Margaret had her own merits, & we shall not see her like. What a basis of earnest love of knowledge & love of character! Her decided selection so sagacious generally of her friends; in some instances, her election anticipates for some years any personal intercourse, & her fidelity to them, & generous forgiving appreciation.—She estimates society & its opinion, very well, —far better than so many people of talent. Her expensiveness creates tragic relation & feeling to it, and thence with ill health comes all the unworthy sentimentalism of Destiny, Daemon, gold, & the cross.

Yet I draw from this warm refreshening of faded tints on the canvas of the past admonitions always needed, that what spoke to the best minds among the young in those years, 1838 to 1842, was the spontaneous & solitary thought, & not the Birmingham Lacker, and though Whiggism & cities condemn now, so did they then, & yet this somewhat more real & strong than Whigs or cities, made itself a place & name, & compelled the reiterated visit & inquest of these, though they still pronounce it imposture, & will require new visit & inquest, until at last it is stamped as good whiggism & municipality.

It is curious that Margaret made a most disagreeable impression on her friends at first,—created a strong prejudice which she had then to conquer. It was so with Elizabeth H., with Sarah Clarke, & with me.

—

Alcott's bonhommie & sympathy would certainly have made him servile, but for his exacting ideal which makes the rich Bostonians & their belongings very commonplace.

A Journal is to the author a book of constants, each mind requiring, (as I have so often said,) to write the whole of literature & science for itself.

—

Charlestown Versatility

Several years ago, how much we were entertained with Mr Tyler, whom I knew only because he had rare books, & the only copy in this country, of Taylor's Aristotle in the "Nobleman's Edition." But when, one day, he stopped at my door, his feats were by no means exclusively platonic. He was hale, stout, & ruddy; said he could lift a barrel of flour, & carry it farther than any of his men. He was immersed in politics, & knew how the elections were going, & was stumping it every night for Gen. Harrison. He was an efficient member of an Engine-Company, was a thriving broker, & had lately been on a visit to some religious relations in New Hampshire, where he met with a Baptist from Plaistow, who was so edified by his talk, that he mistook T. for a clergyman, & invited him to come over to Plaistow, & speak at a Conference;—an invitation, which T. accepted, to the horror of his cousins, went over on the appointed day, spoke an hour & twenty minutes, left all the audience in tears, & heard, two days after, that he had awakened a revival in the town!

—

Kinds or specialties. Besides the genealogists; Besides sheriffs, like the Dartmouth man; and antiquaries or pamphlet-collectors like Mr Chandler; and Dead-men's-men like Mr Walker of London;—I recall the man who so amused the stagecoach once from Middleborough with his contrivances for defending his own coffin in his grave from bodysnatchers. He had contrived a pistol to go off pop from this end, & a pistol pop from that end (of the coffin,) & he was plainly spending his life in the sweets of the revenge he was going to take hereafter on the young doctors that should creep to his graveyard.

—

18 Dec.

Charles Newcomb came, & yesterday departed, but I do not ask him again to come. He wastes my time. 'Tis cruel to think of. Destroyed three good days for me! The Pythagoreans would have built a tomb for him—the unique, inspired, wasted genius!

—

Complained that life had lost its interest. 'Tis very funny, be sure, to hear this. For most of us the world is all too interesting, *l'embarras de richesses.* We are wasted with our versatility; with the eagerness to grasp on every possible side, we all run to nothing. I cannot open an agricultural paper without finding objects enough for Methusalem. I jilt twenty books whenever I fix on one. I stay away from Boston, only because I cannot begin there to see those whom I should wish, the men, & the things. I wish to know France. I wish to study art. I wish to read laws.

Talleyrand at 15 years had discovered that the secret of governing men lay in selfcommand.

> "Augustus Caesar at nineteen years put on the dissimulation, which he never put off." *Gibbon.*

Napoleon III. acquired such skill in the art of lying, that "the journals complained you could not depend on the exact contrary of that which he stated."

Poet,—no, prosewriter is un orateur manqué. Did not old Goethe say, that Byron's poems were, undelivered parliamentary speeches? Much more is it manifest, my dear Carlyle, that your rage at stumporatory is inverted love.

—

Tennyson's *In Memoriam* is the commonplaces of condolence among good unitarians in the first week of mourning. The consummate skill of the versification is the sole merit. The book has the advantage that was Dr Channing's fortune, that all the merit was appreciable. He is never a moment too high for his audience. But to demonstrate this mediocrity I was forced to quote those moral sentences which make the fame of true bards such as

"In whose pure sight all Virtue doth succeed,"

of Wordsworth;

"'Tis crown enough to Virtue, still, her own applause,"

of Ben Jonson; or

"It was for Beauty that the world was made."

B. J.

or

"Unless above himself he can
Erect himself, how poor a thing is man."

of Daniel

or

"The sum of Virtue is to know & dare;"
of Donne

and then to ask, Now show me one such line in this book of Tennyson?

"The recluse hermit oft times more doth see
Of the world's inmost wheels than worldlings can
As man is of the world, the heart of man
Is the epitome of God's great book
Of Creatures, & men need no further look."
Donne

Turner

The fact that the creator of beauty in English art, the man who has all his life been shedding lustre & loveliness in profuse works of his industrious pencil, is a poor hunks sulking in a lonely house with his woman Jessica, a miser too, who never asked anybody to dine, & has made £300 000 by his works,—is not a dead fact, but significant of the compensations of nature; significant that every old crooked curmudgeon has a soft place in his heart; & not without comfort too, that when one feels the drawbacks & diseases & disgraces of his temperament & activity, he recalls, that still he too may not be useless or pestiferous if he steadily retires on his task of even a sad, crusty, churlish, expiatory devotion to art & beauty, like J.M.W. Turner's.

Brave comme l'épée qu'il porte.

The principal thing that occurs now is the might of the law which makes slavery the single topic of conversation in this Country. A great wrong is attempted to be done & the money power is engaged to do it. But unhappily because it is criminal the feeble force of conscience is found to set the whole world against it. Hallelujah!

Edith says, Father, I have very bad dreams, that way that the houses grow larger & smaller.

Diamonds, I read, appear the same in a bowl of water, as out of it, whilst glass loses its light.

—

In the streets I have certain darkenings which I call my nights.

I found when I had finished my new lecture that it was a very good house, only the architect had unfortunately omitted the stairs.

—

15 January

Last night, at the Club it was urged that persons were much hurt who had failed to be elected, &c. & the committee of nomination which brings one candidate, out of all the list, before the Club, was thought most invidious. And much was said on the natural indignation which the rejected candidates feel at having a better man preferred to those who stood prior to him in time of application; &c. To which, two conclusive answers seemed to rise. If, when a vacancy occurs, there be several names and the first in order of time is a blameless candidate, but young & nowise clubable; &, next below him, is the name of a man who tells the best story in the county, & is as full of fun & information as Judge Warren or Harry Lee, or the like excellent talker,—is it not a cruel wrong to the Club to deprive it, perhaps for years, of such a member?

Then, secondly, I have no sympathy with the wounded feelings of candidates who wish to be preferred to a better man, or who count themselves injured when an older or better man is chosen. Let them sympathize with the Club, & with good sense, instead of sympathizing with themselves.

—

Eloquence

Bad air, unfriendly audience, faint heart & vacant thought in the orator are things of course, and incident to Demosthenes, to Chatham, to Webster, as inevitably as to the gentlemen who address the stifling Concord Vestry this week. But here & there fell the bolt of genius astounding & dazzling out of this very fog & stench, burned them all up, melted away bad air, rowdy mob, coldness, aversion, partisanship, sterility, in one blaze of wonder, sympathy, & delight, and the total consumption of all this fuel, is the proof of Eloquence.

Helix oblonga, from Rio Janeiro, I saw in Salem at Mrs Barstow's, with white eggs, about the size of a robin's egg, which the fish lays.

October, 1851 *Littaea geminiflora*, a beautiful plant of the agave species, looking like a gigantic orchis 11 or 12 feet high, I saw in full flower at the Horticultural Shop.

—

To every reproach, I know now but one answer, namely, to go again to my own work.
"But you neglect your relations."
Yes, too true; then I will work the harder.
"But you have no genius." Yes, then I will work the harder.
"But you have no virtues." Yes, then I will work the harder.
"But you have detached yourself & acquired the aversation of all decent people. You must regain some position & relation." Yes, I will work harder.

—

I must try to recall here where I sit by the edge of Seneca Lake, my conversation yesterday with Albert H. Tracy of Buffalo. He believed that Europe was effete beside America & fancied that the office of men here was in many ages to bring the material world into subserviency to the moral. And, that, if one should expect only such a future as the past, nations & man might well despair. Nor that yet were even the means of change apparent and that it was utterly futile to hope anything from such arrangements or philanthropies as might now organize; for they begin by saying, now let us make a compact, which is a solecism inasmuch as it implies a sentimental resistance to the gravities & tendencies which will steadily by little & little pull over your air-castle. There is nothing to tie it to. He believes in a future of great equalities; but all our experience, he sees, is of inequalities.

—

Some persons are thrown off their balance, when in society; others are thrown on to balance; the excitement of company & the observation of other characters corrects their biases. Margaret Fuller always appeared to unexpected advantage in conversation with a circle of persons, with more commonsense

& sanity than any other,—though her habitual vision was through coloured lenses.

Mr Moseley at Buffalo described Webster's attitude when in the senate seeking for a word that did not come. "He pauses, puts his hand to his brow,—you would think then there was a mote in his eye. Still it comes not; then he puts his hands—American fashion first into his breast under his waistcoat, deeper than I can, then,—to the bottom of his fobs, bends forward,—then the word is bound to come, he throws back his head, & out it comes with a leap, &, I promise you, it has its full effect on the Senate."

All national brag in English or American is mean, & betrays want of real power. Just as far as the sympathy of the company goes with you, you may value your English, French, or Dutch traits, but when old Dr Gardiner or Fanny Kemble or my little Kingston begins to assume airs on modern England, going beyond any perception of facts that we have, it is about as respectable as the admiration of a Freshman at College of his class. "My country," forsooth, makes me sick, Madam or Sir.

—

Chasles thinks the rage for *illustrated Journals* all over Europe & the United States, a decided symptom of the decline of literature. Exciting novels, & pictures, in the room of ideas, have made literature a sensual pleasure.

Fourier's Criticism on modern civilization, is, "An accountant was required, & a dancer got the place."

—

The country boys & men have in their mind the getting a knowledge of the world as a thing of main importance. The New Hampshire man in the cars said that. Somebody grew up at home & his father whipped him for several years,—he would fall on him in the field & beat him as he would his cattle. But one day the boy faced him, & held his hands. Then the boy had never been to school, & he thought he would go to California. There he was, a man grown, good, stout, well-looking fellow, six feet, but as ignorant as a horse; *he had never had any chance*; how could he know anything? So he went to

California, & stayed there a year, & has come back.—He looks well, he has much improved in his appearance, but he has not got a ninepence.

And really New Hampshire & Vermont look on California, & railroads, as formerly they did on a peddling trip to Virginia, —as their education, as *giving them a chance* to know something.

—

Nothing so marks a man as bold imaginative expressions. A complete statement in the imaginative form of an important truth arrests attention & is repeated & remembered. A phrase or two of that kind will make the reputation of a man. Pythagoras's golden sayings were such; and Socrates's, & Mirabeau's & Bonaparte's; and, I hope I shall not make a sudden descent, if I say, that, Henry Thoreau promised to make as good sentences in that kind as any body.

—

Bad times. We wake up with a painful auguring, and after exploring a little to know the cause find it is the odious news in each day's paper, the infamy that has fallen on Massachusetts, that clouds the daylight, & takes away the comfort out of every hour. We shall never feel well again until that detestable law is nullified in Massachusetts & until the Government is assured that once for all it cannot & shall not be executed here. All I have, and all I can do shall be given & done in opposition to the execution of the law.

Mr. Hoar has never raised his head since Webster's speech in last March, and all the interim has really been a period of calamity to New England. That was a steep step downward. I had praised the tone & attitude of the Country. My friends had mistrusted it. They say now, It is no worse than it was before; only it is manifest and acted out. Well I think *that* worse. It shows the access of so much courage in the bad, so much check of virtue, terror of virtue, withdrawn. The tameness is shocking. Boston, of whose fame for spirit & character we have all been so proud. Boston, whose citizen intelligent people in England told me they could always distinguish by their culture among Americans. Boston, which figures so proudly in Adams's diary, which we all have been reading: Boston, through the personal influence of this New Hampshire man, must bow its proud spirit in the dust, & make us irretrievably ashamed. I would hide the fact if I could, but it is done, it is debased. It is now as disgraceful to be a Bostonian as it was hitherto a credit.

Boston, we have said with so much lofty confidence,—no fugitive slave can be arrested here—. And now we must transport our vaunt to the country, & say with a little less confidence, no fugitive man can be arrested there, at least we can brag so until tomorrow, when the farmers also are corrupted, & the cowardice & unabashed selfishness of New York & Boston has infected the total population.
The tameness is edifying. There is not a gentleman left in Massachusetts. I am told the only haste in Boston is who shall first sign the list of volunteers. One is only reminded of the Russian poltroonery,—a nation without character where when they cheat you, & you show them that they cheat, they reply—"Why you did not think we were Germans surely; we are only Russians;" that is, *we all cheat.* I met an episcopal clergyman, & allusion being made to Mr Webster's treachery, he replied "Why, do you know I think that the great action of his life?" I am told, they are all involved in one hot haste of terror, presidents of colleges & professors, saints & brokers, insurers, lawyers, importers, jobbers, there is not an unpleasing sentiment, a liberal recollection, not so much as a snatch of an old song for freedom dares intrude.

I am sorry to say it, But New-Hampshire has always been distinguished for the servility of its eminent men. Mr Webster had resisted for a long time the habit of men of his *compatriots*, I mean no irony, & by adopting the spirited tone of Boston had recommended himself—as much as by his great talents to the people of Massachusetts; but blood is thicker than water, the deep servility of New Hampshire politics which have marked all prominent statesmen from that district, with the great exception of Mr Hale, has appeared late in life with all the more strength that it had been resisted so long, & he has renounced what must have cost him some perplexity all the great passages of his past career on which his fame is built. His great speeches are, his discourse at Plymouth denouncing Slavery; his speech against Hayne & Southern aggression; his Eulogy on Adams

& Jefferson; a speech which he is known by & in which he stands by the Fathers of the Revolution for the very resistance which he now denounces; and lastly his speeches & recent writings on Hungarian liberty. At this very moment attitude assumed as foreign secretary in his letter to Mr Hulsemann is printed in all newspapers before the people in the most aukward contradiction to his own domestic position, precisely like that of the French President between French liberty & Roman tyranny; or like *Hail Columbia*, when sung at a slave-auction.

I opened a paper today in which he pounds on the old strings in a letter to the Washington Birth Day feasters at N. Y. "Liberty! liberty!" Pho! Let Mr Webster for decency's sake shut his lips once & forever on this word. The word *liberty* in the mouth of Mr Webster sounds like the word *love* in the mouth of a courtezan.

The fame of Everett is dear to me, & to all his scholars, & I have watched with alarm his derelictions. Whenever his genius shone, it of course was in the instinct of freedom, but one of his old Scholars cannot but ask him whether there was no sincerity in all those apostrophes to freedom & adjurations of the dying Demosthenes: was it all claptrap? And as to the name of New England Societies, which Mr Choate, Mr Webster, & Mr Foote, Mr Clay, & Mr Everett address, & are responded to with enthusiasm, it is all a disgusting obsequiousness.

Their names are tarnished: what we have tried to call great, is little; and the merely ethnographic fact remains that an immense external prosperity is possible, with pure cowardice & hollowness in all the conspicuous official men. I cannot read longer with any comfort the local good news, even "Education in Massachusetts."
Art union
Revival of religion

E. H. finds the life of Campbell to send her back with new force of attachment to her Temperance friends in America. Every life of an European artist shows her that they have no self-command. Their tears are maudlin, for they are the tears of wine. But the ocean & the elements are at the back of the brave old puritans of the world when all the Websters are putrid.

The little fact comes out more plainly that you cannot rely on any man for the defence of truth who is not constitutionally of that side. Wolf, however long his nails have been pared, however neatly he has been shaved, & tailored, & taught & tuned to say 'Virtue' & 'religion', cannot be relied on when it comes to a pinch, he will forget his morality, & say morality means sucking blood. The man only can be trusted to defend humanity. And women are really the heart & sanctuary of our civilization.

The impudence of this pretension is enormous. Mr Choate, whose talent consists in a fine choice of words which he can hang indiscriminately on any offender, has pushed the privilege of his profession so far as to ask hypocritically "What would the puritans of 1620 say to the trashy sentimentalism of modern reformers?" And thus the stern old fathers of Massachusetts who Mr Choate knows would have died at the stake for freedom before soiling themselves with this damnation are made to repudiate the trashy sentimentalism of the Ten Commandments. The joke is too impudent.

The profession of the law has the old objection that it makes the practitioner callous & skeptical. The practice of defending criminals of all dyes of guilt & holding them up with vehement protestations that they are injured but honest men, firm Christians, models of virtue only a little imprudent & open to practices of

It is the need of Mr Webster's position that he should have an opinion; that he should be a step in advance of everybody else, & make the strongest statement in America; that is vital to him. He cannot maintain himself otherwise.

Mr Webster has deliberately taken out his name from all the files of honour in which he had enrolled it, from all association with liberal, virtuous, & philanthropic men, and read his recantation on his knees at Richmond & Charleston. He has gone over in an hour to the party of force, & stands now on the precise ground of the Metternicks, the Castlereaghs, & the Polignacs, without the excuse of hereditary bias & of an ancient name & title which they had. He has undone all that he has spent his years in doing; he has discredited himself.

He to talk of liberty, & to rate an Austrian? He would dragoon the Hungarians, for all his fine words. I advise Kossuth after his experience of Gorgey not to trust Webster. He would in Austria truckle to the Czar, as he does in America to the Carolinas; and hunt the Hungarians from the Sultan as he does the fugitives of Virginia from the Massachusetts. He may bluster. It is his tactics. We shall make no more mistakes. He has taught us the ghastly meaning of liberty in his mouth. It is kidnapping & hunting to death men & women, it is making treason & matter of fine & imprisonment & armed intervention of the resistance of

N

I said the subject of education, of art, of religion, had come to appear bitter mockeries. The newspaper is only a proclamation & detail of our shames. The very question of property, the house & land we occupy, have lost all their sunlight. And a man looks gloomily on his children & thinks what have I done that you should begin life in dishonour?

I may then add *the Union*. Nothing seems to me more bitterly futile than this bluster about the Union. A year ago we were all lovers & prizers of it. Before the passage of that law which Mr Webster made his own, we indulged in all the dreams which foreign nations still cherish of American destiny. But in the new attitude in which we find ourselves, the degradation & personal dishonour which now rests like miasma on every house in Massachusetts, the sentiment is entirely changed. No man can look his neighbor in the face. We sneak about with the infamy of crime in the streets, & cowardice in ourselves and frankly once for all the Union is sunk, the flag is hateful, & will be hissed.

The Union! o yes, I prized that, other things being equal; but what is the Union to a man self condemned, with all sense of self respect & chance of fair fame cut off,—with the names of conscience & religion become bitter ironies, & liberty the ghastly nothing which Mr Webster means by that word? The worst mischiefs that could follow from secession, & new combination of the smallest fragments of the wreck were slight &

medicable to the calamity your Union has brought us. Another year, and a standing army officered by Southern gentlemen, to protect the Commissioners & to hunt the fugitives will be illustrating the new sweets of Union in Boston, Worcester, & Springfield. It did not appear & it was incredible that the passage of the Law would make the Union odious; but from the day it was attempted to be executed in Massachusetts, this result has appeared that the Union is no longer desireable. Whose deed is that?

One more consideration occurs—the mischief of a legal crime. The demoralization of the Community. Each of these persons who touches it is contaminated. There has not been in our lifetime another moment when public men were personally lowered by their political action. But here are gentlemen whose names stood as high as any, whose believed probity was the confidence & fortification of all who by fear of public opinion, or by that dangerous ascendency of Southern manners have been drawn into the support of this nefarious business, and have of course changed their relations to men. We poor men in the country who might have thought it an honor to shake hands with them, would now shrink from their touch; nor could they enter our humblest doors. Can the reputed wealth of Mr Eliot restore his good name? Can Mr Curtis reinstate himself, or could Mr Webster obtain now a vote in the state of Massachusetts for the poorest municipal office? Well, is not this a loss inevitable to a bad law?—a law which no man can countenance or abet the execution of, without loss of all self respect, & forfeiting forever the name of a gentleman. We therefore beg you to stand so far the friends of yourselves & of poor well meaning men, your constituents, as not to suffer them to be put in a position where they cannot do right without breaking your law or keep the law without corrupting & dishonouring the community.

The College, the churches, the schools, the very shops & factories are discredited. Every kind of property & every branch of industry & every avenue to power suffers injury, and the value of life is reduced.—I had hardly written this before my friend said, "If this law should be repealed, I shall be glad that I have lived; if not, I shall be sorry that I was born." What kind of law is that which extorts this kind of language for a free civilized people?

I am surprised that lawyers can be so blind as to suffer the law to be discredited. The law rests not only in the instinct of all people, but, according to the maxims of Blackstone & the jurists, on equity, and it is the cardinal maxim that a statute contrary to natural right is illegal, is in itself null & void. The practitioners should guard this dogma well, as the palladium of the profession, as their anchor in the respect of mankind. Against this all the arguments of Webster make no more impression than the spray of a child's squirt.

The fame of Webster ends in this nasty law.

And as for the Andover & Boston preachers, Dr Dewey & Dr Sharpe who deduce kidnapping from their Bible, tell the poor dear doctor if this be Christianity, it is a religion of dead dogs, let it never pollute the ears & hearts of noble children again. O bring back then the age when valour was virtue, since what is called morality, means nothing but pudding. Pardon the spleen of a professed hermit.

Mr Webster cannot choose but regret his loss. Tell him that those who make fame, accuse him with one voice: those to whom his name was once dear & honoured as the manly statesman, to whom the choicest gifts of nature had been accorded, —eloquence with a simple greatness; those who have no points to carry that are not those of public morals & of generous civilization, the obscure & private who have no voice & care for none as long as things go well, but who feel the infamy of his nasty legislation creeping like a fever into all their homes & robbing the day of its beauty. Tell him that he who was their pride in the woods & mountains of New England is now their mortification; that they never name him; they have taken his picture from the wall & torn it—dropped the pieces in the gutter; they have taken his book of speeches from the shelf & put it in the stove. & he cannot choose but feel the change; and all the fribble of the Daily Advertiser & of its model the N.Y. Journal of Commerce will not quite compensate him. I have no fear that any roars of New York mobs will be able to drown this voice in Mr Webster's ear. It can outwhisper all the salvos of their cannon. If it were Mr Cass, it might be different; but Mr Webster has the misfortune to know the voice of truth from the stupid hurrahs of New York.

It will be his distinction to have changed in one day by the most detestable law that was ever enacted by a civilized state, the fairest & most triumphant national escutcheon the sun ever shone upon, the free, the expanding, the hospitable, the irresistible America, home of the homeless & pregnant with the blessing of the world, into a jail or barracoon for the slaves of a few thousand Southern planters & all the citizens of this hemisphere into kidnappers & drivers for the same. Is that a name will feed his hungry ambition?

I question the civilization when I see that the public mind had never less hold of the strongest of all truths. I cannot think the most "judicious tubing" a compensation for metaphysical debility.

inconceivable levity of the public mind, an unbroken prosperity the cause.

There are or always were in each country certain gentlemen to whom the honour & dignity of the community were confided, persons of elevated sentiments, relieved perhaps by fortune from the necessity of injurious application to arts of gain, and who used that leisure for the benefit of their fellow citizens in the study of elegant learning, the learning of liberty & in their forwardness on all emergences to lead with courage & magnanimity against any peril in the state. I look in vain for such a class among us. And that is the worst symptom in our affairs. There are persons of fortune enough and men of breeding & of elegant learning but they are the very leaders in vulgarity of sentiment. I need call no names. The fact stares us in the face. They are full of sneers & derision & their reading of Cicero & of Plato & of Tacitus has been drowned under grossness of feeding and the bad company they have kept. It is the want perhaps of a stern & high religious training, like the iron Calvinism which made their fathers seventy five years ago. But though I find the names of old patriots still resident in

Boston, it is only the present venerable Mr Quincy who has renewed the hereditary honour of his name by scenting the tyranny in the gale. The others are all lapped in after dinner dreams and are as obsequious to Mr Webster as he is to the gentlemen of Richmond & Charleston. The want of loftiness of sentiment in the class of wealth & education in the University too is deplorable. I am sorry to say I predict too readily their feeling. They will not even understand the depth of my regret & will find their own supercilious & foppish version. But I refer them back to their Cicero & Tacitus & to their early resolutions.

It was always reckoned even in the rudest ages the distinction of the gentleman, the oath of honour of the knight, to speak the truth to men of power or to angry communities, and uphold the poor man against the rich oppressor. Will the educated people of Boston ask themselves whether they side with the oppressor or the oppressed? Yet I know no reason why a gentleman, who is I take it a natural formation, should not be true to his duties in Boston in 1850, as haughtily faithful & with as sovereign superiority to all hazards as his fathers had in 1770, or as Mr Hampden or Mr Eliot in London in 1650, or Arundel, or More, or Milton,

I do not value any artificial enthusiasm of protest got up by individuals in corners, which, however vehement, tells for nothing on the public mind; but I look eagerly and shall not have to look long for a spontaneous expression of the injured people,—in fault of leaders creating their own, & shaking off from their back these degenerate & unworthy riders. I make no secret of my intention to keep them informed of the baseness of their accustomed leaders. It is well to quote Cicero & Tacitus when doing the deed of Chiffinch & of Buckingham.

The first act as it was very natural was a little hesitating, but the next was easier, & the glib officials will I daresay in a few weeks be quite practised & handy at stealing men. When the session is over Mr Webster on his return to Boston can have call at the wardroo

In the weakness of the Union the law of 1793 was framed, and much may be said in palliation of it. It was a law affirming the existence of two states of civilization or an intimate union between two countries, one civilized & Christian & the other barbarous, where cannibalism was still permitted. It was a little gross, the taste for boiling babies, but as long as this kind of cookery was confined within their own limits, we could agree for other purposes, & wear one flag. The law affirmed a right to hunt their human prey within our territory; and this law availed just thus much to affirm their own platform,—to fix the fact, that, though confessedly savage, they were yet at liberty to consort with men;—though they had tails, & their incisors were a little long, yet it is settled that they shall by courtesy be called men; we will all make believe they are Christians; & we promise not to look at their tails or incisors when they come into company. This was all very well. The convenient equality was affirmed, they were admitted to dine & sup, & profound silence on the subject of tails & incisors was kept. No man in all New England spoke of Ghilanes in their presence. But of course on their part all idea of boiling babies in our caboose was dropt; all idea of hunting in our yards fat babies to boil, was dropt; & the law became, as it should, a dead letter. It was merely there in the statute-book to soothe the dignity of the maneaters. And we Northerners had, on our part, indemnified & secured ourselves against any occasional eccentricity of appetite in our confederates by our own interpretation, & by offsetting state-law by state-laws. It was & is penal here in Massachusetts for any sheriff or town- or state-officer to lend himself or his jail to the slavehunter, & it is also settled that any slave brought here by his master, becomes free. All this was well. What Mr Webster has now done is not only to re-enact the old law, but *to give it force*, which it never had before, or to bring down the free & Christian state of Massachusetts to the cannibal level.

—

Now this conspiring to hold up a bad law, and intimate correspondence of leading gentlemen mutually engaging to run to New York & to Cambridge, & dine in public on poor Washington's birthday, & the reading of the riot-act & of Washington's Legacy, & obtaining the preaching of Rev. Drs. Sharpe & Dewey, seems for the moment successful; & I do not know but Mr Fillmore & Mr Webster & Everett flatter themselves that the difficult Massachusetts is somehow managed, & that they had really overestimated the traditionary rebellion of the town of Boston. Once for all the best lie has this insuperable objection. They are always at the mercy of a truth speaker. It does very well as long as all the spectators agree to make believe with them, but the first unlucky boy that calls things by their names will ruin the cheat. Unless they can coax the good Creator not to make any more men or to make them of the pattern of the Ghilanes unless he will hoodwink them all.

My dear sir, Thomas Melville is gone, Mr Cabot is dead, Mr Otis of the Hartford Convention is dead, Mr Quincy is old; the turbulent Quincy Adams is at last still; and though there is an unlucky book of the old Adams printing about these times, yet, north or south, we don't hear of any body who will not be peaceable. I think you may venture it.

Ah Mr President trust not the information. The gravid old Universe goes spawning on; the wombs conceive & the breasts give suck to thousands & millions of hairy babes formed not in the image of your statute, but in the image of the Universe, too many to be bought off, too many than that they can be rich, & therefore peaceable, and necessitated to express first & last by one or another every truth of nature. You can keep no secret, for whatever is true, some of them will say, however unseasonably. You can commit no crime for they are created in their nature & sentiments conscious of & hostile to it: and unless you can suppress the English tongue in America, & hinder boys from declaiming Webster's Plymouth speech, & pass a law against libraries,—

This dreadful English speech is saturated with songs, proverbs & speeches that flatly contradict & defy every line of Mr Mason's Statute. Then sir there is England itself,—faults of her own undoubtedly,—but unhappily now so clean on this question,—that she will give publicity to every vice & trick of ours. There is France,—There is Germany, but worst a thousand times worse than all, there is this yeaning America, the yeaning northwest, millions of souls to accuse us. If the thing were to be carried in a close corporation, all the persons might be sounded & secured. Even in a senate, even in a House, they can calculate the exact amount of resistance; but this is quite impossible in a country. For one, only one truth speaker will ruin them.

This affectation of using sacred days & names,—Washington's birthday forsooth, & the Pilgrims' day, for the effusion of all this rancid oil of eloquence on compromises seems to be a hint borrowed from the adepts at Rochester, where Mrs Tubbs & Mr Potts very familiarly summon the Spirit of the deceased Dr Channing's & of Goethe, & of Swedenborg, to affirm the respectability & transparent honour of Madam Tubbs & of Master Potts.

What is the use of logic & legal acumen if it be not to demonstrate to the people what is metaphysically true? The fact that a criminal statute is illegal—is admitted by lawyers and, that fact once admitted by the people, the whole structure of this new tyranny falls to the ground. Why do not the lawyers who are professionally its interpreters put this home to the people? There is for every man a statement possible of that truth which he is most unwilling to receive, a statement possible, so pungent & so ample that he cannot get away from it, but must either bend to it or die of it. Else, there would be no such word as eloquence, which means this. Mr Webster did that thing in his better days for Hayne. Mr Hayne could not hide from himself that something had been shown him & shown the whole world which he did not wish to see. He left public life & retired, &, it is said, died of it. Mr Webster has now in his turn chosen evil for good, & less innocently than Mr Hayne, and Mr Hayne is avenged. For it is certain that he will be cast & ruined. He fights with an adversary not subject to casualties.

Tout est soldat pour vous combattre.

Everything that can walk, turns soldier to fight this down.

It is said, that, events within a few years have shown a levity in the morals of the population; that the persons who can be relied on to stick to what they have said & agreed are few & fewer.

*

Mr Webster unfortunately is the most remarkable example. The Whig Conventions plead his example & almost come up with it.

But Aristotle's reply to the question, What advantage a man may gain by lying? is still true; "not to be believed when he speaks the truth," much more, 'not to be believed when he lies again.'

Webster & Choate think to discredit the higher law by personalities; they insinuate much about transcendentalists & abstractionists & people of no weight. It is the cheap cant of lawyers & of merchants in a failing condition, & of rogues. These classes usually defend an immorality by the practice of men of the world, & talk of dreamers & enthusiasts; every woman has been debauched by being made to believe that it is the mode, it is custom & none but the priest & a few devout visionaries ever think otherwise. People never bring their history into politics, or this thin smoke would deceive nobody.

It is the most impolitic of all steps, this demoralization of the people. "Poets are the guardians of reverence in the hearts of the people." It must always happen that the guiding counsels of ages & nations should come not from statesmen or political leaders, always men of scared consciences, 'half villains', who, it has been said, are more dangerous than whole ones, [Mr Webster would be very sorry if this country should take his present counsel, for any but this particular emergency] but from contemplative men aloof by taste & necessity from these doubtful activities, and really aware of the truth long before the contemporary statesman because more impressionable. Mr Webster never opened a jury case without praising the law-abiding disposition of this people. But he knows that they owe this

Mr Everett, a man supposed aware of his own meaning, advises pathetically a reverence for the Union. Yes but hides the other horn under this velvet? Does he mean that we shall lay hands on a man who has escaped from slavery to the soil of Massachusetts & so has done more for freedom than ten thousand orations, & tie him up & call in the marshal, and say,—I am an orator for freedom; a great many fine sentences have I turned,—none has turned finer, except Mr Webster,—in favour of plebeian strength against aristocracy; and, as my last & finest sentence of all, to show the young men of the land who have bought my book & clapped my sentences & copied them in their memory, how much I mean by them,—Mr Marshal, here is a black man of my own age, & who does not know a great deal of Demosthenes, but who means what he says, whom we will now handcuff and commit to the custody of this very worthy gentleman who has come on from Georgia in search of him; I have no doubt he has much to say to him that is interesting & as the way is long I don't care if I give them a copy of my Concord & Lexington & Plymouth & Bunker Hill addresses to beguile their journey from Boston to the plantation whipping post? Does Mr Everett really mean this? that he & I shall do this? Mr Everett understands English, as few men do who speak it. Does he mean this? Union is a delectable thing, & so is wealth, & so is life, but they may *all* cost too much, if they cost honour. If

It is very remarkable how rare a bad law, an immoral law, is. Does Mr Everett know how few examples in Civil history there are of bad laws? I do not think it will be easy to parallel the crime of Mr Webster's law. But the crime of kidnapping is on a footing with the crimes of murder & of incest and if the Southern states should find it necessary to enact the further law in view of the too great increase of blacks that every fifth manchild should be boiled in hot water,—& obtain a majority in Congress with a speech by Mr Webster to add an article to the Fugitive Slave Bill,—that any fifth child so & so selected, having escaped into Boston should be seethed in water at 212° will not the mayor & alderman boil him? Is there the smallest moral distinction between such a law, & the one now enacted? How can Mr E. put at nought all manly qualities, all his claims to truth & sincerity, for the sake of backing up this cowardly nonsense?

Does he mean this, that he & I shall do this, or does he secretly know that he will die the death sooner than lift a finger in the matter, he or his son, or his son's son, and only hopes to persuade certain truckmen & constables to do this, that rich men may enjoy their estates in more security?

*

The historian tells us that "Thrasymachus's sophistry was political, & his aim the destruction of freedom, by extinguishing that sense of justice, on which it must ever be based." J. A. St John p 258

If

Mr Webster is fond of fame. His taste is likely to be gratified. For there is not a man of thought or ingenuity, but at every dinner table, in every private letter, in every newspaper I take up, is forced to say some thing biting of this enemy of the honour of Massachusetts. He has the curse of all this Country which he has afflicted.

One way certainly the Nemesis is seen. Here is a measure of pacification & union. What is its effect? that it has made one subject, one only subject for conversation, & painful thought, throughout the Union, Slavery. We eat it, we drink it, we breathe it, we trade, we study, we wear it. We are all poisoned with it, & after the fortnight the symptoms appear, purulent, making frenzy in the head & rabidness

What a moment was lost when Judge Shaw declined to affirm the unconstitutionality of the Fugitive Slave Law!

The present crisis is not analogous to the Revolution. No liberty of the controlling classes is now threatened. If the South, or if the Federal Government threatened the liberty of any class, I doubt not, there would be as violent reaction as was then. This is merely a case of conscience, not of anger, a call for compassion, a call for mercy,

That is one thing; now it is not less imperative that this nation should say, this Slavery shall not be, it poisons & depraves everything it touches.

There can never be peace whilst this devilish seed of war is in our soil. Root it out. Burn it up. Pay for the damage & let us have done with it. It costs a hundred millions. Twice so much were cheap for it. Boston is a little city, & yet is worth near 200 millions. Boston itself would pay a large fraction of the sum, to be clean of it. I would pay a tithe of my estate with joy; for this calamity darkens my days. It is a local accidental distemper, & the vast interests of a continent cannot be sacrificed for it.

Lord John Russell in Parliament, spoke to this effect; "I know there are gentlemen in this House who think that the conquests of England cost too much, that the colonies ought to be abandoned, and the army & navy reduced, & the whole expense of this Empire put on the narrowest economy. Perhaps they are right; but let not me be the instrument of bringing down the glories of England to this humiliation."

I wish Mr Webster could have had the like fine sense of personal honour,—he who had asked "if there was not to be a North," he who had pledged himself to resist all extension of slave area, all Compromise.

It is contrary to the sense of Duty; and therefore all human beings, in proportion to their power of thought & their moral sensibility, are, as soon as they are born, the natural enemies of this statute.

Evils of a bad law are sure to appear. Fitchburg Road evades the manifest intention of their Charter, & calls what is merely *its second track from Acton to Concord* a part of the *Sterling Branch Road*. Well, it obtains a sanction in the legislature for this fraud. Now comes a petition for a Northboro & Sterling Road infringing the Fitchburg privileges by a ruinous competition & lapping, & the Fitchburg men say, "This is robbery." But their case excites no pity, but only a sneer of "*Aha! Robbery is it, this time?*"

Hosmer says, Sims came on a good errand; for Sumner is elected, Rantoul & Palfrey are likely to be; the state of Massachusetts ought to buy that fellow.

I find it has made every student a student of law.
The destiny of America, the Union, yes, great things, dear to the heart & imagination, & not to be put at risk by every young ranter.

*

But a larger state, a prior union, still dearer to heart & imagination, & much longer to be our country is the World. We will not levy war against that, to please this New Hampshire strapper, nor the Carolinas.

We will buy the slaves at a hundred millions. It will be cheaper than any of our wars. It will be cheap at the cost of a national debt like England's.—

But we must put out this poison, this conflagration, this raging fever of Slavery out of the Constitution. If Webster had known a true & generous policy, this would have made him. He is a spent ball. It is the combined wealth behind him that makes him of any avail. And that is as bad as Europe.

from
CO
1851

The worst of antislavery, like war, I find, is, that it spoils conversation; and it is disgraceful to find one's self saying after the newspapers.

The old woman who was shown the telegraph & the railroad, said, "Well, God's works are great, but man's works are greater!"

The wonderful machinery has inspired old Tantalus with a new hope of somehow contriving to bottle the wave.

> "The man who is his own master knocks in vain at the doors of poetry." Plato

The old guide knows the passes from mountain to mountain, the bridges over gorge & torrent; & the salvation of numberless lives is in his oaken staff: and my guide knew not less the difficult roads of thought, the infinitely cunning transitions from law to law in metaphysics; in the most hopeless mazes, he could find a cheerful road, leading upward, & lighted as by the midday sun.

A topic of the "Conduct of Life" under the head of *Prudence*, should be how to live with unfit companions: for, with such, life is, for the most part, spent: and Experience teaches little better than our earliest instinct of selfdefence, namely, not to engage, not to mix yourself in any manner with them, but let their madness spend itself unopposed; You are You, & I am I.

—

I notice, in the road, that the landscape is uninteresting enough, but a little water instantly relieves the monotony. For it is no matter what objects are near it;—a grey rock, a little grass, a crab-tree, or alder-bush, a stake,—they instantly become beautiful by being reflected. It is rhyme to the eye, & explains the charm of rhyme to the ear, & suggests the deeper rhyme or translation of every natural object into its spiritual sphere.

—

Where is nature? Where shall we go to study her interior aspects? She is hard to find. The botanist after completing his herbarium remains a dry doctor, no poet. The lumberer in Maine woods by Moosehead Lake does not get into the forest to any purpose, though he drives logs with his feet in the water all day. The poet goes untimely into a dozen inviting dells, & finds himself not yet admitted, but a poor excluded dilettante. He makes many desperate attempts to throw the brush at the picture, but rarely makes a good hit. Ah when! Ah how rarely! can he draw a true Aeolian note from the harp.—And then comes some fine young gentleman like Milton or Goethe, who draws on his good London boots, and in coat of newest tailoring, with gold-headed cane, marches forth into the groves & straight as if he were going to his Club, to the secret sacred dell, where all the Muses & the shyest gods, fauns, & naiads, have their home. So also did Collins, & so did Spenser: nay, Walter Scott himself sheriff of Selkirkshire, is admitted in full suit to the crag & burn.
My texts are

Moonlight caves when all the fowls
Are safely housed save bats & owls
&c &c

Mountains on whose barren breast &c

Bubbling runnels joined the sound

Shakspeare's threnes

The railroad & telegraph are great unionists. Frank Browne told me that, whilst he was at Savannah, they were telegraphing to the President at Washington, every hour, news of the Cuban invaders.

—

Too much guano. The German & Irish nations, like the Negro, have a deal of guano in their destiny. They are ferried over the Atlantic, & carted over America to ditch & to drudge, to make the land fertile, & corn cheap, & then to lie down prematurely to make a spot of greener grass on the prairie.

But it does not seem to me much better, when the gross instincts are a little disguised, and the oestrum, gadfly, or brize of sex takes sentimental forms. I like the engendering of snails better than the same masquerading in Watts's psalms to the Church, the bride of Christ, or an old girl forming sentimental friendships with every male thing that comes by, under the pretence of "*developing a new side.*"

In feeble individuals, the sex & the digestion are all, absorb the entire vitality; and, the stronger these are, one would say, the individual is only so much the weaker. Of course, the more of these drones perish, the better for the hive. Later, perhaps they give birth, to some superior individual who has sufficient force to add to this animal a new aim, & an apparatus of means to work it out. Instantly all the ancestors become guano. Thus most men are mere bulls & most women cows; with however now & then an individual who has an Æolian attachment or an additional cell opened in his brain as an architectural or a musical or a philological knack; some stray taste or talent, as, a love of flowers, or of chemistry, or pigments, or a narrative talent, a good hand for chess, or a good foot for dancing, &c.—which skill nowise alters the life of himself or the people, nowise alters their rank in the scale of nature, but merely serves to pass the time,—the bulling & milking going on as before. At last, however, these tastes or talents, which nature has hitherto exhibited only as hints & tendencies, get fixed, & in one or in a succession of individuals each appears with steadiness, & absorbs so much food & force as to become itself a new centre & counteraction. The new talent draws off so rapidly the whole spirit & life of the plant, that nothing remains for animal functions, & hardly enough for health, so that, though in the first instance, these individuals have reserved enough juice for digestion & for reproduction, yet, in the second generation, if the like genius appear, the ill health is visibly deteriorated, & the generative force impaired.

M. F. to C. S. Prov. 2 Nov., 1837. "I could not but laugh at your catalogue of the things you must not have,—nothing striped, diamonded, or (above all things) *square.* That is driving me to close quarters I think."

Dualism.

I see but one key to the mysteries of human condition, but one solution to the old knots of Fate, Freedom, & foreknowledge;—the propounding, namely, of the double consciousness. A man is to ride alternately on the horses of his private & his public nature, as the Equestrians in the circus throw themselves nimbly from horse to horse, or plant one foot on the back of one, & the other foot on the back of another: so, when a man is the victim of his fate, has a hump-back, and a hump in his mind; a club foot & a club in his wit; (for there is nothing outward that was not first within) or is ground to powder by the vice of his race;—he is to rally on his relation to the Universe, which his ruin benefits. From the demon who suffers, he is to take sides with the God.

—

Lidian proposes to found a Dormitory, and to preach on almshouses, from the text, "The tender mercies of the wicked are cruel." Abraham, Isaac, & Jacob, are to adorn the walls *couchant*, & in night caps, and the portrait of the Foundress is to be taken fast asleep.

—

Our people mean, that men of thought shall be dilettanti; ornamental merely; if they dare to be practical with their ideas of beauty, it is on their peril. Everett is ornamental with liberty & dying Demosthenes, &c. but when he acts, he comes with the planter's whip in his buttonhole—& Eliot writes "history of liberty," & votes for South Carolina. & the University, Mr Sparks, & Mr Felton carry Demosthenes & General Washington clean for Slavery.

—

Every god is still there sitting in his sphere. The young mortal comes in & on the instant & incessantly fall snowstorms of illusions. Among other things he fancies himself nobody & lost in a crowd. There is he alone with them alone,—they pouring their grand persuasions—proffering to lead him to Olympus—he baffled, dazzled, distracted by the snowing illusions and when, by & by, for an instant the air clears, & the cloud lifts a little, there they are still sitting around him on their thrones.

—

It will hereafter be noted that the events of culture in the nineteenth century were, the new importance of the genius of Dante, Michel Angelo, & Raffael, to Americans; the reading of Shakspeare, &, above all, the reading of Goethe. Goethe was the cow from which all their milk was drawn. They all took the "European complaint" & went to Italy. Then there was an uprise of Natural History and in London if you would see the fashionable & literary celebrities, you must go to the soirées of the Marquis of Northampton, President of the Royal Society, or, to the Geological club at Somerset House.

It seems, however, as if all the young gentlemen & gentlewomen of America spent several years in lying on the grass & watching "the grand movements of the clouds in the summer sky," during this century.

—

The absence of moral feeling in the whiteman is the very calamity I deplore. The captivity of a thousand negroes is nothing to me.

—

Webster truly represents the American people just as they are, with their vast material interests, materialized intellect, & low morals. Heretofore, their great men have led them, have been better than they, as Washington, Hamilton, & Madison. But Webster's absence of moral faculty is degrading to the country.

Of this fatal defect of course Webster himself has no perception. He does, as immoral men usually do, make very low bows to the Christian church, & goes through all the decorums of Sunday, but when allusion is made to Ethics, & the sanctions of morality, he very frankly replies, as at Albany the other day,—"Some higher law somewhere between here & the third heaven, I do not know where."

—

Margaret had the attributes of a lady, a courtesy so real & sincere that it reached the chambermaid, the mantuamaker, and all who served her for money.

The use made of Fate in society is babyish; put your finger in your eye. It should rather be to bring up our conduct to the loftiness of nature. The Englishman & Frenchman may have the November desolation emptiness which cannot see a lamp post or a dangling rope without temptation to suicide, but to a charged, healthful, preoccupied manly mind, night & storm & cold are not grim, but sternly cheerful even. Rude & invincible except by themselves (or their own law) are the elements. So let him be. Let him empty his breast of all that is superfluous & traditional, of all dependence on the accidental, on money, on false fame, falsehood of any kind; & speak wild truth, & by manners & actions as unaffected as the weather, let him be instead of God to men, full of God, new & astonishing & nothing of the Edinburgh Review, of England, of France, or Greece, or Rome, or Fine Arts, or Church, or American Constitution, or any other bit of old hypocritical trumpery.

I suppose I need not go to St Louis to know the flavor of Southern life; there is not only St Louis, but all Avernus, in a fiery cigar. Goethe kept his Acherontian experiences in a separate bag; & said, if he himself should happen to fall into that bag, he should be consumed, bones & all.

London

I read that Sir John Herschel had found London to be the centre of the physical globe. What does that mean? the centre of the terraqueous hemisphere perhaps? The Greeks looked upon Delphi as the navel of the Earth.

I read also that the Crystal Palace was built in six months, & cost £150 000.

—

I noticed a little boy in the company whose speech in talking with his mates never went out as a mendicant from him, engaging him to what was said, but he remained quite entire when his speech was gone. So will it be when he is a man.

—

Never was truer fable than the Sibyl's writing on leaves which the wind scatters. A. asked me if the thought clothes itself in words? I answer, yes; but they are instantly forgotten. The difference between man & man is, that, in one, the memory with inconceivable swiftness flies after & *re-collects* these leaves;—flies on wing as fast as that mysterious whirlwind; & the envious Fate is baffled.

—

In the youth I heard last Sunday a sort of rattle of thunderbolts behind there in the back of his head. He threatened in every sentence to say somewhat new, bright, fatal. And that is the charm of eloquence, its potency. Here is mere play, play of genius, improvisation for the artist's own delight, & out of the midst of it he hurls a winged word that becomes a proverb of the world & conquers kings, & clothes nations in its colours.

I liked that Margaret Fuller should see in Napoleon's head his mighty future, &, for all the beautiful, even voluptuous mouth, should find mountains of the slain & the snows of Russia not irrelevant.

I read somewhere that Dalton did not wait for empirical confirmation of his "law," but promulgated it, struck by its internal evidence.

—

The gross lines are legible to the dull; the cabman is phrenologist so far; he looks in my face to see if his shilling be sure. A dome of brow denotes one thing, a pot belly another, a squint and mats of hair betray character.

—

It will happen easily that twenty mistakes will be made. People often talk most of that which they do not represent. Boston talks of Union, & fevers into proslavery, but the genius of Boston is seen in her real independence, productive power, & *northern* acuteness of mind, πολυτροπος Οδυςςευς, which is generically antislavery. Boston Common, Boston Athenaeum,

Lowell Institute, Railroads, & the love of German literature—these are the true Boston, & not an accidental malignity, or a momentary importance of a few pugnoses, people too slight to sail in any but the fairest weather, and therefore by their very importance praising the great prosperity of Boston. "If it were always such weather as this," my Captain Ellis used to say, "Women might take his ship to sea."

Vasari affirms of the city of Florence, that "the desire for glory & honour is powerfully generated by the air of that place in the men of every profession, & whereby all who possess talent are impelled to struggle that they may not remain in the same grade with those whom they perceive to be only men like themselves," &c, &c, which see, *Bohn's Vasari, Vol. II, p. 308*

I recall today in conversation with W.H.C. the impression made by Wilkinson. He seemed full of ability, power of labor, acute vision, marvellous power of illustration, of great learning in certain directions, having also the power I so value & so rarely meet of *expansion*, expansion, such as Alcott shines with;—but all this spoiled by a certain levity. He held himself cheap. There was no sacredness, no poetry, about him. He was changing his sphere from Swedenborg-mysticism to French Fourierism, with shocking levity, & had forgotten or did not care longer for his past studies. He was surrounded by inferior people, doctors, socialists, Educationists, &c. whom he seemed to value. I fancied I read "For Sale", on all his great talents, & was not flattered even by his kind & encomiastic reception of me. He was tall & largelimbed, looking like our Rev. Thos. Worcester, and wanted the expression of refinement. He was a man of that kind of waste strength that he could easily run for diversion into Icelandic literature, as it seems he is doing.

I should say of him that as we see children at school often expend a prodigality of memory & of arithmetical power, which, occurring in an adult subject, would make a Porson, Parr, or Lacroix—& see it in such children without respect,—mere boarding school rattle,—because it does not seem solid & enduring or known to the mind itself, & so secured, but merely as this year's grass, or annual plants, which a single night in November will annihilate. So I believe that all this unrealized ability seemed insecure. As soon as he himself has said, These weapons are mine, and lo! by them I possess the Universe, as yonder Astronomer does the stars by his tube & chart: O joy, I cannot live, I am too happy. Hold back thy thunderbolt, Jove, envy me not my near approach:—then we should sympathize with the terror & beauty of his gifts & he would be sacred to himself & to us.

It did not seem that he was enamoured of his thoughts, as all good thinkers ought to be. A fair ample house with excellent windows, but no fireplace.

This experience is surely very familiar, that things are valued by pairs, & that either alone is naught. Salt enhances the egg, which without it is naught. Money is good for nothing at Juan Fernandez, but London is not London without it. Refinement of person & manners is inestimable to a person of real force: But one who wants that is only a nice man. And force fails, & is ever in Coventry, for want of refinement. A remarkable example of a man of great proportions failing yet to be great.

Edward Everett had in my youth an immense advantage in being the first American Scholar who sat in the German Universities & brought us home in his head their whole culture, method, & results,—to us who did not so much as know the names of Heyne, Wolf, Hug, & Ruhnken. He dealt out his treasures too with such admirable prudence, so temperate & abstemious that our wonder & delight were still new. It seems to me as if our new lecturer had the like advantage. He has a deal of talent, reads well, distributes well, & keeps fast to the central thesis of his discourse, has a good deal of *popular profoundness*, shall I say, or just that degree of depth which his audience can swim in, without any real originality except in his rhetoric; but suggests to me continually the conjecture, or the probability, that he is repeating after some good master or masters, to us unknown, in Halle, or Gottingen. I think his lectures excellent for our young men, & instructive to old craftsmen, as specimens of good lecturing.

Edward Everett was a Manco Capac.

*

America. Emigration.

In the distinctions of the genius of the American race it is to be considered, that, it is not indiscriminate masses of Europe, that are shipped hitherward, but the Atlantic is a sieve through which only or chiefly the liberal adventurous sensitive *America-loving* part of each city, clan, family, are brought. It is the light complexion, the blue eyes of Europe that come: the black eyes, the black drop, the Europe of Europe is left.

—

1851, July 22. Yesterday, Eddy & Edie going with me to bathe in Walden, Eddy was very brave with a sharp bulrush, & presently broke into this rhyme—

"With my sharp-pointed sword
I will conquer Concórd."

Kleinstadtisch thinks all the rest of the world is a heap of rubbish.

Nationality is babyishness for the most part.

Is it not a convenience to have a person in town who knows where penny royal grows, or sassafras or punk for a slowmatch; or Celtis,—the false elm; or cats-o-nine-tails; or wild cherries; or wild pears; where is the best appletree, where is the Norway pine, where the beech, or Epigaea, or Linnaea, or sanguinavia, or orchis pulcherrima, or drosera, or lauras benzoin, or pink huckleberry, or shag barks, where is the best chestnut grove, hazelnuts, where are trout, where woodcocks, where wild bees, where pigeons, or who can tell where the stakedriver (bittern) can be heard, who has seen & can show you the Wilson's plover?

—

Thoreau wants a little ambition in his mixture. Fault of this, instead of being the head of American Engineers, he is captain of a huckleberry party.

—

I think Horace Greeley's career one of the most encouraging facts in our Whiggish age. A white haired man in the city of New York has adopted every benevolent crotchet, &

maintained it, until he commands an army of a million now in the heart of the United States. Here we stand shivering on the North wall of opposition, we New-England idealists,—& might have taken Boston long ago, "had we had the pluck of a louse," to use the more energetic than elegant expression of my travelling friend.

Conversation.

Whenever the Muses sing, Pan spirts poppy-juice all about, so that no one who hears them can carry any word away.

True of fine conversation.

—

H. T. will not stick
he is not practically renovator. He is a boy, & will be an old boy. Pounding beans is good to the end of pounding Empires, but not, if at the end of years, it is only beans.

I fancy it an inexcusable fault in him that he is insignificant here in the town. He speaks at Lyceum or other meeting but somebody else speaks & his speech falls dead & is forgotten. He rails at the town doings & ought to correct & inspire them.

In Webster the past the letter
the animal orgies, falls back on that
protection of property

—

His rhetoric has got purged of the word liberty for Fate has been too strong for him.
All the drops of his blood have eyes that look downward.
But not by such as he have the steps for mankind been taken.

—

We want an exploding Bonaparte who could take forward steps instead of these crabs.
Webster values the Union then only as a large farm property.

Now Columbus was no crab, nor John Adams, nor Patrick Henry, nor Jefferson,
nor Martin Luther nor Copernicus

*

And the American idea is no crab but a man incessantly advancing as the shadow of the dial or the heavenly body that casts it.

—

S. Ward thinks 'Twill do for Carolina to be unreasonable & nullify. But not so with Massachusetts, which is the head: the toe may nullify, but the head must not nullify.

—

As soon as the Constitution enacts a criminal law, disunion already exists. "*'Tis you that say it, not I; you do the deeds.*"

—

M. F. said one day to S W & A W "I have not seen any intellect that would compare with my own."

If these 30 nations cannot do what they would, who can? Is it not time for them to do something beside ditching & draining? beside making land friable, & hay & corn cheap? beside getting money?
Every race has done somewhat generous. What have you done?

One thing or the other. If it is ascertained that the commissioner is only a notary to surrender the black man to his hunter, then infamy attaches to the post. No man of right sentiments can sit on that bench. It belongs to a class from which the turnkey & the hangman & the informer are taken. The dislike & contempt of Society very properly attaches to the officer.

—

The fugitives
You may say the slaves are better off as they are, & that nothing will tempt them to exchange their condition. This amiable argument falls to the ground in the case of the fugitive. He has certified, as distinctly as human nature could, his opinions.
And to take him back is to steal.

We are glad at last to get a clear case, one on which no shadow of doubt can hang. This is not meddling with other people's affairs,—this is other people meddling with us. This is

not going crusading after slaves who it is alleged are very happy & comfortable where they are: all that amiable argument falls to the ground, but defending a human being who has taken the risks of being shot or burned alive, or cast into the sea, or starved to death or suffocated in a wooden box,—taken all this risk to get away from his driver & recover the rights of man. And this man the Statute says, you men of Massachusetts shall kidnap & send back again a thousand miles across the sea to the dog-hutch he fled from. And this filthy enactment was made in the 19th Century, by people who could read & write.
I will not obey it, by God.

A voyage! yes; but I do not like that craft which requires that we should stand all hours at the pump.

Intellect strips, affection clothes. If the good God would perfect his police on any day he has only to open that upper chamber in each man's & woman's brain which is his or her determinate love, & on the instant chastity is secured by an impregnable guard, as if all the population lived like naked children in one nursery.

Doctrine of Leasts.

Nature makes everything Cheap: the smallest amount of material; the low-price, the low-fare system, is hers. Least action, least pain.

Liberty.

I think this matter of liberty is one of those rights which requires fine sense to appreciate, & with every degree of civility it will be more truly felt & defined. A barbarous tribe will by means of their best heads secure substantial liberty, but where there is any weakness in a race as is in the black race & it becomes in any degree matter of concession & protection from their stronger neighbours, the incompatibility & offensiveness of the wrong will of course be most evident to the most cultivated.

For it is, is it not, the very nature of courtesy, of politeness, of religion, of love, to prefer another, to postpone one's self, to protect another from one's self. That is the distinction of the gentleman,—to defend the weak & redress the injured, as it is of the savage & the brute, to usurp & use others.

—

As Vishnu in the Vedas pursues Maya in all forms, when, to avoid him, she changes herself into a cow, then he into a bull; she into doe, he into a buck; she into a mare, he into a stallion; she into a hen, he into a cock, & so forth; so our metaphysics should be able to follow the flying force through all transformations, & name the new pair, identical thro' all variety. For Memory, imagination, Reason, sense, are only masks of one power; as physical & spiritual laws are only new phases of limitation.

—

Autobiography too. I am never beaten until I know that I am beaten. I meet powerful people to whom I have no skill to reply. They think they have defeated me. It is so published in the journals. I am defeated in this external way, perhaps, on a dozen different lines. My Leger may show that I am in debt, cannot make my ends meet, & vanquish the enemy so. My race may be not prospering, we are sick, ugly, obscure, unpopular: My children may be worsted; I seem to fail in my protegés too. That is to say in all the encounters that have yet chanced I have not been weaponed for that particular occasion, & have been historically beaten, & yet I know all the time that I have never been beaten, have never yet fought, shall certainly fight when my hour comes, & shall beat.

All eloquence is a war of posts. What is said is the least part of the oration. It is the attitude taken, the unmistakeable sign never so casually given (in the tone of voice, or manner, or word,) that a greater spirit speaks from you than is spoken to in him.

—

It is not so strange as we say that races mix. We make a great ado about pure races, but strange resemblances meet us everywhere. Not strange that Malay & European, Celt & Saxon, Roman & Tartar should mix, when we see the descent of the beasts of the forest in our human form, that the barriers of the races are not so firm but that some spray sprinkles us from the most distant seas.

We are superstitious.

What we think & say is wonderfully better for our spirits & trust, *in another's mouth.*

Of course, the fact of my discontent with Webster's speech, which reaches to total aversion, does not yet advertise me that it weakens his position, until I hear another man say "it is base."

We think the event severed from the person, & do not see the inevitable tie. It is like the nudicaulis plant,—the leaf invariably accompanies it, though the stems are connected underground.

I am always taught that not the topic,—the subject,—is important,—but the angle of vision only. Allcot astonishes by the grandeur of his Angle. I tell him he is the Bonaparte of speculators, born to rout the armies of ghosts, the Austrians of the Soul.

Dreams

My dreams are somewhat arch & satirical if I dare give them all the meaning they will bear. If they mean anything, they are surprising hits, yet by no means from a divine plane, but from a great sagacity on the Franklin level. This confusion in counting New Hampshire bills was an example. They had a varying value, twenty different figures on the corners.

—

Shakspeare.

One listens to the magnifying of Goethe's poem by his critic, & replies, "Yes, it is good, if you all agree to come in, & be pleased;" and you fall into another company & mood, & like it not. It is so with Wordsworth. But to Shakspeare alone God granted the power to dispense with the humours of his company: They must needs all take *his.* He is always good; & Goethe knew it, & said, "It is as idle to compare Tieck to me, as me to Shakspeare." I looked through the first part of Faust today, & find it a little too modern & intelligible. We can make such a fabric at several mills, though a little inferior. The miraculous, the beauty which we can manufacture at no mill, can give no account of, it wants;—the cheerful, radiant, profuse beauty of which Shakspeare, of which Chaucer, had the secret.—

The Faust on the contrary abounds in the disagreeable. The vice is prurient, learned, Parisian. In the presence of Jove, Priapus may be allowed, but he should have the least to say. But here he is an equal hero. The egotism, the wit is calculated. The book is undeniably made by a great master, & stands unhappily related to the whole modern world, but it is a very disagreeable chapter of history, & accuses the author.

—

Expansions is still the name for that game which Alcott's talk permits, more than anybody's. Other people, all good people, give you leave,—give you hint, & scope; but he more purely. One would use him for that, tho' others would afford it; just as we prefer litmus as a chemical reagent, tho' other substances will do.

—

E.P.P. ransacks her memory for anecdotes of Margaret's youth, her selfdevotion, her disappointments which she tells with fervency, but I find myself always putting the previous question. These things have no value, unless they lead somewhere. If a Burns, if a De Stael, if an artist is the result, our attention is preengaged; but quantities of rectitude, mountains of merit, chaos of ruins, are of no account without result,—'tis all mere nightmare; false instincts; wasted lives.

Now, unhappily, Margaret's writing does not justify any such research. All that can be said, is, that she represents an interesting hour & group in American cultivation; then, that she was herself a fine, generous, inspiring, vinous, eloquent talker, who did not outlive her influence; and a kind of justice requires of us a monument, because crowds of vulgar people taunt her with want of position.

—

ABA said of W.E.C. that he had the keen appetite for society with extreme repulsion, so that it came to a kind of commerce of cats, love & hate, embraces & fighting.

*

Carlyle is a better painter in the Dutch style than we have had in literature before. It is terrible—his closeness & fidelity: he copies that which never was seen before. It is like seeing your figure in a glass. It is an improvement in writing, as strange as Daguerre's in picture, and rightly fell in the same age with that; and yet, there is withal an entire reserve on his own part, & the hiding of his hand. What do we know of his own life? The courage which is grand, the courage to feel that nature who made me may be trusted, & one's self painted as also a piece of nature, he has not.

Beauty.

Once open the sense of beauty,—& vulgar manners,—tricks, bad eating, loud speaking, yelps, and all the miscreation of ugliness, become intolerable, and we are reconciled to the intense selfishness & narrowness of "good society," thinking that, bad as it is, the better alternative, as long as health lasts.

Privilege. Beauty.

It is a privilege. The handsome youth may stoop as from the clouds, & snatch up the fairest maid. Indeed, all privilege is that of Beauty, for there are many Beauties: 1. of face; 2. of form; 3. of manner, not less prevailing. 4. of brain or method: the sphere changes with the mode, and the sphere of brain or method is elemental, & lasts long:—Shakspeare's, Raphael's, Michel Angelo's is this Beauty of Brain or Method.

In my memoirs, I must record that I always find myself doing something less than my best task. In the spring, I was writing politics; now am I writing a biography, which not the absolute command, but facility & amiable feeling prompted.

—

Jesus said, "When he looketh on her, he hath already committed adultery". But he is an adulterer already, *before yet he has looked on the woman*, by the superfluity of animal, & the weakness of thought, in his constitution. Who meets him, or who meets her, in the street, sees at once, they are ripe to be each other's victim.

—

Symbol

Yes, History is a vanishing allegory, and repeats itself to tediousness, a thousand & a million times. The *Rape of the Sabines* is perpetual, and the fairest Sabine virgins are every day pounced upon by rough victorious Romans, masquerading under mere New Hampshire & Vermont & Boston names, as Webster, Choate, Thayer, Bigelow or other obscurity.

Ellery thinks these waterside cottages of Nahant & Chelsea & so on, never see the sea. There, it is all dead water, & a place for dead horses, & the smell of Mr Kips' omnibus stable. But go to Truro, & go on to the beach there, on the Atlantic side, & you will have every stroke of the sea like the cannon of the "Sea-Fencibles". There is a solitude, which you cannot stand more than ten minutes.

He thinks the fine art of Goethe & company very dubious, & 'tis doubtful whether Sam Ward is quite in his senses in his value of that book of prints of old Italian School, Giotto & the rest. It may do for very idle gentlemen, &c &c. I reply, There are a few giants who gave the thing vogue by their realism,—Michel Angelo & Ribiera & Salvator Rosa, and the man who made the old Torso Hercules, & the Phidias,—man or men, who made the Parthenon reliefs,—had a drastic style which a blacksmith or a stonemason would say, was starker than their own. And I adhere to Van Waagen's belief, that there is a pleasure from works of art, which nothing else can yield.

—

Where is the New Metaphysics? We are intent on Meteorology to find the law of the Variable Winds to the end that we may not get our hay wet. I also wish a Farmer's Almanac of the Mental Moods that I may farm my mind. There are undulations of power & imbecility & I lose days sitting at my table which I should gain to my body & mind if I knew beforehand that no thought would come that day. I see plainly enough that ordinarily we take counters for gold, that our eating & trading & marrying & learning are mistaken by us for ends & realities, whilst they are only symbols of true life; and, as soon as we have come by a divine leading into the inner firmament, we are apprised of the unreality or representative character of what we had esteemed solidest. Then we say, here & now!

We then see that before this terrific beauty nature too is cheap; that geometry & astronomy also are its cheap effects, before this pure glory. Yet Ah! if we could once come in & plant our instruments, & take some instant measurement & inventory of this Dome, in whose light forms, & substances, & sciences are dissolved. But we never so much as enter,—'tis a glimpse; 'tis a peeping through a chink; the dream in a dream. We play at Bopeep with Truth, and cannot write the Chapter of Metaphysics. We write books, "How to Observe," &c yet the Kant or the Plato of the Inner World, which is Heaven, has not come. To describe adequately, is the high power & one of the highest enjoyments of man. This is Art.

'Tis indifferent whether you say, all is matter, or, all is spirit; & 'tis plain there is a tendency in the times to an identity philosophy. You do not degrade man by saying, Spirit is only finer body; nor exalt him by saying, Matter is phenomenal merely; all rests on the affection of the theorist,—on the question whether his aim be noble.

Here & there were souls which saw through peaches & wine, politics, money, & women, saw that these as objects of desire were all alike, & all cheats; that the finest fruit is dirty, & must be seen by the soul as it is seen by the provision-dealer; and that all the other allurements that infatuate men, & which they play for, are the selfsame thing, with a new gauze or two of illusion overlaid. But the soul is distinguished by its aim,—what is its end? This reacts, this far future consummation which it seeks, reacts through ages, & enobles & beatifies every modern moment, & makes the individual grand among his coevals, though they had every advantage of skill, force, & favor. Here & there is a soul which is a seed or principle of good, a needle pointing to the true north, thrown into the mountains of foolishness, & desarts of evil, & therefore maligned & isolated by the rest. This soul has the secret of power, this soul achieves somewhat new & beautiful which endears heaven & earth to mankind, & lends a domestic grace to the sun & the stars.

Edith's opinion

Edith, when a little girl, whimpered when her mother described the joys of Heaven. She did not want to go there, she wanted to "stay" (& she looked round the room,) "where there was a *door*, & folks, and *things.*"

Ellery thinks that he is the lucky man who can write in bulk, forty pages on a hiccough, ten pages on a man's sitting down in a chair; like Hawthorne, &c, that will go.

I have lately in E.P.P.'s letter this passage. "Hawthorne always said, that Lloyd F. explained the faults of Margaret. I don't know if you ever saw that creature. He seems to be the Fuller organization, Fullerism unbalanced, unmixed with the over-soul, which sweetens & balances the original demon, & yet he is unquestionably what the Scotch people call an "innocent;" for he is so self sufficient, & exacting, & insolent, unawares, unconsciously, & in the purest good faith. He acts & feels according to his Constitution, & God is responsible for his ugliness. He was sent, perhaps, as a sign what original ugliness could be overcome by a glorious spirit, which had a vision of the good & true & beautiful, with a will & determination to conquer. Margaret's life was the result of this strange association."

—

The Americans accept any work that falls in their way, & will be sailors, farmers, judges, presidents, or authors, as need & opportunity command, just as the farmer makes no choice of his work because he likes to husk or to thresh or to plant, but accepts the task of the day from the state of the crop & the weather,—hays in a hay day, gathers each fruit when it is ripe, winnows in a windy day, fishes in a wet one, goes on to his meadow in December.

The housewife's proverb is "There are a thousand things to everything."

—

Once again in celebration of the Intellect, it is true, that the world is wrong, & we are right; that our conversation once or twice with our mates has apprized us, that we belong to better circles than we have yet beheld; that there is a music somewhere awaiting us, that shall make us "forget the taste of meat;" a mental power whose generalizations are more worth for joy

& for avail than anything that is now called philosophy or literature; that the poets, that Homer & Milton & Shakspeare, do not content us; they have not dared to offer us this food. No, the most they have done is to have put themselves in symmetry with this, to betray their belief that such discourse as this is possible to the like of them.

There is something,—our brothers over the sea do not know it or own it,—Scott & Southey, Hallam & Macaulay, Carlyle & Dickens would all deny & blaspheme it,—which is setting them all aside, & the whole world also, & planting itself forever & ever.

All men know the truth, but what of that? it is rare to find one that knows how to speak it. A man tries to speak it, & his voice is like the hiss of a snake; the truth is not spoken, but injured. The same thing happens in power to do the right. His rectitude is ridiculous. His organs do not play him true. By & by comes by a facility, a walking facility. He can move the mountain, & carry off yonder star, as easily as he carries the hair on his head. Yet who is he, & whence? God knows; his brother is an ideot, his father is a pawn-broker, his mother is a cow.

Culture. Plainly, a man can spare nothing; he wants blackest night & whitest day, sharp eye, fleet foot, strong hand, head of Jove, health, sleep, appetite, & conscience like a clock. The finest artist, the tenderest poet, wants the ferocity of cannibals,—only transmuted into his milder instruments,—as battery or magazine to furnish out his long drawn sweetness.

—

Oct. 14. Today is holden at Worcester the "Woman's Convention."

I think that, as long as they have not equal rights of property & right of voting, they are not on a right footing. But this wrong grew out of the savage & military period, when, because a woman could not defend herself, it was necessary that she should be assigned to some man who was paid for guarding her. Now in more tranquil & decorous times it is plain she should have her property, &, when she marries, the

parties should as regards property, go into a partnership full or limited, but explicit & recorded.
For the rest, I do not think a woman's convention, called in the spirit of this at Worcester, can much avail. It is an attempt to manufacture public opinion, & of course repels all persons who love the simple & direct method. I find the Evils real & great. If I go from Hanover street to Atkinson street,—as I did yesterday,—what hundreds of extremely ordinary, paltry, hopeless women I see, whose plight is piteous to think of. If it were possible to repair the rottenness of human nature, to provide a rejuvenescence, all were well, & no specific reform, no legislation would be needed. For, as soon as you have a sound & beautiful woman, a figure in the style of the Antique Juno, Diana, Pallas, Venus, & the Graces, all falls into place, the men are magnetised, heaven opens, & no lawyer need be called in to prepare a clause, for woman moulds the lawgiver. I should therefore advise that the Woman's Convention should be holden in the Sculpture Gallery, that this high remedy might be suggested.

"Women," Plato says, "are the same as men in faculty, only less." I find them all victims of their temperament. "I never saw a woman who did not cry," said E. Nature's end of maternity,—maternity for twenty years,—was of so supreme importance, that it was to be secured at all events, even to the sacrifice of the highest beauty. Bernhard told Margaret that every woman (whatever she says, reads, or writes) is thinking of a husband. And this excess of temperament remains not less in Marriage. Few women are sane. They emit a coloured atmosphere, one would say, floods upon floods of coloured light, in which they walk evermore, & see all objects through this warm tinted mist which envelopes them. Men are not, to the same degree, temperamented; for there are multitudes of men who live to objects quite out of them, as to politics, to trade, to letters, or an art, unhindered by any influence of constitution.

I remember meeting with a misogynist, who looked on every woman as an impostor.

—

Fenimore Cooper said to a lady in conversation, "I can make any woman blush." The lady blushed with natural resentment. "I can lay it on deeper than that, madam," said the pitiless talker. Out of vexation at her own selfdistrust the lady crimsoned again to her neck & shoulders. —the power of impudence.
Mr Mackay said to little Marny Storer, "Why, Marny! What is the matter with your eyes?" "Nothing is the matter with my eyes," said the little beauty, looking up earnestly. "Why Marny," said Mr Mackay, "they are getting to look deeper & deeper, and, by & by, I fear, they will be so deep, that somebody will fall in."

A man serves his work, and loves to feel his liberty. He likes his dram & his segar for that, because they make him kick & fling, & the strait jacket is loosened a little. A man serves his work. A man is a housekeeper,—yea, verily, he builds a house, & it is his task thenceforward whilst he lives to paint, shingle, repair, enlarge, & beautify that house. The house finds him in employment as long as he lives. A man buys a piece of land:— Who buys? who is bought? Is it the land? or the man? Year by year will testify.

I knew a man who had a claim on Mexico. He was a good Quaker, &, like the liberal of his sect, a little transcendental in his notions. But he left all, & prosecuted this claim, & it took him no whither. He learned to lie & steal, & to take the name of his God, in vain. A man writes a lecture, & is carted round the Country at the tail of his lecture, for months, to read it.
A man inherits a fortune, & leaves all his ideas & tendencies to husband & spend it; & it spends him. It makes him a fribble.

Roots are made by trees best, when the leaves & wood are made best. Saliency & inertia

I believe in the flowing power. Whigs believe only in the stagnant.

*

27 October

It would be hard to recall the rambles of last night's talk with H. T. But we stated over again, to sadness, almost, the Eternal loneliness. I found, that, though the stuff of Tragedy & of Romances is in a moral Union of two superior persons, and the confidence of each in the other, for long years, out of sight & in sight, and against all appearances, is at last justified by victorious proof of probity, to gods & men, causing a gush of joyful emotion, tears, glory, or whatnot,—though there be for heroes this *moral union*,—yet they too are still as far off as ever from an intellectual union, & this moral union is for comparatively low & external purposes, like the cooperation of a ship's company, or of a fire-club. But how insular & pathetically solitary, are all the people we know! Nor dare we tell what we think of each other, when we bow in the street. 'Tis mighty fine for us to taunt men of the world with superficial & treacherous courtesies. I saw yesterday Sunday whilst at dinner my neighbor H. creeping into my barn. At once it occurred, 'Well, men are lonely, to be sure, & here is this able, social, intellectual farmer under this grim day, as grimly, sidling into my barn, in the hope of some talk with me, showing me how to husband my cornstalks. Forlorn enough!'

It is hard to believe that all times are alike & that the present is also rich. When this annual project of a Journal returns, & I cast about to think who are to be contributors, I am struck with a feeling of great poverty; my bareness! my bareness! seems America to say.

There are several persons who would be inestimable to it, if you could attach to them a selfacting siphon, that would tap & draw them off, as they cannot do by themselves. Alcott & Channing, in chief. Lane would be valuable, year in, & year out, in spite of his bad writing; for he is real sturdy, quantitative, & his sharp speaking creates dramatic situations, & brings out good things from himself & others. Unspeakable meannesses, to be sure—but he can afford them.

Certainly concert exasperates people to a certain fury of performance, they can rarely reach alone. A Journal can behave well, when a man cannot behave well. The same sentence is more weighty from the old Journal, than from a new writer.

And a truth-speaking institution thus seems possible, out of a society of editors who singly cannot quite speak the truth.

Beware of Engagements. Learn to say no, & drop resolutely all false claims. I suppose, I have a letter, each week, asking an autograph; one, each quarter, asking antislavery lecture; one yesterday asking particulars of the life of Mr Carlyle, &c. &c. And every day is taxed by the garden, the orchard, the barn.

Faith shall be justified. Live for the year, not for the day. Let logic, let character rule the hour. That is never vulgar.

But can really every man afford to procure his proper tools?

October

In reading Carlyle's "Life of Sterling," I still feel, as of old, that the best service C. has rendered is to Rhetoric, or the Art of Writing. Now here is a book in which the vicious conventions of writing are all dropped; you have no board interposed between you & the writer's mind, but he talks flexibly, now high, now low, in loud hard emphasis, then in undertones, then laughs outright, then calmly narrates, then hints or raises an eyebrow, & all this living narration is daguerreotyped for you in his page. He has gone nigher to the wind than any other craft. No book can any longer be tolerable in the old husky Neal-on-the-Puritans model. But he does not, for all that, very much uncover his secret mind.

A personal influence towers up in memory the only worthy force when we would gladly forget numbers or money or climate, gravitation, & the rest of Fate. Margaret, wherever she came, fused people into society, & a glowing company was the result. When I think how few persons can do that feat for the intellectual class, I feel our squalid poverty.

Massive figures, sitting never so poorly clothed or sheltered, not ashamed of themselves, or of their hands, or feet, or faces.

*

Undoubtedly if a Concord man of 1750 could come back, & walk in our street, today, from the meetinghouse to the Depot, he would recognize all the people as if they were his own Contemporaries. Yes, that is a Buttrick; and that a Flint; & that Barrett or Minot: Here an Erskine, there a Rowe, for no doubt a regent atom or monad constrains all the other particles to take its feature & temperament.

from

Journal at the West

1850–1853

1850, 25 May at Fort Ancient, Warren County, Ohio. All these alleged *remains* of the departed American race of 3000 years ago seem at first nothing more than the familiar "ridges" of Massachusetts such as I know in Concord woods, in Mount Auburn Cemetery, or, on the Ridge Road in Groton. Geologists call them *Osars* or *horsebacks.* Here, however, they are continued to a great extent, between 4 & 5 miles in circuit, & return into the system; keep too about the same elevation from the interior plane or level of the Fort, & so present a very fort-like appearance. Very old trees stand on the very summit of this long-drawn parapet. A few well-defined mounds are here & there in the line of the works, and two or three piles of stones are found. No other trace of man is here. The forest is a magnificent colonnade of tulip-trees, rock maple, white oak, shagbark, black walnut, & beech. The fallen columns form natural bridges over every ravine, and enormous grapevines depend like cables from the trees. In this sylvan Persepolis, I spent my birthday with a very intelligent party of young men, James, Blackwell, Goddard, Spofford, Mathews, Collins, & was often reminded of my visit to Stonehenge with Carlyle in June 1848.

The Kentuckian sits all day on his horse. You shall see him at the door of a country store. There he sits & talks & makes his bargains for hours, & never dismounts. When all is done, he spurs up his steed, & rides away.—The path of a tornado is traced through the forest, of the same width for miles. They tell of a child who was carried five miles by one. This was too good to leave alone. So we presently heard of a tornado which drove a plough through a field, & turned as pretty a furrow all round the field as you ever saw. This, of course, suggested a storm in Havana where the wind blew so hard, that a man was left clinging to an iron lamp-post, with nothing on him but his stock & his spurs.

—

J. E. Goodson reads his favourite scores without any piano, & says, that, lying on his bed, he thinks them over, & enjoys them more than in any performance, so many faults belong to any execution. "Bach's music has the stability of a spur of the Rocky mountains;" Beethoven always verges on the supernatural. Do not believe too much, it seems to say, in the force of gravitation. I will lift you presently.

Nothing is deep without religion.

The people do not let the Ohio river go by them without using it as it runs along. The waterworks supply the city abundantly, &, in every street, in these dusty days, it is poured on to the pavement. The water offered you to drink is as turbid as lemonade, & of a somewhat greyer hue. Yet it is freely drunk, & the inhabitants much prefer it to the limestone water of their wells.

—

At St Louis only Missouri water is drunk. The waters of the two streams are kept unmixed, the Missisippi on the east bank, the Missouri on the west until 40 miles below St Louis.
18 June. Under a bright moon about 9 o'clock pm I reached the mouth of the Missouri. Very sorry not to see this confluence by day. But at night it was very easy to see the two volumes of water by their different colour, one muddy, & one black, & the force with which from its mighty mouth the Missouri drove the Missisippi towards the Illinois bank. I asked the Captain if the mouth of the Ohio were not as wide? "Perhaps it is but there is not so much water comes out of it. It pours in a high water, but it does not last but a little while." How deep is the water here? "From 20 to 50 feet." How fast is the current? "Three miles an hour." How fast do you go against it? "Six, six and a half, and seven." And ten miles down stream? Can you keep ten all day? "Yes."

*

Steamboat disasters are as common as musquitoes. At St Louis, 47 boats were burned between 17 May, 1849, and 17 May 1850.

In 1834–8 when Captain Ward first went up the Missisippi he carried *produce*. Now the River loads him with exports.

—

7 February 1851. Rochester

Mr J A Wilder made me acquainted with the University of R. which was extemporising here like a picnic. They had bought a hotel, once a railroad terminus depot, for $8,500, turned the diningroom into a chapel by putting up a pulpit on one side, made the barroom into a Pythologian Society's Hall, & the chambers into Recitation rooms, Libraries, & professors' apartments, all for $700. a year. They had brought an Omnibus load of professors down from Madison bag & baggage — Hebrew, Greek, Chaldee, Latin, Belles Lettres, Mathematics, & all Sciences, called in a painter, sent him up a ladder to paint the title "University of Rochester" on the wall, and now they had runners on the road to catch students. One lad came in yesterday; another, this morning; "thought they should like it first rate", & now they thought themselves ill used if they did not get a new student every day. And they are confident of graduating a class of Ten by the time green peas are ripe.

—

Their eyes are all dangerous, & I wonder that life is so safe as it is. They announce in the St Louis papers that only two men were killed in the streets during the last week. But this morning I notice a fatal affray the last night. They are made of sulphur & potash. Yet Memphis is the gunpowder point.

An age or generation in Ohio, is 3 years.

Mr Greene says, "Sir I have held that opinion three weeks."

How did you get on with your goods? "O you know the Pawnees pitched into me & I was glad to get off with my scalp." Well, you know he was humbugging me but only that word Pawnee was enough & I thought I had just as lief be killed by a Pawnee, as sit here at a desk every day, from 9 o'clock till 7.

—

Dr Wing of Collinsville, Ill. remarked that the strength of Slavery consisted in the support it found in the New England States.

He said, what I have heard from others, that you can form no conclusion to depend upon, from what a man says, he will do, in this country. He says he will come, he will not come; he says he will bring twenty hands; perhaps he will bring three.

Entire want of punctuality & business habit. One principal cause of this is the uncertainty of health. The miasma takes the laborers.

The Illinoians were called *Suckers*, from the circumstance, that the first settlements were in the Southern part of the state, & the settlers used to come up to Galena, to work in the mines, about the time when the Suckers came up the river, in the spring & return when they returned.

Jan. 8. 1853. Left St Louis, & came up the river to Alton, 25 miles, at the rate of 10 miles the hour on the steampacket Cornelia. The other boat, the Altona, is faster, & has made it in 1h. 40′. The meeting of the Missouri & Missisippi is a noble landscape & the town of Alton (6 or 7000 pop.) on the high limeston bluff shows well over the widewatered shore.

At Alton, we took the train for Springfield, 72 miles. Senator Breese & Mr Young of U.S. Congress, Gov. Edwards, & other railroad men were in the train, & made an agreeable party *in the baggage car*, where they had a box of brandy, a box of buffalo tongues, & a box of soda biscuit. They showed me eight or ten deer flying across the prairie, with their white tails erect, disturbed by the train; then, presently, one who stood & looked at us; then a fire on the prairie. The corn was not yet gathered, & a farmer told us, that they had not yet been able to get upon the land to gather it,—too much mud for horse & wagon.—It does not usually get all gathered until March. Gov. Edwards had been at St Louis in 1815 or 1816 when there was but one brick house in the place. And until lately any man

arriving there & seeing the dilapidated old French houses, their posts all rotted away at bottom & swinging from the piazza above, would have been more struck with the air of decay than of growth.
At Springfield, found the mud of the deluge. Mr B. had said of a bread & butter pudding at the hotel, "It was a fraud upon Lazarus;" & told the story of the London milk-man, who, being indicted for adulterating milk, got off by proving that there was no particle of milk in the composition. A man brought patent churns here, & somebody there said, "You take Peters's milk, & if you can make a particle of butter out of that, you shall have not only a patent, but a deed of the State of Illinois!" Meanness of politics, low fillibusterism, dog-men, that have not shed their canine teeth; well, don't be disgusted; 'tis the work of this River, this Missisippi River that warps the men, warps the nations, they must all obey it, chop down its woods, kill the alligator, eat the deer, shoot the wolf, "follow the river," mind the boat, plant the Missouri-corn, cure, & save, & send down stream the wild foison harvest tilth & wealth of this huge mud trough of the 2 000 miles or 10 000 miles of river. How can they be high? How can they have a day's leisure for anything but the work of the river? Every one has the mud up to his knees, & the coal of the country dinges his shirt collar. How can he be literary or grammatical? The people are all kings: out on the prairie the sceptre is the driving-whip. And I notice an extraordinary firmness in the face of many a drover, an air of independence & inevitable lips, which are worth a hundred thousand dollars: No holding a hat for opinions. But the politicians in their statehouses are truckling & adulatory.

In California, there is much insanity. A man is getting out of his digging 20.00 a day, &, next beside him, another is getting out $1000. per day, and the men in the one work like dogs, because they are expecting every hour that they will strike on the same vein. How can their heads or bodies stand such excitement?

As soon as one is sick all is over with him, he pays an ounce to the doctor for every visit, say three times a day, then for

nursing at high rates, so that he pays 50 to 75 dollars a day while he is sick, which soon empties his pocket.
A man goes to the tavern & says to the landlord "I have no money." "It makes no difference" says the landlord, "go to the table." For the case is common & they know that every man who will work will soon "make a raise," as they call it, as any mechanical work will pay six dollars a day. Judge Shattuck of Pennsylvania with his two sons tried law, but got no money. Judge Henry lent him some. Then he said, "I only lose so. Here is a man advertises that he wants a cellar dug. I shall take that job" & he & his sons went to work & dug the hole. Somebody came & found him there digging, & told him what a case he had in court. "Now, do you let your sons finish that hole, & you come to court." He went, & tried it, & won it. Then he bought land, & raised vegetables for the market, with his sons, and now is worth half a million. San Francisco is as well built a town as Saint Louis; has 60,000 people, & as good living at the Oriental, or Tehama hotels, as at any hotel in the States;—says my Californian doctor, who means to go to the Sandwich Islands to live. The energy of the States is there, & the humanity too. 5,000,000, a month in gold comes to the States.

Church members are apt to misbehave in San Francisco, & freethinkers are apt to be very moral men there.
And he believes himself safer with money about him in San F. than in St Louis or New York because of the summary justice that is executed there.

Springfield is set down here in a prairie bottom in the richest corn-belt, but in a bottom land, & not a rolling prairie. Therefore, they cannot build cellars under the houses, & there is mud such as I never beheld. The Capitol, a costly limestone building, sinks & cracks its walls. I walk to the end of the streets on each side the town, & look out, but dare not step into the immeasureable mud. After walking the deck, thus, for a sufficient time, as I hope, to secure sleep, I remove some pounds of mud from my overshoes, & creep into my cabin.

Yesterday I went over to the Statehouse, with Judge Breese (U.S. Senator.) & called on the Governor. (French) Whilst I was paying my respects to his Excellency the Secretary of State came into the room, & the Governor introduced me to him. "Governor," said the Secretary, "did you take my screw-driver out of my room?" The Executive of Illinois acknowledged the fact, & asked the clerk in the room to find it. They are all poor country people & live hard.

Senator Douglass (newly re-elected,) gives an entertainment to his friends in the Representative Chamber on Thursday night, for which 800 cards have been issued. Mr Douglass is at Washington, but is to pay the bills, &, 'tis said here, the entertainment is to cost $3000. Tomorrow night the Legislature is invited to Alton, to celebrate the new road, & the desired improvements of that town. The old heroes came in with 100 cannon & 10 000 troops, the leaders of today conquer with 100 champagne bottles & 20 boxes segars.

At St Louis, they talk St Louis incessantly, in all companies. And 'tis said, that, after people have been out here in the West for ten years, nothing would induce them to live in one of the old states. Mr Wolcott of Jacksonville says, his eyes ache for mountains, but when, ten years ago, he went back to Connecticutt, he found he could not breathe there, or, as he persisted in saying, a man was nothing there, could not make his mark. He has the care of keeping the track in order between Springfield & Jacksonville, he in working-clothes, and is a graduate of Yale College. At Springfield the American House is a poor house enough but was full of governors, judges, senators, secretaries, & treasurers, Gov French, the retiring Gov, Matteson, the acceding Executive, Gov Reynolds, the new Speaker of the House, & Gov. Edwards, an old pioneer. When I visited them at their rooms, I found them allowanced with no more square inches of chamber than myself, & with only one chair apiece.

—

Between Jacksonville & Springfield I passed a field of corn containing 1000 acres. A little to the north of us was a field as large belonging to Mr Strawn, who lives 4 miles out of J. & who owns 40 000 acres, lives in the saddle, manages all himself, & is of course a man of prodigious energy. They said he eats mush & milk with two spoons & his ideal of beauty is a fine steer & his ideal of a great man the man who stands in the gap when a great herd of cattle are to be separated, these for market & those to remain for pasture. Of course the man who stands in the gap is to choose on the instant by their looks which to let through the gate & which to keep off the other way as they come up and he must be of such a size & look too as that the cattle shall not run over him. His picture at full length, in his house, exhibits him as standing among cattle with a huge driving whip under his arm. The work is done here by a roving tenantry of natives, of Irish & of Dutchmen, one man being able to till 30 to 40 acres. Mr King represented the whole State as being used for nothing but to raise the greatest quantity of grease.— They raise vast amounts of corn to feed millions of hogs.

from

DO

1852–1854, 1856, 1858

"At mihi succurit pro Ganymede manus."
Martial.

Do you think death or skulls or hospitals fit subjects for cabinet pictures? I do not. I think the pietà or the crucifixion must be treated with more genius than I have seen in all the masters of Italian or Spanish art,—to be a proper picture for houses or churches. And so with dead Romeos, & dead princes & battles. Nature does not so. See how carefully she covers up the skeleton. The eye shall not see it, the sun shall not shine on it, she weaves muscle & tendon & flesh & skin, & down, & hair & beautiful colours of day over it, & forces death down under ground, & makes haste to cover it with leaves & vines, & wipes carefully out every trace by new creation.

The best in us is our profound feeling of interest in the whole of nature. Every man feels that every thing is his cousin, that he has to do with all. Blot out any part of nature, & he too would lose. The great words of the world such as *Analogy*;—what a step mankind took when Plato first spoke that word! Analogy is identity of ratio, & what civilization, what mounting from savage beginnings does it not require! the primary & secondary senses, the several planes or platforms on which the same truth is repeated. So the word of ambition, the proud word of modern science is *homology*.

—

'Tis wonderful how transparent is the creature, how incessantly the creation is in sight. We are like Geneva watches with crystal faces which expose the whole movement. We carry with us this liquor of life flowing up & down in these beautiful bottles & announcing each instant to the curious eye precisely how it is with us.

—

Hannah More scented of violets when a child. Alexander the Great had a natural perfume. It is not uncommon. Children's breath is sweet. My mother in old age had never any ill scent in her chamber, however close it was. The southwind I once found made the hands & hair sweet smelling—

Of HDT. He who sees the horizon, may securely say what he pleases of any tree or twig between him & it.

Genius finds that people are non-conductors.

The day will come when no badge, uniform, or star will be worn, when the eye which carries in it planetary influences from all the stars will indicate rank fast enough by exerting power. For it is true that the stratification of crusts in geology is not more precise than the degrees of rank in minds. A man will say, 'I am born to this position. I must take it, & neither you nor I can help or hinder me. Surely then, I need not fret myself to guard my dignity.'

I find one state of mind does not remember or conceive of another state. Thus I have written within a twelvemonth verses ("Days") which I do not remember the composition or correction of, & could not write the like today, & have only for proof of their being mine, various external evidences as, the MS. in which I find them, & the circumstance that I have sent copies of them to friends, &c &c. Well, if they had been better, if it had been a noble poem, perhaps it would have only more entirely taken up the ladder into heaven.

—

Tin pan.

I am made happy by a new thought, & like to put myself in the conditions to get it, namely, with a person who gives me thoughts in which I find my own mind; or with one who excites my own activity to that point that I think freely & newly. But how rare are these persons! Not one in all Wall street. Yet, while this thought glitters newly before me, I think Wall street nothing. I accurately record the thought, & think I have got it. After a few months, I come again to the record, & it seems a mere bit of glistering tin or tinsel, and no such world wisdom. In fact, the Universe had glowed with its eternal blaze, & I had chipped off this scale, through which its light shone, thinking this the diamond, & put it in my jewel box, & now it is nothing but a dead scale.

—

Fault of Alcott is that he has no memory; therefore, though he built towns, towers, & empires, in his talk of yesterday,—tomorrow, he cannot find a vestige, but must begin again from the Sandy Sahara.

—

On Wednesday, 19 May, I saw Miss Delia Bacon, at Cambridge, at the house of Mrs Becker, & conversed with her on the subject of Shakspeare. Miss B. thinks that a key will yet be found to Shakspeare's interior sense; that some key to his secret may yet be discovered at Stratford; &, I fancy, thinks the famous epitaph, "Good friend for Jesus' sake forbear" protects some explanation of it. Her skepticism in regard to the authorship goes beyond the skepticism of Wolf in regard to Homer or Niebuhr to Latin history.

The multitude of translations from the Latin & Greek classics that have been lately published, have made great havoc with the old study of those languages. At Cambridge, every student is provided with a Bohn's translation of his author, & much the same effect is produced as when lexicons were first introduced. The only remedy would be a rage for prosody, which would enforce attention to the words themselves of the Latin or Greek verse.

—

Smith, in "Divine Drama," rightly sees the unconventionality of the Supreme Actor. And I find in my platoon contrasted figures; as; my brothers, and Everett, & Caroline, & Margaret, & Elizabeth, and Jones Very, & Sam Ward, & Henry Thoreau, & Alcott, & Channing. Needs all these and many more to represent my relations. Besides, what we ask daily is to be conventional; supply this defect in my address, or in my form, or in my fortunes, which puts me a little out of the ring; supply it, & let me be like the rest, & on good terms with them. But the wise gods say, No: We have better things for thee. By humiliations, by defeats, by loss of sympathy, & gulfs of disparity, learn a wider truth & humanity than that of a city gentleman. A Beacon street gentleman is not the highest style of man, and though many fine gentlemen have figured as poets, yet the ethnical man must not be protected, but must himself sound the depths, as well as soar to joys. Saadi & Aesop & Cervantes & Ben Jonson had, I doubt not, the tinker element & tinker experience, which Miss Bacon wishes to ward off from Shakspeare, but which he must also have, as well as the courtly, which she wishes to claim for him. A rich man was never insulted in his life, but Saadi must be stung. A rich man was never in danger from cold, or war, or ruffians, and you can see he was not, from the tameness & dulness of his ideas. But Saadi, or Aesop, or Cervantes, or Regnard, has been taken by corsairs, left for dead, sold as a slave, & knows all the realities of human life.

—

Henry Thoreau's idea of the men he meets, is, that they are his old thoughts walking. It is all affectation to make much of them, as if he did not long since know them thoroughly.

"There is more good in toads, & more harm in frogs, than you can think of," say the countryboys.

—

Adirondac 1858

Aug. 7

Follansbee's Pond. It should be called Stillman's henceforward, from the good camp which this gallant artist has built, & the good party he has led & planted here for the present at the bottom of the little bay which lies near the head of the lake.

The lake is 2 miles long, 1 to ½ mile wide and surrounded by low mountains. Norway pine & white pine abound.

On the top of a large white pine in a bay was an osprey's nest around which the ospreys were screaming, 5 or 6. We thought there were young birds in it, & sent Preston to the top. This looked like an adventure. The tree must be 150 ft. high at least; 60 ft. clean straight stem, without a single branch &, as Lowell & I measured it by the tape as high as we could reach, 14 ft 6 inches in girth. Preston took advantage of a hemlock close by it & climbed till he got on the branches, then went to the top of the pine & found the nest empty, though the great birds wheeled & screamed about him. He said he could climb the bare stem of the pine "though it would be awful hard work." When he came down, I asked him to go up it a little way, which he did, clinging to the corrugations of the bark. Afterwards Lowell watched long for a chance to shoot the osprey, but he soared magnificently, & would not alight.

The pond is totally virgin soil without a clearing in any point, & covered with primitive woods, rock-maple, beech, spruce, white cedar arbor vitae.

We have seen bald eagles, loons, ravens, kingfishers, ducks, tatlers,

We have killed 2 deer yesterday, both in the lake, & otherwise fed our party with lake trout & river trout. The wood thrush we heard at Steph. Bartlett's camp, but not since, & no other thrush.

River, lake, & brook trout cannot be scientifically discriminated, nor yet male from female.

Lowell, next morning, was missing at breakfast, & when he came to camp, told me he had climbed Preston's pine tree.

The midges, blackflies, & musquitoes are looked upon as the protectors of this superb solitude from the tourists, and also —— Creek leading from Raquette river to F. Lake. There is no settler within 12 miles of our camp. Every man has his guide & boat & gun.

—

Abolition

If you can get Russian tactics into your political representation, so as to ensure the fidelity of your representative to the sentiment of the constituency, by making him more afraid of his constituents than he is of his opponents, you will get your will done.

But the secret, the esoterics of abolition,—a secret, too, from the abolitionist,—is, that the negro & the negro-holder are really of one party, & that, when the apostle of freedom has gained his first point of repealing the negro laws, he will find the free negro is the type & exponent of that very animal law; standing as he does in nature below the series of thought, & in the plane of vegetable & animal existence, whose law is to prey on one another, and the strongest has it.

Geology destroys the prestige of antiquity by its larger scale.

The Orientals allow the insane to run with wild animals.

One immense exception each makes in his love of the canon of nature, one reserve,—namely, of all his own rights.

August 3, 1853.

At Lenox, Miss B. S. congratulated herself that Caroline T. had settled down into sensible opinions & practices, like her neighbors. I asked her, if she thought her two sisters who had complied with sensible notions & practices, had quite succeeded? that I perhaps did not think quite as respectfully as she did of Boston & New York, that what she called a success seemed to me a poor thing, &, as those examples betrayed, a mere fetch, or a dose of brandy to drown thought; but only the more degrading those who succeeded. Had New York succeeded? Were the gentlemen of N.Y. entirely satisfied with their manly performance? As far as I am informed, they are ruled by some rowdy aldermen who are notorious rogues & blacklegs. They must feel very clean in going down Wall-street, whilst Mr Rhynders cows them. Is their political conscience sweet & serene, as they find themselves represented at Albany & at Washington? As for these people, they have miserably failed, & 'tis very fine for them to put on airs. The veriest monk in a college is better than they. As to C. I was far from thinking she had ended her experiments. It is her glory that she takes her life in her hand, & is ready for a new world.

In N.Y. Henry James quoted Thackeray's speeches in society, "He liked to go to Westminster Abbey to say his prayers," &c "It gave him the comfortablest feeling." At the same time, he is immoral in his practice, but with limits, & would not commit adultery. H.J. thought Thackeray could not see beyond his eyes, & has no ideas; & merely is a sounding-board against which his experiences thump & resound: He is the merest boy.

These New Yorkers & Lenox people think much of N.Y.; little of Boston. The Bostonians are stiff, dress badly, never can speak

French with good accent; the New Yorkers have exquisite millinery, tournure, great expense, &, on being presented, the men look at you, & instantly see whether your dress & style is up to their mark; if not, (and expense is great part of the thing) they never notice you. "These girls—any one of them,—" (said Thackeray at a party, to a German prince in N.Y.) "has more diamonds on her back than are in all your principality."

And C. said, that it was difficult to go into any society in N.Y. without you were in condition to give parties too. The artists, she said, were very worldly, and will not go anywhere unless they are to have suppers & champagne. She told Hicks she had heard more about money from him & them, than ever before.

H. J. found all these artists poor things, vain, conceited, nobodies.

And E. H. finds in Boston the question of society is that of who gives dinners?

The Boston women spend a great deal of money on rich & rare dresses, and have no milliner of taste who can say, 'this stuff, this color, this trimming, this ensemble does not suit you.' In N.Y. the milliners have this skill. Mrs Perkins, at the Opera, heard a dressmaker say, "how dowdy all the Boston ladies are! Mrs Perkins is dowdy."

Cheering amidst all this trifle was the reading of Charles Newcomb's letters: the golden age came again, the true youth, the true heroism, the future, the ideal.

I could hardly sit to read them out. I was penitent for having ever mistrusted him, for having chided his impatience; and resolved at once to write him, & assure him of my loyalty. Swedenborg rose too, & all the gods out of earth & air & ocean,—if only they would reconcile the two worlds, & make us fit for & contented with either. Only of Charles I would give much to know how it all lies in his mind; I would know his utmost sincerity; know what reserves he makes when he talks divinely.—I would rather know his real mind, than any other person's I have ever met. For it is still true that each makes one immense exception in his love and homage to the canon of nature,—one reserve,—namely, of all his own rights & possibilities.

I told Alcott that I should describe him as a man with a divination or good instinct for the quality & character of wholes; as a man who looked at things in a little larger angle than most other persons; & as one who had a certain power of transition from thought to thought, as by secret passages, which it would tax the celerity & subtlety of good metaphysicians to follow. But he has the least shopvalue of any man. He were a very bad Englishman. He has no wares, he has not wrought his fine clay into vases, nor his gold dust into ingots. All the great masters finish their works to the eye & hand, as well as to the Divine Reason; to the shop, as well as to the gods.

But he is an inestimable companion, because he has no obligations to old or new; but is free as if newborn. But he is not careful to understand you. If he get a half meaning that serves his purpose, 'tis enough.

—

H. T. sturdily pushes his economy into houses & thinks it the false mark of the gentleman that he is to pay much for his food. He ought to pay little for his food. Ice,—he must have ice! And it is true, that, for each artificial want that can be invented & added to the ponderous expense, there is new clapping of hands of newspaper editors, & the donkey public. To put one more rock to be lifted betwixt a man & his true ends. If Socrates were here, we could go & talk with him; but Longfellow, we cannot go & talk with; there is a palace, & servants, & a row of bottles of different coloured wines, & wine glasses, & fine coats.

—

The Americans have the underdose. I find them not spiced with a quality. What poor *mots*,—what poor speeches, they make! 'Tis all like Miss Joanna's stories, wherein all the meaning has to be imputed. "O if you could only have heard him say it!"—"Say what?"—"Why he said '*Yes*,' but with so much intelligence!" Well, John Adams said "Independence forever!" and Sam Adams said, "O what a glorious morning is this!" and Daniel Webster said "I still live," & Edward Everett will say, when he comes to die, "O dear!" & General Cushing will say, "O my!" And Genl Butler will say, "Damn!" & however brilliant in the first & second telling these speeches may be, they somehow lack the Plutarch virility.

—

Cape Cod. Sept 5, 1853.

Went to Yarmouth Sunday 5; to Orleans Monday, 6th; to Nauset Light on the back side of Cape Cod. Collins, the keeper, told us he found obstinate resistance on Cape Cod to the project of building a light house on this coast, as it would injure the wrecking business. He had to go to Boston, & obtain the strong recommendation of the Port Society. From the high hill in the rear of Higgins's, in Orleans, I had a good view of the whole cape & the sea on both sides. The Cape looks like one of the Newfoundland Banks just emerged, a huge tract of sand half-covered with poverty grass, & beach grass & for trees abele & locust & plantations of pitchpine. Some good oak, & in Dennis & Brewster were lately good trees for ship-timber & still are well wooded on the east side. But the view I speak of looked like emaciated orkneys,—Mull, Islay, & so forth, made of salt dust, gravel, & fishbones. They say the Wind makes the roads, &, as at Nantucket, a large part of the real estate was freely moving back & forth in the air. I heard much of the coming railroad which is about to reach Yarmouth & Hyannis, &, they hope, will come to Provincetown. I fancied the people were only waiting for the railroad to reach them in order to evacuate the country. For the stark-nakedness of the country could not be exaggerated. But no, nothing was less true. They are all attached to what they call *the soil.* Mr Collins had been as far as Indiana; but, he said, hill on hill,—he felt stifled, & longed for the Cape, "where he could see out." And whilst I was fancying that they would gladly give away land to anybody that would come & live there, & be a neighbor: no, they said, all real estate had risen, all over the Cape, & you could not buy land at less than 50 dollars per acre. And, in Provincetown, a lot on the Front street of forty feet square would cost 5 or 600 dollars.

Still I saw at the Cape, as at Nantucket, they are a little tender about your good opinion: for if a gentleman at breakfast, says, he don't like Yarmouth, all real estate seems to them at once depreciated 2 or 3 per cent.

They are very careful to give you directions what road you shall take from town to town; but, as the country has the shape of a piece of tape, it is not easy to lose your way. For the same reason it behoves every body who goes on to the Cape to behave well, as he must stop on his return at all the same houses, unless he takes the packet at Provincetown for Boston, 6 hours in good weather, & a week in bad.

The sand grinds the glass at Nauset light, & soon makes it unfit for use. The sand grinds the tires of the wheels of the stage coach.

I found at Yarmouth the deerberry, *Vaccinium Stamineum*; and at Dennis, the *Chrysopsis*.

—

Quotation instantly confesses inferiority. 'Tis boswellism. If Ld Bacon appears in the preface I go & read the Instauratio & leave the new author.

—

At N.Y. Tabernacle, on the 7 March, I saw the great audience with dismay, & told the bragging secretary, that I was most thankful to those who stayed at home; Every auditor was a new affliction, & if all had stayed away, by rain, or preoccupation, I had been best pleased.

H.D.T. charged Blake, if he could not do hard tasks, to take the soft ones, & when he liked anything, if it was only a picture or a tune, to stay by it, find out what he liked, & draw that sense or meaning out of it, & do *that*: harden it, somehow, & make it his own. Blake thought & thought on this, & wrote afterwards to Henry, that he had got his first glimpse of heaven.

Henry was a good physician.

E. H. said, the reason why mother's chamber was always radiant, was that the pure in heart shall see God: and she wished so much to show this fact to the frivolous little woman who pretended sympathy when she died.

Dr Frothingham told me that the Latin verse which he appended to his obituary notice of my mother was one which he had read on the tomb of the wife of Charlemagne, in a chapel at Mayence, & it struck him as very tender. He had never seen it elsewhere.

"Spiritus haeres sit patriae quae tristia nescit."

—

The lesson of these days is the vulgarity of wealth. We know that wealth will vote for the same thing which the worst & meanest of the people vote for. Wealth will vote for rum, will vote for tyranny, will vote for slavery, will vote against the ballot, will vote against international copyright, will vote against schools, colleges, or any high direction of public money.

Plainly Boston does not wish liberty, & can only be pushed & tricked into a rescue of a slave. Its attitude as loving liberty is affected & theatrical. Do not then force it to assume a false position which it will not maintain. Rather let the facts appear, & leave it to the natural aggressions & familiarities of the beast it loves, until it gets well bitten & torn by the dear wolf, perchance it may not be too late to turn & to kill its deceiver.

The invisible gas that we breathe in this room we know if pent, has an elasticity that will lift the Apalachian Range as easily as a scrap of down; and a thought carries nations of men & ages of time on its shoulders.

Is there no difference between you & the rest? Mr Pierce said to me at Chicago, why do these members at Washington pair off? Suppose at Thermopylae, the three hundred Spartans had paired off with three hundred Persians!—

Southworth told me, that when he was in California, there was the purest state of law & order he had ever met; every tent had pans of gold lying open & drying before it; a piece of land as big as your hand was worth a hundred dollars; yet no man pilfered or encroached, though the people were pirates & ruffians of the worst kind. For, every man in California wore pistols & knife, & the first act of violence & thieving was sure to be followed with death in twelve hours by jury & rope.

*

1852

Our four powerful men in the virtuous class in this country are Horace Greeley, Theodore Parker, Henry Ward Beecher, & Horace Mann.

—

A good brain, A. said, was not got so: did not come without preparation & virtues: it came through several descents; it rode all the way on the top; it was the foam, & not the mud.

Poet sees the stars, because he makes them. Perception makes. We can only see what we make, all our desires are procreant. Perception has a destiny. So Fourier's attractions proportioned to destinies.

I notice that all poetry comes or all becomes poetry when we look from within & are using all as if the mind made it.

Poet fundamental

—

Races. Nature every little while drops a link. How long before the Indians will be extinct? then the negro? Then we shall say, what a gracious interval of dignity between man & beast!

Given the conditions, a race of men instantly appears; as in Alps, you find alpine plants, lichens, &c which you lose in descending, & find again in ascending Himmaleh, & again in Andes.

The Bible will not be ended until the creation is.

If I knew only Thoreau, I should think cooperation of good men impossible. Must we always talk for victory, & never once for truth, for comfort, & joy? Centrality he has, & penetration, strong understanding, & the higher gifts,—the insight of the real or from the real, & the moral rectitude that belongs to it; but all this & all his resources of wit & invention are lost to me in every experiment, year after year, that I make, to hold intercourse with his mind. Always some weary captious paradox to fight you with, & the time & temper wasted.

from

GO

1852–1853

"Prisca juvent alios, ego me nunc denique natum
Gratulor." *Ovid.*

"Sit nulla fides augentibus omnia musis"

June 7, 1852. We had a good walk, W.E.C. & I, along the Bank of the North Branch to the swamp, & to the "Harrington Estate." C.'s young dog scampered & dived & swam at such a prodigal rate, that one could not help grudging the youth of the Universe (the animals) their Heaven. They must think us poor pedants in petticoats, as poet Cowper is painted in the Westall Editions. How much more the dog knows of nature than his master, though his master were an Indian. The dog tastes, snuffs, rubs, feels, tries, every thing, everywhere, through miles of bush, brush, grass, water, mud, lilies, mountain, & sky.

At present, however, at night, I am haunted by the lines,

"The stars are in the quiet sky," &c.

which I first heard sung under the mimick stars of the Mammoth Cave, in Kentucky. But there is a charm in the line for my ear & fancy, & I must inquire for the song.

In our walk, we came to Ellery's garden of lupines,—a quarter of an acre covered over with a wild bed of lupines, which, when the sun shone, looked like saloons of beauties in mousseline de laines.

Nature's best feat is enamouring the man of these children, like kissing the knife that is to cut his throat,—they sucking, fretting, mortifying, ruining him, & upsetting him at last, because they want his chair, & he, dear old donkey, well pleased to the end.

—

June 12, 1852. Yesterday a walk with Ellery C. to the Lincoln Mill-Brook, to Nine Acre Corner, & Conantum. It was the first right day of summer. Air, cloud, river, meadow, upland, mountain, all were in their best. We took a swim at the outlet of the little brook at Baker-Farm. Ellery is grown an accomplished Professor of the Art of Walking, & leads like an Indian. He likes the comic surprise of his botanic information which is so suddenly enlarged. Since he knew Thoreau, he carries a little pocket-book, in which he affects to write down the name of each new plant or the first day on which he finds the flower. He admires viburnum & cornel, & despises dooryards with foreign shrubs. Mr Lee's farm at Nine Acre Corner, he thinks the best situated house in Concord:—Southern exposure, land rising behind close to the river, which lies in front, crossed by the bridge, & with wide out-look to the south & south west.

The view of the river from the top of the hill Mine Hill we found lovely, & had much to think of Mr Gilpin all the afternoon. The river just filled its banks to the brim, a rare sight.

Another fine picture from the top of Conantum, where a view of Concord village has newly been opened by cutting away the wood, last winter. The red sorrel gives the rich hue to the pastures. At Conantum, we visited the "Arboretum," where we found sassafras, bass, cornel, viburnum, ash, oak, slippery elm in close vicinity. Ellery has much to say of the abundance & perfection of lemon-yellow in nature which he finds in potentilla, ranunculus, cistus, yellow star of bethlehem, &c and which chemistry cannot well produce. M. Bouvieres, (I believe it is) spent his life in producing a good yellow pigment.

Miss Bridge, a mantuamaker in Concord, became a *Medium*, & gave up her old trade for this new one; & is to charge a pistareen a spasm, and nine dollars for a fit. This is the Rat-revelation, the Gospel that comes by taps in the wall, & thumps in the table-drawer. The spirits make themselves of no reputation. They are rats & mice of Society. And one of the demure disciples of the rat-tat-too, the other day, remarked, "that this, like every other communication from the spiritual world, began very low." It was not ill said; for Christianity began in a manger, & the Knuckle dispensation in a rat-hole.

—

6 July 1852

The head of Washington hangs in my diningroom for a few days past, & I cannot keep my eyes off of it. It has a certain Apalachian strength, as if it were truly the first-fruits of America, & expressed the country. The heavy leaden eyes turn on you, as the eyes of an ox in a pasture. And the mouth has a gravity & depth of quiet, as if this man had absorbed all the serenity of America, & left none for his restless, rickety, hysterical countrymen. Noble aristocratic head, with all kinds of elevation in it, that come out by turns. Such majestical ironies, as he hears the day's politics, at table. We imagine him hearing the letter of General Cass, the letter of Gen. Scott, the letter of Mr Pierce, the effronteries of Mr Webster, recited. This man listens like a god to these low conspirators.

—

Henry T. rightly said, the other evening, talking of lightning-rods, that the only rod of safety was in the vertebrae of his own spine.

—

What Aeschylus will translate our heaventempting politics into a warning ode, strophe & antistrophe? A slave, son of a member of Congress, flees from the plantation-whip to Boston, is snatched by the marshal, is rescued by the citizens; an excited population; a strong chain is stretched around the Court House. Webster telegraphs from Washington urgent orders to prosecute rigorously. Whig orators & interests intervene. Whig wisdom of waiting to be last devoured. Slave is caught, tried, marched at midnight under guard of marshals & pike & sword-bearing police to Long Wharf & embarked for Baltimore. "Thank-God-Choate" thanks God five times in one speech; Boston thanks God. Presidential Election comes on. Webster triumphant, Boston sends a thousand rich men to Baltimore: Convention meets: Webster cannot get one vote, from Baltimore to the Gulf,—not one. The competitor is chosen. The Washington wine sour, dinners disturbed. The mob at Washington turns out, at night, to exult in Scott's election. Goes to Webster's house & raises an outcry for Webster to come out & address them. He resists; the mob is violent,—will not be refused. He is obliged to come in his night-shirt, & speak from his window to the riff-raff of Washington in honor of the election of Scott. Pleasant conversation of the Boston delegation on their return home! The cars unusually swift.

Webster, (earlier, in Bowdoin Square,) exhorts the citizens to conquer their prejudices, to put down agitation; it is treason to feed or defend this young mulatto, son of his friend, the member of Congress, & who has escaped to Boston, from his pursuers.

I think the piece should open by an eulogy of Webster by an ardent youth first scholar at Cambridge, reciting the sentences he chiefly admires from his speeches at Plymouth, at New Hampshire Festival, at Congress & Faneuil Hall.

—

A man avails much to us, like a point of departure to the seaman, or his stake & stones to the surveyor. I am my own man more than most men, yet the loss of a few persons would be most impoverishing;—a few persons, who give flesh to what were, else, mere thoughts, and which, now, I am not at liberty to slight, or, in any manner, treat as fictions. It were too much to say that the Platonic world I might have learned to treat as cloud-land, had I not known Alcott, who is a native of that country, yet I will say that he makes it as solid as Massachusetts to me. And Thoreau gives me in flesh & blood & pertinacious Saxon belief, my own ethics. He is far more real, & daily practically obeying them, than I; and fortifies my memory at all times with an affirmative experience which refuses to be set aside.

I live a good while & acquire as much skill in literature as an old carpenter does in wood. It occurs, then, what pity, that now, when you know something, have at least learned so much good omission, your organs should fail you; your eyes, health, fire & zeal of work, should decay daily. Then I remember that it is the mind of the world which is the good carpenter, the good scholar, sailor, or blacksmith, thousandhanded, versatile, all-applicable, in all these indifferent channels entering with wild vigor, excited by novelty, in that untried channel, confined by dikes of pedantry; works out the proper results of that to the end, & surprises all with perfect consent, *alter et idem*, to every other excellence. Lexicography or Aristotelian logic being found consentaneous with music, with astronomy, with roses, with love. In you, this rich soul has peeped, despite your horny muddy eyes, at books & poetry. Well, it took you up, & showed you something to the purpose; that there was something there. Look, look, old mole! there, straight up before you, is the magnificent Sun. If only for the instant, you see it.— Well, in this way it educates the youth of the Universe; in this way, warms, suns, refines every particle; then it drops the little channel or canal, through which the Life rolled beatific, —like a fossil to the ground,—thus touched & educated by a moment of sunshine, to be the fairer material for future channels & canals, through which the old Glory shall dart again, in new directions, until the Universe shall have been shot through & through, *tilled* with light,

—

Alcott went to Fruitlands again after Palmer had possession. The old beggar went barefoot, & busied himself very much with his toes, as they sat together in the house. Poor Alcott with his inborn elegance, I suppose, found it hard not to be disgusted: but he pushed him off mentally,—it was Pan, Satyr, man in sympathy with his toes,—& thus having found a word for him, disposed of him in literature,—he was relieved once for all of the nasty old beggar.

Lovejoy the preacher came to Concord, & hoped Henry T. would go to hear him. "I have got a sermon on purpose for him."—"No," the aunts said, "we are afraid not." Then he wished to be introduced to him at the house. So he was confronted. Then he put his hand behind Henry, tapping his back, & said, "Here's the chap who camped in the woods." Henry looked round, & said, "And here's the chap who camps in a pulpit." Lovejoy looked disconcerted, & said no more.

Margaret Swan said to Miss Osgood, "I wish it were possible for me to find words small enough to pass through my lips which might convey the grand unspeakable views of heaven enjoyed by me in this state" (clairvoyant).

She thought, "nothing was to be learned of Mesmerism through the action of magnetisers on their patients: the true discoveries are to be obtained through those in whom the affection is spontaneous, because in them the powers of the mind in this high state are exhibited separate from all external influence."

Margaret Swan, of Medford, Masstts

"The thoughts that rushed upon me were unutterable: they seemed like the sound,—I say sound,—of a cataract of light. Ask me not what they were; I should perish in trying to give language to them," said this new pythoness.

"Thoughts that fill my mind are like consuming flames, & I am obliged to interpose a strong human will between myself & them, to sheathe my mind, as it were, against them, & admit them slowly, little by little." "Words," she added, "are the embroidered curtain which then veils for me the Holy of Holies x x x x x After the burning thoughts not to be uttered," (again an awestruck look,) "my mind seems a *shower* of words in all languages: they sail through it like little boats of light."

—

July 18

H T makes himself characteristically the admirer of the common weeds which have been hoed at by a million farmers all spring & summer & yet have prevailed, and just now come out triumphant over all lands, lanes, pastures, fields, & gardens, such is their pluck & vigor. We have insulted them with low names too, pig-weed, smart-weed, red-root, lousewort, chickweed. *He* says that they have fine names: amaranth, ambrosia.

—

I waked at night, & bemoaned myself, because I had not thrown myself into this deplorable question of Slavery, which seems to want nothing so much as a few assured voices. But then, in hours of sanity, I recover myself, & say, God must govern his own world, & knows his way out of this pit, without my desertion of my post which has none to guard it but me. I have quite other slaves to free than those negroes, to wit, imprisoned spirits, imprisoned thoughts, far back in the brain of man,—far retired in the heaven of invention, &, which, important to the republic of Man, have no watchman, or lover, or defender, but I.—

—

In July, 1852, Mr A. went to Connecticut to his native town of Wolcott; found his father's farm in possession of a stranger; found many of his cousins, still, poor farmers in the town; the town itself unchanged since his childhood, whilst all the country round has been changed by manufactures & railroads: Wolcott, which is a mountain, remains as it was, or with a still less population (10 000 dollars, he said, would buy the whole town, & all the men in it,) and now tributary entirely to the neighboring town of Waterbury which is a thriving factory village. A. went about & invited all the people, his relatives & friends, to meet him at 5 o'clock at the schoolhouse, where he had once learned, on Sunday evening. Thither they all came, & he sat at the desk, & gave them the story of his life. Some of the audience went away discontented, because they had not heard a sermon, as they hoped.

Greenough called my contemplations, &c. "the masturbation of the brain."

—

18 August

Horatio Greenough came here & spent a day:—an extraordinary man—"Forty seven years of joy," he says, "he has lived"; and is a man of sense, of virtue, & of great elevation. He makes many of my accustomed stars pale by his clear light. His magnanimity, his idea of a great man, his courage, & cheer, & self-reliance, & depth, & self-derived knowledge, charmed & invigorated me, as none has, who has gone by, these many months. I told him, I would fife in his regiment. His democracy is very deep, &, for the most part, free from crotchets,—not quite,—& philosophical. He finds every body believer in two gods, believer in the devil. He is not. Again, everything is generative, & everything connected. If you take chastity apart, & make chastity a virtue, you create that sink of obscenity a monk. The old ages seeing that circumstances pinched them, & they got no divine man, tried to lift up one of their number out of the press, & so gain a right man. But, it turned out, that the new development really obtained, was abnormal; they got a bloated belly. Then they tried to take twenty or fifty out, & see if they could do better so. But no, instead of one huge kingly paunch, they got twenty or fifty with a round belly. The whole theory has been,—out of a prostrate humanity as out of a bank & magazine, to draw the materials for culture to a class. All a lie, & had the effect of a lie. Take religion out, & make religion separate. Still a lie & ruin. 'Tis all experimenting on nature. Whenever there is a wrong, the response is pain. The rowdy eyes that glare on you from the mob say plainly, that they feel that you are doing them to death; you, you, have got the chain somehow round their limbs, &, though they know not how, war, inter-necine war, to the knife, is between us & you. Your six per cent is as deadly a weapon as the old knife & tomahawk.

In the old Egyptian, & in the Middle age architecture, he sees only "cost to the constituency," prodigious toil of prostrate humanity. In the Greek alone, beauty. His idea of beauty, is, the first form of action, the true prophet of function, and, just as far as function is preparing, beauty will appear; then, (2.) in action the whole is resolved: then, (3.) into character. But everything of beauty for beauty's sake is embellishment: that is false, childless & moribund.

He complains of England, that it never did or can look at Art, otherwise than as a commodity it can buy. Of England, he thinks ill,—its tactics is to live *au jour à la journée*,—perpetual makeshifts.—And he has the party crotchet of the democrats of attributing deeplaid plots of policy to England; forgetful of Defoe's true words

> "In close intrigue their faculty's but weak,
> For, generally, what they know they speak."

—

The farmer said, he should like to have all the land that joined his own. Bonaparte who had the same appetite, endeavoured to make the Mediterranean a French lake. The Russian czar Alexander was more expansive, & wished to call the Pacific *My ocean*, and the Americans were obliged to resist energetically his attempts to make it a close sea. But if he got the earth for his cowpasture & the sea for his fishpond, he would be a pauper still. He only is rich who owns the day.

—

The prohibitions of society make perhaps the sexual appetite morbid, & the abortive generation, or, the death of a large fraction of the population before 3 years, proves it. The way to reach the healthy limits of the census is to have wise chastity & not forced, to have affection & not embargoed routine. I feel the antipodes & the pole, they are mine, as much as the drops of my blood. The powers of man are to be measured by the instrument he is.—

—

As soon as a deviation for the sake of a variety, for a luxurious variety, is allowed, it is easy to see that the whole race of depravation will be run. Therefore Greenough will not allow so much as a supporter to a porch to be varied by a parabola instead of a straight line.

—

The church is there for check of trade. But on examination all the deacons, ministers, & saints of this church are steering with all their sermons & prayers in the direction of the Trade. If the city says, "Freedom & no tax," they say so, & hunt up plenty of texts. But if the city says, "Freedom is a humbug. We prefer a strong government," the pulpit says the same, & finds a new set of applicable texts. But presently Trade says, "Slavery too has been misunderstood: it is not so bad; nay, it is good; on the whole, it is the best possible thing." The dear pulpit & deacons must turn over a new leaf, & find a new string of texts, which they are forward to do. And Sampson Reed, & Orville Dewey, & Moses Stewart, & Park street, & Andover, will get up the new march of the Hypocrites to Pudding, for the occasion.

—

To plow a field with oxen, to cross deep water with oars or sail, are actions requiring goodsense; therefore the giantess rightly says, when her daughter picks up husbandman, plough, & "kittens," & brings them to her in her apron,—'Take them back where you found them; they belong to a race that can inflict great injury to the giants.'

Last Sunday I was at Plymouth on the beach, & looked across the hazy water,—whose spray was blowing on to the hills &

orchards,—to Marshfield. I supposed, Webster must have passed, as indeed he had died at 3 in the morning. The sea, the rocks, the woods, gave no sign that America & the world had lost the completest man. Nature had not in our days, or, not since Napoleon, cut out such a masterpiece. He brought the strength of a savage into the height of culture. He was a man in equilibrio. A man within & without, the strong & perfect body of the first ages, with the civility & thought of the last. "*Os, oculosque Jovi par.*" And, what he brought, he kept. Cities had not hurt him, he held undiminished the power & terror of his strength, the majesty of his demeanour.

He had a counsel in his breast. He was a statesman, & not the semblance of one. Most of our statesmen are in their places by luck & vulpine skill, not by any fitness. Webster was there for cause: the reality; the final person, who had to answer the questions of all the faineants, & who had an answer.

But alas he was the victim of his ambition; to please the South betrayed the North, and was thrown out by both.

The worst of charity, is, that the lives you are asked to preserve are not worth preserving. The calamity is the masses. I do not wish any mass at all, but honest men only, facultied men only, lovely & sweet & accomplished women only; and no shovel-handed Irish, & no Five-Points, or Saint Gileses, or drunken crew, or mob, or stockingers, or 2 millions of paupers receiving relief, miserable factory population, or lazzaroni, at all.

—

Abolition

The argument of the slaveholder is one & simple: he pleads Fate. Here is an inferior race requiring wardship,—it is sentimentality to deny it. The argument of the abolitionist is, It is inhuman to treat a man thus.

Then, for the Fugitive Slave Bill, we say;—I do not wish to hold slaves, nor to help you to hold them. If you cannot keep them without my help, let them go.

Such provisions as you find in the Constitution for your behoof make the most of. You could not recover a load of hay, a barrel of potatoes by such law. The Constitution has expressly guaranteed your barrel of potatoes. No, the Courts would say, it has not named them. If it especially & signally wished by

compromise to protect your potato crop, it would have said so. Laws are to be strictly interpreted, & laws of all things are understood to say exactly what they mean. But how then can you maintain such an incredible & damnable pretension as to steal a man on these loose inuendoes of the law that would not allow you to steal his shoes? How, but that all our northern Judges have made a cowardly interpretation of the law, in favor of the crime, & not of the right? The leaning should be, should it not? to the right against the crime. The leaning has been invariably against the slave for the master.
But Thoreau remarks that the cause of Freedom advances, for all the able debaters now are freesoilers, Sumner, Mann, Giddings, Hale, Seward, Burlingam

—

The Democrats carry the country, because they have more virility: just as certain of my neighbors rule our little town, quite legitimately, by having more courage & animal force than those whom they overbear. It is a kind of victory like that of gravitation over all upraised bodies, sure, though it lie in wait for ages for them. I saw in the cars a broad featured unctuous man, fat & plenteous as some successful politician, & pretty soon divined it must be the foreign Professor, who has had so marked a success in all our scientific & social circles, having established unquestionable leadership in them all;—and it was Agassiz.

Uriah Boyden obtains, by his hydraulic inventions, 96 per cent of the power of a waterfall. The French had only obtained 70 per cent,—the English, before that, only 60. Lowell mills at one time paid him 30 000 dollars for the use of his turbines; Lawrence 16 000. America exceeds all nations in hydraulic improvements. Ingenuity against cheap labor is our reliance. America lives by its wits. Englishman cannot travel out of his road, Erastus B. Bigelow is paid by Crossley of Halifax, Engd, 4(?) cents on every yard of carpet woven on his looms. And in this country Clinton Company draws 1 cent, & Bigelow 3 cts on every yard woven on his looms throughout America.

—

England never stands for the cause of freedom on the continent, but always for her trade. She did not stand for the freedom of Schleswig Holstein, but for the K. of Denmark. She did not stand for the Hungarian, but for Austria. It was strange that with Palmerston's reputation for liberalism, he went out because he favoured Louis Napoleon's usurpation. England, meantime, is liberal, but the power is with the Aristocracy, who never go for liberty, unless England itself is threatened. Few & poor chances for European Emancipation: the disarming; the army; & the army of office-holders, are the triple wall of monarchy. Then consider that the people don't want liberty,—they want bread; &, though republicanism would give them more bread after a year or two, it would not until then, & they want bread every day. Louis Napoleon says, I will give you work,—& they believed him. In America, we hold out the same bribe, "Roast Beef, & two dollars a day." And our people will not go for liberty of other people, no, nor for their own, but for annexation of territory, or a tariff, or whatever promises new chances for young men, more money to men of business.

In either country, they want great men, & the cause of right can only succeed against all this gravitation or materialism by means of immense personalities. But Webster, Calhoun, Clay, Benton, are not found to be philanthropists, but attorneys of great & gross interests.

—

Mr Dean believed with Jacobi, that, when a man did not write his poetry, it escaped in all directions through him, instead of in the one direction of writing, and, that poets had nothing poetical except in their writing. At the south, he noticed more "ideality" than at the north; the millinery & bonnets of Baltimore were better fancied than of Philadelphia, & the behaviour of the people, though they could not write so well, was more ideal.

The Saxons good combiners; &, though an idealist always prefers to trace a discovery or a success home to one mind, yet we must acquiesce in 19 Century Civilization, & accept the Age of Combined working, or joint-stock Companies. I liked to hear that Mr Saml Lawrence invented the Bay State Shawl, which saved the so-called mills when all other manufacturing companies failed. But no: Mr Lawrence gave the grand project—we must make a shawl. & even brought a pattern shawl to his designer. The designer, named Edward Everett, not of Cambridge, but of Lowell, prepared designs. They had an excellent dyer, who could give them fast colors & rich. They had looms, which they could & did adapt to this fabric. But the twisting the fringes would cost 30 cents a shawl:—'tis too much. So Mr —— invented a machine to twist fringes; &, putting all these advantages together, they succeeded.

—

It is the distinction of "Uncle Tom's Cabin," that, it is read equally in the parlour & the kitchen & the nursery of every house. What the lady read in the drawing-room in a few hours, is retailed to her in her kitchen by the cook & the chambermaid, as, week by week, they master one scene & character after another.

Fanny Kemble read Shakspeare better than any body else, & made her fortune. Jenny Lind sung better than any one else, & made hers.

At Solingen, they manufacture swords, called *eisenhauers*, which will cut gunbarrels in two. (London) Examiner.

—

Fate

"The classes & the races too weak to master the new conditions of life must give way." Cor. of the Tribune Karl Max

Politeness was invented by wise men to keep fools at a distance.

Walk with Ellery to Lincoln. Benzoin laurus, rich beautiful shrub in this dried up country. Particolored warbler. E. laughed at Nuttall's description of birds: "on the top of a high tree the bird pours all day the lays of affection," &c. Affection! Why what is it? a few feathers, with a hole at one end, & a point at the other, & a pair of wings: affection! Why just as much affection as there is in that lump of peat.
Thoreau is at home; why he has got to maximize the minimum; that will take him some days.

We went to Bear Hill & had a fine outlook. Descending E got sight of some labourers in the field below. Look at them, he said, those four! four daemoniacs scratching in their cell of pain! Live for the hour. Just as much as any man has done, or laid up, in any way, unfits him for conversation. He has done something, makes him good for boys, but spoils him for the hour. That's the good of Thoreau, that he puts his whole sublunary capital into the last quarter of an hour; carries his whole stock under his arm.

At home, I found H. T. himself who complained of Clough or somebody that he or they recited to every one at table the paragraph just read by him & by them in the last newspaper & studiously avoided every thing private. I should think he was complaining of one H.D.T.

from

VS

1853–1854

English Poetry.

The English genius never parts with its materialistic tendency, &, even in its inspirations is materialistic. Milton, Shakspeare, Chaucer, Spenser, Herbert, who have carried it to its greatest height, are bound to satisfy the senses & the Understanding, as well as the Reason. If the question is asked whether the English repudiate thought, we remember there is always a minority in England who entertain whatever speculations the highest muse has attempted. No brain has dallied with finer imaginings than Shakspeare (yet with mathematical accuracy). No richer thoughted man than Bacon, no holier than Milton or Herbert. We have found English for Behmen,—& English for Swedenborg & readers for both.

—

The Heimskringla is the Iliad & Odyssey of English history. Homeric, I may well say, and all individualized like that.—No masses fight here, but groups of single heroes, every one of whom is named, & personally & patronymically described. A very sparse population gives this high worth to every man; which is fit. They are frequently characterised too as "very handsome persons," which trait only brings the story nearer to the English race. Then the respectable material interest predominates. They are not knights; no vaporing as in the continental chivalry of France & Spain, has corrupted them; but they are all substantial farmers, whom circumstances have forced to defend their own property, & they have weapons, & use them in a determined & business-like manner, not for the sake of fight, but for the sake of property.

But I wish the scald had bethought him once in a while to say something about the ways in which they spent their days when at home in peace, whether they farmed, & what they planted. As we writers today never hint how we get our living, neither

did the scald. Kail & herrings & furs, wadmal, & ale are, however, never at a great distance.
Sentiment is already materialized;—that same dear excellence of English intellect,—*materialized intellect*, like kyanized wood,—has already come into fashion.

—

The quakers create a quaker face especially in old women.

—

It is a bitter satire on our social order, just at present, the number of bad cases. Margaret Fuller having attained the highest & broadest culture that any American woman has possessed, came home with an Italian gentleman whom she had married, & their infant son, & perished by shipwreck on the rocks of Fire Island, off New York; and her friends said, 'Well, on the whole, it was not so lamentable, & perhaps it was the best thing that could happen to her. For, had she lived, what could she have done? How could she have supported herself, her husband, & child?' And, most persons, hearing this, acquiesced in this view, that, after the education has gone far, such is the expensiveness of America, that, the best use to put a fine woman to, is, to drown her to save her board. !!
Well, the like or the stronger plight is that of Mr Alcott, the most refined & the most advanced soul we have had in New England, who makes all other souls appear slow & cheap & mechanical; a man of such a courtesy & greatness, that, (in conversation,) all others, even the intellectual, seem sharp & fighting for victory, & angry,—he has the unalterable sweetness of a muse,—yet because he cannot earn money by his pen or his talk, or by schoolkeeping or bookkeeping or editing or any kind of meanness,—nay, for this very cause, that he is ahead of his contemporaries,—is higher than they,—& keeps himself out of the shop-condescensions & smug arts which they stoop to, or, unhappily, need not stoop to, but find themselves, as it were, born to,—therefore, it is the unanimous opinion of New England judges that this man must die; we shall all hear of his death with pleasure, & feel relieved that his board & clothes also are saved! We do not adjudge him to hemlock, or to garrotting,—we are much too hypocritical & cowardly for that;—but we not less surely doom him, by refusing to protest against this doom, or combine to save him, &

to set him on employments fit for him & salutary to the state, or to the Senate of fine Souls, which is the heart of the state.

In Boston, is no company for a fine wit. There is a certain *poor-smell* in all the streets, in Beacon street & Park & Mt Vernon, as well as in the lawyers' offices, & the wharves, the same meanness & sterility, & *leave-all-hope-behind*, as one finds in a boot manufacturer's premises, or a bonnet-factory; vamps, pasteboard, millinette, and an eye to profit. The want of elevation, the absence of ideas, the sovereignty of the abdomen, reduces all to the same poorness. One fancies that in the houses of the rich, as the temptation to servility is removed, there may chance to be generosity & elevation; but no; we send them to Congress, & they originate nothing and on whatever question they instantly exhibit the vulgarity of the lowest populace. An absence of all perception & natural equity. They have no opinions, & cringe to their own attorney, when he tells the opinion of the Insurance Offices.

But you can never have high aristocracy, without real elevation of ideas somewhere; otherwise, as in Boston, it turns out punk & cheat at last.

—

'Tis very costly, this thinking for the market in books or lectures: As soon as any one turns the conversation on my "Representative men," for instance, I am instantly sensible that there is nothing there for conversation, that the argument is all pinched & illiberal & popular.

Only what is private, & yours, & essential, should ever be printed or spoken. I will buy the suppressed part of the author's mind; you are welcome to all he published.

—

The seaserpent may have an instinct to retire into the depths of the sea when about to die, & so leave no bones on the shores for naturalists. The seaserpent is afraid of Mr Owen; but his heart sunk within him when, at last, he heard that Barnum was born.

—

"Troilus & Cressida" contains many of those sentences which have procured a fame for Shakspeare at least as high as his dramatic genius: sentences which, in their clear & disengaged expression, their universal aptness, imply the widest knowledge of men & one would say such experience & such easy command as only courts, & intimate knowledge of affairs, & habits of command could bestow. It requires the habits of Leicester & Essex, of Burleigh & Buckingham, to speak the expressed essence of life in so large & so easy a phrase.

—

John Bull Englishman is made-up; is blunt; is stubborn; is veracious; staid; utilitarian; nautical; staunch; law-abiding, has the cimmerian conservatism of the Druids, combining; is a trifler, minds trifles. Is habitual; ('Lord bless you, sir, it's the old way, it was always so' is a final argument with him.) is a voracious hunter: is averse to show that he is amused in public: is strong, & has all the modifications that belong to strength, namely, justice, pity, generosity; is clumsy, insular, parochial, illiberal; lays up money; sticks to his traditions & usages; has vowel sounds of his own, which the American can't make.

—

"Whatever is known only to one's self, is always of very great value." *Runic Chapter of the Hava-mal*

Mallet. p 372

"I am possessed of songs such as no son of man can repeat; one of them is called the Helper: it will help thee at thy need, in sickness, grief, & all adversities."

"I know a song which I need only to sing when men have loaded me with bonds: when I sing it, my chains fall in pieces, & I walk forth at liberty."

The Welsh bard "wished that each beam of the sun might be a dagger to pierce the heart of that man who was fond of war."

—

June 10 1853. Yesterday a ride to Bedford with Ellery, along the "Bedford Levels" & walked all over the premises of the Old Mill,—King Philip's Mill,—on the Shawsheen River;—old mill, with sundry nondescript wooden antiquities,—Boys with bare legs were fishing on the little islet in the stream; we crossed & recrossed, saw the fine stumps of trees, rocks, & grove, & many collot views of the bare legs, beautiful pastoral country, but needs sunshine. There were millions of light today,—so all went well,—(all but the dismal tidings which knelled a funeral-bell through the whole afternoon, in the death of Susan Sturgis.—) Rich democratic land of Massachusetts; in every house well-dressed women with air of town-ladies: in every house a clavecin & a copy of the *Spectator*; & some young lady a reader of Willis. Lantara did not like the landscape; too many leaves,—one leaf is like another leaf—& apt to be agitated by east wind. On the other hand, "Professor," (Ellery's dog,) did; he strode gravely as a bear through all the sentimental parts, & fitted equally well the grave & the gay scenes. He has a stroke of humor in his eye, as if he enjoyed his master's jokes. (Mem. to tell E. that Miss Minott has set up an opposition to him. On the last day of tulips, Lidian sent the children to invite her to come & see her garden-show, & Miss M. "sent her love to her, & would come *in a week or two.*") Ellery "thinks England a flash in the pan;" as English people, in 1848, had agreed that "Egypt was humbug." I am to put down among the monomaniacs the English agriculturist who only knows one revolution in political history, the rape-culture. But, as we rode, one thing was clear, as oft before, that it is favorable to sanity,—the occasional change of landscape. If a girl is mad to marry, let her take a ride of ten miles, & see meadows & mountains she never saw before; two villages, & an old mansion house; & the odds are, it will change all her resolutions. World is full of fools who get a-going & never stop: set them off on another tack, & they are half-cured. From Shawsheen we went to Burlington; & E. reiterated his conviction, that the only art in the world is landscape-painting. The boys held up their fish to us from far;—a broad new placard on the walls announced to us that the Shawsheen-mill was for sale; but we bought neither the fish nor the mill.

—

H is military

H seemed stubborn & implacable; always manly & wise, but rarely sweet. One would say that as Webster could never speak without an antagonist, so H. does not feel himself except in opposition. He wants a fallacy to expose, a blunder to pillory, requires a little sense of victory, a roll of the drums, to call his powers into full exercise.

—

In Belgium & other countries, I have seen reports of model farms: they begun with downs or running sands, it makes no difference what bottom, mere land to lay their basket of loam down upon. Then, they proceed from beach grass, or whatever & rye & clover;—manuring all the time,—until they have formed a soil 14 inches deep. Well, so I conceive, it is in national generi-culture, as in agriculture. You must manage to set up a rational will.

You must find a land like England, where temperate & sharp northern breezes blow, to keep that will alive & alert; markets on every possible side, because it is an island; the people tasked & kept at the top of their condition by the continual activity of seafaring & the exciting nature of sea-risks, & the deep stimulus of gain: the land not large enough, the population not large enough, to glut the market, & depress one another; but so proportioned is it to the size of Europe & of the world, that it keeps itself healthy & bright, and, like an immense manufactory, it yields, with perfect security & ease, incredible results.

Many things conduce to this. Over them all works a sort of Anima-mundi or soul of the island,—the aggregation by time, experience, & demand & supply of a great many personalities, —which fits them to each other, & enables them to keep step & time, cooperate as harmoniously & punctually as the parts of a human body; just as New Bedford is invincible in whale fishery, because, there the whole fitting of a whaleship can, by long accumulation of stocks & skills, be cheaper & better achieved, than in any other town. The coopers hug an oilcask like a baby, & put it on or off the wharf, with dexterity; so England is a gang of riggers, sailors, makers, & merchants, who play perfectly together. Power begets & educates power; & success makes courage; a great part of courage is the consciousness of

—

A.D. 810. One day when Charlemagne had halted in a city of Narbonnese Gaul, some Scandinavian pirate barks entered the very port. He knew them by their light build: "They are not merchants, he said, but cruel enemies." They were pursued & escaped; but the Emperor, rising from table, stood at the window looking towards the east, & remained a very long time, with his face bathed in tears; "I am tormented with sorrow," he said, "when I foresee the evils they will bring on my posterity & their subjects." *Mon. Sangall. II* 22 ap. *Michelet*

—

Sylvan could go wherever woods & waters were & no man was asked for leave. Once or twice the farmer withstood, but it was to no purpose,—he could as easily prevent the sparrows or tortoises. It was their land before it was his, & their title was precedent. S. knew what was on their land, & they did not; & he sometimes brought them ostentatiously gifts of flowers or fruits or shrubs which they would gladly have paid great prices for, & did not tell them that he took them from their own woods.

Moreover the very time at which he used their land & water (for his boat glided like a trout everywhere unseen,) was in hours when they were sound asleep. Long before they were awake he went up & down to survey like a sovereign his possessions, & he passed onward, & left them before the farmer came out of doors. Indeed it was the common opinion of the boys that Mr T. made Concord.

Ellery affirms that Adams the cabinet maker has a true artistic eye; for he is always measuring with his eye the man he talks with for his coffin.

—

The sons of clergymen are lawyers & merchants, & the keenest hunters in all the pack, as if a certain violence had been done them in their abstinence in the last generation, & this was the violence of the recoil.
As if there the cat had a retractile claw, which could be kept folded back during a whole lifetime & reappear sound & sharp in the kitten.

—

The game of intellect seems the perception in lucid moments that whatever befalls or can be stated, is a universal proposition; and, contrariwise, that every general statement is poetical again by being particularised or impersonated.

Freedom, yes, but that is a thing of degrees. Is one of the slaveholders free? Not one. Is any politician free? Not one. See the snakes wriggle & wind. Is a man free, whose conscience accuses him of thefts & lies & indulgences without number? No. Is he free whom I see, when my eyes are anointed, to be always egotistical, & blinded by his preference of himself? A humble man can see, but a proud man & a vain man are patients for Dr Eliot, the oculist.

—

20 July 1853 *Short way with Slaveholders.*
I read last night a letter from Lewis Tappan to Lincoln Fearing, stating that he had learned from a scientific person that sulphate of copper, commonly called Blue Vitriol, used in small quantities in the manufacture of wheat flour, had important effects in increasing the docility of the people who eat it: And he proposed to introduce such manufacture on a large scale into the southern states, with a view to reduce the stubbornness of the population, to the end of an easier removal of Slavery: He therefore asks Mr Fearing at what price he can supply him with 240 tons of this article, in the autumn, with a prospect of a much larger purchase hereafter. He proceeds to say that great caution must be used in the introduction of this article, & that a number of bakers must be sent with instructions to use it, & that the project should be confidential. Would like also to have Mr Fearing take the opinions of Abbott Lawrence, and Senator Everett, and others, who may have information as to the use of this article in Europe.

Mr Fearing sent the letter to Dr C. T. Jackson, who replied, that the use of the article is an outrageous fraud, & is forbidden on high penalties in England & France, as it is rank poison.

The sad side of the Negro question.
The abolitionist (theoretical) wishes to abolish slavery, but because he wishes to abolish the black man. He considers that it is violence, brute force, which, counter to intellectual rule, holds property in Man; but he thinks the negro himself the very representative & exponent of that brute base force; that it is the negro in the white man which holds slaves. He attacks Legree, Macduffie, & slaveholders north & south generally, but because they are the foremost negroes of the world, & fight the negro fight. When they are extinguished, & law, intellectual law prevails, it will then appear quickly enough that

the brute instinct rallies & centres in the black man. He is created on a lower plane than the white, & eats men & kidnaps & tortures, if he can. The Negro is imitative, secondary, in short, reactionary merely in his successes, & there is no origination with him in mental & moral sphere.

It is a great loss to lose the confidence of a class; yet the scholar, the thinker goes on losing the ear & love of class after class who once sustained him.
The scholar isolates himself by the sweet opium which he has learned to chew, & which he calls *muses*, & memory, & philosophy. Now & then, he meets another scholar, & then says, 'See, I am rewarded for my truth to myself & calling, by the perfect sympathy I here find.' But, meantime, he is left out more & more, & at last utterly, by society, & his faculties languish for want of invitation, & objective work; until he becomes that very thing which they taunt him with being, a selfindulgent dreamer. In an intellectual community, he would be steeled & sharpened & burnished to a strong Archimedes or Newton. Society makes him the imbecile it accuses him of being.

On the rocks of Nahant the chemical texture of the world appeared, & statistics is also a rock-of-Nahant to show that the world is a crystal, & God a Chemist.

In America, everything looks new & recent, our towns look raw, & the makeshifts of emigrants, & the whole architecture tent-like.

But one would say, that the effect of geology so much studied for the last forty years must be to throw an air of novelty & mushroom speed over history. The oldest Empires, all that we have called venerable antiquity, now that we have true measures of duration, become things of yesterday; and our millenniums & Kelts & Copts become the first experimental pullulations & transitional meliorations of the Chimpanzee. It is yet all too early to draw sound conclusions.

*

England.

My belief is that nobody landed on this island with impunity; that the popular fable of spellbound homes of enchanters, was fact in England; the climate & conditions, labor & rough weather, transformed every adventurer into a laborer & each vagabond that arrived submitted his neck to the yoke of avarice & ambition, or found the air too tense for him to exist in. The race avails much, but the genius of the place also is despotic, & will not have any frivolous persons.

from

HO

1853–1854

Horses

Bayard, horse of Renaud de Montauban which Roland nephew of Charlemagne tried to obtain, understood his master's speech as if he had been his son,—beat the earth with his forefeet as if it had been a harp; ran away from Charlemagne, and still in the forest of Ardennes neighs loud & clear to be heard all over France on St John's day.

Arnaud de Gascoigene's horse could at the age of 100 years make 100 leagues in a day without stopping & without blowing. On the whole, in the stories of the Round Table, the horses show rather more good sense & conduct than their riders.

—

Being once present at the Creation, I saw that from each man as he was formed, a piece of the clay of which he was made was taken, & set apart for him as goods or property; and it was allowed him to receive this in whatever form he desired, whether as wife, friend, son, daughter, or as house, land, warehouses, merchandizes, horses, libraries, gardens, ships. Also, he might have it, now in one of these forms, & at his will it was converted into another. But because it was one & the same lump out of which all these were fashioned, and as that was the clay of his own body, all these things had one & the same taste & quality to him, & he died at last of ennui.

—

Poetry

My quarrel with poets is that they do not believe in their own poetry. Wordsworth himself, if his Ode is cited in conversation, says "ah, but that is poetry." But the only poet in this country I know is Alcott, for he believes in his images, he exists to see & multiply them, & translate by them ever more history natural & civil, & all men & events, into laws.

—

Melancholy marks the deep mind of this race which has dedicated itself in every age to abstractions with a passion which has given vast results, & made with their bodies the bridge on which their posterity step easily to power.

There's a necessity on them to be logical. They are as stiff & tough in their texture as oxen are, & they speak as oxen would speak, if oxen could. English have no fancy, but delight always in strong earthy expressions not mistakeable or adornable as a Greek expression would be into a myth, but in back & belly true to animal man.

—

The ego partial makes the dream, the Ego total the interpretation; and when we have penetrated the secret of dreams, then say, But life also is a dreaming.

Men are bothered by their talents, & withdrawn from the healthy wholeness; they are rightly airballs in the atmosphere, bubbles in the sea, & must not be allowed to exaggerate their film of individualism. Man is a reader. Shakspeare is nothing to nature, but much to the reader.

All the authors are enchanted men; intoxicated plainly, with that stray drop of nectar of idealism they have imbibed; Bacon rich with lustres and powers stolen somehow from the upper world, & inevitably wonderful to men; but he has this plunder of ideas, or this degree of fine madness, to no purpose: he does nothing with it: it leads him nowhere; he is a poor mean fellow all the while; and in fine examples,—in Milton, it is not much better. It is not yet blood,—this drop of ichor that tingles in them, & cannot lift the whole man to the digestion & function of ichor,—that is, of godlike action. Time will be when they shall drink nectar like water; when *Ichor* will be their blood, when their glimpses & aspirations shall take place as the routine of the day.

Yet it is not wholly useless,—poetry & ideas: They are forerunners, & announce the dawn. Men are rushing into the mire, and their religions & superstitions, their Shakspeares & Platos, their respect for dignified & powerful people, their novel & their newspaper, even, are hosts of ideals—if impure ideals,—a whole cordage of ropes that hold them from sinking in the mire.

Poetry inestimable as a lonely faith, a lonely protest in the uproar of atheism which civilization is.

Once more I thought these fellows are spoiled by their bad company. We degrade & infect each other. If a divine physician could come & say Ah you are hurt,—you are bleeding to death,—not out of your body, but, far worse, out of your mind. You that are reckoned the pink of amiable & discreet men:—You are in a raging typhoid, already comatose, blind, & deaf. All the worse that you do not know it. Men run away from the small pox. But see the small pox of small society,—the vermin, the tapeworm of politics, & of trifling city life, is eating your vitals.—Save yourself. I call you to renunciation of trifles, of display, of custom. I lead you to an upright & simple friend who knows what truth means. See that one noble person dwarfs a nation of underlings, makes the day beautiful, and him self venerable, and you shall not fear to wake in the morning.

—

The University wholly retrospective. Milton, Juvenal, Homer, & the rest are old cups of which one cannot drink without some loss & degradation. The happy youth drinks at the Fountain.

Elizabeth Hoar said, 'Tis necessary, when you strike a discord, to let down the ear by an intermediate note or two to the accord again, & that Bloomer dress is very good & reconcilable to men's taste, if only it be not offensively sudden; so a woman may speak, & vote, & legislate, & drive coach, if only it comes by degrees. Swallower of formulas must also strike intervening notes.

—

ABA was here. A baker who bakes a half a dozen worlds as easily as the cook so many loaves: the most obstinate Unitarian that ever existed. He only believes in Unity. Plato is dualist to him. Preexistence is as familiar & essential in his mind as hydrogen or sulphur in a chemist's laboratory. Metachemistry his philosophy might be called with some show of truth. He believes in cause & effect & comes out of such vast caverns up to the surface of conversation that he has to rub his eyes & look about him not to break the proprieties of this trifling world.

He relies on Nature forever—wise, omnific, thousand-handed Nature, equal to every emergency, which can do very well without colleges, and if the Latin & Greek & Algebra & Art were in the parents, is sure it will be in the children without being pasted on outside.

—

A. tells me that Mr Hedge is to write an Essay on the importance of a liturgy. I propose to add an Essay on the importance of a rattle in the throat. Afraid of a pope, afraid of a musk-melon.

How difficult to deal with them. You must interfere continually to steer their talk or they will be sure if they meet a button or a thimble to run against it & forget all in the too powerful associations of the worktable & the pantry. Can't keep it impersonal. Can't keep it afloat in the stream.

Alcott & I bemoaned our common mishap in the change of the Masonic Temple. He has been rabbited out to make room for the mysteries of masonry & I from the Hall to make room for pianos.

—

H.D.T. says he values only the man who goes directly to his needs, who, wanting wood, goes to the woods & brings it home; or to the river, & collects the drift, & brings it in his boat to his door, & burns it: not him who keeps shop, that he may buy wood. One is pleasing to reason & imagination; the other not.

Quotation

"Talking of Sheridan's borrowing other people's jokes, Hallam mentioned some one having said, 'I don't know how it is, a thing that falls flat from me seems quite an

> excellent joke when given at second hand by Sheridan. I never like my own *bon mots* till he adopts them.' "
> Moore's Diary. vol. 4, p. 144

How true, & may well be illustrated by Dumont, who was exalted by being used by Mirabeau; & by Sir P. Francis, who was less than his own Junius; and by James Hogg, who owes his fame to his idealized self in Blackwood; and by Miss Bacon's remark on the superior meaning of Shakspeare read under the light of another authorship Thus;

> "You see yourself how much this idea of the authorship controls our appreciation of the works themselves; & what new worlds *such* an authorship would enable us to see in them."

Hence an argument in favor of combination of wits in a magazine or in a work of imagination.

Quotation

Admirable mimicks have nothing of their own. And in every kind of parasite, when Nature has finished an excellent sucking-pipe to tap another animal, the self-supplying organs wither & dwindle as being superfluous.

> "et quand ils cessent d'etre le personnage qu'ils ont choisi, et qui vous amuse tant, ils deviennent insipides et tristes, parce qu'ils ne sont plus qu'eux."
> *Grimm* Partie. vol 1. 434

I often need the device of ascribing my sentence to another in order to give it weight. Carlyle does so with Teufelsdrock, &c.

—

Intellect

For poppy leaves are strewn when a generalisation is made, for I can never remember the circumstances to which I owe it, so as to repeat the experiment, or put myself in the conditions.

I call those persons who can make a general remark, provided also they have an equal spirit, Aristocrats. All the rest, in palaces or in lanes, are snobs, to use the vulgar phrase. Thus

Picard who knows how to measure a degree on the earth's surface; Vauban, who knows how to make a river & the rain avail to make fountains at Versailles, Cuvier who sees his thought classify the Creation anew, Geoffroi St Hilaire, Laplace, Napoleon, I call nobles. All the grand seigneurs who prate after them, are rabble. I call these fellows nobles because they know something originally of the world. If the sun were extinguished & the solar system deranged they could begin to replace it.

The town is the unit of the Republic. The New England states found their constitutions on towns, & not on committees, which districting leads to & is. And thus are politics the school of the people, the game which every one of them learns to play. And therefore they are all skilful in California, or on Robinson Crusoe's Island, instantly to erect a working government, as French & Germans are not. In the Western states & in New York & Pennsylvania, the town system is not the base, & therefore the expenditure of the legislature is not economical, but prodigal. By district or whatever throws the election into hands of committees men are elected, who could not get the votes of those to whom they are best known.

—

We can do nothing without the shadow. The sun were insipid if the universe was not opaque. Art lives & thrills in ever new use & combining of contrasts, & is digging into the dark ever more for blacker Pits of night. What would painter do, or what would hero & saint, but for crucifixions & hells? and evermore in the world is this marvellous balance of beauty & disgust, magnificence & rats. Then let the ghost sit at my side, closer, closer, dear ghost! if glory & bliss only so can press to the other cheek. And to point how well said Haydon's washerwoman "The more trouble, the more lion,—that's my principle"

There's more memory in the world than we allow for; other things remember, as well as you. Gold always remembers how it was got, & curses or blesses according to the manner of its coming.

—

Wendell Holmes when I offered to go to his lecture on Wordsworth, said, "I entreat you not to go. I am forced to study effects. You & others may be able to combine popular effect with the exhibition of truths. I cannot. I am compelled to study effects." The other day, Henry Thoreau was speaking to me about my lecture on the Anglo American, & regretting that whatever was written for a lecture, or whatever succeeded with the audience was bad, &c. I said, I am ambitious to write something which all can read, like Robinson Crusoe. And when I have written a paper or a book, I see with regret that it is not solid, with a right materialistic treatment, which delights everybody. Henry objected, of course, & vaunted the better lectures which only reached a few persons. Well, yesterday, he came here, &, at supper, Edith, understanding that he was to lecture at the Lyceum, sharply asked him, "Whether his lecture would be a nice interesting story, such as she wanted to hear, or whether it was one of those old philosophical things that she did not care about?" Henry instantly turned to her, & bethought himself, & I saw was trying to believe that he had matter that might fit Edith & Edward, who were to sit up & go to the lecture, if it was a good one for them.

When some one offered Agassiz a glass of water, he said that he did not know whether he had ever drank a glass of that liquid, before he came to this country.

—

Contempt grows in great cities.

Sickness expensive.
I hate sickness. It is a selfish cannibal, eats up all the life & youth it can lay hold of; uses & absorbs its own sons & daughters. I figure it as a pale screaming wailing distracted phantom, absolutely selfish, heedless of all that is good & real, attentive only to its own sensations, & not only losing its own soul, but wasting the sacred youth & life of others in listening to its meanness & mopings & in ministration to its restless voracity of trifles. "When I am old," said the wise woman, "do not fail to rule me."

—

Poetry is the linguist who can speak this tongue only for generous delight.

—

Of Phillips, Garrison, & others I have always the feeling that they may wake up some morning & find that they have made a capital mistake, & are not the persons they took themselves for. Very dangerous is this thoroughly social & related life, whether antagonistic or *co*-operative. In a lonely world, or a world with half a dozen inhabitants, these would find nothing to do. The first discovery I made of P., was, that while I admired his eloquence, I had not the faintest wish to meet the man. He had only a *platform*-existence, & no personality. Mere mouthpieces of a party, take away the party & they shrivel & vanish.

They are inestimable for workers on audiences; but for a private conversation, one to one, I much prefer to take my chance with that boy in the corner.

The "Liberator" is a scold. A sibyl is quite another thing.

—

There is nobody in Washington who can explain this Nebraska business to the people,—nobody of weight. And nobody of any importance on the bad side. It is only done by Douglass & his accomplices by calculation on the brutal ignorance of the people, upon the wretched masses of Pennsylvania, Indiana, Illinois, Kentucky, & so on, people who can't read or know anything beyond what the village democrat tells them. But what effrontery it required to fly in the face of what was supposed settled law & how it shows that we have no guards whatever, that there is no proposition whatever, that is too audacious to be offered us by the southerner. Perhaps it will be five years,—perhaps only one,—before the law that forbids   will be rescinded.

And how absurd are these Abbot Lawrences & Everetts, after throwing their whole weight into the slavery scale, & bringing in this very state of things, now when it is too late, to quarrel with the issue.

I found, in Wisconsin, that the world was laid down in large lots. The member of Congress there, said, that, up in the Pine Country, the trees were so large, & so many of them, that a man could not walk in the forest, & it was necessary to wade up the streams. Dr Welsh at Lasalle told me that the prairie grass there was over the tops of carriages, or higher than the head of a man riding on horseback, so that really a man not accustomed to the prairie could easily get lost in the grass!

—

Metres.

I amuse myself often, as I walk, with humming the rhythm of the decasyllabic quatrain, or of the octosyllabic with alternate sexsyllabic or other rhythms, & believe these metres to be organic, or derived from our human pulse, and to be therefore not proper to one nation, but to mankind. But I find a wonderful charm, heroic, & especially deeply pathetic or plaintive in the cadence, & say to myself, Ah happy! if one could fill these small measures with words approaching to the power of these beats.

The theory of Poetry is the generation of matter from thought, and Swedenborg & Plato are the expounders of this; & the moralists, like Zeno & Christ, are the didactic poets; & heroes are practical poets. But shall we say the brains are so badly formed, so unheroically, brains of the sons of *fallen* men, that the doctrine is most imperfectly received. Psychology is fragmentarily taught. One man sees a sparkle or shimmer of the truth, & reports it, & his saying becomes a legend or golden proverb for all ages; and other men report as much; but no man wholly & well. Poems! we have no poem. The Iliad is a poor ballad grinding—whenever the Poet shall appear!

The man thinks he can know this or that, by words & writing. It can only be known or done organically. He must plunge into the universe, & live in its forms,—sink to rise. None any work can frame unless himself become the same.

The first men saw heavens & earths, saw noble instruments of noble souls; we see railroads, banks, & mills. And we pity their poverty. There was as much creative force then as now, but it made globes instead of waterclosets. Each sees what he makes.

Realism.

We shall pass for what we are. Do not fear to die, because you have not done your task. Whenever a noble soul comes, the audience awaits. And he is not judged by his performance, but by the spirit of his performance. We shall pass for what we are. The world is a masked ball & every one hides his real character, & reveals it by hiding. People have the devil's-mark stamped on their faces, & do not know it, & join the church & talk virtue, and we are seeing the goat's foot all the time.

—

The Unitarians, you say, are a poor skeptical egotistic shopping sect. The Calvinists serious, still darkened over by their Hebraistic dream. The Saxon race has never flowered into its own religion, but has been fain to borrow this old Hebraism of the dark race. The Latin races are at last come to a stand, & are declining. Merry England & saucy America striding far ahead. The dark man, the black man declines. The black man is courageous, but the white men are the children of God, said Plato. It will happen by & by, that the black man will only be destined for museums like the Dodo. Alcott compassionately thought that if necessary to bring them sooner to an end, polygamy might be introduced & these made the eunuchs, polygamy, I suppose, to increase the white births.

Realism in literature

I have no fear but that the reality I love will yet exist in literature. I do not go to any pope or president for my list of books. I read what I like. I learn what I do not already know. Only those above me can give me this. They also do as I,—read only such as know more than they: Thus we all depend at last on the few heads or the one head that is nearest to the stars, nearest to the fountain of all science, & knowledge runs steadily down from class to class down to the lowest people, from the highest, as water does.

—

I believe, the races, as Celtic, Norman, Saxon, must be used hypothetically or temporarily, as we do by the Linnaean classification, for convenience simply, & not as true & ultimate. For, otherwise, we are perpetually confounded by finding the best settled traits of one race, claimed by some more acute or ingenious partisan as precisely characteristic of the other & antagonistic. It is with national traits as with virus of cholera or plague in the atmosphere, it eludes the chemical analysis, and the air of the plague hospital is not to be discriminated by any known test from the air of Mont Blanc. Thus, read what M. Ernest Renan, in *Revue des deux Mondes*, has to say on Celtic marks. As, for example, the love of family & private virtue, in the Celt, as distinguishing him from the Germanic races. No patriotism in the Celt, but deep individualism, says this writer, citing the Mabinogion.

from

IO

1854

The existence of evil & malignant men does not depend on themselves or on men, it indicates the virulence that still remains uncured in the universe, uncured & corrupting & hurling out these pestilent rats & tigers, and men rat-like & wolf-like.

—

Hallam

Hallam leaves out all those writers I read. His Latimer is not the good bishop, but I know not what writer of Latin. Jordano Bruno, Behmen, Van Helmont, Digby, Lord Herbert, George Herbert, Henry More, Swedenborg,—in vain you look in his pages for adequate mention of these men, for whose sake I want a history of literature: All these he passes, or names them for something else than their real merit, namely, their originality & faithful striving to write a line of the real history of the world.

—

It was the Chapel of King's College, Cambridge, of which the legend runs, that Sir C. Wren went thither once a year to see it, & said, "If any man will show me where to lay the first stone, I will build such another."

—

You can't use a man as an instrument, without being used by him as an instrument.

—

Of reading.

I once interpreted the law of Adrastia "that he who had any truth shd. be safe from harm until another period;" as pronounced of originators. But I have discovered that the profound satisfactions—which I take to be the sentence of Adrastia itself,—belong to the truth received from another soul, come to us in reading, as well as in thinking.

—

I have already written once my belief that the American votes rashly & immorally with his party on the question of slavery, with a feeling that he does not seriously endanger anything. He believes that what he has enacted he can repeal, if he do not like it; & does not entertain the possibility of being seriously caught in meshes of legislation. But one may run a risk once too often,

Those who stay away from the election think that one vote will do no good: 'tis but one step more to think one vote will do no harm. But if they should come to be interested in themselves, in their career, they would no more stay from the election than from honesty or from affection.

—

What's the use of telegraph? what of newspapers? (what of waiting to know what the Convention in Ohio, what that in Michigan, is ready to do?) To know how men feel in Wisconsin, in Illinois, in Minnesota, I wait for no mails, I read no telegraphs. I ask my own heart. If those men are made as I am, if they breathe the same air, eat the same wheat or corn-bread, have wives & children, I know their resentment will boil at this legislation. I know it will boil until this wrong is righted. The interest of labor, the self-respect of mankind, that engages man not to be to man a wolf, secures their everlasting hostility to this shame.

—

May, 1854

If Minerva offered me a gift & an option, I would say give me continuity. I am tired of scraps. I do not wish to be a literary or intellectual chiffonier. Away with this jew's rag-bag of ends & tufts of brocade, velvet, & cloth of gold; let me spin some yards or miles of helpful twine, a clew to lead to one kingly truth, a cord to bind wholesome & belonging facts.

The Asmodaean feat be mine
To spin my sand heaps into twine.

—

Thoreau thinks 'tis immoral to dig gold in California; immoral to leave creating value, & go to augmenting the representative of value, & so altering & diminishing real value, &, that, of course, the fraud will appear.

I conceive that work to be as innocent as any other speculating.

Every man should do what he can; & he was created to augment some real value, & not for a speculator. When he leaves or postpones, (as most men do,) his proper work, & adopts some short or cunning method, as of watching markets, or farming in any manner the ignorance of people, as, in buying by the acre to sell by the foot, he is fraudulent, he is malefactor, so far; & is bringing society to bankruptcy. But nature watches over all this, too, & turns this malfaisance to some good. For, California gets peopled, subdued, civilised, in this fictitious way, & on this fiction a real prosperity is rooted & grown. 'Tis a decoy-duck, a tub thrown to the whale; whereby real ducks, & real whales, are caught. And, out of Sabine rapes, & out of robbers' forays, real Romes & their heroisms come in fulness of time.

The world is divided on the fame of the Virgin Mary. The Catholics call her "Mother of God," the Skeptics think her the natural mother of an admirable child. But the last agree with the first in hailing the moral perfections of his character, & the immense benefit his life has exerted & exerts.

—

It does seem as if a vow of silence coupled with systematic lessons might teach women the outline & new direction of the philosopher, but they give themselves no leisure to hear. They are impatient to talk.

There is no theology now.

If I were rich, said Alcot, I should buy all books only for the pictures, & cut these out & save them.

Mr E., he said, has a right to everything.

The title-pages of the old books he finds more significant, &, if he cannot have the book, thinks it much to have the title.

—

Do! what can Englishman & steam not do? He can clothe the shingle-mountains of Scotland with shipoaks. He can scoop out Aetna with a ladle. He can make swordblades that will cut gunbarrels in two. He can divide a line to a millionth of an inch. By his aid has been able to bring rain again into Egypt after 3000 years by scientific planting. I suppose he will be able to skim the sea with a spoon for whales.

Between 300, & 400,000 000 of hands, is the steampower in Engd.

French

Heine thinks the office of the French language to test the sense that is in any philosophy or science. Translate it into French, & you dispel instantly all the smoke & sorcery, & it passes for what it is.

—

The fathers made the blunder in the convention in the Ordinance of 10 July, 1787, to adopt population as basis of representation, & count only three fifths of the slaves, and to concede the reclamation of fugitive slaves for the consideration of the prohibition that "there shall be neither slavery nor involuntary servitude in the said (Northwest) Territory, unless in punishment of crimes." The bed of the Ohio river was the line agreed on east of the Missisippi.

In 1820 when New territory west of the Missisippi was to be dealt with, no such natural line offered and a parallel of latitude was adopted, & 36.30 n. was agreed on as equitable.

The Fathers made the fatal blunder in agreeing to this false basis of representation, & to this criminal complicity of restoring fugitive slaves: and the splendor of the bribe, namely, the magnificent prosperity of America from 1787, is their excuse before God & men, for the crime. They ought never to have passed the Ordinance. They ought to have refused it at the risk of making no Union; &, if no solution could be had, it would have been better that two nations, one free & one slaveholding, should have started into existence at once. The bribe, if they foresaw the prosperity we have seen, was one to dazzle common men. And I do not wonder that most men now excuse & applaud it. But crime brings punishment, always so much crime, so much ruin. A little crime a minor penalty; a great crime, a great ruin; and now, after 60 years, the poison has crept into every vein & every artery of the State.

—

'Tis wonderful the swift & secret channels through which thought can pass & appear at either pole & at the antipodes. The signs of this present time the very nightmares as they go, can read. All this neology, where did it come from? All the bewitched tables rap out Swedenborg.

—

Modern Manners

Why count stamens, when you can study the science of men? The clergy are as like as peas. I can not tell them apart. It was said, they have bronchitis, because of reading from their paper sermon with a near voice, & then, looking at the audience, they try to speak with their far voice, & the shock is noxious. I think they do the same, or the reverse, with their thought. They look into Plato or into the mind, & then try to make parish & unitarian mince-meat of the amplitudes & eternities; & the shock is noxious. Macready thought the falsetto of their voicing gave them bronchitis. See the story of the Buddhist Subking in Σ 99.

—

Cleverness the English Prize

They love syllogisms but they love best the not mistaking the minor & major proposition, the never losing sight of that, & they pardon everything to him who escapes out of the net of his own logic to affirm & enact the major proposition. They love Sam. Johnson, who, master of logic, would jump out of his syllogism the instant his major proposition was in danger, to save that, at all hazards. So Cromwell, so Nelson—

—

Friends do not shake hands. I talk with you, & we have marvellous intimacies, & take all manner of beautiful liberties. After an hour, it is time to go, & straightway I take hold of your hand, & find you a coarse stranger, instead of that musical & permeable angel with whom I have been entertained.

—

Heaven takes care to show us that war is a part of our education, as much as milk or love, & is not to be escaped. We affect to put it all back in history, as the Trojan War, the War of the Roses, the Revolutionary War. Not so; it is *Your* War. Has that been declared? has that been fought out? & where did the Victory perch? The wars of other people & of history growl at a distance, but your war comes near, looks into your eyes, in Politics, in professional pursuit, in choices in the street, in daily habit, in all the questions of the times, in the keeping or surrendering the controul of your day, & your house, & your opinion, in the terrors of the night, in the frauds & skepticism of the day, the American independence! that is a legend. *Your Independence*! that is the question of all the Present. Have you fought out that? & settled it once & again, & once for all in the minds of all persons with whom you have to do, that you & your sense of right, & fit & fair, are an invincible indestructible somewhat, which is not to be bought or cajoled or frighted away? That done, & victory inscribed on your eyes & brow & voice, the other American Freedom begins instantly to have some meaning & support.

—

Rome, says Bacon, was a state without paradoxes.

—

A man can only write one book. That is the reason why everybody begs readings & extracts of the young poet until 35. When he is 50, they still think they value him, & they tell him so; but they scatter like partridges, if he offer to read his paper. They think, it is because they have some job to do. But they never allowed a job to stand in the way, when he was 25.

—

I suppose, every one has favorite topics, which make a sort of Museum or privileged closet of whimsies in his mind, & which he thinks it a kind of aristocracy to know about. Thus, I like to know about lions, diamonds, wine, and Beauty: And Martial, & Hafiz.

—

Le style, c'est l'homme, said Buffon, and Goethe said, that, as for poetry, &c he had learned to speak German; and I say of Burrill's 50 languages, that I shall be glad if he knows one. If I be asked how many masters of English idiom I know, I shall be pestered to count three or four among living men.

A good head cannot read amiss. In every book he finds passages which seem confidences or asides, hidden from all else,

& unmistakeably meant for his ear. No book has worth by itself; but by the relation to what you have from many other books, it weighs.

—

Quotation.

It is curious what new interest an old sentence or poem acquires in quotation. Hallam is never deep, but he is a fair mind, able to appreciate poetry, unless it becomes deep, (& to be sure always blind & deaf to imaginative & analogy-loving souls, like the Platonists, like Behmen, like Donne, Herbert, Crashaw,) and Hallam cites a sentence from Bacon or Sydney, or distinguishes a lyric of Edwards or Vaux, & straightway it commends itself to me as if it had received the Isthmian crown.

—

Hooker & his coevals show the power of an ideal dogma. Christianity was an idealism which did a world of good in the materialism of old Rome, & of the robbers & pirates of the Middle Age. It was a noble heart-warmer with the range & play it gave to thought & imagination, in opening the doctrine of love. These old fellows ranged like poets in these ethereal fields, & only quoted a text now & then, to give a *quasi*-authority to their fancies. But 'tis wonderful the difference between their range, & the straitwaistcoat & close corners of our priests. They quote condescendingly, & out of gentleman-like good humour, a text,—not needing it out of any poverty, for they have as good of their own; but ours in a cowed & servile way, never matching it by anything as good.
Then I notice the freedom with which they fill up the faint outline map which the Christian hypothesis affords them with a bold mythology of their own. Thus the Heaven, on the sparsest hint, they populate with Angels in rank & degree, (borrowed I believe out of Dionysius), & exercise their fancy very freely & well in this rhetoric, which, to the next age, or to the next writer, becomes instantly authority, & is repeated over, like Holy Writ, from one to another, till it becomes believed by being often said.
Hooker, however, it must be owned, calls, "this present age, full of tongue & weak of brain"—

Elizabeth Hoar.

The last night talked with Elizabeth the wise, who defined Commonsense as the perception of the inevitable laws of existence. The philosophers considered only such laws as could be stated; but *sensible* men, those also which could not be stated;—a very just distinction, which, I find, with contentment that I had recognized in my paragraph about Dr Johnson, but had not rightly laid down beforehand. I find also in her a certain forward motion of the mind when at last, through a thousand silences & delays, she begins to speak, which is excellent, as being the mind's own motion, through beauty & sweetness of the thing perceived, & without any manner of reflection or return on one's self.—Her illustration of the common laws was, 'You must count your money. For, if you call it petty, & count it not, "through greatness of soul," it will have its revenge on your soul, by coming in thither also, in the sequel, with injurious suspicions of your best friends & other disquietudes.'

—

Genius.

Temperance in love: and the child of the god is the superfluity of strength. Temperance in art: and the poet is never the poorer for his song. The masters painted & carved for joy, & knew not that virtue had gone out of them. A.B.A. thought the father of the Hebrew Boy must have been superior to his son.

Genius.

The few poems appear to have been written between sleeping & waking; irresponsibly; "forms that men spy with the half-shut eye in the beams of the setting sun." And what W.E.C. said, that Rubens & these old masters "painted a landscape as one smokes a cigar." They could not paint the like again in cold blood. So the Lovelaces, Sucklings, Dorsets, & Wallers, wrote their songs: it was a fine efflorescence of fine powers "the charming accident of their more charming lives," as was said of French Women.

"I could not replace myself," said Napoleon when they talked of his son's filling his place; "I am the child of Destiny"

Universities are, of course, hostile to geniuses, which, seeing & using ways of their own, discredit the routine. Churches & Monasteries for the like reason uniformly persecute saints. Yet we all send our sons to college & though he be a genius he must take his chance.

Last night talking with W.E.C. it appeared still more clear—the two nations in England,—one in all time fierce only for mincepie,—the old granniest beef-eating solemn trifler, a Cheap-side prentice, & growing to be a Cheapside lord;—the other a fine, thoughtful, religious, poetical believer,—fit for hero, fit for martyr, deriving in his flights only the solidity, & square elbows, & method, from his Cheapside brother, & rewarding him with puritanism, with drama, with letters & liberty.

It would be well to begin the story with notice of first visit to England. I was then more ignorant than now. I am ignorant enough now, Heaven knows,—nay I am of the hopelessly ignorant class, to whom the knowledge of scholars is always a marvel,—fault of some method in my mind. But I was ignorant enough then to wish to go to Europe only to see three or four persons,—Wordsworth, Coleridge, Landor, & Carlyle. I should have wished to see Goethe in Germany, but he was then just dead.

—

I praise the expansive, the still generalizing, because it seems as if *transition*, shooting the gulf, were the essential act of life. Nature forever aims & strives at a better, at a new degree, the same nature in & out of man, the same nature in a river-drop & in the soul of a hero.

One class of minds delighting in a bounded fact, & the other class in its relations or correspondency to all other facts.

The art of conversation or the qualification for a good companion, is, a certain self-controul, which now holds the subject, now lets it go, with a respect to the emergencies of the moment.

—

Oct. 11. Never was a more brilliant show of coloured landscape than yesterday afternoon—incredibly excellent topaz & ruby at 4 o'clock, cold & shabby at 6.

—

Intellect

I notice that I value nothing so much as the threads that spin from a thought to a fact, & from one fact to another fact, making both experiences valuable & presentable, which were insignificant before, & weaving together into rich webs all solitary observations.

—

I wish to know the nomenclature of botany & astronomy. But these are soulless both, as we know them; vocabularies both. Add astrology to astronomy, & 'tis somewhat. Add medicine & magic to botany, & that is something. But the English believe that by mountains of facts they can climb into the heaven of thought & truth: so the builders of Babel believed. But the method of truth is quite other, & heaven descends, when it will, to the prepared soul. We must hold our science as mere convenience, expectant of a higher method from the mind itself.

—

Swedenborg is the theosophist of the present age. 'Tis very fine for England & America, Boston & London, refined circles, to affect a scorn. Some theory must be at the bottom; & these surface-creatures might be shown that they are Swedenborgians, or else skeptics. They hate,—all men hate skepticism, &, when shown what kind of rotten underpinning they are strutting upon, they will kiss the robe of Swedenborg.

from

NO

1855

Some thoughts have paternity & some are bachelors. I am too celibate.

—

Rome, N.Y., 18 Feb. 1855. What occurred this morng touching the imagination? In meeting a new student, I incline to ask him, Do you know any deep man? Has any one furnished you with a new image? for to see the world representatively, implies high gifts.

The face, how few inches, yet all the hours, all the passions, sentiments, truths, destinies, use it as their index, inscribe their decrees.

—

Dance

Under the soul of the world, "the bodies are moved in a beautiful manner, as being parts of the whole: but certain things are corrupted, in consequence of not being able to sustain the order of the whole. Just as if, in a great dance, which is conducted in a becoming manner, a tortoise being caught in the middle of the progression, should be trod upon, not being able to escape the order of the dance; though, if the tortoise had arranged itself with the dance, it would not have suffered from those that composed it." Plotinus.

—

Utica, Feb. 11—

Ah! how few things! a warm room, and morning leisure. I sit by the Holy River, & watch the waves. Will it not cease to flow for me! I need not ask for more. Let them ask for results & externals, they who have not this source. Minima pars sui puella, —they who are not substance, have need of the compensation of costume. I do not know that I am ready, like my Dervish, in

his more total devotion, to throw my babes into the stream. No, I am householder, and father, & citizen, far too much for that. But what blazing evidence his vices (so esteemed) afford to the pure beauty that intoxicates him!
How far better his outward shiftlessness & insensibility to what are reckoned the primary Claims, than the Bulwer view of intellect, as a sort of bill of exchange easily convertible into fine chambers, wine, & cigars. Of him, that is, of the Dervish by the River, I think, this morning, most respectfully, when I remember his magnanimity, unparalleled I think among men of his class,—that he truly loves the thought, & wishes its widest publication, and gladly hears his own from the lips of other men.

What a fact, too, that when Higginson went to the Courthouse having made up his mind that he should not return thence, the only man that followed him into it was Alcott!

—

The rule of Positive & Superlative is this: as long as you deal with sensible objects in the sphere of sense call things by their right names. But (it is known to us all that) every man may be, (& some men are,) raised to a platform whence he sees beyond sense to moral & spiritual truth; when he no longer sees snow as snow, or horses as horses, but only sees or names them representatively for those interior facts which they signify. This is the way the prophets, this is the way the poets use them. And in that exalted state, the mind deals very easily with great and small material things, and strings worlds like beads upon its thought. The success with which this is done can alone determine how genuine is the inspiration.

The very failure of Coleridge, a man of catholic mind all related with a hunger for ideas with vast attempts, but most inadequate performings, failing to accomplish any one masterpiece, seems to mark the closing of an era. And the genius of Wordsworth has capital defects.
Then what to say of Hallam? He is too polite by half, but with deficient sympathy, writing the history of literature with resolute generosity, but unable to see the deep value that lies in the mystics, & which often outweighs as a seed of power & a source of revolution all the correct writers of their day. He is

sure to dismiss with a kind of contempt the profounder writers.

—

Men ride on a thought, as if each bestrode an invisible horse, which, if it became visible all their seemingly mad plunging motions would be explained.

When my eyes opened I found I was jogging between the narrowest walls, & seeing nothing else, & that I had mistaken those walls of the lane for England.

—

Queteletism

I saw in Bowdoin Square (did I record it already?) men swinging a stone of the size of Stonehenge stones, with a common derrick,—& the men were common masons, with paddies to help, and did not think they had done anything extraordinary; and yet we wonder how Stonehenge was built & forgotten. 'Tis plain we love to wonder.

—

Quotation

What I said in one of my Saadi scraps of verse, I might say in good sooth, that—

Thus the high Muse treated me
Directly never greeted me,
But when she spread her dearest spells
Feigned to speak to some one else:
I was free to overhear,
Or I might at will forbear;
But that casual word
Thus at random overheard,
Was the symphony of spheres,
And proverb of a thousand years,

My best thought came from others. I heard in their words my own meaning, but a deeper sense than they put on them: And could well & best express my self in other people's phrases, but to finer purpose than they knew.

"He that borrows the aid of an equal understanding," said Burke, "doubles his own: he that uses that of a superior, elevates his own to the stature of that he contemplates."

—

Our Concord mechanics & farmers are very doubtful on the subject of Culture, & will vote against you: but I notice they will all send their children to the dancing-school.

They are rather deaf on the subject of mental superiority; but they value the multiplication-table, & decimal fractions, & theodolites, & surveying & navigation. They value reading & writing.

—

Philip Randolph was surprised to find me speaking to the politics of Antislavery, in Philadelphia. I suppose, because he thought me a believer in general laws, and that it was a kind of distrust of my own general teachings to appear in active sympathy with these temporary heats.
He is right so far as that it is becoming in the scholar to insist on central soundness, rather than on superficial applications. I am to give a wise & just ballot, though no man else in the republic doth. I am not to compromise or mix or accommodate. I am to demand the absolute right, affirm that, & do that; but not push Boston into a false, showy, & theatrical attitude, endeavoring to persuade her she is more virtuous than she is. Thereby I am robbing myself, more than I am enriching the public. After twenty, fifty, a hundred years, it will be quite easy to discriminate who stood for the right, & who for the expedient. The vulgar, comprising ranks on ranks of fine gentlemen, clergymen, college presidents & professors, & great democratic statesmen bellowing for liberty, will of course go for safe degrees of liberty,—that is, will side with property against the Spirit, subtle & absolute, which keeps no terms.

—

Munroe seriously asked what I believed of Jesus & prophets. I said, as so often, that it seemed to me an impiety to be listening to one & another, when the pure Heaven was pouring itself into each of us, on the simple condition of obedience. To listen to any second hand gospel is perdition of the First Gospel. Jesus was Jesus because he refused to listen to another, & listened at home.

—

Οι ρεοντες

For flowing is the secret of things & no wonder the children love masks, & to trick themselves in endless costumes, & be a horse, a soldier, a parson, or a bear; and, older, delight in theatricals; as, in nature, the egg is passing to a grub, the grub to a fly, and the vegetable eye to a bud, the bud to a leaf, a stem, a flower, a fruit; the children have only the instinct of their race, the instinct of the Universe, in which, *Becoming somewhat else* is the whole game of nature, & death the penalty of standing still.

'Tis not less in thought. I cannot conceive of any good in a thought which confines & stagnates. Liberty means the power to flow. To continue is to flow. Life is unceasing parturition.

—

House-hunting.

Every thing is on the street: highways run through nature, as, in the human body, the veins percolate to every spot; you cannot prick with the finest needle anywhere but you draw blood. The young people do not like the town, do not like the seashore, they will go inland, find a dear cottage deep in the mountains, secret as their hearts. They set forth on their travels in search of a home: they reach Berkshire, they reach Vermont, they look at the farms, good farms, high mountain sides, but where is the seclusion? The farm 'tis near this, 'tis near that. They have got far from Boston, but 'tis near Albany, or near Burlington, or near Montreal. They explore this farm, but the house is small, old, thin: discontented people lived there, & are gone:—there's too much sky, too much out-doors, too public: this is not solitude. The youth aches for solitude; he must leave home; he must hide in the forest; he departs for Katahdin, or Moosehead Lake: he cannot get enough alone to write to his friend, to worship his beloved. He finds, after much search, that Italy flies faster than he; he chases a rainbow. When he comes to the house, he passes through the house: that does not make the deep recess he sought. "Ah now, I perceive," he says, "it must be deep with persons: friends only can give depth." Yes, but there's a great dearth, this year, of friends; hard to find, & hard to have, when found; they are just going away: they also are in the whirl of this flitting world, &

have engagements & necessities; they are just starting for Wisconsin; have letters from Bremen: see you again, soon.
Slow, slow to learn the lesson, that there's but one depth, but one interior, and that is,—his purpose. When Joy or Genius or Calamity or Crime shall show him *that*, then woods, then farms, then noisy Boston, then shopmen & cab drivers, indifferently with holiest prophet or dearest friend, will mirror back to him its unfathomable heaven, its populous solitude.

—

It is on the completeness with which metrical forms have covered the whole circle of routinary experience, that improvisation is possible to a rhymer familiar with this cyclus of forms, & quick & dexterous in combining them. Most poetry, stock poetry we call it, that we see in the magazines, is nothing but this mosaic-work done slowly.
But whether is improvisation of poetry possible, as well as this ballad mongering?
Yes, no doubt, since geniuses have existed, we will not be disloyal or hopeless. But beside the strange power implied of passing at will into the state of vision & of utterance, is required huge means, vast health, vigor, & celerity.

Ellery Channing's poetry has the merit of being genuine, & not the metrical commonplaces of the Magazine, but it is painfully incomplete. He has not kept faith with the reader, 'tis shamefully indolent & slovenly. He should have lain awake all night to find the true rhyme for a verse, & he has availed himself of the first one that came; so that it is all a babyish incompleteness.

Walter Scott is the best example of this mastery of metrical commonplaces that makes vulgar Improvisation.

—

Yet nothing but thought is precious. And we must respect in ourselves this possibility, & abide its time. Jones Very, who thought it an honor to wash his own face, seems to me less insane than men who hold themselves cheap.
Let us not be such that our thoughts should disdain us.
If I could find that a perfect song could form itself in my brain, I should indulge it & pamper it as bees their queen.

—

Thor has washed his face, shorn his beard, & entered Parliament, sat down at the desk in India House he has graciously lent Miollnir to Birmingham for a steamhammer. He has entered Oxford & the printing-houses, with the Edda in his hand, & with Miollnir he smashes down colleges & scatters libraries, as superfluous. Every word of the Edda, he says, is the sound of a hammer stroke. Let there be none other than such.

—

Margaret Fuller had rhythm in her speech. And her speech was improvisation.

—

The English have no national religion, & have imported the Hebrew. If one penetrated the cants, what would he find their real faith? They do believe in Shakspeare's genius; in commerce; pit-coal; & the steam-engine.

—

Most men are rubbish, & in every man is a good deal of rubbish. What quantities of fribbles, paupers, bed-ridden or bed-riding invalids, thieves, rogues, & beggars, of both sexes, might be advantageously spared!

But Quetelet Fate knows better; keeps everything alive, as long as it can live; that is, so long as the smallest thread of public necessity holds it on to the tree Igdrasil. The sparks & barkeepers & thief class are allowed, as proletaries; their virility being useful, & every one of their vices being the excess or acridity of a virtue. The mass are animal, in pupilage, & near chimpanzee. Well, we are used as brute atoms, until we think; then we use all the rest. Nature turns all malfaisance to good. California gets peopled & subdued by the general gaol-delivery that pours into it.

—

Books are the destruction of literature. "The golden age of the Greek literature was that in which no book grew under the stylus or the calamus, but these merely served as aids (& not probably until after lapse of centuries,) to the precarious tradition of the nation, & the overladen memory of the poetical singers & narrators." Niebuhr. Letters III 217

—

A. thought he had not a lecture or a book, but was himself an influence. He justified himself by naming or letting you name an ideal assembly of Socrates, Zoroaster, Pythagoras, Behmen, Swedenborg, &, if such were bodily present, he should not be shamed, but would be free of that company. I hinted that all these were exact persons, severe with themselves, & could formulate something. Could he formulate his dogma?

I proposed to lock him up in prison, so that he might find out what was memory, what fancy, what instinct, what analysis?

A horse doctor could give a prescription to cure a horse's heel. Had he no recipe for a bad memory, or a sick angel? To all which he replied, that he must have a scribe to report his thoughts which now escaped him.

But I dread autobiography which usurps the largest part, sometimes the whole of the discourse of very worthy persons whom I know.

—

We are forced to treat a great part of mankind like crazy persons. We readily discover their mania & humor it, so that conversation soon becomes a tiresome effort. We humor a democrat, a whig, a rich man, an antiquary, a woman, a slaveholder, & so on. All Dr J.'s opinions are incipient insanities, & not very incipient either.

—

The mind delights in the contemplation of immense time. All great natures are lovers of stability & permanence. And in spiritualist 'tis only transfer to a stabler stability.

Just as man is conscious of the law of vegetable & animal nature so he is aware of an Intellect which overhangs his consciousness like a sky; of degree above degree; & heaven within heaven.

Number is lost in it. Millions of observers could not suffice to write its first law.

Yet it seemed to him as if gladly he would dedicate himself to such a god, be a fakeer of the intellect, fast & pray, spend & be spent, wear its colors, wear the infirmities, were it pallor, sterility, celibacy, poverty, insignificance, were these the livery of its troop, as the smith wears his apron & the collier his smutted face, honest infirmities, honorable scars, so that he be rewarded by conquest of principles; or by being purified & admitted into the immortalities, mount & ride on the backs of these thoughts, steeds which course forever the ethereal plains.

Time was nothing. He had no hurry. Time was well lavished, were it centuries & cycles, in these surveys. It seemed as if the very sentences he wrote, a few sentences after summers of contemplation, shone again with all the suns which had gone to contribute to his knowing. Few, few were the lords he could reckon: Memory, & Imagination, & Perception: he did not know more for living long. Abandon yourself, he said, to the leading, when the Leader comes, this was the sum of wisdom & duty. Shake off from your shoes the dust of Europe & Asia, the rotten religions & personalities of nations. Act from your heart where the wise temperate guidance is instantly born.

—

Melancholy people see a black star always riding through the light & colored clouds in the sky overhead: waves of light pass over & hide it a moment, but the black star keeps fast in the zenith.

Dungeons in the air

—

The new professions
The phrenologist
the railroad man
the landscape gardener
the lecturer
the sorcerer, rapper, mesmeriser, medium.
the daguerrotypist

—

At Amherst the learned professors in the parlor were pleased that the plurality of worlds was disproved, as that restored its lost dignity to the race of men, & made the old Christian immortality valid again, & probable. I said, this was a poor mechanical elevation, & all true elevation must consist in a new & finer possession, by dint of finer organization, in the same things in which buffalo & fox had already a brutish, & Indian & paddy a semi-brute possession.

—

1855 August 27. Edward says; Father, today I have done three things for the first time; I have swum across the river; I have beat Walter Lewis at the bowling alley; and I have jumped over a stick two feet high.

—

The melioration in pears, or in sheep, & horses, is the only hint we have that suggests the creation of man. Every thing has a family likeness to him. All natural history from the first fossil points at him. The resemblances approach very near in the satyr to the negro or lowest man, & food, climate, & concurrence of happy stars, a guided fortune, will have at last piloted the poor quadrumanous over the awful bar that separates the fixed beast from the versatile man. In no other direction, have we any hint of the *modus* in which the infant man could be preserved. The fixity or unpassableness or inconvertibility of races, as we see them, is a feeble argument, since all the historical period is but a point to the duration in which nature has wrought. Any the least & solitariest fact in our natural history has the worth of a *power* in the opportunity of geologic periods. All our apples came from the little crab.

from

RO

1855–1856

It must be believed that St George when he conquered the dragon absorbed his nature.

—

Morals
'Tis wonderful where the moral influences come from, since no man is a moralist. 'Tis like the generation of the atmosphere, which is a secret.

Coleridge is one of those who save England from the reproach of no longer possessing in the land the appreciation of what highest wit the land has yielded, as, Shakspeare, Spenser, Herbert, &c. But for Coleridge, and a lurking taciturn or rarely-speaking minority, one would say that, in Germany, & in America, is the best mind of England rightly respected. And that is the sure sign of national decay, when the Bramins can no longer read & understand the Braminical science & philosophy.

—

Why need you vote? If new power is here, if a character which solves old tough questions, which puts me & all the rest in the wrong, tries and condemns our religion, customs, laws, & opens new careers to young receptive men & women, you can well leave voting to the old dead people. Those whom you teach, & those whom you half teach, will fast enough make themselves considered & strong with their new insight, & votes will follow from all the dull.

Marriage is bad enough, but is far the best solution that has yet been offered of the woman's problem. Fourierism, or Mormonism, or the New York Socialism, are not solutions that any high woman will accept as even approximate to her ideas of well-being.

—

The policy of defending their property is good; and if the women demand votes, offices, & political equality as an Elder & Eldress are of equal power in the Shaker Families, refuse it not. 'Tis very cheap wit that finds it so funny. Certainly all my points would be sooner carried in the state if women voted.

Woman.

"Take the first advice of a woman, & not the second."

Women more than all are the element & kingdom of illusion. They see only through Claude Lorraine & how dare anyone—I dare not—pluck away the coulisses, stage effects, & ceremonies, by which they live.

—

Premium on Individualism

In each change of industry, whole classes & populations are sacrificed like caterpillars; as when cotton takes the place of linen, or railroads of turnpikes. Or by the inclosing of a common by land lords. Then society is admonished of the mischief of the division of labor, which makes one man a pin- or a buckle-maker, or any other specialty; & all are ruined except such as are proper individuals, capable of thought, and of new choice & application of their talent to new labor.

—

Our fear of death is like our fear that summer will be short, but when we have had our swing of pleasure, our fill of fruit, & our swelter of heat, we say, we have had our day; & rest of brain & affection please.

If life was a disease, then death will be only a varioloid.

—

The English poet must be as large as London, by no means in the commercial or economic way,—large producer, shipper, jobber, or banker,—but in a real way, drawing as much water, consuming as much oxygen, physical, & metaphysical, as any the ablest-bodied, strongest-willed commander in the market, exchange, law courts, or shipyards of the Metropolis.

When I see the waves of Lake Michigan toss in the bleak snow storm, I see how small & inadequate the common poet is. But Tennyson with his eagle over the sea, has shown his sufficiency.

—

Alcott had much to say of there being more in a man than was contained in his skin; as I say, a man is as his relatedness. But I was struck with the late superiority he showed. The interlocutors were all better than he; he seemed childish & helpless, not apprehending or answering their remarks aright, they masters of their weapons. But by & by, when he got upon a thought like an Indian seizing by the mane & mounting a wild horse of the desart, he overrode them all & showed such mastery & took up time & nature like a boy's marble in his hand as to vindicate himself.

Oct. 4

Last night a dream within a dream. I fancied I woke up, & found myself out walking in my cornfield. James was disturbed, & came out & called, who's there? I, though a little confused how I came there, answered, "it was I." Presently, I walked off, & found I had lost my way. I inquired what town it was, & was told *Lisbon*. I was got by & by into a railroad car; but was a long way from home; &c &c—& was furthermore astonished again to wake really.

Imperfection or want that we suffer from in dreams, as, to go on a journey without a hat, or be in a large assembly without your coat, what is the theory of that? o professor of Metaphysics!

Wide the gulf between genius & talent. The men we know deal with their thoughts as jewellers with jewels which they sell but must not wear; like carpenters with houses too fine for such as they to live in. The mystic is as good as his gold & jewels, good as his house that he builds, goes always in purple apparel, a glistering angel.

In the solitary man of whom I wrote elsewhere, who must walk miles & miles to get the twitchings out of his face, the starts & shoves out of his arms & shoulders, is to be noted the remorse running to despair of his social gaucheries, and he exclaimed, "God may forgive sins, but awkwardness has no forgiveness in heaven or on earth."

—

I have crossed the Missisippi on foot three times.

Soft coal which comes to Rock Island from about 12 miles,

sells for 16 cents a bushel: wood at 6.00 per cord. They talk "quarter sections." I will take a quarter section of that pie. Leclaire being a halfbreed of the Sacs & Foxes (& of French Canadian) had a right to a location of a square mile of land & with a more than Indian sagacity of choosing his warpath, he chose his lot one, above the rapids, & the other below the rapids, at Rock Island. He chose his lot 30 years ago, & now the *railroad to the Pacific runs directly through his log-house*, which is occupied by the company for wood & other purposes. His property has risen to the value of 5 or 600 000 dollars. He is 57 years old, & weighs 308 pounds.

—

In Dixon I talked with Mr Dixon the pioneer founder of the city. His full length portrait was hanging in the town-hall where we were. He is 80 years old & a great favorite with the people, his family have all died, but some grand-children remain. He who has made so many rich is a poor man, which, it seems, is a common fortune here; Sutter the Californian discoverer of gold, is poor. It looks as if one must have a talent for misfortune to miss so many opportunities as these men who have owned the whole township & not saved a competence. He is a correct quiet man, was first a tailor, then a stage owner, & mail agent, &c. I went down the Galena river, once Bean river, Fève, then Fever, now Galena River, four or five miles in a sleigh, with Mr McMasters to the Marsden Lead, so called, a valuable lead mine, & went into it. Marsden, it seems, was a poor farmer here; & sold out his place, & went to California; found no gold, & came back, & bought his land again, &, in digging to clear out a spring of water, stumbled on this most valuable lead (leed), as they call it, of lead-ore. They can get up 7000 lb. of the ore in a day (by a couple of laborers), and the smelters will come to the spot, & buy the ore at 3 cents a pound; so that he found California here. He at once called in his brothers, & divided the mine with them. One of them sold out his share, one sixth, ("foolishly") for 12 000 dollars; the others retain theirs.

Mr Shetland said, 75 or 100 000 dollars had already been derived from this mine, & perhaps as much more remains.

Hon. Mr Turner of Freeport said to me, that it is not usually the first settlers, who become rich, but the second comers: the first, he said, are often visionary men, the second are practical. The first two settlers of Rockford died insolvent, & he named similar cases in other town, I think Beloit. I read at the bottom of a map of Wisconsin, that the motto of the State-seal of Wisconsin, is, "*Civilitas successit Barbarum.*"

An idealist, if he have the sensibilities & habits of those whom I know, is very ungrateful. He craves & enjoys every chemical property, and every elemental force, loves pure air, water, light, caloric, wheat, flesh, salt, & sugar, the blood coursing in his own veins, and the grasp of friendly hands; & uses the meat he eats to preach against matter as malignant, & to praise mind, which he very hollowly & treacherously serves. Beware of hypocrisy.

1856, Jan 9, Beloit.

I fancied in this fierce cold weather, mercury varying from 20 to 30 degrees below zero, for the last week, that Illinois lands would be at a discount, and the agent who at Dixon was selling great tracts, would be better advised to keep them for milder days, since a hundred miles of prairie in such days as these are not worth the poorest shed or cellar in the towns. But my easy landlord assured me "we had no cold weather in Illinois, only now & then Indian Summers & cool nights." He looked merrily at his windowpanes, opaque with a stratum of frost, & said, that his was a fashionable first class hotel, with window-lights of ground glass.

This climate & people are a new test for the wares of a man of letters. All his thin watery matter freezes; 'tis only the smallest portion of alcohol that remains good. At the lyceum, the stout Illinoian, after a short trial, walks out of the hall. The Committee tell you that the people want a hearty laugh, & Stark, & Saxe, & Park Benjamin, who give them that, are heard with joy. Well I think with Gov. Reynolds, the people are always right, (in a sense,) & that the man of letters is to say, these are the new conditions to which I must conform. The architect who is asked to build a house to go upon the sea, must not build a parthenon or a square house, but a ship. And Shakspeare or Franklin or Aesop coming to Illinois, would say, I must give my wisdom a comic form, instead of tragics or elegiacs, & well I know to do it, and he is no master who cannot vary his forms, & carry his own end triumphantly through the most difficult.

Mr Sweet, a telegraph agent on the Chicago & Rock River line, said, he can tell the name of the operator, by the accent of his dispatch, by the ear, just as readily as he knows the handwriting of his friends. Every operator has his own manner or accent. An operator usually reads more correctly & quickly by the ear, than by the eye. Some good operators never learn to read by the ear. Boys make the best operators, and, in six months, a boy of 16 was worth 45 dollars a month in an office at Chicago. The rule of their experience is never to establish a telegraph line until after a railroad is built. It cannot sooner pay.

At Beloit, on Tuesday night, 8 Jany the mercury was at 27 & 28 below Zero. It has been bitterly cold for a fortnight. A cold night they call a singer.

The hard times of Illinois were from 1837 to 1845 & onward, when pork was worth 12 shillings a hundred, & men journeyed with loads of wheat & pork a hundred miles or more to Chicago, & sold their wheat for 26 cents a bushel, & were obliged to sell their team to get home again. Mr Jenks, a stage agent & livery stable keeper, told us of his experiences & when he left Chicago to go eastward he would not have given $3.00 for a warranty deed of the State of Illinois.

Hoosier meant Southerner. Hoosiers & Yankees would fight for the land. Yankees when fighting men would fight by the day: the Hoosiers are good to begin, but they *cave*.

Judge Emmons Esq of Michigan said to me that he had said he wished it might be a criminal offence to bring an English law-book into a court in this country, so foolish & mischievous is our slavery to Eng. precedent. The word commerce has had only an Eng meaning & has been made to follow only the petty exigences of Eng. experience but the commerce of rivers & the commerce of roads & the commerce of air balloons must add an American extension to the pondhole of "admiralty."

There are times when the intellect is so active, that every thing seems to run to meet it. Its supplies are found without much thought as to studies. Knowledge runs to the man, & the man runs to knowledge. In spring, when the snow melts, the maple trees run with sugar, & you cannot get tubs fast enough. But it is only for a few days. The hunter on the prairie at the right season, has no need of choosing his ground. East, west, by the river, by the timber, near the farm, from the farm, he is everywhere by his game.

Here is a road, *Michn Southern*, which runs through four sovereign states, a judicial being, which has no judicial sovereign. Ohio, Ind., Mich., Ill.
Franchise has to yield to eminent domain, & the remedy is appraisal & payment of damages. But unfortunately, when, as now, the Mich. Central is to be bereaved of its monopoly, which it had bought & paid for, the jury to appraise the damage done is taken from the population aggrieved by the Mich. Central. I asked, why not take a jury from other states?

People here are alive to a benefaction derived from railroads which is inexpressibly great, & vastly exceeding any intentional philanthropy on record. What is the benefit by a Howard or a Bell & Lancaster or an Alfred or an Elizabeth Fry or any lover less or larger compared with the involuntary blessing wrought on nations by the selfish capitalists who built the Illinois Central & the Mich. Central?
Meantime, my banker here at Adrian, Mr Lyon, is of opinion, that, to run on a bank for gold, is a criminal offence, & ought to be punished by the state's prison! He delights, he frankly told me, to make such people pay 3 & 4 percent a month for money.

Seek things in their purity. Well, we try, on each subject we accost, to ascend to principles; to dip our pen in the blackest of the pot; and, to be sure, find the cause of the trait in some organ, as spleen, or bone, or blood. We are not nearer. We are still outside. Nature itself is nothing but a skin, and all these but coarser cuticles. A god or genius sits regent over every plant & animal, and causes this, & knits this to that, after an order or plan which is intellectual. The botanist, the physicist is not then the man deepest immersed in nature, as if he were ready to bear apples or to shoot out four legs, but one filled with the lightest & purest air who sympathizes with the creative spirit, anticipates the tendency, & where the bird will next alight,—being himself full of the same tendency.

—

My friend had great abilities, & a genial temper, & no vices, but he had one defect which ruined all. He could not speak in the tone of the people. There seemed to be some paralysis on his will, that, when he met men on common terms, he spoke weakly, & from the point, like a silly girl. His consciousness of the fault only made it worse. He envied every woodsawyer & drover in the bar room their manly speech.

But Mirabeau had *le don terrible de la familiarité*. He whose sympathy goes lowest, dread him, o kings!

from SO

1856–1857

1856, Dec. 3. I have been reading some of Trench's translations of Calderon, and I miss the expected power. He has not genius. His fancy is sprightly, but his construction is merely mechanical. The mark of genius, is, that it has not only thoughts, but the copula that joins them is also a thought. It does not take some well-known fable, & use it, if a little more prettily, yet to the same predictable ends, as others; but its fable & its use & end are unpredictable & its own. 'Tis the difference between the carpenter who makes a box, & the mother who bears a child. The box was all in the carpenter; but the child was not all in the parents. They knew no more of the child's formation than they did of their own. They were merely channels through which the child's nature flowed from quite another & eternal power. And the child is as much a wonder to them, as to any: &, like the child Jesus, shall, as he matures, convert & guide them as if he were the Parent.

C. N. Emerson, Esq. of Great Barrington told me a good college story. His father, Rev. Sam. E. of Manchester, was at Williamstown College, I think; at all events, the thing occurred there. It was the custom for the senior class to choose by ballot the Valedictorian orator, as he was called, that is, the one of their number who should have the first honors at Commencement. The class wished to choose Baldwin, who, though otherwise deserving, had received some college censure, and, I believe, had been suspended. The government brought all their influence to bear to secure the election of Justin Edwards. The result of the ballot was 15 for Baldwin, 15 for Edwards; Baldwin voting for Edwards, & Edwards not voting at all. Several ballotings were had with the same result. The President sent for Edwards, & told him that the government thought it altogether proper that he should be elected.

But how to secure it? Edwards said, that he could not vote for himself. The President thought it proper that Edwards should vote for himself. Edwards said, Baldwin would find it out, & then would not vote for him, & then there would still be a tie. The President told him to say nothing about it. And, at the next ballot, Edwards voted for himself, and the ballot stood 16 against 15, & he was elected. Edwards had the oration, but his class absented themselves at the delivery. Mr Emerson said, that his father told him that in his lifetime he never would go to hear Dr Edwards, (who became the head of the Andover Institution) preach, and used to say to him, "My son, whatever you do, never do anything mean." Baldwin, on the following year, was coming to Commencement at Williamstown, & stepping to the door of the tavern at Pittsfield, to see a thunder-shower, was struck by lightning, & killed.

—

1857. January, Chicago, Tremont House.
"In 1838," said Dr Boynton, "I came here to Waukegan & there were not so many houses as there are towns now." He got in to the train at Evansville, a town a year & a half old, where are now 600 inhabitants, a Biblical Institute, or Divinity School of the Methodists, to which a Mrs Garrett lately gave some land in Chicago appraised at $125,000, but which, when they came to sell it, the worser half brought $160 000, & the value of the whole donation, 'tis thought, will be half a million. They had in the same town a College,—a thriving institution, which unfortunately blew down one night,—but I believe they raised it again the next day, or built another, & no doubt in a few weeks it will eclipse Cambridge & Yale! 'Tis very droll to hear the comic stories of the rising values here, which, ludicrous though they seem, are justified by facts presently. Mr Corwin's story of land offered for 50 000, and an hour given to consider of it. The buyer made up his mind to take it, but he could not have it; it was five minutes past the hour, & it was now worth $60,000. After dinner, he resolved to give the price, but he had overstayed the time again, & it was already 70,000; & it became 80,000, before night,—when he bought it. I believe it was Mr Corwin's joke, but the solemn citizen who stood by, heard it approvingly, & said, "Yes, that is about the fair growth of Chicago *per* hour." How-

ever a quite parallel case to this, I am told, actually occurred in the sale of the "American House" lot, which rose in a day from perhaps $40 000 to 50, 60, 70, 80, or 90,000, at which price it was sold. Mr Foster of Evansville, when I asked about the once rival towns which competed with Chicago, said, "Yes, at New City they once thought there was to be the great centre, & built 60 houses." "Was there not a river & harbor there?" "O yes, there was a guzzle out of a sandbank, but now there are still the 60 houses, &, when he passed by the last time, there was one owl, which was the only inhabitant."

Mr W. B. Ogden told me that he came here from New York 21 years ago. In N. Y. he had in association with some others made a large purchase here to the amount of $100,000. He had never been here, but wished to have a reason for coming, beyond merely seeing the country; had never then been beyond Buffalo westward. He arrived here one morning 11 June, 1836. He learned that one of the parties of whom he had purchased, was in the house, on his arrival at the tavern or fort, & this person sent for him to come up & see him. This Mr Bronson had heard some rumor that his brother had sold the land to a company in N. Y. but hoped it was not so. Mr O. showed him his deed. Bronson said it was all right, but it was injudicious in his brother. O. said he was glad to hear that, for he had feared he had made a foolish bargain. While he was in B.'s room, somebody tapped at the door, & wished to know if the man who represented *block no. 1*, was here? Mr O. knew nothing of it; but B. told the man, yes, Ogden represented that purchase. "Well, will you sell Block no. 1?" O. replied, "he knew nothing of it, but after breakfast he would go & see the land." After breakfast, they crossed in a little boat, & looked about in the swamp & woods, & came to a stake. "Here" said Bronson, "is Block no. 1." Well, they were followed by several persons, &, among others, the one he had seen. These came up, & the man said, "What will you take for this property?" O. said, "he knew nothing of its value, but if they would make him an offer, he would inform himself, & answer." The man said, "We will give you $35,000. for eight blocks from No. 1 to No. 8." O. said "I never altered a muscle of my face, but I looked him in the face, to see if he were joking, & expected they would all laugh; but they all looked solemn, & the speaker no more crazy than the rest. So I took Bronson's arm, & walked apart, & said, is this a joke, or are they crazy? or is this the value of the land?" "Yes this is the supposed value." "Is it worth more?" "Perhaps, but you must wait." "So I went back, & said as gravely as I could, that I would take it; but I expected them to laugh, but that would not harm me." But the man said, "Well we will pay 10 per cent down, & we will pay it now." But I said we will go back to the tavern. But the man was uneasy, & wished to pay now. "I said, 'I shall not vary from what I have said.' But the man inclined to pay now. So he took out of his pocket ten $1000. notes of the U.S. Bank, & I put them in my waistcoat pocket." And from that time Mr Ogden proceeded to sell piece after piece of the land (about 150 acres) till in one year he had nearly sold the whole for $1,000,000.

—

Woman should find in man her guardian. Silently she looks for that, & when she finds, as she instantly does, that he is not, she betakes her to her own defences, & does the best she can. But when he is her guardian, all goes well for both.

Your subject is quite indifferent, if you really speak out. If I met Shakspeare, or Montaigne, or Goethe, I should only aim to understand correctly what they said: they might talk of what they would. When people object to me my topics of England, or France, or Nat. History, 'tis only that they fear I shall not think on these subjects, but shall consult my ease, & repeat commonplaces. The way to the centre is everywhere equally short.

"A general has always troops enough, if he only knows how to employ those he has, & bivouacs with them," said Bonaparte. Every breath of air is the carrier of the universal mind. Thus, for subjects, I do not know what is more tedious than Dedications, or pieces of flattery to Grandees. Yet in Hafiz, it would not do to skip them, since his dare-devil muse is never better shown.

A practical man is the hobby of the age. Well, when I read German philosophy, or wrote verses, I was willing to concede

there might be too much of these, & that the western pioneer with axe on his shoulder, & still moving west as the settlements approached him, had his merits. But when I went to Illinois, they told me that the founders of the towns as of Dixon, of Rockford, of San Francisco, St Louis, were visionary men, & always remained poor; that, after them, came practical men, who made fortunes.
On further consideration of this practical quality, by which our people are proud to be marked, I concede its excellence; but practice or practicalness consists in the consequent or logical following out of a good theory.*

—

A.B.A. saw the *Midsummers Night's dream*, played, & said, it was a phallus to which fathers could carry their daughters, & each had their own thoughts, without suspecting that the other had the same.

—

Eugene Sue, Dumas, &c., when they begin a story, do not know how it will end; but Walter Scott when he began the Bride of Lammermoor had no choice, nor Shakspeare in Macbeth. But Mme George Sand, though she writes fast & miscellaneously, is yet fundamentally classic & necessitated: and I, who tack things strangely enough together, & consult my ease rather than my strength, & often write *on the other side*, am yet an adorer of the *One*.

To be classic, then, *de rigueur*, is the prerogative of a vigorous mind who is able to execute what he conceives.

The classic unfolds; the romantic adds.
The discovery of America is an antique or classic work.

—

The property proves too much for the man, and now all the men of science, art, intellect, are pretty sure to degenerate into selfish housekeepers dependent on wine, coffee, furnace, gaslight, & furniture. *Then* things swing the other way, & we suddenly find that civilization crowed too soon, that what we bragged as triumphs were treacheries; that we have opened the

*See *Atlantis* Feb. 1855 p 109

wrong door, and let the enemy into the castle; that civilization was a mistake; that nothing is so vulgar as a great warehouse of rooms full of furniture & trumpery; that, in the circumstances, the best wisdom were an auction or a fire; since the foxes & birds have the right of it, with a warm hole to fend the weather, and no more; that a pent-house to fend the sun & wind & rain, is the house which makes no tax on the owner's time & thought, and which he can leave when the sun reaches noon.

—

Monochord
M M E cannot sympathize with children. I know several persons whose world is only large enough for one person, and each of them, though he were to be the last man, would, like the executioner in Hood's poem, guillotine the last but one. 'Tis A's misfortune, & T's,

E H said of M.M.E., she thinks much more of her bonnet & of other peoples' bonnets than they do, & sends E. from Dan to Beersheba to find a bonnet that does not conform; while Mrs. H., whom she severely taxes with conforming, is satisfied with anything she finds in the shops. She tramples on the common humanities all day, & they rise as ghosts & torment her at night.

Kings & Nobles

"Tycho Brahe refused (1574) for a long time to publish his observations upon the remarkable star in Cassiopeia, lest he should thus cast a stain upon his nobility." *Brewster. Life of* Newton. I. p. 259.

—

What a barren witted pate am I, says the scholar; I will go see whether I have lost my reason. He seeks companions, he seeks intelligent persons, whether more wise or less wise than he, who give him provocation, and, at once, & very easily, the old motion begins in his brain, thoughts, fancies, humors, flow, the horizon broadens, the cloud lifts, & the infinite opulence of things is again shown him. But the right conditions must be observed. Principally he must have leave to be him-

self. We go to dine with M. & N. & O. & P. And, to be sure, they begin to be something else than they were, they play tricks, they dance jigs, they pun, they tell stories, they try many fantastic tricks, under some superstition that there must be excitement & elevation, and they kill conversation at once. It is only on natural ground that they can be rich. Keep the ground, feel the roots, domesticate yourself.
I think of Andrews Norton who did not like toasts & sentiments because they interfered with the hilarity of the occasion.

—

In music, it was once the doctrine, the text is nothing, the score is all, and even, the worse the text, the better the score; but Wagner said the text must be fixed to the score, & from the first must be inspired with the score.

So in Chemistry, Muldar said For a good chemist, the first condition is, he shall know nothing of philosophy; but Oersted & Humboldt saw & said, that Chemistry must be the handmaid of moral Science. Do you not see how nature avenges herself of the pedantry? The wits excluded from the academies met in clubs & threw the academy into the shade.

—

"I can well wait," said E. H., "all winter, if sure to blossom an apple tree in spring; but not, if, perhaps, I am dead wood, & ought to burn now."

—

Whipple said of the author of "Leaves of Grass," that he had every leaf but the fig leaf.

—

Subject for lecture, is, the art of taking a walk. I would not ask W.E.C., like the little girl, "Mamma wishes, Sir, you would begin to be funny." Indeed quite the reverse; for his written fun is very bad—and as to his serious letter, the very best, that to Ward in Europe, is unreproducible. Would you bottle the efflux of a June noon, & sell it in your shop? but if he could be engaged again into kindly letters, he has that which none else could give. But 'tis rare & rich compound of gods & dwarfs, & best of humanity, that goes to walk. Can you bring home the summits of Wachusett & Monadnoc, &

the Uncanoonuc, the savin fields of Lincoln, & the sedge & reeds of Flint Pond, the savage woods beyond Nut brook towards White Pond? He can.

Do you think I am in such great terror of being shot, I, who am only waiting to shuffle off my corporeal jacket to scud away into the *back* stars, & put diameters of the solar system & millions of sidereal orbits between me & all souls, there to wear out ages in solitude, & forget memory itself, if it be possible?

In the conversation, what helpless callow birds we are, each waiting for other,—total inadequacy of power to reach the walls of the vast sky that compasses us in, until at last a thought, a principle appears, from some more active mind; then, each catches by the mane one or other of these strong goers, like horses of the prairie, & rides up & down among worlds & natures.

It is curious that Thoreau goes to a house to say with little preface what he has just read or observed, delivers it in lump, is quite inattentive to any comment or thought which any of the company offer on the matter, nay, is merely interrupted by it, &, when he has finished his report, departs with precipitation.

—

Probability of the Eng. tongue becoming the universal language

—

The comfort of Alcott's mind is, the connexion in which he sees whatever he sees. He is never dazzled by a spot of colour, or a gleam of light, to value that thing by itself; but forever & ever is prepossessed by the undivided One behind it & all. I do not know where to find in men or books a mind so valuable to faith. His own invariable faith inspires faith, in others. I valued Miss Bacon's studies of Shakspeare, simply for the belief it showed in cause & effect; that a first-rate genius was not a prodigy & stupefying anomaly, but built up step by step as a tree or a house is, with a sufficient cause, (and one that, with diligence, might be found or assigned,) for every difference & every superiority to the dunce or average man. For every opinion or sentence of Alcott, a reason may be sought & found, not in his will or fancy, but in the necessity of nature itself, which has daguerred that fatal impression on his susceptible soul. He is as good as a lens or a mirror, a beautiful susceptibility, every impression on which, is not to be reasoned against, or derided, but to be accounted for, &, until accounted for, registered as an (indisputable) addition to our catalogue of natural facts. There are defects in the lens, & errors of refraction & position, &c. to be allowed for, and it needs one acquainted with the lens by frequent use, to make these allowances; but 'tis the best instrument I have ever met with.

Every man looks a piece of luck, but he is a piece of the mosaic accurately measured & ground to fit into the gap he fills, such as Parker or Garrison, or Carlyle, or Hegel is, and with good optics, I suppose, we should find as nice fitting, down to the bores & loafers.

I admire that poetry which no man wrote, no poet less than the genius of humanity itself, & which is to be read in a mythology, in the effect of pictures, or sculptures, or drama, or cities, or sciences, on me.

My son is coming to get his latin lesson without me. My son is coming to do without me. And I am coming to do without Plato, or Goethe, or Alcott.

—

Conversation

In a parlor, the unexpectedness of the effects. When we go to Faneuil Hall, we look for important events; facts, thoughts, & persuasions, that bear on them. But in your parlor, to find your companion who sits by your side start up into a more potent than Demosthenes, &, in an instant, work a revolution that makes Athens & England & Washington Politics—old carrion & dust-barrels,—because his suggestions require new ways of living, new books, new men, new arts & sciences,—yes the lecture & the book seem vapid. Eloquence is forever a power that shoves usurpers from their thrones, & sits down on them by allowance & acclaim of all.

*

Conversation or eloquence, it is to be remembered, is an art in which a man has all mankind for his competitors; for it is that which all are practising every day, while they live.

Conversation.

These black coats never can speak until they meet a black coat; then their tongues are loosed, & chatter like blackbirds. The "practical" folks in the rail-car meet daily, & to their discourse there is no end.

How can a man be concealed?

Conversation

A man cannot utter many sentences, without announcing to intelligent ears exactly where he stands in life & thought, namely whether in the kingdom of the senses & the understanding; in that of truths & the reasoning; or in that of ideas & imagination; in the realm of the intuitions & duty.

Once more for Alcott it is to be said, that he is sincerely & necessarily engaged to his task & not wilfully or ostentatiously or pecuniarily.

Mr Johnson at Manchester said, of him, "he is universally competent. Whatever question is asked, he is prepared for."

—

I shall go far, & see many, before I find such an extraordinary insight as Alcott's. In his fine talk, last evening, he ran up & down the scale of powers, with as much ease & precision as a squirrel the wires of his cage, & is never dazzled by his means, or by any particular, & a fine heroic action or a poetic passage would make no impression on him, because he expects heroism & poetry in All. Ideal purity, the poet, the artist, the man, must have. I have never seen any person who so fortifies the believer, so confutes the skeptic. And the almost uniform rejection of this man by men of parts, Carlyle & Browning inclusive, & by women of piety, might make one despair of society. If he came with a cannonade of acclaim from all nations, as the first wit on the planet, these masters would receive him, & he would sustain the reputation: or if they could find him in a book a thousand years old, with a legend of miracles appended, there would be churches of disciples: but now they wish to know if his coat is out at the elbow, or whether some body did not hear from somebody, that he had got a new hat, &c. &c. He has faults, no doubt, but I may safely know no more about them than he does; and some that are most severely imputed to him are only the omissions of a preoccupied mind.

—

My friend A.H.B.W. refuses to tell her children whether the act was right or wrong, but sends them away to find out what *the little voice* says, and at night they shall tell her.

—

I have but one military recollection in all my life. In 1813 or 1814, all Boston, young & old, turned out to build the fortifications on Noddle's Island; and, the Schoolmaster at the Latin School announced to the boys, that, if we wished, we might all go on a certain day to work on the Island. I went with the rest in the ferry boat, & spent a summer day; but I cannot remember that I did any kind of work. I remember only the pains we took to get water in our tin pails, to relieve our intolerable thirst. I am afraid no valuable effect of my labor remains in the existing defences.

—

21 May

Yesterday to the Sawmill Brook with Henry. He was in search of yellow violet (pubescens) and menyanthes which he waded into the water for. & which he concluded, on examination, had been out five days. Having found his flowers, he drew out of his breast pocket his diary & read the names of all the plants that should bloom on this day, 20 May; whereof he keeps account as a banker when his notes fall due. rubus triflora, guerens , vaccinium , &c. The cypropedium not due 'till tomorrow. Then we diverged to the brook, where was viburnum dentatum, arrowhead. But his attention was drawn to the redstart which flew about with its *cheah cheah chevet*, & presently to two fine grosbeaks, rosebreasted, whose brilliant scarlet "made the rash gazer wipe his eye," & which he brought nearer with his spy glass, & whose fine clear note he compares to that of a "tanager who has got rid of his hoarseness," then

he heard a note which he calls that of the nightwarbler, a bird he has never identified, has been in search of for twelve years; which, always, when he sees, is in the act of diving down into a tree or bush, & which 'tis vain to seek; the only bird that sings indifferently by night & by day. I told him, he must beware of finding & booking him, lest life should have nothing more to show him. He said, "What you seek in vain for half your life, one day you come full upon all the family at dinner.—You seek him like a dream, and as soon as you find him, you become his prey." He thinks he could tell by the flowers what day of the month it is, within two days. We found saxifraga Pennsylvanica and chrysosplenium oppositifolium, by Everett's spring, and stellaria & cerastium and arabis rhemboidea & veronica anagallis, which he thinks handsomer than the cultivated *veronica, forget me not. Solidago odora*, he says, is common in Concord, & penny royal he gathers in quantity as *herbs* every season. *Shad blossom* is no longer a *pyrus*, which is now confined to choke berry. Shad blossom is Amelanchier botryapium & A. , Shad blossom because it comes when the shad come.
Water is the first gardener; he always plants grasses & flowers about his dwelling. There came Henry with music-book under his arm, to press flowers in; with telescope in his pocket, to see the birds, & microscope to count stamens; with a diary, jack-nife, & twine, in stout shoes, & strong grey trowsers, ready to brave the shrub oaks & smilax, & to climb the tree for a hawk's nest. His strong legs when he wades were no insignificant part of his armour. Two Alders we have, and one of them is here on the northern border of its habitat.

I am impressed at the Indignation Meeting last night, as ever, on like occasions, with the sweet nitrous oxide gas which the speakers seem to breathe. Once they taste it, they cling like mad to the bladder, & will not let it go. And it is so plain to me that eloquence, like swimming, is an art which all men might learn, though so few do. It only needs, that they should once be pushed off into the water, overhead, without corks, and after a mad struggle or two, they find their poise, & the use of their arms, & henceforward they possess this new & wonderful element. The most hardfisted disagreeably virile & thought-paralyzing companion turns out in a public assembly to be the most fluent, various, & effective orator. Now you find what all that excess of power which so chafed & fretted you tête a tête, is for.

Affectation also has its place in a fine character, namely, of cordiality to your blood relations.

Sumner's attack is of no importance. It is only a leaf of the tree, it is not Sumner who must be avenged, but the tree must be cut down. But this stroke rouses the feeling of the people, & shows every body where they are. All feel it. Those who affect not to feel it must perforce share the shame, nor will hiding their heads & pretending other tasks & a preoccupied mind, deceive themselves or us. We are all in this boat of the State, & cannot dodge the duties.
This history teaches the fatal blunder of going into false position.
Let us not compromise again, or accept the aid of evil agents.
Our position, of the free states, very like that of covenanters against the cavaliers.
Massachusetts uniformly retreats from her resolutions.
Suppose we raise soldiers in Masstts.
Suppose we propose a Northern Union.

—

2 June. The finest day the high noon of the year, went with Thoreau in a wagon to Perez Blood's auction; found the myrica flowering; it had already begun to shed its pollen one day, the lowest flowers being effete; found the English hawthorn on Mrs Ripley's hill, ready to bloom; went up the Asabet, & found the *Azalea Nudicaulis* in full bloom, a beautiful show, the *viola muhlenbergi*, the *ranunculus recurvatus*; saw *swamp white oak*, (chestnut-like leaves) *white maple*, *red maple*,—no *chestnut oak* on the river— Henry told his story of the *Ephemera*, the manna of the fishes, which falls like a snow storm one day in the year, only on this river, not on the Concord, high up in the air as he can see, & blundering down to the river,—(the shad-fly,) the true angler's fly; the fish die of repletion when it comes, the kingfishers wait for their prey. Around us the pepeepee of the king bird kind was noisy. He showed the history of the river from the banks, the male &

female bank, the pontederia keeps the female bank, on whichever side.

—

The hour is coming when the strongest will not be strong enough.

I go for those who have received a retaining fee to this party of freedom, before they came into this world. I would trust Garrison, I would trust Henry Thoreau, that they would make no compromises. I would trust Horace Greeley, I would trust my venerable friend Mr Hoar, that they would be staunch for freedom to the death; but both of these would have a benevolent credulity in the honesty of the other party, that I think unsafe.

The vote of a prophet is worth a hundred hands.

If he knows it to be the true vote, it will be decisive of the question for his country.

The want of profound sincerity is the cause of failures. South Carolina is in earnest.

I see the courtesy of the Carolinians, but I know meanwhile that the only reason why they do not plant a cannon before Faneuil Hall, & blow Bunker Hill monument to fragments, as a nuisance, is because they have not the power. They are fast acquiring the power, & if they get it, they will do it.

There are men who as soon as they are born take a bee-line to the axe of the inquisitor, like Jordano Bruno.

—

June 14.

12 June, at our Kansas relief meeting, in Concord, $962. were subscribed on the spot. Yesterday, the subscription had amounted to $1130.00 and it will probably reach 1200. or one per cent on the valuation of the town.

—

I was to say at the end of my narrative of Wordsworth, that I find nothing in the disparaging speeches of the Londoners about him, that would not easily be said of a faithful scholar who rated things after his own scale, & not by the conventional. He almost alone in his generation has treated the mind well.

—

When I said of Ellery's new verses that "they were as good as the old ones"; "Yes," said Ward, "but those were excellent promise, & now he does no more."

He has a more poetic temperament than any other in America, but the artistic executive power of completing a design, he has not. His poetry is like the artless warbling of a vireo, which whistles prettily all day & all summer in the elm, but never rounds a tune, nor can increase the value of melody by the power of composition & cuneiform determination. He must have construction also.

23 July. Returned from Pigeon Cove, where we have made acquaintance with the sea, for seven days. 'Tis a noble friendly power, and seemed to say to me, "Why so late & slow to come to me? Am I not here always, thy proper summer home? Is not my voice thy needful music; my breath, thy healthful climate in the heats; my touch, thy cure? Was ever building like my terraces? Was ever couch so magnificent as mine? Lie down on my warm ledges and learn that a very little hut is all you need. I have made thy architecture superfluous, and it is paltry beside mine. Here are twenty Romes & Ninevehs & Karnacs in ruins together, obelisk & pyramid and Giants' Causeway here they all are prostrate or half piled."

And behold the sea, the opaline, plentiful & strong, yet beautiful as the rose or the rainbow, full of food, nourisher of men, purger of the world, creating a sweet climate, and, in its unchangeable ebb & flow, and in its beauty at a few furlongs, giving a hint of that which changes not, & is perfect.

—

At Niagara, I noticed that as quick as I got out of the wetting of the Fall, all the grandeur changed into beauty. You cannot keep it grand, it is so quickly beautiful. And the sea at Pigeon

Cove gave me daily the same experience. It is great & formidable when you lie down in it among the rocks; but on the shore, at one rod's distance, it is changed instantly into a beauty as of gems & clouds.

—

Demonology

There are many things of which a wise man would wish to be ignorant, and this is one of them. Shun them, as you would shun the secrets of the undertaker, of the butcher, the secrets of the jakes & the dead-cart. The adepts are they who have mistaken flatulence, for inspiration. If this drivel which they report as the voice of spirits were really such, we must find out a more decisive suicide.

—

Nov. 15. Walk with Ellery, who finds in nature, or man, that whatever is done for beauty or in sport, is excellent; but the moment there's any use in it or any kind of talent, 'tis very bad & stupid. The fox sparrows & the blue snowbirds pleased him & the watercresses which we saw in the brook, but which, he said, were not in any botany.

There are people who give you their society in large saturating doses.

—

I speak badly whilst I speak for feats. Feats are no measure of the heaven of intellect. It is profoundly solitary, it is unprofitable, it is to be despised & forgotten of men. If I recall the happiest hours of existence, those which really make man an inmate of a better world, it is a lonely & undescribed joy; but it is the door to joys that ear hath not heard nor eye seen.

To answer a question so as to admit of no reply, is the test of a man, to touch bottom every time.

—

Tracy

A.H.T. said, "Masstts was full of rhetoricians." I forgot to tell him, that every twelfth man in Massachusetts was a shoemaker, & that Erastus Bigelow, Uriah Boyden, Nathaniel Bowditch and Mason of Taunton were not rhetoricians, & the rail-road projectors all over U.S. & the merchants who planned so many voyages of vessels which distribute their cargoes at New York, & make so much of the importance of that city, did not so much create speeches, as business.—

—

"And then, Mr John Wistar, pray tell me for what purpose Jesus Christ came into the world?"—
"My dear sir, 'tis very hard to say for what purpose any man came into the world," replied the Quaker.

from

VO

1857–1858

The turtles in Cambridge, on the publication of this book of Agassiz, should hold an indignation meeting, & migrate from the Charles River, with Chelydra serpentina marching at the head, and "Death to Agassiz!" inscribed on their shields.

Naturalists.

No matter what savants say, tortoise, or shark, or sheep, or ostrich, it is always man they have in their thought, both professor & public are surreptitiously studying man whom they would gladly read directly, if they could. 'Tis a vast Aesop's Fable, which prates about lions & foxes & storks, but means you & me from beginning to end.

The important fact in his book, is, that, when the turtle is born, its ovary is already full of eggs.

If natural philosophy is faithfully written, moral philosophy need not be, for it will find itself expressed in these *theses* to a perceptive soul.

—

Captain John Brown of Kansas gave a good account of himself in the Town Hall, last night, to a meeting of Citizens. One of his good points was, the folly of the peace party in Kansas, who believed, that their strength lay in the greatness of their wrongs, & so discountenanced resistance. He wished to know if their wrong was greater than the negro's, & what kind of strength that gave to the negro?

He believes on his own experience that one good, believing, strong-minded man is worth a hundred, nay twenty thousand men without character, for a settler in a new country; & that the right men will give a permanent direction to the fortunes of a state. For one of these bullying, drinking rowdies,—he seemed to think cholera, smallpox & consumption were as valuable recruits.

The first man who went in to Kansas from Missouri to interfere in the elections, he thought, had a perfect right to be shot.

He gave a circumstantial account of the battle at Black-Jack, where 23 Missourians surrendered to 9 abolitionists.

He had 3000 sheep in Ohio, & would instantly detect a strange sheep in his flock. A cow can tell its calf by secret signal, he thinks, by the eye, to run away or to lie down & hide itself. He always makes friends with his horse or mule, (or with the deer that visit his Ohio farm) & when he sleeps on his horse, as he does as readily as in his bed, his horse does not start or endanger him.

Brown described the expensiveness of war in a country where every thing that is to be eaten or worn or used by man or beast must be dragged a long distance on wheels.

"God protects us in winter," he said; "No Missourian can be seen in the country until the grass comes up again."

—

Men's conscience, I once wrote, is local in spots & veins, here & there, & not in healthy circulation through their system, so that they are unexpectedly good in some passage, & when you infer that they may be depended on in some other case, they heavily disappoint you. Well, so is their thought. Albert Tracy dazzles with his intellectual light, but is a wretched hunker in politics, & hunks in social & practical life. And I learn from the photograph & daguerre men, that almost all faces & forms which come to their shops to be copied, are irregular & unsymmetrical, have one eye blue & one grey, the nose is not straight, & one shoulder is higher than the other. The man is physically as well as metaphysically a thing of shreds & patches, borrowed unequally from his good & bad ancestors,—a misfit from the start.

The democratic party is the party of the Poor marshalled against the Rich. They are sure they are excluded from rich houses & society, & they vote with the poor against you. That is the sting that exasperates them, & makes a strong party. But they are always officered by a few self-seeking deserters from the Rich or Whig Party. They know the incapacity of their own rank & file, and would reject one of their own nobodies as a leader. A few rich men or Whigs are therefore always ready to accept the place of Captain & Major & Colonel & President, & wear their colors for the rewards which are only to be given to the officers, & never to rank & file. But these leaders are Whigs, & associate with Whigs, that is, they are the dining, drinking, & dancing & investing class, & by no means the digging & hoeing class.

But 'tis of no use to tell me, as Brown & others do, that the Southerner is not a better fighter than the Northerner,—when I see, that uniformly a Southern minority prevails, & gives the law. Why, but because the Southerner is a fighting man, & the Northerner is not.
1857.

—

Skeptic
I find no more flagrant proof of skepticism than the toleration of slavery. Another is, this running of the girls into popery. They know nothing of religions, & the grounds of the sects; they know that they do like music, & Mozart's masses; & Bach's, & run into the Catholic Church, where these are. Another is, this mummery of rapping & pseudo spiritualism.

—

Power of opinion
'Tis a small part of the guarding that police & armies do; the main guard is, the fear & superstition of men themselves. The reverence for the Bible has saved a million crimes, which the people were bad enough to commit. "Thou shalt not kill," guards London.

Art.
You cannot make a cheap palace.

Because our education is defective, because we are superficial & ill-read, we were forced to make the most of that position, of ignorance; to idealize ignorance. Hence America is a vast Know-Nothing Party, & we disparage books, & cry up intuition. With a few clever men we have made a reputable thing of that, & denouncing libraries & severe culture, & magnifying the motherwit swagger of bright boys from the country colleges, we have even come so far as to deceive every body, except ourselves, into an admiration of un-learning and inspiration forsooth.

—

Shakspeare's Plays published in 1623, three years after Plymouth Colony. If they had been published first, the good forefathers had never been able to come away.

We are called a very patient people. Our assemblies are much more passive in the hands of their orators than the English. We do not cough down or roar down the heaviest proser, nor smother by dissent the most unpalatable & injurious. 'Tis a pity that our decorum should make us such lambs & rabbits in the claws of these wolves & foxes of the caucus. We encourage them to tear us by our tameness. They drop their hypocrisy quite too early, & are not at the pains to hide their claw under velvet,—from the dear innocents that we are.

—

2 May.

Walk yesterday first day of May with Henry T. to Goose Pond, & to the "Red chokeberry Lane." Found sedge flowering, & *salix humilis* later than s. discolor; found Lycopodium dendroides & lucidulum; found *Chimaphila maculata* the only patch of it in town. Found *Senecio* & even *solidago* in the water already forward, & the Sawmill-brook much adorned with hellebore *veratrum viride.* Saw the white-throated sparrow with a strong white stripe on the top of his head.

Saw a stump of a canoe-birch-tree newly cut down, which had bled a barrel. From a white birch, H. cut a strip of bark to show how a naturalist would make the best box to carry a plant or other specimen requiring care. & thought the woodman would make a better hat of birch-bark than of felt, yes, & pantaloons too,—hat, with cockade of lichens, thrown in.—I told him the Birkebeiners of the Heimskringla had been before him.

We will make a book on walking, 'tis certain, & have easy lessons for beginners. "Walking in ten Lessons." Pulsifer, &, it seems, Collier, have already taken ground. Thoreau, Channing,

Rice, Pulsifer, Collier, & I. H. had found, he said, lately a fungus which was a perfect Phallus; & in the books one is noted *Obscoenum.*

1865. I have since seen this very undesirable neighbor under my study window.

—

1857

October 14th, the New York & Boston Banks suspended specie payment. And, as usual in hard times, there are all sorts of petty & local reasons given for the pressure, but none that explain it to me. I suppose the reasons are not of yesterday or today; that the same danger has often approached & been avoided or postponed. 'Tis like that destruction of St Petersburgh, which was threatened by Kohl, which may come whenever a great freshet in the Neva shall coincide with a long prevalence of Northwest (?) wind. 'Tis like the jam which the ice or the logs make in our rivers: There is ample room for all the ice & all the logs to go down stream,—was, & is, & shall be;—but, by unfavorable circumstances, they are heaped together in a dead lock, so as to dam up the back water, till it accumulates to a deluge, & bursts at last, carrying bridges, houses, & half towns, to destruction.

But I take it as an inevitable incident to this money of civilization. Paper-money is a wonderful convenience, which builds up cities & nations, but it has this danger in it, like a camphene lamp, or a steam-boiler, it will sometimes explode. So excellent a tool we cannot spare, but must take it with its risks. We know the dangers of the railroad but we prefer it with its dangers to the old coach. & we must not forego the high civility of paper & credit, though once in twenty years it breaks the banks, & puts all exchange & traffic at a stand.

—

Receptivity.

'Tis the receptivity that is rare, 'tis this I value, the occasions I cannot scientifically tabulate; the motive or disposing circumstances I could never catalogue; but now one form, or color, or word, or companion, or book, or work, & now another strikes the mystic invisible string, I listen with joy. And the day is good that has the most perceptions.

—

The financial panic has the value of a test. Nobody knows how far each of these bankers & traders blows up his little airball on what infinitely small supply of soap & water. They all float in the air alike as balloons or planets, if you will, until they strike one another, or any house.—But this panic is a severer examiner than any committee of Bank Commissioners to find out how much specie all this paper represents, & how much real value.

These enjoyers have abdicated all high claims; they saw early in the course that they stood no chance for coming in for the plate, & they decline the strife, & say, well, we will keep ourselves for the "scrub-race." "The man," said Proclus, "who has not subdued his passions, the universe uses him as a brute." And these fellows squalidly accept their tavern joys.

—

A man signing himself Geo. Ross (of Madison, Wis.) & who seems to be drunk, writes me, that "the secret of drunkenness, is, that it insulates us in thought, whilst it unites us in feeling."

Victor Hugo said, "An idea steeped in verse, becomes suddenly more incisive & more brilliant; the iron becomes steel."

—

19 May, 1857. I saw Peter Kaufmann in N. Y., a man of much intellectual power, and of expansive moral sympathy & purposes; another Benjamin Franklin in his practical skill & tastes. Unhappily, he is without imagination, the more to be regretted, that his life has kept him invariably *bourgeois.* His bonhommie & philanthropy occasionally changed his face to a wonderful degree, as if a young man looked out of an old mask.

1874, February,
On looking—I fear too late—into the singular Diary which Kaufmann sent me many years ago, I grieve that I neglected it until now. It is very imaginative & doubtless sincere, & indicates a far more intellectual person than I suspected in our short & singular meeting in New York. Alas I have never heard

from him, or of him, since, & I fear that this total silence on my part must have pained & alienated him.

25 May.
Yesterday, at the Cliff, with a family party, & H.D.T. & Ricketson, found the trailing Arbutus, & the Corydalis. H.D.T. has found new willows, & has a natural *Salictum*, where the seeds gather and plant themselves, near the railroad. Saw the *Salix rostrata; discolor; humilis*; I think, he finds 14.—At this time of the year, the old leaves of the forest are gone, & the new not yet opened, & for a few days the view of the landscape is more open.

At home, D. Ricketson expressed some sad views of life & religion. A thunderstorm is a terror to him, and his theism was judaical. Henry thought a new pear-tree was more to purpose, &c. but said better, that an ecstasy was never interrupted. A theology of this kind is as good a meter or yardstick as any other. If I can be scared by a highwayman or a thunderclap, I should say, my performances were not very high, & should at once be mended.

1857
Thursday, 28 May. We kept Agassiz's fiftieth birthday at the Club. Three or four strangers were present, to wit, Dresel, Felton, Holmes, & Hillard. For the rest, we had Agassiz, Pierce, Ward, Motley, Longfellow, Lowell, Whipple, Dwight, Woodman, & J. Cabot was due, but did not come. Agassiz brought what had just been sent him, the last coloured plates to conclude the First Volume of his "Contributions, &c", which will now be published incontinently. The flower of the feast was the reading of three poems, written by our three poets, for the occasion. The first by Longfellow, who presided; the second, by Holmes; the third, by Lowell; all excellent in their way.

May 30. Walk this PM with Henry T. Found the *perfoliate uvularia* for the first time in Lincoln by Flint's Pond, found the *chestnut sided warbler*, which, I doubt not, I have seen already, & mistaken for the *particolored*. Heard the note of the latter, which resembles a locust-sound. Saw the cuckoo. Examined the young oak leaves by way of comparing the black, scarlet, & red, & think the penetrating the bark of the first to find the yellow quercitrum must be for me the final test. Found the chestnut-oak, in Lincoln, on Thompson's land, not far from his boat-house, near large old chestnuts. Saw the two poplars, grandidentata, & tremuliforma, which are both good for the powder-mills. Henry thinks, that planting acres of barren land by running a furrow every four feet across the field, with a plough, & following it with a planter, supplied with pine seed, would be lucrative. He proposes to plant my Wyman lot so. Go in September, & gather white-pine cones with a hook at the end of a long pole, & let them dry & open in a chamber at home. Add acorns, & birch-seed, & pitch-pines. He thinks, it would be profitable to buy cheap land & plant it so. Edward Gardner at Nantucket sells the land at an advanced price as soon as he has planted it. It is a woodlot. Henry says, that the Flora of Massachusetts embraces almost all the important plants of America. We have all the willows but one or two, all the oaks but one or two.

Furrows 8 feet apart & stick a pine along each at every 4 feet.

Παντα ρει, said Heraclitus.

I do not count the hours I spend in the woods, though I forget my affairs there & my books. And, when there, I wander hither & thither; any bird, any plant, any spring, detains me. I do not hurry homewards for I think all affairs may be postponed to this walking. And it is for this idleness that all my businesses exist.

I do not count the hours I spend
In wandering by the sea

—

Scholar & Times

Could I make you feel your indispensableness,—& yet it behoves first to show you the joy of your high place. You have the keys. You deal with design & the methods. Here lies this wide aboriginal Nature, old beyond figures, yet new & entire, the silver flame which flashes up the sky,—no aeons can date it,

yet there it burns as delicately as the passing cinder of the firefly with the lightness of a new petal. Here you rest & work in this element of Space, whose bewildering circuits make all the Universe a dot on its margin, dwarfing the gods.
To teach us the first lesson of humility, God set down man in these two vastitudes of Space and Time, yet is he such an incorrigible peacock that he thinks them only a perch to show his dirty feathers on.

—

What we accept in generals, we deny in particulars.
But the applicability is not capricious, this applicability by which planets subside & crystallize & clothe themselves with forests & animate themselves with animals & men will not stop; but will continue into finer particulars, & from finer to finest evermore.

—

There are more belongings to every creature than his lair & his food. He is full of instincts that must be met, & he has predisposing power that bends & fits all that is near to his use. He is not possible until the invisible things are right for him as well as the visible. What changes then in sky & earth, & in finer skies & earths than ours, does not the appearance of some Dante or Columbus apprize us of!

—

Against Whigs. Zoologists may dispute whether horse hairs in the water change to worms, but I find that whatever is old corrupts, & the past turns to snakes. The reverence for the deeds of our ancestors is a treacherous sentiment. Their merit, was, not to reverence the old, but to honor the present moment. & we falsely cite them as examples of the very habit which they hated & defied. Memory is bitter.

Wednesday, 8 July, 1857. This morning I had the remains of my mother & of my son Waldo removed from the tomb of Mrs Ripley to my lot in "Sleepy Hollow." The sun shone brightly on the coffins, of which Waldo's was well preserved—now fifteen years. I ventured to look into the coffin. I gave a few white-oak leaves to each coffin, after they were put in the new vault, & the vault was then covered with two slabs of granite.

*

There is certainly a convenience in the money scale in the absence of finer metres. In the South a slave is bluntly but accurately valued at 500 to 1000 dollars, if a good working field hand; if a mechanic, as carpenter or smith, at 12, 15, or 20 hundred. A Mulatto girl, if beautiful, rises at once very naturally to high estimation. If beautiful & sprightly-witted, one who is a joy when present, a perpetual entertainment to the eye, &, when absent, a happy remembrance, $2500 & upwards of our money.

Clubs

In the East, they buy their wives at stipulated prices. Well, shall I not estimate, when the finer anthropometer is wanting, my social properties so? In our club, no man shall be admitted who is not worth in his skin 500,000. One of them, I hold worth a million; for he bows to facts, has no impertinent will, & nobody has come to the bottom of his wit, to the end of his resources. So, in my house, I shall not deign to count myself by my poor taxable estate 20 or 30 thousand, but each of my children is worth, on leaving school, a hundred thousand, as being able to think, speak, feel & act correctly,—able to fill the vacant hours, & keep life up to a high point. Bonaparte was right in saying, "I have three hundred millions in my treasury, & I would give them all for Ney."

Sunday, 19 July, 1857. A visit to Josiah Quincy, Jr., on his old place at Quincy, which has been in the family for seven generations since 1635, and the deed by which the place is holden is an *order* on the first page of the Records of the Town of Boston, "*Ordered*, that Edmund Quincy & (one other named party) lay out 800 acres at Mount Wollaston." There lives the old President, now 85 years old, in the house built by his father in 1770; & Josiah Jr. in a new house built by Billings, 7 years ago. They hold 500 acres, & the land runs down to the sea. From the piazza in the rear of the house of J.Q. Jr. you may see every ship that comes in or goes out of Boston, and most of the islands in the harbor. 'Tis the best placed house I know. The old man I visited on Saturday evening, & on Sunday he came & spent the evening with us at his son's house. He is the most fortunate of men. Old John Adams said that of him; & his good fortune has followed to this hour. His son said to me, "My father has thrown ten times, & every time got doublets." Yet he was engaged to a lady whose existence he did not know of, 7 days before, & she proved the best of wives. I made a very pleasant acquaintance with young Josiah 3d, the poet of "Lyteria." And I like him better than his poem. Charles Francis Adams also was there in the Sunday Evening. Old Quincy still reads & writes with vigor & steadiness 2 or 3 hours every night after tea till ten. He has just finished his "Life of J. Q. Adams."

Montaigne's story of the man who learned courage from the hare weighs with me. 'Tis the best use of Fate to teach us courage like the Turk. Go face the burglar, or the fire at sea, or whatever danger lies in the way of duty, knowing you are guarded by the omnipotence of Destiny. If you believe in Fate to your harm, believe it, at least, for your good. And, one more lesson learn,—to balance the ugly fact of temperament & race, which pulls you down,—this, namely, that, by that cunning co-presence of the two elements, which we find throughout nature, what ever lames you, or paralyzes you, drags in with it the divinity in some form to repay.

Peirce at Cambridge Observatory told me, that what we call a fine night is often no good night for the telescope; that the sky is not clear for astronomical observation, perhaps more than one night in a month. Of course, they hate to be annoyed by visiters at such times & I can well believe it. My days & hours for observation & record are as few: not every undisturbed day is good for the Muse. The day comes once in a month, & 'tis likely on that day the idle visiter drops in, thinking his coming no intrusion.

—

Every man tries his hand at poetry somewhere, but most men don't know which their poems are.

26 July

Ellery Channing thinks that these frogs at Walden are very curious but final facts; that they will never be disappointed by finding themselves raised to "a higher state of intelligence."*

*The "Sacontala" ends with a prayer of the King,—

He persists in his bad opinion of orchards & farming; declares, that the only success he ever had with the former, was, that he once paid a cent for a russetin apple; and farming, he thinks, is an attempt to outwit God with a hoe: that they plant a great many potatoes, with much ado; but it is doubtful if they ever get the seed again.

28 July. Yesterday the best day of the year we spent in the afternoon on the river. A sky of Calcutta, light, air, clouds, water, banks, birds, grass, pads, lilies, were in perfection, and it was delicious to live. Ellery & I went up the South Branch, & took a bath from the bank behind Cyrus Hubbard, where the river makes a bend. Blackbirds in hundreds; swallows in tens sitting on the telegraph lines; & one heron (ardea minor) assisted. In these perfect pictures, one thinks what weary nonsense is all this painful collection of rubbish,—pictures of rubbish masters,—in the total neglect of this & every lovely river valley, where the multitudinous life & beauty makes these pictures ridiculous cold chalk & ochre. Ellery complains of the new pedantry in T., as a dry rot, which consumes, as the famed Yacht "America" perishes now in Liverpool, for all its fine model.—

—

Thoughts.

Will he coax & stroke these deities? I do. I can no more manage these thoughts that come into my head than thunderbolts. But once get them written down, I come & look at them every day, & get wonted to their faces, & by & by, am so far used to them, that I see their family likeness, & can pair them & range them better, & if I once see where they belong, & join them in that order they will stay so.

—

August 2. Yesterday with Ellery at Flint's Pond. The pond was in its summer glory, the chestnuts in flower, two fishermen in a boat, thundertops in the sky, and the whole picture a study of all the secrets of landscape. "A place for every thing, &

"And may the purple selfexistent God,
Whose vital energy pervades all space,
From future transmigrations save my Soul!"

everything in place;" "No waste & no want;" "Each minds his own part, & none overdo & none interfere,"—these & the like rules of good householding are kept here in nature. The great afternoon spends like fireworks, or festival of the gods, with a tranquil exultation, as of a boy that has launched his first boat, or his little balloon, & the experiment succeeds.
E said, You must come here to see it! It can never be imagined. You must come here to see it, or you have lost your day.

'Tis an objection, I said, to astronomy, that you light your candle at both ends. After you have got through the day & 'tis necessary you should give attention to the business of sleeping, all hands are called; here come Canopus, Aldebaran, & all stars, & you are to begin again.

The woods were in their best, high grown again, & flecked with spots of pure sunshine everywhere,—paths for Una & her lamb; say better, fit for the stoutest farmers & the greatest scholars.

Reading is a languid pleasure and we must forget our books to see the landscape's royal looks.

Inspired we must forget our books,
To see the landscape's royal looks.

"What can be done with a man," says the biographer of Beaumarchais, "who converts successively five censors into five advocates?"

The Indian can call a muskrat swimming in the river to the side where he stands, & make him land. "See muskrat, me go talk with em." He can go into the lakes, & be paddled round & round ten or twenty times & then can go off in straight line "to camp," or to Oldtown. White man cannot; & Indian can't tell how he does it. He can give you a new tea every night, & a soup every day; lily soup; hemlock tea; tea from the snowberry, chiogenes hixpidula, is best. He can cut a string from spruce root, as you cannot. Joseph Polis is the hunter who went with Henry T. & Edward Hoar.

An Indian has his knowledge for use, & it only appears in use. Most white men that we know have theirs for talking purposes.

Cornus Sericeus is the ***kinnik kinnik.***

—

Sept. 4. Yesterday with Henry T. at the Estabrook Farm & Ebba Hubbard's swamp, to see the yellow birches, which grow larger than I have seen them elsewhere. The biggest measured, at 5 ft. from the ground, 10 feet, 5 inches in circumference. We found bass, black ash, a large old white thorn (Crataegus) tree, fever-bush abounding, a huge ivy running up from the base round a   tree, to the height of 20 or 30 feet, like a hairy snake, Osmunda regalis, white mint, penny royal, calamint, aster corymbosa, the bay-berry, Amphicarpaea, botrychium onoclea, brake tripartite,

A valuable walk through the savage fertile houseless land, where we saw pigeons & marsh-hawks, &, ere we left it, the mists, which denote the haunt of the elder Gods, were rising.

Henry said of the railroad whistle, that nature had made up her mind not to hear it, she knew better than to wake up. And, "the fact you tell, is of no value, 'tis only the impression."

Curious that the best thing I saw in Mammoth Cave, was an illusion.

But I have had many experiences like that & many men have. Our conversation with nature is not quite what it seems. The sunset glories are not quite so real as childhood thought them, & the part that our organization plays in them is too large. The same subjectiveness interferes everywhere.

—

The doses of heaven are homoeopathic. How little it is that differences the man from the woman; the animal from the plant; the most like, from the most unlike things!

—

Surfaces. Good writing sips the foam of the cup. There are infinite degrees of delicacy in the use of the hands; and good workmen are so distinguished from laborers; & good horsemen, from rude riders; & people of elegant manners, from the vulgar. In writing, it is not less. Montaigne dwells always at the surface, & can chip off a scale, where a coarser hand & eye finds only solid wall.

—

We read the orientals, but remain occidental. The fewest men receive anything from their studies. The abolitionists are not better men for their zeal. They have neither abolished slavery in Carolina, nor in me. If they cannot break one fetter of mine, I cannot hope they will of any negro. They are bitter sterile people, whom I flee from, to the unpretentious whom they disparage.

—

The eye is final; what it tells is the last stroke of nature. Beyond color we cannot go.

Gauss, I believe it is, who writes books that nobody can understand but himself, & himself only in his best hours. And Pierce & Gould & others in Cambridge are piqued with the like ambition. But I fancy more the wit of Defoe, & Cervantes, & Montaigne, who make deep & abstruse things popular. & I like the spirit of Kean who said, "the boxes, say you? a fig for the boxes;—the Pit rose to me," and of Mrs Stowe who had three audiences for "Uncle Tom," the parlor, & the kitchen, & the nursery.

Henry avoids commonplace, & talks birch bark to all comers, & reduces them all to the same insignificance.

Alcott returns to the lunar theory & thinks we must justify the ancients.
talked well of the Atlantic.

Good novels, O yes, but never a marriage, no new quality, no change of character, no marriage, have not baked a loaf. Ideas have not yet got possession, though they say they have. Does J. P. hold his money for the public benefit? does he establish a press for the dissemination of truth? or sustain men apt for that? Who holds wealth for the public good? No, but all for themselves or some worthless son. The publishers dictate, & do not yet know their places.

A journal is an assuming to guide the age—very propre & necessary to be done, & good news that it shall be so.—But this

Journal, is this it? His solar eye looked over the list, without much comfort. This the Dodona? this the Sais? Has Apollo spoken? In this, the sentiment of freedom is the sting which all feel in common. A northern sentiment, the only tie; & the manifest conveniency of having a good vent for such wares as scholars have.

There is this discrepancy in the nature of the thing. Each of the contributors is content that the thing be to the largest aims; but when he is asked for his contribution, he considers where his strength lies: he has certain experiences which have impressed him lately, & which he can combine, but no choice, or a very narrow choice among such. And the best the Editor can do, is, to see that nothing goes into the Book but important pieces. Every chapter must be something sterling; some record of real experiences. It suffices that it be weighty. It matters not whether 'tis upon Religion, or Balloons, or kneebuckles, so only that there was nothing fantastic or factitious in the subject & writing. Great scope & illumination ought to be in the Editor, to draw from the best in the land, & to defy the public, if he is only sure himself that the piece has worth, & is right. Publics are very placable, & will soon find out when they have a Master. The value of money-Capital is to be able to hold out for a few months, & go on printing, until the discerning minority of the public have found out that the Book is right, & must be humbly & thankfully accepted, & abandon themselves to this direction, too happy that they have got something good & wise to admire & to obey.

Alcott makes his large demand on the *Lecture*, that it is the University of the people, & 'tis time they should know at the end of the season what their professors have taught this winter: & it should be gathered by a good reporter in a book what Beecher, Whipple, Parker, Bellows, King, Solger, & Emerson, have taught. But the Lecturer was not allowed to be quite simple, as if he were on his conscience to unfold himself to a college class. But he knew his audience, & used the "adulatory" & "confectionary" arts, (according to Plato,) to keep them in their seats. He treats them as children; and Mercantile Libraries & Lyceums will all vote, if the question be virtually put to them,—we prefer to be entertained, nay, we must be entertained.

Alcott.

My friend has magnificent views, & looks habitually to the government of the County; of the state; of Nature. Nothing less. His natural attitude explains Plato. When has Plato found a genial critic? No, always a silly village wondering what he could be at? What he said about women? Did he mean Athens, or Hippias, or the Thirty? None of it at all, but just what you mean, when you come to the morning mountains, & say, the soul made the world, & should govern it, and the right radiancy of the soul from the centre outward, making nature, & distributing it to the care of wise souls, would be thus & thus. Here is my sketch; speaking really or scientifically, & not in your conventional gabble.

Alcott thinks Socrates would not have known his own remark when Plato repeated it!

People do not see that their opinion of the world is a confession also of character. We can only see what we are, and if we misbehave, we suspect others.

'Tis a proverb that "the air of Madrid will not put out a candle," that is to say, it will kill a man.

What an obstinate illusion is that which in youth gives respect to the old! And, presently, whilst we are yet young, & all our mates are mere youths & boyish, one Dick or Harry among them prematurely sports a bald head, or a grey one, which does not deceive us, who know how frivolous he is, but does not less deceive his juniors & the public, who presently treat him with a most inadequate respect: & this lets us into the secret, that the venerable forms we knew in our childhood were just such impostors.

Dreams.

I owe real knowledge & even alarming hints to dreams, & wonder to see people extracting emptiness from mahogany tables, when there is vaticination in their dreams. For the soul in dreams has a subtle synthetic power which it will not exert under the sharp eyes of day. It does not like to be watched or looked upon, & flies to real twilights, as the rappers do in their wretched mummeries. If in dreams you see loose & luxurious pictures, an inevitable tie drags in the sequel of cruelty & malignity.

If you swallow the devil's bait, you will have a horizon full of dragons shortly.

When I higgled for my dime & half dime in the dream, & lost,—the parrots on the chimney tops & church pinnacles scoffed at me, Ho! ho!

The shooting complexion, like the cobra capello & scorpion, grows in the South. It has no wisdom, no capacity of improvement: it looks, in every landscape, only for partridges, in every society, for duels. And, as it threatens life, all wise men brave or peaceable run away from the spider-man, as they run away from a black spider: for life to them is real & rich, & not to be risked on any curiosity as to whether spider or spider-man can bite mortally, or only make a poisonous wound. With such a nation or a nation with a predominance of this complexion, war is the safest terms. That marks them, &, if they cross the lines, they can be dealt with as all fanged animals must be.

The contrary temperament. The wrong thing always mounts to their lips, & they raise their voices at the moment when the person they are disparaging chances upon them.

Is there no check to this class of privileged thieves that infest our politics? We mark & lock up the petty thief or we raise the hue & cry in the street, and do not hesitate to draw our revolvers out of the box, when one is in the house. But here are certain well dressed well-bred fellows, infinitely more mischievous, who get into the government & rob without stint, & without disgrace. They do it with a high hand, & by the device of having a party to whitewash them, to abet the act, & lie, & vote for them. And often each of the larger rogues has his newspaper, called "his organ," to say that it was not stealing, this which he did; that if there was stealing, it was you who stole, & not he. There is no abominable act which these men will not do, & they are not abominated. No meanness below their stooping; yet is there no loathsomeness which their party & the "organ" will not strain its elastic larynx to swallow, & then to crow for it. I knew some of these robbers born within sound of church bells, & rejoicing in good Christian New England names such as Douglas, Pierce, Cushing, Govr Gardner. There is a serious objection to hounding them out,—that they are nasty prey, which the noble hunter disdains. A good dog even must not be risked on such. They "spoil his nose."

I took such pains not to keep my money in the house, but to put it out of the reach of burglars by buying stock, & had no guess that I was putting it into the hands of these very burglars now grown wiser & standing dressed as Railway Directors.

—

Wonders of Arnica. I must surely see the plant growing. Where's Henry? If Louis XVI had only in his pocket a phial of arnica, Father Edgeworth could have attached his falling head to his body, & with a little arnica made all whole again, & altered the fate of Europe.

It was a sublime sounding fact which we used to hear of Egyptian temples, that the foundation stones showed carving on their under sides, showing that old as they were, they were ruins of an older civilization. And I found in Sicily, that the church in Syracuse, was an antique temple of Diana; but that was a mushroom to the Egyptian. But Geology will show that first primaeval carved stone to have been a stratum precipitated & crystallized in what far aeons of uncounted time! Neither then were the particles & atoms new & raw, but mellowed & charred & decomposed from older mixtures, when, when, & where to reach their youth? A particle of azote or carbon is & remains azote & carbon, "nothing can in the least wear it." Well, the like aerugo, sacred rust & smell of an immeasurable antiquity, is on all with which we deal or of which we are.

"And the ruby bricks
Of the human blood
Have of old been wicks
In God's halls that stood."

as Wilkinson huskily sings.

Do we suppose it is newer with our thoughts? Do they come to us as for the first time? these wandering stars & sparks of truth that shone for eternity, & casually beamed this instant on us? The memory is made up of older memories, the blaze of genius owes its depth to our delighted recognition of the truth, as something older than the oldest, & which we knew aforetime, whether in the body or out of the body we cannot tell, God knoweth.

—

We should no more complain of the obstructions which make success in poetry, oratory, or in character difficult, than we should complain of the iron walls of the gun which hinder the shot from scattering here & there. It was walled round with iron tube with that purpose to give it irresistible force in one direction. I hate these cheap successes of every idle whimsical boy & girl. I like the successes of George Stephenson, & Columbus, well-won, hard-earned, by 50 years of work, a sleepless eye & an invincible will. Do you not know that "wisdom is not found in the hands of those who live at their ease?" (*Job*)

—

If a true metaphysician should come, he would accompany each man through his own (the student's) mind, & would point at this treasure-crypt, & at that, indicating immense wealth lying here & there, which the student would joyfully perceive, & pass on from hall to hall, from recess to recess, ever to more interior & causal forces, being minded to come over again on the same tracks by himself, at future leisure & explore more nearly the treasures now only verified. But such as we now call metaphysicians, the Lockes, & Reids, & Stewarts, &c., are no more than the *valets de place* & *custodi* who lead travellers through the curiosities of Rome or Verona, & say over by rote the legends that have been repeated from father to son, "Molto antico, signore;" "un tempio," "c'era battaglia," &c. &c.

Why does the name of a chapter "on Memory," shoot a little chill to the mind of each auditor?

There are few facts known on the subject of Memory. In the minds of most men it is nothing but a calender. On such a day, I paid my note: on the next, my cow calved: on the next, I cut my finger: on the next, the Banks suspended payment. But another man's memory is the history of science & art & civility & thought. & there are men whose memory is the history of their country during their active life. And still another's memory deals with laws & perceptions that are the platonic reminiscence of the Cosmos. "You may perish out of your senses, but not out of your memory & imagination," said Alcott. But he says nothing satisfactory about either of these two immense powers. All that is good is his ranking them so high. I tell him, that no people have imagination. 'Tis the rarest gift. Imagination is the nomination of the causal facts,—the laws of the soul,—by the physical facts. All physical facts are words for spiritual facts, & Imagination, by naming them, is the Interpreter, showing us the Unity of the world.

Most men are cowed by society, & say good things to you in private, but will not stand to them in public. And we require such a solitude as shall hold us to our order when we are in the street or in palaces.

These wonderful horses need to be driven by fine hands. The conditions are met, if we keep our independence, yet are not excluded. We must come to the club, yet in boots & spurs ready to depart on the instant our private alarm-clock strikes.

I listen to every prompting of honor, believing that it can deliver itself through all the maze of relations to the end of nature.

Nature does not like criticism. There is much that a wise man would not know. See how she never shows the skeleton, but covers it up, weaves her tissues & folds & integuments, the sun shall not shine on it, the eye shall not see it. Who & what are you that would lay it bare? & what a ghastly grinning

fragment have you got at last, which you call a man! That is criticism.
And jokes are of the same bastard kind. As soon as the company betray the delight in jokes, we shall have no Olympus. Nothing comes of it but vacancy & self reproach. True wit never made us laugh.

—

'Tis curious what the show of nature does for us. We find ourselves expressed in it, but we cannot translate it into words. 'Tis easier to read Greek, to read Sanscrit, to cipher out the arrowheaded character, than to interpret these familiar symbols of snow & grass, animals, rocks, seas, & skies. 'Tis even much to name these very things. Thus Thomson's "Seasons" and the best parts of many old & many new poets, are nothing but simple enumerations, by a person who felt the beauty of the common sights & sounds, without the least attempt to draw a moral, or affix any meaning to them. The charm of the Hindoo writings is a lively painting of these elements of fire, water, winds, clouds, without a hint of what they signify.

—

The saddest fact I know under the category of *Compensation*, is, that, when we look at an object, we turn away from every other object in the universe.

Answer. The redress is that we find every other object in that.

My philosophy holds to a few laws, 1. *Identity*, whence comes the fact that *metaphysical faculties & facts are the transcendency of physical.* 2. Flowing, or transition, or shooting the gulf, the perpetual striving to ascend to a higher platform, the same thing in new & higher forms.

High Criticism.

You must draw your rule from the genius of that which you do, & not from by-ends. Don't make a novel to establish a principle of polit. economy. You will spoil both. Do not set out to make your school of design lucrative to the pupils: you will fail in the art & in the profit. Don't set out to please,—you will displease. Don't set out to teach theism from your Nat. History, like Paley & Agassiz. You spoil both. The Augsburg

Allgemeine Zeitung deprecates an Observatory founded for the benefit of Navigation!*

—

The ballads got their excellence, as perhaps Homer & the Cid did, by being conventional stories conventionally treated, with conventional rhymes & tunes & images, done over & over, until, at last, all the strokes were right, & the faults were thrown away. Thus Logan got his "sought him east, & sought him west," &c. Somebody even borrowed "*Parcite dum propero, mergite dum redeo.*" See Child's Edition Vol II p 176

—

If men should take off their clothes, I think the aristocracy would not be less, but more pronounced than now.

If men were as thick as snowflakes,——millions of flakes, but there is still but one snowflake: but every man is a door to a single deep secret.

The ancients to make a god added to the human figure some brutal exaggeration, as the leonine head of Jove, the bull-neck of Hercules; and Michel Angelo added horns to give mysterious strength to the head of Moses. So Webster impressed by his superb animality, & was strong as a nature, though weak in character. His understanding & his demonstrative talents were invigorated from these low sources, but he had the vulgar ambition, & his power was only that of a lawyer,† & it perished utterly, even before his death. What is called his fame—only marks the imbecility of those who invoke it.

Sentiment is always color, as thought is form. When I talked with Goodson, on a Sunday morning, in Cincinnati, of Catholic Churches, how warm & rich & sufficient was the hour & conversation: as the colors of the sunset, whilst we gaze, make life so great; but now no memory remains of conversation or sunset.

—

**March, 1874*. That Observatory has been established to the great benefit of Navigators.

†No, he was a skilful statesman & a great orator.

I found Henry T. yesterday in my woods. He thought nothing to be hoped from you, if this bit of mould under your feet was not sweeter to you to eat, than any other in this world, or in any world. We talked of the willows. He says, 'tis impossible to tell when they push the bud (which so marks the arrival of spring) out of its dark scales. It is done & doing all winter. It is begun in the previous autumn. It seems one steady push from autumn to spring. I say, How divine these studies! Here there is no taint of mortality. How aristocratic, & of how defiant a beauty! This is the garden of Edelweisen. He says, Wachusett is 27 miles from Fairhaven, and Monadnoc about 50.

I want animal spirits.

I have not oil enough for my wheels.

Bonaparte asked Talleyrand what they meant by this term non-intervention? Talleyrand replied, "It means about the same as intervention"

Perhaps it would be a safe episode to the Intellect chapters, to give an account of the gentleman in search of the Practical, as illustrated by the history of the turbine, which is valued here at $100 000, & there is discarded as useless, and on which there seems no settled verdict to be had. J. Bright of Rochdale said, the use of machinery in America & in England went by fancy: & my search for the pioneers in Illinois & Wisconsin,—"they were visionary men, not practical, & all bankrupted." And my western banker, at Adrian, & Mr Hooper's at Lexington, may serve to show what practical people are.

—

When a dog barks on the stage of a theatre, the audience are interested. What acting can take their attention from the dog? But if in the real action which their scene represents, a dog had barked, it would not have been heard.

"Thou art roaring ower loud, Clyde water!
Thy streams are ower strang;
Make me thy wreck, when I come back,
But spare me when I gang."

Parcite dum propero, mergite dum redeo.

People who caught cold in coming into the world, & have increased their cold ever since.

The politics of Massachusetts are cowardly. O for a Roman breath, & the courage that advances & dictates! When we get an advantage, as in Congress, the other day, it is because our adversary has made a fault, & not that we have made a thrust.

Why do we not say, We are abolitionists of the most absolute abolition, as every man that is a man must be? Only the Hottentots, only the barbarous or semibarbarous societies are not. We do not try to alter your laws in Alabama, nor yours in Japan, or the Fee Jee Islands; but we do not admit them or permit a trace of them here. Nor shall we suffer you to carry your Thuggism north, south, east, or west into a single rod of territory which we control. We intend to set & keep a *cordon sanitaire* all around the infected district, & by no means suffer the pestilence to spread.

At Springfield, I told Lamoureux that I thought metaphysics owed very little to the French mind. What we owe is not to the professors, but to the incidental remarks of a few deep men, namely, to Montaigne, Malebranche, Pascal, & Montesquieu.* The analytic mind will not carry us far. Taking to pieces is the trade of those who cannot construct. In a healthy mind, the love of wholes, the power of generalizing, is usually joined with a keen appreciation of differences. But they are so bent on the aim & genius of the thing, that they don't mind the surface faults. But minds of low & surface power pounce on some fault of expression, of rhetoric, or petty mis-statement of fact, and quite lose sight of the main purpose. I knew a lady who thought she knew she had heard my discourse before, because the word "*Arena*" was in both of the two discourses.

The English think, if you add a hundred facts, you will have made a right step towards a theory; if you add a thousand, so

*[Yet we must remember DesCartes & Malebranche; if Cousin is only a pupil of Hegel.]

much the nearer. But these lines never meet. A good mind infers from two or three facts, or from one, as readily as from a legion. Witness Kepler, Newton, Dalton, &c., who are born with a taste for the manners of nature, & catch the whole tune from a few bars.

It is impossible to be a gentleman, & not be an abolitionist. For a gentleman is one who is fulfilled with all nobleness, & imparts it; is the natural defender & raiser of the weak & oppressed; like the Cid. But these are snobs. In the southern country, their idea of a gentleman is a striker. There are abundance of their gentlemen garrotting &c in N. Y. streets.

—

Wordsworth's "Prelude" is not quite solid enough in its texture: it is rather a poetical pamphlet; though proceeding from a new & genuine experience. It is like Milton's "*Areopagitica*," an immortal pamphlet.

Many of Tennyson's poems, like "Clara Vere de Vere," are only the sublime of magazine poems,—admirable contributions for the "Atlantic Monthly" of the current month, but not classic & eternal.

—

Milton would have raised his eyebrow a little at such pieces. But the "Ulysses" he would have approved.

The quaking earth did quake in rhyme
Seas ebbed & flowed with clanging chime

The sun athwart the cloud thought it no sin
To use my land to put his rainbows in

Eloquence
What unreckoned elements the orator carries with him, for example, silence. He performs as much or more with judicious pauses, as by his best stroke.

We can't afford to take the horse out of Montaigne's Essays.

*

11 May

Yesterday with Henry T. at the pond saw the creeper *vesey vesey vesey. Yorick is the veery, or Wilson's Thrush.* The lamprey-eel was seen by Wetherell building the pebble nest in the river. The dead sucker so often seen in the river needs a great deal of air & hence perhaps dies when detained below. The trout was seen to kill the pickerel by darting at him & tearing off a fin every time. I hear the account of the man who lives in the wilderness of Maine with respect, but with despair. It needs the doing hand to make the seeing eye, & my imbecile hands leave me always helpless & ignorant, after so many years in the country. The beauty of the spectacle I fully feel, but 'tis strange that more than the miracle of the plant & any animal is the impression of mere mass of broken land & water, say a mountain, precipices, & water-falls, or the ocean side, and stars. These affect us more than anything except men & women. But neither is Henry's hermit, 45 miles from the nearest house, important, until we know what he is now, what he thinks of it on his return, & after a year. Perhaps he has found it foolish & wasteful to spend a tenth or a twentieth of his active life with a muskrat & fried fishes. I tell him that a man was not made to live in a swamp, but a frog.* The charm which Henry T. uses for bird & frog & mink, is patience. They will not come to him, or show him aught, until he becomes a log among the logs, sitting still for hours in the same place; then they come around him & to him, & show themselves at home. Peabody-bird; *Pee-pee*, pee pee pee, five bars,—that is the note of the *myrtle bird*. Penetrating and like the note of the meadow lark.

—

We are all better in attack than in defence. It is very easy to make acute objections to any style of life, but the objector is quite as vulnerable. Greenough wittily called my speculations *masturbation*; but the artist life seems to me intolerably thin & superficial. I feel the reasonableness of what the lawyer or merchant or laborer has to allege against readers & thinkers, until I look at each of their wretched industries, and find them without end or aim.

*If God meant him to live in a swamp, he would have made him a frog.

monotone
Chicadee dee, says the titmouse; *pēē pēē* pee pee pee, says the myrtle bird, "Peabody bird" each as long as he lives; & the man who hears, goes all his life saying his one proverb too.

My dear Henry,
A frog was made to live in a swamp, but a man was not made to live in a swamp. Yours ever,
R.

Nature overloads the bias, overshoots the mark, to hit the mark. Her end of reproduction & care of young is so dear to her, that she demoralizes the universe of men with this immense superfluity of attraction in all directions to woman: & see what carnage in relations results! Nothing is so hypocritical as the abuse in all journals,—& at the South, especially,—of Mormonism & Free-Love Socialism. These men who write the paragraphs in the "Herald" & "Observer," have just come from their brothel, or, in Carolina, from their Mulattoes. How then can you say, that, in nature is always a minimum of force to effect a change? It is a maximum.

Nature has two ways of hiding her things, by light, & by darkness. We never see mosses, lichens, grasses, birds, or insects, which are near us every day, on account of our preoccupied mind. When our attention is at last called to them, they seem the only things worth minding.

1858
8 June. I spent the evening of 7th June at the American House, with J. S. Babcock, the carpenter, Mr Rowse's friend—a man of much reading, & a very active & independent mind, with an exclusive respect for intellectual power, not much sensibility to morals, though meaning to be fair, & of little hope for the race. The bully, he thinks, the great god of the people, &, if Sumner had killed Brooks, he thought the people would have worshipped Sumner. Now, all the west despised him. I tried to show him how much the genius of Burke was indebted to his affection; what insight good will gives, & what eyewaters all the virtues are, as humility, love, courage, &c & what a blindman's

buff self-conceit makes. And he was candid enough. I told him, that, whatever was dreary & repels, is not power, but the lack of power,—which he allowed. He struggled hard for Webster, who is his idol. He thought the masses admire Cushing, Burlingame, Wise, or any man who has done the feat,—who has succeeded.

His opinions on books,—which he has read a good deal,—were his own, & just.

from

AC

1858–1859

I owe to Genius always the same debt of lifting the curtain from the Common, & showing me that gods are sitting disguised in this seeming gang of gypsies & pedlers.

—

To M. P. Forbes

I send you back "Counterparts," a talismanic book, full of secrets guarded so well that no profaner eye can read. For the gem will, I doubt not, be taken by most for a dull pebble, whilst you are sure you have seen it shoot rays of green, blue, & rosy fire. I don't know when a novel has contained so many searching glances into the house of life, & given the reader this joy of sincere conversation rightly made the culmination of interest. Genius always treats us well, & we are not turned rudely out of doors at the end of the story, by a prosperity exclusively the hero's, but are delighted to find he means *us*. What a discovery to know there is an Author of "Counterparts" hidden among these slow British people! Send to Caroline T. to meet you at an Evening with the Author of "Counterparts," in London.— Feb. 14, 1859.

—

Want of reference to thought: I dreamed I stood in a city of beheaded men, where the decapitated trunks continued to walk about.

—

Miscellany.

For the chapter on Quotation, much is to be said on the matter of originality. We have said all our life, whoever is original, I am not. What have I that I have not received? Let every creditor take his own, & what would be left? 'Tis the sea again, which, if you stop all the rivers, Amasis can drink up.

Yet this is true, & not true. Every man brings a certain difference of angle to the identical picture which makes all new.

But this makes originality, that the beholder of this particular knot of things or thoughts has the habit of recurrence to Universal views. The boy in the school or in the sitting room at home sits there adorned with all the color, health, & power which the day spent out of doors has lent him. The man interests in the same way, not for what he does in our presence, at the table, or in his chair, but for the authentic tokens he gives us of powers in the landscape, over ships, railroads, cities, or other outdoor organizations. The girl charms us with the distant contributions which she reconciles. She has inherited the feature which manly joy & energy of her ancestors formed long ago, softened & masked under this present beauty, & she brings the hint of the romance of fields & forests & forest brooks, of the sunsets, & music, & all-various figures that deck it. A white invalid that sits in a chamber is good for nothing. To be isolated, is to be sick, & so far dead. That is, the life of the *All* must stream through us, to make the man & the moment great. And the same law takes place in thought that the mind has gone out of its little parlor into the great sky of Universal truths, & has not come back the same it went, but ennobled, & with the necessity of going back habitually to the same firmament & importing its generosities into all its particular thought. He who compares all his traditions with this eternal standard—He who cannot be astonished by any tinsel or claptrap or smartness or popgun; for the immensities & eternities, from which he newly came, to which he familiarly returns, have once for all put it out of his power to be surprised by trifles: That man conveys the same ecstasy in which he lives, in some degree, into every thing he says; it is in his manners & feeds the root of his life. It is the magic of nature, that the whole life of the universe concentrates itself on its every point.

—

Edward says, that Cicero was a postmaster who kept in with the strongest side.

'Tis very important in writing that you do not lose your presence of mind. Despair is no muse, & he who finds himself hurried, & gives up carrying his point this time, writes in vain. Goethe had the "*urkraftige behagen*," the stout comfortableness, the stomach for the fight, and you must.

Correspondence of the mind to the world. Obedience of the mind to the laws. Vital obedience or sympathy. Then, in the Perfection of this correspondence or expressiveness, the health & force of man consists.

Hence intellect is Aesculapian.

—

The *va et vient*, the ebb & flow, the pendulum, the alternation, the fits of easy transmission & reception, the pulsation, the undulation which seems to be a fundamental secret of nature, exists in intellect. Nature masks under ostentatious subdivision & manifold particulars the poverty of her elements, the rigid economy of her rules.

—

Doses of heaven are homoeopathic.

—

The fool in Goethe's "Helena" when paper currency was invented, said, "what do you say—this is money? I will go & buy me a farm"; and Mephistopheles points to the fact that the fool is the only one of the set who does a wise thing. I saw the same thing occur the other day, when the two girls passed me. The accomplished & promising young man chose, with the approbation of all surrounding society, the pretty girl, who went through all her steps unexceptionably. But the real person, the fine hearted witty sister, fit for all the range of real life, was left, & to her a foolish youth passionately attached himself, & said, "I shall be wretched & undone, but you I must have." And he was right, & the other not.

Ripple Pond

The rippling of the pond under a gusty south wind gives the like delight to the eye, as the fitful play of the same wind on the Aeolian harp to the ear. Or the darting & scud of ripples is like the auroral shootings in the night heaven.

W.E.C.'s poetry is wanting in clear statement. Rembrandt makes effects without details, gives you the effect of a sharp nose or a gazing eye, when, if you look close, there is no point to the nose, & no eye is drawn. W. Hunt admires this, & in his own painting, puts his eye in deep shadow; but I miss the eye,

& the face seems to nod for want of it. & Ellery makes a hazy indefinite impression, as of miscellaneous music, without any theme or tune. Still, it is an autumnal air & like the smell of the herb "Life Everlasting" & syngenesious flowers.

"Near Home" is a poem which would delight the heart of Wordsworth, though genuinely original, & with a simplicity of plan which allows the writer to leave out all the prose. 'Tis a series of sketches of natural objects, such as abound in N. England, enwreathed by the thoughts they suggest to a contemplative pilgrim,

> "Unsleeping truths by which wheels on
> Heaven's prime."

There is a neglect of superficial correctness, which looks a little studied, as if perhaps the poet challenged notice to his subtler melody. & strokes of skill which recall the great Masters. There is nothing conventional in the thought, or the illustration, but "thoughts that voluntary move harmonious numbers," & pictures seen by an instructed eye.

Jefferson says in a letter to Judge Roane "The great object of my fear is the federal judiciary. That body, like gravity, ever acting with noiseless foot & unalarming advance, gaining ground step by step, & holding what it gains, is ingulphing insidiously the special governments into the jaws of that which feeds them." Jefferson's works Vol VII. p 212

Illusions.
One is the belief that W —— is large & cosmical, does not strut nor pinch his lips, but hospitably receives you with laughter & intimate graces, and you set him down so on your table of constants. The fact is he is *timed* to you; and to the next man he meets though as apprehensive as yourself, he is not *timed*, and is stilted, struts, & pinches his lips.

I am a natural reader, & only a writer in the absence of natural writers. In a true time, I should never have written.

*

The village of Amherst is eagerly discussing the authorship of a paper signed Bifid which appeared in the College Magazine. 'Tis said, if the Faculty knew his name, the author would be expelled from the college. Ten miles off, nobody ever heard of the magazine, or ever will hear of it. In London 'tis of equal interest today whether Lord Palmerston wrote the leader in Wednesday's Times.

In literary circles they still discuss the question who wrote Junius,—a matter of supreme unimportance, like the others. But in the whole world none discuss the question who wrote Hamlet & Lear and the Sonnets, which concerns mankind.

You can always tell an English book by the confusion of ideas; a German, by the ideal order. Thus an English speculator shows the wonders of electricity, & talks of its leaving poetry far behind, &c, or, perhaps, that it will yet show poetry new materials, &c.

Illusion. See above, no poetry without illusion— Yet poetry is in nature just as much as carbon is: love & wonder & the delight in suddenly seen analogy exist as necessarily as space, or heat, or Canada thistles; and have their legitimate functions: and where they have no play, the impatience of the mind betrays precisely the distance from the truth,—the truth which satisfies the mind & affections, & leaves the real & the ideal in equilibrium which constitutes happiness.

I have now for more than a year, I believe, ceased to write in my Journal, in which I formerly wrote almost daily. I see few intellectual persons, & even those to no purpose, & sometimes believe that I have no new thoughts, and that my life is quite at an end. But the magnet that lies in my drawer for years, may believe it has no magnetism, and, on touching it with steel, it shows the old virtue; and, this morning, came by a man with knowledge & interests like mine, in his head, and suddenly I had thoughts again.

Races. There are female races, which, mixing with male races, produce a better man.

The solid men complain that the idealist leaves out the fundamental facts; the poetic men complain that the solid men leave the sky out.

Among the words to be gazetted pray insert the offensive Americanism "*balance*" for *remainder*, and, what always accompanies it in this Albany Hammond's book, "*lay*" for lie.
"I am very particular"
Sneak

Pace παντα ρει

The world is reckoned by dull men a dead subject, whilst it is quick & blazing. The house & farm are thought fixed & lasting, whilst they are rushing to ruin every moment. The difference between skilful & unskilful men is,—that the one class are timed to this movement, & move with it, can shoot flying, can load as they go, can read as they run, can write in a cab; whilst the heavy men wait for the eagle to alight, for the swallow to roost like a barn fowl, for the river to run by, for the pause in the conversation, which never comes till the guests take their hats.

Rarey can tame a wild horse, but can he make wild a tame horse, it were better.
Channing, who writes a poem for our fields, begins to help us. That is construction, & better than running to Charlemagne & Alfred for subjects.

Secondary men & primary men. These travellers to Europe, these readers of books, these youths rushing into counting rooms of successful merchants, are all imitators, and we get only the same product weaker. But the man who never so slowly & patiently works out his native thought, is a primary person. The girl who does not visit, but follows her native tastes & objects, draws Boston to her. If she do not follow fashion, fashion follows her.

Why do I hide in a library, read books, or write them, & skulk in the woods, & not dictate to these fellows, who, you say, dictate to me, as they should not? Why? but because in my bones is none of the magnetism which flows in theirs. They inundate all men with their streams. I have a reception & a perception, which they have not, but it is rare & casual, and yet drives me forth to watch these workers, if so be I may derive from their performance a new insight for mine. But there are no equal terms for me & them. They all unwittingly perform for me the part of the gymnotus on the fish.

Every man has the whole capital in him, but does not know how to turn it. Every man knows all that Plato or Kant can teach him. When they have got out the proposition at last, 'tis something which he recognizes & feels himself entirely competent. He *was* already that which they say, & was that more profoundly than they can say it. Yet, from the inertness & phlegm of his nature, the seldomness with which a spark passes from him, he exists as a flint, he that should be a sun.

—

We impatient Americans! If we came on the wires of the telegraph, yet, on arriving, every one would be striving to get ahead of the rest.

Ellery said, looking at a golden rod,—"ah! here they are. These things consume a great deal of time. I don't know but they are of more importance than any other of our investments."

—

I have been writing & speaking what were once called novelties, for twenty five or thirty years, & have not now one disciple. Why? Not that what I said was not true; not that it has not found intelligent receivers but because it did not go from any wish in me to bring men to me, but to themselves. I delight in driving them from me. What could I do, if they came to me? they would interrupt & encumber me. This is my boast that I have no school & no follower. I should account it a measure of the impurity of insight, if it did not create independence.

Here came the subsoil plougher H. J.
H. J.'s correspondent is Kimball in Franklin, N. H.

The ease with which people use the word spiritual to cover what is antagonistic to spiritual, suggests the possibility of a searching tuition in that direction. I fancy, that, if you give me a class of intelligent youths & maidens, I could bring them to see the essential distinctions which I see; & could exercise them in that high department, so that they should not let go what they had seen. Spiritual is that which is its own evidence; which is self-executing; which cannot be conceived not to be; that which sets aside you & me, & can very well let us drop, but not we it. The existence & history of Christ are doubted & denied by some learned & critical persons in perfect good faith. Of course, the existence & history of Christ are not a spiritual reality, for they could not deny the existence of justice, of love, of the laws of time & space.

H. J. said of woman, "that the flesh said, it is for me, & the spirit said, it is for me."

—

A man finds out that there is somewhat in him that knows more than he does.
Then he comes presently to the curious question, who's who? which of these two is really me? the one that knows more, or the one that knows less? the little fellow, or the big fellow?

—

Send the divingbell of Memory down,—see the immense relations of every symbol—

—

I value M. Angelo's saying There is something I can do—

I value a man's trust in his fortune, when it is a hearing of voices that call him to his task; when he is conscious of a great work laid on him to do, & that nature cannot afford to lose him until it is done.

—

Believe the faintest of your presentiments against the testimony of all sacred & profane history. A great man is always a contradiction to his age & to foregoing history. If Plato had not been, you would say, no Plato could be. If Jesus had not been, would not the Skeptic deny the possibility of so just a life? And yet steadily in the heart of every man, the possibility of a greater than Plato, of a greater than Jesus, was always affirmed, and is affirmed; for every man carries with him the vision of the Perfect. And the highest actual that fulfils any part of this promise exalts the Ideal just so much higher, & it can no more be attained than he can set his foot on the horizon which flies before him.

—

The greatest benefit of London seems today to be this, that, in such a vast number of persons & conditions, one can believe there is room for such people as we read of in novels to exist, such, for instance, as the heroes & heroines of "Counterparts."

Nobody can read in M.M.E.'s MSS. or in the conversation of old-school people, without seeing that Milton and Young had a religious authority in their mind, & no wise the slight, merely entertaining quality of modern bards. And Plato, Aristotle, Plotinus, how venerable & organic as Nature, they are in M.M.E.'s mind!

What a subject is her mind & life for the finest novel. And I wish I were younger, or that my daughters would aspire to draw this portrait. And when I read Dante, the other day, & his periphrases to signify with more adequateness Christ or Jehovah,—who, do you think, I was reminded of? who but M.M.E, & her eloquent theology?

At every parting with people who interest us at all, how the sense of demerit is forced upon each!

Here dies the amiable & worthy Prescott amid a chorus of eulogies, and, if you believe the American & almost the English newspapers for a year or two back, he is the very Muse of History. And meantime here has come into the country 3 months ago a book of *Carlyle*, History of Frederick, infinitely the wittiest book that ever was written, a book that one would think the English people would rise up in mass to thank him for, by cordial acclamation & congratulate themselves that such a head existed among them, and much-sympathising & on its own account reading-America would make a new treaty extraordinary of joyful grateful delight with England, in acknowledgment of such a donation,—a book with so many memorable & heroic facts, working directly, too, to practice,—with

new heroes, things unvoiced before, with a range of thought & wisdom, the largest & the most colloquially elastic, that ever was, not so much applying as inosculating to every need & sensibility of a man, so that I do not so much read a sterotype page, as I see the eyes of the writer looking into my eyes; all the way, chuckling with undertones & hums & winks & shrugs, & long commanding glances, and stereoscoping every figure that passes & every hill, river, wood, hummock, & pebble in the long perspective, and withal a book that is a Judgment Day, too, for its moral verdict on the men & nations & manners of modern times.
With its wonderful new system of mnemonics, whereby great & insignificant men are ineffaceably ticketed & marked in the memory by what they were, had, & did.
And this book makes no noise: I have hardly seen a notice of it in any newspaper or journal, and you would think there was no such book; but the secret interior wits & hearts of men take note of it, not the less surely. They have said nothing lately in praise of the air, or of fire, or of the blessing of love, and yet, I suppose, they are sensible of these, & not less of this Book, which is like these.

—

"In the morning—solitude," said Pythagoras. By all means, give the youth solitude, that nature may speak to his imagination, as it does never in company; and, for the like reason, give him a chamber alone; and that was the best thing I found in College.

—

When James Burke was driving home from carrying Ellen T. E. in my wagon to the Concord station, the bolt of the wagon broke, & James was thrown out, & the horse ran home with the shafts. James was much hurt, but he thought only of the horse, & picked himself up the best he could, & limped home comforting himself how lucky it was that "it did not happen when Miss Ellen was in the wagon."

Now & then, rarely comes a stout man like Luther, Montaigne, Pascal, Herbert, who utters a thought or feeling in a virile manner, and it is unforgettable. Then follow any number of spiritual eunuchs and women, who talk about that thought,

imply it, in pages & volumes. Thus Novalis said, "Spinoza was a God-intoxicated man." Samuel Hopkins said, "A man must be willing to be damned for the glory of God."
George Fox said, "That which men trample on must be thy food." Swedenborg said, "the older the angels are, the more beautiful."

—

Each of these male words being cast into the apprehension of pious souls delight & occupy them, and they say them over in every form of song, prayer, & discourse. Such is Silesius Angelus, such is Upham, such Alger, such Pusey & his men.

Great bands of female souls who only receive the spermatic aura & brood on the same but add nothing.

Do not spend one moment on the last; they are mere publishers & diluters & critics.

'Tis amusing to see Henry's constant assumption that the science is or should have been complete, & he has just found that they had neglected to describe the seeds, or count the sepals, or mark a variety. The ignorant scoundrels have not been in Concord. I mildly suggest that "what is every body's business is nobody's"; besides, who said they had?—besides, what were you sent for but to make this observation?

—

There are better pleasures than to be first. I keenly enjoyed Caroline's pointed remark, after we had both known Charles Newcomb, that "no one could compare with him in original genius," though I knew that she saw, as I saw, that his mind was far richer than mine, which fact nobody but she and I knew or suspected. Nay, I rejoiced in this very proof of her perception. And now, sixteen years later, we two alone possess this secret still.

The French wittily describe the English on a steamboat as each endeavoring to draw around himself an impassable space detaching him from his countrymen, in which he shall stand alone, clean & miserable. The French pay for their brilliant social cultivation herein, that they all write alike. I cannot tell whose book I am reading without looking on the cover; you would think all the novels & all the criticism were written by one & the same man.

Antony had heard too well the knell of thought & genius in the stertorous voice of the rector to have the smallest inclination to the church.

People live like these boys who watch for a sleigh-ride & mount on the first that passes, & when they meet another that they know, swing themselves on to that, & ride in another direction, until a third passes, & they change again; 'tis no matter where they go, as long as there is snow & company.

—

Shall I blame my mother, whitest of women, because she was not a gipsy, & gave me no swarthy ferocity? or my father, because he came of a lettered race, & had no porter's shoulders?

—

There is no strong performance without a little fanaticism in the performer. That field yonder did not get such digging, ditching, filling, & planting for any pay. A fanaticism lucky for the owner did it. James Burke opened my hay as fiercely on Sunday as on Monday.

Neither can any account be given of the fervid work in M.M.E.'s manuscripts, but the vehement religion which would not let her sleep, nor sit, but write, write, night & day, year after year. And C.K.N. had this *Δαιμων* dazzling his eyes, & driving his pen. Unweariable fanaticism (which, if it could give account of itself to itself, were lost,)—is the Troll that

> "by night threshed the corn
> Which ten day laborers could not end."

Cushing, & Banks, & Wilson, are its victims, &, by means of it, vanquishers of men. But they whose eyes are prematurely opened with broad common-sense views, are hopeless dilettanti, & must obey these madmen.

Bonaparte rightly sighed for his soldiers of 1789.

May 25

The warblers at this season make much of the beauty & interest of the woods. They are so elegant in form & coat, and many of them here but for a short time; the Blackburnian warbler rarely seen by H.D.T—; the trees still allowing you to see far. Their small leaflets do not vie with the spaces of the sky,—but let in the vision high—and (yesterday) Concord was all Sicily.

Glad of Ellery's cordial praise of Carlyle's History, which, he thinks well entitled to be called a "Work," & far superior to his early books. Wonders at his imagination which can invest with such interest to himself these (one would think) hopeless details of German story. He is the only man who knows.—What a reader! how competent to give light now on the politics of Europe!
Today this History appears the best of all histories.

Alcott said, "Jove is in his reserves."

'Tis worth remembering in connexion with what I have so often to say of surface, that our whole skill is in that direction. Carlyle's Friedrich is a great book; opens new extension to history. How much event, personality, nationality, is there disclosed, or hinted at, & will draw multitudes of scholars to its exploring & illustration! So with every new vein that is opened. Wide, east & west, north & south, immense lateral spaces,—but the sum & upshot of all, the aim & theory,—is in few steps, or one; seen in an instant, or never seen. Vast surface, short diameter.

—

Egotism.

'Tis pity to see egotism for its poverty. All must talk about themselves, for 'tis all they know, but genius never needs to allude to his personality, as every person & creature he has seen serves him as an exponent of his private experience. So he communicates all his secrets, and endless autobiography, & never lets on that he means himself. See *MME*, I. p. 50, 73, Remember Dr Chauncey's prayer.

Dante.

Dante cannot utter a few lines but I am informed what transcendent eyes he had, as, for example,

"un foco
Ch' emisperio di tenebre vincia."

How many millions would have looked at candles, lamps, & fires, & planets, all their days, & never noticed this measure of their illuminating force, "of conquering a hemisphere of the darkness." Yet he says nothing about his own eyes.

Inspiration.

What marks right mental action is always newness, ignoring of the past; & the elasticity of the present object,—which makes all the magnitudes & magnates quite unnecessary. This is what we mean when we say your subject is absolutely indifferent. You need not write the History of the World, nor the Fall of Man, nor King Arthur, nor Iliad, nor Christianity; but write of hay, or of cattleshows, or trade sales, or of a ship, or of Ellen, or Alcott, or of a couple of school-boys, if only you can be the fanatic of your subject, & find a fibre reaching from it to the core of your heart, so that all your affection & all your thought can freely play.

Tennyson.

England is solvent, no matter what rubbish & hypocrisy of Palmerstons & Malmesburys & D'Israelis she may have, for here comes Tennyson's poem, indicating a supreme social culture, a perfect insight, & the possession of all the weapons & all the functions of a man, with the skill to wield them which Homer, Aristophanes, or Dante had. The long promise to pay that runs over ages from Chaucer, Spenser, Milton, Ben Jonson,—the long promise to write the national poem of Arthur, Tennyson at last keeps, in these low selfdespising times; Taliessin & Ossian are at last edited, revised, expurgated, distilled. The national poem needed a national man. And the blood is still so rich, & healthful, that, at last in Tennyson a national soul comes to the Olympic games—equal to the task. He is the Pisistratus, who collects & publishes the Homer, ripened at last by the infusion of so many harvests, & henceforth unchangeable & immortal.

from

CL

1859–1861

I learned that the rhyme is there in the theme, thought, & image, themselves. I learned that there is a beyond to every place, & the bird moving through the air by successive dartings taught me.

—

Certain persons utter oracles, as Bettine, as Aunt Mary, as Alcott, & Charles Newcomb. We hear awestruck that the ancients recognized an *omen* or *fatum*, now & then, in chance words spoken; and we cast about & wonder what these oracles were. And we hear some remark which explains our own character, or foible, or circumstance, and it does not occur to us that this is the very chance those ancients considered. This is the omen & *fatum*. But these oracles are simply perceptions of the intellect; &, whenever the intellect acts, there is an oracle. An omen or fatum is that of Pindar;

Nature wishes that woman should attract man, but she has cunningly made them with a little sarcasm in expression, which seems to say, "Yes, I am willing to attract, but to attract a little better kind of man than any I yet see."

—

Bettine is a wise child with her wit, humor, will, & pure inspirations. She utters oracles & is the best critic of Goethe. Her talk about manners & character, is like Charles Auchester's. But he has no wit like her fine things about the "flat seventh." (Vol. I, 282) And Mme. de Stael, & Jacobi. How clearly she sees the defects of his mind & working! How superior she is to him, & cunningly hints it, (See Vol I. p 310) & he never dares own it. He thanks her "for every bright glance into a spiritual life, which, without you, I should perhaps never again have experienced." Never *again*! Mean fellow! As if he had or could anticipate a thought of hers! (Vol II 178)

'Tis easy to see that Carlyle has learned of Goethe his literary manners, & how to be condescending & courteous, & yet to keep himself always in rein.

But when Bettine writes from Vienna her admirable reports of her conversation with Beethoven, Goethe in his reply comes at last out of his shell, & pays a homage to Beethoven he has not expressed for any other; calls himself a "layman" before this "demon-possessed person," and offers to meet him at Carlsbad. &c.

(Vol II. p. 217)

—

Very little reliance must be put on the common stories of Mr Webster's or of Mr Choate's learning, their Greek, or their varied literature. That ice won't bear. Reading! to what purpose did they read? I allow them the merit of that reading which appears in their opinions, tastes, beliefs, & practice. They read that they might know,—did they not? Well, these men did not know: they blundered. They were utterly ignorant of that which every boy & girl of fifteen knows perfectly, the rights of men & women, and this old talking lubber among his dictionaries, & Leipsic editions of Lysias, had lost his knowledge.

—

In reading prose, I am sensible as soon as a sentence drags, but in reading poetry, as soon as one word drags.

Of Adam Smith, "but had I known that he loved rhyme as much as you say he does, I should have hugged him;" said Johnson.

Boswell p. 118

—

It is true there is but one institution. It is true that the University & the Church, which should be counterbalancing institutions & independent, do now express the sentiment of the popular politics, & the popular optimism, whatever it be. Harvard College has no voice in Harvard College, but Statestreet votes it down on every ballot. Every thing will be permitted there which goes to adorn Boston Whiggism; is it geology,

Astronomy, Poetry, antiquities, art, rhetoric, but, that which it exists for,—to be a fountain of novelties out of heaven,—a Delphi uttering warning & ravishing oracles to elevate & lead mankind,—*that* it shall not be permitted to do or to think of. On the contrary every generosity of thought is *suspected*, & gets a bad name. And all the young men come out decrepit Bostonians; not a poet, not a prophet, not a daemon, but is gagged & stifled, or driven away. All that is sought in the instruction is drilling tutors, & not inspirers.

—

Aug. 16. I saw Dr. H. J. Bigelow's bird Mino, about the size of a cat-bird, black, with a yellow collar. His speech was articulate as a man's. "What's your name?" "How d'ye do?" "Go way," "Doctor Bigelow," "Mino," and a loud whistle, like a locomotive's, were his utterances.

παντα ρει. You think a farm & broad acres a solid property but its value is flowing like water. It requires as much watching as if you were decanting wine from a hogshead. Bent the farmer knows what to do with it, & decants wine; but a blunderhead Minns comes out of Cornhill & it all leaks away. So is it with houses as with ships. What say you to the permanent value of an estate invested in railroad stocks?

The secret of the charm which English castles & cathedrals have for us is in the conviction they impress that the art & the race that made these is utterly gone. 'Tis fine to tell us, that chemically diamond is identical with coal-cinder, if there is no science in the world that can re-form such a crystal; and I must respect the men who built Westminster Abbey, since they have left no posterity who can do the like.

Beatitudes of Intellect.

Am I not, one of these days, to write consecutively of the beatitude of intellect? It is too great for feeble souls, and they are overexcited. The wineglass shakes, & the wine is spilled. What then? The joy which will not let me sit in my chair, which brings me bolt upright to my feet, & sends me striding around my room, like a tiger in his cage, and I cannot have composure & concentration enough even to set down in

English words the thought which thrills me—is not that joy a certificate of the elevation? What if I never write a book or a line? For a moment, the eyes of my eyes were opened, the affirmative experience remains, & consoles through all suffering.

For art, for music, overthrilled
The wineglass shakes, the wine is spilled

Him art, him music overthrilled,
The wine glass shakes, the wine is spilled

—

What is the poetic interest of the lost Pleiad for so many minds? Each nun or hermit in the country-towns has heard, that there were once seven stars, & now the eye can count but six. (No matter about the fact; it is a numerous cluster, & more or fewer can be counted, as your eyes are better or worse.) But the legend is, as I have said, & each nun or hermit is struck with the circumstance & writes solitary verses about it. What is the charm of the incident? I think because it is to each a symbol of lost thoughts.

The pace of nature is so slow. Why not from strength to strength, from miracle to miracle, & not as now with this retardation, as if Nature had sprained her foot, & makes plenteous stopping at little stations.

The correct writer will have a wide effect, as if he had written a dictionary for his people.

The privilege of thought is that it dates from itself. Winckelmann dates from Pericles or Augustus or the Renaissance; Hallam from the Revival, or the Reformation; Coleridge from Shakspeare; but the intellect from itself. We like a person of will & of thought because there is nobody behind his chair. It is the year one, and the Emperor is here.

The right answer to Archimedes's "Δος που οτω," &c, is Who couldn't?

—

one wrong step.

On Wachusett, I sprained my foot. It was slow to heal, & I went to the doctors. Dr H. Bigelow said, "a splint, & absolute rest;" Dr Russell said, "rest yes; but a splint, no." Dr Bartlett said, "neither splint nor rest, but go & walk." Dr Russell said, "Pour water on the foot, but it must be warm." Dr Jackson said, "stand in a trout brook all day."

The philanthropies are all duns, & hated as duns. But art is worse.

When I sprained my foot I soon found it was all one as if I had sprained my head, if I must sit in my chair. Then I thought nature had sprained her foot; and that King Lear had never sprained his, or he would have thought there were worse evils than unkind daughters. When I see a man unhappy, I ask, has a sprained foot brought him to *this* pass?

Aug. 20

Home is a good place in August. We have plenty of sopsavines, & Moscow Transparents, & the sweet apple we call Early Bough (?). Our Early pears—(Madeleine) are past, but Bloodgoods are ripe & ripening. And apricot plums, (if we had more trees than the one survivor!) are mature.

All knowledge gives superiority, & it makes so little difference in what direction. 'Tis so wonderful to expound an Assyrian inscription! but 'tis not less to know a Greek or German word that I do not know; or to see through a galvanic battery, or a chemical combining, or a binomial theorem, which I see not at all.

Dread the collectors. Whether of books, of shells, of coins, of eggs, of newspapers, they become alike trustless. Their hunger overrides their honesty. A *forte* always makes a foible.

Remember Norton's story of the gentleman who passed the antique coin which he believed to be an unique around his dinner-table, & lost it. One guest alone refused to be searched, and, after it was found on the floor, excused his refusal by announcing that he had a duplicate of the coin at that moment in his pocket.

—

The tired traveller who sees the Atlantic covers, says Well here comes the Autocrat to bring me one half hour's absolute relief from the vacant mind. And to Perception wherever it appears I hail the inextinguishable mystery with joy. Who is Wendell Holmes? if it shines through him, it is not his, it belongs to all of us, & we hail it as our own.

I find Haydon's Autobiography one of the best books. He admired Boswell's Johnson, & his book is precious like that. His estimate of himself & his sanguine folly of hoping important results from every compliment or polite look with which any of his great men smoothed their leave-taking, reminds me of Alcott's Journals fifty times. How weak & how strong these English are!

—

Mr Crump Aug., Sept., 1859.

The unfortunate days of August & September, when the two cows were due from the Temple Pasture, & did not arrive, & we learn that they strayed on the way, & are lost. When the Muster approached bringing alarms to all housekeepers & orchard-owners. When the foot was lame, & the hand was palsied, & the foot mending was lame again. When a strong southwest wind blew in vicious gusts, all day, stripping every loaded pear-tree of its fruit, just six weeks too early. The beggars arrive every day, some on foot, the Sardinians & Sicilians, who cannot argue the question of labor & mendicity with you, since they do not speak a word of English; then the Monumentals, who come in landaus or barouches, & wish your large aid to Mt Vernon; Plymouth; Ball's Webster; or President Quincy in marble; then the chipping lady from the Cape who has three blind sisters, & I know not how many dumb ones, & she had been advised to put them in the Poor House. No, not she. As long as she had health, she would go about & sell these books for them, which I am to buy, and she tosses her head, & expects my praise & tears for her heroic resolution; though I had a puzzled feeling, that, if there was sacrifice anywhere it was in me, if I should buy them; & I am sure I was very little inclined to toss my head on the occasion.

Mr Crump remarked that he hated lame folks: there was no telling how hypocritical they were. They are dreadful lame when you see them, but the lamest of them, if he wants something, & there's nobody will help him to it, will manage to get it himself, though it were a mile off; *if you are not by.*

But the fortnight of vexations is not over. I receive a letter, last night, to tell me that Phillips & Sampson will fail in a week.

—

Mrs Thrale quoted with pleasure Garrick's line "I'd smile with the simple, & feed with the poor." Johnson said, "what folly! who would feed with the poor that could help it? No, no, let me smile with the wise, & feed with the rich."

The inconceivable frivolity of people, a ribband, a cigar, rum, a muster, it makes no difference what the bawble is, they are drunk with delight if they have it, they are peevish if they want it.

Johnson said of a Jamaica gentleman then lately dead, "He will not, whither he is now gone, find much difference either in the climate or the company." Piozzi

N. tried to look as much like a piece of meat as she could.

Mr W. W. said to me "All genial men are insincere."

Mrs Piozzi says of Johnson "and whatever work he did, seemed so much below his powers of performance, that he appeared the idlest of all human beings."

—

Old age is comely enough in the country, but if you look at the faces of the people in Broadway, there is depression or indignation in the old ones,—a determination not to mind it,—a sense of injury. Old age is not disgraceful, but immensely disadvantageous.

The newspaper says, that Dr Burnap was in the prime of life, being in his 57th year.

—

We live, late in life, by memory, and in our solstices, or periods of stagnation, we live on our memories; as the starved camel lives on his humps.

—

Aristotle said, that there was the same difference between one learned & unlearned as between the living & the dead. Boswell p 433

M.M.E.

Dr Johnson is a good example of the force of temperament. 'Tis surprising how often I am reminded of my Aunt Mary E. in reading Boswell lately. Johnson impresses his company as she does, not only by the point of the remark, but also when the point fails, because he makes it. Like hers, his obvious religion or superstition, his deep wish that they should think so or so, weighs with them, so rare is depth of feeling, or a constitutional value for a thought or opinion, among the lightminded men & women who make up society. And this, though in both cases, their companions know that there is a degree of shortcoming, & of insincerity, & of talking for victory.—Yet the existence of character and habitual reverence of principles over talent or learning is felt by the frivolous.

—

Ellen Hooper's passionate inquiry twenty years ago was, What is the place & use of common people? or I suppose what Tennyson also meant by "Reflections of a sensitive second class mind."

Let this Question take the first page in the new Edition of "Notes & Queries."

The physicians wisely say, that fevers are self-limiting; so are all diseases, sprains, & headaches, & passions; and all errors, like Jupiter's moons, periodical.

The resistance to slavery,—it is the old mistake of the slaveholder to impute the resistance to Clarkson or Pitt, to Channing or Garrison, or to some John Brown whom he has just captured, & to make a personal affair of it; & he believes, whilst he chains & chops him,—that he is getting rid of his tormentors; and does not see that the air which this man breathed is liberty, & is breathed by thousands & millions; that men of the same complexion as he, will look at slave-holders as felons who have disentitled themselves to the protection of law, as the burglar has, whom I see breaking into my neighbor's house; and therefore no matter how many Browns he can catch & kill, he does not make the number less, for the air breeds them, every school, every church, every domestic circle, every home of courtesy, genius, & conscience is educating haters of him & his misdeeds.

—

Anna Ward was at a loss in talking with me, because I had no church whose weakness she could show up, in return for my charges upon hers. I said to her, Do you not see that though I have no eloquence & no flow of thought, yet that I do not stoop to accept any thing less than truth? that I sit here contented with my poverty, mendicity, & deaf & dumb estate, from year to year, from youth to age, rather than adorn myself with any red rag of false church or false association? My low & lonely sitting here by the wayside, is my homage to truth, which, I see is sufficient without me; which is honored by my abstaining, not by superserviceableness. I see how grand & selfsufficing it is; how it burns up, & will none of your shifty patchwork of additions & ingenuities.

You can always see in the eyes of your companion whether your argument hits him.

High courage, or a perfect will superior to all events, makes a bond of union between two enemies. Inasmuch as Gov. Wise is a superior man, he distinguishes John Brown. As they confer, they understand each other swiftly, each respects the other; if opportunity allowed, they would prefer each other's society, & desert the rest; enemies would become affectionate. Rivals & enemies, Hector & Achilles, Wellington & Soult, become aware that they are nearer & liker than any other two, &, if their nation & circumstance did not keep them apart, would fly into each other's arms.

See too what contagion belongs to it. It finds its own with magnetic affinity, all over the land. Heroic women offer themselves as nurses to the brave veteran. Florence Nightingale brings lint, & the blessing of her shadow. The troop of infantry that cut him down ask leave to pay their respects to the prisoner; Poetry & Eloquence catch the hint. Everything feels the new breath, excepting the dead old doting politicians, whom the trumpet of resurrection cannot waken.

—

Brown shows us, said H.D.T, another school to send our boys to,—that the best lesson of oratory is to speak the truth. A lesson rarely learned—To stand by the truth. We stand by our party, our trade, our reputation, our talent, but these each lead away from the truth. That is so volatile & vital, evanescing instantly from all but dedication to it.
And yet inspiration is that, to be so quick as truth; to drop the load of Memory & of Futurity, Memory & Care, & let the moment suffice us: then one discovers that the first thought is related to all thought & carries power & fate in its womb.

Mattie Griffith says, if Brown is hung, the gallows will be sacred as the cross.

—

Ideas make real societies and states. My countryman is surely not James Buchanan, nor Caleb Cushing, nor Barnum, nor Governor Gardner, nor Mrs Gardner the poisoner, nor Lot Poole, nor Fernando Wood; but Thoreau & Alcott & Sumner & whoever lives in the same love & worship as I; every just person, every man or woman who knows what truth means.

It will always be so. Every principle is a war-note. Who ever attempts to carry out the rule of right & love & freedom must take his life in his hand.

> "Varius Sucronensis ait, Aemilius Scauras negat; Utri creditis Quirites" *Val Max* iii, 7.

Queenie's private earthquake. We had disputed about the duration of the vibrations, which I thought lasted 12 seconds, and she insisted returned at intervals of two minutes. Of course our accounts could not agree; but, yesterday, it chanced to turn out, that her earthquake was *in the afternoon*, & that of the rest of the world at 6 in the morning.

1860. Earthquake 17 Oct. at 6 a.m.

Pierre d'Auvergne, troubadour of 12th century, sings

"I will sing a new song which resounds in my breast x x x Never was a song good or beautiful which resembled any other" *Fauriel II. 13*

"Since the air renews itself, & softens, So must my heart renew itself &, what buds in it, buds & grows outside of it."

"The nightingale glitters on the bough"

—

Intellect pure of action is skeptical. *Being*, & so *doing*, must blend, before the eye has health to behold through sympathy & through presence, the Spirit. Then all flows, & is known without words. Power even is not known to the pure. Power indicates weakness & opposition. Health exists & unfolds in the rose, in the sea, in the circular & endless astronomy. The electricity is not less present in my body & my joy, for twenty years, that I never saw or suspected it, than in the twenty first, when I drew by art a spark from my knuckle.

—

John Brown.
He drew this notice & distinction from the people among whom he fell from the fact that this boy of 12 had conducted his drove of cattle a hundred miles alone.

—

Culture
Books. The Indian who carried a letter from the French governor through the forest, hid it when he would eat, or do any unsightly office. Atahualpa caused a Spaniard to write "Dio"

on his thumbnail, & when Pizarro could not read it, despised him. What a wonder we make of Cadmus, or of whatever inventor of letters: And what an ado about the invention of printing: This month again on Franklin's birthday!
Then what a debt is ours to books. How much we owe to imaginative books! the boy has no better friend or influence than his Scott, Shakspeare, Plutarch, & Homer. And if, in Arkansaw or Texas, I should meet a man reading Horace, I were no stranger, & should forget the dreary land.
Yet there is a limit to this influence also. After reading Adam Smith or Linnaeus, I am no better mate for Mr Hosmer or Mr Potter.

And one book crowds out another, so that, after years of study, we are not wiser. Then books can't teach motherwit, sagacity, presence of mind, & humanity.

—

At Kalamazoo, I had a humpbacked driver who took me to Grand Rapids & back. His name is Church, & his father is a noted lawyer at Syracuse; but this dwarf prefers to be an ostler. He talks to his horses all the way & praises them. "Ha, ha; Jimmy, what are you looking after? ha, ha, ha, take care Jimmy!" st! st! John! "John takes it easy," he says, "but whenever he's called on, he's on hand, ha! ha!" He says, he slept for years in the same stall with the seed-horse, "Sir Henry," which killed its Dutch ostler, & was ironed, but Church took the irons off, & gave it a barrel of sugar.
Flora Temple trotted for a purse of 3000 dollars at Kalamazoo, & made the shortest time ever made in the Union, "Two minutes, nineteen seconds, *& a half*." "She flew." But, he thinks, the "Princess" which was beaten, the handsomer & the better horse.

—

'Tis trite enough, but now & then it is seen with explaining light, that nature is a mere mirror, & shows to each man only his own quality.

Illusions. Color is illusion, you say; but how know I that the rock & mountain are more real than its hue & gleam?

*

"Pardon me, but the moral impression (of Everett's Φ B K Oration) is nothing to Cicero's. Could he with sincerity but once, if only once, have raised his gifted voice to the Aegis of our salvation! He would then better resemble Burke, who descended from a higher sphere, when he would influence human affairs." M. M. E. 1825.

Then for Culture, can Solitude be spared? Solitude, the safeguard of mediocrity, is to genius the stern friend, the cold obscure shelter where moult the eagle wings which will bear one farther than suns & stars. Byron & Wordsworth there burnished their pens. Ah! that you could be disunited from travelling with the souls of other men,—of living, breathing, reading, & writing, with one livelong timefated yoke,—their opinions.

—

The costliest benefit of books is that they set us free from themselves also.

Classification a necessity of the human mind, and one of its main joys. It masters the mind, & makes rogues & thieves of learned men. A professor of theology at Berlin ? has just been convicted of stealing books from the Library of the University. All Collectors tend to this foible. W. S. Shaw, the founder of the Boston Athenaeum, used to steal from the private libraries of his friends any book he coveted to make his darling Athenaeum complete.
Collectors of shells steal orangias from Mr Grinnell's mantelpiece & Mrs Coffin's(?) house at Siasconset.
All autograph names of distinguished persons are cut out of the books of the Cambridge College Library.

May 1860
Mellish Motte told me, that the books stolen from the Boston Athenaeum are mostly from the *Theological department*, so that they are forced to lock that up, as they do the Fine-Arts alcoves. As an offset to this, Mr Jewett, the Librarian, assured me at the "*City Library*," that it was necessary to guard in securest manner the 100 vols of "Patent Reports" sent by the British Govt, for lawyers who had a case requiring

the use of one of these books, were utterly reckless, & would borrow & never return, or would cut out the plate or diagram they wanted.

Thoreau.

Agassiz says, "There are no varieties in nature. All are species." *Thoreau* says, "If A. sees two thrushes so alike that they bother the ornithologist to discriminate them, he insists they are two species; but if he see Humboldt & Fred. Cogswell, he insists that they come from one ancestor."

April 1860

Somebody said in my hearing lately, that a house in Concord was worth half as much again as a house in any other town, since the people had shown a good will to defend each other.

—

Cassius M. Clay gave Wendell Phillips his audience at New Haven, by closing his own agricultural address at 7½ & went himself to attend P's lecture at 7¾, and the whole audience with him. So Phillips opened his lecture with some compliment to him, & referred to the fact that Clay had said, that, in a fight between the negroes & the whites, his own part would be taken with the whites. The audience gave 3 cheers for Mr Clay. "Well," said Phillips, "This, then, we must reckon the rollcall on that side,—this distinguished leader and the white population in the slave states." The Audience instantly repeated their cheers. Phillips thought himself in a bad plight, but rescued himself by saying, "Well, gentlemen, now let us see the muster on the other side. Thomas Jefferson says, that, '*in this contest, the Almighty has no attribute but must take part with the slave.*' Mr Clay & the Southern gentlemen on one side, & all the attributes of the Almighty on the other." The audience were utterly silenced,—& Phillips proceeded with his speech.

—

Duc de Brancas said, "Why need I read the Encyclopédie? Rivarol visits me." I may well say it of Theodore Parker.

Theodore Parker has filled up all his years & days & hours. A son of the energy of New Engd: restless, eager, manly,

brave, early old, contumacious, clever. I can well praise him at a spectator's distance, for our minds & methods were unlike, —few people more unlike.
All the virtues are solidaires. Each man is related to persons who are not related to each other, and I saw with pleasure that men whom I could not approach were drawn through him to the admiration of that which I admire.

'Tis vain to charge him with perverting the opinions of the new generation. The opinions of men are organic. Simply, those came to him who found themselves expressed by him; and had they not found this enlightened mind in whom they found their own opinions combined with zeal in every cause of love & humanity, they would have suspected their opinions, & suppressed them; & so sunk into melancholy or malignity: a feeling of loneliness & hostility to what was reckoned respectable.

He was willing to perish in the using. He sacrificed the future to the present, was willing to spend & be spent, felt himself to belong to the day he lived in, & had too much to do than that he should be careful for fame.—
He used every day, hour, & minute; he lived to the latest moment, & his character appeared in the last moments with the same firm control as in the day of strength.

—

I am a matchmaker, & delight in nothing more than in finding the husband or mate of the trivial fact I have long carried in my memory, (unable to offer any reason for the emphasis I gave it,) until now, suddenly, it shows itself as the true symbol or expressor of some abstraction.

Advantages of old age.
I reached the other day the end of my fifty seventh year, and am easier in my mind than hitherto. I could never give much reality to evil & pain. But now when my wife says, perhaps this tumor on your shoulder is a cancer, I say, what if it is? It would not make the gentleman on his way in a cart to the gallows very unhappy, to tell him that the pain in his knee threatened a white swelling.

—

Plutarch, the elixir of Greece & Rome, that is the book which nations went to compose.—If the world's library were burning, I should as soon fly to rescue that, as Shakspeare & Plato, or next afterwards.

Clough says, "Plutarch's best life is Antony, I think."

—

11 Sept. 1860

Fine walk yesterday with Ellery to Estabrook Farm. Finest day in the year, & best road, almost all the way "through the lots." Birds singing;—got over their summer silence—sunlight full of gnats; crickets in full cry; goldfinches (carduelis) on the thistle eating the seed, scattering the awns. Boulder field: cooper's hawk: rock of Sinai, all books & tables of law, wonderful hedges, barberry, apple, elder, viburnum, ivy, cornel, woodbine, grape, white thorn, the brook through the wood—. Benzoin. The big birch. Largeness of the estate.
Nobody can buy. Came out at Capt Barrett's & through the fields again out at Flint's. A cornucopia of golden joys. E. says, that he & H. T have agreed that the only reason of turning out of the mowing, is, not to hurt the feelings of the farmers; but it never does, if they are out of sight. For the farmers have no imagination. And it doesn't do a bit of hurt. Thoreau says, that, when he goes surveying, the farmer leads him straight through the grass.

'Tis strange. The bluebirds' song brings back vividly the cold spring days when we first hear them; those days were so sour & unlovely, & now seem so sweet!

There is one trap into which the most cautious avoider of North Street and Broadway may fall. How unsuspectingly a quiet conservative assembly allows a man to speak to them! They would have called in the police, if he had come in with a club, but, the moment he opens his mouth, he begins to unseat them, bereave them of their property, their position, their reasons, their self-respect, to take them out of their possession, & into his, & if he is the man I take him for, they will not soon be their own men again.
They manage things better in the South which is quite right in

sticking to its gag-laws.— The poor gentlemen go out of the meeting, when this outlaw ends his speech, &, rallying to recover their disturbed associations, they fancy that all is as it was when they came; that, if they suspected a kind of threat & thunder in this strange harangue, probably the odd things dropped by the speaker were not noticed or understood by most people, & will be forgotten tomorrow. At all events, themselves will forget them as fast as they can, & Faneuil-Hall-Market, and the Brokers' Exchange, and the Banks, stand where they did, & will help to blot out these impertinences very soon. Never believe it. Younger people & stronger than they, heard them also; and, above all, the speaker was very well convinced himself, and is already today taking more outrageous positions; and the speech of men & women, & the fingers of the Press, are doing their utmost to give his words currency & experiment.

Eloquence is forever a power that shoves usurpers from their thrones, & sits down on them by allowance & acclaim of all.

The feat of the Imagination is in showing the convertibility of every thing into every other thing. Facts which had never before left their stark common sense, suddenly figure as Eleusinian mysteries. It is as if my boots & chair & candlestick are found out to be fairies in disguise, are meteors & constellations. All the facts in nature are nouns of the intellect, & signify what befalls in the eternal world. Every word has a double, treble, or centuple use & meaning. I cry you mercy, good shoebox! I did not know you were a jewel-case.
Rubbish & dust sparkle with elemental energies & the laborer at my sawhorse is the Lord of Nature. Now when I go to the Pyramid or to Fountain Abbey or to Stonehenge, I find the sentiment of ancient peoples, their delight in their gods, & in the future, their humanity, expressed in this patience of labor that staggered under the toil of hewing & lifting these grey rocks into scientific symmetry. That sentiment of their hope & love touch me, & our associations (which are most pliant & placable) persuade the eye to forget its mathematics & reconcile it to angles & distortions. The rainbow, the sky, Niagara, the rose, a tone of music, have in them something which is not

individual, but public & universal, & speak to me of that central benefit which is the soul of Nature, & thereby are beautiful. And, in men & women, I find somewhat in manners, in form, in speech, which is not of their person or family, but is of a public & human character, but is of a solar & supersolar greatness, and I love them as the sky. Alcott yonder never learned in Connecticut or in Boston what he sees & declares to me, & his face & manners are sublime at times. The wonder of men is that the reason of things comes to my side moulded into a person like myself & full of universal relations.

This power of imagination, the making some familiar object as fire, or rain, or a bucket, or shovel, do new duty as an exponent of some truth or general law, bewitches & delights men; it is a taking of dead sticks & clothing about with immortality, it is music out of creaking & scouring.

All opake things are transparent, and the light of heaven struggles through.

Oct. 9. Henry James thinks the upper powers don't care so much for talent now as once. It was once the great point to civilize & lead by these gods of the mind. Now they are putting the material activities right, to sustain & order the masses of life.—Perhaps the Fourierists have had a reaction upward. *Chacun a son tour.*

He talked well about Louis Napoleon, who is absolute master of all the crowned heads, because he has the revolution in his hand, & can at any time cry *Histaboy*! to the dogs, & pull them all down. And he knows that England is necessary to him, & has no thought of breaking with it, but likes the prestige which these great crybabies in England by their terror give him with the French & with Europe.

Then of Science: Mansel's Limits of Knowledge. The blunder of the savans is to fancy science to be a finality; that it contains & is not contained; but a scientific fact is no more than the scratching of a nail if it stops. All the life of it is in its relatedness, its implication of the All.

Only the poetic savant is right, for it is not as a finality, but as a convertibility into every other fact & system, & so indicative of First Cause, that the mind cares for it.

The games of Greece were in the interest & honor of manhood. They called out every personal virtue & talent. Ho! everyone who can wrestle, run, lift, ride, fight, sing, narrate, or so much as look well!

Imagination transfigures, so that only the cosmical relations of the object are seen.

The persons who rise to beauty must have this transcendency.

The calm sky hides all wisdom & power in Beauty.

That haughty force of form, *vis superba formae*, which poets praise,—this is that: Under calm precise outline, the immeasureable & divine.

It is as if new eyes were opened so that we saw under the lilac bush or the oak or the rock or the tiger, the spiritual cause of the lilac, oak, stone, or tiger, the genius of that kind, & so could rightly & securely use the name for the truth it stood for in the human mind, & still again under this genius, its origin in a generic law, & thence its affinities to cosmical laws, & to myriads of particulars, & then again deeper causes below & so on ad infinitum.

—

An old woman standing by the sea, said, "she was glad to see something that there was enough of."

1860

Nov. 15. The news of last Wednesday morning (7th) was sublime, the pronunciation of the masses of America against Slavery. And now on Tuesday 14th I attended the dedication of the Zoological Museum at Cambridge, an auspicious & happy event, most honorable to Agassiz & to the State. On Wednesday 7th, we had Charles Sumner here at Concord & my house. Yesterday eve I attended at the Lyceum in the Town Hall the Exhibition of Stereoscopic views magnified on the wall, which seems to me the last & most important application of this wonderful art: for here was London, Paris, Switzerland, Spain,

&, at last, Egypt, brought visibly & accurately to Concord, for authentic examination by women & children, who had never left their state. Cornelius Agrippa was fairly outdone. And the lovely manner in which one picture was changed for another beat the faculty of dreaming. Edward thought that "the thanks of the town should be presented to Mr Munroe, for carrying us to Europe, & bringing us home, without expense." An odd incident of yesterday was that I received a letter or envelope mailed from Frazer, Pennsylvania enclosing no letter but a blank envelope containing a Ten dollar bank note.

from

DL

1860–1866

The mind in conversation is perpetually provoked to see how all things reflect or image her momentary thought.
Whenever this resemblance is real, not playful, & is deep, or pointing at the causal identity, it is the act of imagination: if superficial, & for entertainment, it is Fancy.

—

Beware of the minor key!

When Napoleon asked Laplace why there was no mention of God in the "Mécanique Celeste,"— "Sire, je n'avais pas besoin de cette hypothèse."

You perceive the theory?—
But the facts contradict it.—
So much the worse for the facts.

> "In 1837, the same Academy offered a prize of 3000 francs to any one who could read through a board. No one gained the prize" Buchner, "*Force & Matter*" p. 153

Thoreau's page reminds me of Farley, who went early into the wilderness in Illinois, lived alone, & hewed down trees, & tilled the land, but retired again into newer country when the population came up with him. Yet, on being asked, what he was doing? said, he pleased himself that he was preparing the land for civilization.

—

"Hell itself may be contained within the compass of a spark."
Thoreau.

*

Use the low style. Build low. Mr. Downer said the "snuggeries" in Dorchester kept their tenants; the airy houses on the hills soon lost them.

I have heard that Col. Wainwright, (was it, or what gay gentleman?) took Allston out to ride one day; Allston painted out of that ride three pictures.

Faraday's subjects were, a tea-kettle, a chimney, a fire, soot, ashes, &c.

—

It is impossible to extricate oneself from the questions in which our age is involved. You can no more keep out of politics than out of the frost.

—

Elliott Cabot's paper on "Art" has given emphasis to one point among others, that people only see what they are prepared to see. Thus who sees birds, except the hunter? or the ornithologist? How difficult it is to me to see certain particulars in the dress of people with whom I sit for hours, and after I had wished to know what sort of waistcoat, or coat, or shirt-collar, or neckcloth they wore.
I have gone to many dinners & parties with instructions from home & with my own wish to see the dress of the *men*, & can never remember to look for it.

Who teaches manners of majesty, of frankness, of grace, of humility? who but the adoring aunts & cousins that surround a young child? The babe meets such courting & flattery as only kings receive when adult, &, trying experiments every day, & at perfect leisure with these posture masters & flatterers, all day,—he throws himself into all the attitudes that correspond to theirs: are they humble? he is composed; are they eager? he is nonchalant; are they encroaching? he is dignified & inexorable.—And this in humble as well as high houses; that is my point.

—

Thoreau's Letter.

"Do you read any noble verses? For my part, they have been the only things I remembered, or that which occasioned them, when all things else were blurred and defaced. All things have put on mourning but they; for the elegy itself is some victorious melody in you escaping from the wreck. It is a relief to read some true books, wherein all are equally dead, equally alive. I think the best parts of Shakspeare would only be enhanced by the most thrilling & affecting events. I have found it so. And so much the more, as they are not intended for consolation."

Letter to Mrs Brown from H.D. Thoreau.

—

Old Age. I told Richard Fuller that he would soon come to a more perfect obedience to his children, than he had ever been able to obtain from them.

M. Babinet informs us, that the problem of aerial navigation is on the point of being solved. I am looking, therefore, for an arrival of the remainder of the Prisoners of War from the Libby & Atlanta prisons, by the balloon, descending at some point in Pennsylvania by a night-voyage from the South.

—

Lowell told me, that, when Mrs Stowe was invited to dine with the Atlantic Club, she refused to drink wine, & it was banished for that day. But Lowell said, "Mrs Stowe, you took wine with the Duke of Argyle, when you visited him?" She acknowledged that she did. And now do you mean to treat us as if we were not as good as he? "No," she said. "Bring some Champagne," cried Lowell, & Mrs Stowe & the company drank. "And how did you know," I asked, "that she did take wine at the Duke's?"—"O, I divined that," he said, "Of course she did."

—

I suppose I must read Renan, *Vie de Jesus*, which I fancied was Frenchy. It is a pregnant text, & a key to the moral & intellectual pauses & inactivity of men,—"The creature is subject to Vanity." There is none almost who has not this misleading egotism. The efficient men are efficient by means of this Flanders horse. But it destroys them for grandeur of aim, & for highest conversation. They all gravitate to cities. God, the inward life, is not enough for them: they must have the million mirrors of other minds, must measure wit with others for mastery, and must have the crowns & rewards of wit that cities

give. Yet up & down in every nation, are scattered individual souls with the grace of humility. Geo. Fox, Behmen, Scougal, the Mahometan Saint Rabbia, and the Hindoos, have the art to cheapen the world thereby. So Ossian's "Cathmore dwelled in the wood to avoid the voice of praise." Jesus was grand where he stood, and let Rome & London dance after Nazareth. But the thinkers or litterateurs of humility are not humble. Thus Alcott, Thoreau, & I, know the use & superiority of it, but I can't praise our practice.
Every saint as every man comes one day to be superfluous.

Who can doubt the potences of an individual mind, who sees the shock given to torpid races, torpid for ages, by Mahomet, a vibration propagated over Asia & Africa, & not yet exhausted. What then of Menu? What of Buddh?

The single word *Madame* in French poetry, makes it instantly prose.

Scholar

Montaigne had rather take Europe into his confidence than to tell so much to a French lord; as one may move aukwardly in a parlor, who walks well enough in a crowd. I heard Bandmann read Hamlet's soliloquy, the other day, at Bartol's. In conversation, he was polite & expansive enough, but plainly enjoyed the new expansion that the reading gave him. He stood up, & by musing distanced himself, then silences all the company, & gets out of doors, as it were, by a cheerful cry of a verse or two, & acquires a right to be the hero, & abounds in his own sense, & puts it despotically upon us, in look, manner, & elocution. He brought out the broad meaning of the soliloquy truly enough, but, as all actors will, with an *overmuch*, with emphasis & mouthing. They cannot let well alone: but must have the merit of all the refinements & second senses they have found or devised, & so drive it too finely. It is essential to reach this freedom, or gay self-possession, but temperance is essential too.

H.D.T. wrote in 1840, "a good book will not be dropped by its author, but thrown up. It will be so long a promise that he will not overtake it soon. He will have slipped the leash of a fleet hound."

—

I wrote to Arnold, & should have said; I have heard that the engineers in the locomotives grow nervously vigilant with every year on the road, until the employment is intolerable to them; and, I think, writing is more & more a terror to old scribes.

Of Wordsworth Blake writes; "This is all in the highest degree imaginative, & equal to any poet, but not superior; I cannot think that real poets have any competition. None are greatest in the kingdom of heaven. It is so in poetry."

—

I find no mention of tobacco in Shakspeare, neither pipes nor snuff, which, one would have said the dates permitted. 'Tis a remarkable case, like Goethe's chronologic relation to steam locomotives.

—

One of Agassiz's introductory speeches was; "Many years ago, when I was a young man, I was introduced to a very estimable lady in Paris, who, in the conversation said to me, that she wondered how a man of sense could spend his days in dissecting a fish. I relied, 'Madam, if I could live by a brook which had plenty of gudgeons, I should ask nothing better than to spend all my life there.' But, since I have been in this country, I have become acquainted with a club, in which I meet men of various talents; one man of profound scholarship in the languages; one of elegant literature; or a high mystic poet; or one man of large experience in the conduct of affairs; one who teaches the blind to see, and, I confess, that I have enlarged my views of life; & I think, that, besides a brook full of gudgeons, I should wish to meet once a month such a society of friends."

—

When I read Shakspeare, as lately, I think the criticism & study of him to be in their infancy. The wonder grows of his long obscurity;—how could you hide the only man that ever wrote, from all men who delight in reading?—then, the courage with which, in each play, he accosts the main issue, the highest problem, never dodging the difficult or impossible, but addressing himself instantly to that,—so conscious of his secret competence; and, at once, like an aeronaut fills his balloon with a whole atmosphere of hydrogen that will carry him over Andes, if Andes be in his path.

—

Shakspeare puts us all out. No theory will account for him. He neglected his works. Perchance he did not know their value? Aye, but he did; witness the sonnets.

He went into company as a listener, hiding himself, ὁ δ᾽ ἤιε νυκτι εοικως. Was only remembered by all as a delightful companion. Alcott thinks "he was rhetorician, but did not propound new thoughts."—aye, he was rhetorician, as was never one before, but also had more thoughts than ever any had.

Say first, the greatest master of language, who could say the thing finer, nearer to the purity of thought itself, than any other and with the security of children playing, who talk without knowing it. [and, to this point, what can Carlyle mean by saying what he does of Voltaire's superiority to all men in speech.

Life of Frederic IV. p. 382]

I admire his wealth. I watch him when he begins a play, to see what simple & directest means he uses; never consulting his ease, never, in the way of common artists, putting us off with ceremonies or declamations; but, at once addressing himself to the noblest solution of the problem, having the gods, & the course of human life in view.

The wonder of his obscurity in his life-time is to be explained by the egotism of literary men. To me the obscurity of Alcott is a like wonder.

Pub. & Priv. Education

Shakspeare should be the study of the University. In Florence Boccacio was appointed to lecture on Dante. But in English Oxford, or in Harvard College, I have never heard of a Shakspeare Professorship. Yet the students should be educated not only in the intelligence of but in the sympathy with the thought of great poets.

The *Sonnets* intimate the old Aristotelian Culture, & a poetic Culture that we do not easily understand whence it came,—smacks of the Middle Ages, & Parliaments of love & poesy, (and I should say, that the string of poems prefixed to Ben Jonson's or Beaumont & Fletcher's plays, by their friends, are more seriously-thought than the pieces which would now in England or America be contributed to any call of literary friendship.) And yet if Whittier, Holmes, Lowell, Channing, Thoreau, Bryant, Sanborn, Wasson, Julia Howe, had each made their thoughtful contribution, there might be good reading.

I must say that in reading the plays, I am a little shy where I begin; for the interest of the story is sadly in the way of poetry. It is safer therefore to read the play backwards.

To know the beauty of Shakspeare's level tone, one should read a few passages of what passes for good tragedy in other writers, & then try the opening of "Merchant of Venice," Antonio's first speech—

I am inquisitive of all possible knowledge concerning Shakspeare, & of all opinions: yet how few valuable criticisms, how few opinions I treasure!—How few besides my own! And each thoughtful reader, doubtless, has the like experience.

—

The Cannon will not suffer any other sound to be heard for miles & for years around it. Our chronology has lost all old distinctions in one date,—*Before the War, and Since.*

—

It is, I own, difficult not to be intemperate in speaking of Shakspeare; and most difficult, I should say, to the best readers. Few, I think none, arrive at any intelligence of his methods. His intellect does not emit jets of light, at intervals, but is incessant, always equal to the occasion, & addressing with equal readiness a comic, an ingenious, or a sublime problem. I find him an exceptional genius. If the world were on trial, it is the perfect success of this one man that might justify such expenditure of geology, chemistry, fauna, & flora, as the world was. And, I suppose, if Intellect perceives & converses "in climes beyond the solar road," they probably call this planet, not Earth, but "*Shakspeare.*" In teleology, they will come to say, that the final cause of the creation of the Earth was Shakspeare,

—

Yesterday, 23 May, we buried Hawthorne in Sleepy Hollow, in a pomp of sunshine & verdure, & gentle winds. James F. Clarke read the service in the Church & at the grave. Longfellow, Lowell, Holmes, Agassiz, Hoar, Dwight, Whipple, Norton, Alcott, Hillard, Fields, Judge Thomas, & I, attended the hearse as pall bearers. Franklin Pierce was with the family. The church was copiously decorated with white flowers delicately arranged. The corpse was unwillingly shown,—only a few moments to this company of his friends. But it was noble & serene in its aspect,—nothing amiss,—a calm & powerful head. A large company filled the church, & the grounds of the cemetery. All was so bright & quiet, that pain or mourning was hardly suggested, & Holmes said to me, that it looked like a happy meeting.

Clarke in the church said, that, Hawthorne had done more justice than any other to the shades of life, shown a sympathy with the crime in our nature, &, like Jesus, was the friend of sinners.

I thought there was a tragic element in the event, that might be more fully rendered,—in the painful solitude of the man,—which, I suppose, could not longer be endured, & he died of it.

I have found in his death a surprise & disappointment. I thought him a greater man than any of his works betray, that there was still a great deal of work in him, & that he might one day show a purer power.

Moreover I have felt sure of him in his neighborhood, & in his necessities of sympathy & intelligence,—that I could well wait his time,—his unwillingness & caprice,—and might one day conquer a friendship. It would have been a happiness, doubtless to both of us, to have come into habits of unreserved intercourse. It was easy to talk with him,—there were no barriers;—only, he said so little, that I talked too much, & stopped only because,—as he gave no indications,—I feared to exceed. He showed no egotism or self-assertion, rather a humility, &, at one time, a fear that he had written himself out.—One day, when I found him on the top of his hill, in the

woods, he paced back the path to his house, & said, "*this path is the only remembrance of me that will remain.*" Now it appears that I waited too long.
Lately, he had removed himself the more by the indignation his perverse politics & unfortunate friendship for that paltry Franklin Pierce awaked,—though it rather moved pity for Hawthorne, & the assured belief that he would outlive it, & come right at last.

I have forgotten in what year, (Sept. 27, 1842,), but it was whilst he lived in the Manse, soon after his marriage, that I said to him, "I shall never see you in this hazardous way; we must take a long walk together. Will you go to Harvard & visit the Shakers?" He agreed, & we took a June day, & walked the twelve miles, got our dinner from the Brethren, slept at the Harvard Inn, & returned home by another road the next day. It was a satisfactory tramp; we had good talk on the way, of which I set down some record in my journal.

"The Nineteenth Century is an Age of progress, & every one soon will be in his right place." *London "Reader."* 14 May, 1864

Reginald Taylor, a child of six years, was carried to see his mother's kinsman, President Day. On his return home, he said, "Mother, I think that old man loves God too much. You know I say my prayers when I go to bed: well he talks just so all the time."

It is said, that, in the Western courts, it is a rule, that, "a town is a place where they sell whisky."

—

We see the dawn of a new era, worth to mankind all the treasure & all the lives it has cost, yes, worth to the world the lives of all this generation of American men, if they had been demanded.

It is commonly said of the War of 1812, that it made the nation honorably known: it enlarged our politics, extinguished narrow sectional parties.

*

But the States were young & unpeopled. The present war, on a prodigiously enlarged scale, has cost us how many valuable lives; but it has made many lives valuable that were not so before, through the start & expansion it has given. It has fired selfish old men to an incredible liberality, & young men to the last devotion. The journals say, it has demoralized many rebel regiments, but also it has *moralized* many of our regiments, & not only so, but *moralized* cities & states. It added to every house & heart a vast enlargement. In every house & shop, an American map has been unrolled, & daily studied,—& now that peace has come, every citizen finds himself a skilled student of the condition, means, & future, of this continent.

—

Our success sure; its roots in poverty, Calvinism, schools, farms, thrift, snow, & east wind.

The war has made the Divine Providence credible to a good many people. They did not believe that Heaven was quite honest.

I think it a singular & marked result, that it has established a conviction in so many minds that the right will get done; has established a chronic hope for a chronic despair.

This victory the most decisive. This will stay put. It will show your enemies that what has now been so well done will be surely better & quicker done, if need be, again.

—

When I ask Ellen if she has made out what "the leopard," what "the wolf," and what "Lucia," in the "*Inferno*," signify? she says "No, & I do not wish to: To me they mean leopard, wolf, & Lucia, & any second & interior meaning would spoil all for me."

—

Therienism.

Enfant du peuple. That fair, large, sound, wholesome youth or maid whom we pick out in a whole street full of passengers as a model of native strength, is not to be raised by rule in schools or gymnasia. It is the Vermont or New Hampshire farm, & a series of farmers laboring on mountain & moor, that produced this rare result. When a good head for ciphering, trade, & affairs is turned out, he drifts to the city counting-room, or perhaps to the law-school, & brings thither a constitution able to supply resources to all the demand made on him, & easily goes ahead of all competitors, has a firm will, cool head, &, in the sequel, plants a family which becomes marked through two or three generations for force & beauty, until luxury corrupts them, as it had destroyed those whom they displaced.

—

1865
Augt. 13th. A disaster of this year has been the loss of six or seven valuable pear trees by the pear-blight. I think, in preceding years, single boughs have withered & died, but these have not attracted much notice; but now I cut off half of each tree with its coppery leaves & the mournful smell of the sick bark, & shall not save them so.

The difference between writers is that one counts forms, & the other counts powers. The gazetteer, in describing Boston, reckons up the schools, the churches, & the Missionary Societies; but the poet remembers the alcoves of the Athenaeum, or the Bates Library, certain wise & mannered men, certain fair women, & the happy homes in which he saw them. The friend,—he is the power that abode with us: & the book, which made night better than day,—that may be well counted.

Read some sentences yesterday in Macmillan for August (?) (in an article on Grote's Book on Plato,) which I must read again;—a paper by Baine, but of no great merit. Looked thro' a superior article in the Quarterly Review on Carlyle's Friedrich,—a good example of the excellent criticism which in England is always to be found, whilst poetry is so rare.

Then in the Revue des D. M. found a paper on the Future Life, which suggested the thought, that one abstains,—I abstain, for example,—from printing a chapter on the Immortality of the Soul, because, when I have come to the end of my statement, the hungry eyes that run through it will close disappointed; *That is not here which we desire:* & I shall be as much wronged by their hasty conclusion, as they feel themselves by my omissions. I mean, that I am a better believer, & all serious souls are better believers in the Immortality, than we give grounds for. The real evidence is too subtle, or is higher, than we can write down in propositions, & therefore Wordsworth's Ode is the best modern Essay on the subject.

—

It is curious to see how fast old history is the counterpart of our own, as soon as we are intimately let into knowledge of it. Thus I am just now surprised by finding Michel Angelo, Vittoria Colonna, Savonarola, Contarini, Pole, Occhino, & the superior souls near them to be the religious of that day, drawn to each other, & under some cloud with the rest of the world, as the Transcendentalists of 20 years ago in Boston. They were the reformers, the Abolitionists, the radicals of the hour, separated, to be sure, by their intellectual activity & culture, from the masses who followed Luther & Savonarola, yet on their side in sympathy against the corruptions of Rome.

—

In how many people we feel the tyranny of their talent as the disposer of their activity.
In Wendell Phillips, now the "seul homme d'état in America," I feel that his patriotism or his moral sentiment are not primarily the inspiration of his career, but this matchless talent of debate, of attack, of illustration, of statement,—this talent which was in him, & must be unfolded, that drove him, in happy hours, under most fortunately determining auspices, into the lists, where kings were to be competitors, & nations spectators.

Our best allies, from the beginning of the war until now, are still the Southerners! Our foolish good nature & facility cannot ruin us utterly, before these people will contrive some outrage that will exasperate even us into resolution again. We may well say *not unto us*, and yet it would be odd to say, not unto the Lord, but unto the Devil in the Southerner, be the praise!—

The conduct of intellect must respect nothing so much as preserving the sensibility. That mind is best which is most impressionable. There are times when the cawing of crows, a flowering weed, a snowflake, a boy's willow whistle or a porter's wheelbarrow is more suggestive to the mind than the Yosemite Gorge or the Vatican would be in another hour. In like mood, an old verse, or particular words gleam with rare significance. How to keep, how to recover at will this sensibility?

Manners.

There are things whose hour is always a little over or not quite come, as, for example, the rule that you shall not go out to dine too well-dressed: which means, that a certain slovenliness fits certain persons, but requires perfect aplomb, & clear sensible manners & conversation. Cold scholars cannot afford these liberties.

—

Mr B. P. Hunt said, that a young man of good position in Philadelphia went to the war, & accepted the colonelcy of a colored regiment. On his return lately to Phila., all his acquaintances cut him. Judge H. said to me, that he had long ago made up his mind that the cutting was to be from the other side: that this country belonged to the men of the most liberal persuasion.
This world belongs to the energetical.

—

Now in the time of the Fugitive Slave-law, when the best young men who had ranged themselves around Mr Webster were already all of them in the interest of freedom, & threw themselves at once into opposition, Mr Webster could no longer see one of them in the street; he glared on them but knew them not; his resentments were implacable. What did they do? Did they sit down & bewail themselves? No; Sumner & his valiant young contemporaries set themselves to the task of making their views not only clear but prevailing. They proclaimed & defended them & inoculated with them the whole population, & drove Mr Webster out of the world. All his mighty genius, which none had been so forward to acknowledge & magnify as they, availed him nothing: for they knew that the spirit of God & of humanity was with them, and he withered & died as by suicide. Calhoun had already gone, as Webster, by breaking his own head against the nature of things.

—

November 5, 1865

We hoped that in the Peace, after such a war, a great expansion would follow in the mind of the country: grand views in every direction,—true freedom in politics, in religion, in social science, in thought. But the energy of the nation seems to have expended itself in the war, and every interest is found as sectional & timorous as before. The Episcopal church is baser than ever,—perfect Yahoo; the Southerner just the same Gambia negro chief,—addicted to crowing, garotting, & stealing, as ever: the Democrat as false & truckling; the Union party as timid & compromising, the scholars pale & expectant, never affirmative;
only Phillips & Frank Bird, only Wilson & Sumner unreconciled, aggressive, & patriotic still.

Apropos to what I wrote of French Bohemians, I read in my Publishers' Circular's French correspondent (Oct. 16, 1865) "How short-lived is the last generation of literary men & artists here!" The Lamartines, Hugos, Saint Beuves, are young as ever, but their juniors poisoned by nicotine, absinthe, & reckless licentiousness, are all dead.

Nov. 14. Williamstown. I saw tonight in the Observatory, through Alvan Clark's telescope, the Dumb-Bell nebula in the Fox & Goose constellation;
the four double stars in Lyra;
the double stars of Castor;
the 200 stars of the Pleiades;
the nebula in (Perseus?)

Mr Button, Professor Hopkins's assistant, was our starshowman & J. H. Stanbrough & Hutton, who have been my Committee of the "Adelphic Union", inviting me here, carried me thither. I have rarely been so much gratified.

Early in the afternoon Prof. Bascom carried me in a gig to the top of the West Mountain, & showed me the admirable view down the Valley in which this town & Adams lie, with Greylock & his attendant ranges towering in front: then we rose to the crest, & looked down into Rensellaer County, New York,

& the multitude of low hills that compose it. This was the noted Anti-rent country, & beyond, in the horizon, the mountain range to the West.

Of all tools, an observatory is the most sublime. And these mountains give an inestimable worth to Williamstown & Massachusetts. But for the mountains, I don't quite like the proximity of a college & its noisy students. To enjoy the hills as poet, I prefer simple farmers as neighbors.

The dim lanthorn which the astronomer used at first to find his object-glasses, &c. seemed to disturb & hinder him, preventing his seeing his heavens, &, though it was turned down lower & lower, he was still impatient, & could not see until it was put out. When it had long been gone, and I had looked through the telescope a few times, the little garret at last grew positively lightsome, & the lamp would have been annoying to all of us. What is so good in a college as an observatory? The sublime attaches to the door & to the first stair you ascend, that this is the road to the stars. Every fixture & instrument in the building, every nail & pin has a direct reference to the Milky-Way, the fixed stars, & the nebulae. & we leave Massachusetts & the Americas & history outside at the door, when we came in.

Dec. 10, Doctor Jackson shone in the talk on Thanksgiving Day, explaining many things so successfully,—the possibility of the balloon by the aid of gun-cotton (one of whose principal merits, he asserted, was, that it does not foul the barrel or engine as powder does), the Ocean Telegraph, which he thinks far less practicable, & certainly less desireable to us, than the Siberian. Then the fact that the patents of the telegraph companies do not really protect the monopoly, for what is patented they no longer use, as, the system of "marks on paper", of Morse's patent; for the telegraph is everywhere conducted without paper, being read by the ear. He thinks the U.S. Post Office should take possession of the Telegraph as part of the Postal Arrangement, pay a compensation to the Companies, & give its use to the people at a cent a word, & so save the immense transportation of letters, by this imponderable correspondence. He told the story of the Rumford medal voted to Ericson, by the American Academy, & the money voted to Roper & Co. for valuable improvements on Ericson; from which last he anticipates very great practical benefit, the Union or double-union engine.

—

I. T. Williams told me that the last time he saw Albert H. Tracy, he told him, that, when he & Cass were in Congress, they became very intimate, & spent their time in conversation on the Immortality of the soul, & other intellectual questions, & cared for little else. When he left Congress, they parted, &, though Mr Cass passed through Buffalo twice, he did not come near him, and he never saw him again until 25 years afterward, they saw each other through open doors at a distance, in a great party at the President's House, in Washington. Slowly they advanced towards each other as they could, & at last met, said nothing, but shook hands long & cordially. At last, Cass said, "Any light, Tracy?" "None," answered Tracy, and then said, "Any light, Cass?" "None," replied he. They looked in each others' eyes, gave one shake more each to the hand he held, & thus parted for the last time.

When I was a senior in College, I think,—Saml Barrett whom I had known in Concord was about to be ordained in the Chamber-street Church and I called upon him in his room in College.—I think he must have been a proctor. We talked about the vices & calamities of the time,—I don't recall what the grim shadows were, or how we came on them,—but when I rose to go, & asked him what was the relief & cure of all this? he replied with cheerful ardor, "Nothing but Unitarianism." From my remembrance of how this answer struck me, I am sure that this antidote must have looked as thin & poor & pale to me then, as now. I was never for a moment the victim of "Enlightenment," or "Progress of the Species" or the "Diffusion-of-Knowledge-Society."

Carlyle.

I have neglected badly Carlyle, who is so steadily good to me. Like a Catholic in Boston, he has put himself by his violent anti-Americanism in false position, & it is not quite easy to deal with him. But his merits are overpowering, & when I read "Friedrich," I forget all else. His treatment of his subject is ever so masterly, so original, so self-respecting, so defiant allowing himself all manner of liberties & confidences with his hero, as if he were his hero's father or benefactor, that he is proud of him, & yet checks & chides & sometimes puts him in the corner, when he is not a good boy, that, amid all his sneering & contempt for all other historians, & biographers, & princes, & peoples, the reader yet feels himself complimented by the confidences with which he is honored by this free-tongued, dangerous companion, who discloses to him all his secret opinions, all his variety of moods, & varying estimates of his hero & everybody else. He is as dangerous as a madman. Nobody knows what he will say next, or whom he will strike. Prudent people keep out of his way. If Genius were cheap, we should do without Carlyle; but, in the existing population, he cannot be spared.

The Tribune says of Winter Davis,—"with that power of continuous thought which is essential to every man who has to do with the affairs of the forum or the street."

January 5, 1866. I thought, last night, as so often before, that when one has a task before him in which literary work becomes *business*,—undertaken, that is, for money,—any hearing of poetry or any intellectual suggestion, (as e.g. out of J. H. Stirling's book lately,) brings instant penitence, and the thoughts revert to the Muse, and, under this high invitation, we think we will throw up our undertaking, & attempt once more this purer, loftier service. But if we obey this suggestion, the beaming goddess presently hides her face in clouds again. We have not learned the law of the mind, cannot control & bring at will or domesticate the high states of contemplation & continuous thought. "Neither by sea nor by land canst thou find the way to the Hyperboreans:"—Neither by idle wishing, nor by rule of three or of thumb. Yet I find a mitigation or solace of the alternative which I accept (of the paid lectures, for instance,) by providing always a good book for my journey, as, Horace, or Martial, or the "Secret of Hegel," some book which lifts quite out of prosaic surroundings, & from which you draw some lasting knowledge.

The Tribune says, "It is time, since the sale of women & children on the auction-block has been banished from our country, that the sale of legislators, whether by the lot or piece, should be banished from our State."

In the "Funeral" of Steele, Sable the undertaker reproaches the too cheerful mute, "Did I not give you ten, then fifteen & twenty shillings a week to be sorrowful? And the more I give you, I think the gladder you are."

—

The power of manners is a principal agent in human affairs. The rich & elegant & the strong-willed not so much talk down as look down & silence the well-disposed middle class. 'Tis fine that the scholar or the red republican defies these people, or writes against them: he cannot get them out of his thoughts. When he meets them in the street, he cannot deny them his bow; & when he meets them in clubs or in drawing-rooms, he prizes their attentions, & easily leaves his own set on any advances from theirs. In England Sir Robert Peel & Thackeray are only two out of manifold examples. I myself always fall an easy prey to superior manners. I remember how admirable in my youth were to me the southern boys. Andrew Johnson, wont to look up to the planters as a superior race, cannot resist their condescensions & flatteries &, though he could not be frightened by them, falls an easy victim to their caresses. This result was explicitly foretold by M. D. Conway & Fred. Douglass.

The remedy of this political mischief should be to train youth in poverty to a nobler style of manners than any palace can show him, by Plato & Plutarch, by the Cid, & Sydney, & George Herbert, & Chaucer.

Quick people touch & go, whilst heavy people insist on pounding. 'Tis in vain to try to choke them off, & change the conversation to avoid the slaughter-house details. Straightway they begin at the beginning, & thrice they slay the slain. Society shall be distressing, & there's an end of it.

from

GL

1861–1862, 1863

The persons generally most praised & esteemed are not those whom I most value, for the world is not receptive or intelligent of Being, but of Intellect. But heroes are they who value Being. Being cannot be told, & is left alone not only because little appreciated, but that its influence is silent & quiet. The world is awed before the great, & is subdued without knowing why.

—

The best thing I heard yesterday was Henry James's statement, that, in the spiritual world, the very lowest function was Governing. In heaven, as soon as one wishes to rule, or despises others he is thrust out at the door.

Another fine spiritual statement which he made, was, to the effect, that all which men value themselves for as religious progress,—going alone, renouncing, & self-mortifying, to attain a certain religious superiority,—was the way *from*, not the way *to* what they seek; for, it is only as our existence is shared, not as it is self-hood, that it is divine.

—

"But Cathmor dwelt in the wood, to avoid the voice of praise," says Ossian.

Destitution is the Muse of M.M.E.'s genius, Destitution & Death. We have said that her epitaph ought to be, "Here lies the Angel of Death." And wonderfully as she varies & poetically repeats that image in every page & day, yet not less fondly & sublimely she returns to the other, the grandeur of humility & privation, as thus; "The chief witness which I have had of a God-like principle of action & feeling is the disinterested joy felt in others' superiority." "For the love of superior virtue is mine own gift from God."

"To obey God is joy, though no hereafter." "Where were thy own intellect, if greater had not lived."

—

As soon as one sees that life is one, & God does not create, but communicates his life, all is right. This self-love is much in our way. A wise man, an open mind, is as much interested in others, as in himself; they are only extensions of himself. They stand on a hilltop, & see exactly what he would see if he were there. He cannot be offended by an honest partiality in others. Alcott said of his company, "I can offend them at any moment."

Perfect health is the subjugation of matter to be the servant, the instrument of thought & heart; so that matter is not felt as matter, but only as opulence, & light, & beauty, & joy. As soon as we know a particle of matter for itself it is obstruction & defect of health.

It is not my duty to prove the immortality of the Soul. That secret is hidden very cunningly;—perhaps the archangels cannot find the secret of their existence, as the eye cannot see itself, —but, ending or endless, to live while I live.
Yet I find the proofs noble, wholesome, & moral.

Pay every debt. If you cannot, you may be bankrupt, & content with bankruptcy. Tomorrow try again. 'Tis not your duty to pay the debt, but to try to pay the debt. Do all with a clear & perfect intent. Call in the Universe to witness & sanction, & not skulk into a corner. If it is your part to kill, kill in the face of day, & with the plaudits of the Universe.
Other world! there is no other world. The God goes with you,—is here in Presence. What is here, that is there. & it is by his only strength that you lift your hand.

—

Subjective Life

We are partial & only pick, like birds, a crumb here & there. Tho' the world is full of food, we can take only the crumbs fit for us. The air rings with sounds, but only a few vibrations can reach our tympanum, deaf to all the thunders around us. Perhaps creatures live with us which we never see, because their motion is too swift for our vision; and 'tis familiar that people

pass out of the world unknown, being too good, or too high, or too subtle, for the appreciation of their bystanders. I know three or four men, Charles Newcomb, and Alcott, & Channing, who are concealed, as Swedenborg was. These are buried in light, as the stars are by day. I might add Jones Very.
I have elsewhere added Samson Reed, & Bailey.

I know no more irreconcileable persons ever brought to annoy & confound each other in one room than are sometimes actually lodged by nature in one man's skin. Thus I knew a saint of a woman who lived in ecstasies of devotion, "a pensive nun devout & pure," and who, moved by pity for a poor schoolmistress, undertook one day to give her a little vacation which she sorely needed, & took her place in the school: but, when the children whispered, or did not mind their book, she stuck a pin into their arms, & never seemed to suspect the cruelty. I knew a gentle imaginative soul, all poetry & sympathy, who hated every inmate of his house, & drove away his dog, by starving him. Rousseau left his children at the Foundling Hospital. Mrs Ripley at Brook Farm, said the hard selfishness of the socialists ruined the Community. Hawthorne, I believe, sued the members for their debt to him. Howard the great philanthropist was harsh to his children, & Sterne the sentimentalist had a bad name for hardness to his mother(?)

—

We are experimenters. We try out every appetite, passion, & desire that urges us;—make it strong with opinion & crowds &

Guns at Springfield, watches at Waltham, are made—part by part—the parts being of one uniform size & structure, so that any screw or ring or wheel missing can be instantly supplied. 'Tis a hint borrowed from nature, as shown in budding & grafting, & transfusion of blood, only that, in nature, it is unity in the particles, instead of the parts.

I watched the fair boy & girl, one as fair & sweet as the other, both surprised with a new consciousness, which made every hour delicious, each laying little traps for the admiration of the other, & each jumping joyfully into the traps.

*

Overture of the Quintette Club last evening.

Tuttle tuttle lira
tuttle tuttle liro
tuttle tuttle polywog po
tuttle tuttle up the stairs
tuttle tuttle out the window
tuttle tuttle all the world over
tuttle tuttle arms akimbo
tuttle tuttle all go smash.

Because I have no ear for music, at the concert it looked to me as if the performers were crazy, and all the audience were making-believe crazy, in order to soothe the lunatics, & keep them amused.

—

"These are facts that must be caught flying, & by a flying spectator."—*Alcott.*

What magical merit belongs, over all the details of any work, to the grand design! The performance of steam & iron locomotive on an iron road, is wonderful anywhere for a few rods or a mile, but is then only a toy; but continued or repeated for many miles, tens or hundreds, & directed on Boston or New York, acquires suddenly an incredible grandeur. All the details are performed by very narrow ordinary people, but the total effect seems quite out of the reach of any one man, and a godlike gift.

I remember seeing in my first visit to Baltimore a pulpit in the Catholic church, which was moveable on the floor from the side to the centre of the church, and as I doubt not was much older than any railroad and should have suggested it.

George Stephenson made the first locomotive in 1814. died 1848.

The doctrine of the Imagination can only be rightly opened by treating it in connection with the subject of Illusions. And the Hindoos alone have treated this last with sufficient breadth in their legends of the successive Maias of Vishnu. With them, youth, age, property, condition, events, persons, *self*, are only successive Maias, through which Vishnu mocks & instructs the Soul.

—

I saw at Augusta Mr Wilds, a civil-engineer, whom I had met at Grand Rapids, & who works for the mining companies at Lake Superior. His associate is Edward Emerson of Portland. He told me that at Lake Superior, last year (I think) they came, in their excavations, upon a mass of copper of (3? or 6?) tons standing on end, & on wooden wedges with a wooden bowl or pan near it, & some stone axes or chisels lying around it. Trees had grown above it since it was thus lifted, and they counted on these trees 390 rings.

He told me that his friend Mr Foster who lives at Montreal, when building the Eastern railroad at Kennebunk, had found a nest of bird's eggs ten feet below the surface, in the solid rock, and that they turned out a toad in the rock at the same place. He Wilds himself was present, & he & the others thought that they saw the toad gasp on being thrown out. Foster has the eggs now at Montreal.

—

Do the duty of the day. Just now, the supreme public duty of all thinking men is to assert freedom. Go where it is threatened, & say, 'I am for it, & do not wish to live in the world a moment longer than it exists.'

Phillips has the supreme merit in this time, that he & he alone stands in the gap & breach against the assailants. Hold up his hands. He did me the honor to ask me to come to the meeting at Tremont Temple, &, esteeming such invitation a command, though sorely against my inclination & habit, I went, and, though I had nothing to say, showed myself. If I were dumb, yet I would have gone & mowed & muttered or made signs. The mob roared whenever I attempted to speak, and after several beginnings, I withdrew.

—

I read many friendly & many hostile paragraphs in the journals about my new book, but seldom or never a just criticism. As long as I do not wince, it cannot be that the fault is touched. When the adept applies his galvanic battery now to this part, then to that, on the patient's head, the patient makes

no sign, for lungs are sound, & liver, & heart: but, at last, he touches another point, & the patient screams, for it seems there is bronchitis, or is hip disease.
And when the critics hit you, I suppose you will know it. I often think I could write a criticism on Emerson, that would hit the white.

—

27 Feb., 1861. Long peace makes men routinary & gregarious. They all walk arm in arm. Poverty, the sea, the frost, farming, hunting, the emigrant, the soldier, must teach self reliance, to take the initiative, & never lose their head.
In the South, slavery & hunting & horsemanship & the climate, & politics, give the men self-reliance; & the South is well officered, &, with some right, they despise the peaceful north people, leaning on the law, & on each other. In proportion to the number of self-reliant persons, will the power & attitude of the state be.

Theodore Parker was our Savonarola.

Liberty, like religion, is a short & hasty fruit of rare & happy conditions.

—

For really every object in nature is a little window through which the whole universe may be seen. For, every one, say, a cat, or a partridge, or a pickerel, has relations to all other things, to the state of land & water, to the climate, &, of course, to latitude & longitude, to the atmosphere, to the bulk of the planet, & the system of animals, &, from this single specimen, a Naturalist might gradually make out the *systema Naturae.*

Detachment by illumination is the gift of genius, as I have somewhere written. The poet sees some figure for a moment in an expressive attitude & surroundings, &, without hesitating, because it is a mere purposeless fragment, he paints out that figure with what skill & energy he has.

Poetry will never be a simple means, as when history or philosophy is rhymed, or laureate odes on state occasions, are used,

Poetry must be the end to which it is written, or it is nought.

See Spenser's delight in his art for his own skill's sake, in the Muiopotmos

—

I like dry light, & hard clouds, hard expressions, & hard manners.

—

Only our newest knowledge works as a source of inspiration & thought, as only the outmost layer of liber in the tree.

Not what you see imports, but with what idea. The most tender, the most radiant, the most sublime landscape is stark as tombstones, except seen by the thoughtful.

What came over me with delight as I sat on the ledge in the warm light of last Sunday, was the memory of young days at College, the delicious sensibility of youth, how the air rings to it! how all light is festal to it! how it at any moment extemporizes a holiday! I remember how boys riding out together on a fine day looked to me! ah there was a romance! How sufficing was mere melody! The thought, the meaning was insignificant; the whole joy was in the melody. For that I read poetry, & wrote it; and in the light of that memory I ought to understand the doctrine of Musicians, that the words are nothing, the air is all.

What a joy I found, & still can find, in the Aeolian harp! What a youth find I still in Collins's "Ode to Evening," & in Gray's "Eton College"! What delight I owed to Moore's insignificant but melodious poetry! That is the merit of Clough's "Bothie," that the joy of youth is in it. Ah the power of the spring! and, ah the voice of the bluebird! And the witchcraft of the Mount Auburn dell, in those days! I shall be a Squire Slender for a week.

Greenough said, the Elgin marbles taken together put the horse through all his paces, so that one feels as if he had seen the motion; as in the phanakistiscope. So is it with nature, as seen by botanist or zoologist, if poetical.

For sources of inspiration, all poetic men will agree in a respect for fact-books, and more or less skill to turn them to an account least thought-of by those who wrote them:

Fact books,
dictionaries,
new poetry, by which I mean chiefly, old poetry that is new to me, are the preparatives of the poet for his hour.

—

One thing strikes me in all good poetry, that the poet goes straight forward to say his thought & the words & images fly to him to express it, whilst colder moods are forced to hint the matter, or insinuate, or perhaps only allude to it being unable to fuse & mould their words & images to fluid obedience.

The place which I have not sought, but in which my duty puts me, is the right place. I feel with pleasing awe the immensity of the chain of which I hold the last link in my hand, & am led by it.

—

M M E speaks of her attempts in Malden "to wake up the soul amid the dreary scenes of monotonous sabbaths, when nature looked like a pulpit."

Ralph Emerson in Paris, in 1833, said to me that he possessed a certain advantage there, in business, from the settled belief of other Americans that there was some magic in speaking French, & not, like all other arts, mere iteration, a step at a time, like learning a trade. So is it with public speaking, as Dr Blair might have told Mr Alexander: and so, I must not doubt, with music & mathematics. The order of logical learning is one, & the order of wonder or of exhibition, quite another. See what I have written of *Pace*, & of Wilkie's picture.

March 16. I have seldom paid money with so much pleasure as today to Dr Barrett, fifty cents, for taking with a probe a little cinder out of my left eye, which had annoyed me for a week.

—

I told the School Company at the Town Hall, this P. M., that I felt a little like the old gentleman who had dandled ten sons & daughters of his own in succession on his knee, when his grandchild was brought to him, "No," he said, "he had cried kitty-kitty long enough." And yet when I heard now recitations & exercises, I was willing to feel new interest still.

—

Yesterday I saw Rarey's exhibition in Boston. What a piece of clean good sense was the whole performance, the teaching & the doing! An attack on the customary nonsense of nations in one particular. The horse does not attack you till you attack him. He does not know his own strength, until you teach it him. Just keep yourself then in such position that he always finds you the strongest, & he believes you invincible. Make him not resist you, by always stroking & conciliating him. Hold the drum, or strap up to his nose, let him get acquainted with it, & he will not fear it. When he shies whip him & he will shy again the more, because he has not only the terror of the object, but the terror of the whip, associated.

—

March 26, 1861.

Yesterday wrote to F. G. Tuckerman to thank him for his book, & praised Rhotruda. Ellery C. finds two or three good lines & metres in the book, thinks it refined & delicate, but says, the young poets run on a notion that they must name the flowers, talk about an orchis, & say something about Indians; but, he says, "I prefer passion & sense & genius to botany."

Ellery says of Tennyson, "What is best, is, the things he don't say."

Most men believe that their goodness is made of themselves. Others have the converse opinion. What a probity has W. E. It shines in all his face & demeanor. He has never analysed or inquired into it. But if he thinks at all, he thinks it is a part of him. But, in reality, he exists from that, & all of him, but that, is caducous.

—

One capital advantage of old age is the absolute insignificance of a success more or less. I went to town & read a lecture yesterday. Thirty years ago it had really been a matter of importance to me whether it was good & effective. Now it is of none in relation to me. It is long already fixed what I can & what I cannot do, & the reputation of the man does not gain or suffer from one or a dozen new performances. If I should in a new performance rise quite beyond my mark, & do somewhat

extraordinary & great, that, to be sure, would instantly tell; but I may go below my mark with impunity. 'O, he had a headach, or lost his sleep for two nights,'
Great are the benefits of old age!
See Swift's Letter on old age; also,
old age is frowzy.

—

In youth, the day is not long enough. I well remember my feeling (say in 1823, or 4,) that a day of 18 hours would accommodate my plans of study & recreation much better than our poor Copernican astronomy did.

Apr. 18
Art. Yesterday I read my lecture on Art. I add;
There are as many orders of architecture as creatures or tenants or reasons for erecting a building; a seashell, a bird's nest, a spider's web, a beaver-dam, a muskrat's house, a gopher's, a rabbit warren, a rock spider's silver counterpane over its eggs; a cocoon; a woodpecker's hole in a tree; a field-mouse's gallery, wasp-paper, a beehive, a lamprey's pyramid are examples. So a tree, so the shape of every animal, is the structure, the architecture, which nature builds for a purpose which rules the whole building & declares itself at sight.

Some animals have a spare set of legs as a ship carries two suits of sails. Agassiz cut all the legs off of his lizard in succession, & all the legs grew out again as good as new.

I delight to see boys, who have the same liberal ticket of admission to all shops, factories, armories, town meetings, caucuses, mobs, target shootings, as flies have; quite unsuspected, coming in as naturally as the janitor; known to have no money in their pockets; & themselves not suspecting the value of their privilege, putting nobody on his guard but seeing the inside of the show, hearing all the asides; there only for fun, & not knowing that they are at School as much or more than they were an hour ago in the arithmatic class. They know truth from counterfeits as quick as chemistry. They detect weakness in your eye & behavior a week before you open your mouth,

& have given you the benefit of their opinion quick as wink. There are no secrets from them. They know everything, all that befalls in the fire company, the merits of every engine, & every man at the brakes,—how to work it, & all the names & all the conditions of the practice, & are very swift to try their hand at every part; & so the merits of every engineer, & every engine, & locomotive on the rails. & will coax good John to let them ride on the engine, & even pull the handles, when it goes into the engine-house. They know every man in the rifle corps & in the artillery, & brag the prowess, & imitate it, of their favorite Samson.

Try them on horses, & see how much they know of racers. Try them on pugilists, on theatres, on regattas, on jumping, climbing, pitching quoits.

They make no mistakes, and have no pedantry yet; but unaffected belief on experience. The elections in the cricket-game, base & football, and the boat, are right, & not liable to mistake: they put the round post in the round hole & the square post in the square, & no log-rolling, no managing to put an imbecile on the county who can't be elected in his own town, ever happens. Wo wo to the man who never was a boy! They don't pass for swimmers until they can swim, nor for stroke-oar until they can row:

and I desire to be saved from their infinite contempt. If I can pass with them, I can manage well enough with their fathers.

—

The country is cheerful & jocund in the belief that it has a government at last. The men in search of a party, parties in search of a principle, interests & dispositions that could not fuse for want of some base,—all joyfully unite in this great Northern party, on the basis of Freedom. What a healthy tone exists! I suppose when we come to fighting, & many of our people are killed, it will yet be found that the bills of mortality in the country will show a better result of this year than the last, on account of the general health; no dyspepsia, no consumption, no fevers, where there is so much electricity, & conquering heart & mind.

So in finance, the rise of wheat paid the cost of the Mexican War; & the check on fraud & jobbing & the new prosperity of the West will pay the new debt.

—

Mem. Feb. 9, 1825. I went to Cambridge, & took a chamber in Divinity College.
Feb. 8. my last day in Canterbury.

Southerners do not shrink from the logical conclusion of their premises because it is immoral: neither will they shrink from the practical result, because it is degrading.

—

August 5. The war goes on educating us to a trust in the simplicities, and to see the bankruptcy of all narrow views. The favorite pet policy of a district, the *épicier* party of Boston or N York, is met by conflicting *épicier* party in Philadelphia, another in Cincinnati, others in Chicago & St Louis, so that we are forced still to grope deeper for something catholic & universal, wholesome for all. Thus war for the Union is broader than any State policy, or Tariff, or Maritime, or Agricultural, or Mining interest. Each of these neutralizes the other. But, at last, Union Party is not broad enough, because of Slavery, which poisons it; and we must come to "emancipation with compensation to the Loyal States," as the only broad & firm ground. This is a principle. Every thing else is an intrigue.
I wrote to Cabot, that, huge proportions as the war had attained from despicable beginnings, it is felt by all as immensely better than the socalled Integrity of the Republic, as amputation is better than cancer: and we find it out by wondering why we are so easy at heart, in spite of being so beaten & so poor.

A rush of thoughts is the only conceivable prosperity that can come to me. Fine clothes, equipages, villa, park, & social consideration cannot cover up real poverty & insignificance from my own eyes, or from others like mine.

Hodsdon's Life, like this war, this teaching war, is a good chapter of the Bible which the nations now want. Self-help; trust against all appearances,—against all privations, in your own worth, & not in tricks or plotting. Lose the good office, lose the good marriage, lose the coveted social consideration, that seem within your reach, if they do not constitutionally belong to you, but must be won by any shadow of intrigue, any departure from that utterly honest, solid & reverable self-existency which you are. Honor shall walk with me, though the footway is too narrow for Friendship or Success, or what is called Power; and the great sacrifices which directly become necessary in such a resolution, force us on new & grander thoughts, open the eyes to the Angels who attend us in phalanxes.

All the pleasure & value of novels is in the exhibition of this poetic justice, the triumphs of being over appearance.

In talking with Alcott of ontology, &c. I said that few people were entitled to make the catalogue of the powers & the order of Genesis; that the great primal powers will not sit for their portraits, and are ever melting into each other,—dodging, one might almost say, behind each other. And it is only a Plato, a Bacon, or a Kant, that may presume to rank them, nor he but delicately & diffidently. Alcott said, "Yes he must use a ladder of lightning, & efface all the steps as he passed up or down."

There is always a larger consideration, just ahead, which the mind can be stimulated to apperceive, & which is the consolation & the energy which in dulness & despair we need.

If we Americans should need presently to remove the capitol to Harrisburg, or to Chicago, there is almost nothing of rich association with Washington City to deter us. More's the pity. But excepting Webster's earlier eloquence, as against Hayne, & John Quincy Adams's sublime behaviour in the House of Representatives, & the fine military energy of Jackson in his Presidency, I find little or nothing to remember.

Doctrine of Leasts

Resources. If you want Plinlimmon in your closet, Caerleon, Provence, Ossian, & Cadwallon,—tie a couple of strings across a board, & set it in your window, & you have a windharp that no artist's harp can rival. It has the tristesse of nature, yet, at the changes, a festal richness ringing out all kinds of loftiness. Sounds of the animals & of the winds, waters, & forest, are for the most part triste,—whippoorwill, owl, veery, night-hawk, cricket, frog, & toad,—but the thrush, songsparrow, oriole, Bobolink, & others are cheerful.

—

But to me the first advantage of the War is the favorable moment it has made for the cutting out of our cancerous Slavery. Better that war & defeats continue, until we have come to that amputation.

President Lincoln said, "When we are swimming the river, 'tisn't a good time to swap horses."

I suppose, if the war goes on, it will be impossible to keep the combatants from the extreme ground on either side. In spite of themselves, one army will stand for slavery pure; & the other for freedom pure.
"Famâ bella stant." *Q. Curtius*

—

I am at a loss to understand why people hold Miss Austen's novels at so high a rate, which seem to me vulgar in tone, sterile in invention, imprisoned in the wretched conventions of English society, without genius, wit, or knowledge of the world. Never was life so pinched & narrow. The one problem in the mind of the writer in both the stories I have read, "Persuasion," and "Pride & Prejudice," is marriageableness. All that interests in any character introduced is still this one, Has he or she money to marry with, & conditions conforming? 'Tis "the nympholepsy of a fond despair," say rather, of an English boarding-house. Suicide is more respectable.

When the troops left at Fort Hatteras wake up the next morning, they look out at their conquest with new eyes. If their commander knows what to do with it, the feeling of victory continues;—but if not, they already are the timorous apprehensive party. A day in Carolina or elsewhere is a splendor of beauty & opportunity to a rational man; to an ox, it is hay, grass, & water; 'Tis heavy to an idle empty man, for it will defeat him. The physician, if he apply blister or external inflammation, gives a drop or pill internally for the sake of reaction and a day is an inflammation of nature, which requires an idea or purpose in the man to counteract. In the midst of stupendous difficulties, Napoleon is cheerful & fat, because he sees clearly what to do, & has it to do.

Sept. 9. Last night a pictorial dream fit for Dante. I read a discourse somewhere to an assembly, & rallied in the course of it to find that I had nearly or quite fallen asleep. Then presently I went into what seemed a new house, the inside wall of which had many shelves let into the wall, on which great & costly Vases of Etruscan & other richly adorned pottery stood. The wall itself was unfinished, & I presently noticed great clefts, intended to be filled with mortar or brickwork, but not yet filled, & the wall which held all these costly vases, threatening to fall. Then I noticed in the centre shelf or alcove of the wall a man asleep, whom I understood to be the architect of the house. I called to my brother William who was near me, & pointed to this sleeper as the architect, when the man turned, & partly arose, & muttered something about a plot to expose him.

When I fairly woke, & considered the picture, & the connection of the two dreams,—what could I think of the purpose of Jove who sends the dream?

War the searcher, of character, the test of men, has tried already so many reputations, has pricked so many bladders. 'Tis like the financial crises, which, once in ten or twenty years, come to try the men & institutions of trade; using, like them, no ceremony, but plain laws of gravity & force to try tension & resistance. Scott, McDowell, Maclellan, Fremont, Banks, Butler, & I know not how many more, are brought up, each in turn, dragged up irresistibly to the anthropometer, measured & weighed, & the result proclaimed to the universe.
With this dynamometer, & not so much that as *rack* to try the tension of your muscles & bones, standing close at hand, everybody takes the hint, drops much of brag & pretension, & shortens his speeches. The fop in the street, the beau at the ball feels the war in the air,—the examiner, the insatiate demand for reality,—& becomes modest & serious. The writer is less florid, the wit is less fantastical. The epicure & the man of

pleasure put some check & cover on their amusements. Everybody studies retrenchment & economy.

Every body bethinks himself how he shall behave, if worst should come to worst. It will not always serve, or may not, to stand aloof & contribute money. Shall we carry on a war by subscription and politely? They will conquer who take up the bayonet, or leave their other business & apply themselves to the business of the war.

The war searches character, & acquits those whom I acquit, whom life acquits, those whose reality & spontaneous honesty & singleness appear. Force it requires. 'Tis not so much that you are moral, as that you are genuine, sincere, frank, & bold. I do not approve those who give money, or give their voices for liberty, from long habit, & the feminine predominance of sentiment; but the rough democrat who hates Garrison, but detests these southern traitors. The first class will go in the right way, but they are devoured by sentiments, like premature fruit ripened by the worm.
The "logic of events" has become a household word.

—

1861 October
Lately I find myself oft recurring to the experience of the partiality of each mind I know. I so readily imputed symmetry to my fine geniuses, on perceiving their excellence in some insight. How could I doubt, that, Thoreau, that Charles K. N., that Alcott, or that H. James, as I successively met them, was the master-mind, which, in some act he appeared. No, he was only master-mind in that particular act. He could repeat the like stroke a million times, but, in new conditions, he was inexpert; & in new company, he was dumb.

—

H. T. forgot himself once.

Men assume their own existence.

"Severity is almost always a defect of memory." *Gasparin.*

*

Originality. How easy it is to quote a sentence from our favorite author, after we have once heard it quoted! how unthought of before! Il n'y a que le premier pas qui coute. 'Tis like our knowledge of a language. We can read currently in German, but if you ask me what is German for horse, or spade, or pump, I cannot tell.

The revolving light resembles the man who oscillates from insignificance to glory, & every day, & all his life long. So does the waxing & waning moon.

If you see, what often happens, a dull scholar outstripping his mates, & coming into high stations, you will commonly find, on inquiry, that the successful person possesses some convivial talent; like B. S.

Originality

I am not sure that the English religion is not all quoted. Even Jeremy Taylor, Fuller, even George Herbert,—Catholics all,—are only using their fine fancy to blazon & illuminate their memory. 'Tis Judaea & not England which is the ground. So with the mordant Calvinism of Scotland & America. But the Stoic, M. Antoninus, Zeno, but Pythagoras, but the Hindoo;—these all speak out their own mind, & do not quote. George Fox, Jones Very speak originally.

I find conversation so magnetic an affair, that I think two persons are easily deceived as to the genius of each other. Each hears from the other a better wisdom than any other party will ever hear from either.

M.M.E.

Aunt Mary wished everybody to be a Calvinist except herself.*

—

Good writing how rare! Conway writes affectedly or secondarily with all his talent & heat of purpose; so Kingsley, & Hepworth Dixon, & others of Carlyle's imitators. But the old

*Like Dr Johnson's minister in the Hebrides who wished him to believe in Ossian, but did not himself believe in him.

Psalms & Gospels are mighty as ever: showing that what people call religion is literature; that is to say,—here was one who knew how to put his statement, & it stands forever, & people feel its truth, as he did, & say, *Thus said the Lord*, whilst it is only that he had the true literary genius, which they fancy they despise. In the old grand books, there will be now & then a falsetto, as, in "the Cid," a Moor who makes a malediction on Valencia, before its fall: which is inflated, has no inspiration. But in Taliessin, the chants of Merlin or T. are good.
A great deal of what is called luck, in literature,—not only in men, but in particular works. Thus Hogg's Kilmeny is a true inspiration wonderful as a chant of Merlin, or sonnets of Shakspeare & how strange that it should have been written by such a muddlepate as James Hogg, who has written nothing else that is not second or third rate. And our Alcott (what a fruit of Connecticut!) has only just missed being a seraph. A little English finish & articulation to his potences, & he would have compared with the greatest.

—

Old Age

I ought to have added to my list of benefits the general views of life we get at 60 when we penetrate show & look at facts.

—

Jan. 9, 1862. *Memory*

We should so gladly find the law of thought unmechanical: but 'tis a linked chain,—drop one link, & there is no recovery. When newly awaked from lively dreams, we are so near them, still agitated by them, still in their sphere;—give us one syllable, one feature, one hint, & we should re-possess the whole;—hours of this strange entertainment & conversation would come trooping back to us; but we cannot get our hand on the first link or fibre, and the whole is forever lost. There is a strange wilfulness in the speed with which it disperses, & baffles your grasp.

I ought to have preserved the Medical Journal's notice of R.W.E. in Philadelphia, that, of all the persons on the platform, Mr E. was the least remarkable looking, &c.,—which I could very often match with experiences in hotels, & in private circles, as at the Mayor Elgie's in Worcester, England.

Besides, I am not equal to any interview with able practical men. Nay, every boy out-argues, out-states me, insults over me, & leaves me rolling in the dirt. Each thinks that 'tis he who has done it, & I know that every body does or can as much.

J. T. Payne of Charlestown said to me that he had noticed that Englishmen never presume to go behind the workman whom they employ. If they order a coat, or a trunk, or a house, or a ship, they call in the proper person to make it, & they accept what he gives them; whilst an American makes himself a very active party to the whole performance.

Cannot we let people be themselves, & enjoy life in their own way? You are trying to make that man another *you*. One's enough.

Go out of doors & get the air. Ah, if you knew what was in the air! See what your robust neighbor, who never feared to live in it, has got from it;—strength, cheerfulness, talent, power to convince, heartiness, & equality to each event.

Sympathy, yes, but not surrender. When I fancy that all the farmers are despairing in the drought, or the frost, I meet Edmund Hosmer, & find him serene, & making very slight account of the circumstance. In the cars, we all read the same fool bulletin, & smile or scowl all as one man, & they who come to ask my opinion, find me only one flat looking-glass more; when I ought to have stayed at home in my mind, & to have afforded them the quite inestimable element of a new native opinion or feeling,—of a new quality.

John Quincy Adams engraved on his seal, *Haeret*.

The use of "occasional poems" is to give leave to originality. In a game-party or a picnic poem, the writer is released from all the solemn poetic traditions under which he writes at other times, & which suffocate his fancy & spirit, & now amuses himself & indulges his nature, & the result is, that you get often a poem that is in a new style, & hints a new literature. Yet the writer holds it cheap, & could do the like all day. 'Tis like acting in tragedy & comedy. The tragedy is very tedious; for all the players are on stilts, & mouth it like masks. But, in comedy, the same players delight you by their *naturel*; for they understand the part, & play it as in undress.

sources of inspiration.
1, sleep is one, mainly by the sound health it produces; incidentally also, & rarely, by dreams, into whose farrago a divine lesson is sometimes slipped.
2. solitary converse with nature is a second, (or perhaps the first,) and there are ejaculated sweet & dreadful words never uttered in libraries. Ah the spring days, summer dawns, & October woods.
3. New poetry; what is new to me, whether in recent manuscript or in Caxton black letter
4 Conversation
I know where to find songs new & better than any I have heard.

—

Talent without character is friskiness. The charm of Montaigne's egotism & of his anecdotes is that there is a stout cavalier, a seigneur of France at home in his Chateau, responsible for all this chatting, and if it could be shown to be a jeu d'esprit of Scaliger, or other scribacious person, written for the booksellers, & not resting on a real *status* picturesque in the eyes of all men, it would lose all its value. But Montaigne is essentially unpoetic.—

Jan. 16

It occurred yesterday after my conversation with the chicadee that the Illusions are many & sure, Each has his own, & all are tripped up by one or the other. The men of hard heart & iron will, old merchants & lawyers fall an easy prey to Mother Deb Saco, & Hume, & the rappers. & converse with their dead aunts, like Dr Hare & Mr Shaw & H. Meanwhile the subtlest intellectualist Alcott runs about for books, which he does not understand, & which make a dilettante of him, & making scholars thus his inferiors his superiors, and forfeiting his immense & unique genius, to which all books are trivial.

Then again the question recurs daily, how far to respect the illusions? You cannot unmask or snub them with impunity. I know the hollowness & superstition of a dinner. Yet a certain health & good repair of social status comes of the habitude & well informed chat there which have great market value, though none to my solitude.

The War is a new glass to see all our old things through, how they look. Some of our trades stand the test well. Baking & butchering are good under all skies & times. Farming, haying, & wood chopping don't go out of vogue. Meat & coal & shoes we must have; but coach painting & bronze match-holders we can postpone for a while yet. Yet the music was heard with as much appetite as ever, and our Quintettes had only to put the "Starspangled Banner" into the Programme, to gain a hurra beside; but the concert could have prospered well without. And so if the Union were beaten, & Jeff Davis ruled Massachusetts, these flutes & fiddles would have piped & scraped all the same, & no questions asked. It only shows that those fellows have hitched on their apple-cart to a star, & so it gets dragged by might celestial. They know that few have thoughts or benefits, but all have ears; that the blood rolls to pulsebeat & tune, that the babe rhymes & the boy whistles, & they throw themselves on a want so universal, and as long as birds sing, ballad singers will, & organ grinders will grind out their bread.

—

Jan. 17

We will not again disparage America, now that we have seen what men it will bear. What a certificate of good elements in the soil, climate, & institutions is Lowell, whose admirable verses I have just read! Such a creature more accredits the land than all the fops of Carolina discredit it.

Long ago I wrote of "Gifts," & neglected a capital example. John Thoreau, Jr. one day put up a bluebird's box on my barn fifteen years ago, it must be,—and there it is still with every summer a melodious family in it, adorning the place, & singing his praises. There's a gift for you which cost the giver no money, but nothing he could have bought would be so good. I think of another quite inestimable. John Thoreau, Junior, knew how much I should value a head of little Waldo, then five years old. He came to me, & offered to carry him to a daguerrotypist who was then in town, & he, Thoreau, would see it well done. He did it, & brought me the daguerre which I thankfully paid for. In a few months after, my boy died, and I have ever since had deeply to thank John Thoreau for that wise & gentle piece of friendship.

To a perfect foot no place is slippery.

Old Age
As we live longer, it looks as if our company were picked out to die first, & we live on in a lessening minority. In England, I have lost John Sterling, Samuel Brown, David Scott, Edward Forbes, Arthur Clough; in Rome, Paul Akers, Mrs Browning, Margaret Fuller; Giles Waldo,
Here dies, last week, the excellent Mary H. Russell; and I am ever threatened by the decays of Henry T.

from
WAR

1862–1864

Though practically nothing is so improbable or perhaps impossible a contingency for me, yet I do not wish to abdicate so extreme a privilege as the use of the sword or the bullet. For the peace of the man who has forsworn the use of the bullet seems to me not quite peace.

—

Happily we are under better guidance than of statesmen. We are drifting in currents, and the currents know the way. It is, as I said, a war of Instincts.

Then I think the difference between our present & our past state, is in our favor; it was war then & is war now, but war declared is better than undeclared war.

—

Governments are mercantile, interested, & not heroic. Governments of nations of shopkeepers must keep shop also. There is very little in our history that rises above commonplace. In the Greek revolution, Clay & Webster persuaded the Congress into some qualified declaration of sympathy. Once we tendered Lafayette a national ship, gave him an ovation and a tract of public land (200 000 acres?). We attempted some testimony of national sympathy to Kossuth & Hungary. We subscribed & sent out corn & money to the Irish famine. These were spasmodic demonstrations. They were ridiculed as sentimentalism, they were sentimentalism, for it was not our natural attitude. We were not habitually & at home philanthropists. No, but timorous sharp shopmen, and each excuses himself if he talks politics, for leaving his proper province, & we really care for our shop & family, & not for Hungary & Greece, except as an opera, private theatricals, or public theatricals. And so of slavery. We have only half a right to be so good; for Temperament cracks the whip in every Northern kitchen.

Interests were never persuaded. Can you convince the shoe interest or the iron interest by reading Milton & Montesquieu?

Govt. has no regard for men until they become property; then, it has the tenderest.

The thinking class are looked at inquisitively in these times by the actors, as if some counsel were expected from them. But the thinker seldom speaks to the actor in his time, but ever to actors in the next age. Milton & Algernon Sidney were not listened to in their own time, but now are consulted with profit, & have just authority. The philosopher speaks over the heads of the contemporary audience to that advancing assembly he sees beyond; as Dr Reed of Bridgewater, after he was blind, preaching one day in his church, saw the congregation, nor did it occur to him that it was strange that he should see them until he left the Church; then he asked his son if he had said or done anything unusual today. His son said he had observed nothing more than that he spoke with unusual animation. But the Doctor bethought him that he had seen the Congregation, yet that the persons composing it were strange to him, & not his old acquaintances of the town;—and asked himself if it were perhaps an audience of persons in the spiritual world?

—

England has no higher worship than Fate. She lives in the low plane of the winds & waves, watches like a wolf a chance for plunder; values herself as she becomes wind & wave in the low circle of natural hunger & greed: never a lofty sentiment, never a Duty to civilization, never a generosity, a moral self-restraint. In sight of a commodity, her religion, her morals are forgotten. Why need we be religious? Have I not bishops & clergy at home punctually praying, & sanctimonious from head to foot? Have they not been paid their last year's salary?

—

The govt is not to be blamed. The govt with all its merits is to be thanked & praised for its angelic virtue compared with anything we have known for long. But the times will not allow us to say more in compliment. I wish I saw in the people that inspiration, that, if the govt could not obey the same, it would leave the government far behind, & create on the moment the means & heroes it wanted. Better the war should more deeply threaten us, threaten fracture in what is still whole, punish us with burned capitals & slaughtered armies, & so exasperate us to energy & exasperate our sectionalism, esprit du corps, nationality. There are scriptures written invisibly in men's hearts whose letters do not come out until they are enraged. They can be read by the light of war fires by eyes in peril.

—

It is impossible to disengage oneself from the questions in which your age is involved. You can no more keep out of politics than you can keep out of the frost.

Shall it be said of America, as of Russia, "it was a fine fruit spoiled before it had ripened"?

The peace of the world is kept by striking a new note, when classes are exasperated against each other. Instantly, the units part, and form in a new order, and those who were opposed, are now side by side.

For slavery, extirpation is the only cure.

—

We have not yet found a kerosene lamp to supersede the sun. Hitch your wagon to a star. Do the like in your choice of tasks. Let us not fag in paltry selfish tasks which aim at private benefit alone. No god will help. We shall find all the teams going the other way,—Charles's Wain, the Great Bear, Orion, Leo, Hercules, every god will leave us. Let us work rather for those interests which the gods honor & promote, justice, love, utility, freedom, knowledge.

The evil spirits also serve a wise & just govt. It taxes the vices.

—

Visit to Washington.

31 January, 1862.

At Washington, 31 January, 1 Feb, 2d, & 3d, saw Sumner, who on the 2d, carried me to Mr Chase, Mr Bates, Mr Stanton, Mr Welles, Mr Seward, Lord Lyons, and President Lincoln. The President impressed me more favorably than I had hoped. A frank, sincere, well-meaning man, with a lawyer's habit of mind, good clear statement of his fact, correct enough, not vulgar, as described; but with a sort of boyish cheerfulness, or that kind of sincerity & jolly good meaning that our class meetings on Commencement Days show, in telling our old stories over. When he has made his remark, he looks up at you with great satisfaction, & shows all his white teeth, & laughs. He argued to Sumner the whole case of Gordon, the slave-trader, point by point, and added that he was not quite satisfied yet, & meant to refresh his memory by looking again at the evidence.

All this showed a fidelity & conscientiousness very honorable to him.

When I was introduced to him, he said, "O Mr Emerson, I once heard you say in a lecture, that a Kentuckian seems to say by his air & manners, "*Here am I; if you don't like me, the worse for you.*"

In the Treasury Building I saw in an upper room a number of people, say, 20 to 30 seated at long tables all at work upon Treasury Notes, some cutting & some filling up, &c, but the quantity under their multitudinous operation looked like paper-hangings, & when I saw Mr Chase, I told him I thought the public credit required the closing of that door on the promenaders of the gallery. Mr Hooper told me that in the manufacture of a million notes (I think,)—$66. disappeared. Mr Staunton, who resembles Charles R. Train, though a heavier & better head & eye, made a good impression, as of an able determined man, very impatient of his instruments, &, though he named nobody, I thought he had Maclellan in mind. When somewhat was said of England, he said England is to be met in Virginia.—" 'Mud'! O yes, but there has been mud before. Ah the difficulty is n't outside,—'tis inside." He had heard that Gov. Andrew had come to the city to see him about the Butler-

Andrew difficulty. Well, why doesn't he come here? If I could meet Gov. Andrew under an umbrella at the corner of the street, we could settle that matter in five minutes, if he is the man I take him for. But I hear he is sitting on his dignity, & waiting for me to send for him. And, at that rate, for I learn there are 70 letters, I don't know that anything can be done. Both Sumner & I assured him that Gov. Andrew was precisely the man to meet him cordially & sensibly without parade & offhand.

Mr Seward received us in his dingy State Department. We spoke as we entered the anteroom, or rather in the corridor, with Gov. Andrew & Mr. Forbes, who were waiting. Sumner led me along, & upstairs, & into the Secretary's presence. He began, "Yes I know Mr E. The President said yesterday, when I was going to tell him a story, 'Well, Seward, don't let it be smutty.' And I remember when a witness was asked in court, 'Do you know this man?' 'Yes, I know him.'—'How do you know him?' 'Why I know him. I can't say I have carnal knowledge of him, &c——' "

Well, with this extraordinary exordium, he proceeded to talk a little more, when Sumner said, "I met Gov. Andrew waiting outside. Shan't I call him in?" "O yes," said Seward. Sumner went out & brought in him & Mr Forbes. Mr Seward took from the shelf a large half smoked cigar, lighted & pulled at it. Sumner went into a corner with Andrew, & Mr F. seized the moment to say to the secretary, that he saw there was an effort making to get Gordon the slavetrader pardoned. He hoped the Govt. would show to foreign nations that there was a change, & a new spirit in it, which would not deal with this crime as heretofore. Seward looked very cross & ugly at this; twisted his cigar about, &, I thought, twisted his nose also, & said coarsely, "Well, perhaps you would be willing to stand in his place," or something like that, & rather surprised & disconcerted Mr Forbes, but, Mr Forbes seeing that, though we had risen to go, Sumner still talked with Andrew, he went up to him, put his hands about him, & said, "don't you see you are obstructing the public business?", or somewhat to that effect, & so we made our adieus. Mr Seward came up to me, & said, "will you come & go to church with me tomorrow, at 10¼, & we will go home afterwards, & get some lunch or dinner." I accepted. &

Sumner then carried me into some of the chambers of the Department, into the office of Mr Hunter, who has been chief clerk, I believe, he said for 14 or 15 years, into the Library, where Mr Derby presided, & where I found Gurowski at his desk, growling; into the chamber where the Treaties with foreign nations, some of them most sumptuously engrossed & bound, & inclosed, were shown us, as the Belgian treaty,—and a treaty with the French Republic, signed by Buonaparte, countersigned by Talleyrand;—and, far richer than all, the Siamese Treaty, & presents,—Siamese,—I think,—not Japanese treaty, tied up with rich red silken ropes & tassels, & the sublime of tea-caddy style, written as on moonlight.

Then, in another chamber, the Washington Papers, bought of Judge Washington by Congress for $20 000, were shown us. We opened several volumes to see the perfect method & clerical thoroughness with which Washington did all his work. I turned to the page on which the opinion of Marquis de Lafayette was given in answer to a requisition of the General, before the battle of Yorktown, &c &c.

All these vols. of original letters, &c., of Washington preserved in plain wooden cabinets here on the ground floor, not defended from fire; and any eager autograph-hunter might scale the windows, & carry them off.

—

The next morning, at 10¼, I visited Mr Seward, in his library, who was writing, surrounded by his secretary & some stock brokers.——After they were gone, I said, "you never come to Massachusetts." "No," he said, "I have neither had the power nor the inclination." His father died early, & left him the care, not only of his own family, but of his cousins' property, three fiduciary trusts, and he had much on his hands. Then he early saw, that, whatever money he earned was slipping away from him, & he must put it in brick & stone, if he would keep it, & he had, later, obtained a tract of land in Chatauque (?) County, which, by care & attention, had become valuable, & all this had occupied him, until he came into public life, & for the last 15 (?) years, he had been confined in Washington.

—

We went to Church. I told him "I hoped he would not demoralize me; I was not much accustomed to churches, but trusted he would carry me to a safe place." He said, he attended Rev. Dr Pyne's Church. On the way, we met Gov. Fish, who was also to go with him. Miss Seward, to whom I had been presented, accompanied us.

I was a little aukward in finding my place in the Common-Prayer Book, & Mr S. was obliging in guiding me, from time to time. But I had the old wonder come over me at the Egyptian stationariness of the English church. The hopeless blind antiquity of life & thought,—indicated alike by prayers & creed & sermon,—was wonderful to see, & amid worshippers & in times like these. There was something exceptional too in the Doctor's sermon. His church was all made up of secessionists; he had remained loyal, they had all left him, & abused him in the papers: And in the sermon he represented his griefs, & preached Jacobitish passive obedience to powers that be, as his defence. In going out, Mr S. praised the sermon. I said that the Doctor did not seem to have read the Gospel according to San Francisco, or the Epistle to the Californians; he had not got quite down into these noisy times.

Mr S. said, "Will you go & call on the President? I usually call on him at this hour." Of course, I was glad to go.

We found in the President's chamber his two little sons,—boys of 7 & 8 years perhaps,—whom the barber was dressing & "whiskeying their hair," as he said, not much to the apparent contentment of the boys, when the cologne got into their eyes. The eldest boy immediately told Mr Seward, "he could not guess what they had got." Mr Seward "bet a quarter of a dollar that he could.—Was it a rabbit? was it a bird? was it a pig?" he guessed always wrong, & *paid his quarter* to the youngest, before the eldest declared it was a rabbit. But he sent away the mulatto to find the President, & the boys disappeared. The President came, and Mr Seward said, "You have not been to Church today." "No," he said, "and, if he must make a frank confession, he had been reading for the first time

Mr Sumner's speech (on the Trent affair)." Something was said of newspapers, & of the story that appeared in the journals, of some one who selected all the articles which Marcy should read, &c, &c,

The President incidentally remarked, that for the N.Y. Herald, he certainly ought to be much obliged to it for the part it had taken for the Govt. in the Mason & Slidell business. Then Seward said somewhat to explain the apparent steady malignity of the "London Times." It was all an affair of the great interests of markets. The great capitalists had got this or that stock: as soon as anything happens that affects their value, this value must be made real, and the "Times" must say just what is required to sell those values. &c. &c. The Government had little or no voice in the matter. "But what news today?" "Mr Fox has sent none. Send for Mr Fox." The servant could not find Mr Fox.

The President said, he had the most satisfactory communication from Lord Lyons; also had been notified by him, that he had received the order of the Bath, & he, the President, had received two communications from the French minister. France, on the moment of hearing the surrender of the prisoners, had ordered a message of gratification to be sent, without waiting to read the grounds: then, when the dispatches had been read, had hastened to send a fresh message of thanks & gratulation. Spain also had sent a message of the same kind. He was glad of this that Spain had done. For he knew, that, though Cuba sympathized with secession, Spain's interest lay the other way. Spain knew that the Secessionists wished to conquer Cuba.

Mr Seward told the President somewhat of Dr Pyne's sermon, & the President said, he intended to show his respect for him some time by going to hear him.

—

In the Congressional Library I found Spofford Assistant Librarian. He told me, that, for the last twelve (?) years, it had been under Southern domination, & as under dead men. Thus the Medical department was very large, and the Theological very large, whilst of modern literature very imperfect.

There was no copy of the "Atlantic Monthly," or of the "Knickerbocker," none of the "Tribune," or "Times," or any

N.Y. Journal. There was no copy of the "London Saturday Review" taken, or any other live journal, but the "London Court Journal," in a hundred volumes, duly bound.
Nor was it possible now to mend matters, because no money could they get from Congress, though an appropriation had been voted.

1864 March. Captain O. W. Holmes tells me, that the Army of the Potomac is acquiring a professional feeling, & that they have neither panics nor excitements, but more selfreliance.

—

He who does his own work frees a slave, He who does not his own work, is a slave-holder.

—

Strange that some strong-minded president of the Womans' Rights Convention should not offer to lead the Army of the Potomac. She could not do worse than General Maclellan.

—

Negro Soldiers

If the war means liberty to you you should enlist. It does mean liberty to you in the opinion of Jeff Davis for the South says, we fight to plant slavery as our foundation. And of course we who resist the South, are forced to make liberty of the negro our foundation. I speak for the forces above us those issues which are made for us over our heads, under our feet, paramount to our wills. If you will not fight for your liberty who will? If you will not, why then take men as they are and the Universe of men will say you are not worth fighting for. Go & be slaves forever & you shall have our aid to make you such. You had rather be slave than freemen. Go to your own place.

Plainly we must have a worthy cause for such soldiers as we send to battle or they shall not go. Do you think such lives as this city & state have yielded up already, the children of this famed city, the children of our public schools, the children of Harvard College, the best blood of our educated counties, objects of the most romantic hope & love, poets & romancers themselves—I attended the funeral of one of them & heard with hearty assent the voice that said that the whole state of S Carolina was not worth that one life—that these precious young men Lander, Lowell, Putnam, Dwight, Willard, the voice will choke to name them are given up to bring back into the Capitol of Washington the reckless politicians who had reeled out of it with threats to destroy it, or come back into it to rule again? Never. Better put gunpowder under its foundations & plough up the ground where its streets stand than they die for the disgraceful dynasty which had brought our freedom to be a lie & our civilization & wealth to dishonor as a partnership of thieves.

—

I am not black in my mind
But born to make black fair:
On the battlefield my master find,—
His white corpse taints the air.

Perhaps only his period is larger, & his return to light requires a better medium than our immoral civilization allows.

—

West Point Academy makes a very agreeable impression on me. The innocence of the cadets, the air of probity, of veracity, & of loyalty to each other struck me, & the anecdotes told us confirmed this impression. I think it excellent that such tender youths should be made so manly & masterly in rough exercises of horse & gun & cannon & mortar, so accurate in French, in Mathematics, geology, and engineering, should learn to draw, to dance, & to swim.

I think their ambition should be concentrated on their superiority in Science,—being taught, that, whoever knows the most must command *of right,* & must command *in fact*, if just to himself. Let them have no fears, then, of prejudices against West Point. "West Point a hot bed of aristocracy," is a word of some political hack, which seems to rankle in their memories. Rather let them accept it, and make West Point a true aristocracy, or "the power of the Best," best scholars, best soldiers, best engineers, best commanders, best men,—and they will be indispensable to their government & their country; will be, as they ought, the nucleus of the army, though it be three fourths or nine tenths volunteers;—they will be the shop of power, the source of instruction, the organization of Victory. Watt said, "he sold power in his shop." Ah! that is what all men wish to buy, if they can only have the pure article. Something finer, I think, than Watt meant, or had. Or if he had it, he forgot to tell us the number of the shop. In regard to the points to which the attention of the Board was called, the "Administration" appeared to me judicious, & more mild in fact than the printed rules led us to look for. Thus, on inquiry for the "dark prison," we found there was none, the room once used for this, having been for some years appropriated to other uses.

One fact appeared plainly, that this Academy was free of the bête noir of colleges, namely, criminal justice.
Here they are once & forever freed from every question by means of martial law. Every cadet is instantly responsible to his superior officer, for his behavior, & is sent to the guard-house, or has one or two hours' patrol-duty added to his day's work, or, is put down a long row of steps on his ladder of merit, or, if the offence is grave, is discharged from the Academy.

I think that the point of competitive examinations should be urged on the Congress, and that a severer preliminary test should be required for admission. The Academy should be relieved of the task of teaching to spell & parse English. Thus the course of study might be less superficial, or the application of science might be carried into detail in other schools.

The discipline is yet so strict, that these military monks, in years, never pass the limits of the post, & know nothing of the country immediately around them. It is pleasant to see the excellence & beauty of their fences, which cost nothing & need no repairs, namely, the Hudson River on one or two sides, & the mountains on the other sides. There is nothing beyond the post, no village, no shops, no bad company. It is two miles to Cozzens' new Hotel, but over a desart road, & there any cadet would be under dangerous observation.

—

At West Point, I entered some of the chambers of the cadets in the barracks, & found two cadets in each, standing as if on guard. Each chamber was perfectly clean, & every article orderly disposed. The mattrass on the camp iron bed was rolled up into a scroll. "Who makes your bed?" "I do." "Who brings your water?" "I do." "Who blacks your shoes?" "I do." In the battery drill, I saw each handsome dainty boy whom I had noticed in the Examination, flying over the field in the caissons, or loading or working the gun, all begrimed with powder. In the mortar practice, in the siege battery drill, each was promptly performing his part in the perfect exercise.

Lincoln We must accept the results of universal suffrage, & not try to make it appear that we can elect fine gentlemen. We shall have coarse men, with a fair chance of worth & of manly ability, but not polite men, not men to please the English or French.

You cannot refine Mr Lincoln's taste, or clear his judgment; he will not walk dignifiedly through the traditional part of the President of America, but will pop out his head at each railroad station & make a little speech, & get into an argument with Squire A. & Judge B.; he will write letters to Horace Greeley, and any Editor or Reporter or saucy Party committee that writes to him, & cheapen himself. But this we must be ready for, and let the clown appear, & hug ourselves that we are well off, if we have got good nature, honest meaning, & fidelity to popular interest, with bad manners, instead of an elegant roué & malignant selfseeker.

If our brothers or children are killed in the battle, we owe to them the same courage & selfrenunciation in bearing well their death, which they showed us in sacrificing themselves.

They who come today to his funeral, tomorrow will tread in his warpath, & show to his slayers the way to death.

—

Of Wordsworth's poem "To H. C. six years old," William Blake writes; "This is all in the highest degree imaginative, & equal to any poet, but not superior. I cannot think that real poets have any competition. None are greatest in the kingdom of heaven. It is so in poetry." "Natural objects always did & now do weaken, deaden, & obliterate imagination in me. Wordsworth must know that what he writes valuable is *not* to be found in Nature." *Wm Blake*. See *Life* Vol I p 345

He adds to this last remark—"Read Michael Angelo's sonnet, Vol 2, p. 179. of this Edition."

Blake spoke of the Spirits, & had talked with Voltaire. "I asked," says Crabbe Robinson, "in what language Voltaire spoke: he answered, 'To my sensations it was English. It was like the touch of a musical key: he touched it probably French, but to my ear it became English.' "

—

Renan writes "*Vie de Jesus.*" Many of his contemporaries have no doubt projected the same theme. When I wrote "Representative Men," I felt that Jesus was the "Rep. Man" whom I ought to sketch: but the task required great gifts,—steadiest insight & perfect temper; else, the consciousness of want of sympathy in the audience would make one petulant or sore, in spite of himself. Theodore Parker, of course, wished to write this book; so did Maria Child in her Book of Religions, and Miss Cobb, and Alcott, and I know not how many more.

—

Words used in a new sense & figuratively, dart a diamond lustre that delights; & *every* word admits a new use, & heaven beyond heaven. Almost it is not even friends, but this power of words that is best.

Barriers of man impassable. They who should be friends cannot pass into each other. Friends are fictions founded on some single momentary experience.

Thoughts let us into realities. Nothing of religious tradition, not the immortality of the soul is incredible, after we have experienced an insight, a thought. But what we want is consecutiveness. 'Tis with us a flash of light, & then a long darkness, & then a flash again. This separation of our days by a sleep almost destroys identity. Ah! could we turn these fugitive sparkles into an astronomy of Copernican worlds!
Scarcely a link of memory holds yesterday & today together, with most men; I mean, in their minds. Their house & trade & families serve them as ropes to give a coarse continuity. But they have forgotten the thoughts of yesterday, and they say today what occurs to them, & something else tomorrow.

—

from *VA*

1862–1863

HDT

Broadest philosophy narrower than the worst poetry.

Criticism on him in 1851.

Perhaps his fancy for Walt Whitman grew out of his taste for wild nature, for an otter, a wood-chuck, or a loon.
He loved sufficiency, hated a sum that would not prove: loved Walt & hated Alcott.

"It were well if the false preacher of Xy were always met & balked by a superior more living & elastic faith in his audience just as some missionaries in India are balked by the easiness with which the Hindoos believe every word of miracle & prophecy only surprised that they are much less wonderful than those of their own scriptures which also they implicitly beleive" *H.D.T.*

The vital refinements are the moral & intellectual steps. The appearance of the Seven Wise Masters, of the Stoic Zeno, of the acute & loyal Socrates, of Anacharsis, of Moses, the Essenes, of Jesus, of Buddh, and, in modern Christendom, of the realists, Savonarola, Huss, & Luther, are the causal facts which carry forward nations, & the race to new self examination & conviction, & raise the universal standard, compelling all to mend or affect to mend their behavior.

This morale civilization we neglect, and measure our advance by percussion-caps, lucifer-matches, rubber-shoes, gas-light & steam-power; but it is security & freedom & exhilaration, depending on a healthy morale in the Society, that leaves the mind alert, self-helping, & inventive.

Therien came to see Thoreau on business, but Thoreau at once perceived that he had been drinking; and advised him to go home & cut his throat, and that speedily. Therien did not well know what to make of it, but went away, & Thoreau said, he learned that he had been repeating it about town, which he was glad to hear, & hoped that by this time he had begun to understand what it meant.

The old school of Boston citizens whom I remember in my childhood had great vigor, great noisy bodies or I think certain sternutatory vigor, the like whereof I have not heard again. When Major B, or old Mr T. H. took out their pocket handkerchiefs at church, it was plain they meant business; they would snort & roar through their noses, like the lowing of an ox, & make all ring again. Ah, it takes a Northender to do that!

—

Holmes came out late in life with a strong sustained growth for two or three years, like old pear trees which have done nothing for ten years, & at last begin & grow great. The Lowells come forward slowly. & H. T. remarks, that men may have two growths like pears.

March 3, 1862. The snow still lies even with the tops of the walls across the Walden road, and, this afternoon, I waded through the woods to my grove. A chicadee came out to greet me, flew about within reach of my hands, perched on the nearest bough, flew down into the snow, rested there two seconds, then up again, just over my head, & busied himself on the dead bark. I whistled to him through my teeth, and, (I think, in response,) he began at once to whistle. I promised him crumbs, & must not go again to these woods without them. I suppose the best food to carry would be the meat of shagbarks or castille nuts. Thoreau tells me that they are very sociable with wood-choppers, & will take crumbs from their hands.

Voices have their various manners also. I remember when Greenwood began to preach, though he indulged a playful fancy that had perhaps caught its trick from Everett, yet the effect of that fine bass voice was, as if he were a rocky cliff, & these pretty descriptions only flowers & colors thereon. He could well afford them—they might bloom or fade—he remained fast. Other Speakers have nothing left, but put themselves entirely into their speech, as Phillips.

Some voices are warnings: some voices are like the bark of a dog.

"les caresses de sa parole."

—

La Nature aime les croisemens.

Blair rightly thinks, that, Chase, because he was always a Whig, will not have nerve. The Unitarians, born unitarians, have a pale shallow religion; but the Calvinist born & reared under his rigorous, ascetic, scowling creed, & then ripened into a Unitarian, becomes powerful, as Dr Channing, Dewey, Horace Mann, Wasson, Garrison, & others. So is it in politics. A man must have had the broad audacious Democratic party for his nursing-mother, and be ripened into a Free soiler, to be efficient; as Jackson, as Benton, as Potter, Wade, Blair, Hickman, Johnson, & Boutwell, were.

—

Freedom does not love the hot zone. The snow-flakes are the right stars of our flag, & the Northern streamers the stripes.

Latimer's story, that his father taught him not to shoot with his arms, but to lay his body to the bow, should be remembered by writers. The labial speech instead of the stomachic, afflicts me in all the poetry I read, even though on a gay or trifling subject. Why has never the poorest country college offered me a professorship of rhetoric? I think I could have taught an orator, though I am none.

*

24 March

S. Staples yesterday had been to see Henry Thoreau. Never spent an hour with more satisfaction. Never saw a man dying with so much pleasure & peace. Thinks that very few men in Concord know Mr Thoreau; finds him serene & happy.

Henry praised to me lately the manners of an old, established, calm, well-behaved river, as perfectly distinguished from those of a new river. A new river is a torrent; an old one slow & steadily supplied. What happens in any part of the old river relates to what befals in every other part of it. 'Tis full of compensations, resources, & reserved funds.

—

April 2, 1862. Yesterday I walked across Walden Pond. Today I walked across it again. I fancied it was late in the season to do thus; but Mr Thoreau told me, this afternoon, that he has known the ice hold to the 18th April.

April 9. The cold days have again arrested the melting of the ice, & yesterday I walked again across the middle of Walden, from one side to the other.

April 10. Today, I crossed it again on foot.

I believe it broke up on the 19th 20th.

—

Resources

In *GL* pp 292, 175 I have indicated some of my pastimes instead of whist & hunting. The chapter of these however is much longer, & should be most select. The first care of a man settling in the country should be to open the face of the earth to himself by a little knowledge of nature, or a great deal of knowledge, if he can, of birds, plants, & astronomy, in short, the art of taking a walk. This will draw the sting out of frost, dreariness out of November & March, & drowsiness out of August. To know the trees is, as Spenser says of the ash, "for nothing ill." Shells, too, how hungry I found myself the other day at Agassiz's Museum, for their names.

But the uses of the woods are many, & some of them for the scholar high & peremptory. When his task requires the wiping out from memory "all trivial fond records that youth &

observation copied there," requires self-communion & insights: he must leave the house, the streets, & the club, & go to wooded uplands, to the clearing, & the brook. Well for him if he can say with the old Minstrel, 'I know where to find a new song.'

—

May, 1862.

Of the most romantic fact the memory is more romantic.

—

Compensation.

Much mischief from the negro race. We pretended to christianize them but they heathenized us.

The Supreme Court under Southern dictation pronounced, that, "the negro had no rights which the white man was bound to respect." Today, by the rebellion, the same rule holds & is worked against the Southerner; "The rebel has no rights which negro or white man is bound to respect." The world is upside down when this dictum comes from the Chief Justice of the Supreme Court of the United States of America.

Resources or feats. I like people who can do things. When Edward & I struggled in vain to drag our big calf into the barn, the Irish girl put her finger into the calf's mouth, & led her in directly. When you find your boat full of water at the shore of the pond & strive to drag it ashore to empty it, Tom puts a round stick underneath, & 'tis on wheels directly.

Romance

June 6, 1862. If we could tell accurately the evanescing effects of an imaginative book on us as we read! Thus Milman's Translation of "Nala & Damayanti" is nearer to my business & bosom than is the news in today's "Boston Journal." And I am admonished & comforted, as I read. It all very nearly concerns me. We are elevated by beauty. I walk in marble galleries & talk with kings the while.

—

I told Alcott, who read me his paper "on the Garden," that it was written in the unnecessary vagabond style of Burton's "Anatomy of Melancholy," stringing together all unchosen possible things that might, could or would be said, and therefore requires leisure & lassitude of the desart in order to be read. Nobody in busy trading political, much more in scientific literary eras, could find days or hours to read it in. Such must be intercalated by idle gods for idle men in monasteries or English Colleges. 'Tis inexcusable in a man who has messages to men, who has truths to impart, to scribble these flourishes. He should write that which cannot be omitted, every sentence a cube, standing on its bottom like a die, essential & immortal. When cities are sacked & libraries burned, this book will be saved,—prophetic, sacred, a book of life,

For, truly considered, the work of writers is like that of capitalists. Suppose in London, Amsterdam, or New York, a company of proprietors should agree to found a bank or treasury for lending money at fixed rates, and, each having subscribed what amount he would contribute to the stock, they should begin bringing in their strongboxes; one brings his keg of ten thousand doubloons; one, his box of Spanish dollars; one, his bag of gold Napoleons; one, his uncoined box of nuggets; & so on: At last one gentleman brings in some sheets of beautifully engraved bank notes with very handsome vignettes of Liberty, & Commerce, & Agriculture, each note "promising to pay a thousand dollars," but all counterfeit. What will the other partners say?

Carlyle's III vol. of Friedrich a masterpiece. Now sovereignly written, above all literature, dictating to the world below, to citizens, statesmen, scholars & kings, what they shall think & accept as fatal & final for their salvation. It is mankind's Bill of Rights, the *Magna Charta*, or Declaration of Independence, or right royal Proclamation of the Intellect ascending the throne, announcing its good pleasure that hereafter, *as heretofore*, & now once for all, the world shall be governed by common sense & law of morals, or shall go to ruin.

But the manner in which the story is told, the author sitting like the supreme Demiurgus, & trotting out his heroes & heroines like puppets, coaxing & bantering them, amused with their good performance, patting them on the back, talking down to them as naughty dolls when they misbehave, communicating his information always in measure, just as much as the

young reader can understand, hinting the future when it would be useful, recalling now & then some illustrative antecedents of the actor, and impressing the reader with the conviction that he is in possession of the entire history centrally seen, that his diligence & investigation have been exhaustive, & that he has descended on the petty plot of Prussia from higher & cosmical surveys.
Then the soundness & breadth of his sense & the absolute independence of the tone is one to put kings in fear. And as every reader of this book shares, according to his intelligence, the haughty tone of this genius, & shares it with delight, we recommend to all governors,—English, French, Austrian & other, to double their guards, & look carefully to the censorship of the press, during the next twenty years.

—

I read a good sentence of General Scott's in the newspaper, that "resentment is a bad basis for a campaign."

Henry T. remains erect, calm, self-subsistent, before me, and I read him not only truly in his Journal, but he is not long out of mind when I walk, and, as today, row upon the pond. He chose wisely no doubt for himself to be the bachelor of thought & nature that he was,—how near to the old monks in their ascetic religion! He had no talent for wealth, & knew how to be poor without the least hint of squalor or inelegance. Perhaps he fell, all of us do, into his way of living, without forecasting it much, but approved & confirmed it with later wisdom. And I find myself much approving lately the farmer's scale of living, over the villager's. Plain plenty without luxury or show. This draws no wasteful company, & escapes an army of cares. What a ludicrous figure is a village gentleman defending his few rods of clover from the street boys who lose their ball in it once a day!

I am so sensible to cold, that one of the abatements of the displeasure of dying is the pleasure of escaping the east winds & north winds of Massachusetts.

—

Henry Thoreau writes, "Journal of July 1852"
"The youth gets together his materials to build a bridge to the

moon, or, perchance, a palace or temple on the earth, &, at length, the middle aged man concludes to build a woodshed with them."

"There is sport in the boy's water-mill, which grinds no corn, & saws no logs, & yields no money,—but not in the man's."
H.D.T. *Journal* 1852

He loved the sweet fragrance of Melilot.

The bass at Conantum 16 July.

Peter Robbins assured Henry, that yesterday's rain had not reached the potatoes after all. "Exorbitant potatoes!" H. adds, "it takes very serious preaching to convert them"

He is very sensible of the odor of waterlilies

> "no one has ever put into words what the odor of the waterlily expresses. A sweet & innocent purity. The perfect purity of the flower is not to be surpassed"

"Every poet has trembled on the verge of science"

Thinks at Becky Stow's swamp of the Revue des deux Mondes.
1852 Augt. 6. "Hearing that one with whom I was acquainted had committed suicide, I said, I did not know when I planted the seed of that fact, that I should hear of it."—*Thoreau*

If there is a little strut in the style, it is only from a vigor in excess of the size of his body. His determination on natural history is organic: he sometimes felt like a hound or a panther &, if born among Indians, would have been a fell hunter: restrained, modified by his Massachusetts culture he played out the game in this mild form of botany & ichthyology.

H D T.'s *Journal* 1852 p. 23
He examined "the heaps of small stones about the size of a walnut, more or less, which line the river shallows,—one every rod or two. The recent ones frequently rising by more than half their height above the water at present, i.e. a foot or

1½ feet & sharply conical, the older flattened by the elements & greened over with the thread-like stem of *Ranunculus filiformis.*
Some of these heaps contain two cartloads of stones, & as, probably, the creature that raised them took up one at a time, it must have been a stupendous labor."

I see many generals without a command, besides Henry.

—

Ah! the inconvertibility of the sentimentalist, the soul that is lost by mimicking soul. Cure the drunkard, heal the insane, sweeten the morose, mollify the homicide, civilize the Pawnee. But what lessons for the debauchee of sentiment? Was ever one converted? A deep aping or mimicry that has adhered like a parasite, until it sucks the vital juices, & makes the malformations as of false flowers on shrubs, which are found to be stingings of insects, or the warts on the plum tree.

The innocence & ignorance of the patient is the first difficulty. A rough realist or a neighborhood of realists would be prescribed, but that is like proposing to mend your bad road with diamonds. Then poverty, war, imprisonment, famine, Labrador with mercury at Zero, would lop the garrulity & check the grimacing. In a world where a remedy exists for every mischief if it were only a boy's cracker to silence cats under dormitory windows.

The way to have large occasional views, as in a political or social crisis, is to have large habitual views. When men consult you, it is not that they wish you to stand on your toes & pump your brains, but to apply your wisdom to the present question.

I defend myself against failure in my main design by making every inch of the road to it pleasant.

The points that glowed a little in yesterday's conversation, were, that the North must succeed. That is sure, was sure for 30 or 60 years back, was in the education, culture, & climate of our people;—they are bound to put through their undertakings. The exasperations of our people by the treacheries &

savageness of the Southern warfare are most wholesome disinfectants from the potent influence of Southern manners on our imagination. It was certain also that the Southerner would misbehave; that he will not keep his word; that he will be overbearing, rapacious. Slavery corrupts & denaturalizes people, as it has done Anna Barnard. There is no more probity in a slaveholder than truth in a drunken Irishman. Our success is sure. Its roots are in our poverty, our Calvinism, our schools, our thrifty habitual industry, in our snow, & east wind, & farm-life, & sea-life. These able & generous merchants are the sons & grandsons of farmers, & mechanics & sailors.

Logic of Events. Yes. President Lincoln, S. thought, must fail as inevitably as President Davis.

We insulted the abolitionist, but he instructed us.

There is who can afford to wait.

Party heats are so much whiskey, & simply intoxicate.

—

Reading.

I wish only to read that which it would be a serious disaster to have missed. Now how many foreign or domestic opinions on our war shall I suffer for not knowing? I do not know that Lord Palmerston or Lord Russell's opinion or existence is of the least importance. Not that fly of less.

The human mind cannot be burned, nor bayonetted, nor wounded, nor missing.

Henry Thoreau fell in Tuckerman's Ravine, at Mount Washington, and sprained his foot. As he was in the act of getting up from his fall, he saw for the first time the leaves of *Arnica Mollis!* the exact balm for his wound.

Thoreau

"Every poet has trembled on the verge of Science."

"If you would obtain insight, avoid anatomy."

"It requires so much closer attention to the habits of the birds, that, if for that reason only, I am willing to omit the gun."

Thoreau

By what direction did Henry entirely escape any influence of Swedenborg? I do not remember ever hearing him name Swedenborg.

If we should ever print Henry's journals, you may look for a plentiful crop of naturalists. Young men of sensibility must fall an easy prey to the charming of Pan's pipe.

—

Thoreau

"I look back for the era of this creation, not into the night, but to a dawn for which no man ever rose early enough."

"*Field Notes.*" Jan. 1853 p 38

"We cannot well afford not to see the geese go over a single spring, & so commence the year regularly." *Ib.* p 103

"If you make the least correct observation of nature this year, you will have occasion to repeat it with illustrations the next, & the season, & life itself is prolonged." *Ib.* 124

H. D. Thoreau

"'Trench says, a wild man is a willed man.' Well, then, a man of will, who does what he wills or wishes,—a man of hope, & of the future tense,—for not only the obstinate is willed, but far more the constant & persevering. The obstinate man, properly speaking, is one who will not. The perseverance of the saints is positive willedness, not a mere passive willingness. The fates are wild, for they will, and the Almighty is wild above all—as fate is."

Field Notes, Jan. 1853. p. 46

"A large fresh stone-heap 8 or 10 inches above water, just below there, quite sharp, like Teneriffe."

H.D.T. June, 1854, p. 307

"Men may talk about measures till all is blue & smells of brimstone, & then go home, & sit down, & expect their measures to do their duty for them. The only measure is integrity & manhood."

1854. June 19, p. 309.

"I am not so much reminded of former years as of existence prior to years," 1854 p 376

See his account of snapping-turtles, in "*Field Notes.*" August, 1854, p. 430, 453,

"They thus not only continue to live after they are dead, but begin to live before they are alive." Sept. 2, 1854.

"The day is short,—it seems to be composed of two twilights merely."

Dec. 1854, p. 92

"Ah how I have thriven on solitude & poverty,—I cannot overstate this advantage." Jan. 1855 p. 48

"I buy but few things, & those not till long after I begin to want them, so that when I do get them, I am prepared to make a perfect use of them & extract their whole sweet."

(this of buying a spy-glass) Apr. 10, 1854(?)

"If I would preserve my relation to Nature, I must make my life more moral, more pure, and innocent. The problem is as precise & simple as a mathematical one. I must not live loosely, but more & more continently."

Nov. 23, 1853 p 279

"The air over these fields is a foundry fill of moulds for casting bluebirds' warbles." 1857. Feb. 18

"How can we expect a harvest of thought who have not had a seed time of character. Already some of my small thoughts,—fruit of my spring life,—are ripe, like the berries which feed the first broods of birds, & other game are prematurely ripe & bright, like the lower leaves of herbs which have felt the summer's drought."

1854 Aug. 7

(*Of the seasons, & Winter.*)

"It is solid beauty. It has been subjected to the vicissitudes of millions of years of the gods, & not a single superfluous ornament remains. The serverest & coldest of the immortal critics shot their arrows at & pruned it, till it cannot be amended." 1856 Dec. 7

"Again & again I congratulate myself on my so-called poverty." Feb. 1857

"When I have only a rustling oak-leaf, or the faint metallic cheep of a tree-sparrow for variety in my winter walk, my life becomes continent & sweet as the kernel of a nut." Mss. 1857. Feb. 8

"The woodfrog had 4 or 5 dusky bars which matched exactly when the legs were folded, showing that the painter applied his brush to the animal when in that position." 1857, Sept. 12

—

"A broad leech on a turtle's sternum,—apparently going to winter with it." 1857 Dec. 2.

"There's as great an interval between the thrasher & the woodthrush, as between 'Thomson's Seasons' & Homer." 1853. June 14. p 333

"At this season (10 May) the traveller passes thro' a golden gate on causeways where these willows are planted, as if he were approaching the entrance of Fairy Land. & there will surely be found the yellowbird,—and already from a distance is heard his note, a *tche tche tche—tcha tchar tcha*. Ah willow willow, ah, could not *he* truly arrange for us the difficult family of the willows better than Boner or Barrett of Middletown!"
1853. p. 169

July, 1862. I suppose the war does not recommend slavery to any body. If it cost ten years of war, & ten to recover the general prosperity, the destruction of slavery is worth so much. But it does not cost so much time to get well again. How many times France has been a war-field! Every one of her towns has been sacked; the harvest has been a hundred times trampled down by armies: And yet, when you suppose, as after the first Napoleon's time, that the country must be desolate a year's labor, a new harvest, almost the hours of one perfect summer day create prodigious wealth, & repair the damage of ten years of war. What was it Goethe said of Nature's tilth? "This field has been reaped for a thousand years, but lo! a little sun & rain and all is green again."

—

Fact-books, if the facts be well & thoroughly told, are much more nearly allied to poetry than many books are that are written in rhyme.

—

All M.M.E.'s language was happy but inimitable as if caught from some dream.

I read with great satisfaction of the epoch in Art when ugly people were painted for Saints.

The art of the writer is to speak his fact & have done. Let the reader find that he cannot afford to omit any line of your writing, because you have omitted every word that he can spare. You are annoyed—are you?—that your fine friends do not read you: they are better friends than you knew, & have done you the rarest service. Now write so that they must. When it is a disgrace to them that they do not know what you have said, you will hear the echo.

—

Alcott brings me his Essay on the Garden. It has the old faults, false taste, sentimentalism, ambition of fine writing, ever so many ventures, in the hope that each may turn out a good one. I tell him that he is not to write anything but necessary words. He is not to write anything that I can afford not to read, can omit & never miss it. He had better never write a line to the end of the world than write thus. But he is incorrigible. You shall write what must be said, not what may be said.

When you write, you are to have the same resistless momentum that any good workman has in his work. Something is to be done which is worth doing, & it must be done now. You must not lose your presence of mind. Despair is no muse, he who finds himself hurried & gives up carrying his point now, writes in vain. Goethe had *urkraftige behagen*, stout comfortableness, stomach for the fight.

He that made the world lets that speak, & does not also employ a town-crier.

26 Aug., 1862.

Little Waldo, when I carried him to the circus, & showed him the clown & his antics, said, "It makes me want to go home," and I am forced to quote my boy's speech often & often since. I can do so few things, I can see so few companies, that do not remind me of it! Of course, if I had the faculty to meet the occasion, I should enjoy it. Not having it, & noting how many occasions I cannot meet, life loses value every month, & I shall be quite ready to give place to whoso waits for my chair.

—

When I compare my experience with that of my own family & coevals, I think, that, in spite of the checks, I have had a triumphant health.

The aphorism of the lawyers *non curat de minimis praetor*, like most of their wisdom is to be reversed; for the truth is, *in minimis existit natura*. In Nature, nothing is insignificant because it is small. The bee is essential to the marriage of the plants.

I believe in the perseverance of the saints. I believe in effectual calling. I believe in life Everlasting.

—

Henry said, "I wish so to live as to derive my satisfactions & inspirations from the commonest events, so that what my senses hourly perceive, my daily walk, the conversation of my neighbors may inspire me, & I may dream of no heaven but that which lies about me."

—

"We *condescend* to climb the crags of earth." H.D.T. May 23, 1854

—

If we were truly to take account of stock before the Last Court of Appeals,—that were an inventory. What are my resources? A few moral maxims, confirmed by much experience, would stand high on the list, constituting a supreme prudence. Then the knowledge, unutterable, of my strength, of where it lies, of its accesses, & facilitations, & of its obstructions; my conviction of principles,—that is great part of my possession. Having them, 'tis easy to devise or use means of illustrating them,—I need not take thought for that. Certain thoughts, certain observations, long familiar to me in night-watches & daylights, would be my capital, if I remove to Spain, or China, or, by stranger translation, to the planet Jupiter or Mars, or to new spiritual societies.

To work by your strength,—never to speak, or act, or behave, except on the broad basis of your *Naturel*,—constitution,

—

Thoreau in a rainstorm on the river with Channing, lands his boat, draws it ashore, turns it over in a twinkling against a clump of alders with cat-briars which keep up the lee side, crawls under it, & lies there for an hour on the ground, delighted with his stout roof.

Nov. 1853. p 247

Dr C. T. Jackson silences cats under his window at night by throwing out a lighted Indian cracker.

How remarkable the principle of iteration in rhetoric! We are delighted with it in rhyme, in poetic prose, in song, above all, allowing a line to be not only a burden to the whole song, but, as in Negro melodies, to be steadily repeated 3 or 4 times in immediate succession. Well, what shall we say of a liturgy? what of a litany? What of a Lord's Prayer, the burial service which is echoed & reechoed from one end of man's life to the other?

In optics no number of reflections of the same object displeases; and, in acoustics, no number of echoes displeases, rather in both the more the better.

Wren said, a portico may be continued ad infinitum. Irish

woman, as soon as she has told her fact, tells it again; & Wm Prescott, Esq repeated his argument once for every juror.

—

A singer cares little for the words of the song, he will make any words glorious. I think the like rule holds of the good reader. I call him only a good reader who can read sense & poetry into any hymn in the hymn-book.

—

From our boat in Walden Pond we saw the bottom at great depth, the stones all lying covered with moss or lichen as they looked of a greenish gray color. Ellery said, There is antiquity. How long they have lain there unchanged!

The country seems to be ruined not so much by the malignity as by the levity of people. A vast force of voters allow themselves by mere compliments & solicitations of a few well-dressed intriguers to promise their support to a party whose wish is to drag back slavery into the Government of the Union.

Great is the virtue of the Proclamation. It works when men are sleeping, when the Army goes into winter quarters, when generals are treacherous or imbecile.

—

People's Party.

The Proclamation has defined every man's position. In reading every speech, or any sentence of any speech, but a few words show at once the *animus* of the men, shows them friends of Slavery; shows us that the battleground is fast changing from Richmond to Boston. They unmask themselves, &, though we tried to think them freemen, they are not. Look where they rage, at Sumner. They find not Lincoln, for they do not think him really antislavery, but the abolitionist they can find is Sumner, and him they hate. If Sumner were pro-slavery, there would be no chemical analysis & magnifying glass needed to exhibit his foibles.

It seems to promise an extension of the war. For there can be no durable peace, no sound Constitution, until we have fought this battle, & the rights of man are vindicated. It were to patch a peace to cry peace whilst this vital difference exists.

And you are fond of music. How delightful! my brother is a musician, & we can send for him to entertain you at any time. And what instrument does he play on? On the bass drum.

1 November. Yesterday, 31 October, I found the foliage more richly colored, I think, in the woods, than on any day of this season. Earlier at the time when we usually find the richest color, some warm misty weather seemed to rob it prematurely, &, when the sun came out again, the landscape was rusty. Yesterday & today the mildest, most poetic of days, and, as usual, this equilibrium of the elements seems to be the normal state, and the northeast wind the exception.

A flock of fine large sparrows (?) flew in such perfect time as if the globed flock were one ball, forward, forward, swift & steadily,—that I thought no drill of cavalry could ever reach that perfection of manoeuvre.

—

Wendell Phillips gives no intimation of his perfect eloquence in casual intercourse. How easily he wears his power, quite free & disengaged, nowise absorbed in any care or thought of the thunderbolt he carries concealed. I think he has more culture than his own, is debtor to generations of gentlemen behind him. Conway says, that, when Phillips speaks, Garrison observes delighted the effect on the audience & seems to see & hear everything except Phillips, is the only one in the audience who does not hear & understand Phillips.

But I think Phillips is entirely resolved into his talent. There is not an immense residuum left as in Webster.

—

Well, yes, all our political disasters grow as logically out of our attempts in the past to do without justice, as thistles & nettles out of their seeds. One thing is plain; a certain personal virtue is essential to freedom, & it begins to be doubtful whether our corruption in this country has not gone a little over the mark of safety, and now, when canvassed, we shall be found to be made up of Fernando Woods, Joel Parkers, & Mayor Wightmans, the divine knowledge has ebbed out of us, & we do not know enough to be free.

There never was a nation great except through trial. A religious revolution cuts sharpest, & tests the faith & endurance. A civil war sweeps away all the false issues on which it begun, & arrives presently at real & lasting questions.

—

G F Train said in a public speech in New York, "Slavery is a divine institution." "So is hell," exclaimed an old man in the crowd.

—

In poetry, the charm is of course in the power of the thought which enforces beautiful expression. But the common experience is, fine language to clothe commonplace thoughts, if I may say thoughts. And the effect is, dwarfs on stilts.
'Tis a fine expression of Arnold's "the lyrical cry," though the examples he gives are not well chosen.

When we build, our first care is to find good foundation. If the surface be loose, or sandy, or springy, we clear it away, & dig down to the hard pan, or, better, to the living rock, & bed our courses in that. So will we do with the state. The War is serving many good purposes. It is no respecter of respectable persons or of worn out party platforms. War is a realist, shatters everything flimsy & shifty, sets aside all false issues, & breaks through all that is not real as itself, comes to organize opinions & parties, resting on the necessities of man, like its own cannonade comes crushing in through party walls that have stood fifty or sixty years as if they were solid. The screaming of leaders, the votes by acclamation of conventions, are all idle wind. They cry for mercy but they cry to one who never knew the word. He is the Arm of the Fates and as has been said "nothing prevails against God but God." Everything must perish except that which must live.

Well, this is the task before us, to accept the benefit of the War: it has not created our false relations, they have created it. It simply demonstrates the rottenness it found. We watch its course as we did the cholera, which goes where predisposition already existed, took only the susceptible, set its seal on every putrid spot, & on none other, followed the limestone, & left the granite. So the War. Anxious Statesmen try to rule it, to slacken it here & let it rage there, to not exasperate, to keep the black man out of it; to keep it well in hand, nor let it ride over old party lines, nor much molest trade, and to confine it to the frontier of the 2 sections. Why need Cape Cod, why need Casco Bay, why need Lake Superior, know any thing of it? But the Indians have been bought, & they come down on Lake Superior; Boston & Portland are threatened by the pirate; more than that, Secession unexpectedly shows teeth in Boston, our parties have just shown you that the war is already in Massachusetts, as in Richmond.

Let it search, let it grind, let it overturn, &, like the fire when it finds no more fuel, it burns out. The war will show, as all wars do, what wrong is intolerable, what wrong makes & breeds all this bad blood. I suppose that it shows two incompatible states of society, freedom & slavery. If a part of this country is civilized up to a clear insight of freedom, & of its necessity, and another part is not so far civilized, then I suppose that the same difficulties will continue; the war will not be extinguished; no treaties, no peace, no Constitutions can paper over the lips of that red crater.

Only when, at last, so many parts of the country as can combine on an equal & moral contract,—not to protect each other in polygamy, or in kidnapping, or in eating men,—but in humane & just activities,—only so many can combine firmly & durably.

I speak the speech of an idealist. I say let the rule be right. If the theory is right, it is not so much matter about the facts. If the plan of your fort is right it is not so much matter that you have got a rotten beam or a cracked gun somewhere, they can by & by be replaced by better without tearing your fort to pieces. But if the plan is wrong, then all is rotten, & every step adds to the ruin. Then every screw is loose, and all the machine crazy. The question stands thus, reconstruction is no longer matter of doubt. All our action now is new & unconstitutional, & necessarily so. To bargain or treat at all with the rebels, to make arrangements with them about exchange of prisoners or hospitals, or truces to bury the dead, all unconstitutional & enough to drive a strict constructionist out of his wits. Much more in our future action touching peace, any & every arrangement short of forcible subjugation of the rebel country, will be flat disloyalty, on our part.

Then how to reconstruct. I say, this time, go to work right. Go down to the pan, see that your works turn on a jewel. Do not make an impossible mixture.

Do not lay your cornerstone on a shaking morass that will let down the superstructure into a bottomless pit again.

Leave slavery out. Since (unfortunately as some may think,) God is God, & nothing satisfies all men but justice, let us have that, & let us stifle our prejudices against commonsense & humanity, & agree that every man shall have what he honestly earns, and, if he is a sane & innocent man, have an equal vote in the state, and a fair chance in society.

And I, speaking in the interest of no man & no party, but simply as a geometer of his forces, say that the smallest beginning, so that it is just, is better & stronger than the largest that is not quite just.

This time, no compromises, no concealments, no crimes that cannot be called by name, shall be tucked in under another name, like, "persons held to labor," meaning persons stolen, & "held", meaning held by hand-cuffs, when they are not under whips.

Now the smallest state so formed will & must be strong, the interest & the affection of every man will make it strong by his entire strength, and it will mightily persuade every other man, & every neighboring territory to make it larger, and it will not reach its limits until it comes to people who think that they are a little cunninger than the maker of this world & of the consciences of men.

—

Nov. 29. 1862 Great harvest this year of apples & pears. I suppose I have sold a hundred barrels of apples, when I add the August & September sales to the winter apples.—Beurre Diels have been our excellent fruit for the last month, & were still perfect at Thanksgiving. Passe Colmans perfect also on that day. We had a profusion of Seckels & of Louise Bonnes. We had 2 to 3 barrels of Bonnes Louises, & not less than 4 barrels of Glout Morceaux (which proved excellent from 22 Dec. to 6 January); and now to 6 February

What a convivial talent is that of Wendell Holmes! He is still at his Club, when he travels in search of his wounded son; has the same delight in his perceptions, in his wit, in its effect, which he watches as a belle the effect of her beauty; would still hold each companion fast by his spritely, sparkling, widely-allusive talk, as at the Club-table: tastes all his own talent, calculates every stroke, and yet the fountain is unfailing, the wit excellent, the *savoir vivre & savoir parler* admirable.

Isaac Hecker, the Catholic priest, came to see me, & desired to read lectures on the Catholic Church, in Concord. I told him that nobody would come to hear him, such was the aversation of people, at present, to theological questions; & not only so, but the drifting of the human mind was now quite in another direction than to any churches. Nor could I possibly affect the smallest interest in anything that regarded his church. We are used to this whim of a man's choosing to put on & wear a painted petticoat, as we are to whims of artists who wear a mediaeval cap or beard, & attach importance to it; but, of course, they must say nothing about it to us, & we will never notice it to them, but will carry on general conversation, with utter reticence as to each other's whimsies: but if once they speak of it, they are not the men we took them for, & we do not talk with them twice. But I doubt if any impression can be made on Father Isaac. He converted Mrs Ward, &, like the lion that has eaten a man, he wants to be at it again, & convert somebody.

—

I write laboriously after a law, which I see, & then lose, & then see again. And, I doubt not, though I see around me many men of superior talent, that my reader will do me the justice to feel that I am not contriving something to surprise or to tickle him, but am seriously striving to say that which is.

We used, forty years ago, religious rites in every house, which have disappeared. There is no longer, in the houses of my acquaintances, morning or evening family prayer, or grace said at table, or any exact observance of the Sunday, except in the houses of clergymen.

I have long ceased to regret this disuse. It is quite impossible to put the dial-hand back. The religion is now where it should be. Persons are discriminated as honest, as veracious, as generous & helpful, as conscientious, or having public & universal regards; are discriminated according to their aims, & not by these ritualities.

—

I should have noted whilst they were fresh in mind the consternation & religious excitement caused in my good grandfather & his companions by the death of one soldier at Bunker Hill. Let us believe it was the first or it would discredit the history of the carnage. Similar was the impression made by a death in their neighborhood on the family of Samuel Moody, as appeared in a letter which Ellen read to me. One would think that nobody ever died before, or, that our great grandfathers were the longliving patriarchs of Shem & Seth & Enoch's time.

A Lyceum needs three things, a great deal of light, of heat, & of people. At Pittsburgh we wanted all three, and usually we lack one or the other.

—

I am a bard least of bards.

I cannot, like them, make lofty arguments in stately continuous verse, constraining the rocks, trees, animals, & the periodic stars to say my thoughts,—for that is the gift of great poets; but I am a bard, because I stand near them, & apprehend all they utter, & with pure joy hear that which I also would say, &, moreover, I speak interruptedly words & half stanzas which have the like scope & aim.

from
FOR

1863

> "There are some living creatures that can out of their own natures raise up a light in the dark when they are inflamed with desire." *Swed.*

I suppose the reference is to fireflies & glowworms.

But how shall weakness write of force?

—

We affirm & affirm, but neither you nor I know the value of what we say. Every Jersey wagon that goes by my gate moves from a motive & to an end as little contemplated by the rider as by his horse.

—

The delight in the first days of spring, the "wish to journeys make," seems to be a reminiscence of Adam's Paradise, & the longing to return thither.

> 'Tis that which sets all mortals a roving
> in the month of May.

—

Family likeness in the Greek Gods. Socrates says, "the Laws below are sisters of the laws above." So really are the material elements of close affinity to the moral elements. But they are not their cousins, but they are themselves. They are the same laws acting on superior & inferior planes. On the lower plane, it is called Heat; on the higher, Love. Whenever you enunciate a physical law, I hear in it a moral rule.

Swedenborg's genius is the perception of the doctrine of inspiration, that "the Lord flows into the spirits" of angels & men. *παντα ρει*

—

In the beauty of the boy, I detect somewhat passagère, that is, that will not stay with *me*.

—

Affirmative & Negative

"You tell me a great deal of what the devil does, & what power he has: when did you hear from Christ last?" asked Father Taylor of some Calvinistic friends.

When Thoreau heard a cricket or a blue bird, he felt he was not far from home after all. He found confirmation of all his human hopes in the smell of a water lily.—But the froth or spittle on the alders & andromedas in June made the walk disagreeable to him.

—

April, 1863—

This running into the Catholic Church is disgusting, just when one is looking amiably round at the culture & performance of the young people, & fancying that the new generation is an advance on the last. Sam. Ward says, the misfortune is that when the young people have this desire, there is nothing on the other side to offer them instead. And it is true that stoicism, always attractive to the intellectual & cultivated, has now no temples, no Academy, no commanding Zeno or Antoninus. It accuses us that it has none,—that pure Ethics is not now formulated & concreted into a *cultus*, a fraternity with assemblings & holy days, with song & book, with brick & stone.

Why have not those who believe in it, & love it, left all for this, & dedicated themselves to write out its scientific scripture to become its Vulgate for millions? I answer for one, that the inspirations we catch of this law are not continuous & technical, but joyful sparkles & flashes, and are recorded for their beauty,—for the delight they give,—not for their obligation; and that is their priceless good to men that they charm & uplift, not that they are imposed. These words out of heaven are imparted to happy uncontrollable Pindars, Hafizes, Shakspeares, & not to Westminster Assemblies of divines.

And yet it must be confessed that the new world lies in chaos & expectation until now; that this mad war has made us all mad, that there was no minority to stand fast for eternal truth, & say, cannons & bayonets for such as already knew nothing stronger: but we are here for immortal resistance to wrong: we resist it by disobedience to every evil command, and by incessant furtherance of every right cause.

But in regard to Ward's remark, cited above p. 814, it must be said, that *there is the eternal offset of the moral sentiment.* The Catholic religion stands on morals & is only the effete state of formalism; & morals are ever creating new channels & forms.

—

1863 April 15. I find Walden entirely open, and I have failed to know on what day; probably on Saturday 11 & Sunday 12th.

—

April 17. Alcott defended his thesis of personality, last night; but it is not a quite satisfactory use of words. We speak daily of a government, of power used to personal ends. And I see profound need of distinguishing the First Cause as superpersonal. It deluges us with power; we are filled with It, but there are skies of immensity between us & it. But Alcott's true strength is in the emphasis he gives to partnership of power against the doctrine of Fate. There is no passive reception: the receiver to receive must play the God also. God gives, but, it is God, or, it takes God, also, to receive. He finds or fancies Goethe priest of Fate, &, writing Faust he never liberates, because he is prisoner himself.

Of me, Alcott said, "some of the organs were free, some fated; the voice was entirely liberated; And my poems or Essays were not rightly published, until I read them!"

—

20 April, 1863.

Abraham Jackson, Esq. was here yesterday, & speaks of his old experience of the College at Cambridge. He owed more to Jones Very, who was Greek Tutor, than to almost any or all others in the faculty. Any enthusiasm, any literary ambition or attempt was sure to be snubbed by teachers, as well as by the public opinion of the classes. Only expense, only money, was respectable. He remembers Dr Walker with respect, and Doctor Beck, but not Felton. In the Law School, he had better experience, from Judge Story, Mr Greenleaf, & Charles Sumner.

*

And now, when the question arises—how shall money be bestowed for the benefit of learning?—his recollection of the University does not appear edifying.

—

The "Herald's" correspondence from Washington, N.C. (Gen Foster) speaks of the negroes seen with a musket in one hand, & a spelling book in the other.

"Some of them lie behind the breast-works, with a spelling book in one hand, & a musket in the other."

—

I have never recorded a fact which perhaps ought to have gone into my sketch of "Thoreau," that, on the 1 August, 1844, when I read my Discourse on Emancipation, in the Town Hall, in Concord, and the selectmen would not direct the sexton to ring the meeting-house bell, Henry went himself, & rung the bell at the appointed hour.

It were worth while to notice the jokes of Nature, she so rarely departs from her serious mood. The "punch" faces in the English violets is one; the parrot is one; the monkey; the lapwing's limping, & the like petty stratagems of other birds.

Saladin caused his shroud to be made & carried it to battle as his standard. Aunt Mary has done the like all her life, making up her shroud, & then thinking it pity to let it lie idle, wears it as night-gown or day-gown until it is worn out; (for death, when asked, will not come;) then she has another made up, &, I believe, has worn out a great many. And now that her release seems to be really at hand, the event of her death has really something so comic in the eyes of everybody that her friends fear they shall laugh at the funeral.

Hannah Parsons relates, that, for years M M E had her bed made in the form of a coffin; and delighted in the figure of a coffin made daily on her wall by the shadow of a church.

—

We can easily tell of Whittier or Longfellow or Patmore, what suggestion they had, what styles of contemporaries have affected their own. We know all their possible feeders. But of Donne, of Daniel, of Butler, we do not, & read them as self-educated & originals, imputing to them the credit of now forgotten poets. Still more is this true of Saadi & Cervantes.

4 May, 1863. On Friday morning 1 May, at 3 o'clock, died Mary Moody Emerson, at Williamsburg, New York, aged 88 years, 8 months. Hannah Haskins Parsons, her niece, who has, since her childhood, been in some sort dedicated to the care & nursing of her Aunt, has for the last four years taken entire charge of her, &, having with incredible patience & tenderness attended her throughout her long decline, & closed her eyes, now attended the remains to Concord, & arrived here on Saturday Night. This afternoon (Monday) the body was taken from the Receiving Tomb to the grave in my lot in Sleepy Hollow, & deposited in a vault therein, in the presence of Elizabeth Hoar, Elizabeth Ripley, Mary Emerson Simmons, Lidian Emerson, Ellen Tucker Emerson, Edith Emerson and myself. The day was cloudy & warm, with mist resting over the South, & the rain waited until an hour after she was laid in the ground.

I said, we have never a right to do wrong.

—

"The coldest weather" (writes MME in her journal, Concord 1821) "ever known. Life truly resembles a river, always the same, never the same. And perhaps a greater variety of internal emotions would be felt by remaining with books in one place, than pursuing the waves which are ever the same. Is the melancholy bird of night, covered with the dark foliage of the willow & cypress, less gratified than the gay lark amid flowers & suns?"

"It is mortifying to fluctuate in our opinions respecting anything which is not novel, especially one's self. Yet as to mind & heart, I alter very much. Yet how stationary that little self! How many stars have set & risen, suns perhaps expired, & angels lost their glory, since I have droned in this place!"

Ennui

"The pursuit of planting a garden or raising a nation occupies the mind, but, at bottom of the heart remains a void which we do not like to feel or complain of. The same ennui may be felt when the pursuits are intellectual or religious, but not in measure. One bustles, & is illuded by the hope of doing good, & stifles this gnawing discontent for higher objects in the spiritual world. How much happier to be employed with those very objects which are already above!" Jan. 31.

—

The Southerner says with double meaning, "Cotton is King," —intimating that the art of command is the talent of their country. We reply, 'Very likely, but we prefer a republic.'

—

At Washington, in 1862, I met Governor Andrew, who had Mr Forbes, Mr Ward, & Mr Amory, with him: he said, he had particularly solicited them to go along with him, since a single man at Washington was nobody, & was thrust aside. I had not expected to find a Governor of Massachusetts playing the part of unprotected female. And he too one of the most industrious & devoted patriots the war has brought out.

A benefit of War is, that the appeal not being longer to letter & form, but now to the roots of strength in the people, the moral aspect becomes important, & is urgently presented & debated. Whilst, in preceding quiet times, custom is able to stifle this discussion as sentimental, & bring in the brazen devil himself.

Certain it is that never before since I read newspapers, has the morale played so large a part in them as now.

—

In reading Henry Thoreau's Journal, I am very sensible of the vigor of his constitution. That oaken strength which I noted whenever he walked or worked or surveyed wood lots, the same unhesitating hand with which a field-laborer accosts a piece of work which I should shun as a waste of strength, Henry shows in his literary task. He has muscle, & ventures on & performs feats which I am forced to decline. In reading him, I find the same thought, the same spirit that is in me, but he takes a step beyond, & illustrates by excellent images that which I should have conveyed in a sleepy generality. 'Tis as if I went into a gymnasium, & saw youths leap, climb, & swing with a force unapproachable,—though their feats are only continuations of my initial grapplings & jumps.

—

My feeling about Henry James's book is that he is a certain Saul among the prophets. The logical basis of his book a certain pure & absolute theism:—there is but one Actor in the Universe,—there is no self but devil;—all must be surrendered to ecstasy of the present Deity. But the tone in which all this is taught is in perpetual contemptuous chiding & satire.

The Arabs measure distance by horizons, and scholars must.

'Twas odd that I woke at midnight, & mused on the indifference of all subjects to genius. Not dainty & fastidious is he, but accosts the nearest fact, high or humble. Like General Lee, "he carries his base with him," & shows you that God & his eternities are equally near to every point of humanity.

—

Inspiration alternated
Sometimes the electrical machine will not work; no spark will pass; then, presently, the world is all a cat's back, all sparkle & shock. Sometimes there is no sea-fire; and again the sea is all aglow. Sometimes the Aeolian harp is dumb all day in the window; & again it is garrulous, & tells all the secrets of the world. In June, the mornings are noisy with birds; & in July, already they are getting old & silent. Il n'y a que le matin
Napoleon's 1806 & 1807

Channing thinks Carlyle does not recognize the people, in "Life of Friedrich".
July 16 Rode this p.m. with Channing in wagon to White Pond. 'Tis perhaps ten years ago since I was there with him before, and in the reflections of the larger grown trees in the lake noticed the same peculiarities. The trees were all done in minute squares, as in the crochet work of girls; the colors of the foliage, russet & ruddy, added to the beauty. Pines on the distant shore, of which we saw only the short stem veiled above by the branches,—in the water showed the stem of the tree to the top! We were on the farther side of the pond at the

"Cove," & talked with a party,—a young man & three young women from Sudbury 3½ miles distant. They left the shore in a boat. C. & I agreed that a picnic is like a "revival," it changes a man in an instant, & he forgets his home & habits, & thinks he will come & live with Nature. But he returns to his village to put up his horse, stops at the Post Office, takes tea with his family, and does not for ten years get a glance at the Paradise again. After a bath in the Pond came home by the beautiful road through Nine-Acre-Corner, where the farms were in richest array. An old hemlock tree in one field should teach every body to plant and guard a hemlock, that it may some day be old.

—

Ellery Channing always speaks of the landscape as of a painting.

—

I went to Dartmouth College, and found the same old Granny system which I met there 25 years ago. President Lord has an aversion to emulation, as injurious to the character of the pupils. He therefore forbids the election of members into the two literary societies by merit, but arranges that the first scholar alphabetically on the list shall be assigned to the Adelphi, & the second to the Mathesians, the third to the Adelphi, & the fourth to the Mathesians; and so on, every student belonging to the one or the other.—"Well, but there is a first scholar in the class, is there not, & he has the first oration at Commencement?" "O no, the parts are assigned by lot."—The amiable student who explained it, added, that it tended to remove disagreeable excitement from the societies. I answered, Certainly and it would remove more if there were no college at all. I recommended morphine in liberal dose, at the College Commons. I learn, since my return, that the President has resigned;—the first good trait I have heard of in the man.

—

Hawthorne unlucky in having for a friend a man who cannot be befriended; whose miserable administration admits but of one excuse, imbecility. Pierce was either the worst, or he was the weakest of all our Presidents.

I was to write that our people have false delight in talent, in a showy speech, a lawyer who can carry his point, in Webster,

Choate, Butler, Banks, in Macaulay, & in innumerable Goughs & Dunlaps without considering their soundness or truth. But the measure in art & in intellect is one; To what end? Is it yours to do? Are you bound by character & conviction to that part you take? The very definition of Art is, the inspiration of a just design working through all the details. But the forsaking the design to produce effect by showy details, is the ruin of any work. Then begins shallowness of effect; intellectual bankruptcy of the artist. All goes wrong. Artist & public corrupt each other. Now the public are always children. The majority are young & ignorant, unable to distinguish tinsel from gold, ornament from beauty. But the scholar must keep faith with himself. His sheet-anchor is sincerity; and, when he loses this, he loses really the talent of his talent.

Mem. Aug. 25. Coombs worked ⅔ of a day on the apple trees grubbing out borers, & declared it was the best time in the year for it.

—

Carlyle has sacrificed to force of statement. One would say, none has ever equalled his executive power in the use of English. He makes an irresistible statement, which stands, & which every body remembers & repeats. It is like the new Parrott guns. There were always guns & powder. But here today are latest experiments & a success which exceeds all previous performance in throwing far, & in crushing effect. Much is sacrificed for this, but this is done. So with Carlyle's projectile style.

—

School-keeping is a dreary task, only relieved by the pleasure the teacher takes in two or three bright & beautiful pupils. The majority of the children will be infidels,—and the consoler is—the appearance of genius & noble nature in one or another.

—

'Tis strange, that it is not in vogue to commit hari-kari as the Japanese do at 60. Nature is *so* insulting in her hints & notices, does not pull you by the sleeve, but pulls out your teeth, tears off your hair in patches, steals your eyesight, twists your face into an ugly mask, in short, puts all contumelies upon you, without in the least abating your zeal to make a good appearance, and all this at the same time that she is moulding the new figures around you into wonderful beauty which, of course is only making your plight worse.

—

The miller is an idle man & makes the brook or the wind do his work. The poet is an idler man, hates the trouble of consecutive thinking, but observing that these tempestuous passions of his search all his knowledge, all his thought, all his sentiment, in their fury;—he fastens pens on the end of these, & they write songs, prophecies, tragedies & lampoons, that last till the morning of the Resurrection.
The daily problem is how to get force.
Borrowed the hint of the selfregistering thermometer.

—

It needs this & that incessant nudge of necessity or of passion to drive us from idleness & bring the day about, but what prodigious force must that spring have, whose impulsion reaches through all the days, through all the years, & keeps the old man constant to the same pursuits as in youth! 'Tis like the diurnal, annual, & centennial variations of the magnet.

For Alcott, I have always the feeling, that the visiter will not rightly see him; for he is like a piece of Labrador spar, which is a dull stone enough until you chance to turn it to the particular angle where its colors appear, & it becomes a jewel.

Men that are great only to one or two men.

Railroad.

The railroad justifies its monopoly of a strip of land 100 miles long suddenly & inconveniently taken from every man's cornfield or house lawn, or between his house & barn, or through his bedchamber, with the greatest violence to his private comfort,—through its constant occupation of it all day, all night by successive loaded trains.

Good out of evil.

One must thank the genius of Brigham Young for the creation of Salt Lake City,—an inestimable hospitality to the Overland Emigrants, and an efficient example to all men in the vast desart, teaching how to subdue & turn it to a habitable garden. And one must thank Walt Whitman for service to American literature in the Apalachian enlargement of his outline & treatment.

—

My interest in my Country is not primary, but professional. I wish that war as peace shall bring out the genius of the men. In every company, in every town, I seek intellect & character; & so in every circumstance. War, I know, is not an unmitigated evil: it is a potent alterative, tonic, magnetiser, reinforces manly power a hundred & a thousand times. I see it come as a frosty October, which shall restore intellectual & moral power to these languid & dissipated populations.

On the whole, I know that the cosmic results will be the same, whatever the daily events may be. The Union may win or lose battles, win or lose in the first treaties & settlement: Sutlers & pedlers may thrive on some abuse, but Northwest trade, & Northeastern production, & Pennsylvania coalmines, and New York shipping, and white labor, though not idealists, gravitate in the ideal direction. Nothing less large than justice to them all can keep them in good temper.

—

The reward which his puritan conscience brought to Samuel Hoar to indemnify him for all it had cost him, was, that his appearance in court for any party in a suit at once conciliated court, jury, & bystanders, to that side which the incorruptible man defended.

—

It was an excellent custom of the Quakers, (if only for a school of manners) the silent prayer before meals. When the table is ready, & the family have taken their places, they compose themselves, & sit for the space of a minute quite still, then open their napkins, & begin to eat. It has the effect to stop mirth & idle talking, & introduce a moment of reflection. After this pause, all begin again their usual intercourse from a vantage-ground. It would rebuke those violent manners which many people bring to the table, of wrath, & whining, & heat in trifles.

—

Do I not know how to play billiards & whist? Do I not know the violin & flute? yet I will throw myself on those bayonets.

—

Washington & Cromwell,—one using a moral, the other a revolutionary policy. The Govt. of Algiers & of Turkey is, tho' it last for ages, revolutionary. If we continued in Boston to throw tea into the bay at pleasure, that were revolutionary. But our *revolution* was in the interest of the moral or anti-revolutionary. Slavery is Algiers or perpetual revolution. Society upside down, head over heels, & man eating his breakfast with pistols by his plate. It is man degraded to cat & dog. & Society has come to an end, and all gentlemen die out.

—

Originality
A well-read man can always find the opinion & thesis of a new writer, be he who he will, & however original,—already printed in an old book. Thus Madame du Deffand had Carlyle's horror at eloquence. Every new writer is only a new crater of an old volcano.

Having penetrated the people & known their unworthiness, we can well cease to respect their opinion, even their contempt, & not go to war at our disadvantage for the avoiding of this. Who are they that they should despise?——these people who cringe before Gortchakoff & Napoleon. Let us remember the wise remark of General Scott, "Resentment is a bad basis for a campaign." I am not sure of the wisdom of Burke's saying, "Contempt is not a thing to be despised."

—

In poetry, Nature bears the whole expense. In prose, there must be concatenation, a mass of facts, and a method. 'Tis very costly; only a capitalist can take hold of it; but, in poetry, the mere enumeration of natural objects suffices. Nay, Tennyson is a poet, because he has said, "the stammering thunder," or, "the wrinkled sea beneath him crawls" & Longfellow "the plunging wave".

—

Boutwell said to me, the other day, "It makes no difference whether we gain or lose a battle, except the loss of valuable lives: we gain the advantage from month to month." There has been no example like ours of the march of a good cause as by gravitation, or rather, by specific levity, against particular defeats. It is like the progress of health in sleep. You have removed the causes of disease, (& one of them is your restless doing,) & all mends of itself. It is like the replacement of the dislocated bone, as soon as you have removed the obstruction. The vanity of no man is gratified: the Abolitionist would so willingly put in his claim. The sublime God puts him back into the same category of egotism with the Copperhead.

I remember when I feared—what one still newly escaped shudders to think of,—that a little more success, a wiser choice of candidate by the Southern party,—say, of Jefferson Davis, instead of Pierce or Buchanan,—had enabled them by a coup d'état to have strained the whole organism of the government to the behoof of Slavery,—to have insisted, by all the courts, marshals, & army & navy of the Union, on carrying into effect a right of transit with Slaves from state to state. It had then only been necessary for rich democrats in N Y, Pennsylvania & Connecticut to buy slaves, & it is not easy to see how the ardent abolitionists—always a minority hated by the rich class,—could have successfully resisted. The effect however would have been to put the *onus* of resistance on the North, and, at last, the North would have seceded. We had been the rebels, & would have had the like difficulty to put our states into secession as the Southerners had.

—

Boston.
The Boston of Franklin, Adams, Otis, Quincy, Warren, Horatio Greenough, of Wendell Phillips, of Jonathan Phillips, of Edward Everett, of Allston, of Brook Farm, of Edward Taylor, of Daniel Webster, of Samuel Dexter, of Buckminster, Channing, Greenwood, of Charles Sprague, of Starr King, of Billings the architect, of Mrs Julia Howe, Margaret Fuller, of a class of forgotten but wonderful young men, burning too fast to live long, but who marked not less the powers of the air & soil, John Everett, Clark Harris the Orientalist, Edward Lowell, Edward & Charles Emerson, Fisk, who wrote his Greek grammar in his bed; not having clothes enough: the Boston of

Beecher, of Horace Mann, Parker, Sumner, Lowell, Holmes, Agassiz, Longfellow, Pierce, Dana, Ward, Hoar, Hunt, Henry James, Peter Hunt, Newcomb, the Boston which animates other souls born of it, or adopted spiritually into it, &, in all quarters of their dispersion, drawing inspiration from it;—Furness, Beecher, Channing, Fremont, even, Bryant, Greeley
Nay, the influences are so wide, & the names crowd on me so fast, that I must take the Boston Directory or the National Census to exhaust them. The neighborhood of Thanksgiving Day makes me look at our cousins of New York with a kinder eye, and I remember that the Germans say, that, Vienna is the first German city, Berlin the second, & New York the third: and I shall say, that New York is the second city of Bostonians; and, whenever we shall so far have inoculated that centre of nations, by our crowding immigration from New England, that they shall give a republican vote, I will concede, that it is the first.

—

Beecher at Exeter Hall is superb:—his consciousness of power shown in his jocular good humor & entire presence of mind; the instant surrender of the English audience, as soon as they have found a master; he steers the Behemoth,—sits astride his very snout, strokes his fur, tickles his ear, & rules him; secures the English by the method & circumstantiality of statement which they love, by figures, and then by downright homely illustration of important statements. His compliment to Wendell Phillips as the first orator of the world,—did he not say so?—recalls Byron's line

"And Jura answers from his misty shroud
Back to the joyous Alps that call to him aloud."

They write better, but we read more out of their books than they do. They have better blowpipe, (we have not yet narrowed our heat to a focus. A continent full of coal.)
England possesses drastic skill, always better artists than we: Carlyle a better writer, Gladstone or Bright a better debater, I suppose, than any of ours. Tennyson a better poet; but is the scope as high? is the material of Tennyson better, or does not our dumb muse see stars & horizons they do not? In England, in France, in Germany, is the popular sentiment as illuminated as here? As I wrote the other day,—our native politics are ideal.

These women, old wives sitting by the chimney side here, shrill their exclamations of impatience & indignation, shame on Mr Seward, shame on the Senate, &c, for their want of humanity, of mere morality;—they stand on the ground of simple morality, & not on the class feeling which narrows the perceptions of English, French, German people, at home. We are affirmative. They live under obstructions & negations. England's six points of Chartism are still postponed. They have all been granted here to begin with. England has taken in more partners, & stands better on its legs, than once, but still has huge load to carry. See how this moderates the ferocity incident elsewhere to political changes. We, in the midst of a great Revolution, still enacting the sentiment of the Puritans, and the dreams of young people 30 years ago; we, passing out of the old remainders of barbarism into pure Christianity & humanity, into freedom of thought, of religion, of speech, of the press, & of trade, & of suffrage, or political right; & working through this tremendous ordeal which elsewhere went by beheadings, & massacre, & reigns of terror,—passing through all this & through states & territories, like a sleep, & drinking our tea the while. 'Tis like a brick house moved from its old foundations & place, & passing through our streets, whilst all the family are pursuing their domestic work inside.

I hate to have the egotism thrust in with such effrontery. This revolution is the work of no man, but the effervescence of nature. It never did not work. But nothing that has occurred but has been a surprise, & as much to the leaders as to the hindmost. And not an abolitionist, not an idealist, can say without effrontery, I did it. It is the fly in the coach, again. Go boost the globe, or Scotch the globe, to accelerate or retard it in its orb. It is elemental, it is the old eternal gravitations: beware of the swing, & of the recoil! Who knows, or has computed, the periods? A little earlier, & you would have been burned or crazed; a little later, you are unnecessary. If I had attempted in 1806, what I performed in 1807, said Napoleon, I had been lost. Fremont was superseded in 1861, for what his superseders are achieving in 1863. And many the like examples. The Republicans of this year were the Whigs & democrats of 1856. Mazzini & Kossuth 'tis fine for them to sit in committee in London, & hope to direct revolution in Italy, Hungary, & Poland. Committees don't manage revolutions. A revolution is a volcano, and from under every body's feet flings its sheet of fire into the sky. More than that, let not the old thinker flatter himself. 'You may have your hour at 30,' says Jove, '& lay for a moment your hand on the helm, but not at 60. I draft only between the ages of 20 & 45. Only Quincy Adams in a whole generation of men do I allow to lay an iron hand on the helm at 75.'

—

Mere "Natural objects always did & do weaken, deaden & obliterate imagination in me," said W. Blake.

"One thought fills immensity." *Blake*

"The tigers of wrath are wiser than the horses of instruction." Blake

from

KL

1864–1865

I too am fighting my campaign.

So many things require the top of health, the flower of the mind, the engraver must not lay stone walls, nor the king's lapidary pave streets. 'Tis fine health that helps itself with lucky expressions & fit images:—All things offer themselves to be words & convey its meaning. But lassitude has nothing but prose.

What omniscience has music! So absolutely impersonal, & yet every sufferer feels his secret sorrow soothed.

Within, I do not find wrinkles & used heart, but unspent youth.

—

Inspiration

I have found my advantage in going to a hotel with a task which could not prosper at home. I secured so a more absolute solitude, for it is almost impossible for a housekeeper who, in the country, is also a small farmer, & who has guests in the house, to exclude interruptions & even necessary orders, though I bar out by system all I can, & resolutely omit to my constant loss all that can be omitted. In the hotel, I have no hours to keep, no visits, & can command an astronomic leisure. At home the day is cut up into short strips. In the hotel, I forget rain, wind, & cold, heat. At home, I remember in my library the wants of the farm, & have all too much sympathy. I envy the abstraction of some scholars I have known, who might sit on a curb-stone in state street & solve their problem. I have more womanly eyes. All the conditions must be right for my success, slight as that is. What untunes is as bad as what cripples or stuns me. Therefore I extol the prudence of Carlyle, who, for years, projected a library at the top of his house, high above the orbit of all housemaids, and out of earshot of door-bells. Could that be once secured,—a whole floor,—room for books, & a good bolt,—he could hope for six years of history. And he kept it in view till it was done. And I remember that Henry Thoreau, with his cynic will, yet found certain trifles disturbing the delicacy of that health which composition exacted,—namely, the slightest irregularity or the drinking too much water on the preceding day. And George Sand's love of heat agrees with mine. Even the steel pen is a nuisance.

—

Inspiration
And the first rule for me would be to defend the morning. Keep all its dews on. *Il n'y a que le matin en toutes choses.*

Goethe thanks the flies that waked him at dawn as the Musagetes.

And where shall I find the record of my brag of places, favorite spots in the woods & on the river, whither I once went with security for a poetic mood?

—

Inspiration
M. M. E. writes, "How sad, that atmospheric influences should bring to dust the communions of soul with the Infinite!"—meaning, how sad that the atmosphere should be an excitant. But no, she should be glad that the atmosphere & the dull rock itself should be deluged with deity,—should be theists, Christian, Unitarian, poetic.

Inspiration
Shall I add to my list of electrics, after Sleep, Conversation, New Poetry, Fact-books, &c., certain localities, as, mountain-tops, the shores of large bodies of water, or of rapid brooks, as excitants of the muse? And yet the experience of some good artists would prefer the smallest & plainest chamber with one chair & one table to these picturesque liberties.

—

When Renan speaks of France, or any Englishman Macaulay of England, or any American of America, I feel how babyish they are.

I suppose hardly Newton, or Swedenborg, or Cervantes, or Menu, can be trusted to speak of his nationality.

—

The grief of old age is, that, now, only in rare moments, & by happiest combinations or consent of the elements can we attain those enlargements & that intellectual *élan*, which were once a daily gift.

—

I have more enjoyed, in the last hours of finishing a chapter, the insight which has come to me of how the truths really stand, than I suffered from seeing in what confusion I had left them in my statement.

June, 1865

St Francis rode all day along the border of the Lake of Geneva, &, at night, hearing his companions speak of the lake, inquired What lake?

—

"We can never compete with English in manufactures, because of the low price of labor in Europe,"—say the merchants, day by day. Yet, this season, half or two thirds of our laborers are gone to the war, and we have reaped all the hay by the use of the horse-mower & the horse-rake; the wheat, by MacCormick's reaper; &, when the shoemakers went, then, by the use of the new pegging machine & scrap-machine, we make 600 pairs of shoes every day at Feltonville, & can let Weymouth send away 100 shoemakers to the war in the regiment that has just departed. We make horseshoes by machine as well at Pittsburg. We can spare all the whalemen to the navy, for we draw oil out of the rocks in Pennsylvania; we can spare the Cuba sugar, for we made 7 000 000 gallons of sorghum molasses in 1860, though the article was not known here in 1850.

—

Want of scale appears in this; each of the masters has some puerility, as Carlyle his proslavery whim; Tennyson, English class feeling; University men, churchmen, not humanity, heroism, truth. Our faculties are of different ages. The Memory is mature, sometimes the imagination adult, & yet the Moral sense still swaddled & sheathed. Yet on the credit of their talent, these masters are allowed to parade this baby faculty, all fits & folly, in the midst of grown company.

We have freedom, are ready for truth, but have not the executive culture of Germany. They have good metaphysics,—have made surveys, sounding every rod of way, set their foot on every rock, and where they felt the rock they planted a buoy & recorded it. Kant, Hegel, Schelling, are architects. Scope is not sufficient. We have scope, but we want the Copernicus of our inward heaven. Let us be very mum at present about American literature. One of these ages, we too will set our feet on Andes' tops.

We lack repose. As soon as we stop working, or active thinking, we mope: there is no self-respect, no grand sense of sharing the Divine presence. We are restless, run out & back, talk fast, & overdo.

Nothing in the universe so solid as a thought.

Use of towns I considered in an old Journal in many points. But we are far from having the best aesthetics out of them. The French & Italians have made a nearer approach to it. A town in Europe is a place where you can go into a café at a certain hour of every day, buy *eau sucrée*, or a cup of coffee, for six sous, &, at that price, have the company of the wits, scholars & gentlemen fond of conversation. That is a cheap & excellent club, which finds & leaves all parties on a good mutual footing. That is the fame of the "Café Procope," the "Cafe Grec" of Rome, the "Cafe de Trinità" of Florence, & the principle of it exists in every town in France & Italy. But we do not manage it so well in America. Our clubbing is much more costly & cumbersome.

The test of civilization is the power of drawing the most benefit out of cities.

—

A true nation loves its vernacular tongue. A completed nation does not import its religion. Duty grows everywhere, like children, like grass, and we need not go to Asia to learn it.

—

When I go to talk with Alcott it is not so much to get his thoughts as to watch myself under his influence. He excites me, & I think freely. But he mistakes me, & thinks, if J. is right, that I come to feed on him.

It is mortifying that all events must be seen by wise men even, through the diminishing lens of a petty interest. Could we have believed that England should have disappointed us thus? that no man in all that civil, reading, brave, cosmopolitan country, should have looked at our revolution as a student of history, as philanthropist, eager to see what new possibilities for humanity were to begin,—what the inspirations were; what new move on the board the Genius of the world was preparing. No, but every one squinted; Lords, Ladies, statesmen, scholars, poets, all squinted,—like Borrow's gipsies when he read St. John's Gospel. Edinburg, Quarterly, Saturday Review, Gladstone, Russell, Palmerston, Brougham, nay Tennyson; Carlyle, I blush to say it; Arnold. Every one forgot his history, his poetry, his religion, & looked only at his shoptill, whether his salary, whether his small investment in the funds, would not be less: whether the stability of English order might not be in some degree endangered. No Milton, no Bacon, no Berkeley, no Montesquieu, no Adam Smith was there to hail a new dawn of hope & culture for men, to see the opportunity for riddance of this filthy pest which dishonored human Nature; to cry over to us, "Up & God with you! And for this slavery,— Off with its head! We see & applaud; the world is with you; such occasion does not come twice. Strike for the Universe of Men!"
No; but, on the other hand, every poet, every scholar, every great man, as well as the rich, thought only of his pocket book, & to our astonishment cried, *Slavery forever! Down with the North! Why does not England join with France to protect the slaveholder?* I thought they would have seized the occasion to forgive the Northerner every old grudge; to forget their dislike of his rivalry, of his social short-comings; forget, in such a moment, all petty disgusts & would see in him the honored instrument of Heaven to destroy this rooted poisontree of five thousand years.

We shall prosper, we shall destroy slavery, but by no help of theirs. They assailed us with mean cavils, they sneered at our manners, at our failures, at our shifts, at the poverty of our treasury, at our struggles & legal & municipal irregularities, in the presence of mortal dangers. They cherished our enemies, they exulted at the factions which crippled us at home; whenever the allies of the rebels obstructed the great will & action of the Government, they danced for joy.

—

The War.

The War has cost us many valuable lives; but perhaps it has compensated us, by making many lives valuable that were not so before,—through the start & expansion it has given them. It has demoralized many rebel regiments; but I hold that it has *moralized* many of ours.

—

When a man writes descriptions of the sun as seen through telescope, he is only writing autobiography, or an account of the habit & defects of his own eyes.

Henry Thoreau found the height of the cliff over the river to be ft. 231.09.

—

1864

24 September. Yesterday with Ellery walked through "Becky Stow's Hole," dry-shod, hitherto a feat for a muskrat alone. The sky & air & autumn woods in their early best. This year, the river meadows all dry & permeable to the walker. But why should nature always be on the gallop? Look now & instantly, or you shall never see it: Not ten minutes' repose allowed. Incessant whirl. And 'tis the same with my companion's genius. You must carry a stenographic press in your pocket to save his commentaries on things & men, or they are irrecoverable. I tormented my memory just now in vain to restore a witty criticism of his, yesterday, on a book.

Room! room! breathing space! play ground! horizon! Ah! in him were chambers in the brain, halls, palaces, champaigns heaven-wide.

Though Love recoil, & reason chafe,
There came a voice without reply,
''Tis man's perdition to be safe,
When for the Truth he ought to die.'

—

But in all the living circle of American wits & scholars is no enthusiasm. Alcott alone has it.

—

M.M.E. & her contemporaries spoke continually of Angels & Archangels, with a good faith, as they would have spoken of their parents, or their late minister. Now the word palls,—all the credence gone.

The War at last appoints the Generals, in spite of parties & Presidents. Every one of us had his pet, at the start, but none of us appointed Grant, Sherman, Sheridan, & Farragut,—none but themselves. Yet these are only shining examples. The fruit of small powers and virtues is as fixed. The harvest of potatoes is not more sure than the harvest of every talent.

Great difference in life of two consecutive days. Now it has grip, tastes the hours, fills the horizon, & presently it recedes, has little possession, is somnambulic.

We read often with as much talent as we write. The retrospective value of a new thought is immense. 'Tis like a torch applied to a long train of powder.

A page of M.M.E. (vol II. 212) gives much to think of the felicity of greatness on a low ground of condition, as we have so often thought a rich Englishman has a better lot than a king. "No fair object but affords me gratification, and with common interests." And, (on p 201) she writes, "they knew by hearsay of Apes of men, vampire despots, crawling sycophants—"

See, however, what she writes of middle class virtue (Vol II p. 219–220)!

Criticism. I read with delight a casual notice of Wordsworth in the "London Reader," in which, with perfect aplomb, his

highest merits were affirmed, & his unquestionable superiority to all English poets since Milton, & thought how long I travelled & talked in England, & found no person, or none but one, & that one, Clough, sympathetic with him, & admiring him aright in face of Tennyson's culminating talent & genius in melodious verse. What struck me now was the certainty with which the best opinion comes to be the established opinion. This rugged rough countryman walks & sits alone, assured of his sanity & his inspiration, & writes to no public,—sneered at by Jeffrey & Brougham, branded by Byron, blackened by the gossip of Barry Cornwall & DeQuincey, down to Bowring,—for they all had disparaging tales of him, yet himself no more doubting the fine oracles that visited him than if Apollo had brought them visibly in his hand:
and here & there a solitary reader in country places had felt & owned them, & now, so few years after, it is lawful in that obese material England, whose vast strata of population are nowise converted or altered, yet to affirm unblamed, unresisted, that this is the genuine, & the rest the impure metal. For, in their sane hours, each of the fine minds in the country has found it, & imparted his conviction, so that every reader has somewhere heard it on the highest authority:

"And thus the world is brought
To sympathy with hopes & fears it heeded not."

—

How often I have to say, that every man has material enough in his experience to exhaust the sagacity of Newton in working it out. We have more than we use. We know vastly more than we digest. I never read poetry, or hear a good speech at a caucus, or a cattle-show, but it adds less stock to my knowledge, than it apprises me of admirable uses to which what I knew can be turned. I write this now on remembrance of some *structural* experience of last night,—a painful waking out of dream as by violence, & a rapid succession of quasi-optical shows following like a pyrotechnic exhibition of architectural or grotesque flourishes, which indicate magazines of talent & invention in our structure, which I shall not arrive at the control of, in my time, but perhaps my great grandson will mature & bring to day.

—

I have often occasion to recall Horace Walpole's remark that nothing will stay in his memory but the names of men & women. (Equivalent is De Stael's "Mes opinions politiques sont des noms propres.") I look over this desart of Frothingham's metaphysics, & see the names of Carlyle, Ruskin, Emerson, & can hope to find some shed & life on the wide prairie at these points.

—

Oct. 19. Yesterday as I passed Shannon's field, robins, blackbirds, bluebirds & snowbirds (fringilla hiemalis) were enjoying themselves together.

Bryant has learned where to hang his titles, namely, by tying his mind to autumn woods, winter mornings, rain, brooks, mountains, Evening winds, & wood-birds. Who speaks of these is forced to remember Bryant.
American. Never despaired of the Republic. dared name a jay & a gentian, crows.
His poetry is sincere. I think of the young poets that they have seen pictures of mountains & seashores but his that he has seen mountains & has the staff in his hand

—

1864. October 25 Power of certain States of the sky. There is an astonishing magnificence even in this low town, & within a quarter of a mile of my doors, in the appearance of the Lincoln hills now drest in their colored forest, under the lights & clouds of morning, as I saw them at 8 o'clock. When I see this spectacle so near, & so surprising, I think no house should be built quite low, or should obstruct the prospect by trees.

—

native American
Bryant sincere
balanced mind had the enthusiasm which perception of nature inspires but it did not tear him; only enabled him; gave him twice his power; he did not parade it, but hid it in his verse.
his connection with party usque ad aras.
simple, True bard but simple,
I fear he has not escaped the infirmity of fame, like the Presidential malady, a virus once in, not to be got out of the system:

he has this, so cold & majestic as he sits there,—has this to a heat which has brought to him the devotion of all the young men & women who love poetry, & of all the old men & women who once were young. 'Tis a perfect tyranny. Talk of the people, shopmen who advertise their drugs or cosmetics on the walls & on the palisades & huge rocks along the railways. Why this man more cunning by far has contrived to levy on all American Nature & subsidized every solitary forest & monument mountain in Berkshire or the Katskills, every waterfowl, every partridge, every gentian & goldenrod, the prairies, the gardens of the desart, the song of the stars, the Evening wind,—has bribed every one of these to speak for him, so that there is scarcely a feature of day & night in the country which does not, whether we will or not,—recall the name of Bryant. This high-handed usurpation I charge him with, & on the top of this, with persuading us & all mankind to hug our fetters & rejoice in our subjugation.

Rev. Dr P. talked the other day, at Cambridge as if he had been much corrupted by society, since I knew him a young man already much courted, but with his manly simplicity still unspoiled. Now he grimaces, & had the pulpit airs of a court preacher. Perhaps a bad dentist had served him ill, & had given him fashionable teeth for his own honest grinders. Yet I felt, while he spoke, that it was easy, or at least possible, to open to the audience the thesis which he mouthed upon, how the Divine Order "pays" the Country for the sacrifices it has made & makes in the war.—War ennobles the Country; searches it; fires it; acquaints it with its resources; turns it away from false alliances, vain hopes, & theatric attitudes; puts it on its mettle; "in ourselves our safety must be sought"; gives it scope & object; concentrates history into a year, invents means; systematizes everything. We began the war in vast confusion; when we end it, all will be in system.

—

1865 Concord 13 Feb
Home from Chicago & Milwaukee. Chicago grows so fast that one ceases to respect civic growth: as if all these solid & stately squares, which we are wont to see as the slow work of a cen-

tury, had come to be done by machinery, as cloth & hardware is made, & was therefore shoddy architecture, without honor.

'Twas tedious the obstructions & squalor of travel. The advantage of their offers at Chicago made it needful to go. It was in short this dragging a decorous old gentleman out of home, & out of position, to this juvenile career tantamount to this; "I'll bet you fifty dollars a day for three weeks, that you will not leave your library & wade & freeze & ride & run, & suffer all manner of indignities, & stand up for an hour each night reading in a hall:" and I answer, "I'll bet I will," I do it, & win the $900.

—

'Tis far the best that the rebels have been pounded instead of negociated into a peace. They must remember it, & their inveterate brag will be humbled, if not cured. George Minott used to tell me over the wall, when I urged him to go to town meeting & vote, that "votes did no good, what was done so wouldn't last, but what was done by bullets would stay put." General Grant's terms certainly look a little too easy, as foreclosing any action hereafter to convict Lee of treason, and I fear that the high tragic historic justice which the nation with severest consideration should execute, will be softened & dissipated & toasted away at dinner-tables. But the problems that now remain to be solved are very intricate & perplexing, & men are very much at a loss as to the right action. If we let the southern States in to Congress, the Northern democrats will join them in thwarting the will of the government. And the obvious remedy is to give the negro his vote. And then the difficult question comes,—what shall be the qualification of voters? We wish to raise the mean white to his right position, that he may withstand the planter. But the negro will learn to write & read, (which should be a required qualification,) before the white will.

—

The assassin Booth is a type man of a large class of the Southern people. By the destruction of Slavery, we destroy the stove in which the cockatrice eggs are hatched.

—

For "inspiration," the experience of writing letters is one of the best keys to the *modus* of it. When we have ceased for a long time to have any fulness of thoughts that once made a diary a joy as well as a necessity, & have come to believe that an image or a happy turn of expression is no longer at our command, in writing a letter, we may find that we rise to thought, & to a cordial power of expression that costs no effort, & it seems to us that this facility may be indefinitely applied & resumed. The wealth of the mind in this respect, *of seeing*, is like that of a looking-glass which is never tired or worn by any multitude of objects which it reflects. You may carry it all round the world, it is ready & perfect as ever for new millions. So is the mind of Shakspeare.

Inspiration is like yeast. 'Tis no matter in which of half a dozen odd ways you get the infection of yeast,—you can apply it equally well to your purpose, & get your loaf of bread. When I wish to write on my topic, 'tis of no consequence what kind of book or man gives me a hint or a motion, nor how far off that is from my topic.

—

President Lincoln.

Why talk of President Lincoln's equality of manners to the elegant or titled men with whom Everett or others saw him? A sincerely upright & intelligent man as he was, placed in the Chair, has no need to think of his manners or appearance. His work day by day educates him rapidly & to the best. He exerts the enormous power of this continent in every hour, in every conversation, in every act;—thinks & decides under this pressure, forced to see the vast & various bearings of the measures he adopts: *he* cannot palter, he cannot but carry a grace beyond his own, a dignity, by means of what he drops, e.g. all pretension & trick, and arrives, of course, at a simplicity, which is the perfection of manners.

—

Alcott thinks there was an infusion of Theodore Parker in Jesus which he could spare.

—

Southern Morality.

I charge the Southerner with starving prisoners of war; with massacring surrendered men; with the St Albans' raid; with plundering railroad passenger-trains in peaceful districts; with plots of burning cities; with advertising a price for the life of Lincoln, Butler, Garrison, & others; with assassination of the President, & of Seward; with attempts to import the yellow fever into New York; with the cutting up the bones of our soldiers to make ornaments, & drinking-cups of their skulls.

—

I am an old writer, & yet I often meet good English words which I never used once. Thus I met just now the word *wainscot.*

—

Admirable fairness of Elizabeth Hoar's mind. I think no one who writes or utilizes his opinions, can possibly be so fair. She will see finer *nuances* of equity which you would never see if untold. She applied the Napoleon *mot*, "Respect the burden," so well to Lincoln *quoad* Wendell Phillips.
And one may say, there is a genius for honesty, as well as for poetry, and nobody can anticipate the directness & simplicity of the true man.

The best in argument is not the accosting in front the hostile premises, but the *flanking* them by a new generalization which incidentally disposes of them.

It should be easy to say what I have always felt, that Stanley's "Lives of the Philosophers" or Marcus Antoninus are agreeable & suggestive books to me, whilst St Paul or Saint John are not, & I should never think of taking up these to start me on my task, as I often have used Plato or Plutarch. It is because the bible wears black cloth. It comes with a certain official claim against which the mind revolts. The book has its own nobilities,—might well be charming, if it was left simply on its merits, as the others; but this "you must,"—"it is your duty"—repels. 'Tis like the introduction of martial law into Concord. If you should dot our farms with picket lines, & I could not go or come across lots without a pass, I should resist, or else emigrate. If Concord were as beautiful as Paradise, it would be detestable at once.

And then were Concord plain as fair
As Eden when high God had blest it,
I should abandon & detest it.

—

May 28
In the acceptance that my papers find among my thoughtful countrymen, in these days, I cannot help feeling how limited is their reading. If they read only the books that I do, they would not exaggerate so wildly.

from

LN

1866–1868

1866 March 24.
I often think of uses of an Academy, though they did not rapidly appear when Sumner proposed his Bill. And perhaps if it was national, & must meet in Washington, or Philadelphia,—or even New-York would be a far away place for me,—such benefits as I crave, it could not serve. But today I should like to confide to a proper committee to report on what are called the "sentences of Zoroaster," or "the Chaldaic oracles;" to examine & report on those extraordinary fragments,—so wise, deep,—some of them poetic;—& such riddles, or so frivolous others,—& pronounce shortly, but advisedly, what is their true history.

Zoroaster has a line saying "that violent deaths are friendliest to the health of the soul." Attribute that among his good fortunes to Lincoln. And in the same connection remember the death of Pindar. Add Jones Very's washing his face to the title of Humility.

—

Not Niebuhr only lost his power of divination, but every poet has on the hills counted the Pleiads, & mourned his lost star. Ah the decays of memory, of fancy, of the saliency of thought! Who would not rather have a perfect remembrance of all I thought & felt in a certain high week, than to read any book that has been published.

When I read a good book, say, one which opens a literary question, I wish that life were 3 000 years long. Who would not launch into this Egyptian history, as opened by Wilkinson, Champollion, Bunsen, but for the *memento mori* which he reads on all sides. Who is not provoked by the temptation of the Sanscrit literature? And, as I wrote above, the Chaldaic oracles tempt me. But so also does Algebra, and astronomy, & chemistry, & geology, & botany. Perhaps, then, we must increase the appropriation, & write 30 000 years. And, if these years have correspondent effect with the 60 years we have experienced, some earnest scholar will move to amend by striking out the word "years," & inserting "centuries."

—

It is plain that the War has made many things public that were once quite too private. A man searches his mind for thoughts, & finds only the old commonplaces; but, at some moment, on the old topic of the day's politics, he makes a distinction he had not made; he discerns a little inlet not seen before. Where was a wall, is now a door. The mind goes in & out, & variously states in prose or poetry its new experience. It points it out to one & another, who, of course, deny the alleged discovery. But repeated experiments & affirmations make it visible soon to others. The point of interest is here, that these gates once opened never swing back. The observers may come at their leisure, & do at last satisfy themselves of the fact. The thought, the doctrine, the right, hitherto not affirmed, is published in set propositions, conversation of scholars & at last in the very choruses of songs.

The young hear it, &, as they have never fought it, never known otherwise, they accept it, vote for it at the polls, embody it in the laws. And this perception, thus satisfied, re-acts on the senses to clarify them, so that it becomes more indisputable. Thus it is no matter what the opposition may be of presidents or kings or majorities, but what the truth is as seen by one mind.

I copy a scrap copy of my letter sent to Mrs C. T., when in Europe, (perhaps never sent) which I pick up today. "I have let go the unreturning opportunity of which your visit to Germany gave me to acquaint you with Gisela Von Arnim, & Herman Grimm her husband, & Joachim the violinist. —and I who prize myself only on my endurance, that I am as good as new when the others are gone,—I to be slow, derelict, & dumb to you, in all your absence! I shall regret this as long as I live. How palsy creeps over us with gossamer first, & ropes afterwards! And you have the prisoner when you have once put your eye on him, as securely as after the bolts are drawn.—How strange that C.K.N., whose secret you & I alone have, should come to write novels. Holmes's genius is all that is new,—nor that to you. The worst is that we can do without it. Grand behavior is better, if it rest on the axis of the world."

Hegel seems to say, Look, I have sat long gazing at the all but imperceptible transitions of thought to thought, until I have seen with eyes the true boundary. I know what is this, and that. I know it, & have recorded it. It can never be seen but by a patience like mine added to a perception like mine. I know the subtile boundary, as surely as the mineralogist Hauy knows the normal lines of his crystal, & where the cleavage must begin. I know that all observation will justify me, and to the future metaphysician I say, that he may measure the power of his perception by the degree of his accord with mine.

—

American Politics.

I have the belief that of all things the work of America is to make the advanced intelligence of mankind in the sufficiency of morals practical; that, since there is on every side a breaking up of the faith in the old traditions of religion, &, of necessity, a return to the omnipotence of the moral sentiment, that in America this conviction is to be embodied in the laws, in the jurisprudence, in international law, in political economy. The lawyers have always some glaring exceptions to their statements of public equity, some reserves of sovereignty, tantamount to the Rob Roy rule that might makes right. America should affirm & establish that in no instance should the guns go in advance of the perfect right. You shall not make coups d'etat, & afterwards explain & pay, but shall proceed like William Penn, or whatever other Christian or humane person who treats with the Indian or foreigner on principles of honest trade & mutual advantage. Let us wait a thousand years for the Sandwich islands before we seize them by violence.

—

June 14 But the surprise & dazzle of beauty is such, that I thought today, that if beauty were the rule, instead of the exception, men would give up business.

—

Here is Ralph has got a hammer, & is creeping with all his might in a bee-line for the pier-glass.

—

I suspect Walt Whitman had been reading these Welsh remains when he wrote his "Leaves of Grass."
Thus Taliesin sings,

"I am water, I am a wren;
I am a workman, I am a star;
I am a serpent;
I am a cell, I am a chink;
I am a depositary of song, I am a learned person."

Nash, p. 183

—

Read M.M.E.'s mss. yesterday—many pages. They keep for me the old attraction; though, when I sometimes have tried passages on a stranger, I find something of fairy gold;—they need too much commentary, & are not as incisive as on me. They make the best example I have known of the power of the religion of the Puritans in full energy, until fifty years ago in New England. The central theme of these endless diaries, is, her relation to the Divine Being; the absolute submission of her will, with the sole proviso, that she may know it is the direct agency of God, (& not of cold laws of contingency &c) which bereaves & humiliates her. But the religion of the diary, as of the class it represented, is biographical; it is the culture, the poetry, the mythology, in which they personally believed themselves dignified, inspired, judged, & dealt with, in the present & in the future. And certainly gives to life an earnestness, & to nature a sentiment, which lacking, our later generation appears frivolous.

July 2. 1866. I went with Annie Keyes & Mr Channing on Wednesday, 27th June, to Troy, thence to the Mountain House in wagon, &, with Edward & Tom Ward who had come down to meet us, climbed the mountain. The party already encamped were Story, Ward, & Edward, for the men; & Una Hawthorne, Lizzie Simmons, & Ellen E. for the maidens. They lived on the plateau just below the summit, & were just constructing their one tent by spreading & tying India-Rubber blankets over a frame of spruce poles large enough to hold the four ladies with sleeping space, & to cover the baggage. The men must find shelter, if need is, under the rocks. The mountain at once justified the party & their enthusiasm. It was romance enough to be there, & behold the panorama, & learn one by one all the beautiful novelties. The country below is a vast champaign,—half cleared, half forest,—with forty ponds in sight, studded with villages & farmhouses, &, all around the horizon, closed with mountain ranges. The eye easily traces the valley followed by the Cheshire railroad, & just beyond it the valley of the Connecticut river, then the Green Mountain chain: in the north the White Hills can be seen; &, on the East, the low mountains of Watâtic & Wachusett. We had hardly wonted our eyes to the new Olympus, when the signs of a near storm set all the scattered party on the alert. The tent was to be finished & covered, & the knap-sacks piled in it. The Wanderers began to appear on the heights, & to descend, & much work in camp was done in brief time. I looked about for a shelter in the rocks, & not till the rain began to fall, crept into it. I called to Channing, & afterwards to Tom Ward, who came, & we sat substantially dry, if the seat was a little cold, & the wall a little dripping, &, pretty soon, a large brook roared between the rocks, a little lower than our feet hung. Meantime, the thunder shook the mountain, & much of the time was continuous cannonade.

The storm refused to break up. One & another adventurer rushed out to see the signs, & especially the sudden torrents, little Niagaras, that were pouring over the upper ledges, & descending upon our plateau. But everybody was getting uncomfortably wet, the prospect was not good for the night, &, in spite of all remonstrance on the part of the young ladies, I insisted that they must go down with me to the "Mountain-House," for the night. All the four girls at last were ready, & descended with Storey & me,—thus leaving the tent free to be occupied by Mr Channing, Tom. W., & Edward. The storm held on most of the night, but we were slowly drying & warming in the comfortable inn. Next day, the weather slowly changed, & we climbed again the hill, and were repaid for all mishaps by the glory of the afternoon & evening. Edward went up with me to the summit, up all sorts of giant stairs, & showed the long spur with many descending peaks on the

Dublin side. The rock-work is interesting & grand;—the clean cleavage, the wonderful slabs, the quartz dikes, the rock torrents in some parts, the uniform presence on the upper surface of the glacial lines or scratches, all in one self-same direction. Then every glance below apprises you how you are projected out into stellar space, as a sailor on a ship's bowsprit out into the sea. We look down here on a hundred farms & farm-houses, but never see horse or man. For our eyes the country is depopulated, around us the arctic sparrow, *fringilla nivalis*, flies & *peeps*, the ground-robin also; but you can hear the distant song of the wood-thrushes ascending from the green belts below. I found the picture charming & more than remunerative. Later, from the plateau, at sunset, I saw the great shadow of Monadnoc lengthen over the vast plain, until it touched the horizon. The earth & sky filled themselves with all ornaments,—haloes, rainbows, and little pendulums of cloud would hang down till they touched the top of a hill, giving it the appearance of a smoking volcano. The wind was north, the evening cold, but the camp fire kept the party comfortable, whilst Story, with Edward for chorus, sang a multitude of songs, to their great delectation. The night was forbiddingly cold;—the tent kept the girls in vital heat, but the youths could hardly keep their blood in circulation, the rather, that they had spared too many of their blankets to the girls & to the old men. Themselves had nothing for it but to rise & cut wood, & bring it to the fire, which Mr Channing watched & fed. & this service of fetching wood was done by Tom Ward once to his great peril during the night. In pitching a formless stump over into the ravine, he fell, &, in trying to clear himself from the stump now behind him, flying & falling, got a bad contusion.

I see with joy the Irish emigrants landing at Boston, at New York, & say to myself, There they go—to school.

Hazlitt, Lovelace's Editor, says, "Wither's song, 'Shall I, wasting in despair,' is certainly superior to the *Song to Althea*." —I will instantly seek & read it.—I have read it, & find that of Lovelace much the best.

*

I find my window looking west has a certain occult way of looking east also, & has surprised me again & again with noting arrivals or domestic incidents which I ought to know, occurring on the other side of the house. Such is the trick of the spectacles.

—

We say as a reproach, that a man lives on Memory; but Genius on the inspiration of the moment. And it is essential mark of poetry, that it betrays in every word instant activity of mind, shown in new uses of every fact & image, in preternatural quickness or perception of relations.
A presence of mind that gives a miraculous command of all means of uttering the thought & feeling of the moment. The poet squanders on the hour an amount of life that might furnish the seventy years of the man that stands next him.

In classes of men, what a figure is Charles Lamb! so much wit lodged in such a saccharine temperament.

—

Dr Channing took counsel, in 1840?, with George Ripley & Mrs Ripley, to find whether it were possible to bring cultivated thoughtful people socially together. He had already talked with Dr Warren on the same design, who made, I have heard, a party, which had its fatal termination in an oyster supper. Mrs Ripley invited a large party, but I do not remember that Dr Channing came. Perhaps he did, but it is significant enough of the very moderate success, that I do not recall the fact of his presence, or indeed any particulars but of some absurd toilettes.

I think there was the mistake of a general belief at that time, that there was some concert of doctrinaires to establish certain opinions, & inaugurate some movement in literature, philosophy, & religion, of which the supposed conspirators were quite innocent; for there was no concert, & only here & there, two or three men or women who read & wrote, each alone, with unusual vivacity. Perhaps they only agreed in having fallen upon Coleridge, Wordsworth, Goethe, & then upon Carlyle, with pleasure & sympathy. Otherwise, their education & reading were not marked, but had the American superficialness, & their studies were solitary. I suppose all of them were surprised at this rumor of a school or sect, & certainly at the name of Transcendentalism, which nobody knows who gave, or when it was first applied. As these persons became, in the common chances of society, acquainted with each other, there resulted certainly strong friendships, which, of course, were exclusive in proportion to their heat, & perhaps those persons who were mutually the best friends were the most private & had no ambition of publishing their letters, diaries or conversation. Such were Charles Newcomb, Saml G. Ward, & Caroline Sturgis,—all intimate with Margaret Fuller. Margaret with her radiant genius & fiery heart was perhaps the real centre that drew so many & so various individuals to a seeming union. Hedge, Clarke, W. H. Channing, W. E. Channing, jr., Ripley, James Clarke & many more then or since known as writers, or otherwise distinguished, were only held together as her friends. Mr A Bronson Alcott became known to all these as the pure idealist, not at all a man of letters, nor of any practical talent, & quite too cold & contemplative for the alliances of friendship, but purely intellectual, with rare simplicity & grandeur of perception, who read Plato as an equal, & inspired his companions only in proportion as they were intellectual, whilst the men of talent, of course, complained of the want of point & precision in this abstract & religious thinker. Elizabeth Hoar & Sarah Clarke, though certainly never summoned to any of the meetings which were held at George Ripley's, or Dr Francis's, or Stetson's, or Bartol's or my house, were prized & sympathetic friends of Margaret & of others whom I have named, in the circle. The "Dial" was the only public or quotable result of this temporary society & fermentation: and yet the Community at Brook Farm, founded by the readers of Fourier, drew also inspirations from this circle. A little later than at our first meetings, Theodore Parker became an active, &, of necessity, a leading associate: And in the logic of events, the "Twenty Eighth Congregation" & its "Fraternity," might be claimed as a robust result. I have seen Brownson & Father Taylor & Charles Sumner in the company.

—

In a warmer & more fruitful climate Alcott & his friends would soon have been Buddhists.

An important fact in the sequel was the plantation of Mr Lane & Mr Alcott at Stillriver, "Fruitlands." The labor on the place was all done by the volunteers; they used no animal food; they even for a time dressed themselves only in linen; but there were inherent difficulties: the members of the community were unused to labor, & were soon very impatient of it: the hard work fell on a few, & mainly on women. The recruits whom they drew were some of them partly, some of them quite insane. And the individuals could not divest themselves of the infirmity of holding property. When the winter came, & they had burned all the dry wood they could find, & began to burn green wood, they could not keep themselves warm, & fled to the Shakers for their warm fires.

What a saint is Milton!
How grateful we are to the man of the world who obeys the morale, as in humility, & in the obligation to serve mankind. True genius always has these inspirations.

Humanity always equal to itself. The religious understand each other under all mythologies, & say the same thing. Homer & Aeschylus in all the rubbish of fables speak out clearly ever & anon. the noble sentiments of all ages.

Calvinism was as injurious to the justice, as Greek myths were to the purity of the gods. Yet noble souls carried themselves nobly, & drew what treasures of character from that grim system.

We want heat to execute our plans. The good will, the knowledge, the whole armory of means are all present, but a certain heat, that long since used not to fail, refuses its office: And all is vain, until this capricious fuel is supplied. It seems a certain semi-animal heat, as if tea, or wine, or sea-air, or mountains or a new thought suggested in book or conversation could fire the train, wake the fancy, & the clear perception. Pitcoal! where to find it. 'Tis of no use that your engine is made like a watch, that you are a good workman, & know how to drive it, if there is no coal. What said Bettine to Goethe, "Go to ruin with your sentiments! Tis the senses alone that work in art, as in love, & nobody knows this better than you."

I find it a great & fatal difference whether I court the Muse, or the Muse courts me: That is the ugly disparity between age & youth.

July 30. 1866. This morn came again the exhilarating news of the landing of the Atlantic telegraph cable at Heart's Content, Newfoundland, & we repeat the old wonder & delight we found on the Adirondac, in August 1858. We have grown more skilful, it seems, in electric machinery, & may confide better in a lasting success. Our political condition is better, &, though dashed by the treachery of our American President, can hardly go backward to slavery & civil war. Besides, the suggestion of an event so exceptional & astounding in the history of human arts, is, that this instant & pitiless publicity now to be given to every public act must force on the actors a new sensibility to the opinion of mankind, & restrain folly & meanness.

—

The religion of seventy years ago was a belt to the mind, giving it a concentration & force. Notable men were kept respectable by the determination of thought on the Eternal world. Now men fall abroad, want polarity, & suffer in character & intellect. Perhaps it is the result of the temporary anarchy from the now hypocritical respect that is paid to Christianity, & a sort of scientific acceptance, without Enthusiasm, of the Moral Law. We are civil to Christianity, & have not learned to abandon ourselves to the all sufficiency & beatitude of Ethics. But this is temporary, & when the awful nature & origin of the sentiment is frankly declared, it will give at once the balance & the magnanimity.

Our thoughts on affairs, of course, are all pitched on the measure of human life. If we had the longevity of a redwood tree, or of a stone, we should not despond under bad politics. We have made a disastrous mistake in the election of a rebel as President. But the blunder is only noxious for the time, & discloses so soon the natural checks & cures, that it would cause no anxiety in a patriot who should live to the age of the antediluvians.

—

"The early Friends had not confidence in their own convictions, & fell under the debasing influence of authority. They whom no prisons appalled, who yielded to no cruelty, were not strong enough to maintain their own simple views" against the bigoted traditions. W. L. Fisher

When the Quakers settled in France, (in the early part of the French Revolution,) asked of the National Assembly to be released from military duty, Mirabeau (President) replied, "The Assembly will in its wisdom consider your requests, but, whenever I meet a Quaker, I shall say, 'My brother, if thou hast a right to be free, thou hast a right to prevent any one from making thee a slave: as thou lovest thy fellow-creature, suffer not a tyrant to destroy him; it would be killing him thyself.' "

—

What fanatics in politics we are! There are far more important things than free suffrage; namely, a pure will, pure & illumined.

August 12. Last night in conversation with the N. Y. ladies, Alcott appeared to great advantage, & I saw again, as often before, his singular superiority. As pure intellect, I have never seen his equal. The people with whom he talks do not even understand him. They interrupt him with clamorous dissent, or what they think verbal endorsement of what they fancy he may have been saying, or with, "Do you know Mr Alcott, I think thus & so,"—some whim or sentimentalism; & do not know that they have interrupted his large & progressive statement, do not know that all they have in their baby brains is spotty & incoherent, that all that he sees & says is like astronomy, lying there real & vast, & every part & fact in eternal connection with the whole. And that they ought to sit in silent gratitude, eager only to hear more, to hear the whole, & not interrupt him with their prattle. It is because his sight is so clear, commanding the whole ground, & he perfectly gifted to

state adequately what he sees, that he does not lose his temper, when his glib interlocutors bore him with their dead texts & phrases. Another who sees in flashes, or only here & there a land-mark, has the like confidence in his own truth, & in the infinitude of the soul, but none in his competence to show it to the bores; &, if they tease him, he is silent. Power is not pettish, but want of power is. A.'s activity of mind is shown in the perpetual invention & felicity of his language: the constitutionality of his thought, apparent in the fact, that last night's discourse only brought out with new conviction the old fundamental thoughts which he had, when I first knew him.
The moral benefit of such a mind cannot be told. The world fades: men, reputations, politics shrivel: the interests, power, future of the soul beam a new dayspring. Faith becomes sight.

—

Dhruva said; Enveloped by the divine Maya, I see distinctions, like a man who dreams. &, in presence of another being, who has meantime no real existence, I suffer from grief in thinking that this being, who is my brother, is my enemy. p 51

—

On 31 August visited Agassiz by invitation with Lidian & Ellen, & spent the day at his house & on the Nahant rocks. He is a man to be thankful for, always cordial, full of facts, with unsleeping observation, & perfectly communicative. In Brazil he saw on a half mile square 117 different kinds of excellent timber,—& not a saw mill in Brazil. A country thirsting for Yankees to open & use its earth. In Brazil is no bread: Manioca in pellets the substitute, at the side of your plate. No society, no culture; could only name three men; the Emperor, M. Coutinho, & M. Couteau.

governor of a province, Tom Ward's friend. For the rest, immense vulgarity: and, as Longfellow said, the Emperor wished he could swap places with Agassiz, & be a professor,—which A. explained, that the Emperor said, 'Now you, when you leave your work, can always return into cultivated society, I have none.'—Agassiz says, the whole population is wretchedly immoral, the color & features of the people showing the entire intermixing of all the races. Mrs Agassiz found the women ignorant, depressed, with no employment but needle-work, with no future, negligent of their persons, shabby & sluttish at home, with their hair about their ears, only gay in the ball room: The men well dressed.

Ida A. Higginson says, the bats in Georgia are covered with bedbugs.

I don't remember how long the "Brook Farm" existed, I think about six or seven years—the society then broke up, & the Farm was sold, &, I believe all the partners came out with loss. Some of them had spent on it the accumulations of years. I suppose they all at the moment regarded it as a failure. I do not think they can so regard it at this time, but probably as an important chapter in their experience, which has been of life-long value. What knowledge of themselves & of each other, what various practical wisdom, what personal power, what studies of character, what accumulated culture many of the members must have owed to it!

—

I can find my biography in every fable that I read.

—

Geometry, masonry, must make the basis of a poem also.

—

If one had the experience that when he sat in the boughs of a certain tree he could write his thoughts with more clearness, & not only so, but thought better— —

The promise of literature amazes, for none reads in a book in happy hour without suggestion of immensities on the right hand & on the left,—without seeing that all recorded experience is a drop of dew before the soliciting universe of thought.

—

Thought is more ductile than gold, more expansive than hydrogen gas; nations live on one book, &, in active states, one thought, one perception, discloses endless possibilities. It is ever as the attention, as the activity of the mind, & not as the number of thoughts or sensations, that the result is.

—

Egypt.

There is a good deal of stick in all the pictures. The masters beat the workmen.

—

What a boon of civilization & culture is a Dictionary! For a scholar's closet, his dictionaries are the solid indispensable companions, & he can almost spare the rest of his library, or find it for his occasion in another house. Liddell & Scott, Spiers, Grimm, Flugel, & Worcester, & Lemprière, the American Encyclopaedia, & the Biographie Générale, & the "Art of verifying dates," would reconcile a mature man to the sale of all his books, & to content himself with consulting them at the libraries as his occasion required. For these dictionaries are the result & condensation of the history of nations, the true history of the mind, and every word a theme for thought. Of course I must add to the above list a good Atlas, a Botany, an astronomy, &c.

Alcott said, "the Dictionary requires abandonment."

Genius itself is glad of a dictionary, as "the King himself is served by the field."

—

Dr Jackson said he was at Pulpit rock, Lake Superior, when he heard music, like rhythmical organ or vocal chanting, & believed it to come from some singers. But going on a little further, it ceased; in another direction, heard it again; & by & by perceived that it was the beating of the waves on the shore deprived of its harshness by the atmosphere.
He has never seen the subject treated scientifically, he thinks, except in a paper on sound by Dr Wollaston.

—

Greatness.
M. M. E. again (in II. p 200) has a vision of her Saint crowned, & the adorers "still ignorant that in this race could exist a capacity to find higher purer enjoyment than belonged to this martyr who was publicly crowned for his labors & motives,—that there were those in whom lived a higher aspiration, who felt there might be a secret union & derivation from the Infinite, without external forms or performances. Society made only for this influx. O where is he hid? In fathomless decrees? He will pass retiring Angels & hide himself under the wing of

the Absolute. Who cannot shake him off from his own gifts & emanations which Jesus revealed." &c. &c. *M. M. E.* II. 202

Poetry teaches the enormous force of a few words, & in proportion to the inspiration checks loquacity. The reading of a new poet frees the mind, teaches the power of the old names & symbols, & shames us again into new compression. Always to begin, to give a new glance at the fact or subject, & from the deepest centre,—is the rule, & to abhor counters, or lines, or words, to fill up.

It is with a book as it is with a man. We are more struck with the merits of a man who is well-mannered, well-drest, & well-mounted, than with those of my neighbor in shoddy; and I am a little ashamed to find how much this gay book in red & gold with a leaf like vellum & a palatial page, has opened my eyes to the merits of the poet whose verses I long since coldly looked over in newspapers or monthlies or in small cloth-bound volumes.

—

Oct. 12.

Dreams are more logical sometimes than waking thought. Last night, a robust dream of an insurrection of the American St Antoine quarter. The insurgent masses filled the grand palatial street, brought lumber, filled it with wooden barricade from side to side, entered thus all the palaces, by the upper windows, & drove out the tenants,

Every word in the language has once been used happily. The ear caught by that felicity retains it, & it is used again & again, as if the charm belonged to the word, & not to the life of thought which so enforced it. These profane uses of course kill it, & it is avoided. But a quick wit can, at any time, reinforce it, & it comes into vogue again.

—

Dreams. Oct. 24.

I have often experienced, & again last night, in my dreams, the surprise & curiosity of a stranger or indifferent observer to the trait or the motive & information communicated. Thus some refractory youth, over whom I had some guidance or authority, expressed very frankly his dissent & dislike, disliked my way of laughing. I was curious to understand the objection, & endeavored to penetrate & appreciate it, &, of course, with the usual misfortune, that, when I woke & attempted to recover the specification, which was remarkable, it was utterly forgotten. But the fact that I, who must be the author of both parts of the dialogue, am thus remote & inquisitive in regard to one part, is ever wonderful.

—

I don't know but I value the name of a thing, that is, the true poet's name for it, more than the thing. If I can get the right word for the moon, or about it,—the word that suggests to me & to all men its humane & universal beauty & significance then I have what I want of it, & shall not desire that a road may be made from my garden to the moon, or that the gift of this elephant be made over to me.

Cunning egotism. If I cannot brag of knowing something, then I brag of not knowing it. At any rate, Brag.

—

The negro, thanks to his temperament, appears to make the greatest amount of happiness out of the smallest capital.

—

Diderot was the best natured writer I have read of, who, to help a poor devil who had written a book against him, wrote a dedication to a pious duke of . He should stand in the same file of fame as the monk, my type of humility, who, when the Devil came into his cell, rose & gave him his only chair to sit in.

—

You complain that the negroes are a base class. Who makes & keeps the jew or the negro base, who but you, who exclude them from the rights which others enjoy?

Telegraph. I remember when somebody came to Mr R. G. Shaw, senior, & wished his aid to a system of telegraph by which he might instantly know in his counting-room when his ships approached the coast: he replied, "My ships come soon enough for me when the captain arrives in this room. It is all I can do to attend to them then."

If I were rich, I should get the education I have always wished by persuading Agassiz to let me carry him to Canada; & Dr Gray to go to examine the trans-Mississippi Flora; & Wyman should find me necessary to his excavations; and Alvan Clark should make a telescope for me too, & I can easily see how to find the gift for each master that would domesticate me with him for a time. Wise were the American boys who, in Berlin, engaged Dr Waagen, the Superintendent of the Royal Gallery, to attend them on their visits to the works of art in the city, & explain them.

I thought as the train carried me so fast down the east bank of the Hudson River, that Nature had marked the site of New York with such rare combination of advantages, as she now & then finishes a man or woman to a perfection in all parts, & in all details, as if to show the luxuriant type of the race;—finishing in one what is attempted or only begun in a thousand individuals. The length & volume of the river; the gentle beauty of the banks, the country rising immediately behind the bank on either side; the noble outlines of the Katskills; the breadth of the bays at Croton? & Tarrytown? then West Point; then, as you approach N. York, the sculptured Palisades;—then, at the city itself, the meeting of the waters; the river-like Sound; & the ocean at once,—instead of the weary Chesapeake & Delaware Bays.

—

Ellen reminds me that, years ago, when I had given her some memorandum of an account or other paper important to keep, & she had mislaid it, & could not find it when it was much wanted,—it happened that one night she dreamed where she had put it in a book, & on waking in the morning, went directly to the place, & found it.

—

M.M.E. read Tasso in 1826. The story hurries her along, but she has "too little imagination now to relish the inventions, & all the time thinks of Homer's Iliad. Alas! how narrow the limits of human invention. The 'Paradise Lost' gains in the comparison, yet had *that* never been, were it not for these. The moderns write better, but the readers are too wise to enjoy as in an unphilosophical age. A few pulsations of created beings, a few successions of acts, a few lamps held out in the firmament, enable us to talk of *time*, make epochs, write histories,—to do more—to date the revelations of God to man. But these lamps are held to measure out some of the moments of eternity, to divide the history of God's operations as in the birth & death of nations,—of worlds. It is a goodly name for our notions of breathing, suffering, enjoying, acting. We personify it. We call it by every name of fleeting, dreaming, vaporing imagery. Yet it is nothing. We exist in eternity; dissolve the body, & the night is gone,—the stars are extinguished, & we measure duration by the number of our thoughts, by the activity of reason, the discovery of truths, the acquirement of virtue, the approach to God."

—

In old Boston, a feature not be forgotten was John Wilson, the town crier, who rung his bell at each street corner,—"*Lost!* A child strayed this morning from 49 Marlborough Street; four years old; had on check apron, &c,
Auction! Battery-March-Square, &c &c." He cried so loud, that you could not hear what he said, if you stood near.

—

Reading.

I suppose every old scholar has had the experience of reading something in a book which was significant to him, but which he could never find again. Sure he is that he read it there; but no one else ever read it, nor can he find it again, though he buy the book, & ransack every page.

—

Original power in men is usually accompanied with assimilating power: and I value in Coleridge his excellent knowledge & quotations, perhaps as much, possibly more, than his original suggestions. If you give me just distinctions, if you give me inspiring lessons, imaginative poetry,—it is not important to me whose they are. If I possess them, & am fired & guided by them, I know you as a benefactor, & shall return to you as long as you serve me so well. I may like well to know what is Plato's, & what is Goethe's part, & what thought was always dear to you: but their very worth consists in their radiancy, & equal fitness to all intelligence. They fit all my facts like a charm. I respect myself (the more) that I know them.

Next to the originator of a good sentence is the first quoter of it. Many will read the book before one thinks of quoting a passage. As soon as he has done this, that line will be quoted east & west.

Warren Burton used to come to my room in College days, & said, he did not like to read, & did not remember what he read, but what I read or quoted to him he remembered, & never forgot.

—

But Dante still appears to me, as ever, an exceptional mind, a prodigy of imaginative function, executive rather than contemplative or wise. Another Zerah Colburn or Blind Tom, undeniable force of a peculiar kind, a prodigy, but not like Shakspeare, or Socrates, or Goethe, a beneficent humanity. His fames & infamies are so capriciously distributed,—What odd reasons for putting his men in inferno! The somnambulic genius of Dante is dream strengthened to the tenth power,—dream so fierce that it grasps all the details of the phantom spectacle, &, in spite of itself, clutches & conveys them into the waking memory, & can recite what every other would forget.

What pitiless minuteness of horrible details! He is a curiosity like the mastodon, but one would not desire such for friends & contemporaries. Abnormal throughout like Swedenborg. But at a frightful cost these obtain their fame. A man to put in a museum, but not in your house. Indeed I never read him, nor regret that I do not.

—

There is no saying of Rochefoucauld which is so bitter a satire on humanity as our religious Doctor Johnson's, when some one lamented the death of a friend; "We must either outlive our friends, you know, or our friends must outlive us; and I see no man who would hesitate about the choice." See *Piozzi* p. 123

Johnson, with his force of thought & skill of expression, with his large learning & his true manliness, with his piety & his obstinate narrow prejudices, & withal his rude impulses, is the ideal or representative Englishman.

Note also the sharp limitations of his thought. I never can read a page of Piozzi without being reminded of Aunt Mary.

—

In that Newtonian experiment we wrote of above, there is surprise & delight of finding identity, which the deep mind always anticipates. The child is perpetually amused by a new object, by a chip or a wad of wool or a rope or a bed-key,—each of a hundred objects, if before unseen, amuses him for a few moments, & he is long in learning, as the man is long in learning, that each is the old toy in a new mask; that, as Ellery said, he found in his youth in the confectioner's shop, that they had but two flavors in all the sweetmeats, peppermint & checkerberry.

—

I rarely take down Horace or Martial at home, but when reading in the Athenaeum, or Union Club, if I come upon a quotation from either, I resolve on the instant to read them every day. But,—at home again, homely thoughts.

Quotation—yes, but how differently persons quote! I am as much informed of your genius by what you select, as by what you originate. I read the quotation with your eyes, & find a new & fervent sense: as my reading of Shakspeare's Richard II. has always borrowed much of its interest from Edmund Kean's rendering: though I had that play only at second hand from him, through William Emerson, who heard him in London. When I saw Kean in Boston, he played nothing so high. The reading of books is, as I daily say, according to the sensibility of the scholar, & the profoundest thought or passion sleeps as in a mine, until an equal mind or heart finds & publishes it. The passages of Shakspeare that we most prize were never quoted within this century: & Bacon & Milton's prose,—& even Burke have their best fame within it. Every one, too, remembers his friends by their favorite poetry or other reading as I recall Shakspeare's "Make mouths at the invisible event," always from M.M.E.'s lips. & so many of Antoninus's & Milton's sentences.

—

Certain resemblances in nature, or unexpected repetitions of form, give keen pleasure when observed; as the figure of the oak leaf on the under shell of the tortoise; the figure of the acanthus leaf in the flame of burning wood; or, better as W. E. C. said, that the oak wood burning gives again the form of the oak leaf. So the vegetable form of frost on the window pane suggesting the identity of vegetation with crystallization.

So the piping of the hylas in the early days of April sounds at a little distance like the jingle of sleigh bells.

And Quatremere de Q's theory of Art is resemblance in the work to something of a different kind.

And why not in the repetition in nature of her scents, as of the orange in the little Sarothra; of black birch & chequerberry,

In this old matter of Originality & Quotation, a few points to be made distinctly.

The apparently immense amount of debt to the old. By necessity & by proclivity, & by delight, we all quote. We quote books, & arts & science, & religion, & customs, & laws, Yes, & houses, tables & chairs. At first view, 'tis all quotation,—all we have. But presently we make distinction. 1. By wise quotation. Vast difference in the mode of quotation. One quotes so well, that the person quoted is a gainer. The quoter's selection honors & celebrates the author. The quoter gives more fame than he receives aid. Thus Coleridge. Quoting is often merely of a suggestion which the quoter drew but of which the author is quite innocent.

For good quoting, then, there must be originality in the quoter,—bent, bias, delight in the truth, & only valuing the author in the measure of his agreement with the truth which we see, & which he had the luck to see first.

And originality, what is that? It is being; being somebody, being yourself, & reporting accurately what you see & are. If another's words describe your fact, use them as freely as you use the language & the alphabet, whose use does not impair your originality. Neither will another's sentiment or distinction impugn your sufficiency. Yet in proportion to your reality of life & perception, will be your difficulty of finding yourself expressed in others' words or deeds.

And yet—and yet—I hesitate to denounce reading, as aught

inferior or mean. When visions of my books come over me, as I sit writing, when the remembrance of some poet comes, I accept it with pure joy, & quit my thinking, as sad lumbering work; & hasten to my little heaven, if it is then accessible, as angels might. For these social affections also are part of Nature & being, and the delight in another's superiority is, as M. M. E. said, "my best gift from God." For here the moral nature is involved, which is higher than the intellectual.

—

The moral law preserves its eternal newness, & appears to each age new-born: almost abolishing memory by the splendor it lends to the passing moment.

Admirable chapter of Harriet Martineau, in her "Eastern Life, Present & Past." Vol. I. p. 230. One would think it had never been read, or that the minds of the readers had been instantly dipped in Lethe. It needs instant republication, & the advertisement to be cried in the churches.

It plays into my chapter of Quotation to find this necessity of repetition. If man takes any step, exerts any volition, initiates anything, no matter what, it is law of fate that another man shall repeat it, shall simply echo it. The Egyptian legend got this tyrannical currency, ploughed itself into the Hebrew captives.

The Henchman is possible only in the savage or semi savage state. Our age is not intelligent of the Jew. His religion was in every drop of his blood. The Americans cannot understand these Japanese, who must obey their Tycoon or whatever superior, if he commands *hari-kari*: It is in their heart & head & body to obey, & they say, their head bursts at the dismay into which they are thrown at thought of disobedience. Ourselves are our keys to find out Americans or English by; but they will not quite unlock Chinamen or Japanese. It is not our fault but theirs. They are remains of earlier & now almost extinct formations.

—

I have no knowledge of trade & there is not the sciolist who cannot shut my mouth & my understanding by strings of facts that seem to prove the wisdom of tariffs. But my faith in freedom of trade, as the rule, returns always. If the Creator has made oranges, coffee, & pineapples in Cuba, & refused them to Masstts, I cannot see why we should put a fine on the Cubans for bringing these to us,—a fine so heavy as to enable Massachusetts men to build costly palm-houses & glass conservatories, under which to coax these poor plants to ripen under our hard skies, & thus discourage the poor planter from sending them to gladden the very cottages here. We punish the planter there & punish the consumer here for adding these benefits to life.

Tax opium, tax poisons, tax brandy, gin, wine, hasheesh, tobacco, & whatever articles of pure luxury, but not healthy & delicious food.

—

An advantage of the mechanical improvements, is, that it has made old age more possible, more tolerable, & more respectable. What with spectacles, artificial teeth, preservation of the hair, trusses, overshoes, drop-lights & sleeping-cars, we can hold this dissolving body staunch & fit for use ten or twenty years longer than our ancestors could.

I wish the American Poet should let old times go & write on Tariff; Universal suffrage; Woman's suffrage; Science shall not be abused to make guns. The poet shall bring out the blazing truth, that he who kills his brother commits suicide. The gold was not hid in the Black Mountains that one man should own it all. The telegraph shall be open as writing is to all men. The grape is fertile, this year, that men may be genial & gentle, & make better laws, & not for their set alone. Thus shall the harvest of 1868 be memorable. The laws shall sternly hold men to their best, & fools shall not be allowed to administer what requires all the wisdom of the wisest.

—

Extremes meet, & there is no better example than the haughtiness of humility. No aristocrat, no porphyrogenet, can begin to compare with the self-respect of the saint. M. M. E. in her vision of her place in heaven looks very coolly at her "Divine Master." "I approached no nearer the person of my Divine Master—but the Infinite must forever & ever surround me. I had too proud a spirit, too elate, too complacent from constitution, may be, ever to have that affinity to Jesus which his better holier ones have." See *M.M.E. 4th*; p 277–8.

It is simply the consciousness, however yet obscure & undefined, of resting on Deity, that destroys all other dignities, or so called divinities, & can well afford to be disgraced & degraded in their presence. "To have less than an angel" (writes MME.) "write only from benevolence, I cannot." See MME. I. 23,
Jones Very, in his constant sense of the divine presence, thought it an honor to wash his own face.

Among the men who fulfil the part of the American Gentleman, I place gladly Theodore Lyman, who went in a right spirit to the War, & who now works so faithfully & beneficently in this charge of establishing the pisciculture in Massachusetts.

I understand Dr C.T.J. in talk yesterday to say that the balloon can never be relied on as a machine for travel, since the attempt to resist the wind, & sail against it will tear the balloon to pieces: that there must be wings invented to fly against the wind; and, that gun-cotton which is so light, &, especially, which does not soil the barrel, is the best force yet found. The reliance on a permanent west wind in the upper region of the atmosphere, may hold only over the land, & not over the sea. In the region of the tradewinds, the balloon may be applicable. The project has ceased to be presumptuous, since the ocean telegraph has become a fact.

—

18 March.
Charles Newcomb said, he liked Catholics born to it, but American Catholics were disgusting. And I have never seen any such converts who did not seem to me insane. As to the stories told yesterday of the vast tolerance of the New York Jesuits, &c. 'tis the mere gabble of the auctioneer to sell his wares. 'Tis all a trade in mummy.

I suppose that what Richard Owen told me in London of Turner's coming to him to ask him to give him the natural history of the mollusk on which the whale fed, he wishing to understand it *ab ovo* thoroughly, because he was going to paint "the Whale-ship", was just that chance of suggestion which I sought for my "Song of Boston" in going down the harbor, to Nantasket, & in my visit not yet made to Bunker-Hill Monument. We cannot give ourselves too many advantages, & a hint to the centre of the subject may spring from these pensive strolls around the walls.

—

In an earlier page in this book I wrote some notes touching the so called Transcendentalists of Boston in 1837. Hawthorne drew some sketches in his Blithedale Romance, but not happily, as I think: rather, I should say quite unworthy of his genius. To be sure I do not think any of his books worthy of his genius. I admired the man, who was simple, amiable, truth loving, & frank in conversation: but I never read his books with pleasure.—they are too young.

In & around Brook Farm, whether as members, boarders, or visiters, were many remarkable persons, whether for character, or intellect, or accomplishments. There was Newcomb, one of the subtlest minds,—I believe I must say—the subtlest observer & diviner of character I ever met,—living, reading, writing, talking there, as long, I believe, as the colony held together: Margaret Fuller, whose rich & brilliant genius no friend who really knew her could recognize under the dismal mask which, it is said, is meant for her in Hawthorne's story. C. S. too was known to them all, & I believe a frequent, certainly an honored guest. G.P.B. purest & genialest & humblest of men, with all his Culture. The Curtises,—with their elegance & worth—were within the fold: Theodore Parker & the Russells were just outside. Mrs Alvord I never knew, but she was a lady in high esteem. There were some devout persons, & many too of varied worth & talent. And, at the head, the integrity, devotion & ability of George & Sophia Ripley. Out of all this company could no better sketches be gained than that poor novel?

from

NY

1868–1870

Greatness.

The appearance of a great man draws a new circle outside of our largest orbit, & surprises & commands us. It is as if to the girl fully occupied with her paper dolls, a youth approaches & says, 'I love you with all my heart, come to me.' Instantly she leaves all—dolls, dances, maids, & youths, & dedicates herself to him. Or, as California in 1849, or the war in 1861, electrified the young men, & abolished all their little plans & projects with a magnificent hope or terror requiring a whole new system of hopes & fears & means. Our little circles absorb & occupy us as fully as the heavens: we can minimise as infinitely as maximise & the only way out of it is, (to use a country phrase,) to kick the pail over, & accept the horizon instead of the pail, with celestial attractions & influences, instead of worms & mud pies. Coleridge, Goethe, the new Naturalists in astronomy, geology, zoology, the correlations, the Social Science, the new readings of history through Niebuhr, Mommsen, Max Muller, Champollion, Lepsius astonish the mind, & detach it effectually from a hopeless routine. 'Come out of that,' they say, 'you lie sick & doting, only shifting from bed to bed.' And they dip the patient in this Russian bath, & he is at least well awake, & capable of sane activity. The perceptions which metaphysical & natural science cast upon the religious traditions, are every day forcing people in conversation to take new & advanced position. We have been building on the ice, & lo! the ice has floated. And the man is reconciled to his losses, when he sees the grandeur of his gains.

—

As I was told in Venice that there were plenty of people who never stirred out of it to the main land, &, as my Mrs Holbrook, with whom I went from Boston to Malta, never went on deck or saw the sea; so it is in sea-ports; the wharves are practically as far from the ocean as are the mountains. A boy born in Boston may often wander with boys down to the wharves, see the ships, boats, & sailors, but his attention is occupied by the rough men & boys, very likely by the fruit ships & their cargoes: specially the molasses casks. His eye may never get beyond the islands & the light house, to the sea. He remains a cockney, &, years later, chances to visit far from his town, the shore where the ocean is not hidden by ships & the wharf population, but fills the horizon: he realizes its wonder for the first time, its chill breath comes to him a snuff of defiance & now first beholds the maker of cities & of civilization, & may come to understand how Greece came to exist, & Tyre, & England.

It takes twenty years to get a good book read. For each reader is struck with a new passage & at first only with the shining & superficial ones, & by this very attention to these the rest are slighted. But with time the graver & deeper thoughts are observed & pondered. New readers come from time to time,—their attention whetted by frequent & varied allusions to the book,—until at last every passage has found its reader & commentator.

—

Mrs Hunt wished me to admire *George Eliot*'s "Spanish Gypsy", but on superficial trial by hearing passages, I refused. It was manufactured, not natural poetry. Any elegant & cultivated mind can write as well, but she has not insight into nature nor a poetic ear. Such poetry satisfies readers & scholars too at first sight,—does not offend,—conciliates respect, & it is not easy to show the fault. But let it lie awhile, & nobody will return to it. Indeed time, as I so often feel, is an indispensable element of criticism. You cannot judge of Nahant, or Newport, or of a gallery, or a poem, until you have outlived the dismay or over-powering of a new impression.

I took a volume of Wordsworth in my valise, & read for the first time, I believe, carefully "The White Doe of Rylstone"; a poem on a singularly simple & temperate key, without ornament or sparkle, but tender, wise, & religious, such as only a true poet could write, honoring the poet & the reader.

—

There are critics who cannot tell a glass from a stone.

Write that I may know you. Style betrays you as your eyes do. We detect at once by it whether the writer has a firm grasp on his fact or thought,—exists at the moment for that alone,—& so has a new possession to offer us, or, whether he has one eye apologising, deprecatory, turned on his reader. In proportion always to your possession of the thought is your defiance of your readers. There is no choice of words for him who clearly sees the truth. That provides him with the best word.

—

Tennyson's Sangrail

When Lycidas has been written, you shall not write an elegy on that key, unless you can do better than Lycidas. And so in each style of images or fables, after a best has been shown, you must come up to that, or pass it, or else abstain from the writing. Tennyson has abundant invention, but contents himself with the just enough. He is never obscure or harsh in a new or rare word. Then he has marked virility, as if a surgeon or practical physiologist had no secrets to teach him, but he deals with these as Abraham or Moses would & with out prudery or pruriency. His inventions are adequate to the dignity of the fable. The gift of adequate expression is his. Bacchic phrenzy in right words in right places—e.g. "is the immediate jewel of their souls".

Maud.—A nightingale drunken with his overflowing melody. An animal heat in the verse, & its opulent continuations. The priest is astonished to find a holiness in this Knight-errant which he himself never knew, & rubs his eyes. The fine invention of Tennyson is in crowding into an hour the slow creations & destructions of centuries.

It suggests besides in the coming & vanishing of cities & temples what really befalls in long durations on earth. How Science of Ethnology limps after these enchantments!

Miracles of cities & temples made by Merlin, like thoughts. 1 Jan. 1870.

—

What I wrote on the last leaf concerning Tennyson is due perhaps to the first reading,—to the new wine of his imagination,—& I may not enjoy it, or rate it so highly again.

—

When I remember how easily & happily I think in certain company,—as, for instance, in former years, with Alcott, & Charles Newcomb, earlier with Peter Hunt, though I must look far & wide for the persons & conditions—which yet were real,—& how unfavorable my daily habits & solitude are for this success, & consider also how essential this commerce is to fruitfulness in writing,—I see that I cannot exaggerate its importance among the resources of inspiration. Gurney seemed to me in an hour I once spent with him a fit companion. Holmes has some rare qualities. Horatio Greenough shone, but one only listened to him. So Carlyle, Henry Hedge, George Ward especially, & if one could ever get over the fences, & actually on even terms, Elliot Cabot. But I should like to try George E. Tufts, my brilliant correspondent of three letters; & William B. Wright, of the "Highland Rambles." There is an advantage to being somewhat *in the Chair* of the company,—a little older & better-read,—if one is aiming at searching thought. And yet, how heartily I could sit silent,—purely listening, & receptive, beside a rich mind!

—

June 16, 1868.

In reading these fine poems of Morris, I see but one defect, but that is fatal, namely, that the credence of the reader no longer exists.

I wrote thus last night, after reading "King Acrisius"; but, this evening, I have read "The Proud King," wherein the fable is excellent, & the story fits this & all times.

The negro should say to the government, your principle is, no tax without representation; but as long as you do not protect me at home & abroad, you do not give me the value for which I have paid.

—

1868

16 August. Came home last night from Vermont with Ellen. Stopped at Middlebury on the 11th, Tuesday, & read my

discourse on *Greatness, & the good work & influence of heroic scholars.* On Wednesday, spent the day at Essex Junction, & traversed the banks & much of the bed of the Winooski River, much admiring the falls, & the noble mountain peaks of Mansfield, & Camel's Hump, (which there appears to be the highest,) & the view of the Adirondacs across the Lake. In the evening, took the stage to Underhill Centre. And, the next morning, in unpromising weather, strolled away with Ellen towards the Mansfield mountain, 4 miles off; &, the clouds gradually rising & passing from the summit, we decided to proceed toward the top, which we reached, (with many rests at the Half-way House, & at broad stones on the path,) a little before 2 o'clock, & found George Bradford at the Mountain House. We were cold & a little wet, but found the house warm with stoves. After dinner, Ellen was thoroughly warmed & recruited lying on a settee by the stove, & meanwhile I went up with Mr Bradford & a party to the top of "the Chin," which is the highest land in the State,—4 400 feet. I have, later, heard it stated 4 389 ft. Lake Champlain lay below us, but was a perpetual illusion, as it would appear a piece of yellow sky, until careful examination of the islands in it, & the Adirondac summits beyond brought it to the earth for a moment; but, if we looked away an instant, & then returned, it was in the sky again. When we reached the summit, we looked down upon the "Lake of the Clouds," & the party which reached the height a few minutes before us, had a tame cloud which floated by a little below them. This summer, bears & a panther have been seen on the mountain, & we peeped into some rocky caves which might house them. We came, on the way, to the edge of a crag, which we approached carefully, & lying on our bellies; & it was easy to see how dangerous a walk this might be at night, or in a snowstorm. The White Mountains—it was too misty to see; but "Owl's Head," near Lake Memphremagog, was pointed out. Perhaps it was a half mile only from the House to the top of "the Chin," but it was a rough & grand walk. On such occasions, I always return to my fancy that the best use of wealth would be to carry a good professor of Geology, & another of Botany, with you.

In the House were perhaps twenty visiters besides ourselves, a Mr Taylor of Cincinnati,—a very intelligent gentleman,—

with excellent political views, republican & free-trader: George Bartlett was there with a gay company of his friends, who had come up from Stowe, where he had given a theatrical entertainment of amateurs, the night before. In the evening, they amused us mightily with charades of violent fun. The next morning a man went through the house ringing a large bell, & shouting "Sunrise," & every body dressed in haste, & went down to the piazza. Mount Washington & the Franconia mountains were clearly visible, & Ellen & I climbed now the *Nose*, to which the ascent is made easy by means of a stout rope firmly attached near the top, & reaching down to the bottom of the hill, near the House. Twenty people are using it at once at different heights. After many sharp looks at the heavens & the earth, we descended to breakfast.

—

At Monadnoc, the final cause of towns appears to be, to be seen from mountains.

—

The only place where I feel the joy of eminent domain is in my wood lot. My spirits rise whenever I enter it. I can spend the entire day there with hatchet or pruning-shears making paths, without a remorse of wasting time. I fancy the birds know me, & even the trees make little speeches or hint them. Then Allah does not count the time which the Arab spends in the chase.

Ah what a blessing to live in a house which has on the ground-floor one room or one cabinet in which a Worcester's Unabridged; a Liddell & Scott; an Andrews & Stoddard; Lempriere's Classical; a "*Gradus Ad*"; a Haydn's "Dictionary of Dates"; a "Biographie Generale;" a Spiers' French, & Flugel's German Dictionary, even if Grimm is not yet complete;—where these & their equivalents, if equivalents can be, are always at hand.—And yet I might add, as I often do,—Ah! happier, if these or their substitutes have been in that house for two generations or for three,—for Horace's Metres & Greek literature will not be thoroughly domesticated in one life: a house, I mean where the seniors who are at fault about school questions, can inquire of the juniors with some security of a right answer. This is one of my dreams for the American house. Another is the use of wealth in buying for the adult the companionship, if it be only occasional, as on a journey, of the master of that science we are hungering to know.

—

A man never gets acquainted with himself, but is always a surprise. We get news daily of the world within, as well as of the world out side, & not less of the central than of the surface facts. A new thought is awaiting him every morning.

—

Books—Men read so differently with purpose so unlike. I had read in Cudworth from time to time for years, & one day talked of him with Charles W. Upham, my classmate,—& found him acquainted with Cudworth's argument, & theology; & quite heedless of all I read him for,—namely, his citations from Plato & the philosophers; so that, if I had not from my youth up loved the man, I suppose we might have "inter-despised," as De Quincy said of Wordsworth, & (perhaps) Mackintosh.

—

Nov. 11. Yesterday was well occupied in accompanying W. R. Ware to the Church he is building for the First Church Society, in Berkeley street. It has a completeness & uniformity of strength, richness, & taste, perfect adaptation to its present purpose, & an antiquity in all its ornamentation that give delight. It seemed to threaten ruin to the Radical Club, retroaction in all people who shall sit down in its sumptuous twilight. I lamented for my old friend Dr Frothingham his loss of sight, once more, that he could not enjoy this faultless temple.

—

9 December 1868.

In poetry, tone. I have been reading some of Lowell's new poems, in which he shows unexpected advance on himself, but perhaps most in technical skill & courage. It is in talent rather than in poetic tone, & rather expresses his wish, his ambition, than the uncontrollable interior impulse which is the authentic mark of a new poem, & which is unanalysable, & makes the merit of an ode of Collins, or Gray, or Wordsworth, or Herbert, or Byron,—& which is felt in the pervading tone, rather than in brilliant parts or lines; As if the sound of a bell, or a certain cadence expressed in a low whistle or booming, or humming, to which the poet first timed his step, as he looked at the sunset, or thought, was the incipient form of the piece, & was regnant through the whole.

Wordsworth is manly, the manliest poet of his age. His poems record the thoughts & emotions which have occupied his mind, & which he reports because of their reality. He has great skill in rendering them into simple & sometimes happiest poetic speech. Tennyson has incomparable felicity in all poetic forms, & is a brave thoughtful Englishman, exceeds Wordsworth a hundredfold in rhythmic power & variety, but far less manly compass; and Tennyson's main purpose is the rendering, whilst Wordsworth's is just value of the dignity of the thought.

—

Conversation
As I wrote lately there is for your thought & expression a certain advantage in occupying the Chair in your company, or talking down. We can talk better on our own ground to intelligent young men than to our equals. Remember Pepys's description of Lord Clarendon's fine superiorities of talk. I think sometimes I could give useful lessons or hints to a class of young writers, who were yet able & sympathetic.

No doubt at Brook Farm there was in many a certain strength drawn from the fury of dissent. George Ripley told Theodore Parker, that "John Dwight would hoe corn all Sunday, if he would let him, but all Massachusetts could not make him do it on Monday." Told me by Mr Hewins.

—

In this proposition lately brought to me of a class, it occurs that I could by readings show the difference between good poetry & what passes for good; that I could show how much so-called poetry is only eloquence; that I could vindicate the genius of Wordsworth & show his distinctive merits. I should like to call attention to the critical superiority of Arnold, his excellent ear for style, & the singular poverty of his poetry, that in fact he has written but one poem, "Thyrsis," & that on an inspiration borrowed from Milton. I might give, too, the catalogue of the *Poets of one Poem*, the Single-speech men. A topic also would be this Welsh genius (& Arnold too has been attracted to that,) which I recognized today in reading this new translator, Skene. And which I find, as long ago, far more suggestive, contagious, or I will say, more inoculating the reader with poetic madness, than any poet I now think of, except Hafiz. I can easily believe this an idiosyncrasy of mine, & to describe it more accurately, I will add that I place these as not equal, but *of like kind* in genius & influence with the Zoroastrian sentences, & those of the Bhagavat Geeta & the Vishnu Purana.

There is always a height of land which, in a walk for pleasure or business, the party seek as the natural centre or point of view; & there is in every book, whether poem, or history, or treatise of philosophy, a height which attracts more than other parts, & which is best remembered. Thus, in Morte d'Arthur, I remember nothing so well as Merlin's cry from his invisible inaccessible prison. To be sure, different readers select by natural affinity different points. In the proposed class, it would be my wish to indicate such points in literature, & thus be an "old guide", like Stephen, who shows, after ten years daily trudging through the subterranean holes, the best wonders of the Mammoth Cave.

—

There are so many men in the world, that I can be spared to work a great while on one chapter;—so long, that, when at last it is finished & printed, & returns to me, I can read it without pain, & know that others can.

—

In 1821 I heard Edward Everett preach a sermon to the Howard Benevolent Society in the Old South Church. One passage I keep in memory to this day.—"I have known a woman in this town go out to work with her own hands to pay for the wooden coffin which was to inclose the body of her only child. I prayed with her when there was none to stand up by her but he who was to bear that body to the tomb."

—

Of immortality, I should say, that it is at least equally & perhaps better seen in little than in large angles: I mean, that, in a calm & clear state of mind, we have no fears, no prayers, even, that we feel all is well; we have arrived at an enjoyment so pure, as to imply & affirm its perfect accord with the Nature of things, so that it alone appears durable, & all mixed or inferior states accidental & temporary.

—

In my visit to New York I saw one remarkable person new to me, Richard Hunt, the Architect. His conversation was spirited beyond any that I could easily remember, loaded with matter, & expressed with the vigor & fury of a member of the Harvard boat or ball club, relating the adventures of one of their matches; inspired, meantime, throughout, with fine theories of the possibilities of art. Yet the tone of his voice & the accent of his conversation so strongly reminded me of my rural neighbor S. S. as to be in ludicrous contrast with the Egyptian & Greek grandeurs he was hinting or portraying. I could only think of the immense advantage which a thinking soul possesses when horsed on a robust & vivacious temperament. The combination is so rare of an Irish laborer's nerve & elasticity with Winckelmann's experience & cultivation, as to fill one with immense hope of great results, when he meets it in the New York of today.

—

R. wakes from a sound sleep, has an excellent breakfast, and inquires if this is not a jolly universe?

no more irreconcileable persons brought to annoy & confound each other in one room, than are sometimes actually lodged by nature in one man's skin,

Memory.

It sometimes occurs that Memory has a personality of its own, & volunteers or refuses its informations at *its* will, not at mine. I ask myself, is it not some old Aunt who goes in & out of the house, & occasionally recites anecdotes of old times & persons, which I recognize as having heard before,—&, she being gone again, I search in vain for any trace of the anecdotes?

*

March 29.

Alcott came, & talked Plato & Socrates, extolling them with gravity. I bore it long, & then said, that was a song for others, not for him. He should find what was the equivalent for these masters in our times: for surely the world was always equal to itself, & it was for him to detect what was the counter-weight & compensation to us. Was it natural science? Was it the immense dilution of the same amount of thought into nations? I told him to shut his eyes, & let his thoughts run into reverie or whithersoever,—& then take an observation. He would find that the current went outward from man, not to man. Consciousness was up stream.

—

July 1, 1869.

Judge Hoar in his speech at the Alumni dinner at Cambridge yesterday, was a perfect example of Coleridge's definition of Genius, "the carrying the feelings of youth into the powers of manhood"; And the audience were impressed & delighted with the rare combination of the innocence of a boy with the faculty of a hero.

—

Sumner collects his works. They will be the history of the republic for the last 25 years, as told by a brave perfectly honest & well-instructed man, with large social culture & relations to all eminent persons. He is a diligent & able workman, with rare ability, without genius, without humor, but with persevering study, wide reading, excellent memory, & high sense of honor, disdaining any bribe, any compliances, & incapable of falsehood. His singular advantages of person & of manners & a statesman's conversation impress every one favorably. He has the foible of most public men, the egotism which seems almost unavoidable at Washington.

I sat in his room once at Washington whilst he wrote a weary succession of letters,—he writing without pause as fast as if he were copying. He outshines all his mates in historical conversation & is so public in his regards, that he cannot be relied on to push an office seeker, so that he is no favorite with politicians; but wherever I have met with a dear lover of the country, & its moral interests, he is sure to be a supporter of Sumner.

—

At Walden, the other day, with G. P. B., I was struck, as often, with expression of refinement which Nature wears often in such places:—the bright sunshine reflected by the agreeable forms of the water, the shore-line, & the forest; the soft lapping sound of the water.

At my Club, I suppose I behave very ill in securing always, if I can, a place by a valued friend, &, though I suppose (though I have never heard it,) that I offend by this selection, sometimes too visible, my reason is, that I, who see in ordinary rarely select society, must make the best use of this opportunity, having, at the same time, the feeling that

"I could be happy with either,
Were the other dear charmer away."

—

Humboldt one of those wonders of the world like Aristotle, like Crichton, like Newton, appearing now & then as if to show us the possibilities of the Genus Homo, the Powers of the eye, the range of the faculties; whose eyes are natural telescopes & microscopes & whose faculties are so symmetrically joined that they have perpetual presence of mind, & can read nature by bringing instantly their insight & their momentary observation together; whilst men ordinarily are, as it were, astonished by the new object, & do not on the instant bring their knowledge to bear on it. Other men have memory which they can ransack, but Humboldt's memory was wide awake to assist his observation. Our faculties are a committee that slowly, one at a time, give their attention & opinion,—but his, all united by electric chain,—so that a whole French Academy travelled on his shoes. You could not put him on any sea or shore, but his instant recollection of the past history of every other sea & shore illuminated this, & he saw in this confirmation or key of the old fact. You could not lose him. He was the man of the world, if ever there was one. You could not lose him; you could not detain him; you could not disappoint him. The tardy Spaniards were months in getting their expedition ready & it was a year that he waited; but Spain or Africa or Asia were all harvest fields to this armed eye, to this Lyncaeus who could see through the earth, & through the ocean, who knew how mountains were built, & seas drained.

Humboldt with great propriety named his sketch of the results of Science Cosmos.
His words are the mnemonies of science, "volcanic paps", "magnetic storms," &c.

Agassiz never appeared to such advantage as in his Biographical Discourse on Humboldt, at the Music Hall in Boston, yesterday. What is unusual for him, he read a written discourse, about two hours long; yet all of it strong, nothing to spare, not a weak point, no rhetoric, no falsetto;—his personal recollections & anecdotes of their intercourse, simple, frank & tender in the tone of voice too, no error of egotism or of self assertion, & far enough from French sentimentalism. He is quite as good a man as his hero, & not to be duplicated, I fear. I admire his manliness, his equality always to the occasion, to any & every company,—never a fop, never can his manners be separated from himself.

—

I read a good deal of experimental poetry in the new books. The author has said to himself, '*Who knows but this may please, & become famous? Did not Goethe experiment? Does not this read like the ancients?*' But good poetry was not written thus, but it delighted the poet first; he said & wrote it for joy, & it pleases the reader for the same reason.

Oct. 21. I wish I could recall my singular dream of last night with its physics, metaphysics, & rapid transformations,—all impressive at the moment, that on waking at midnight I tried to rehearse them, that I might keep them till morn. I fear 'tis all vanished. I noted how we magnify the inward world, & emphasize it to hypocrisy by contempt of house & land & man's condition, which we call shabby & beastly. But in a few minutes these have their revenge, for we look to their chemistry & perceive that they are miracles of combination of ethereal elements, & do point instantly to moral causes. I passed into a room where were ladies & gentlemen, some of whom I knew. I did not wish to be recognised because of some disagreeable task, I cannot remember what. One of the ladies was beautiful, and I, it seemed, had already seen her, & was her lover. She looked up from her painting, & saw, but did not recognize me;—which I thought wrong,—unpardonable. Later, I reflected that it was not so criminal in her, since I had never *proposed*. Presently the scene changed, & I saw a common street-boy, without any personal advantages, walking with an air of determination, and I perceived that beauty of features signified nothing,—only this clearness & strength of purpose made any form respectable & attractive.—'Tis all vain,—I cannot restore the dream.

Concord. Friday, 22 October, 1869. This morning at 5h. 25m. I perceived that the house was shaken by an earthquake. I think the motion was prolonged for a minute. I got out of bed, lit a match, & looked at the clock. I heard no other noise than the wave-like shaking of the house would make. At breakfast, I found that Mrs Small had also observed it, & thought it an earthquake.

—

Tides in men & children. A wave of sanity & perception comes & they are on a level instantly with adults,—perfectly reasonable & right; out goes the wave, & they are silly intolerable miscreants. 'Tis all the difference between the bright water with the ships & the sun thereon, & the empty bay with its mud.

M. M. E held a relation to good society not very uncommon. She was strongly drawn to it as to the reputed theatre for genius, but her eccentricity disgusted it, & she was quite too proud & impulsive to sit & conform. So she acquiesced, & made no attempt to keep place, & knew it only in the narratives of a few friends like Mrs George Lee, Mrs Mary Schalkwic, Miss Searle, &c. with whom she had been early intimate & who for her genius tolerated or forgave her oddities. But her sympathy & delight in its existence daily appear through all her disclaimers & fine scorn.

Good Writing

All writing should be selection in order to drop every dead word. Why do you not save out of your speech or thinking only the vital things,—the spirited *mot* which amused or warmed you when you spoke it,—because of its luck & newness. I have just been reading, in this careful book of a most intelligent & learned man, any number of flat conventional words & sentences. If a man would learn to read his own manuscript severely,—becoming really a third person, & search only for what interested him, he would blot to purpose,—& how every page would gain! Then all the words will be sprightly, & every sentence a surprise.

Dr Hedge tells us, that the Indian asked John Eliot, "why God did not kill the devil?" One would like to know what was Eliot's answer.

In the heavy storm I heard the cathedral bells squeaking like pigs through the snout.

Good Writing.
I will tell you what it is to be immortal,—this namely, that I cannot read Plutarch without perpetual reminders of men & women whom I know.

—

Calvinism
There is a certain weakness in solemnly threatening the human being with the revelations of the Judgment Day, as Mrs Stowe winds up her appeal to the executors of Lady Byron. An honest man would say, why refer it? All that is true & weighty with me has all its force now.

We meet people who seem to overlook & read us with a smile, but they do not tell us what they read.

Now & then we say things to our mates, or hear things from them, which seem to put it out of the power of the parties to be strangers again. Especially if any one show me a stroke of courage, a piece of inventive wit, a trait of character, or a pure delight in character when shown by others, henceforward I must be that man's or that woman's debtor, as one who has discovered to me among perishing men somewhat more clean & incorruptible than the light of these midnight stars. Indeed

the only real benefit of which we are susceptible is (is it not?) to have man dignified for us.
Very fine relations are established between every clear spirit & all bystanders.

I find myself always harping on a few strings which sound tedious to others, but, like some old tunes to common people, have an inexhaustible charm to me. We are easily tired of a popular modish tune, but never of the voice of the wind in the woods.

—

Memory. A man would think twice about learning a new science or reading a new paragraph, if he believed that the magnetism was only a constant amount, & that he lost a word therefore for every word he gained. But the experience is not quite so bad. In reading a foreign language, every new word added is a lamp lighting up related words, & so assisting the memory & the apprehension; & so is it with each fact in a new science.

The words are mutually explaining, & every one adds transparency to the whole mass.

"To declare war against length of time." *Simonides.*

Compensation of failing memory in age by the increased power & means of generalization

A member of the Senior Class in College asked me on Saturday, "whether, when I was in Europe, I had met with Spinosa?" I told him that I did not; that Spinoza must now be pretty old, since he was born in 1632.

—

I asked Theodore Lyman on Saturday how it was exactly with Agassiz's health. He said, "that no further paralysis had appeared, & that he seemed not threatened. It was not apoplexy but a peculiarity of his constitution, these turns of insensibility which had occurred. It was *hysteria.*" I replied, that I had often said that Agassiz appeared to have two or three men rolled up into his personality, but I had never suspected there was any woman also in his make. Lyman insisted that he had himself seen hysteria oftener in men than in women.

1870. 3 February. The last proof-sheet of "Society & Solitude" comes back to me today for correction.

Mr Charles Ware tells Edward, that the night before the Cambridge Commemoration Day, he spent the night at Mr Hudson's room, in Cambridge, & woke from a dream which he could not remember, repeating these words,—

And what they dare to dream of, dare to die for.

He went to the Pavilion Dinner, & there heard Mr Lowell read his Poem, and when he came to the lines

"Those love her best who to themselves are true
And what— —"

Ware said, now I know what's coming,—but it won't rhyme, & Mr Lowell proceeded—

"And what they dare to dream of, dare to do."

—

Feb. 24.
A prudent author should never reprint his occasional pieces, which, of course, must usually be based on such momentary events & feelings as certainly to conflict with his cooler habitual mundane judgments.

The dead live in our dreams.

Bettine in Varnhagen's Diary reminds me continually of M.M.E. though the first is ever helping herself with a lie, which the other abhorred. But the dwelling long with grief & with genius on your wrongs & wrong-doers, & exasperating the offender with habitual reproaches puts the parties in the worst relation & at last incapacitates the complaining woman from seeing what degree of right or of necessity there is on the side of her offender, & what good reason he has to complain of her wrath & insults. This ever-increasing bias of the injured party has all the mischief of lying.

—

How dangerous is criticism. My brilliant friend cannot see any healthy power in Thoreau's thoughts. At first I suspect of course that he oversees me who admire Thoreau's power. But when I meet again fine perceptions in Thoreau's papers, I see that there is defect in his critic that he should under-value them. Thoreau writes, in his "*Field Notes*," "I look back for the era of this creation not into the night, but to a dawn for which no man ever rose early enough."

a fine example of his affirmative genius.

March 15. My new book sells faster, it appears, than either of its foregoers. This is not for its merit, but only shows that old age is a good advertisement. Your name has been seen so often that your book must be worth buying.

—

March 16. *Musagetes.*

After the Social Circle had broken up, last night, & only two remained with me, one said that a cigar had uses. If you found yourself in a hotel with writing to do,—fire just kindled in a cold room,—it was hard to begin; but light a cigar, & you were presently comfortable, & in condition to work. Mr Simon Brown then said, that he had never smoked, but as an editor (of the New England Farmer) he had much writing, & he often found himself taking up a little stick & whittling away on it, and, in a short time, brought into tune & temper by that Yankee method.

Alvan Crocker gave me in the cars a history of his activity in the matter of the Fitchburg Railroad beginning, I think, in 1837. He is the author of the road. He was a paper manufacturer & could not get the material for making paper for less than 8 cents a pound, whilst in Boston & elsewhere it could be got for 2, 3, or 4 cents. He must find a way to bring Fitchburg nearer to Boston. He knew the country round him & studied the possibilities of each connection. He found he must study the nearest practicable paths to tide water. No man but he had faith in the rivers. Nashua River

After studying the Hoosac Mountains well, he decided that the mountain must be perforated. He must see Loammi Baldwin, who was the best engineer in the state. He could not get at that busy man. He knew that his own mother's dearest friend had been the lady who was now Mr Baldwin's wife. To her he went, & told her who he was, & that he wished of all things to see Mr B. The lady said, "I loved your mother dearly, but I know nothing of you: but for her sake, I will take care that you shall see him. Come here, say, next Sunday after dinner, about 3 o'clock,—that is the right time, & I will see that Mr B. shall answer all your questions." He did so.

Dream.

The waking from an impressive dream is a curious example of the jealousy of the gods. There is an air as if the sender of the illusion had been heedless for a moment that the Reason had returned to its seat, & was startled into attention. Instantly, there is a rush from some quarter to break up the drama into a chaos of parts, then of particles, then of ether, like smoke dissolving in a wind: it cannot be disintegrated fast enough or fine enough. If you could give the waked watchman the smallest fragment, he could reconstruct the whole; for the moment he is sure he can & will; but his attention is so divided on the disappearing parts, that he cannot grasp the least atomy, & the last fragment or film disappears before he could say, I have it.

Lidian thinks that the claim made, & properly, for Christianity, is that it took away the fear of death. But, thanks to Calvinism, it is plain that no people on earth now or heretofore were so haunted with fear of death as the Christians. Hell-fire for sin, hell-fire for not accepting the creed of our Church, hell-fire for babes, if they died before there was time to baptize them.

—

The scholar who abstracted himself with pain to make the analysis of Hegel is less enriched than when the beauty & depth of any thought by the wayside has commanded his mind & led to new thought & action: for this is healthy, & these thoughts light up the mind: he is made aware of the walls, & also of the open way leading outward & upward, whilst the other analytic process is cold & bereaving, &,—shall I say it?—somewhat mean as spying.

I heard on the day when I graduated at Cambridge, in 1821, Sampson Reed, who on that day took his Master's degree, deliver his oration on Genius. It was poorly spoken, as A. Adams said, "in a meeching way," & the audience found it very dull & tiresome. John Quincy Adams who sat on the platform (his son George Washington A. graduating on that day) clapped Reed's oration with emphasis, & I doubt if any one joined him. But I was much interested in it, &, at my request, my brother William, of Reed's class, borrowed afterwards the manuscript, & I copied the whole of it, & kept it as a treasure. In 1826, he published "The Growth of the Mind," which I heartily prized & admired, &, in 1833, sent to Carlyle, as a specimen of American thought. In 1830, I became much acquainted with Reed, who talked very seriously with me, both at his counting room & at my own house. In 1851,* after Webster's March Speech in the U.S. Senate pronouncing for the Fugitive Slave Law, I met Sampson Reed in the Boston Athenaeum, & deplored to him this downfall of our great man, &c. He replied, that "he thought it his best speech, & the greatest action of his life." So there were my two greatest men both down in the pit together.

—

Henry Thoreau was well aware of his stubborn contradictory attitude into which almost any conversation threw him, & said in the woods, "When I die, you will find swamp oak written on my heart." I got his words from Ellery Channing today.

—

Churches are good for nothing except when they are poor. When the New Jerusalem Church was new in Boston they wrote an admirable magazine. Since they have grown rich, not a thought has come from them. Churches are best in their beginnings.

—

Plutarch rightly tells the anecdote of Alexander (badly remembered & misrelated usually), that he wept when he heard from Anaxarchus that there was an infinite number of worlds; and his friends asking if any accident had befallen him, he replied, "Don't you think it a matter for my lamentation, that, when there is such a vast multitude of them, I have not yet conquered one?" *Plut. Morals.* I. 134

*September.

Were I professor of Rhetoric, I would urge my class to read Plutarch's "Morals" in English, & Cotton's Montaigne for their English style.

—

Poetry is a free manner of speaking by one in a larger horizon than is his wont, free, therefore, to help himself with many more symbols for his thoughts, & consciously playing this game, delighting in this liberty & whim to magnify & dwarf things alternately, by using many symbols never before so used.

—

The reason of a new philosophy or philosopher is ever that a man of thought finds that he cannot read in the old books. I can't read Hegel, or Schelling, or find interest in what is told me from them, so I persist in my own idle & easy way, & write down my thoughts, & find presently that there are congenial persons who like them, so I persist, until some sort of outline or system grows. 'Tis the common course: Ever a new bias. It happened to each of these, Heraclitus, or Hegel, or whosoever.

The part of each one of the class is as important & binding as that of the professor: they are like the baseball players where the catcher & the bat & the pitcher are equally important.

—

I cannot but please myself with the recoil when Plutarch tells me, that, "the Athenians had such an abhorrence of those who accused Socrates, that they would neither lend them fire, nor answer them any question, nor wash with them in the same water, but commanded the servants to pour it out as polluted, till these sycophants, no longer able to bear up under the pressure of this hatred, put an end to their own lives." *Plut. Mor.* II. 96.

—

July 14, 1870.

Here at Nantasket Beach, with Ellen, I wonder that so few men do penetrate what seems the secret of the inn-keeper. He runs along the coast, & perceives, that by buying a few acres well-chosen of sea-shore, which cost no more or not so much as good land elsewhere, & building a good house, he shifts upon nature the whole duty of filling it with guests, the sun, the moon, the stars, the rainbow, the sea, the islands, the whole horizon,—not elsewhere seen,—ships of all nations. All of these, (& all unpaid,) take on themselves the whole charge of entertaining his guests, & filling & delighting their senses with shows; and it were long to tell in detail the attractions which these furnish. Every thing here is picturesque;—the long beach is every day renewed with pleasing & magical shows, with variety of color, with the varied music of the rising & falling water, with the multitudes of fishes & the birds & men that prey on them; with the strange forms of the radiates sprawling on the beach; with shells; with the beautiful variety of sea-rolled pebbles,—quartz, porphyry, sienite, mica, & limestone. The man buys a few acres, but he has all the good & all the glory of a hundred square miles, by the cunning choice of the place; for the storm is one of the grand entertainers of his company; so is the sun, & the moon, & all the stars of heaven, since they who see them here, in all their beauty, & in the grand area or amphitheatre which they need for their right exhibition, feel that they have never rightly seen them before. The men & women who come to the house, & swarm or scatter in groups along the spacious beach, or in yachts, or boats, or in carriages, or as bathers, never appeared before so gracious & inoffensive. In these wide stretches, the largest company do not jostle one another. Then to help him, even the poor Indians from Maine & Canada creep on to the outskirts of the hotel to pitch their tents, & make baskets & bows & arrows to add a picturesque feature. Multitudes of children decorate the piazza, & the grounds in front, with their babble & games; and in this broad area every individual from least to largest is inoffensive & an entertaining variety. To make the day complete, I saw from the deck of our boat this morning, coming out of the bay the English steamer which lately made the perilous jump on Minot's Ledge, & this afternoon saw the turret monitor, *Miantonomok*, sailing into Boston.

The parlors, chambers, & the table of the Rockland House were all good, but the supreme relish of these conveniences was this superb panorama which the wise choice of the place, on which the house was built, afforded. This selection of the site gives this house the like advantage over other houses that an astronomical observatory has over other towers,—namely, —that this particular tower leads you to the heavens, & searches depths of space before inconceivable.

July 21.

I am filling my house with books which I am bound to read, & wondering whether the new heavens which await the soul, (after the fatal hour,) will allow the consultation of these?

—

I find my readings of M.M.E. ever monitory & healthful as of old, & for the reason that they are moral inspirations. All the men & women whose talents challenge my admiration from time to time lack this depth of source, & are therefore compartively shallow; they amuse; they may be inimitable; I am proud of them as countrymen & contemporaries; but it is as music or pictures,—& other music & pictures would have served me as well; they do not take rank hold of me as consolers, uplifters, & hinderers from sleep. But the moral Muse is eternal, & wakes us to eternity,—pervades the whole man; Socrates is not distant; Sparta is nearer than New York; Marcus Antoninus is of no age; Plotinus & Porphyry, Confucius & Menu had a deeper civilization than Paris or London; and the deeply religious men & women in or out of our churches are really the Salt of our civilization, & constitute the nerve & tension of our politics in Germany, England & America. The men of talent see the power of principle, & the necessity of respecting it, but they deal with its phenomena, & not with the source. It is learned & wielded as an accomplishment & a weapon. As I have before written, that no number of *Nays* will help;—only one *Yea*, and this is moral.

Strength enters according to the presence of the moral element. There are no bounds to this power. If it have limits, we have not found them. It domesticates. They are not our friends who are of our household, but they who think & see with us. But it is ever wonderful where the moral element comes from.

—

Very much afflicted in these days with stupor:—acute attacks whenever a visit is proposed or made.

from

ST

1870–1877

Old age stands not in years, but in directed activity.

Memory. Among my Mnemonics I record that I went in to France just three hundred years after Montaigne did. He was born 1533; I visited it in 1833.

—

October 6. Last night heard Mrs Dallas Glyn read or act Antony & Cleopatra. A woman of great personal advantages & talent,—great variety of style, & perfect self possession: in dialogue between Antony & Cleopatra, the manly voice & the woman adequately rendered: and the dialogue between the queen & the boy with the asp was perfect. The great passages in which I have always delighted were not duely felt by her, & had therefore no eminence: Some of them quite omitted. She ought to go on to the stage, where the interruption by the other actors would give her the proper relief, & enhance her own part. Her cries & violence were all right,—never vulgar. Her audience was not worthy of her reading, impertinently read newspapers & had a trick of going out. I am afraid they would have done the like to Siddons herself, until they had been told it was Siddons, & so had been afraid of being found out.

1870.

6 October. Today at the laying of the cornerstone of the "Memorial Hall," at Cambridge. All was well & wisely done. The storm ceased for us, the company was large,—the best men & the best women all there, or all but a few;—the arrangements simple & excellent, and every speaker successful. Henry Lee, with his uniform sense & courage, the Manager; the Chaplain, Rev. Phillips Brooks, offered a prayer, in which not a word was superfluous, & every right thing was said.

Henry Rogers, William Gray, Doctor Palfrey, made each his

proper Report. Luther's Hymn in Dr Hedge's translation was sung by a great choir, the cornerstone was laid, & then Rockwood Hoar read a discourse of perfect sense, taste, & feeling, —full of virtue & of tenderness. After this, an original song by Wendell Holmes was given by the choir. Every part in all these performances was in such true feeling, that people praised them with broken voices, & we all proudly wept. Our Harvard soldiers of the war were in their uniforms, & heard their own praises, & the tender allusions to their dead comrades. General Meade was present, & "adopted by the College," as Judge Hoar said, & Governor Claflin sat by President Eliot. Our English guests, Hughes, Rawlins, Dicey, & Bryce, sat & listened.

"I bear no ill will to my contemporaries," said Cumberland. "After you, Maame, is manners," said Swett. The only point in which I regret priority of departure is that I, as every one, keep many stories of which the etiquette of contemporariness forbids the airing, & which burn uncomfortably being untold. I positively resolve not to kill A. nor C. nor N.—but I could a tale unfold like Hamlet's father. Now a private class gives just this liberty which in book or public lecture were unparliamentary, & of course because here at least one is safe from the unamiable presence of reporters. Another point. I set great value in Culture on foreign literature—the farther off the better—much on French, on Italian, on German or Welsh,—more on Persian or Hindu, because if one read & write only English, he soon slides into narrow conventions, & believes there is no other way to write poetry than as Pope or as Milton. But a quite foreign mind born & grown in different latitude & longitude,—nearer to the pole or to the equator,—a child of Mount Heckla, like Sturluson, or of the Sahara, like Averroes, astonishes us with a new nature, gives a fillip to our indolence & we promptly learn that we have faculties which we have never used.

—

Plutarch's style picturesque with his active, objective eyes, seeing every thing that moves, shines, or threatens, in nature, art, or thought, or dreams, superstitions & ghost; believes in the evil eye, but prefers, if you please, to talk of these things in the morning.

He loves apples like our Thoreau, & well praises them *P.M.* III. 362

—

I delight ever in having to do with the drastic class, the men who can do things, as Dr C. T. Jackson; & Jim Bartlett; & Boynton. Such was Thoreau. Once out of doors, the poets paled like ghosts before them. I met Boynton in Rochester, N.Y. & was cold enough to a popular unscientific lecturer on Geology. But I talked to him of the notice I had read of repulsion of incandescent bodies, & new experiments. "O," he said, "nothing is plainer: I have tried it;" &, on my way to Mr Ward's, he led me into a forge, where a stream of melted iron was running out of a furnace, & he passed his finger through the streamlet again & again, & invited me to do the same. I said, Do you not wet your finger? "No," he said, "the hand sweats a little & that suffices."

—

One reason for Parnassus is that I wish a volume on my own table that shall hold the best poems of all my Poets: and shall have nothing that is not poetry.

—

Dec. 26, 1870.

I saw that no pressman could lay his sheets so deftly but that under every one a second sheet was inadvertently laid; & no bookbinder could bind so carefully, but that second sheet was bound in the book; then I saw, that if the writer was skilful, every word he wrote sank into the inner sheet, & there remained indelible; & if he was not skilful, it did not penetrate, & the ink faded, & the writing was effaced.

—

February 10, 1871.

I do not know that I should feel threatened or insulted if a chemist should take his protoplasm or mix his hydrogen, oxygen & carbon, & make an animalcule incontestably swimming & jumping before my eyes. I should only feel that it indicated that the day had arrived when the human race might be trusted with a new degree of power, & its immense responsibility; for these steps are not solitary or local, but only a hint of an advanced frontier supported by an advancing race behind it.

—

The attraction & superiority of California are in its days. It has better days, & more of them, than any other country.

—

In Yosemite, Grandeur of these mountains perhaps unmatched on the Globe; for here they strip themselves like Athletes for exhibition, & stand perpendicular granite walls, showing their entire height, & wearing a liberty cap of snow on their head.

—

At the request of Galen Clark, our host at Mariposa, & who is by State appointment the Protector of the trees, & who went with us to the Mammoth Groves, I selected a Sequoia Gigantea, near Galen's Hospice, in the presence of our party, & named it *Samoset*, in memory of the first Indian ally of the Plymouth Colony, and I gave Mr Clark directions to procure a tin plate, & have the inscription painted thereon in the usual form of the named trees;

Samoset—
12 May.
1871.

& paid him its cost. The tree was a strong healthy one, girth at 2½ feet from the ground, 50 feet.

—

The splendors of this age outshine all other recorded ages. In my lifetime, have been wrought five miracles, namely, 1. the Steamboat, 2. the railroad; 3. the Electric telegraph; 4. the application of the Spectroscope to astronomy; 5. the photograph: five miracles which have altered the relations of nations to each other. Add cheap Postage; and the Sewing machine; &, in agriculture, the Mowing machine & the horse-rake. A corresponding power has been given to manufactures by the machine for pegging shoes, & the power-loom; & the power-press of the printers. And in dentistry & in surgery Dr Jackson's discovery of Anaesthesis. It only needs to add the power which up to this hour eludes all human ingenuity, namely a rudder to the balloon, to give us the dominion of the air, as well as of the sea & the land. But the account is not complete until we add the discovery of Oersted, of the identity of Electricity & Magnetism, & the generalization of that conversion by its application to light, heat, & gravitation. The geologist has found the correspondence of the age of stratified remains to the ascending scale of structure in animal life.

—

Emphasis betrays poverty of thought, as if the man did not know that all things are full of meaning, and not his trumpery thing only.

’Tis one of the mysteries of our condition, that the poet seems sometimes to have a mere talent,—a chamber in his brain into which an angel flies with divine messages, but the man, apart from this privilege, common-place. Wordsworth is an example; (& Channing’s poetry is apart from the man.) Those who know & meet him day by day cannot reconcile the verses with their man.

Ah not to me these dreams belong
A better voice sings through my song.

—

In certain minds thought obliterates memory. I have this example,—that, eager as I am to fix & record each experience, the interest of a new thought is sometimes such that I do not think of pen & paper at all, and the next day I puzzle myself in a vain attempt to recall the new perception that had so captivated me.

—

Channing’s poetry does not regard the reader. It is written to himself; is his strict experience, the record of his moods, of his fancies, of his observations & studies, & will interest good readers as such. He does not flatter the reader by any attempt to meet his expectation, or to polish his record that he may gratify him, as readers expect to be gratified. He confides entirely in his own bent or bias for meditation & writing. He will write as he has ever written, whether he has readers or not. But his poems have to me & to others an exceptional value for this reason. We have not been considered in their composition, but either defied or forgotten, and therefore read them securely as original pictures which add something to our knowledge, & with a fair chance to be surprised & refreshed by novel experience.

—

George Bradford said, that Mr Alcott once said to him "that as the child loses, as he comes into the world, his angelic memory, so the man, as he grows old, loses his memory of this world."

Oct. 18, 1871. Bret Harte's visit.
Bret Harte referred to my Essay on Civilization, that the piano comes so quickly into the shanty, &c. & said, "do you know that on the contrary it is vice that brings them in. It is the gamblers who bring in the music to California. It is the prostitute who brings in the New York fashions of dress there, & so throughout." I told him that I spoke from Pilgrim experience, & knew on good grounds the resistless culture that religion effects.

—

The physicists in general repel me. I have no wish to read them, & thus do not know their names. But the anecdotes of these men of ideas wake curiosity & delight. Thus Hooke's catenary problem, & Hauy's crystals, & Goethe's & Oken's theory of the Skull as a metamorphosed vertebra; & Hunter's "arrested development;" & Oersted's "correlation of forces"; & Hay's theory of the form of vases; & Garbett's & Ruskin's architectural theories; & Vitruvius's relation between the human form & the temple; & Pierce's showing that the orbits of comets (parabolic) make the forms of flowers; & Kepler's relation of planetary laws to music: & our Dr Wyman's hint from the action of the magnet on steel filings to the form of the mammal skeleton; and Tyndall's experiment of the effect of sounds on different gases; & Franklin's kite;

All science must be penetrated by poetry. I do not wish to know that my shell is a strombus, or my moth a vanessa, but I wish to unite the shell & the moth to my being: to understand my own pleasure in them; to reach the secret of their charm for me.

Reality however has a sliding floor.

Look sharply after your thoughts. They come unlooked for, like a new bird seen on your trees, &, if you turn to your usual task, disappear; & you shall never find that perception again; never, I say,—but perhaps years, ages, & I know not what events & worlds may lie between you & its return! In the novel, the hero meets with a person who astonishes him with a perfect knowledge of his history & character, & draws from him a promise that whenever & wherever he shall next find him, the youth shall instantly follow & obey him. So is it with you, & the new thought,

"For deathless powers to verse belong
And they like demigods are strong
On whom the Muses smile."

—

Oct. 31. I recall today, after 50 years, a couplet of W. H. Furness, in college verses, which ran,

"O there are minds whose giant thoughts devise
Deeds whose fulfilment asks eternities."

I doubt if I have recalled it in all the interval.

—

Beware of the minor key.

What a benediction of heaven is this cheerfulness which I observe with delight,—which no wrath & no fretting & no disaster can disturb, but keeps its perfect key & heals insanity in all companies & crises.

An Englishman in Parliament House is a narrow partisan, out in his castle he is a cultivated European gentleman.

How vain to praise our literature, when its really superior minds are quite omitted, & utterly unknown to the public. Sampson Reed is known only to his sect, which does not estimate him. And Newcomb is a subtiller thinker than is any other American. And Philip Randolph a deep & admirable writer, utterly unknown,—died unknown. Thoreau quite unappreciated, though his books have been opened & superficially read. Alcott, the scholars do not know how to approach, or how to discriminate his tentative & sometimes tiresome talking, from his insights. Horatio Greenough has no rightful fame: his genius surpassed all the artists of his time.

*

Like Bacon, who said, "I bequeath my books to my countrymen, when some little time has past;" or Kepler;—

"I can well wait a hundred years for a reader, since God Almighty has been content to wait 6 000 years for an observer like myself."

—

When a boy I used to go to the wharves, & pick up shells out of the sand which vessels had brought as ballast, & also plenty of stones, gypsum, which, I discovered would be luminous when I rubbed two bits together in a dark closet, to my great wonder,—& I do not know why luminous, to this day. That, & the magnetising my penknife, till it would hold a needle; & the fact that blue & gambooge would make green in my pictures of mountains; & the charm of drawing vases by scrawling with ink heavy random lines, & then doubling the paper, so as to make another side symmetrical,—what was chaos, becoming symmetrical; then hallooing to an echo at the pond, & getting wonderful replies.

Still earlier, what silent wonder is waked in the boy by blowing bubbles from soap & water with a pipe.

1872

March 31. Judge French restored to me today my lost wallet which Mr F. D. Ely, Esq. of Dedham, Masstts had brought to him & which had been found by Hannah Ryan, of Dedham. It contained $113.05 & a bank cheque for $5.00 more. The young woman came to Mr Ely with it & said she had found it at the corner of Tremont & Winter streets. He looked for an advertisement, & found that which I had sent to the Herald, & so brought it to Judge French who paid the reward of 20.00, as I had requested him; & I hope to make the acquaintance of Hannah Ryan.

—

1872, May 26. Yesterday, my sixty ninth birthday, I found myself on my round of errands in Summer street, &, though close on the spot where I was born, was looking into a street with some bewilderment and read on the sign *Kingston street*, with surprise, finding in the granite blocks no hint of Nathaniel Goddard's pasture & long wooden fence, & so of my nearness to my native corner of Chauncy Place. It occurred to me that few living persons ought to know so much of the families of this fast growing city, for the reason, that Aunt Mary, whose MSS. I had been reading to Hedge & Bartol, on Friday Evening, had such a keen perception of character, & taste for aristocracy, & I heard in my youth & manhood every name she knew. It is now nearly a hundred years since she was born, & the founders of the oldest families that are still notable were known to her as retail-merchants, milliners, tailors, distillers, as well as the ministers, lawyers, & doctors, of the time. She was a realist, & knew a great man or "a whale hearted woman,"—as she called one of her pets,—from a successful money maker.

If I should live another year, I think I shall cite still the last stanza of my own poem, "The World-Soul."

Walk in the city for an hour, and you shall see the whole history of female beauty. Here are the school girls in the first profusion of their hair covering them to the waist, & now & then one maiden of 18 or 19 years, in the moment of her perfect beauty. Look quick & sharply,—this is her one meridian day. To find the like again, you must meet, on your next visit, one who is a month younger today. Then troops of pleasing well dressed ladies, sufficiently good looking & graceful, but without claims to the prize of the goddess of Discord.

—

We would all be public men if we could afford it. I am wholly private: such is the poverty of my constitution. Heaven "betrayed me to a book, & wrapt me in a gown". I have no social talent, no wealth of nature, nothing but a sullen will, & a steady appetite for insights in any or all directions, to balance my manifold imbecilities.

Men of genius in their rare moments, say things quite beyond their ordinary calibre, or perhaps adopt such sayings of their wisest companions. Thus Mahomet writes in the Koran, "Paradise is under the shadow of swords"; and then, with matchless all-atoning generosity, "Paradise,—whose breadth equals the Heaven & the earth."

*

Goethe.

What proof of Goethe's wealth of mind like the *Sprüche*? which, no doubt, could he have lived twice eighty years, he would have orderly expanded into consecutive chapters & volumes, but, in despair at his shortening days & multiplying aperçus, was forced to string into a magazine of proverbs.

—

I prefer the photograph to any other copy of the living head: the light is the best painter, & makes no mistakes. Truth evermore.

'Tis easy to write the technics of poetry, to discriminate Imagination & Fancy, &c. but the office & power which that word *Poetry* covers & suggests are not so easily reached & defined. What heaven & earth & sea & the forms of men & women are speaking or hinting to us in our healthiest & most impressionable hours,—What fresh perceptions a new day will give us of the old problems of our own being & its hidden source; what is this Sky of Law, & what the Future hides

House burned, Wednesday, 24 July.

—

Naushon, 31 Augt. '72. I thought today, in these rare seaside woods, that if absolute leisure were offered me, I should run to the College or the Scientific school which offered best lectures on Geology, chemistry, Minerals, Botany, & seek to make the alphabets of those sciences clear to me. How could leisure or labor be better employed. 'Tis never late to learn them, and every secret opened goes to authorize our aesthetics. Cato learned Greek at eighty years, but these are older bibles & oracles than Greek. Certainly this were a good *pis aller* if J.E.C. & Athens & Egypt should prove an abortive dream.

I think one must go to the tropics to find any match to this enchanting isle of Prospero. It needs & ought to find its Shakspeare. What dells! what lakelets! what groves! what clumps of historic trees of unknown age, hinting annals of white men & Indians, histories of fire & of storm & of peaceful ages of social growth! Nature shows her secret wonders, & seems to have impressed her fortunate landlords with instant & constant respect for her solitudes & centennial growths. Where else do such oaks & beeches & vines grow, which the winds & storms seem rather to adorn than spoil by their hurts & devastations, touching them as with Fate, & not wanton interference? And the sea binds the Paradise with its grand belt of blue, with its margin of beautiful pebbles, with its watching herons & hawks & eagles, & its endless fleet of barques, steamers, yachts, & fishers' boats.

—

The island compels them—glad to be compelled—to be skilful sailors, yachtsmen, fishermen, & swimmers, thus adding all the charm of the sea to their abode, & adds the surprise & romance of hunting.

—

Shepard's Hotel, Cairo Egypt 30 December, '72.

"Egyptian bride of Anastasius adds 250 false plaits to the 150 which grew from her head, & in forming the joint mass into an edifice so ponderous that a second head merely for use would have been very acceptable." Vol II. pp. 59, 62 See Conder, Vol. I, p 174

—

All this journey is a perpetual humiliation, satirizing & whipping our ignorance. The people despise us because we are helpless babies who cannot speak or understand a word they say; the Sphinxes scorn dunces; the obelisks, the temple-walls defy us with their histories which we cannot spell. Every new object only makes new questions which each traveller asks of the other, & none of us can answer, & each sinks lower in the opinion of his companion. The people whether in the boat, or out of it, are a perpetual study for the excellence & grace of their forms & motion. No people walk so well, so upright as they are, & strong & flexible; and for studying the nude, our artists should come here & not to Paris. Every group of the country people on the shores as seen from our dearbeah, look like the ancient philosophers going to the School of Athens. The women too are as straight as arrows from their habit of carrying every thing on their heads. In swimming, the Arabs show great strength & speed, all using what at Cambridge we used to call the "southern stroke," alternating the right arm & the left.

All the boys & all the babes have flies roosting about their eyes, which they do not disturb, nor seem to know their presence. 'Tis said that the ophthalmia, which is so common here, is thus conveyed from one to another. 'Tis said that it is rare to find sound eyes among them. Blind beggars appear at every landing led about by their children.

—

The magnet is the mystery which I would fain have explained to me, though I doubt if there be any teachers. It is the wonder of the child & not less of the philosopher. Goethe says, "The magnet is a primary phenomenon, which we must only express in order to have it explained. Thereby is it then also a symbol for all besides for which we use to speak no word or name."

—

The enjoyment of travel is in the arrival at a new city, as Paris, or Florence, or Rome,—the feeling of free adventure, you have no duties,—nobody knows you, nobody has claims, you are like a boy on his first visit to the Common on Election Day. Old Civilization offers to you alone this huge city, all its wonders, architecture, gardens, ornaments, Galleries, which had never cost you so much as a thought. For the first time for many years you wake master of the bright day, in a bright world without a claim on you;—only leave to enjoy. This dropping for the first time the doleful bundle of Duty creates, day after day, a health as of new youth. Then the cities know the value of travellers as purchasers in their factories & shops, & receive them gladly.

In Paris, your mere passport admits you to the vast & costly public galleries on days on which the natives of the city can not pass the doors. Household cares you have none: You take your dinner, lunch, or supper where & when you will: cheap cabs wait for you at every corner,—guides at every door, magazines of sumptuous goods & attractive fairings, unknown hitherto, solicit your eyes. Your health mends every day. Every word spoken to you is a wonderful & agreeable riddle which it is a pleasure to solve,—a pleasure & a pride. Every experience of the day is important, & furnishes conversation to you who were so silent at home.

—

Egypt.

Mrs Helen Bell, it seems, was asked "What do you think the Sphinx said to Mr Emerson?" "Why," replied Mrs Bell, "the Sphinx probably said to him, 'You're another.'"

—

I add from my old MSS. the following,—

A reader of profound apprehension has an equality to the greatest poet. The creative seems mere knack. The reader of Shakspeare must be for a time a Shakspeare, or find no joy in the page.

—

I ought to have many notes of my pleasant memories of Abel Adams one of the best of my friends whose hospitable house was always open to me by day or by night for so many years in Boston, Lynn, or West Roxbury. His experiences as a merchant were always interesting to me. I think I must have somewhere recorded the fact which I recall today that he told me that he & two or three merchants had been counting up, in the Globe Bank, out of a hundred Boston merchants how many had not once failed, and they could only count three.

—

Monday night Nov. Parker House

The secret of poetry is never explained,—is always new. We have not got farther than mere wonder at the delicacy of the touch, & the eternity it inherits. In every house a child that in mere play utters oracles, & knows not that they are such, 'Tis as easy as breath. 'Tis like this gravity, which holds the Universe together, & none knows what it is.

—

The death of Francis C. Lowell is a great loss to me. Now for fifty seven years since we entered college together, we have been friends, meeting sometimes rarely, sometimes often; seldom living in the same town, we have always met gladly on the old simple terms. He was a conservative, I always of a speculative habit; and often in the wayward politics of former years, we had to compare our different opinions. He was a native gentleman, thoroughly true, & of decided opinions, always frank, considerate, & kind. On all questions his opinions were his own, & deliberately formed.

—

1877, January.
All writing should be affirmative.

—

I confess that I have inserted some poems for the sake of one verse; nay, possibly for a single happiest word. Tennyson's "the *stammering* thunder"; Shakspeare's "How many a glorious morning have I seen *Flatter* the mountain tops with sovereign eye;" Herrick's "tempestuous petticoat" & Chaucer's language is often as wonderful. I know not in poetry a more pathetic stroke than the plea of Griselda to her husband,

"Let me not like a worm go by the way."

It can only be compared with his own Ariadne's to Theseus,

"Meker than thee, find I the beastès wild."

It was said of Rogers's poem of "Memory," that there was but one good line in it, "All other pleasures are not worth its pains." and one in Scott's "Helvellyn," addressed to the dead traveller's dog, "When the wind waved his garments, how oft didst thou start!"

Wordsworth has secured his fame not only against his critics but against himself, a prey long time to the critics in his puerile poems, I may say infantile, & the self conceit which he could not exclude from his loftier strains. All this he outgrew at the last in the Ode on Immortality, in the poems of Laodamia, Dion, The Happy Warrior, and in some noble sonnets has established his claim to the highest thought in England in his time.

—

Mr Buttrick, father of Steadman B., said to me that he saw Captain Davis on the 19 April, 1775, in the morning, and he looked very much worried: "his face was red as a beet." Afterwards, describing the same fact, he said, "his face was as red as a piece of cloth."

—

Christopher James, of Gold Hill, Nevada, working in the Comstock Lode, a miner, a Welshman by birth, a Comtist in his politics, and about 23 or 24 years old—a good friend of mine, though I have never seen him.
His token brought me by B B Titcomb of Watertown, Mass.

Editor's Afterword

Ralph Waldo Emerson began keeping a journal when he was 16. By the time he was 30, in 1833, he had turned it into his most successful experiment in creating a literary form. He continued writing in that form for most of the rest of his life, with the last datable entry in 1877: "all writing should be affirmative." He left 182 individual volumes, some regular journals and some miscellaneous notebooks, some bought ready-made and some hand-sewn; these together fill 16 volumes in the great Harvard edition of the work, the *Journals and Miscellaneous Notebooks of Ralph Waldo Emerson* (*JMN*), begun in 1960 and completed in 1982. This Library of America edition contains approximately one third of what Emerson wrote in his regular journals, and is the most comprehensive selection ever made from that work.

The editor's goals in making the selection were two-fold: to present Emerson's best and most vital writing, and to retain what was most significant biographically and historically in the journals. Proportionality of representation was not a goal; by and large the selection draws more heavily on the mature journals, those in which Emerson was writing in a form he had mastered, than on the early journals or the very late ones, before Emerson had found his form or after he had lost some of his power.

The fact that Emerson often used passages from the journals in his lectures and in essays has led some to view them as primarily a literary quarry, a mine of rough material to be refined into finished products. But the journals should rather be approached as a great literary work in themselves, a different kind of literary work perhaps: more intimate, conversational, spontaneous, aleatoric, and indecorous than the lectures and essays.

The text of the present edition is based on, and deeply indebted to, the Harvard edition mentioned above, one of the great triumphs of modern scholarship. Our principles of adaptation have been simple. The *JMN* editors devised typographical conventions for showing the reader not only what Emerson wrote but also what he crossed out and what he added later, thus revealing much about the sentence-by-sentence process of Emerson's writing. We have not retained this editorial apparatus. From *JMN*'s densely marked-up process text we have produced clear text, omitting what Emerson crossed out and adding what he added.

This edition's order of presentation reflects *JMN*'s practice. The earlier large-scale edition of Emerson's journals, the 1909–14 *Journals* in ten volumes edited by his son Edward Waldo Emerson and grandson Waldo Emerson Forbes, rearranged the entries in the separate and often overlapping journal volumes into a single chronological sequence, and some previously published selections from the journals have followed the same principle. *JMN* offers, instead, each of Emerson's individual volumes in its original order of pagination, and presents the individual volumes themselves in rough chronological order. The present edition does the same.

A major advantage of keeping the individual journals separate is the opportunity it affords to reveal Emerson's art as a diarist, which was preeminently an art of transition and juxtaposition. The reader's illumination and pleasure in reading the journals lie in watching the movement of Emerson's thought from subject to subject and mood to mood. That such an approach is consistent with Emerson's thinking can be gauged from the compelling claims that he himself made for the aesthetic value of transition: "The experience of poetic creativeness . . . is not found in staying at home, nor yet in travelling, but in transitions from one to the other, which must therefore be adroitly managed to present as much transitional surface as possible" (in this volume, p. 289), he wrote in 1845. The present edition seeks precisely to "present as much transitional surface as possible," to show what Emerson in 1857 called one of his "few laws" in inexhaustibly vivid action: "Flowing, or transition, or shooting the gulf, the perpetual striving to ascend to a higher platform, the same thing to new and higher forms" (in this volume, p. 695).

The present edition is a selection from the journals, not the whole of them. Some of the transitions from one paragraph to the next, therefore, are not Emerson's but ours, produced by the elimination of the material originally separating them. Wherever we have omitted material, the omission is indicated with a centered em-dash, so that the reader can easily see which transitions are Emerson's and which are ours.

Because Emerson was a master of two related forms within the journal—the entry and the paragraph—we have seldom made cuts within entries (although it is, to be sure, not always clear when one entry ends and the next begins) and still more seldom within paragraphs.

A further principle has been to accept the distinction made by the *JMN* editors between regular journal and miscellaneous notebook, and to include only material from the former category. The distinction is fluid, and some individual volumes are hard to classify; but the distinction is broadly applicable and worth applying. It is, moreover, a distinction that Emerson himself seems to have been aware of and to have used; his titles differentiate the one category from the other, as do the epigraphs and concluding passages of most regular journal volumes.

The distinction matters because the miscellaneous notebooks are for the most part *topical* notebooks. In setting them up, Emerson determined in advance his principles of inclusion and exclusion, and limited in advance his freedom of intellectual movement. Often such notebooks are entirely what the regular journals are only secondarily, namely, collections of raw material of which finished essays or speeches are to be made. Often they bring together material written at multiple periods and in multiple volumes; sometimes it is precisely their purpose to accumulate previously written material on a defined subject. There is distinguished new writing in some of these, but in them Emerson is doing something different from what he is doing in the regular journals, and the movement of his mind is less exhilaratingly free and surprising. (Occasionally within a regular journal volume Emerson gets obsessed with a topic, and for a while writes about that topic. These sequences are some of his best writing, and we have sought to retain them; if in the topical notebooks one is reading Emerson the collector, in these intense sequences of reflection, about Thoreau or slavery or friendship, one is reading Emerson possessed.)

In 1841, Emerson offered a prophecy: "novels will give way by and by to diaries or autobiographies; captivating books if only a man knew how to choose among what he calls his experiences that which is really his experience, and how to record truly!" (*Selected Journals 1820–1842*, p. 769) If Emerson was wrong about novels "giving way," he was right about diaries, or at least about his own. Emerson was as good at the tasks he defined—to choose "that which is really his experience, and how to record truly!"—as any diarist before him or since. The present edition of his journals offers a capacious opportunity to watch him explore the full implications of those tasks in the extraordinary form he created.

Chronology

1803 Born May 25, Election Day, in Boston, Massachusetts, the fourth child of William (pastor of Boston's First Church) and Ruth Haskins Emerson, both of English descent. Described by father at age two as "rather a dull scholar." From age three attends nursery and then grammar school.

1811 Father dies May 12 of stomach tumor at age 42, leaving children to be raised by his widow with help from his sister, Mary Moody Emerson, whose idiosyncratic religious orthodoxy and acute critical intelligence were a lifelong influence. Of eight children, only Ralph Waldo and four brothers survive childhood: William (b. 1801), Edward Bliss (b. 1805), Charles Chauncy (b. 1808), and the mentally retarded Robert Bulkeley (b. 1807), named for illustrious ancestor Peter Bulkeley, first-generation Puritan minister and a founder of Concord, Massachusetts.

1812 Enters Boston Public Latin School; begins writing poetry.

1817–21 Attends Harvard College and lives in President Kirkland's lodgings as his "freshman" or orderly; waits on table and teaches during vacations to pay costs. Begins keeping a journal to record his "luckless ragamuffin ideas." By junior year prefers the name Waldo. Wins prizes for oratory and for essays on Socrates and ethical philosophy; graduates 30th in a class of 59 and delivers class poem at graduation after six others decline the honor. Following graduation teaches in brother William's school for young ladies in Boston.

1822 Continues to teach. Dedicates his seventh "Wideworld" journal to "the Spirit of America." Publishes essay on "The Religion of the Middle Ages" in *The Christian Disciple*, a leading Unitarian religious review.

1823 Takes walking trip to the Connecticut Valley. Runs school alone when William departs to study theology in Germany. Childhood dreams, he complains, "are all fading away & giving place to some very sober & very disgusting views of a quiet mediocrity of talents and condition."

1824 Dedicates himself to the study of divinity; complains in journal of his lack of warmth and self-confidence, but hopes "to put on eloquence as a robe."

1825 Closes school. Notes in journal that his "unpleasing boyhood is past" and enters middle class at Harvard Divinity School. When studies are interrupted by eye trouble, resumes teaching, this time in Chelmsford, Massachusetts. Edward sails for Europe for his health; William, back from Germany, decides against ministerial career because of religious doubts.

1826 Begins year with "mended eyes," but afflicted by rheumatism of the hip. Teaches in Roxbury, then opens school in Cambridge (a student later describes him as "not inclined to win boys by a surface amiability, but kindly in explanation or advice"). William and Edward study law, the former on Wall Street and the latter in Daniel Webster's office. Impressed by Sampson Reed's *Observations on the Growth of the Mind*, a treatise that discusses "correspondences" between nature and spirit. Approbated to preach in October, but with onset of lung trouble, voyages to Charleston, South Carolina, financed by uncle Samuel Ripley.

1827 "I am not sick; I am not well; but luke-sick," he writes William in January, complaining of "a certain stricture" in his lungs. Sails for St. Augustine, Florida; establishes friendship with Napoleon's nephew Achille Murat, and is intrigued by this "consistent Atheist." Returns to Boston in spring and continues to preach. In December, while preaching in Concord, New Hampshire, meets Ellen Louisa Tucker.

1828 Edward becomes deranged; Waldo links this collapse to his brother's "preternatural energy" and assures himself that he is protected from a similar fate by the "mixture of *silliness*" in his character. Made honorary member of Phi Beta Kappa. Engaged to Ellen Tucker in December.

1829–30 Invited in January to become junior pastor of Boston's Second Church—the church of the Mathers. Becomes chaplain of state senate, as his late father had been. Although Ellen is ill with tuberculosis, they marry in September. Elected to Boston School Committee in December. In November 1830, Edward, his health failing, sails for Puerto Rico.

1831 Ellen dies on February 8 at age 19. Waldo notes the religious resignation of her last hours and writes, "My angel is gone to heaven this morning & I am alone in the world & strangely happy"; five days later he prays, "God be merciful to me a sinner & repair this miserable debility in which her death has left my soul." Begins walking to her tomb every morning. Charles' health begins to fail, and he sails for Puerto Rico where Edward is employed at the American consulate.

1832 Uneasy with role as minister; feels "the profession is antiquated" and "in an altered age we worship in the dead forms of our forefathers." Writes Second Church governing board requesting changes in communion service and, when denied, decides to resign. Suffers from persistent diarrhea. In September delivers sermon "The Lord's Supper" explaining his objections to the rite and concludes he is "not interested in it." In poor health, sails for Europe on December 25.

1833 Lands in Malta in February much improved in health. Enthusiastically travels north through Italy, spending Easter week in Rome and meeting Walter Savage Landor in Florence; describes religious pomp at Sistine Chapel as "millinery & imbecility," but finds Pope's Easter benediction at St. Peter's "a sublime spectacle." Arrives in Paris in June. Complains it is "a loud modern New York of a place" but enjoys cafés and liveliness; visits Jardin des Plantes and decides to become "a naturalist." In London in July; meets John Stuart Mill, Coleridge, and Wordsworth, and begins lifelong friendship with Carlyle, whom he visits in Craigenputtock, Scotland. Sails for home in September and notes, "I like my book about nature & wish I knew where & how I ought to live." Preaches at Boston Second Church in October and in November lectures on "The Uses of Natural History."

1834 Lectures in Boston on natural history and continues to preach nearly every Sunday; begins to correspond with Carlyle. In spring receives first half of Ellen's estate (about $11,600). In October moves with mother to Emerson family home in Concord (later named by Hawthorne the Old Manse). Decides "not to utter any speech, poem, or book that is not entirely & peculiarly my work." Edward dies in Puerto Rico on October 1.

1835 Lectures in Boston on lives of great men. In January feels "very sober joy" on being engaged to Lydia Jackson of

Plymouth; buys house in Concord for $3,500 and then marries Lydia (whom he calls "Lidian") in September. Declines pastorate in East Lexington, Massachusetts, but agrees to preach there every Sunday or procure a substitute. Delivers address on Concord history for the town's second centennial; begins winter lecture series on "English Literature" in Boston.

1836 Pronounces it a "gloomy epoch" when Charles dies of tuberculosis on May 9. Margaret Fuller visits the Emerson home for three weeks in July. Informal group (later dubbed Transcendental Club)—including Fuller, Orestes Brownson, Theodore Parker, Bronson Alcott, James Freeman Clarke, among others—organized for discussions and continues to meet until 1843. His "little azure-coloured *Nature*" published anonymously, a common practice, in September. Sees American edition of Carlyle's *Sartor Resartus* through press at own expense. (Although advances for this and future American editions of Carlyle's works are a financial hardship, Emerson will eventually recover his investment and send Carlyle nearly $3,000 in profits.) Son Waldo born October 30. Gives lecture series on "Philosophy of History" in winter.

1837 Notes in journal that "the land stinks with suicide" as American economy slides into severe depression. Receives final portion of Ellen's estate, bringing total to about $23,000, yielding an annual income of some $1,200. "Concord Hymn" sung July 4 at unveiling of monument to Revolutionary soldiers. Delivers "The American Scholar" as Harvard's Phi Beta Kappa oration in August and is toasted as "the Spirit of Concord" who "makes us all of One Mind." Lectures in winter on "Human Culture," defined as "educating the eye to the true harmony of the unshorn landscape."

1838 Finding the pulpit a constraint, asks East Lexington church committee to relieve him of responsibilities in February. In April writes open letter to President Van Buren protesting displacement of Cherokee Indians from their ancestral lands. Delivers address at Harvard Divinity School (July 15), subsequently attacked as "the latest form of infidelity." Though defended by George Ripley, Orestes Brownson, J. F. Clarke, and Theodore Parker, he is not invited back to Harvard for nearly 30 years. Dartmouth Oration ("Literary Ethics") delivered July 24. Meets Jones Very and develops close friendship with

Thoreau, with whom he takes walks in the woods. Winter lecture series on "Human Life" includes such topics as "Head," "Home," "Love," "Duty," "Genius," "Demonology," and "Animal Magnetism."

1839 Preaches his last sermon in January. Daughter Ellen born February 24, with Thoreau's mother serving as midwife. Visits from Very, Fuller, Alcott, and Carolyn Sturgis lead Emerson to note his "porcupine impossibility of contact with men," although of Alcott and Fuller he writes, "Cold as I am, they are almost dear." Edits and finds publisher for Very's poems and essays. Lectures on "The Present Age" in winter on a widening circuit.

1840 With Margaret Fuller, brings out first issue of *The Dial* in July, hoping it will be "one cheerful rational voice amidst the din of mourners and polemics." Strives to write "with some pains Essays on various matters as a sort of apology to my country for my apparent idleness." Attends reformers' Chardon Street Convention, but when invited to join Brook Farm community declines "to remove from my present prison to a prison a little larger."

1841 First series of *Essays* published in March, and aunt, Mary Moody Emerson, pronounces it a "strange medly of atheism and false independence"; favorable reviews in London and Paris lay basis for international reputation. Invites Thoreau to join household in spring, offering room and board in exchange for gardening and household chores. In summer delivers "The Method of Nature" at Waterville College in Maine. Daughter Edith born November 22. Lectures on "The Times" in winter.

1842 Devastated by death of five-year-old Waldo from scarlet fever on January 27, avers that he comprehends "nothing of this fact but its bitterness." Succeeds Margaret Fuller as editor of *The Dial* when she resigns. Raises money to send Bronson Alcott to England. Takes walking trip in September with Hawthorne, now living at the Old Manse, to visit Shaker community in village of Harvard, Massachusetts. On lecture tour in New York City—the lecture "Poetry of the Times" is reviewed by young editor Walter Whitman—dines with Horace Greeley and Albert Brisbane and visits between lectures at home of Henry James, Sr.

1843 In spring, finds Thoreau employment in Staten Island as tutor to children of his brother William, now a New York

State district judge. Completes a translation of Dante's *Vita Nuova*. Summer, entertains Daniel Webster at his home and pronounces him "no saint . . . but according to his lights a very true & admirable man."

1844 Last issue of *The Dial* appears in April. Son Edward Waldo born July 10. Purchases land on shore of Walden Pond. Contributes $500 toward land for the Alcott family when they purchase a house in Concord (later Hawthorne's Wayside). Opposes annexation of Texas and war with Mexico: "Mexico will poison us." Delivers address attacking slavery in the West Indies. *Essays: Second Series* published in October.

1845 Gives Thoreau permission to build hut on Walden property. His discourse at Middlebury College provokes a local minister to ask God "to deliver us from ever hearing any more such transcendental nonsense." Refuses to lecture at the New Bedford Lyceum when informed that Negroes are excluded from membership. In winter delivers "Representative Men" lecture series.

1846 April, hears Edward Everett's inaugural discourse as president of Harvard and decries "the corpse-cold Unitarianism & Immortality of Brattle street & Boston." In July feels limited sympathy for Thoreau's night in jail ("this prison is one step to suicide"). *Poems* published in December, including "Threnody," an elegy for his son Waldo.

1847–48 Sails for Liverpool in October, having been invited to lecture in various British industrial cities; Thoreau leaves Walden Pond to take charge of the Emerson household. November to February, lectures extensively on various topics, including "Natural Aristocracy," in an England and Scotland disturbed by political unrest. Sees Carlyle, Wordsworth, Harriet Martineau, Dickens, and Tennyson. May, visits Paris during attempted revolution, where he meets Alexis de Tocqueville. Returns to England in June, dines with Chopin, and visits Stonehenge with Carlyle. Disembarks in Boston in late July.

1849 Offers winter lecture series on "Mind and Manners in the Nineteenth Century," drawing on English experiences, and a spring series on "Laws of the Intellect." Begins smoking cigars. *Nature; Addresses, and Lectures* published in September.

1850 January, *Representative Men* published. Winter–spring, extensive lecturing in New England, New York, Philadelphia, Cleveland, and Cincinnati. July, mourns death of Margaret Fuller Ossoli in shipwreck ("I have lost in her my audience") and sends Thoreau to Fire Island beach to search for her effects. Winter, lectures on "The Conduct of Life."

1851 Outraged by Webster's March 7 speech defending Fugitive Slave Law, fills journal with passionate condemnation of this former hero ("all the drops of his blood have eyes that look downward") and speaks against the law.

1852 Contributes to *Memoirs of Margaret Fuller Ossoli.* Praises *Uncle Tom's Cabin.* During winter, 1852–53, lectures to enthusiastic crowds from Boston to St. Louis, Philadelphia to Maine and Montreal.

1853 Mother dies on November 16 at age 84; she had lived with Waldo and Lidian since their marriage in 1835.

1854 Demanding lecture schedule throughout country includes attack on Fugitive Slave Law in New York City.

1855 Anti-slavery lectures in Boston, New York, and Philadelphia. Writes Whitman praising *Leaves of Grass* ("I give you joy of your free & brave thought. . . . I greet you at the beginning of a great career"). Helps F. B. Sanborn establish the Concord Academy, whose pupils will include the children of Emerson, Hawthorne, and Henry James, Sr. Saturday Club founded, with Emerson as a charter member, for informal literary discussions. Addresses Woman's Rights Convention in Boston.

1856 Lecture schedule ranges from New England to the Middle West. *English Traits* published in August. Speaks in favor of Kansas Relief, a fund raised to help Kansans impoverished by marauding pro-slavery advocates.

1857 Listens approvingly to Captain John Brown's speech in Concord. Moves remains of mother and Waldo ("I ventured to look into the coffin") to Sleepy Hollow Cemetery.

1858 Declares himself an abolitionist "of the most absolute abolition." Spends two weeks in August camping in the Adirondacks with Louis Agassiz, Oliver Wendell Holmes, and others. Calculates his income for the year at $4,162.11.

1859 Brother Bulkeley dies at age 52. Records in journal his fear that he has "no new thoughts, and that [his] life is quite at an end." Much agitated by capture and execution of

John Brown, and predicts that his hanging will make the gallows "sacred as the cross."

1860 Lectures throughout New York, New England, the Middle West, and at Toronto. Walks on Boston Common with Whitman for two hours on a March day trying to persuade him to tone down the "sex element" in *Leaves of Grass.* William Dean Howells visits in August as part of the itinerary of his literary pilgrimage. Declares in November that news of Lincoln's election is "sublime." *Conduct of Life* published in December.

1861 Told to "dry up" by unruly pro-Union crowd while attempting to speak at Massachusetts Anti-Slavery Society ("the mob roared . . . and after several beginnings, I withdrew"). Roused by unity and patriotism of New England following attack on Fort Sumter, visits Charlestown Navy Yard and declares "sometimes gunpowder smells good." Says of war that "amputation is better than cancer."

1862 Lectures on "American Civilization" in Washington and meets Lincoln. Reads address at Thoreau's funeral averring that "the country knows not yet, or in the least part, how great a son it has lost." Celebrates Emancipation Proclamation in an address printed in the *Atlantic Monthly.*

1863 Aunt Mary dies at age 89 on October 3. Appointed to committee to review standards of U.S. Military Academy at West Point. Lectures throughout Midwest.

1864 Attends Hawthorne's funeral and laments "the painful solitude of the man—which, I suppose, could not longer be endured, & he died of it." Lectures on "American Life" and the "Fortune of the Republic," exhorting Americans to "wake" and correct the injustices of the political system "with energy"; declares "this country, the last found, is the great charity of God to the human race." Elected to newly formed American Academy of Arts and Sciences.

1865 Eulogizes martyred Lincoln as "the true representative of this continent." Thinks Grant's terms for Lee's surrender too lenient. Daughter Edith engaged to Col. William Forbes, later president of Bell Telephone Co., son of railroad magnate John Murray Forbes. Lectures 77 times.

1866 Receives honorary Doctor of Laws degree from Harvard. Reads to son Edward Waldo his poem "Terminus" ("It is time to be old, / To take in sail.").

1867 *May-Day and Other Pieces* published in April. Delivers Phi Beta Kappa oration at Harvard, ending 29-year exile. Named an overseer of Harvard College. Lectures 80 times, the peak of his platform career, traveling west twice as far as Minnesota and Iowa.

1868 William dies in New York on September 13.

1870 *Society and Solitude* published in March; writes preface for edition of *Plutarch's Morals.* Lectures at Harvard on "Natural History of Intellect" and is much occupied with university affairs.

1871 Repetition of Harvard course cut short due to fatigue; April–May, travels to West Coast, in a private Pullman car leased by John Forbes, for relaxation and relief with family and friends. Meets naturalist John Muir and notes that California "has better days, & more of them" than any other place. Back in Concord, visited by Bret Harte.

1872 Health declines; suffers lapses of memory while lecturing. House in Concord badly damaged by fire on July 24; James Russell Lowell and other friends raise $17,000 to repair house and send Emerson abroad for a vacation. Travels to Egypt and Europe with daughter Ellen in October. In Paris, Henry James, Jr., guides them through the Louvre; sees Carlyle for last time. Meets Hermann Grimm, Hippolyte Taine, Ivan Turgenev, Robert Browning, Friedrich Max Müller, Benjamin Jowett, and John Ruskin.

1873 Returns in May to cheering crowd in Concord and discovers house has been restored by friends.

1874 Publishes *Parnassus*, an anthology of his favorite poetry (Whitman and Poe are not included).

1875 Ceases writing new entries in his private journals, but rereads and comments on old ones; *Letters and Social Aims* published in December with editorial assistance of Ellen and James Elliot Cabot.

1876 Emma Lazarus visits, and this "real unconverted Jew" creates much interest in household. *Selected Poems* published.

1877–82 Lives last years serenely in mental twilight (at Longfellow's funeral in his own last year, Emerson is reported to have said, "That gentleman was a sweet, beautiful soul, but I have entirely forgotten his name"). Dies of pneumonia on April 27, 1882, in Concord.

Note on the Texts

Emerson's career as a journal writer extended, with few significant periods of inactivity, for almost 60 years. He began his first journal, *Wide World 1*, in January 1820; his last, *ST*, includes an entry dated January 1877. Not counting a few journals known to have been lost, or items such as account books and engagement diaries, he completed 182 journals and miscellaneous notebooks during his lifetime, all but one of these now in the collections of the Houghton Library at Harvard University. Emerson used some of these manuscript volumes exclusively as commonplace books, poetry notebooks, composition books (in which he drafted works for publication), or record books of various kinds; others were journals in the more ordinary sense of the term, to which he added thoughts and observations over time; and in others, he mixed these modes to varying degrees.

The present volume contains selections from 46 manuscript journals, with entries written between 1841 and 1877. A companion volume, *Ralph Waldo Emerson: Selected Journals, 1820–1842*, contains selections from 35 journals. All told, the selections in these two volumes represent approximately a third of the contents of Emerson's regular journals, excluding his miscellaneous notebooks and mixed journals, in which regular journal writing is not the predominant mode. Both volumes present Emerson's manuscript journals as distinct works, in order of the date on which each is known or can be inferred to have been begun; entries within each journal are printed in the order in which they appear in Emerson's manuscripts (except in a few cases, where Emerson left some clear indication that he was writing in continuation of a remotely preceding entry). The resulting order of entries is not strictly chronological, though it is loosely so. Emerson sometimes began a new journal before he had finished a current one and would keep two or more journals at the same time; he also sometimes revisited earlier journals, revising or adding to them. Some entries bear a date, others do not.

Emerson did not attempt to publish his journals, but he drew on them extensively in his other writings, borrowing and adapting phrases, sentences, or longer passages from his journals. For a detailed account of his subsequent use of those parts of the journals included in the present volume, see www.loa.org/emerson-notes.

After Emerson's death, his son Edward Waldo Emerson and nephew Waldo Emerson Forbes collaborated in editing the journals for publication. Their 10-volume *Journals of Ralph Waldo Emerson*

(Boston: Houghton Mifflin, 1909–14) contains much of the text of Emerson's regular manuscript journals but omits passages printed elsewhere, rearranges entries from many separate journals into new chronological and thematic sequences, and also occasionally bowdlerizes.

The text of the journals presented here is a newly prepared clear text, based on the genetic text of Emerson's manuscript journals published in the 16-volume *Journals and Miscellaneous Notebooks of Ralph Waldo Emerson* (Cambridge: Harvard University Press, 1960–82), hereafter *JMN*. Where the editor of the present volume has omitted an entry or entries within the text of a journal, this fact is indicated with a centered em dash. (A centered asterisk at the bottom of a page indicates a line space in Emerson's manuscript journal.) *JMN* represents Emerson's cancellations and revisions and other features of the manuscript journals using a system of editorial marks to indicate rewriting, interlinear and marginal interpolation, original pagination, erasure, and manuscript mutilation. The present volume silently accepts a number of textual emendations included in *JMN* within these editorial marks, such as restored or corrected punctuation; letters or words omitted or repeated by a likely slip of the pen; interlinear insertions; dates supplied for particular entries; matter interpolated from the margins or conjecturally recovered from illegible or damaged sections of the manuscripts. Canceled matter is silently omitted in all but a few cases; whatever text has been restored in these cases is described in the Notes. Also silently omitted in the present volume are *JMN*'s expansions of abbreviated names and other annotative additions, such as the identification of quotations; Emerson's brief cross-references to other journal passages; and uncanceled variant words or phrases. For the identification of abbreviated names or of quotations, see the Notes to the present volume; for further information about Emerson's cross-references and uncanceled textual variants, see www.loa.org/emerson-notes.

The list below offers further detail about the individual volumes of *JMN* from which the texts of the journals in the present volume have been taken. All volumes are reprinted by arrangement with Harvard University Press:

G to *R*: *JMN* VIII (1841–1843), William H. Gilman, J. E. Parsons, eds. (1970).

U to *O*: *JMN* IX (1843–1847), Ralph H. Orth, Alfred R. Ferguson, eds. (1971).

AB to *Xenien*: *JMN* X (1847–1848), Merton M. Sealts, Jr., ed. (1973).

RS to *Journal at the West*: *JMN* XI (1848–1851), A. W. Plumstead, William H. Gilman, eds.; Ruth H. Bennett, assoc ed. (1975).

DO to *NO*: *JMN* XIII (1852–1855), Ralph H. Orth, Alfred R. Ferguson, eds. (1977).
RO to *CL*: *JMN* XIV (1854–1861), Susan Sutton Smith, Harrison Hayford, eds. (1978).
DL to *KL*: *JMN* XV (1860–1866), Linda Allardt, David W. Hill, eds.; Ruth H. Bennett, assoc. ed. (1982).
LN to *ST*: *JMN* XVI (1866–1882), Ronald A. Bosco, Glen M. Johnson, eds. (1982).

This volume presents the texts of *JMN* in clear form, but does not attempt to reproduce every feature of its typographic design, such as its display capitalization, or all representations of holographic features, such as variation in the length of dashes. A small number of emendations have been necessary in the preparation of a clear text from the genetic text of *JMN*, due to the unfinished nature of Emerson's manuscript. In some cases, for instance, Emerson added or canceled a word or phrase but did not subsequently correct a corresponding part of a sentence. Such emendations are listed below. The texts are otherwise presented without change, except for correction of typographical errors. Spelling, punctuation, and capitalization are often expressive features, and they are not altered, even when inconsistent or irregular. The following is a list of emendations and of typographical errors corrected, cited by page and line number: 80.24, selfheal [no period]; 158.36, male. / And; 164.21, easilier; 346.9, or course; 356.14, 566 925 016; 373.2, wonder. ↑of our isle↓; 391.25–26, Parilement; 419.15, that it; 473.20–21, hesitation; 550.19, a apparatus; 612.15, *"in*; 728.3–4, And what . . . birthday [2 lines transposed]; 762.12, palace; 798.23, an boy's; 809.9, Boston our; 871.15, ↑to him.↓:; 878.25, is diligent; 904.21, 1875.

Note on the Illustrations

1. Fredrika Bremer, *Ralph Waldo Emerson* (1850).
   Courtesy Concord Free Public Library.

2. Emerson's second wife, Lidian Jackson, with son Edward, c. 1847.
   Photograph from Emerson family photograph album. Gift from the estate of Amelia Forbes Emerson, 1982.
   Courtesy Concord Free Public Library.

3. Emerson with Edward and his younger daughter Edith, 1858.
   Photograph from Emerson family photograph album. Gift from the estate of Amelia Forbes Emerson, 1982.
   Courtesy Concord Free Public Library.

4. Emerson's elder daughter Ellen, born in 1839.
   Photograph from Emerson family photograph album. Gift from the estate of Amelia Forbes Emerson, 1982.
   Courtesy Concord Free Public Library.

5. Thomas Carlyle, 1846.
   MS Am 1280.235 (706.13). Ralph Waldo Emerson Memorial Association deposit, Houghton Library, Harvard University. Not to be reproduced in whole or in part without permission.
   Reprinted by permission of the Houghton Library, Harvard University.

6. Ralph Waldo Emerson, 1846.
   Courtesy Concord Free Public Library.

7. The Emersons' garden house, "Tumbledown Hall."
   May Alcott, *Concord Sketches: Consisting of Twelve Photographs from Original Drawings* (Boston: Fields, Osgood, 1869).
   Courtesy Concord Free Public Library.

8. "Bush," the Emerson family home in Concord, 1875.
   Courtesy Concord Free Public Library.

9. Henry David Thoreau, 1856.
   Benjamin Maxham, daguerreotype.
   Courtesy Concord Free Public Library.

10. Herbert Wendell Gleason, *Walden from Emerson's Cliff* (c. 1917).
Hand-colored lantern slide.
Courtesy Concord Free Public Library.

11. Margaret Fuller, 1846.
Copy (c. 1850–55) by Southworth & Hawes of an original daguerreotype (1846) by John Plumbe, not now known to be extant.
43.1412. Museum of Fine Arts, Boston. Gift of Edward Southworth Hawes in memory of his father Josiah Johnson Hawes.
Courtesy of the Museum of Fine Arts, Boston.

12. Ellery Channing.
Photograph from Alfred Winslow Hosmer's extra-illustrated copy of *The Life of Henry David Thoreau* (1896 edition), by Henry S. Salt. Gift of Herbert Buttrick Hosmer, 1949.
Courtesy Concord Free Public Library.

13. Elizabeth Hoar with an unidentified child, c. 1850.
Photograph from Emerson family photograph album. Gift from the estate of Amelia Forbes Emerson, 1982.
Courtesy Concord Free Public Library.

14. Bronson Alcott on the steps of the Concord School of Philosophy, c. 1879.
Alfred Winslow Hosmer, photograph.
Courtesy Concord Free Public Library.

15. William Torrey Harris and Elizabeth Palmer Peabody outside the Concord School, c. 1879.
Alfred Winslow Hosmer, photograph.
Courtesy Concord Free Public Library.

16. Emerson with classmates Samuel Bradford and William Henry Furness, 1875.
Frederick Gutekunst, photograph.
Boston Athenaeum. (photo) AA 5 Eme.r.1875.
Courtesy of the Boston Athenaeum.

17. Emerson in his study, 1879.
Autograph File F: Folsom, A.H., photograph. Ralph Waldo Emerson in his study. 1879. Houghton Library, Harvard University.

Reprinted by permission of the Houghton Library, Harvard University.

18. Emerson with his family on the steps of their Concord home, 1879.
Photograph from Emerson family photograph album. Gift from the estate of Amelia Forbes Emerson, 1982.
Courtesy Concord Free Public Library.

Notes

In the notes below, the reference numbers refer to page and line of this volume; the line count includes titles, headings, and thin rules dividing entries, but not blank lines. No note is made for material found in standard desk-reference works. Biblical quotations are keyed to the King James Version. Quotations from Shakespeare are keyed to *The Riverside Shakespeare*, ed. G. Blakemore Evans (Boston: Houghton Mifflin, 1974).

For further information about Emerson's use of his journals in his other literary works, the journals' internal cross-references, and uncanceled variant words and phrases, see www.loa.org/emerson-notes, which presents a detailed account of such uses, references, and variants, keyed to the present volume.

For biographical details about individuals in Emerson's family and his immedicate circle, see the Biographical Notes.

For more detailed notes, references to other studies, and further biographical information than is presented in the Biographical Notes or Chronology, see the 16-volume *Journals and Miscellaneous Notebooks of Ralph Waldo Emerson* (Cambridge: Harvard University Press, 1960–82), and also: Gay Wilson Allen, *Waldo Emerson: A Biography* (New York: Viking Press, 1981); Maurice Gonnaud, *An Uneasy Solitude: Individual and Society in the Work of Ralph Waldo Emerson*, tr. Lawrence Rosenwald (Princeton: Princeton University Press, 1978); Walter Harding, *Emerson's Library* (Charlottesville: University Press of Virginia, 1967); Joel Myerson, *Ralph Waldo Emerson: A Descriptive Bibliography* (Pittsburgh: University of Pittsburgh Press, 1982); Ralph H. Orb et al., eds., *The Topical Notebooks of Ralph Waldo Emerson*, 3 vols. (Columbia: University of Missouri Press, 1990–94); Barbara L. Packer, *Emerson's Fall* (New York: Continuum, 1982) and *The Transcendentalists* (Athens: University of Georgia Press, 2007); Joel Porte, ed., *Emerson in His Journals* (Cambridge: Harvard University Press, 1982); Joel Porte and Saundra Morris, eds., *The Cambridge Companion to Ralph Waldo Emerson* (New York: Cambridge University Press, 1999); Robert D. Richardson Jr., *Emerson: The Mind on Fire* (Berkeley: University of California Press, 1995); Lawrence Rosenwald, *Emerson and the Art of the Diary* (New York: Oxford University Press, 1988); Ralph L. Rusk, *The Life of Ralph Waldo Emerson* (New York: Charles Scribner's Sons, 1949); Stephen E. Whicher, *Freedom and Fate: An Inner Life of Ralph Waldo*

Emerson (Philadelphia: University of Pennsylvania Press, 1953).

from JOURNAL G

2.4 Colombe . . . Hosmer] Antoine Colombe, a French-Canadian laborer, worked for Emerson, his neighbor Edmund Hosmer, and others in Concord.

3.11–12 "When nature . . . Veeshnoo Sarma] See *The Hĕĕtōpadēs of Vĕĕshnŏŏ-Sărmā, in a Series of Connected Fables, Interspersed with Moral, Prudential, and Political Maxims*, tr. Charles Wilkins (1787).

5.1–2 Schleiermacher] Friedrich Daniel Ernst Schleiermacher (1768–1834), German theologian and philosopher.

6.31 C.] Caroline Sturgis (1819–1888), later Caroline Sturgis Tappan.

8.27 Osman] A name Emerson uses variously to refer to himself, to an ideal man or poet, or sometimes to Jones Very (1813–1880), poet and occasional pastor.

8.33–34 "To me . . . with me."] See "The Lay of the Humble" (1833), by poet and Member of Parliament Richard Monckton Milnes (1809–1885).

9.5 Hurry is for slaves.] Emerson included this sentence in one of four notebooks he compiled, collecting the writings and sayings of his aunt Mary Moody Emerson (1778–1863).

10.26 L.] Probably Lidian Jackson Emerson (1802–1892).

11.24–31 Hedge . . . his oration] Unitarian minister Frederic Henry Hedge (1805–1890) delivered the Phi Beta Kappa oration at the Harvard Commencement on August 26, 1841; it was subsequently published in *Conservatism and Reform* (1843).

12.25 Beacon street] A Boston street synonymous with respectability and affluence.

13.34 Landor . . . His book] Walter Savage Landor (1775–1864) published the first two volumes of his *Imaginary Conversations* in 1824.

14.29–30 the picture of Normanby] Christopher Normanby, a character in Landor's "Duke de Richelieu, Sir Fire Coats, and Lady Glengrin," *Imaginary Conversations*, vol. 5 (1829).

14.31 Earl Peterborough] Charles Mordaunt, 3rd Earl of Peterborough (1658–1735), featured in Landor's "William Penn and Lord Peterborough," *Imaginary Conversations*, vol. 2.

15.8–9 In the afternoon . . . afternoon] See "The Lotos-Eaters" (1833), by Alfred, Lord Tennyson (1809–1892).

16.7 but he has] After this point in Emerson's manuscript journal, a torn page interrupts the text.

16.9–10 April 1775 . . . Blood] Abel Davis, Jonas Buttrick, and Thaddeus Blood had all witnessed the Battle of Concord on April 19, 1775; with the Battle of Lexington, it was the first military engagement of the American Revolutionary War. Dr. Ezra Ripley (1751–1841) was Emerson's step-grandfather.

16.18–19 "*the 2 . . . courage*,"] See Count Emmanuel Augustin Dieudonné de Las Cases, *Mémorial de Sainte Hélène. Journal of the Private Life and Conversations of the Emperor Napoleon at Saint Helena* (1823).

19.27 "In the midst of . . . on me,"] From Landor's *Pericles and Aspasia* (1836).

19.36 Elizabeth,] Elizabeth Sherman Hoar (1814–1878), who was engaged to Emerson's brother Charles Chauncy (1808–1836) before his death, and who later worked with Emerson on *The Dial.*

20.27 Osman] See note 8.27.

20.29–31 Wordsworth's Recluse . . . seen"] See *The Excursion* (1814), II, l. 832, by William Wordsworth (1770–1850).

21.8 George P. B.] George Partridge Bradford (1807–1890), a former Divinity School classmate of Emerson's and a Concord schoolteacher.

21.16 Thomas T. Stone's] Thomas Treadwell Stone (1801–1895), a preacher, lecturer, and contributor to *The Dial.*

23.12 Mr Frost] Barzillai Frost (1804–1858), Ripley's assistant minister at the First Church in Concord, 1837–41.

24.1–2 Protogenes . . . painting] According to accounts in Pliny and elsewhere, the fourth-century Rhodian painter Protogenes, dissatisfied with a painting of a dog he had been working on, threw a sponge at it in disgust; by chance, the sponge hit the dog's mouth, producing the foaming effect he had desired.

24.28–29 Wo . . . tomb.] See "The Soldier's Widow" (1827), by Nathaniel Parker Willis (1806–1867).

25.6–7 F King . . . Governor Gore] Frederick Gore King (1801–1828), a Harvard classmate of Emerson's, and Christopher Gore (1758–1827), a governor of Massachusetts and U.S. senator.

25.16–17 "a warrior . . . around him".] See "The Burial of Sir John Moore at Corunna" (1817), by Charles Wolfe (1791–1823).

26.11–13 "Though by constitution . . . *Sand.*] The quotation, ultimately from *Un Hiver à Majorque* (1839) by George Sand (1804–1876), was published in this form in an *Athenaeum* review of Sand's *A Winter in the South of Europe* on September 4, 1841.

26.15–17 "The true coin . . . p 412] Emerson cites *The History of Ancient Philosophy* (1838–1846), by Heinrich Ritter (1791–1869).

26.19 G. R.] Probably George Ripley (1802–1880).

26.23–24 "Ah! if . . . Mrs. Maffit] Ann Maffit, wife of John Newland Maffit (1795–1850), a lecturer and Methodist Episcopal minister.

28.20 Menzel] Wolfgang Menzel (1798–1873), German literary critic and poet.

29.7 the Amistad captive] In 1839, a group of slaves staged a mutiny and successfully overran the Spanish slave ship *La Amistad*. They were captured, brought to New London, and tried for murder. In 1841, their case was argued in the Supreme Court, which affirmed an earlier finding that their transportation had been illegal in the first place; in 1842, they were returned to Sierra Leone.

29.20–22 the Hebrew story . . . people.] See I Chronicles 21:1–30.

29.33–30.2 "It is necessary . . . derived."] See *On the Mysteries of the Egyptians, Chaldeans and Assyrians*, tr. Thomas Taylor (1821), for this version of Iamblichus (c. 245–325).

from JOURNAL H

32.27 the good German] Emerson indexed this quotation under the name of Johann Gottlieb Fichte (1762–1814).

33.37 young Genius.] Emerson indexed this journal entry under the name of his friend, poet William Ellery Channing (1818–1901).

34.2–3 Edward Taylor's] Edward Thompson Taylor (1793–1871) was pastor of Seaman's Bethel in Boston.

34.34 G. W. Tyler] Probably George Washington Tyler (1813–1870), Boston merchant and editor of the Boston *Herald*.

35.29 Queenie] One of Emerson's pet names for his wife, Lidian.

35.32 Burrill Curtis] James Burrill Curtis (1821–1895), a resident of Brook Farm and later Concord along with his brother George William Curtis (1824–1892).

35.38 Cushings & Perkinses] John P. Cushing (1787–1862) and Thomas H. Perkins (1764–1854) were wealthy Boston merchants.

36.13 S.A.R.] Sarah Alden Bradford Ripley (1793–1867), wife of Emerson's half-uncle, the Rev. Samuel Ripley (1783–1847).

36.16 Biot & Bichat] Jean Baptiste Biot (1774–1862), French physicist, and Marie François Xavier Bichat (1771–1802), French physician.

36.22 C. A. Greene] Christopher A. Greene (1816–1853), a teacher and reformer who briefly co-edited a liberal monthly, the *Plain Speaker*.

37.26–27 *Spiraea tomentosa.*] Steeplebush, a perennial shrub.

40.7–8 whether in the body . . . God knoweth] See II Corinthians 12:2.

40.39 the Maelzel secret] Johann Nepomuk Maelzel (1772–1838), a German inventor and showman, toured the United States beginning in 1826 with a "Chess Turk," an ostensible chess-playing automaton. The machine actually housed a human player, a secret revealed by Edgar Allan Poe in his 1836 essay "Maelzel's Chess Player," as well as by other observers.

43.14 The gallipots of Socrates] Francis Bacon (1561–1626) writes in *The Advancement of Learning* (1605) that Plato compared Socrates to "the gallypots of apothecaries, which on the outside had apes and owls and antiques but contained within sovereign and precious liquors and confections."

43.17–18 the Protocols of Vienna & St Petersburg] Diplomatic agreements adopted by multiple parties at the Congress of Vienna in 1815 and by England and Russia at St. Petersburg in 1826.

43.27 "the great seraphic . . . cherubim"] See *Paradise Lost* (1674), I.794, by John Milton (1608–1674).

44.4 "And the more . . . faster on."] From an untitled puzzle poem in "On Riddles" (1825), by Anna Laetitia Barbauld (1743–1825).

44.5 Fanny Elsller . . . Nathalie.] Austrian ballerina Fanny Elssler (1810–1884) appeared in *Nathalie, or la Laitière suisse* (1832), a ballet by Filippo Taglioni (1777–1871).

47.1 The Retreat of the Ten Thousand] The Ten Thousand was an army consisting mostly of Greek mercenaries hired by Cyrus the younger to help him seize the Persian throne from his brother, Artaxerxes II in the late 5th century BCE. Their march through Asia Minor, their defeat at the battle of Cunaxa (401 BCE) and their long retreat home was chronicled by the Greek historian Xenophon (c. 430–354 BCE) in his *Anabasis.*

49.1 canting moths of peace] See Shakespeare, *Othello*, I.iii.256.

49.30 the great Condé] Louis II de Bourbon, Prince de Condé (1621–1686), French general during the Thirty Years War.

50.15 H.] Henry David Thoreau (1817–1862).

50.18 A] A. Bronson Alcott (1799–1888).

52.25–26 No Douglas . . . Cassius] See the poem *The Lady of the Lake* (1810), V.xxiii, by Sir Walter Scott (1770–1832), in which Douglas casts a bar or caber farther than his opponents, and Shakespeare's *Antony and Cleopatra*, II.vi.15, which refers to "pale Cassius" conspiring against Julius Caesar.

52.33 he wets them] At this point in Emerson's manuscript journal, a torn page interrupts the text.

53.25 the Erl King] A poem (1783) by Johann Wolfgang von Goethe (1749–1832), set to music by many composers, most famously in 1815 by Franz Schubert (1797–1828).

54.16 "a being . . . Universe".] See the Introduction to *Conversations with Children on the Gospels* (1836–37) by Alcott, transcribed by Elizabeth Palmer Peabody (1804–1894).

56.1 "Bubb Dodington"] *The Diary of the Late George Bubb Dodington* (1784), English politician and baron who lived from 1691 to 1762.

56.7 Ellen. H.] Probably Ellen Sturgis Hooper (1812–1848), sister of Caroline Sturgis Tappan, both contributors of poetry to *The Dial.*

56.15 C. & M.] Probably Caroline Sturgis and Margaret Fuller (1810–1850).

57.20–22 "Donde hai . . . poet] The remark, reportedly made by Cardinal d'Este (1479–1520) when he received a copy of *Orlando Furioso* (1516) from its author Ludovico Ariosto (1474–1533), is recounted and translated in similar terms in the translator's preface to Book IV of *The Works of Francis Rabelais* (revised and extended edition, 1693), by Peter Anthony Motteux (1663–1718).

57.31 The small red lion] In his "Speech at the Public Dinner, in the Lyceum Room, on Friday, the 30th of August, 1822," George Canning (1770–1827) offered an anecdote about an artist who specialized in painting red lions; asked for something new and striking, he suggested "a *small red lion.*"

58.15–16 "Mr Fox . . . have it."] From *The Diary of the Late George Bubb Dodington.*

from JOURNAL J

60.4 J. V.] Jones Very.

65.1–3 "According to Boehmen . . . p 123] Emerson cites *Histoire de la Philosophie Allemande depuis Leibnitz jusqu'à Hegel* (1836), by Auguste Théodore Hilaire, Baron Barchou de Penhoën (1799–1855).

65.7 at bottom of last page] See the final paragraph on page 64 of the present volume.

66.23 Dear Waldo] The salutation, in Emerson's manuscript journal, is in another hand, probably Elizabeth Hoar's ("Aunt Elizabeth").

69.7–8 "mania . . . Proclus would say.] See *The Six Books of Proclus, the Platonic Successor, on the Theology of Plato*, tr. Thomas Taylor (1816).

70.9 chaos of visiting.] A canceled sentence follows in Emerson's manuscript journal: "Ghostlike we glide through life & should not know the place again."

70.11 Gam. Bradford] Gamaliel Bradford (1795–1839), a physician, essayist, and lecturer, father of Sarah Alden Bradford Ripley.

70.20–23 Our poetry . . . *miow*.] Emerson indexed this journal entry under the name of poet William Ellery Channing.

72.8–9 "the prince . . . of the air."] See Ephesians 2:2.

72.31–33 "It is impossible . . . p. 472] Emerson cites *The Cratylus, Phaedo, Parmenides and Timaeus of Plato*, tr. Thomas Taylor (1793).

73.4 E. H.] Elizabeth Hoar.

73.19–20 Patmos] Greek island where John the Divine, in exile, wrote the Book of Revelation.

73.23 his MS story] "The Two Dolons," by Charles King Newcomb (1820–1894), was published soon after in the July 1842 issue of *The Dial.*

73.28–29 Robert . . . Weiss] Robert Bartlett was a Latin tutor at Harvard, and John Weiss a Harvard Divinity School student.

73.34 Nelly] Ellen Tucker Emerson (1839–1909), Emerson's elder daughter.

75.17 A.] Abby Larkin Adams, adopted daughter of Emerson's business adviser and former parishoner Abel Adams (d. 1867).

75.37–76.1 "this . . . coil."] See Shakespeare, *Hamlet*, III.i.66.

76.36–77.5 Montaigne vol 3 . . . advice."] Emerson's page reference is to "Of Profit and Honesty" in his 1738 edition of Charles Cotton's 1685–86 translation of Montaigne's *Essays.* Dandamys, in Plutarch's life of Alexander, was an Indian sage.

77.35–36 Captain Chandler . . . Farm-School] Daniel Chandler (1788–1847) was superintendent of the Boston Asylum and Farm School for Indigent Boys from 1835 to 1839.

78.7–9 these English Tracts . . . Jack Cade] John Goodwyn Barmby (1820–1881), a Christian socialist reformer, published a periodical series, *New Tracts for the Times*, the first five numbers of which were issued under the title *The Communist Miscellany: A Collection of Tracts, Religious, Political, and Domestic* (1843); like poet Ebenezer Elliot (1781–1849), the "Corn Law rhymer," he was active in the Chartist reform movement. Jack Cade, a leader of Kentish peasants in a 1450 rebellion against Henry VI, appears on a number of occasions in Emerson's journals as an archetype of the radical.

78.13–14 Lane, Owen, Wright, Fry,] Charles Lane (1800?–1870) was coeditor of the *Healthian*, a dietary reform journal, and cofounder with A. Bronson Alcott of the utopian community Fruitlands; Robert Owen (1771–1858), a Welsh social reformer and founder of utopian communities at Orbiston, Scotland, and New Harmony, Indiana; Henry G. Wright (c. 1814–1846), a teacher at Alcott's "Alcott House School" in England who traveled to the United States with Lane in 1842; and Elizabeth Fry (1780–1845), a prison reform activist.

80.21–22 Very often there seems . . . not he.] Emerson indexed this entry in his journal under the name of poet William Ellery Channing.

80.26 Zanoni] A novel (1842) by Edward Bulwer-Lytton (1803–1873).

81.12 Vivian Grey] Novel (1826–27) by Benjamin Disraeli (1804–1881).

81.24 Beckendorf] The prime minister in *Vivian Grey.*

81.27 Bulwer] Edward Bulwer-Lytton.

82.3 Bettine] Elizabeth "Bettina" Brentano von Arnim (1785–1859), author of the fictional *Goethe's Correspondence with a Child* (1839).

83.9 Edmund] Edmund Hosmer, the Emersons' neighbor.

from JOURNAL K

86.10–13 "There is no . . . Sarma] See note 3.11–12.

86.23 Thomas Delf] Delf (1810–1865) was an English editor and literary agent who later wrote several books under the pseudonym Charles Martel.

87.1 "Lord of the Isles"] Long poem (1815) by Walter Scott.

87.13 Charles G. Loring] Loring (1794–1867) was a Boston lawyer who served in the Massachusetts state senate.

88.24–26 *Tecumseh* . . . this poem] George H. Colton (1818–1847), editor of *The American Review*, published *Tecumseh* in 1842.

89.6 Brisbane . . . his Fourierism] Albert Brisbane (1809–1890), a leading American advocate of the socialist theories of Charles Fourier (1772–1837), coedited the Fourierist journal *The Phalanx* (1843–45) and wrote *The Social Destiny of Man* (1840).

90.19–20 New Harmonys] Utopian socialist communities like New Harmony, Indiana, which was founded as "Harmony" by German pietists in 1814 and renamed "New Harmony" by Welsh reformer Robert Owen in 1824.

91.30 his Orphic Sayings] Alcott's "Orphic Sayings" appeared in *The Dial* in July 1840, January 1841, and April 1842.

93.13 "Moral Sam Patch."] Sam Patch (1799–1829), also known as the "Yankee Leaper," was a celebrity daredevil.

93.29 *Sauve qui peut.*] Every man for himself (literally, "save who can").

94.4 F. E.] Fanny Elssler; see note 44.5.

96.18 Edward Palmer] Palmer (1802–1886), a former clergyman, advocated the renunciation of money and refused to accept any for the services he performed.

97.21 this big Meg] Meg Merrilies, a gypsy in Scott's novel *Guy Mannering* (1815).

97.25 G. R. & S. R.] George Ripley & Sophia Ripley.

97.31–32 Theresa . . . make a show."] See Goethe, *Wilhelm Meister's Apprenticeship* (1795–96), Bk. VII, ch. vi.

106.21–22 Mme Guion & Jacob Behmen] Mystics Jeanne-Marie Bouvier de la Motte Guyon (1648–1717) and Jakob Böhme (1575–1624).

107.15 "Every intellect . . . essence."] See note 69.7–8.

107.30–34 I have sometimes . . . peace.] Emerson indexed this journal entry under Thoreau's name.

109.3–5 "Since neither . . . entrance knew"] Sophocles, *Antigone* (c. 442 BCE), lines 455–57, in a 17th-century translation by Samuel White, quoted in "Of Common Conception against the Stoics" in Emerson's 1718 edition of Plutarch's *Morals.*

109.34–35 Mr Phinney . . . Moore] Elias Phinney (1780–1849), a Lexington farmer, was a trustee of the Massachusetts Agricultural Society; Abel Moore (1777–1848), a real estate broker, served as deputy sheriff of Concord.

from JOURNAL N

112.4 E.P.P.] Elizabeth Palmer Peabody.

112.6–7 *l'humanité* from Le Roux] See *De l'Humanité, de son Principe et de son Avenir* (1840), by Pierre Leroux (1797–1871).

113.6 W.H.C.] William Henry Channing (1810–1884), a Unitarian minister and social reformer.

118.5 H. T.] Henry David Thoreau.

121.12–13 C. & H. . . . A.] Ellery Channing & Nathaniel Hawthorne (1804–1864), and Alcott.

122.10 Milnes] Richard Monckton Milnes.

122.38–123.2 Richter said . . . lips"] See the *Life of Jean Paul Frederic*

Richter (1842), tr. Eliza Buckminster Lee (1794–1864), which appends to his autobiography Lee's biographical essay.

124.33 Hug . . . Ruhnken] German philologists and classicists Johann Leonard Hug (1765–1846), Friedrich August Wolf (1759–1824), and David Ruhnken (1723–1798).

127.3 S.G.W.] Samuel Gray Ward (1817–1907), a financier and art patron.

127.7–8 Mr Demond . . . Domett cloths] Calvin Carver Damon (1803–1854) was a local fabric manufacturer who had invented a type of wool-cotton flannel called domett cloth.

127.17–18 *Nunc dimittis me.*] Now let me depart. (Adapted from the Vulgate version of Luke 2:29, "Lord, now lettest thy servant depart in peace," included in the evensong service of the Book of Common Prayer, 1662.)

128.9–10 "huts . . . lie"] See Wordsworth's "Song at the Feast of Brougham Castle" (1807).

129.1–2 Hayraddin Magraber] Hayraddin Maugrabin, a character in Scott's novel *Quentin Durward* (1823).

129.33–35 One of Landor's sentences . . . primary."] See "Roger Ascham and Lady Jane Grey" in Landor's *Imaginary Conversations*, vol. 4.

130.20 this last book of Wordsworth] See Wordsworth's *Poems, Chiefly of Early and Late Years* (1842).

132.14 Dr Channing] Dr. William Ellery Channing (b. 1789), the poet's namesake and uncle, died on October 2, 1842.

135.16 M described E] Probably Margaret Fuller and Ellery Channing.

135.19–20 M. F . . . C. S.] Margaret Fuller; Caroline Sturgis.

136.19 Panurge] One of the main characters in *Pantagruel* (1532), by François Rabelais (c. 1483–1553); a libertine, a coward, and a cheat.

136.34 M Rotch] Mary Rotch (1777–1848), a New Light Quaker and religious schismatic whom Emerson first met in 1833.

137.19–20 Joe Miller] An 18th-century English actor who lent his name to *Joe Miller's Jests: or the Wits Vade-Mecum* (1739), a collection of jokes and witticisms published after his death.

137.31 Bartlett] Probably John Bartlett (1784–1849), pastor of the Second Congregational Church at Marblehead, Massachusetts, and author of *God Not the Author of Sin* (1819) and *Preaching Christ in Love* (1825).

138.13–15 The strangers . . . books.] Charles Lane and Henry G. Wright brought with them, when they traveled to the United States, the library of James Pierrepont Greaves (1777–1842), a school reformer; see note 78.13–14 and page 140 in the present volume.

138.17–18 Then comes . . . University] In 1840, Emerson and Alcott collaborated in envisioning a new university, to be built in Concord.

139.18 G.P.B.'s] George Partridge Bradford's.

139.34–39 "Waste not . . . p 106] Emerson cites *Paracelsus* (1835), by Robert Browning (1812–1889).

140.30–31 C. L. . . . Brownson] Charles Lane and Orestes Brownson (1803–1876), social reformer and editor of the *Boston Quarterly Review.*

from JOURNAL Z[A]

142.6 A. . . . his project] A. Bronson Alcott's utopian community, Fruitlands.

143.21 our friends] Lane, Wright, and Alcott.

144.23 young R.] A "Mr. Richardson" lectured at the Concord Lyceum on December 7, 1842, probably James Richardson Jr., one of Thoreau's classmates.

145.8 W.] Samuel Gray Ward.

145.20 C.'s] Caroline Sturgis's.

146.10 E. H.] Elizabeth Hoar.

147.32–33 "I do not inflame . . . allusion."] See the February 22, 1834, Senate speech by Daniel Webster (1782–1852) regarding "The Removal of Deposits."

147.39 the Hayne debate] A Senate debate between Webster and South Carolina senator Robert Y. Hayne over protectionist tariffs, January 19–30, 1830.

148.21–22 Talleyrand's . . . refreshing] See the *Life of Prince Talleyrand* (1834–36), by Charles Maxine Catharinet de Villemarest (1785–1852).

148.35–37 Stetson . . . guilt."] The Rev. Caleb Stetson (1801–1885) was a Divinity School classmate of Emerson's.

149.4 his speech at Richmond] Webster delivered an address at the Whig Convention in Richmond, Virginia, on October 5, 1840.

149.22 the Knapp trial] Webster was the state prosecutor in the 1830 case against the Knapp brothers for the murder of Captain Joseph White in Salem.

151.28 W.A.T.] William Aspinwall Tappan (1819–1905), who married Caroline Sturgis in 1847.

152.16 H. J. . . . Mrs B.] Probably Henry James Sr. (1811–1882) and New York mystic Rebecca Black.

from JOURNAL R

155.4 Mundt] Theodor Mundt (1808–1861), author of *Geschichte der Literatur der Gegenwart* (1840) and other works of criticism and fiction.

155.11 Sir Everard Home] British physician and anatomist (1756–1832).

155.25 North Americans & Knickerbockers] The *North American Review* and the *Knickerbocker* were literary magazines.

156.9–12 Miss Peabody . . . way to it.] Peabody sold artists' supplies at her Boston bookshop; the potential customers Emerson mentions are the painter Washington Allston (1779–1843) and engraver John Cheney (1801–1885).

156.21 E. H.] Elizabeth Hoar.

157.5–17 SHANG MUNG. . . . void."] See *The Chinese Classical Work, Commonly Called the Four Books*, ed. David Collie (1828).

157.26 ornithorhynchus] Platypus.

158.20–22 The Veeshnoo . . . leather."] See note 3.11–12.

159.8–10 "Aristo said . . . p 339] See "Of Vanity" in Montaigne's *Essays*, tr. Cotton.

159.25 Webster at Concord.] Daniel Webster was one of the defense lawyers in a local embezzlement trial; Emerson entertained him at his home, along with other participants in the proceedings, on August 15, 1843.

160.16 Wyman's character] William Wyman, a bank president, was on trial for embezzlement.

160.34 E.R.H.] Ebenezer Rockwood Hoar (1816–1895), brother of Elizabeth Hoar, served as a defense attorney during the trial.

161.4 R. C.] Rufus Choate (1799–1859), an attorney for the defense.

161.32–34 as Waller the poet . . . returns home."] See *Brief Lives* (first collected as *Letters Written by Eminent Persons in the Seventeenth and Eighteenth Centuries*, 1813), by John Aubrey (1626–1697).

162.30 ABW] Probably Anna Barker Ward (1813–1900), wife of Samuel Gray Ward.

162.38–39 Herr Driesbach . . . caravan.] Lion-tamer Jake "Herr" Driesbach (1807–1877) toured the United States between 1840 and 1854.

163.21–22 Von Amburgh . . . candy] Isaac A. Van Amburgh (1808–1865) was a popular animal trainer and menagerie performer; R. L. & A. Stuart was a successful New York candy-making firm.

163.24 faint heartedness.] A canceled sentence follows in Emerson's manuscript journal: "Dear husband, I wish I had never been born. I do not see how God can compensate me for the sorrow of existence."

163.36–164.5 Two brave chanticleers . . . talons.] Emerson indexed this journal entry under the name of Charles Lane; see note 78.13–14.

164.6–7 C. N. . . . T. P.] Charles Newcomb; Theodore Parker (1810–1860).

166.32 King Réné period] René of Anjou (1409–1480), also known as "Good King René," was a painter, poet, and patron of the arts.

166.35 "Dial . . . piety."] In his journal *AB*, Emerson attributes this quote to Thomas Delf; see note 86.23.

168.18 S.G.W.'s] Samuel Gray Ward's.

168.30 C.K.N. & G.P.B.] Charles King Newcomb and George P. Bradford.

168.34 N. H. . . . Burton] Nathaniel Hawthorne and Warren Burton (1800–1866), Unitarian and Swedenborgian clergyman.

169.34–37 "this . . . Orpheus says."] See note 69.7–8.

171.7–8 Speech on Foot's . . . 182 ;] Webster first spoke on Foot's Resolution, on the subject of public lands, on January 20, 1830.

171.12–17 "It has never . . . Emperor."] See note 157.5–17.

172.38 Flaxman's drawing] Draftsman and sculptor John Flaxman (1755–1826) published his *Compositions for the Tragedies of Aeschylus* in 1795.

174.1 S. S.] Probably Sarah Franklin Stearns (1816–1856), a resident at Brook Farm.

174.10 English visitors] Poet William Cox Bennett (1820–1895) and his wife visited Emerson in May 1843.

174.18–19 G. & S. R.] George and Sophia Ripley (1803–1861).

174.30–31 this book of Carlyle] *Past and Present* (1843), by Thomas Carlyle (1795–1881).

174.35–36 *The gods . . . of men.*] See Acts 14:11.

176.11 Ball] Benjamin West Ball (1823–1896), later the author of *Elfin Land, and Other Poems* (1851).

177.22 My friends . . . town] Alcott and Lane left Concord to start the Fruitlands community on June 1.

177.25 C. L.] Charles Lane.

179.32 J. P.] Jonathan M. Phillips (1778–1861), an early member of the Transcendental Club.

180.12–15 Luther said . . . at us."] See *Colloquia Mensalia; or Dr. Martin Luther's Divine Discourses at His Table*, tr. H. Bell (1652); Martin Luther lived from 1483 to 1546.

182.5–6 Yesterday at Bunker Hill . . . people] The occasion was the unveiling of the Bunker Hill monument in Charlestown, Massachusetts.

183.13 S R.] Probably Sophia Ripley.

from U

189.34 Mr Tuttle's] John L. Tuttle, a Concord farmer.

190.2–3 must have taste.] A canceled sentence follows in Emerson's manuscript journal: "The new gospel is, By taste are ye saved."

190.13 WEC] William Ellery Channing.

191.31 My friend] Caroline Sturgis.

192.5 "vis superba formae"] "Tyranny of beauty"; see Goethe's posthumously published *Maximen und Reflexionen* (*Maxims and Reflections*), which quotes this phrase from Dutch poet Johannes Secundus (1511–1536).

194.11 Borne] Ludwig Börne (1786–1837), German satirist.

195.15 all under cover.] A canceled sentence follows in Emerson's manuscript journal: "Well, I should add to this, grounds that should never require the tenant to take a journey."

196.8–13 the sentence . . . p 152] Emerson cites Cotton's translation of Montaigne.

196.29 Qui facit . . . per se] What a man does through another, he does through himself.

198.31 Os oculosque . . . par.] A mouth and eyes equal to Jove; see *The Anatomy of Melancholy* (1621), part I, section I, by Robert Burton (1577–1640).

198.32 Henry Ware] Henry Ware Jr. (1794–1843), Unitarian clergyman and one of Emerson's mentors, died September 22.

199.14–15 pumpkin-sweeting] A variety of apple.

199.18 G.B.E.] George Barrell Emerson (1797–1881), Emerson's cousin.

200.9–10 like (See Aubrey)] In his lecture "The Young American," printed in *The Dial* in April 1844, Emerson revised the preceding paragraphs of his journal and notes that John Aubrey "has given us an engaging account of the manner in which Bacon finished his own manor at Gorhambury." Aubrey's account appears in his *Brief Lives*.

200.12–13 Saadi's Gulistan . . . I drew] See *The Gulistan, or Flower-*

Garden, of Shaikh Sadī of Shīraz, tr. James Ross (1823), and Emerson's poem "Saadi," later published in *Poems* (1847).

201.19 "Her bed . . . pearl."] From *The Gulistan*.

204.10 Dr C.T.J.] Charles Thomas Jackson (1805–1880), Lidian's brother.

205.16 "Wish . . . England."] See Shakespeare, *Henry V*, IV.iii.30.

206.4 Hesiod's . . . παντος] How much more the half is than the whole; see *Works and Days*, l. 40 (c. 700 BCE).

209.38–39 Vich ian Vohr] A character in Scott's novel *Waverley* (1814).

210.6–7 the calamity . . . Saturday] The death of Emerson's son Waldo (1836–1842).

211.10 "And fools . . . tread."] From the *Essay on Criticism* (1711), l. 625, by Alexander Pope (1688–1744).

217.6–7 this great . . . *proportions!*] Allston began his large canvas *Belshazzar's Feast* around 1817, but decided to repaint it after Gilbert Stuart (1755–1828), in 1820, criticized the perspective; the painting remained unfinished, in spite of longstanding effort, when he died in July 1842.

218.12–33 Very sad . . . the gods.] Emerson indexed this entry in his journal under "Alcott."

219.10–11 Eripitur persona . . . res] See Lucretius, *De Rerum Natura*, III, 230–1: "The mask is torn off, the man remains."

219.17 D W] Daniel Webster.

from V

221.4–5 Tom Appleton . . . Italy & Spain] Thomas Gold Appleton (1812–1884), a Boston lawyer known for his witticisms, took delight in travel, much like the "dilettante" William Thomas Beckford (1760–1844), whose *Italy, with Sketches of Spain and Portugal* was published in 1834.

221.27 Ole Bull] A Norwegian violin virtuoso (1810–1880) who toured North America five times.

223.2 H.'s] Henry David Thoreau's.

224.2 Abbot Samson] Saint Samson of Dol (fl. c. 486–573) founded monasteries in Cornwall and Brittany.

225.23 Mr Hudson] Henry Norman Hudson (1814–1886) lectured on *Macbeth* on January 1, 1845.

226.23 Ellen H.] Ellen Sturgis Hooper.

227.16–19 "He'd harpit . . . none."] See "Glenkindie," in *Popular*

Ballads and Songs from Tradition, Manuscripts, and Scarce Editions (1806), ed. Robert Jamieson (1780–1844).

227.20–23 "O I did get the rose . . . mither's wame."] See "Lord Thomas and Fair Annet," in *Reliques of Ancient English Poetry* (1765), ed. Thomas Percy (1729–1811).

228.33 Mr Hecker] Isaac Hecker (1819–1888), later a Catholic priest, had lived at Fruitlands, Brook Farm, and in the Thoreau household.

231.22 Hugh] Hugh Whelan, the Emersons' gardener.

232.12–13 "Tis . . . gain"] See Wordsworth's *The Excursion*, IV.138–39.

235.4–7 George Sand . . . Faustina] See Sand's *Consuelo* (1842–3); *I Promessi Sposi* (1827), by Alessandro Manzoni (1785–1873); and *Faustina* (1841), by Countess Ida von Hahn-Hahn (1805–1880).

238.2 Clarkson] Thomas Clarkson (1760–1846), English abolitionist.

238.14–17 Buonaparte . . . happy."] See *Private Memoirs of Napoleon Bonaparte* (1830), by Louis Antoine Fauvelet de Bourienne (1769–1834).

239.28 *Cent mille hommes*] One hundred thousand men.

240.1–2 Putnam pleased . . . oration] See *An Oration Delivered at Cambridge before the Phi Beta Kappa Society* (1844), by George Putnam (1814–1872).

240.22 S.A.R.] Sarah Alden Ripley.

242.26–27 what was said . . . they all know it;"] See de Villemarest's *Life of Prince of Talleyrand* (1834–36).

243.28–29 the statues . . . Uncle Toby] *Tam O'Shanter* (1828) by James Thom (1802–1850) and *My Uncle Toby and the Widow Wadman* by Robert Ball Hughes (1806–1868). Literary characters, alone or in small groups, were popular subjects for drawing-room sculpture in 19th-century America.

244.27–31 Bonaparte . . . sword?"] See note 238.14–17.

245.17–21 the Corsican anecdote . . . to sleep.] In an entry in Journal *V* not included in the present volume, Emerson wrote: "The Corsicans in 1769 fought resolutely at the passage of Golo. Not having time to cut down the bridge, which was of stone, they made use of their dead to form an entrenchment." John Aubrey recounts the story of Sir Adrian Scrope in his *Brief Lives*. The Borodino soldier appears in Bayle St. John's "The Gates of Death: A Revelation of the Horrors of the Battle-field," *Bentley's Miscellany*, XVI (1841).

247.1–2 Mr Hoar's visit to S. Carolina] Samuel Hoar had been appointed by the Massachusetts legislature to collect evidence in South Carolina of the imprisonment and sale of free black Massachusetts citizens serving on merchant ships. The South Carolina legislature responded to Hoar's appointment by issuing a resolution to expel him.

247.25–27 Lord Edward . . . more virtuous."] See *The Life and Death of Edward Fitzgerald* (1831), by Thomas Moore (1779–1852).

from W

254.34–36 St. Evremond's . . . sin."] Charles de Saint-Évremond (c. 1610–1703), French soldier and essayist, recounted this confidence of François Bernier (1626–1688), French traveler and physician, in a letter to Anne "Ninon" de Lenclos (1620–1705).

256.25 Cagliostro . . . Edwards] Count Alessandro di Cagliostro, an alias of Giuseppe Balsamo (1743–1795), a forger and swindler; Monroe Edwards (1808–1847), a confidence-man and forger tried in New York in 1842.

257.7–8 My kings . . . St Elwes—.] Hunks was a slang term for miser; John Elwes (1714–1789), a British politician and notorious miser, is believed to be the inspiration for Ebenezer Scrooge.

257.31 W. T] William Tappan (1819–1905), son of abolitionist Lewis Tappan, was shortly to marry Caroline Sturgis.

259.17 "Man is . . . wind"] See *Bussy D'Ambois* (1607), I.i.18, by George Chapman (1559–1634).

260.25 Mrs R.] Probably Sarah Alden Ripley.

263.9–10 the friend . . . month?] Caroline Sturgis.

263.15–19 "If we look . . . Vol II] Emerson cites *The Economy of the Animal Kingdom* (1740–41), tr. James John Garth Wilkinson (1843–44), by Emanuel Swedenborg (1688–1772), which quotes *Exposition anatomique de la structure du corps humain* (1732), by Jakob Benignus Winslow (1669–1760).

264.14–19 And Byron . . . us all."] See the January 1827 issue of *The Quarterly Review*, which prints these lines, from "The Wedding of Maxim Zernojevitz," in a review of *Translations from the Servian Minstrelsy* (1826), an unattributed collection printed in "a very small edition . . . for private circulation" and no longer known to be extant, but probably translated by John Bowring (1792–1872), who soon after published *Servian Popular Poetry* (1827) in collaboration with Vuk Stefanović Karadžić (1787–1864). In his poetry anthology *Parnassus* (1874), Emerson appends the lines to others by George Gordon, Lord Byron (1788–1824), and adds a title, "Hurts of Time."

264.22–27 "Out upon time . . . creatures of clay."] See Byron's *The Siege of Corinth* (1816), lines 499–502.

265.13–15 "To make . . . part."] See "The Lives of Ten Orators: Isocrates" in Plutarch's *Morals.*

266.2 Father Taylor] See note 34.2–3.

273.18 the sad game] The third trial of William Wyman (see note 159.25) in the Concord County Court; a guilty verdict in his second trial had been set aside by the Supreme Court on technical grounds, and he retained the same counsel.

274.16 Cheney] John Milton Cheney, cashier of the Middlesex Institution for Savings.

275.5 Mussey] Probably Benjamin B. Mussey, a Boston publisher.

from Y

278.4 "What's Hecuba to him?"] See Shakespeare, *Hamlet*, II.ii.559.

279.19 "Travelling the path . . . births"] See *The Vishńu Puráńa, a System of Hindu Mythology and Tradition*, tr. H. H. Wilson (1840).

279.33 *Cudworth*] See Ralph Cudworth, *The True Intellectual System of the Universe* (1678).

280.4–5 Theobald's Shakspeare . . . Shakspeare wrote.] In his 1726 *Shakespeare Restored*, and in later editions of Shakespeare, Lewis Theobald (c. 1688–1744) attempted to establish a correct text of Shakespeare's works, removing the errors and misreadings that had been introduced by others.

281.25 Phedo p 202.] Emerson cites *The Cratylus, Phaedo, Parmenidies, and Timaeus of Plato*, and continues a dialogue between Cebes and Simmias and Socrates.

285.13 Peter Parley's story] Beginning in 1827, Samuel Griswold Goodrich (1793–1860) published almost 200 children's books, written by himself and others, under the pseudonym Peter Parley.

286.4–6 Abu Said . . . I see."] See *Practical Philosophy of the Muhammadan People*, tr. W. F. Thompson (1839).

287.29 "I never . . . look for"] Emerson elsewhere attributes this quotation to poet William Ellery Channing.

289.34 "A ride . . . said the ancient.] See "Symposiacs" in Plutarch's *Morals.*

289.36 *La nature* . . . Fourier.] See "Des Demoiselles et Damoiseaux" in Fourier's *Théorie de l'Unité Universelle* (1841): "Nature loves mixtures."

290.1 *tenax propositi*] Steadfast of purpose.

290.11–14 words like these . . . escapes you."] In *Memoirs of Margaret Fuller Ossoli* (1852), Emerson attributes these sentences to Margaret Fuller.

291.26 *volvox globator*] A species of algae that lives in multicellular colonies.

291.39–292.8 Whilst Dhruva sat . . . sunk down."] See note 279.19. The opening couplet is Emerson's.

295.2–3 Dyce & Collier . . . Warburton] Alexander Dyce (1798–1869), John Payne Collier (1789–1883), Edmond Malone (1741–1812), and William Warburton (1698–1779), editors and critics of Shakespeare.

295.16 Revisit'st now . . . Moon] See *Hamlet*, I.iv.53.

295.31–37 my delicate Ariel . . . up change] See *The Tempest*, IV.1.49; *Othello*, III.iii.330 and *Antony and Cleopatra*, I.v.4; *All's Well That Ends Well*, I.i.103; and *Antony and Cleopatra*, V.ii.6.

298.25–26 Locke said . . . the man."] See *An Essay Concerning Human Understanding* (1690), by John Locke (1632–1704).

from O

305.6 Kurouglou] See *Specimens of the Popular Poetry of Persia, as Found in the Adventures and Improvisations of Kurroglou, the Bandit-Minstrel of Northern Persia*, tr. Alexander Chodzko (1842).

305.21 philosopheme] Philosophical principle or proposition.

305.28–29 Kepler . . . world."] See Emerson's poem "Blight," published in *Poems* (1847).

305.29 Si non . . . minus.] See Martial, *Epigrams*, I.xxi: "Had it not erred, it had achieved less."

306.14 Burke . . . Debi Sing] Edmund Burke refers to Devi Singh (fl. 1765–1805), the *diwan* or Indian administrator of a district in Bihar, in speeches given during impeachment proceedings against Warren Hastings (1732–1818), governor-general of Bengal.

306.26 De Foe . . . Mrs. Veal] "A True Relation of the Apparition of Mrs. Veal, after Her Death, to Mrs. Bargrave" (1706), by Daniel Defoe (1660–1731), was written to recommend a new English edition of *Les Consolations de l'âme fidèle contre les frayers de la mort* (1651; translated as *The Christian's Defence against the Fears of Death*), by French Protestant theologian Charles Drelincourt (1595–1669). From beyond the grave, Mrs. Veal claims Drelincourt's book is the best ever written about the afterlife.

306.34 *muscae volitantes*] Literally, "flying flies"; spots or floaters in one's vision.

310.10 tea tray style] A number of pages are torn out of Emerson's manuscript journal after this entry.

310.12–13 The best collection . . . Dr Greenwood's] See *A Collection of Psalms and Hymns for Christian Worship* (1830), compiled by the Rev. Francis William Pitt Greenwood (1797–1843).

310.29 Abbott Lawrence] Lawrence (1792–1855), an industrialist and politician, built textile mills in Lawrence, Massachusetts, a town he helped to found.

311.37–312.1 the "Hebrew Melodies" . . . sword."] Byron's *Hebrew Melodies* was published in 1815, first as a book of songs set to folk music adapted by Isaac Nathan (c. 1792–1864), and then as a book of separate lyrics. Emerson quotes a line from "Song of Saul before his last battle."

313.1 *'Expectatur . . . vernacula,'*] "We expect a speech in the common tongue," a phrase ritually invoked prior to collegiate exercises in English.

313.11 Old Quincy] Josiah Quincy III (1772–1864), the retiring president of Harvard.

313.18–19 The Latin allusions . . . alter,"] Webster alludes to Burton's *Anatomy of Melancholy* on the succession of Richard I ("the sun has set, no night has ensued"), and Winthrop to the *Aeneid*, VI.143–44 ("when the first is torn away, a second fails not, golden too").

313.27–28 Holmes's poem] Oliver Wendell Holmes Sr. (1809–1894) read "A Modest Request, Complied with after the Dinner at President Everett's Inauguration."

313.29–30 Judd . . . "Margaret,"] Sylvester Judd (1813–1853) had recently published a novel, *Margaret* (1845).

318.25 Punch] *Punch, or The London Charivari*, a satirical magazine founded in 1841.

321.19 the Martyr Torrey] Charles Turner Torrey (1813–1846) was arrested in 1844 while aiding fugitive slaves and died in prison.

321.33 Walker of the branded hand] Jonathan Walker (1799–1878) was branded "S.S." ("Slave Stealer") and jailed in the wake of an attempt in 1844 to aid seven fugitive slaves escape from Florida to the British West Indies.

322.29 Carlyle's head (photograph)] See fig. 5 in the present volume.

322.35 Lawrences & Dorsays] Samuel Laurence (1812–1884) and Count Alfred D'Orsay (1801–1852) had painted portraits of Carlyle.

324.27 "The path . . . Porphyry,] See Eusebius' *Praeparatio Evangelica*, which quotes an otherwise lost work, *Philosophy from Oracles*, by Porphyry (234–c. 305).

324.30 Pillsbury] Parker Pillsbury (1809–1898), abolitionist orator.

324.34 John Knox] A Scottish clergyman (c. 1510–1571) and a leader of the Protestant Reformation.

332.16–17 Jenny Lind . . . Elssler] Lind (1820–1887), Swedish opera singer; for Elssler, see note 44.5.

340.25–26 On they came . . . recorders.] See Milton, *Paradise Lost*, I.549–51.

from AB

341.21–22 'Tis merry . . . wag all] See Shakespeare, *2 Henry IV*, V.iii.34.

345.13 N. P. Rogers] Nathaniel Peabody Rogers (1794–1846), former editor of the abolitionist newspaper *Herald of Freedom.*

349.4 Brumoy] See *Le théâtre des Grecs* (1730), by Pierre Brumoy (1688–1742).

350.18 Osman] See note 8.27.

350.24 Guy] See Emerson's poem "Guy" (1847).

351.2–3 Johnson's knocking down Osborne] Thomas Osborne (c. 1704–1767), a London bookseller, had hired Samuel Johnson to assist him in cataloguing and promoting the recently purchased Harleian Library; around 1744, in the course of this work, Osborne accused Johnson of wasting time, and Johnson, enraged, took up a large folio volume and used it to knock him down.

352.5 La Nature . . . Croisements] See note 289.36.

from CD

358.3 Etzlers] John Adolphus Etzler (c. 1796–after 1845) envisioned an earthly paradise hastened by technological innovation; see *The Paradise within the Reach of All Men, without Labor, by Powers of Nature and Machinery* (1833).

358.16–19 "Il faudrait . . . d'Argent] See *Le Mariage d'Argent* (1827), I.iv.99, by Augustin Eugène Scribe (1791–1861).

358.27 Calashes.] Two-wheeled horse-drawn carts.

364.28–34 Song to his . . . cheap to me."] See note 305.6.

365.5–17 Boeckh thinks . . . he did"] See *The Public Economy of Athens* (1842), by August Böckh (1758–1867).

365.16 opson] Food, provision.

366.11–15 In George Sand's . . . law of Vehm.] See Sand's novels *Consuelo* (1842) and its sequel, *La Comtesse de Rudolstadt* (1843).

368.35–369.3 The ship Skidbladnir . . . his bag.] See *The Prose or Younger Edda Commonly Ascribed to Snorri Sturlson*, tr. George Webber Dasent (1842).

369.13–14 Menetrier de Meudon!] A fiddle virtuoso in the *Chansons: nouvelles et dernières* (1833) by Pierre Jean de Béranger (1780–1857).

370.25 Ellery Channing . . . Rome] *Conversations in Rome: Between an Artist, a Catholic, and a Critic* (1847).

372.26–29 O Asa! . . . Thor's hammer] See note 368.35–369.3.

from GH

374.22 in P?] Plymouth.

374.30 Kraitsir] See *Significance of the Alphabet* (1846), by Charles V. Kraitsir (1804–1860).

378.8 The fable of Zohak] See the *Shāhnāmeh* (c. 1000 CE) of Persian poet Ferdowsi (935–1020).

379.24 Ygdrasil;] The "world tree" in Norse mythology; see note 368.35–369.3.

380.4 N.L.F.] Nathaniel Langdon Frothingham (1793–1870), Unitarian minister.

386.15 Rogers] Samuel Rogers (1763–1855), one of whose renowned literary breakfasts Emerson attended on October 29, 1847.

from London

393.32 D. W.] Daniel Webster.

394.4 H. M. . . . W. W.] Harriet Martineau (1802–1876), writer and philosopher; William Wordsworth.

394.26–27 "Taking . . . Froissart.] See "Merry England," in *Sketches and Essays* (1839) by William Hazlitt (1778–1830), which attributes this saying to medieval historian Jean Froissart (c. 1337–c. 1405).

395.3 Tattersall's] A London racehorse auctioneer.

395.17 Chalmers] Thomas Chalmers (1780–1847), a mathematician and leading figure in the Free Church of Scotland.

396.5 Louis Blanc] French politician and historian (1811–1882), author of *Histoire de la Revolution Française* (1847–62).

397.1 Lady G.] Lucie, Lady Duff Gordon (1821–1869), English author.

397.4 Wicksteed] Charles Wicksteed (1810–1885), Unitarian minister.

397.15 Chadwick] Sir Edwin Chadwick (1880–1890), social reformer and author of *The Sanitary Condition of the Labouring Population* (1842), served as London's sewer commissioner in 1848–49.

398.20 "cet affreux . . . en marchant en ligne,—"] The terrible silence that one observes while marching in step.

399.4–8 "Barbarous . . . Jamblichus] See *On the Mysteries of the Egyptians, Chaldeans, and Assyrians*, tr. Thomas Taylor (1821).

399.14 R M] Richard Monckton Milnes; see note 8.33–34.

399.30 My friend A. . . . mystics] Alcott; see note 78.13–14.

400.21–22 Clark's Sartor] Elijah P. Clark, a Boston bank cashier, had assembled an 8-volume extra-illustrated copy of Carlyle's *Sartor Resartus* (1833–34).

400.23 Mr Douce's 20 000 books] The library of Francis Douce (1757–1834).

403.32 Mr Hallam] Henry Hallam (1777–1859), historian.

404.1 Thomas Taylor] Taylor (1758–1835) was a translator of Plato, Aristotle, and other philosophers.

404.7 Hallam] Arthur Hallam (1811–1833), lamented in Tennyson's *In Memoriam* (1850).

411.6–13 Mr. Reid . . . Graveyards."] See *Illustrations of the Theory and Practice of Ventilation* (1844) by David B. Reed (1805–1863), and *Gatherings from Graveyards* (1839), by George Alfred Walker (1807–1884), a doctor known as "Graveyard Walker" for his works on cemeteries and burial practices.

411.24 "It was so . . . wet."] Attributed to Thoreau in Emerson's eulogy "Thoreau," delivered on May 9, 1862, and published as an essay in *The Atlantic*.

412.2 Hudson . . . Cobden] George Hudson (1800–1871), a railroad financier known as "The Railway King"; Sir Walter Trevelyan (1797–1879), a wealthy baronet; Richard Cobden (1804–1865), manufacturer and advocate of free trade.

415.38 Wyman] Jeffries Wyman (1814–1874), curator of Boston's Lowell Institute beginning in 1840.

416.27–29 "The belief . . . Ignorance."] See note 279.19.

422.22 *dogmes* were *malfaisants*] Dogmas were harmful.

428.14–15 impediunt foris.] Encumbrance in the world; see Cicero, *Pro Archia Poeta*, VII.16.

435.17–18 Ben Jonson's . . . thread."] See the tragedy *Sejanus* (1603), by Ben Jonson (1572–1637).

435.22–23 Mr Rae . . . English.] See "Of the Nature of Stock," in *Statement of Some New Principles on the Subject of Political Economy* (1834), by John Rae (1796–1872).

436.26 disparate] This word is illegible in Emerson's manuscript journal.

from England and Paris

441.16 C] Thomas Carlyle.

442.1 C Fellowes] Charles Fellowes (1799–1860), British archaeologist.

from RS

443.10–11 "More are made . . . *Democritus*.] See *The History of Philosophy* (1655–62), by Thomas Stanley (1625–1678).

443.12–13 the election of Ames . . . Jarvis;] Charles Jarvis (1748–1807) unsuccessfully challenged Fisher Ames (1758–1808), a Federalist congressman from Massachusetts, in the election of 1795.

443.15–16 A boy . . . *Laws* p 203] Emerson cites *The Works of Plato*, tr. Floyer Sydenham and Thomas Taylor (1804).

444.5–6 "When the famed . . . sacrificed";] See note 443.10–11.

448.1 C.] Channing.

448.28 C. L.] Probably Charles Lane.

449.1 Chadwick] See note 397.15.

449.28–29 Again must I . . . winter more.] The couplet is Emerson's.

451.25 Tell me . . . Master Brook] See Shakespeare, *The Merry Wives of Windsor*, III.v.60–152.

452.16 Brisbane] See note 89.6.

452.21 young Ward . . . Von Waagen] Samuel Gray Ward (see note 127.3), a banker and art collector, and Gustav Friedrich Waagen (1794–1868), a German art historian.

452.32 George Minott] Minott (1783–1861) was a local farmer; Thoreau described him as "the most poetical farmer . . . that I know."

453.38–39 Downings . . . Capability Browns] Brothers Charles (1802–1885) and Andrew Jackson Downing (1815–1852) were both horticulturalists, the latter also a landscape designer and author of *A Treatise on the Theory and Practice of Landscape Gardening, Adapted to North America* (1841); John Claudius Loudon (1783–1843) was a Scottish botanist and landscape designer and founder of *Gardener's Magazine*; Lancelot ("Capability") Brown (1715–1783) was an English landscape gardener.

454.23–24 Suckling's line . . . newly"] See "A Ballad upon a Wedding" (1641), by John Suckling (1609–1642).

457.3–11 "Hengist had . . . (maggots)] See "Romance of Merlin" in George Ellis's *Specimens of Early English Metrical Romances* (1805).

458.10 "Wykeham's Life"] See *The Life of William of Wykeham, Bishop of Winchester* (1758), by Robert Lowth (1710–1787).

458.11 *conferva rivularis*] A species of algae.

461.32–33 "When Nature . . . survive."] See note 3.11–12.

461.35 C.T.J.] See note 204.10.

462.12 Mitchell] Henry Mitchell (1830–1902), a hydrographer and amateur astronomer.

462.18 The Flying Childers] A celebrated British thoroughbred (1714–1741).

462.23–24 young George Emerson's] A son of Emerson's cousin George Barrell Emerson.

462.25 Clough's poem] *The Bothie of Toper-na-Fuosich* (1848), later retitled *The Bothie of Tober-na-Vuolich.*

from TU

469.9 Philip & Elspie] See Clough's *The Bothie.*

469.26 aversation] Aversion.

470.20 Ellen Hooper's . . . Scott's.] For Ellen Sturgis Hooper, see note 56.7; David Scott (1806–1849) was a Scottish painter, mainly of historical subjects, with whom Emerson sat for a portrait during his 1848 visit to Edinburgh.

473.21 Malleus mediocritatis.] Hammer against moderateness.

474.14–15 Macaulay's two volumes] *The History of England from the Accession of James II* (1849), by Thomas Babington Macaulay (1800–1859).

475.21–23 In New York they . . . *uncochituated*] *Frogpondish*, after a pond in Boston known as the Frog Pond; *uncochituated* from Lake Cochituate, the source of Boston's water.

475.31 σπερματος . . . συντηρησιν] Observation of one's issue.

476.8 Μελετη το παν] Care for the whole.

477.1 Oken] Lorenz Oken (1779–1851), German naturalist.

477.3 what L. read me . . . Love"] Lidian's text was Swedenborg's *Delights of Wisdom Concerning Conjugal Love; after Which Follow Pleasures of Insanity Concerning Scortatory Love* (1843).

477.6 Mr Cushing's Watertown garden] "Bellmont," the Watertown estate of John Perkins Cushing (1787–1862), a wealthy merchant, opened its elaborate gardens to the public once a week.

477.10–15 Dante . . . s'eterna.] "In my memory is fixed, and now goes to my heart, the dear kind paternal image of you, when in the world, hour by hour, you taught me how man makes himself eternal."

479.18 Mr H. G. Otis] Harrison Gray Otis (1765–1848), a former U.S. senator and mayor of Boston.

480.32–33 I found Page . . . canvas.] William Page (1811–1855) completed his *Ruth and Naomi* in 1847.

481.7–10 Lord Brooke's . . . body thought."] See "A Treatise of Humane Learning" (1622–28) by Fulke Greville, Lord Brooke (1572–1631), and "The Second Anniversarie" (1612) by John Donne (1554–1628).

484.18 E.A.K.] *The Economy of the Animal Kingdom* (1740–41); see note 263.15–19.

485.28 the Primer] The New England Primer (1687–90), an early American schoolbook.

487.6–8 "Carve at . . . barred."] See Scott's long poem *The Lay of the Last Minstrel* (1805).

487.28–29 the Banvard . . . Panorama] John Banvard (1815–1891) painted and exhibited a massive panoramic portrait of the Mississippi River valley in the early 1840s.

from AZ

495.29–30 George . . . Barrows] In his manuscript journal, at the end of this list of three, Emerson added a footnote, "See p 25"; his manuscript page 25 appears at 496.22–496.35 in the present volume. "George" and "Edmund" are probably Emerson's neighbors George Minott and Edmund Hosmer.

496.6–7 I value Hyde . . . Mr Ticknor] "Mr Ticknor" is canceled in Emerson's manuscript journal. Hyde may be James Hyde of the Massachusetts Horticultural Society; Alek Therien (1812–1885) is described in Thoreau's *Walden* (1854) as "a Canadian, a woodchopper and post-maker, who can hole fifty posts in a day, who made his last supper on a woodchuck which his dog caught."

498.5 L.'s] Lidian's.

498.17 Chladni's] Ernst Florens Friedrich Chladni (1756–1827), a German physicist and musician.

504.20 N. P. Rogers] Nathaniel Peabody Rogers; see note 345.13.

507.8 Rose Flammock] See Scott's novel *The Betrothed* (1825).

508.37 Lucretia Mott] Lucretia Coffin Mott (1793–1880) was a Quaker abolitionist, feminist, and social reformer.

509.4 Mr] Daniel Neall (1784–1846), a Pennsylvania dentist long active in the abolitionist movement; John Greenleaf Whittier eulogized him in his poem "Daniel Neall" (1846).

510.22–23 "at a market . . . virtues."] See the February 11, 1780, speech before the House of Commons, by Edmund Burke (1729–1797), recommending "A Plan, for the Better Security of the Independence of Parliament, and the Economical Reformation of the Civil and Other Establishments."

510.29 Betaubende] *Betäubende*: narcotizing, numbing, stunning.

512.3–4 "Her heart . . . Goethe,] Attributed to Johann Heinrich Jung (1740–1817) in Carlyle's essay "Schiller" (1831).

512.27 "Margaret & her Friends"] A title suggested by William Henry Channing; Emerson subsequently collaborated with Channing and James Freeman Clarke in editing *Memoirs of Margaret Fuller Ossoli*, published in 1852.

513.20–21 "Nor custom . . . variety"] See *Antony and Cleopatra*, II.ii.234–35.

515.1–3 Lee's . . . singing."] Charles Carter Lee (1798–1871) and John Everett (1801–1826) both delivered Harvard orations; "Licoo" appears in the 1818 "Banquet Song of the Tonga Islanders" later anthologized by Emerson in *Parnassus* (1874), and in Byron's *The Island* (1823); *Lalla-Rookh* (1817) and "The Song of Fionnuala" (1821), source of "When shall the swan . . . ," are by Thomas Moore.

515.35–37 "more fair . . . delight."] See Wordsworth's poem "Dion" (1816).

from BO

520.12 Layard] Austen Henry Layard (1817–1894) British archaeologist, art historian, and diplomat.

523.1 W. L. Fisher] William Logan Fisher (1781–1862), author of *Pauperism and Crime* (1831), *The History of the Institution of the Sabbath Day, Its Uses and Abuses* (1845), and other works.

523.32 *muscae volitantes*] See note 306.24.

524.17 Lacker] Lacquer, finish.

524.36–37 Tyler] Probably George Washington Tyler; see note 34.34.

525.19–20 pamphlet-collectors . . . Mr Walker] Seth Chandler (1806–1889), of Shirley, Massachusetts, and George Alfred Walker (1807–1884; see note 411.6–13).

526.8–9 "Augustus . . . *Gibbon.*] See Chapter III of *The History of the Decline and Fall of the Roman Empire* (1776–88), by Edward Gibbon (1737–1794).

526.26–527.10 "In whose . . . Donne] Emerson quotes these "moral sentences" from Wordsworth's "Brave Schill" (1815); Jonson's "An Ode. To Himself" (1630) and *The Masque of Beauty* (1608); "To the Lady Margaret, Countess of Cumberland" (1600) by Samuel Daniel (1562–1619); and "To the Countess of Bedford" and "Eclogue" (1613), by John Donne.

527.25 Brave . . . porte.] As true as steel.

528.10 the Club] The Social Circle club, founded in 1782, admitted Emerson as a member in 1839.

529.19 Albert H. Tracy] Tracy (1793–1859) had served in the U.S. Congress from 1819 to 1825 and in the New York State Senate from 1830 to 1837.

530.3 Mr Moseley] William Abbot Mosely (1799–1873), a lawyer, served in Congress from 1843 to 1847.

530.21 Chasles] Philarète Chasles (1798–1873), French scholar, librarian, and critic.

533.5 his letter . . . Mr Hulsemann] See *The Austro-Hungarian Question: Correspondence between Mr. Hülsemann, Austrian Chargé d'Affaires, and Mr. Webster* (1851).

535.4–5 Kossuth . . . Gorgey] Artúr Görgey (1818–1916), a Hungarian general, surrendered his army to the Russians at the battle of Világos in 1849, afterward securing amnesty for himself while his officers were court-martialed and executed; Kossuth called him "Hungary's Judas."

536.23 Mr Eliot . . . Mr Curtis] Samuel Atkins Eliot (1798–1862) was a former mayor of Boston; George Ticknor Curtis (1812–1894), the United States Commissioner in Boston, ordered fugitive slave Thomas Sims returned to his master in April of 1851.

538.16 "judicious tubing"] Earlier in Journal *BO*, in a passage not included in the present volume, Emerson writes: "There is and must be a little air-chamber, a sort of tiny Bedlam in even the naturalist's or mathematician's brain who arrives at great results. They affect a sticking to facts; they repudiate all imagination & affection, as they would disown stealing. But Cuvier, Oken, Geoffrey-St-Hilaire, Owen, Agassiz, (Audubon), must all have this spark of fanaticism for the generation of steam, & there must be that judicious tubing in their brain that is in the boiler of the locomotive, or wherever steam must be swiftly generated."

539.30 the deed . . . Buckingham] George Villiers, second Duke of Buckingham (1628–1687), and William Chiffinch (1602–1688) were connected with abuses of power under Charles II.

540.17 Ghilanes] An African tribe whose members were reported by French travel writer Louis du Couret (1812–1867) to have two- or three-inch tails.

545.1–4 The historian . . . p 258] Emerson cites *The History of the Manners and Customs of Ancient Greece* (1842), by James Augustus St. John (1795–1875).

545.19–20 What a moment . . . Fugitive Slave Law!] Judge Lemuel Shaw refused, on April 7, to release Thomas Sims (b. 1834), a fugitive slave, from prison on habeas corpus.

546.28 Rantoul & Palfrey] Robert Rantoul Jr. (1805–1852) and John Gorham Palfrey (1796–1881), anti-slavery politicians.

from CO

549.27–31 Moonlight . . . sound] Emerson quotes from *The Nice Valour, or The Passionate Mad-man* (c. 1615), by Francis Beaumont (1584–1616) and John Fletcher (1579–1625), Milton's "L'Allegro" (1645), and "The Passions: An Ode for Music" (1747), by William Collins (1721–1759).

549.33–36 Frank Browne . . . invaders.] Frank Browne is probably Emerson's nephew, Francis Charles Browne (1829–1900). In April 1850 and August 1851, Narciso Lopez (1797–1851) led expeditions to free Cuba from Spainish rule.

551.20 with the God.] A canceled phrase follows in Emerson's manuscript journal: "who damns him."

551.32–35 Eliot writes . . . Slavery.] Samuel Eliot (1821–1898), author of *Passages from the History of Liberty* (1847) was a historian; Samuel Atkins Eliot (1798–1862), a congressman from Massachusetts who voted for the 1850 Fugitive Slave Law. Jared Sparks (1789–1866), a Harvard president, edited *The Writings of George Washington* (1834–37); Cornelius Conway Felton (1807–1862) was a professor of Greek literature.

553.23 Avernus] An Italian crater believed in antiquity to contain the entrance to the underworld, or any spot emitting noxious vapors.

554.36 πολυτροπος Οδυςςευς] A versatile Ulysses.

555.6 my Captain Ellis] Cornelius Ellis was captain of the brig that Emerson took to Europe in 1832.

555.15 Wilkinson] John James Garth Wilkinson (1812–1899), a scholar of Swedenborg whom Emerson met on his 1848 trip to England.

555.27–28 Rev. Thos. Worcester] Worcester (1795–1878) was first pastor at the Boston Society of New Jerusalem.

555.33–34 Porson . . . Lacroix] Richard Porson (1759–1808) and Samuel Parr (1747–1825) were English classical scholars, and Sylvestre François Lacroix (1765–1843) a French mathematician.

556.23 Heyne . . . Ruhnken] Classicists and philologists Christian Gottlieb Heyne (1729–1812), Friedrich August Wolf (1759–1824), Johann Leonhard Hug (1765–1846), and David Ruhnken (1723–1798).

556.26 our new lecturer] Emmanuel Vitalis Scherb, exiled German patriot and poet.

556.36 a Manco Capac] Legendary founder and law-giver of the Inca dynasty in Peru.

557.15 Kleinstadtisch] *Kleinstädtisch*: provincial.

565.24–25 Von Waagen's . . . yield.] See *Works of Art and Artists in England*, tr. H. E. Lloyd (1838), by Gustav Friedrich Waagen (see note 452.21).

567.9 Lloyd F.] James Lloyd Fuller (1826–1891), Margaret's youngest brother and a one-time resident of Brook Farm.

569.25 Bernhard] Bernhard Domschke (c. 1827–1869), editor of the New York *Deutsche Schnellpost.*

572.22 Neal-on-the-Puritans] See *The History of the Puritans* (1732), by Daniel Neal (1678–1743).

from JOURNAL AT THE WEST

576.8 Mr J A Wilder] John Nichols Wilder, founder and president of the University of Rochester Board of Trustees.

577.24 Gov. Edwards] Possibly John Cummins Edwards (1804–1888), governor of Missouri from 1844 to 1848, or Ninian Wirt Edwards (1809–1889), Illinois superintendent of public instruction and son of former Illinois governor Ninian Edwards (1775–1833).

from DO

582.4–5 "At mihi . . . *Martial.*] See *Epigrams*, II.xliii: "But my own hand is Ganymede to serve me."

584.12 Miss Delia Bacon] Bacon (1811–1859) was the author of *The Philosophy of the Plays of Shakspere Unfolded* (1857), which argues that Raleigh, Spenser, and Bacon wrote Shakespeare's plays.

584.30 Smith . . . Drama,"] James Smith, *The Divine Drama of History and Civilization* (1854).

585.24 Adirondac 1858] In the first two weeks of August 1858, Emerson and other members of the Saturday Club—a recently formed Boston literary society centered around *The Atlantic Monthly*—traveled to painter William J. Stillman's camp on Follensby Pond in the Adirondacks. The party included Stillman (1828–1901), naturalist Louis Agassiz (1807–1873), diplomat and man of letters James Russell Lowell (1819–1891), jurist Ebenezer Rockwood Hoar (1816–1895), and Samuel Gray Ward.

587.8–9 if she thought . . . quite succeeded?] Caroline Sturgis Tappan's sister, Susan Sturgis Bigelow, committed suicide on June 9, 1853; the other sister, Ellen Sturgis Hooper, also died a suicide, in 1848.

587.18–19 Mr Rhynders] Isaiah Rynders (1804–1885), a sportsman, gangster, and Tammany Hall organizer.

591.23 Blake] Harrison Gray Otis Blake (1816–1898), schoolteacher, Unitarian minister, and friend of Thoreau.

591.35–592.4 Dr Frothingham . . . nescit."] Nathaniel Landon Frothingham (1793–1870), pastor of the First Congregational Church of Boston, contributed an obituary of Ruth Haskins Emerson (1768–1853) to the *Christian Examiner* in January 1854. The verse may be translated: "May her soul inherit the land which knows no sorrow."

592.27 Southworth] Albert Sands Southworth (1811–1894), partner in the Boston photographic firm Southworth & Hawes.

from GO

594.4–5 "Prisca . . . *Ovid.*] See *The Art of Love*, III.121–22: "Let ancient times delight other folk: I congratulate myself that I was not born till now."

594.6 "Sit nulla . . . musis"] See Claudian, *De Sexto Consulatu Honorii Augusti*, The Panegyric (XXVIII), 475: "Believe not that the Muses will aid in all things."

594.12–13 poet Cowper . . . Editions.] Richard Westall (1765–1836) illustrated the works of William Cowper (1731–1800).

594.19 "The stars . . . sky,"] See "Night and Love" in Bulwer-Lytton's novel *Ernest Maltravers* (1837).

595.19 Mr Gilpin] William Gilpin (1724–1804), a clergyman and watercolorist, wrote accounts of sketching tours he took throughout England.

596.24 A slave] Thomas Sims; see note 545.19–20.

596.33 "Thank-God-Choate"] Rufus Choate (1799–1859), an orator and leading supporter of Webster.

596.39 Scott's election] General Winfield Scott (1786–1866), Whig Party nominee in the presidential election of 1852.

598.2 *alter et idem*] The other and the same.

598.19 Palmer] Joseph Palmer (1791–1874), a former resident of Fruitlands, had purchased it from Charles Lane in August 1846.

600.19 Greenough] Horatio Greenough (1805–1852), American sculptor famed for his colossal classical sculpture of Washington.

601.28–30 Defoe's true words . . . speak."] See Defoe's satirical long poem "The True-Born Englishman" (1697).

603.9 "*Os . . . par.*"] See note 198.31.

605.25 Mr Dean . . . Jacobi] Emerson met a "W. Dean" while lecturing in Philadelphia in 1853 who introduced him to the theories of theologian Friedrich Heinrich Jacobi (1743–1819).

from VS

608.32 scald] Skald, poet (usually, an ancient Scandinavian poet).

609.4 kyanized] Impregnated with a corrosive sublimate, as a preservative.

611.18–26 "Whatever . . . liberty."] Emerson cites *Northern Antiquities; or, an Historical Account of the Manners, Customs, Religions and Laws, Maritime Expeditions and Discoveries, Language and Literature of the Ancient Scandinavians*, by Paul Henri Mallet (1730–1807), in Bishop Percy's 1847 translation.

611.27–28 The Welsh bard . . . war."] Emerson quotes Charles Claude Hamilton's 1825 translation of the *History of the Conquest of England by the Normans*, by Augustin Thierry (1795–1856).

612.3 Susan Sturgis] See note 587.8–9.

612.12 Miss Minott] Mary Minott, a tailor, was one of the Emersons' neighbors.

612.33 H] Henry David Thoreau.

613.31–32 Power . . . consciousness of] Three leaves have been torn from Emerson's manuscript journal following this fragmentary sentence.

613.36–614.2 "They are not . . . ap. *Michelet*] Emerson cites *Histoire de France* (1835–67), by Jules Michelet (1798–1874).

614.4 Sylvan] Henry David Thoreau.

615.7 *Short way with Slaveholders.*] A title Emerson modeled after that of Defoe's 1702 pamphlet *The Shortest-Way with Dissenters.*

615.8 Lewis Tappan . . . Fearing] Tappan (1788–1873) was an abolitionist and the father-in-law of Caroline Sturgis; Fearing was a Boston merchant and apothecary.

615.22–23 Abbott Lawrence . . . Everett] Lawrence (1792–1855) was a former congressman and Edward Everett (1794–1865) a Unitarian clergyman, first professor of Greek at Harvard, and a sitting senator, whose orations were much admired by the young Emerson.

615.36 Legree, Macduffie] Simon Legree is a Northern-born slave owner in *Uncle Tom's Cabin* (1852), by Harriet Beecher Stowe (1811–1896). George McDuffie (1790–1851), a governor of South Carolina, was a prominent advocate of slavery.

from HO

621.13 Mr Hedge] Frederic Henry Hedge, Unitarian minister and later professor of ecclesiastical history at Harvard Divinity School; see note 11.24–31.

621.34–622.3 "Talking . . . p. 144] Emerson cites Thomas Moore's *Memoirs, Journal and Correspondence* (1853–56).

622.10–13 "You see . . . them."] Emerson quotes a letter he had received from Delia Bacon (see note 584.12).

622.21–24 "et quand . . . vol 1. 434] Emerson cites *Correspondance littéraire, philosophique et critique* (1812), by Friedrich Melchior von Grimm (1723–1807): "And when they have stopped being the character they've chosen, which amuses you so much, they become insipid and sad, because they are no longer anything but themselves."

622.26 Carlyle does . . . Teufelsdrock] See *Sartor Resartus.*

623.31–33 Haydon's washerwoman . . . principle"] See Tom Taylor, ed., *The Life of Benjamin Robert Haydon, Historical Painter, from His Autobiography and Journals* (1853); Haydon lived from 1786 to 1846.

625.20–21 this Nebraska business] Stephen Douglas's Kansas-Nebraska bill proposed that the question of slavery in the new territories be settled by popular referendum, effectively nullifying the Missouri Compromise which forbade slavery north of the latitude 36° 30′. The bill was finally passed on May 25, 1854, after three months of debate.

628.7 Mabinogion.] Title given to a group of 11 narratives drawn from medieval Welsh manuscripts.

from IO

629.9 *Hallam*] See note 403.32.

629.30–31 the law of Adrastia . . . period;"] See *The Six Books of Proclus*, tr. Thomas Taylor (1816). Adrastia, in Greek mythology, was a nymph charged with protecting the infant Zeus from his father, Cronus.

630.34–35 The Asmodaean feat . . . twine.] The couplet is Emerson's.

633.17–18 See the story . . . Σ 99.] Emerson's notebook Σ or *Sigma*, now at the Houghton Library at Harvard, has not been published; it compiles material from other notebooks.

634.35 Burrill's 50 languages] Elihu Burritt (1810–1879), a social reformer known as the "Learned Blacksmith," was hailed as a linguistic prodigy.

635.13–14 Isthmian crown] Victory laurel awarded in the ancient Greek Isthmian games, held during the year before and the year after the quadrennial Olympic games.

635.38–39 "this . . . brain"] See *Of the Lawes of Ecclesiastical Politie* (1594), by Sir Richard Hooker (1554–1600).

636.29–30 "forms that men spy . . . sun."] See chapter 9 of Scott's novel *The Monastery* (1820).

636.35–36 "the charming accident . . . French Women] See "Woman in France: Madame de Sablé," *Westminster Review*, October 1854.

from NO

639.17–26 "the bodies . . . Plotinus.] See *Select Works of Plotinus, the Great Restorer of the Philosophy of Plato*, tr. Thomas Taylor (1817).

639.32 Minima pars sui puella] The girl is the least part of herself. (See Ovid, *Remedia Amoris*, line 344.)

639.34 my Dervish] A. Bronson Alcott.

640.14–15 when Higginson . . . Courthouse] Thomas Wentworth Higginson (1823–1911) and others attempted unsuccesfully to free a fugitive slave, Anthony Burns (1834–1862), from the federal courthouse in Boston on May 26, 1854.

641.11 *Queteletism*] Adolphe Quetelet (1796–1874), a Belgian astronomer and statistician, was a pioneer in the application of statistical models in the social sciences; his 1835 *Treatise on Man, and the Development of His Faculties* proposed the idea of a statistically "average man" as an ideal type.

641.36–38 "He that . . . contemplates."] See Edmund Burke's "Substance of the Speech in the Debate on the Army Estimates, in the House of Commons, on Tuesday, February 9, 1790."

642.10 Philip Randolph] A friend and correspondent of Emerson's since the 1850s, Randolph lived in Philadelphia.

642.31 Munroe] Probably James Munroe, Emerson's publisher.

643.1 Οι ρεοντες] The flowing ones.

645.3 Miollnir] In the *Prose Edda*, and Norse mythology more generally, the hammer of the god Thor.

645.32–37 "The golden . . . Letters III 217] Emerson cites the *Life and Letters* (1852) of Barthold Georg Niebuhr (1776–1831), German historian.

646.21 Dr J.'s] Probably Charles T. Jackson (see note 204.10).

from RO

653.31 Stark . . . Benjamin] William Stark (1825–1873), John Godfrey Saxe (1816–1887), and Park Benjamin Sr. (1809–1864) were all poets who occasionally lectured.

655.21–22 a Howard . . . Elizabeth Fry] English reformers John Howard (1726–1790), Andrew Bell (1753–1832), Joseph Lancaster (1778–1838), John Jebb, who wrote under the pseudonym "Alfred" (1736–1786), and Elizabeth Fry (1780–1845).

656.16 *le don . . . familiarité*] The terrible gift of familiarity.

from SO

657.20 C. N. Emerson] Charles Noble Emerson (1821–1869), a cousin of Emerson's.

662.15 Hood's poem] See "The Last Man" (1826), by Thomas Hood (1799–1845).

662.24–28 *Kings* . . . p. 259.] See *Memoirs of the Life, Writings and Discoveries of Sir Isaac Newton* (1855) by David Brewster (1781–1868).

663.8 Andrews Norton] Norton (1786–1853) was a leading Unitarian theologian and preacher who regarded Emerson's Harvard "Divinity School Address" (1838) as heretical and called Transcendentalism "the latest form of infidelity."

663.26 Whipple] Edwin Percy Whipple (1819–1886), essayist and critic.

664.32 Miss Bacon's . . . Shakspeare] See note 584.12.

667.10 A.H.B.W.] Anna Hazard Barker Ward; see note 162.30.

667.38 "made the rash . . . eye,"] See "Vertue," from *The Temple* (1633), by George Herbert (1593–1633).

668.29 the Indignation Meeting last night] A protest in the wake of the beating of Senator Charles Sumner (1811–1874) in the Senate, on May 22, 1856.

669.24 Perez Blood's] Blood was a Concord farmer.

672.34 A.H.T.] Albert H. Tracy (1793–1859) served as a member of Congress from New York from 1819 to 1825.

672.36–37 Erastus . . . Taunton] Erastus Bigelow (1814–1879), Uriah Boyden (1804–1879) and William Mason (1808–1883) were inventors, and Nathaniel Bowditch (1773–1838) was the author of *The American Practical Navigator* (1802).

from VO

674.4–5 the publication of . . . Agassiz] The first monograph in Louis Agassiz's *Contributions to the Natural History of the United States of America* (1857–62), an elaborate publication to which Emerson subscribed, is about the order Testudinata, which includes turtles and tortoises.

675.24–26 Albert Tracy . . . hunks] Tracy (1793–1859), a former member of Congress and New York state senator, is described as reactionary (a "hunker") and surly or miserly ("hunks").

677.35 Birkebeiners] The Birkebeinars—a Norwegian rebel group described in the *Heimskringla*, an Icelandic saga (c. 1230) by Snorri Sturluson (1179–1242)—were named for their birch-bark leggings.

678.13–14 that destruction of St Petersburgh . . . Kohl] See *Russia: St. Petersburg, Moscow, Kharkoff, Riga, Odessa, the German Provinces on the Baltic, the Steppes, the Crimea, and the Interior of the Empire* (1844), by German travel writer and historian Johann Georg Kohn (1808–1878).

679.23 Peter Kaufmann] Kaufmann (1800–1869), a German-born publisher from Canton, Ohio, and the author of *The Temple of Truth, or the Science of Ever-Progressive Knowledge* (1858), sent Emerson an 80-page autobiographical manuscript in April 1857.

680.4–5 Ricketson] Daniel Ricketson (1813–1898), a friend of Thoreau and Alcott and later the author of *The Autumn Sheaf* (1869), a collection of poems.

680.21–22 the Club] The Saturday Club; see note 585.24.

681.22 Παντα ρει] All things flow.

681.29–30 I do not count . . . sea] From Emerson's poem "Waldeinsamkeit," published in *May-Day and Other Pieces* (1867). (The German title means "Loneliness of the woods.")

684.36 The "Sacontala"] See Kálidása, *Sákoontalá; or, the Lost Ring: An Indian Drama*, tr. Monier Williams (1855).

686.15–16 Una & her lamb] See Book I of *The Faerie Queene* (1590–96), by Edmund Spenser (c. 1552–1599).

686.22–24 "What can be done . . . advocates?"] See *Beaumarchais and His Times*, tr. Henry S. Edwards (1857), by Louis de Loménie (1815–1878).

688.12–14 Gauss . . . Gould] Astronomers Karl Friedrich Gauss (1777–

1855), Benjamin Peirce (1809–1880), and Benjamin Apthorp Gould (1824–1896).

689.2 the Dodona . . . Sais?] Sites of ancient oracles, the former in Greece and the latter in Egypt.

690.7 Hippias . . . Thirty?] Hippias of Elias (c. 460 BCE), a Greek sophist, and the Thirty Tyrants, oligarchs who led Athens after its defeat in the Peloponnesian War (404 BCE), both subjects in Plato's dialogues.

692.19–21 Arnica . . . Father Edgeworth] Several species of the genus *Arnica* are used medicinally and in homeopathy; Henry Essex Edgeworth de Firmont (1745–1807), Louis XVI's confessor, was present at his execution.

693.1–5 "And the ruby . . . sings.] See *Improvisations from the Spirit* (1857), by James John Garth Wilkinson (see note 555.15).

693.12–13 whether . . . knoweth.] See II Corinthians 12:2.

693.21 George Stephenson] An English engineer (1781–1848) and railway pioneer.

693.23–25 "wisdom is not . . . *Job*)] See Kenelm Digby, *Two Treatises: In the One of Which, the Nature of Bodies; in the Other, the Nature of Mans Soule, Is Looked Into* (1645).

696.8–10 Thus Logan . . . p 176] See Francis James Child's *English and Scottish Ballads* (1857–58), which notes the borrowing of lines from the ballad "Rare Willy Drown'd in Yarrow" in the poem "The Braes of Yarrow" (1781) by John Logan (1748–1788), and from Martial's *Epigrams*, XXV, in the anonymous ballad "The Drowned Lovers" (which translates them as "Make me your wrech as I come back, / But spare me as I gang").

697.32–36 "Thou art . . . redeo.] From "Rare Willy Drown'd in Yarrow" and Martial's *Epigrams*; see note 696.8–10.

from AC

703.8–9 M. P. Forbes . . . "Counterparts,"] The novel *Counterparts; or, the Cross of Love* (1854), by English writer Elizabeth Sara Sheppard (1830–1862), was sent to Emerson by Margaret P. Forbes, a sister of railroad magnate John Murray Forbes; Emerson's younger daughter Edith (1841–1929) was married to his son, William Hathaway Forbes.

703.32–33 the sea again . . . Amasis can drink up.] See Plutarch's *Convivium Septem Sapientum*, in which the Pharaoh Amasis is challenged by the king of Ethiopia to drink the sea; the Pharaoh is advised that he should first ask that the Ethiopian stop the rivers adding to it. (The riddle is recounted in Child's *English and Scottish Ballads*; see note 696.8–10.)

705.36 W. Hunt] William Morris Hunt (1824–1879), a painter from Newport, Rhode Island; Emerson's son Edward Waldo (1839–1909) suggests his father had Hunt's 1859 portrait of Chief Justice Lemuel Shaw in mind when he wrote this entry.

706.5–12 "Near Home" . . . prime."] See Channing's *Near Home* (1858).

706.17 "thoughts that . . . numbers,"] See Milton's *Paradise Lost*, III.37–38.

706.19–24 Jefferson says . . . p 212] Emerson cites the 1854 edition of *The Writings of Thomas Jefferson*.

707.9 Junius] The pseudonymous author of a series of letters to the London *Public Advertiser* and other papers between 1769 and 1772.

708.6 this Albany Hammond's book] Jabez Delano Hammond (1778–1855) was the author, most recently, of *On the Evidence, Independent of Written Revelation, of the Immortality of the Soul* (1851).

708.9 παντα ρει] See note 681.22.

708.20 Rarey] John Solomon Rarey (1827–1866), a horse whisperer and rehabilitator.

709.7 gymnotus] An electric eel.

709.33 H. J.] Henry James Sr.

712.29 James Burke] An Irish laborer who worked for the Emerson family.

713.1–6 Novalis said . . . more beautiful."] Emerson quotes Carlyle's essay "Novalis" (*Foreign Review*, July 1829); an account of "A Dialogue Between a Calvinist and a Semi-Calvinist" (c. 1799), by Samuel Hopkins (1721–1803), in *Memoir of the Life and Character of Samuel Hopkins, D.D.* (1852), by Edwards A. Park (1808–1900); the *Journal or Historical Account of the Life, Travels, Sufferings, Christian Experiences and Labour of Love in the Work of the Ministry* (1694), by George Fox (1624–1691); and Swedenborg's *Heaven and Hell* (1758).

713.25 Caroline's] Caroline Sturgis Tappan's.

714.24 Δαιμων] Daemon.

714.27–28 "by night threshed . . . not end."] See Milton's "L'Allegro."

716.1–2 "un foco . . . vincia."] See Dante's *Inferno*, iv, 68–69.

716.22 Tennyson's poem] *Idylls of the King*; the first parts of the finished sequence of poems were published in 1859.

from CL

717.26–27 Charles Auchester's] See the novel *Charles Auchester: A Memorial* (1853), by Elizabeth Sara Sheppard (see note 703.8–9).

717.28–29 "flat . . . 282)] Emerson cites Bettina Brentano von Arnim's *Goethe's Correspondence with a Child* (1839); see note 82.3.

719.16 παντα ρει] See note 681.22.

719.20 Cornhill] A Boston district known for its booksellers and financial institutions.

720.5–8 For art . . . is spilled] See Emerson's "Fragments on the Poet and the Poetic Gift," published in William Ellery Channing's *Thoreau: The Poet-Naturalist* (1873).

720.31 Δος . . . οτω] Give me a place to stand on and I will move the earth.

722.5–9 Atlantic covers . . . Holmes?] The essays in Holmes's *The Autocrat of the Breakfast-Table* (1858) began appearing in *The Atlantic Monthly* in 1857.

722.11 Haydon's Autobiography] See note 623.31–33.

723.10 Phillips & Sampson] Emerson's publishers.

723.12–15 Mrs Thrale . . . rich."] See *The Life of Samuel Johnson* (1791) by James Boswell (1740–1795).

723.20–22 Johnson said . . . Piozzi] See *Anecdotes of the Late Samuel Johnson, LL.D.* (1786), by Hester Piozzi (1741–1821).

724.26 Ellen Hooper's] See notes 56.7 and 587.8–9.

725.31 Gov. Wise] Henry Alexander Wise (1806–1876), governor of Virginia, 1856–1860.

726.22 Mattie Griffith] Emerson described Mattie Griffith in a letter as "a brilliant young lady from Kentucky."

726.34–35 "Varius . . . *Val Max* iii, 7.] See Valerius Maximus, *Factorum Dictorumque Memorabilium*: "Varius Sucronesis affirms, Aemilius Scuaras denies; Which do you believe?"

727.1 Queenie's] Lidian Emerson's; see note 35.29.

727.9–14 "I will sing a new . . . bough"] See *Histoire de la Poésie Provençale* (1846), by Claude-Charles Fauriel (1772–1844).

730.8–9 Fred. Cogswell] Described by Edward Waldo Emerson in his edition of the *Journals* as "a kindly, underwitted intimate of Concord Almshouse."

730.15 Cassius M. Clay] Cassius Marcellus Clay (1810–1903), a Kentucky anti-slavery crusader.

730.34–35 Duc de Brancas . . . me."] See *Men and Women of the Eighteenth Century* (1852), by Arsène Houssaye (1815–1896).

734.31 Mansel's . . . Knowledge.] See "The Limits of Demonstrative Science Considered" (1853) by Longueville Mansel (1820–1871).

from DL

737.11–13 When Napoleon . . . hypothèse."] See *Force and Matter: Empirico-Philosophical Studies, Intelligibly Rendered*, tr. J. Frederick Collingwood (1864), by Ludwig Büchner (1824–1899).

738.14 Elliott . . . "Art"] "On the Relation of Art to Nature," *Atlantic Monthly*, February 1864, by James Elliot Cabot (1821–1903).

739.10 Richard Fuller] Richard Frederic Fuller (1824–1869), one of Margaret Fuller's younger brothers.

739.13–14 M. Babinet . . . solved.] See "Des Tables Tournantes," *Revue des Deux Mondes*, January 15, 1854, by Jacques Babinet (1794–1872), French physicist.

740.4–5 Ossian's . . . praise."] See *The Poems of Ossian* (1760–63) by James MacPherson (1736–1796), which Emerson read in an 1857 collected edition.

740.20–21 Bandmann . . . at Bartol's.] Daniel E. Bandmann (1840–1905), a German actor who had recently immigrated to the United States, at the home of Unitarian clergyman Cyrus A. Bartol (1813–1900), occasional host of the Transcendental Club.

741.4 Arnold] Matthew Arnold (1822–1888), English poet and critic.

741.9–12 Of Wordsworth . . . in poetry."] See *The Life of William Blake* by Alexander Gilchrist (1828–1861), completed by his wife and published in 1863.

742.10–11 ó . . . εοικως] See Homer, *Iliad*, I.47: "and his coming was like the night."

743.35–36 "in climes . . . road,"] See "The Progress of Poesy" (1757), by Thomas Gray (1716–1771).

746.32 Therienism] See note 496.6–7.

747.26–30 in Macmillan . . . Friedrich] Scottish philosopher Alexander Bain (1818–1903) contributed two articles to *Macmillan's* on *Plato, and the Other Companions of Sokrates*, by George Grote (1794–1871), one in July and one in October 1865; a *Quarterly Review* article on "Carlyle's Friederic the Great" was published in July 1865.

747.32–33 in the Revue . . . Future Life] See "Un Nouveau Système sur la vie future," May 15, 1863, by French philosopher Paul Janet (1823–1899).

749.13 Mr B. P. Hunt] Benjamin Peter Hunt (1808–1877), a notable student in Emerson's school at Chelmsford, in 1825, and a subsequent correspondent.

752.2 Ericson] John B. Ericsson (1803–1899), an inventor and mechanical engineer.

753.19–21 The Tribune . . . street."] See the New York *Daily Tribune*, January 1, 1866. Henry Winter Davis (1817–1865), author of *The War of Ormuzd and Ahriman in the Nineteenth Century* (1852), had been a member of Congress from Maryland.

753.25–26 J. H. Stirling's book] See *The Secret of Hegel* (1865), by Scottish philosopher James Hutchinson Stirling (1820–1909).

753.33–34 "Neither by sea . . . Hyperboreans:"] See *The Odes of Pindar*, tr. Dawson W. Turner (1852).

754.3–6 The Tribune . . . our State."] See the New York *Daily Tribune*, January 3, 1866.

754.7–10 In the "Funeral" . . . are."] See *The Funeral; or, Grief a-la-Mode* (1701), I.i.102–4, by Richard Steele (1672–1729).

754.27 M. D. Conway] Moncure Daniel Conway (1832–1907), abolitionist and author.

from GL

755.23–24 "But Cathmoor . . . Ossian.] See note 740.4–5.

757.10–11 "a pensive nun . . . pure,"] See Milton, "Il Penseroso," line 31.

761.30 a Squire Slender] See Shakespeare's *Merry Wives of Windsor* (1602).

762.23–24 as Dr Blair . . . Alexander] See the *Autobiography of the Rev. Dr. Alexander Carlyle, Minister of Inveresk* (1860), which describes a letter in which William Alexander (1729–1819) offered Hugh Blair (1718–1800), a professor of rhetoric, a thousand pounds to teach him the art of public speaking.

763.2 Rarey's exhibition] See note 708.20.

763.16–17 F. G. Tuckerman . . . Rhotruda.] See the *Poems* (1860) of Frederick Goddard Tuckerman (1821–1873).

763.25 W. E.] William Emerson (1801–1868), oldest of the Emerson brothers.

764.5 Swift's Letter on old age] Jonathan Swift (1667–1745) to John Gay, December 2, 1736.

766.11 *épicier*] Grocer.

766.31 Hodsdon's Life] See *Twelve Years of a Soldier's Life in India* (1859), by William Stephen Raikes Hodson (1821–1858).

768.26 "the nympholepsy . . . despair,"] See *Childe Harold's Pilgrimage* (1812–18), IV.cxv.

770.34 "Severity . . . *Gasparin.*] See Agénor Étienne Gasparin, *The Uprising of a Great People: The United States in* 1861, tr. Mary L. Booth (1861).

771.3 Il n'y a . . . coute.] A remark attributed to Marie Anne de Vichy Chamrond, marquise du Deffand (1697–1780), responding to Melchior de Polignac (1661–1742), on the beheaded St. Denis's miraculous two-mile walk, head in hands, to his burial place: "It is only the first step which matters."

772.9 T.] Taliesin; see *Taliesen; or, The Bards and Druids of Britain, a Translation of the Remains of the Earliest Welsh Bards, and an Examination of the Bardic Mysteries* (1858), by David William Nash (1809–1876).

772.11 Hogg's Kilmeny] One of the narrative poems in *The Queen's Wake* (1813), by James Hogg (1770–1835).

773.28 *Haeret.*] Make it stick.

774.30 Mother Deb Saco . . . rappers] Deb Saco (c. 1759–1839) was an itinerant herb seller and fortune teller active around Malden, Massachusetts, and subsequently represented as a type at local fairs; Daniel Douglas Home (1833–1886; commonly also "Hume"), a Scottish-born spiritualist ostensibly capable, during séances, of producing loud "raps" in inanimate objects by his mental powers.

from WAR

780.14–15 the whole case . . . slave-trader] Nathaniel Gordon (c. 1834–1863), a slave trader, was executed on February 21; his ship *Erie* had been captured with a cargo of nearly 1,000 slaves.

780.32 Mr. Staunton . . . Charles R. Train] Edwin M. Stanton (1814–1869) was Secretary of War; Train (1817–1885), a Boston lawyer, served in Congress from 1859 to 1863.

780.35 Maclellan] George B. McClellan (1826–1885), general-in-chief of the Union Army.

780.39–781.1 the Butler-Andrew difficulty.] John A. Andrew (1818–1867), governor of Massachusetts, and his appointee General Benjamin Franklin Butler (1818–1893) quarreled over many issues; in January 1862, Andrew persuaded the War Department to reverse its prior decision giving Butler the authority to recruit soldiers in the New England states along with those states' governors.

782.7 Gurowski] Adam Gurowski (1805–1866), a clerk and translator in the department, later published a controversial *Diary* (1862–66).

784.7 the Mason & Slidell business] In November 1861, Confederate diplomats James Mason (1798–1871) and John Slidell (1793–1871) were captured by Union captain Charles Wilkes (1798–1877) aboard the British mail ship *Trent*; after British protests, the two were released.

786.11–14 I am but black . . . taints the air.] The quatrain is Emerson's.

from VA

791.3 Therien] See note 496.6–7.

792.2–3 Greenwood . . . Everett] Francis W. P. Greenwood, Boston clergyman and Unitarian editor (see note 310.12–13), and Edward Everett (see note 615.22–23).

792.13 La Nature . . . croisemens.] See note 289.36.

792.28 Latimer's story] See the "Sixth Sermon Preached before King Edward the Sixth" (1549), by Hugh Latimer (c. 1485–1555).

793.2 S. Staples] Samuel F. Staples, Concord's town jailer.

793.24 In *GL* pp 292] See page 767.29–35 in the present volume.

793.32–33 as Spenser says . . . ill."] See *The Faerie Queene*, I.ix (1590–96).

794.28–29 Milman's . . . Damayanti"] See *Nala and Damayanti, and Other Poems* (1835), by Henry Hart Milman (1791–1868).

795.25 Carlyle's III vol. of Friedrich] Carlyle's *History of Friedrich II. of Prussia, called Frederick the Great* was published in six volumes between 1858 and 1865.

797.7 Melilot.] Sweet clover.

800.21 "'Trench says . . . man.'] See *On the Study of Words* (1851), a series of lectures by Richard Chenevix Trench (1807–1886).

802.30 Boner . . . Middletown!"] Botanists William Borrer (1781–1862) and Joseph Barratt (1796–1882).

804.21–23 *non curat de . . . existit natura.*] "The magistrate is not concerned with leasts," and "nature works in leasts."

805.37 Wren] Christopher Wren (1632–1723), English architect.

807.35–36 Fernando Woods . . . Wightmans] Fernando Wood (1812–1881), a Tammany Hall mayor who suggested to the New York City Council that New York secede from the Union in order to continue trade with the Confederate States of America; Joel Parker (1816–1888), who as New Jersey governor argued that the Emancipation Proclamation was unconstitutional;

Joseph Milner Wightman (1812–1885), a mayor of Boston who decided, controversially, to divert supplies from a charity set up for Union servicemen to Confederate prisoners newly arrived at Fort Warren.

808.6 G F Train] George F. Train (1829–1904), author of *An American Merchant in Europe, Asia, and Australia* (1851) and *Young America Abroad* (1857).

808.14 Arnold's "the lyrical cry,"] See Matthew Arnold's 1861 lecture series "On Translating Homer."

808.30 "nothing prevails . . . God."] See Goethe's autobiography, *Aus meinem Leben: Dichtung und Wahrheit* ("From My Life: Poetry and Truth," 1811–33.)

812.12 Samuel Moody] Emerson's great-great-grandfather (1676–1747), a minister from York, Maine.

from FOR

813.4–6 "There are . . . *Swed.*] See Swedenborg, *The Economy of the Animal Kingdom.*

813.18–19 'Tis that . . . May.] See Emerson's "May-Day," the title poem of *May-Day and Other Pieces* (1867).

813.30 παντα ρει] All things are in flux.

819.4 Henry James's book] *Substance and Shadow* (1863) by Henry James Sr.

819.24 Il n'y a que le matin] In his essay "Inspiration," published in *Letters and Social Aims* (1876), Emerson comments on the proverbial French phrase as follows: "The French have a proverb to the effect that not the day only, but all things have their morning,—*'Il n'y a que le matin en toutes choses.'* And it is a primal rule to defend your morning, to keep all its dews on, and with fine foresight to relieve it from any jangle of affairs—even from the question, Which task?"

824.17 Madame du Deffand] Marie Anne de Vichy-Chamrond, marquise du Deffand (1697–1780), a patron of the arts; see note 771.3.

824.26–27 Burke's saying . . . despised."] See *Thoughts on the Prospect of a Regicide Peace: In a Series of Letters* (1796).

824.37 Boutwell] George Sewall Boutwell (1818–1905), a former Massachusetts governor; he served in the House of Representatives from 1863 to 1869, and later as senator and Secretary of the Treasury.

826.28–30 Byron's line . . . aloud."] See *Childe Harold's Pilgrimage*, III.xcii.867–68.

828.11–15 "Natural objects . . . Blake] See Gilchrist, *Life of William Blake.*

from KL

830.13 *Il n'y a que . . . toutes choses.*] See note 819.24.

830.14–15 Goethe . . . Musagetes.] See Goethe's poem "The Musagetes" (1798); Apollo, in his role as leader of the muses, was termed "Apollo Musagetes."

835.1–4 Though Love recoil . . . die.'] See Emerson's poem "Sacrifice," published in *May-Day and Other Pieces* (1867).

835.25 A page of M.M.E.] Emerson cites the notebooks in which he compiled his aunt Mary Moody Emerson's sayings and writings.

836.23–24 "And thus the world . . . not."] See "To a Skylark" (1820), by Percy Bysshe Shelley (1792–1822).

837.3–4 De Stael's . . . propres."] See the sketch of Madame de Staël by Charles-Augustin Saint-Beuve (1804–1869) in "Poètes et Romanciers Modernes de la France," *Revue des Deux Mondes* (1835).

837.36 usque ad aras.] Even to the altars; to the last extremity.

838.30 "in ourselves . . . sought"] See *3 King Henry VI*, IV.i.46.

839.15 George Minott] See note 452.32.

from LN

843.6 when Sumner . . . Bill] Charles Sumner (1811–1874) presented the Senate with a bill proposing the formation of a "National Academy of Literature and Art" in June 1864; Emerson's name was among its proposed members.

843.22 Niebuhr] See note 645.32–37.

844.30 Mrs C. T.] Caroline Sturgis Tappan.

846.1 Ralph] Ralph Emerson Forbes (1866–1937), Emerson's grandson.

846.6–12 Taliesin . . . *Nash*, p 183] See note 772.9.

848.34–35 Hazlitt . . . *Althea.*"] See *Lucasta: The Poems of Richard Lovelace, Esq.*, ed. W. Carew Hazlitt (1864); Lovelace lived from 1618 to 1657.

852.1–3 Bettine . . . than you."] See von Arnim, *Goethe's Correspondence with a Child.*

853.4–8 "The early Friends . . . Fisher] Emerson cites *The Nature of War, Together with Some Observations on the Coercive Exactions of Religious Societies* (1862), by William Logan Fisher (1781–1862), Quaker businessman and author.

853.11–16 "The Assembly . . . killing him thyself.'"] See note 853.4–8.

854.16–19 Dhruva said . . . p 51] Emerson cites *Le Bhâgavata Purâna, ou Histoire Poétique de Krychna*, tr. Eugène Burnouf (1840–47), vol. II.

854.31 Tom Ward's] Ward, a son of Samuel Gray Ward and a member of the Harvard class of 1865, had accompanied Agassiz on his 1865–66 expedition to Brazil.

855.3 Ida A. Higginson] Louis Agassiz's daughter.

856.19 Dr Jackson] Charles Thomas Jackson.

856.26 Dr Wollaston.] William Hyde Wollaston (1766–1828), British physicist and chemist.

858.34–35 Mr R. G. Shaw, senior] Probably Robert Gould Shaw, a prosperous shipping merchant and grandfather of Robert Gould Shaw (1837–1863), commander of the African-American 54th Massachusetts Volunteer Infantry.

861.8 Warren Burton] Burton (1800–1886) was a Harvard classmate.

861.15 Zerah Colburn or Blind Tom] Colburn (1804–1839) and Thomas ("Blind Tom") Wiggins (1849–1908) were child prodigies, both of whom toured internationally exhibiting their abilities. Colburn excelled at mathematical calculation, Wiggins at reproducing exactly, by ear, on the piano, music heard only once.

862.6 that Newtonian experiment . . . above] In a longer passage in journal *LN* not included in the present volume, Emerson writes: "Newton, habitually regarding a particular fact in nature as an universal fact,—what happens in one place and time, happens in all places at all times,—happens to see an apple fall, & says to himself, What is the moon but a bigger apple falling also to the earth? What is the earth but a much bigger apple falling to the sun?"

862.36 Shakspeare's . . . event,"] See *Hamlet,* IV.iv.50.

865.34 porphyrogenet] One born into royalty.

866.2 See *M.M.E.* . . . 277–8.] See note 835.25.

866.35–867.3 Turner's . . . "Song of Boston"] See *The Slave-Ship* (1840), a painting by J.M.W. Turner, and Emerson's poem "Boston Hymn" (1863).

867.9 an earlier page in this book] Page 67 in Emerson's journal *LN*, printed at 849.19–28 in the present volume.

869.24 Mrs Hunt] Helen Fiske Hunt (1830–1885), later Helen Hunt Jackson, author of the novel *Ramona* (1884) and other works.

870.14 Sangrail] Holy Grail.

870.26–27 "is the immediate . . . souls".] See *Othello*, III.iii.156.

871.26–30 these fine poems . . . King,"] "King Acrisius" and "The Proud King" both appear in the 1868 first volume of *The Earthly Paradise*, by William Morris (1834–1896).

874.11 Cudworth] Ralph Cudworth (1617–1688), English philosopher.

874.16–18 "inter-despised . . . Mackintosh.] See "Society of the Lakes" (1840), one of the *Recollections of the Lake Poets* (1835–40), by Thomas de Quincey (1785–1859).

874.32–33 Lowell's new poems] *Under the Willows, and Other Poems* (1869), by James Russell Lowell.

876.2–4 this Welsh genius . . . Skene.] See *The Four Ancient Books of Wales, Containing the Cymric Poems Attributed to the Bards of the Sixth Century*, tr. William Forbes Skene (1868).

876.20–23 "old guide" . . . Cave.] Emerson toured Mammoth Cave in Kentucky in 1850, with a guide named Stephen.

877.14–15 my rural neighbor S.S.] Samuel Staples; see note 793.2.

877.20 Winckelmann's] Johann Joachim Winckelmann (1717–1768), German art historian and archaeologist.

877.24 R.] Ralph; see note 846.1.

878.16–18 Coleridge's definition . . . manhood"] See *The Friend* (1809–10, 1812; 1818), essay I, section ii, by Samuel Taylor Coleridge (1772–1834).

878.22 Sumner collects . . . will be] See *The Works of Charles Sumner*, published in 15 volumes between 1870 and 1883.

879.13–14 "I could be . . . away."] See *The Beggar's Opera* (1728) by John Gay (1685–1732).

882.22–23 Mrs Stowe . . . Lady Byron] See Stowe's "The True Story of Lady Byron's Life" (1869) and *Lady Byron Vindicated* (1870).

884.10–16 Mr Lowell . . . dare to do."] See Lowell's "Ode Recited at the Harvard University Commemoration, July 21, 1865."

884.24 Bettine in Varnhagen's Diary] See the 14-volume *Tagebücher* (1861–70) of Karl August Varnhagen von Ense (1785–1858).

885.13 *Musagetes.*] See note 830.14–15.

from ST

892.14 "After you . . . Swett.] See the second dialogue in Jonathan Swift's *Polite Conversation* (1738, published under the pseudonym "Simon Wagerstaff, Esq."): "O! madam; after you is good manners."

893.1 *P.M.*] Plutarch's *Morals.*

893.18 Parnassus] An anthology of poetry edited by Emerson and published in 1874.

895.15–16 Ah not to me . . . song.] The couplet is Emerson's.

897.9–11 "For deathless powers . . . smile."] See Wordsworth's "September 1819" (1820).

899.26 "betrayed me . . . in a gown"] See Herbert's poem "Affliction," from *The Temple.*

900.2 *Sprüche?*] *Sprüche in Prosa* (*Proverbs in Prose*, published posthumously in 1870).

900.29 J.E.C.] James Elliot Cabot, who volunteered as Emerson's secretary for a number of years and later published *A Memoir of Ralph Waldo Emerson* (1887).

901.16–20 "Egyptian bride . . . p 174] Emerson cites an 1830 edition of *The Modern Traveller*, a multivolume compilation of travel writings, edited by Joseph Condor (1789–1859).

902.10–14 Goethe says . . . word or name."] See *Conversations with Goethe* (1836–48), by Johann Peter Eckermann (1792–1854).

904.5 inserted some poems] See Emerson's 1874 anthology *Parnassus.*

Biographical Notes

AMOS BRONSON ALCOTT (1799–1888), the son of poor Connecticut farmers, was largely self-educated. He began working in a local clock factory at age 14, and left home at 17, earning a living as an itinerant peddler in the Carolinas and Virginia. He returned to Connecticut in 1823, and accepted several teaching positions. Soon after his marriage to Abigail May in 1830, he began to set up experimental schools, doing away with rote learning and corporal punishment. The most successful of these, his Temple School (where he was assisted by Elizabeth Peabody and Margaret Fuller), operated from 1835 to 1839; it closed amid controversies over his heretical methods and his admission of an African-American girl. Emerson met Alcott in 1835 and soon after called him "the most extraordinary man, and the highest genius of the time." After the failure of his experiment in communal living, Fruitlands, in 1844, Alcott and his family barely managed to make ends meet (in the mid-1850s, Emerson helped to raise money from local citizens to help support them). These circumstances were relieved in 1859, with his appointment as Concord's superintendent of schools. Though Emerson was sometimes irritated by Alcott's egotism (he "never loses sight of his own personality," he noted), they remained close friends throughout their lives; the day Emerson died, Bronson's daughter Louisa May Alcott wrote in her journal that Emerson had been "the nearest and dearest Friend father has ever had."

GEORGE PARTRIDGE BRADFORD (1807–1890), the youngest of several children of Captain Gamaliel Bradford and Elizabeth Hickling, was raised largely by his older sister, Sarah. In 1818, she married Emerson's uncle, the Rev. Samuel Ripley, of Waltham, Massachusetts, and he moved with her to Waltham. Bradford graduated from Harvard in 1825 and the Divinity School three years later. Forgoing the pulpit (Andrews Norton, a Divinity School professor, told him that one of his sermons was "marked by the absence of every qualification a good sermon ought to have"), he earned a living as a teacher in Plymouth. He was one of the original residents of Brook Farm, where he was assigned the task, with Nathaniel Hawthorne, of milking the cows. When the farm was converted into a Fourierist phalanx, Bradford confessed he was too much a "genuine descendant of the old Puritans" to participate fully in the Brook Farm experiment; he returned to Plymouth, where he worked briefly as a market gardener before returning to teaching. Emerson praised Bradford's "beautiful conscience," and wrote in 1840: "I can better converse with G. B. than with any other."

THOMAS CARLYLE (1795–1881) first attracted Emerson's attention as the anonymous writer of "Germanick new-light" essays in English periodicals; "The State of German Literature" (1827), "Signs of the Times" (1829), and "Characteristics" (1831) so struck him that, after he discovered the author's identity just prior to his 1833 European tour, he went out of his way to visit him at his farm, Craigenputtock, in Scotland. The two men favorably impressed each other. Carlyle, writing to John Stuart Mill, praised Emerson as "a most gentle, recommendable, amiable, wholehearted man." Emerson wrote of Carlyle: "He talks finely, seems to love the broad Scotch, & I loved him very much, at once." Thereafter, the pair began what would become a 38-year correspondence. Beginning in 1835, Emerson helped gather subscriptions for an American edition of *Sartor Resartus*, and wrote a preface. Carlyle had been unable to find an English publisher for his unconventional book; in 1836, Emerson proudly sent him the first edition, printed in Boston. He later served as Carlyle's American literary agent, reading proofs and sending royalty payments. The friendship grew strained after Emerson visited Carlyle during his 1848 lecture tour of England. In his journal, he wrote: "Carlyle is no idealist in opinions, but a protectionist in political economy, aristocrat in politics, epicure in diet, goes for murder, money, punishment by death, slavery, & all the pretty abominations, tempering them with epigrams. His seal holds a griffin with the word, *Humiliate*." In spite of increasing philosophical and political differences, the two continued to correspond and to follow each other's careers. In 1859, the year after its publication, Emerson described Carlyle's *History of Frederick the Great* in his journal as "infinitely the wittiest book that was ever written." A few days before his death, having lost much of his memory, he is reported to have noticed a photograph of Carlyle in his study and to have remarked: "That is my man, my good man!"

WILLIAM ELLERY CHANNING (1780–1842)—sometimes referred to as "Dr. Channing," to distinguish him from his nephew and namesake, poet William Ellery Channing (1817–1901)—was born into a prominent Rhode Island Federalist family and raised by his maternal grandfather, William Ellery, a signer of the Declaration of Independence, after the premature death of his father. He graduated from Harvard in 1798. After spending a miserable year as a tutor in Richmond, Virginia, Channing—now a determined opponent of slavery—returned North, and accepted the ministry of the Federal Street

Church in Boston. Over the coming years, in his essays and sermons, he would outline the central tenets of American Unitarianism. In 1816, he helped found Harvard's Divinity School; in 1820, he organized the Berry Street Conference, a forerunner of the American Unitarian Association. Though reclusive and reserved, Channing exercised a profound influence on the younger generation of Unitarians. Emerson called him "our Bishop" and claimed him, along with his aunt Mary Moody Emerson, as one of his principal early influences.

WILLIAM ELLERY CHANNING (1817–1901)—often known as "Ellery Channing" to distinguish him from his more famous uncle, the prominent Unitarian—was sent to live with relatives after his mother died when he was five. He entered Harvard in the fall of 1834, but dropped out three months later, feeling its attendance regulations constrained his freedom. He tried homesteading in Illinois for a few months, but soon moved to Cincinnati, where he met and married Ellen Fuller, Margaret's sister. In the summer of 1842, Channing came to Concord and met Emerson for the first time; the following spring, his wife joined him and they moved into Red Lodge, the cottage next to Emerson's garden. A frequent contributor of verse to *The Dial*, he published his *Poems* in 1843. (Edgar Allan Poe wrote a lacerating review: Channing's poems were "full of all kinds of mistakes, of which the most important is that of their having been written at all.") Never a consistent breadwinner, Channing often left his family—ultimately including five children—to wander ("whim, thy name is Channing," his friend Bronson Alcott would write in his journal). He worked at the *Tribune* in New York from November 1844 to March 1845, and in 1846 traveled in Europe. Returning to Concord, he spent much of his time rambling through the woods with Alcott, Emerson, and (most frequently) Thoreau. In 1855, he attempted to make amends with his family (his wife had gone to live with her sister-in-law Mary and her husband, Thomas W. Higginson, two years earlier) but Ellen Fuller died that same year; relatives agreed to take care of his children. After the death of Thoreau, his closest friend, he helped, along with Thoreau's sister, Sophie, to prepare Thoreau's *The Maine Woods* (1864) and *Cape Cod* (1865) for publication; in 1873, Channing's biography, *Thoreau, the Poet-Naturalist*, was published. Channing spent his last years living off the income from a trust fund, reading and writing, and dining with the Emersons on Sundays.

WILLIAM HENRY CHANNING (1810–1884), was, like Ellery Channing, a nephew of the theologian William Ellery Channing, who oversaw his education. He graduated from Harvard in 1829 and the Harvard Divinity School in 1833. After serving as the Unitarian minister of the First Congregational Church of Cincinnati, from 1838 to 1841, he moved to New York and became involved in a variety of social reform projects, serving as the head of congregations informed by Christian and Fourierist ideas. He edited two periodicals, *The Present* (1840) and *The Spirit of the Age* (1849–50), while contributing to the Fourierist journals *The Phalanx* and *The Harbinger*. He also lived briefly at Brook Farm in 1846 and in 1850 at the North American Phalanx, a Fourierist community in New Jersey. In 1851 he co-edited, along with Emerson and James Freeman Clarke, the *Memoirs of Margaret Fuller Ossoli*. After ministering to a Unitarian congregation in Rochester, New York, he accepted an appointment to a church in England. Channing returned to America on the outbreak of the Civil War, eventually becoming chaplain to the House of Representatives. Unable to find work after the war, he returned to England where he would live for the rest of his life, coming back to America occasionally for lecture tours.

CHARLES CHAUNCY EMERSON (1808–1836), the youngest of the Emerson brothers, was thought by many during his lifetime—including his aunt Mary Moody—to be the most promising. After graduating from Harvard, where he won the Bowdoin Prize his sophomore year, he studied law and in 1832 took a Harvard law degree. Daniel Webster was impressed enough by his performance to exclaim, when Charles was debating where he should practice, "Let him settle anywhere! . . . the clients will throng after him." Around this time he fell in love with Elizabeth Hoar, the daughter of Samuel Hoar, in whose Concord office he beginning his legal career; a wedding date was set for September 1836. Five months before the scheduled date, Charles died of tuberculosis at his brother William's house in Staten Island. Emerson wrote to his wife, Lidian, soon after: "I can never bring you back my noble friend who was my ornament my wisdom & my pride . . . You must be content henceforth with only a piece of your husband."

EDITH EMERSON (1841–1929), the third child of Emerson and Lidian, married William Hathaway Forbes, a Civil War veteran, in 1865. Forbes eventually became president of Bell Telephone; they raised seven children. She assisted her father in editing his 1874 poetry anthology *Parnassus*, and in 1916 herself edited *Favorites of a Nursery School Seventy Years Ago*.

EDWARD BLISS EMERSON (1805–1834), born two years after his brother Ralph Waldo, excelled at Harvard, where he delivered a commencement oration attended by the Marquis de Lafayette. After his graduation, he entered the law office of Daniel Webster, supplementing his income by teaching. All the while, his health was gradually deteriorating, a year abroad failed to improve his condition. "Edward hardly seems to have the strength necessary for the race he ought to run," wrote brother William. In the spring of 1828, he had a complete mental breakdown and was committed to the McLean Asylum—a "constitutional calamity," Emerson wrote, that "has buried at once so many towering hopes." He eventually recovered his sanity, sailed for Puerto Rico, and got a job as a clerk at the American consulate. He never fully recovered his health, however, and soon died of tuberculosis.

EDWARD WALDO EMERSON (1844–1930), the fourth and last child of Emerson and Lidian, graduated from Harvard in 1866 and Harvard Medical School in 1874. He practiced medicine in Concord from 1874 to 1882. After his father's death, he spent the rest of his life painting, writing, and editing his father's works. His 10-volume *Journals of Ralph Waldo Emerson* was published between 1909 and 1914.

ELLEN TUCKER EMERSON (1811–1831) was raised by her mother and stepfather in Concord, New Hampshire; her father, who owned a rope factory, died prematurely. She met Emerson on the day after Christmas, 1827, through his Harvard classmate Edward Kent, her stepbrother. By the end of the next year they were engaged and were married in September 1829, six months after Emerson was ordained as minister at the Second Church in Boston. They moved into a house in Chardon Street in Boston, and though she was consumptive, lived very happily together. She died of tuberculosis in February 1831. The income from her estate allowed Emerson a measure of financial independence in the years following her death.

ELLEN TUCKER EMERSON (1839–1909) was Emerson and Lidian's second child. She lived a quiet and religious life, assisting her father. Her *Life of Lidian Jackson Emerson* was published posthumously in 1980, followed by *The Letters of Ellen Tucker Emerson*, in two volumes, in 1982.

LIDIAN JACKSON EMERSON (1802–1892), a native of Plymouth, Massachusetts, saw Emerson for the first time in Boston in 1834, during a visit to her sister; after hearing him preach, she told a friend: "that man is certainly my predestined husband." She met him later the same year and they married the next, soon moving into their new Concord home, Bush, where they would spend the rest of their lives. Although an active and sympathetic participant in Emerson's social life (she regularly attended Margaret Fuller's "Conversations," and Emerson's friend Sarah Freeman Clarke called her a "searing transcendentalist"), Lidian was never fully content in Concord. Ellen Emerson, in her biography of her mother, wrote: "In her fifty-seven years of life in Concord she had never taken root there, she was always a sojourner," and that from 40 to 70 "sadness was the ground color of her life."

MARY MOODY EMERSON (1774–1863), Emerson's deeply pious, sharply satirical, and always unconventional paternal aunt, was one of his most formative influences. She was born in Concord to the Rev. William Emerson and Phebe (Bliss) Emerson, but lived after her father's death in 1776 and her mother's remarriage in 1780 with poor relatives in Maine. Though she spent much of her life in Maine—residing sometimes with her sister's family at Elm Vale in Waterford, a property she eventually owned—she also moved frequently, boarding with relatives and acquaintances. At 17, she returned to Concord to help raise her half-siblings. At 37, after the death of Emerson's father, she came to educate her nephews, with whom she also corresponded extensively in her absence. She lived again in the Emerson household for about a year in her early 60s, leaving in 1836. After staying with her in Maine some ten years later, Elizabeth Palmer Peabody called her "an extraordinary creature," but noted "she does stick hard things in all tender places." She quarreled with Emerson as his religious beliefs grew increasingly unorthodox (for his part, he felt that she was "not a Calvinist," only that she "wished everyone else to be one"). But they made amends, and Emerson eventually received from her some of her extensive manuscript writings, which he copied—along with recollections of her conversation—into four notebooks, totaling almost 900 manuscript pages.

ROBERT BULKELEY EMERSON (1807–1859), the second youngest of Emerson's siblings, was mentally retarded; he required constant care and supervision all his life, sometimes by the family, sometimes by hired helpers, and finally at the McLean Asylum. He is seldom mentioned in the journals. In a letter to his brother William describing Bulkeley's funeral, Emerson wrote: "His face was not much changed by death, but sadly changed by life from the comely boy I can well remember . . . it did not seem so odious to be laid down there under the oak trees in as perfect an innocency as was Bulkeleys, as to live corrupt & corrupting with thousands. What a happiness, that, with his infirmities, he was clean of all vices!"

RUTH HASKINS EMERSON (1768–1853), Emerson's mother, was born into a prosperous Boston Episcopalian family. She married William Emerson in 1796, and in 1799 they moved from Harvard, Massachusetts, to Boston. After the death of her husband in 1812, she earned enough money by taking in boarders to send four of her sons (including Ralph Waldo) to Harvard. She moved in with Emerson permanently after his second marriage in 1835. Emerson wrote of her soon after her death that her manners and character were "the fruit of a past age," and praised "her punctilious courtesy extended to every person." In June 1851 she demonstrated this in an extreme way: after falling out of bed in the middle of the night and breaking her hip, she refused to call for help so as not to wake anyone. Emerson wrote to Carlyle following her death: "in my journeyings lately, when I think of home, the heart is taken out."

WALDO EMERSON (1836–1842), Emerson's youngest child, died of scarlet fever soon after his fifth birthday. "His image, so gentle, so rich in hopes," Emerson wrote to Caroline Sturgis a few days later, "blends easily with every happy moment, every fair remembrance, every cherished friendship, of my life." Waldo's death was the occasion of one of Emerson's most famous poems, "Threnody."

WILLIAM EMERSON (1769–1811) died before his son, Ralph Waldo, had reached the age of eight. He was born in Concord, his father a minister; he graduated from Harvard in 1789, taught school for two years, studied divinity, and himself became a minister at the Unitarian church of Harvard, Massachusetts. He married Ruth Haskins in 1796, and besides Ralph Waldo they had seven other children, so he taught school in addition to preaching, and the family took in boarders. In 1799, he accepted the pulpit of Boston's First Church, and began an active literary and civic life in Boston, joining the Massachusetts Historical Society and becoming an overseer of Harvard College, founding the Anthology Club, and editing the *Monthly Anthology*. He published orations and sermons, and was the author of *An Historical Sketch of the First Church in Boston* (1812).

WILLIAM EMERSON (1801–1868), the oldest of Emerson's brothers, graduated from Harvard in 1818, just as Emerson was finishing his freshman year. For five years afterward he taught high school in Kennebunk, Maine, to help support the educations of his younger brothers, who called him "his Deaconship" and "our Sultan." In 1823, William left for Göttingen, Germany, to study theology, but his studies weakened his resolve to be a minister, and he soon returned to America with the intention of pursuing law. He moved to Staten Island, married, and raised a family; Thoreau was briefly a tutor to his children. Eventually he became a judge. He remained close to Emerson to the end of his life.

MARGARET FULLER (1810–1850) was born in Cambridgeport, Massachusetts, the daughter of Margaret Crane Fuller, a teacher, and congressman Timothy Fuller; she studied at Dr. Park's Boston Lyceum for Young Ladies. After her father's death in 1835, she began writing articles and teaching, to help support the family. She succeeded Elizabeth Palmer Peabody as an assistant at Bronson Alcott's controversial Temple School, and then taught in Providence, Rhode Island. Her writings brought her to Emerson's attention, and he invited her to his house for three weeks in the summer of 1836 as he was finishing *Nature*. In the coming years, she introduced Emerson to many of her friends, including Charles King Newcomb and Samuel Gray Ward. In 1839, she published a translation of Johann Eckermann's *Conversations with Goethe*, and in 1840 she became editor of *The Dial*, to which she made extensive contributions. She also began the first of her series of "Conversations for Women" (1839–44), gatherings that addressed the "great questions." Emerson described Fuller at one of these events: "She rose before me at times into heroical and godlike regions, and I could remember no superior woman, but thought of Ceres, Minerva, Proserpine." In 1844, her book *A Summer on the Lakes* prompted Horace Greeley to invite her to serve as literary critic for the *New-York Tribune*. After 18 months there reviewing books and reporting on slum conditions, lunatic asylums, and prisons—and having published her groundbreaking *Woman in the Nineteenth Century* (1845)—she traveled through England and France as a foreign correspondent. In 1847, she arrived in Italy, where she met and fell in love with Giovanni Angelo, Marchese d'Ossoli. In 1848 she had a son and became involved with the Italian revolution of 1848–49, which she described with enthusiasm in articles for the *Tribune*. After the fall of the Roman republic in 1849, she relocated with her family to Florence, and in 1850 they sailed for the United States. Within sight of Fire Island, their ship sank and all three drowned. Emerson, Henry Channing, and James Freeman Clarke immediately set about collaborating on a biography of her, published in 1852 as *Memoirs of Margaret Fuller Ossoli*.

MARTIN GAY (1803–1850) entered Harvard in 1819, when Emerson was a sophomore. Emerson was instantly drawn to this "strange face in the Freshman class" and would chronicle the development of his fascination with Gay over the next two years. After receiving his M.D. degree from Harvard in 1826, Gay became a prominent Boston physician, mineralogist, and chemist, occasionally lecturing on these subjects. He was one of the original members of the Boston Society of Natural History and a fellow of the American Academy of Arts & Sciences.

NATHANIEL HAWTHORNE (1804–1864) was a graduate, along with his friends Henry Wadsworth Longfellow and Franklin Pierce, of

Bowdoin College. His book of stories, *Twice-told Tales* (1837), brought him to the attention of Elizabeth Palmer Peabody, through whom he met his future wife, Sophia, her sister. In 1841, he became a resident at Brook Farm, mainly to save money while writing, but he found that farm work exhausted him and he left later that year. After his marriage to Sophia in 1842, he moved with her to the Old Manse in Concord (built by Emerson's grandfather William). He spent the next several years taking walks with Emerson, Channing, and Thoreau, and writing most of the stories that would be published in *Mosses from an Old Manse* (1846). Of Emerson at this time, he wrote: "It was impossible to dwell in his vicinity without inhaling the mountain-atmosphere of his lofty thought." Emerson was incompletely convinced of Hawthorne's abilities as a writer, but admired him personally: soon after Hawthorne's death, he wrote "I found in him a greater man than any of his works betray."

FREDERIC HENRY HEDGE (1805–1890), one of the leading New England disseminators of German thought, was the son of Levi Hedge, a Harvard professor of Natural Religion and Moral Philosophy. In his early teens, he accompanied historian George Bancroft to Germany, and studied for four years at schools in Hanover and Saxony. He took his bachelor's degree from Harvard in 1825, and graduated from the Divinity School in 1829; in the same year he married Lucy Pierce and was ordained a Congregational minister in West Cambridge. In 1833, he published "Coleridge's Literary Character," an essay sometimes cited as the first recognition of German transcendentalism in the United States; Emerson read it avidly, calling it "a living, leaping logos." In 1836, a year after becoming minister of the Independent Congregational Church in Bangor, Maine, Hedge's return visits to Massachusetts served as occasions for the meetings of Hedge's Club—later known as the Transcendental Club—which met regularly over the next four years at George Ripley's house in Boston. The meetings ended in 1840, Hedge feeling that the younger generation of Unitarians had "slipped their moorings" in abandoning the call for Unitarian church reform. In an 1840 letter to Margaret Fuller, Emerson wrote that though he and Hedge "never quite meet . . . he has such a fine free wit, such accomplishments & talents & then such an affectionate selfhealing nature that I always revere him." Hedge eventually settled in Brookline, Massachusetts, and in 1872 became professor of German at Harvard.

ELIZABETH SHERMAN HOAR (1814–1878) was the oldest child of Samuel Hoar, a wealthy Concord lawyer and politician. After graduating from Concord Academy, she was engaged to Emerson's brother Charles Chauncy, who was then working in her father's firm.

Five months before their wedding, her fiancé died of tuberculosis, but she remained closely connected with the Emersons. When Lidian was sick or indisposed, Hoar would manage the household; Emerson's mother, Ruth, died in her arms, and his children would call her "Aunt Lizzie." In 1841, Emerson wrote of her: "I have no friend whom I more wish to be immortal than she." A love of learning, cultivated at a young age, drew her into the circles of both Margaret Fuller, whose "Conversations" she regularly attended, and Sarah Alden Ripley, with whom she visited frequently after the Ripleys moved to Concord in 1846.

EDMUND HOSMER (1798–1881), a farmer, lived about half a mile east of the Emerson household. According to Edward Emerson, he was "the oracle constantly consulted" by his father and "the ally called in, dealing with the interesting but to him puzzling management of his increasing acres." Emerson was drawn instantly to Hosmer, whom he praised as "a man of strongly intellectual taste . . . of much reading, and of an erect good sense and independent spirit." Hosmer was not only a frequent guest at Emerson's house, but also a welcome visitor to Thoreau's Walden cabin, which he and his sons helped to build.

CHARLES THOMAS JACKSON (1805–1880), Lidian Emerson's brother, expressed an interest in mineralogy from an early age and published his first study (on the minerals of Nova Scotia) in the *American Journal of Science* in 1829, a year after graduating from Harvard Medical School. He studied medicine and mineralogy in Paris, and in 1836, four years after his return and two years after his marriage, he retired from medicine to set up a commercial chemical laboratory in Boston. Jackson later served as state geologist of Maine, New Hampshire, and Rhode Island, and as U.S. geologist for the Lake Superior region. His career was overshadowed, however, by his habit of claiming credit and priority for scientific advances not his own: at various points, he claimed to have discovered the telegraph, guncotton, the digestive action of the stomach, and the medical applications of ether. These and other controversies contributed to a mental breakdown in 1873, after which he was committed to the McLean Asylum, where he lived until his death.

HENRY JAMES SR. (1811–1882)—a recently married writer, lecturer, and Calvinist theologian—attended a lecture of Emerson's in New York in 1842 and sought him out. After they met, Emerson wrote Lidian that James seemed "a very manlike thorough seeing person," and they became lifelong friends, despite James's frustration at Emerson's unwillingness to defend or explain his religious views

("Oh you man without a handle!" he at one point exclaimed in their conversations). In 1844, during an extended trip to England, James experienced a "vastation" and spiritual crisis and turned increasingly to the works of Emanuel Swedenborg for his religious self-understanding. On his return to New York in 1845, he threw himself into social reform, associating with Albert Brisbane and the Fourierist movement and contributing reviews to the Fourierist organ *The Harbinger*. His *Moralism and Christianity* (1850) and other works that questioned conventional ideas of marriage and morality earned him considerable notoriety. James spent the rest of his life expounding Swedenborgian theology in books and articles. Though he continued to correspond with Emerson, their friendship became more distant after the Civil War; in 1868, James wrote his son William that Emerson's writings were "wholly destitute of spiritual flavor, being at most carbonic acid gas and *water*." In spite of philosophical differences, he always praised Emerson the man, writing in 1872: "Mr. Emerson's authority consists, not in his ideas, not in his intellect, not in his culture, not in his science, but simply in himself, in the form of his natural personality."

CHARLES LANE (1800–1870) was a member of the circle centered around James Pierrepont Greaves, an English mystic and former merchant who founded a small community and school in Ham, Surrey, known as "Alcott House" in honor of Bronson Alcott and informed by his progressive writings on education. Lane served as editor of a number of reformist magazines including *The Healthian*, which promoted spiritual enrichment through a wholesome diet, and contributed ten articles to *The Dial*. When Alcott returned from his trip to England in 1842, he brought Lane with him, along with Lane's son and Henry G. Wright, founder of *The Healthian*. In May of 1842, Lane purchased a 90-acre farm near Harvard, Massachusetts, where they founded Fruitlands, an experiment in communal living that forbade all ownership of property, the consumption of animals, animal products, and any liquid but water. It also enforced a rigorous celibacy. After seven months, the farm failed, having attracted no more than a dozen occasional members. After this, Lane lived briefly in the Harvard Shaker community; he eventually returned to England, resuming his job as manager of the *London Mercantile Price Current*.

CHARLES KING NEWCOMB (1820–1894) and his mother moved to Providence, Rhode Island, soon after his father died in 1825. After graduating from Brown in 1837, he abandoned plans to join the navy, then the Episcopal ministry. He met Emerson in 1840 through Margaret Fuller, a friend of his mother who had become a close correspondent. Newcomb's moral and intellectual leanings made him the ideal boarder at Brook Farm, where he lived more or less continuously from May 1841 to December 1845. During his residence there he wrote the only work published during his lifetime, "The Two Dolons," which appeared in the July 1842 issue of *The Dial.* Emerson drew comfort from it in the wake of his son's death, saying it had "more native gold than anything . . . since Sampson Reed's Oration on Genius." Soon after moving back to Providence with his mother, Newcomb began keeping a journal, eventually filling 27 manuscript volumes. This journal, excepting a three-month stint with Tenth Rhode Island Volunteer Infantry in 1862, would become the main focus of his life until he departed for Europe in 1871. Emerson's feelings toward him fluctuated from adoration (in the beginning, he called Newcomb his "key to Shakespeare" and the "brightest star" of the younger generation of Transcendentalists) to extreme impatience (after a visit in 1850, Emerson wrote in his journal, "He wastes my time . . . Destroyed three good days for me!"). In spite of what he felt was wasted potential in Newcomb, Emerson still thought highly enough of him in 1858 to agree with Caroline Sturgis when she said "no one could compare with him in original genius."

THEODORE PARKER (1810–1860), a native of Lexington, Massachusetts, was ordained as a Congregational minister in 1837, a year after graduating from Harvard Divinity School. In the same year he married Lydia Dodge Cabot and associated himself with the Transcendental Club, meeting Emerson and his circle; in 1838, he praised Emerson's controversial "Divinity School Address." His own preaching, influenced by the German higher criticism of the Bible, increasingly offended mainstream Unitarians, and in the wake of his 1841 sermon *The Transient and Permanent in Christianity* and 1842 lecture *A Discourse of Matters Pertaining to Religion*, he was publicly criticized and excluded from church functions. His parishoners opted to secede and in 1845 offered him the pulpit of the newly formed Twenty-Eighth Congregational Society of Boston. His following grew in size and enthusiasm. Parker railed against the political corruption and moral abuses of his day (Emerson called him "our Savonarola"), including slavery and the Mexican War. From 1850 onward, slavery became his central issue: he assisted many fugitive slaves, and was one of the "Secret Six," helping to fund John Brown's raid on Harpers Ferry. In 1857, after years of frenetic activity as a lecturer and writer, he fell ill and gradually withdrew from public life; he died of tuberculosis in Florence.

ELIZABETH PALMER PEABODY (1804–1894), born in Billerica, Massachusetts, moved with her family to Lancaster after her father's dental practice collapsed. Her mother soon set up a school, which Elizabeth at 15 was obliged to help run. Emerson, around this time, tutored her in Greek. From 1834 to 1836, along with Margaret Fuller, she taught at Bronson Alcott's controversial Temple School, where he attempted to arouse children's interest in religion by engaging them in conversation. When she transcribed and published these conversations in 1837 as *Conversations with Children on the Gospels*, some outraged parents pulled their children out of the school. Three years later Peabody opened a bookstore and lending library in the parlor of the family home in Boston; one of the few bookstores in the city that carried a substantial stock of foreign literature, it became, in the words of George Bradford, a "Transcendentalist exchange." She hosted Margaret Fuller's "Conversations," beginning in 1839, and helped plan the publication of *The Dial*, of which she served as business manager; she also published books by her brother-in-law Nathaniel Hawthorne and by the elder William Ellery Channing, under her imprint. Inspired by her reading of Friedrich Froebel, the creator of the Kindergarten, she opened the first English-language kindergarten on Pinckney Street in Boston in 1861. The rest of her life was spent promoting the kindergarten and training young women to teach in it, through books like *Moral Culture of Infancy and Kindergarten Guide* (1866) and *Lectures in Training Schools for Kindergartners* (1888) and her magazine the *Kindergarten Messenger* (1873–77). Miss Birdseye, in the younger Henry James's novel *The Bostonians* (1885–86), was taken by contemporaries as a caricature of Peabody, though James himself disclaimed this intention.

SAMPSON REED (1800–1880), the son of a Unitarian minister, gave up his own plans to join the ministry soon after his graduation from Harvard in 1818, in the wake of his encounter with the writings of Emanuel Swedenborg. Reed's "Oration on Genius," delivered three years later when he received his M.A., was admired by an 18-year-old Emerson, who was in the audience. His *Observations on the Growth of the Mind* (1826), a distillation of Swedenborg's thoughts, affected Emerson even more profoundly; it came to him with "the aspect of a revelation, such is the wealth & such is the novelty of the truth unfolded in it." (Bronson Alcott would later note that *Nature* "reminds me more of Sampson Reed's *Growth of the Mind* than any other work.") Reed apprenticed himself to an apothecary and later opened an apothecary shop in Boston, working in this profession until 1860. Although he would spend his life advancing the cause of the Swedenborgian church, he distanced himself from the Transcendentalists, explicitly denying any connection with them in his preface to the 1838 edition of his *Growth of the Mind*. Reed would prove to be a huge disappointment to Emerson when he came out in support of Daniel Webster and the Fugitive Slave Law of 1850. "There were my two greatest men," Emerson reflected in 1870, "both down in the pit together."

EZRA RIPLEY (1751–1841) was born in Woodstock, Connecticut, the fifth of 19 children. He graduated from Harvard in 1776. Two years later, he was ordained minister of the First Church of Concord, taking over from Emerson's recently deceased grandfather, William, whose widow, Phebe Bliss, he soon married, and whose son—Emerson's father—he would go on to raise. He would serve as pastor of the First Church for almost 63 years. In 1834, he invited Emerson and his mother, Ruth, to live with him in Concord's Old Manse, where Emerson remained until his marriage the next year, working on the essay *Nature* (1836). "He ever reminds one," Emerson noted during his stay there, "both in his wisdom & in the faults of his intellect, of an Indian Sagamore, a sage within the limits of his own observation, a child beyond." After his death, Emerson wrote, "I am sure all who remember . . . will associate his form with whatever was grave and droll in the old, cold, unpainted, uncarpeted, square-pewed meetinghouse."

GEORGE RIPLEY (1802–1880), son of Jerome Ripley, a businessman, and Sarah Franklin, was born in Greenfield, Massachusetts. He entered Harvard in 1819, graduated first in his class, and went on to Divinity School. In 1826, he became a minister at the Purchase Street Church in Boston and married Sophia Willard Dana. In 1836, along with his cousin Emerson, Frederick Henry Hedge, and George Putnam, he met to form an occasional discussion group. Nicknamed Hedge's Club, and later referred to as the Transcendental Club, the group gradually expanded to include Orestes Brownson, William Henry Channing, Margaret Fuller (with whom he worked on *The Dial*, as managing editor), Elizabeth Palmer Peabody, Sophia Ripley, Henry David Thoreau, Jones Very, and others. Also in 1836, after publishing articles that questioned the tenets of Unitarianism, he was attacked in print by theologian Andrews Norton (for whom the Transcendentalist movement was "the latest form of infidelity"), sparking a four-year paper war. He defended Emerson in 1838 after Norton criticized Emerson's "Divinity School Address" as heretical. Looking for a means of support after quitting the ministry in 1840 and wanting to put the Transcendentalists' ideas into practice, he came up with the idea of a community that would "combine the thinker and the worker as far as possible." The result was Brook Farm in West Roxbury, a six-year experiment in communal living that attracted hundreds of boarders, including George Bradford, Nathaniel Hawthorne, Charles King Newcomb, and Caroline Sturgis. In 1844, the Brook Farmers began building a "Phalanstery or Unitary dwelling," inspired by the writings of Charles Fourier; the nearly completed structure burned down in 1846, and the community was finally dissolved in 1847. Afterward, Ripley and his wife moved to New York City, where he found work as a critic for Horace Greeley's *Tribune*, filling a position Margaret Fuller had recently left. He soon established himself as one of New York's leading editors and critics, helping to found *Harper's Magazine* in 1850, and publishing the lucrative *New American Cyclopedia* (1858–63). After his wife, Sophia, died in 1861, he married Louisa Schlossberger; for the remainder of his life he was a convivial fixture of New York's literary scene.

SAMUEL RIPLEY (1783–1847) was born at Concord's "Old Manse," the son of the Rev. Ezra Ripley and Phebe Emerson, and a half-brother of Emerson's father, the Rev. William Emerson, and Emerson's aunt Mary Moody Emerson. He graduated from Harvard in 1804, and in 1809 became minister of the First Congregational Society in Waltham, Massachusetts. He continued to serve his parish there for over three decades. He married Sarah Alden Bradford in 1818, and they had nine children; they also, together, helped local students prepare for college. After his death, Emerson wrote: "I know not where we shall find in a man of his station & experience a heart so large, or a spirit so blameless & of a childlike innocence."

SARAH ALDEN BRADFORD RIPLEY (1793–1867) was the oldest daughter of Gamaliel Bradford, a prison warden and former sea-captain, and Elizabeth Hickling. With her mother incapacitated by tuberculosis, the responsibility for managing the household and six younger siblings often fell to her. Despite this, she learned Latin and Greek and studied physics, chemistry, and botany. When her brothers went to college, she read all of their books and, with the guidance of Mary Moody Emerson (who would later accuse her of leading Emerson into heterodoxy), gave herself a college education. In 1818, she married Emerson's uncle Samuel Ripley, the Unitarian minister at Waltham, Massachusetts, and moved into his parsonage along with four of her brothers and sisters, including George P. Bradford; she tutored in Latin and Greek. In 1846 the family moved to the Old Manse in Concord, recently vacated by the Hawthornes, her husband accepting a post in nearby Lincoln. The younger members of Emerson's circle, including Fuller, Hedge, Parker, Peabody, and Thoreau, were all frequent visitors. Emerson, who had known her since he was 11, wrote that despite her vast learning, she was "absolutely without pedantry." At her burial service, Frederic Henry Hedge said although she'd never written a book, "in the hearts of those who knew her, she wrote a book whose substance they will remember as long as they remember anything, & whose contents are a commentary on the text: 'A perfect woman nobly planned.'"

SOPHIA WILLARD DANA RIPLEY (1803–1861) was born in Cambridge, Massachusetts, to Francis Dana Jr. and Sophia Willard Dana. After graduating from Dr. Park's Lyceum in Boston, she and her sister began teaching in Fay House, a school near Harvard that her mother had opened some years earlier. In 1825, through her extensive network of Unitarian friends, she met George Ripley, whom she married two years later. She became friends with Margaret Fuller in the 1830s, and participated in Fuller's series of "Conversations" (1839–44); she also attended meetings of the Transcendental Club. In 1841, she contributed a letter to *The Dial* on the communistic "Separatists" of Zoar, Ohio, and a feminist essay entitled "Woman"; along with her husband, she formed a joint stock company to procure the funds to purchase Brook Farm. She envisioned the Brook Farm community as a place where she could realize her ideals of womanhood, but the experiment proved a disappointment as the scheme limited her to taking care of sick children and boarders, teaching elementary school, and working at menial chores in the kitchen and around the house. After Brook Farm collapsed she suffered an emotional breakdown, realizing "that I do not love anyone and never did, with the heart, & of course could never have been worthy in any relation." She converted to Catholicism in 1847, partly due to the influence of Orestes Brownson who had himself converted three years earlier. She spent the last decade of her life in New York with her husband, translating devotional tracts, praying, and visiting hospitals, prisons, and lunatic asylums.

GEORGE A. SAMPSON (d. 1834), a Boston merchant, was a parishioner of the Second Church and the closest of Emerson's friends during his pastorate there. Emerson lived briefly in the Sampson household in 1829, and later relied on his advice in business and financial matters. Eulogizing his friend in 1834—in his final sermon at the Second Church—Emerson described Sampson as "a man without a fault—I might almost say—so utterly unable am I, after five years intercourse with him, to remember in him anything to censure."

CAROLINE STURGIS TAPPAN (1819–1888) was the fourth of six children of William Sturgis, a Boston merchant who had built a large trading empire in the Far East, and Elizabeth Marston Davis. She and her sisters were encouraged to think for themselves and read widely in various disciplines. At 13, she met Margaret Fuller, who was deeply impressed by her; Caroline and her sister Ellen would be the first friends Fuller invited to her series of "Conversations," begun in 1839. When *The Dial* began publication, the Sturgis sisters would be among its most frequent contributors. Around this time, Fuller introduced her to Emerson, inaugurating a lifelong friendship. In 1847, Sturgis married William Aspinwall Tappan, the son of New York merchant and abolitionist Lewis Tappan. In 1850, when Sophia and Nathaniel Hawthorne were looking for a house to rent for the summer, the Tappans, now with two children, offered them their home in Lenox, Massachusetts, where Hawthorne would write *The House of the Seven Gables* (1851), *The Blithedale Romance* (1852), and *Tanglewood Tales* (1853). From 1855 to 1861 the Tappans lived in Europe, where they met the young William and Henry James; the latter later described Caroline as being of the "incurable ironic or mocking order." They returned to the United States to support the Union cause during the Civil War, and after ten more years in Europe, moved home permanently in 1880.

EDWARD THOMPSON TAYLOR (1793–1871)—the "Father Taylor" of Emerson's journals—was born in Richmond, Virginia. Orphaned and homeless by age seven, he went to sea as a cabin boy. At 17, he had a religious awakening after hearing a Methodist preacher and developed his own preaching skills as a British prisoner during the War of 1812. He eventually made his way to Boston, where he began preaching to sailors. In 1833, he was installed as pastor of Seaman's Bethel and would hold his pulpit there for almost 40 years. Emerson had sometimes preached at Bethel during his own ministry nearby in Boston's North End and was a great admirer, calling Taylor the "Shakspeare of the sailor & the poor." In a letter to Margaret Fuller, Emerson wrote, "There is beauty in that man & when he is well alive with his own exhortations it flows out from all the corners of his great heart & steeps the whole rough man in its gracious element." Dickens wrote about Taylor in his *American Notes for General Circulation* (1842), and he inspired the character of Father Mapple in Melville's *Moby-Dick* (1851). Taylor, though not impressed with Emerson's particular theological views or Transcendentalism more generally, is reported to have said that Emerson was "more like Jesus Christ than anyone he had ever known"; he had "seen him where his religion was tested, and it bore the test."

HENRY DAVID THOREAU (1817–1862), the son of a pencil manufacturer, was born in Concord. He graduated from Harvard in 1837 and taught briefly at a local school, resigning after he was ordered to flog students against his wishes; he later taught with his brother John at Concord Academy until John fell ill with tuberculosis in 1841. Emerson, greatly impressed by the young Thoreau, introduced him to his Concord circle and encouraged his writing: Thoreau began his ultimately voluminous journals in 1837 at Emerson's suggestion, and published his first essay, on the dramatist Aulus Persius Flaccus, in *The Dial* in 1840. For most of 1841–44, and occasionally thereafter, Thoreau lived in the Emerson household, acting as a tutor to Emerson's children and as a handyman and assistant. (He subsequently worked as a surveyor, and, for much of his life, in his father's pencil factory, suggesting innovations that made Thoreau pencils the best in the country.) In July 1845, Thoreau built his famous cabin on Emerson's land beside Walden Pond and lived there until September 1847, drafting *A Week on the Concord and Merrimack Rivers* (1849) and beginning *Walden, or Life in the Woods* (1854). The friendship between the two men cooled somewhat in 1849, Emerson critical of Thoreau's lack of ambition ("instead of engineering for all America," he later wrote, "he was the captain of a huckleberry party"), and Thoreau unhappy at being considered a mere follower of Emerson. But they continued to meet often for walks and conversation, read each other's works as they appeared, and had many friends in common, including Bronson Alcott and Ellery Channing. Thoreau traveled widely, writing accounts that would be published posthumously in his *Excursions* (1863), *The Maine Woods* (1864), *Cape Cod* (1865), and *A Yankee in Canada* (1866). During the 1850s his involvement in the abolitionist cause intensified; he aided fugitive slaves, spoke publicly, and wrote "Slavery in Massachusetts" (1854) and "A Plea for John Brown" (1859). He died of tuberculosis in 1862.

JONES VERY (1813–1880) was the oldest of six children of Jones Very, a ship's captain, and Lydia Very. He entered Harvard his sophomore year and finished second in his class in 1836, then served as a tutor in Greek while he studied at Harvard Divinity School. In April 1838, he met Emerson through Elizabeth Palmer Peabody. Emerson took an instant liking to him, and wrote to Peabody that he felt "anew" in his company. In the fall of 1838, college authorities decided that Very—overcome with religious enthusiasm—had gone insane, relieved him of his duties, and committed him to the McLean Asylum for a month. Over the next year and a half Very would produce a unique body of religious poetry—all a product, he would claim, of the "holy spirit." In 1839, Emerson selected and edited these poems and saw them through the press; Very's *Essays and Poems* received almost no critical attention at the time but was highly regarded by Emerson and his circle. By the mid-1840s, Very's religious enthusiasm had waned; he moved back in with his family in Salem, filling temporarily vacant pulpits in the neighboring towns when need arose, and continuing to write poetry.

ANNA HAZARD BARKER WARD (1813–1900), the sixth of 12 children, was born into a prosperous Quaker family. Her father moved the family to New Orleans while she was an infant, his insurance company having failed, and he built another fortune there. Barker met Emerson through Margaret Fuller, with whom she had been friendly for several years, in the fall of 1839. "So lovely, so fortunate," he wrote after their first meeting, "and so remote from my own experiences." After her marriage to Samuel Ward the next year, she and her husband moved to a farm in the Berkshires, but they moved back to Boston in the early 1850s so he could run his father's banking firm. Several years later, she suffered an attack of neuralgia following the death of her daughter and traveled to Europe alone to recover. In March 1858, while in Rome, she converted to Catholicism. On receiving this news, Emerson drafted a letter—never sent—lamenting "the chance-wind that has made a foreigner of you—whirled you from the forehead of the morning into the medievals." Samuel Ward accepted his wife's decision, and had a chapel built for her near their country house in Lenox, Massachusetts. After the war, the Wards moved to New York City, where they became prominent patrons of the arts.

SAMUEL GRAY WARD (1817–1907) was the son of banker Thomas Wren Ward and Lydia Gray Ward. After graduating from Harvard in 1836, he traveled in Europe for two years, studying art and architecture; while abroad, he met Anna Hazard Barker, whom he married in 1840. He met Emerson soon after he returned, and the two became fast friends, Emerson eager to draw on the knowledge and judgment of art his friend had acquired in Europe. Ward loaned him sketches and books, and Emerson spent time with Margaret Fuller looking through Ward's portfolios of prints. At Emerson's suggestion, Ward wrote poems and essays for *The Dial*. After his father's retirement in the early 1850s, he took over as the American agent for the London banking house of Baring Brothers, which was to be his main occupation, first in Boston, then in New York City. In 1869, he became one of the founders of the Metropolitan Museum of Art, later serving on its Board of Trustees and eventually becoming its treasurer. Emerson's correspondence with Ward was collected in 1899 as *Letters to a Friend*.

Index

THE LIBRARY OF AMERICA SERIES

Library of America fosters appreciation of America's literary heritage by publishing, and keeping permanently in print, authoritative editions of America's best and most significant writing. An independent nonprofit organization, it was founded in 1979 with seed funding from the National Endowment for the Humanities and the Ford Foundation.

1. Herman Melville: Typee, Omoo, Mardi
2. Nathaniel Hawthorne: Tales & Sketches
3. Walt Whitman: Poetry & Prose
4. Harriet Beecher Stowe: Three Novels
5. Mark Twain: Mississippi Writings
6. Jack London: Novels & Stories
7. Jack London: Novels & Social Writings
8. William Dean Howells: Novels 1875–1886
9. Herman Melville: Redburn, White-Jacket, Moby-Dick
10. Nathaniel Hawthorne: Collected Novels

11 & 12. Francis Parkman: France and England in North America

13. Henry James: Novels 1871–1880
14. Henry Adams: Novels, Mont Saint Michel, The Education
15. Ralph Waldo Emerson: Essays & Lectures
16. Washington Irving: History, Tales & Sketches
17. Thomas Jefferson: Writings
18. Stephen Crane: Prose & Poetry
19. Edgar Allan Poe: Poetry & Tales
20. Edgar Allan Poe: Essays & Reviews
21. Mark Twain: The Innocents Abroad, Roughing It

22 & 23. Henry James: Literary Criticism

24. Herman Melville: Pierre, Israel Potter, The Confidence-Man, Tales & Billy Budd
25. William Faulkner: Novels 1930–1935

26 & 27. James Fenimore Cooper: The Leatherstocking Tales

28. Henry David Thoreau: A Week, Walden, The Maine Woods, Cape Cod
29. Henry James: Novels 1881–1886
30. Edith Wharton: Novels

31 & 32. Henry Adams: History of the U.S. during the Administrations of Jefferson & Madison

33. Frank Norris: Novels & Essays
34. W.E.B. Du Bois: Writings
35. Willa Cather: Early Novels & Stories
36. Theodore Dreiser: Sister Carrie, Jennie Gerhardt, Twelve Men
37. Benjamin Franklin: Writings (2 vols.)
38. William James: Writings 1902–1910
39. Flannery O'Connor: Collected Works

40, 41, & 42. Eugene O'Neill: Complete Plays

43. Henry James: Novels 1886–1890
44. William Dean Howells: Novels 1886–1888

45 & 46. Abraham Lincoln: Speeches & Writings

47. Edith Wharton: Novellas & Other Writings
48. William Faulkner: Novels 1936–1940
49. Willa Cather: Later Novels
50. Ulysses S. Grant: Memoirs & Selected Letters
51. William Tecumseh Sherman: Memoirs
52. Washington Irving: Bracebridge Hall, Tales of a Traveller, The Alhambra
53. Francis Parkman: The Oregon Trail, The Conspiracy of Pontiac
54. James Fenimore Cooper: Sea Tales

55 & 56. Richard Wright: Works

57. Willa Cather: Stories, Poems, & Other Writings
58. William James: Writings 1878–1899
59. Sinclair Lewis: Main Street & Babbitt

60 & 61. Mark Twain: Collected Tales, Sketches, Speeches, & Essays

62 & 63. The Debate on the Constitution

64 & 65. Henry James: Collected Travel Writings

66 & 67. American Poetry: The Nineteenth Century

68. Frederick Douglass: Autobiographies
69. Sarah Orne Jewett: Novels & Stories
70. Ralph Waldo Emerson: Collected Poems & Translations
71. Mark Twain: Historical Romances
72. John Steinbeck: Novels & Stories 1932–1937
73. William Faulkner: Novels 1942–1954

74 & 75. Zora Neale Hurston: Novels, Stories, & Other Writings

76. Thomas Paine: Collected Writings

77 & 78. Reporting World War II: American Journalism

79 & 80. Raymond Chandler: Novels, Stories, & Other Writings

81. Robert Frost: Collected Poems, Prose, & Plays
82 & 83. Henry James: Complete Stories 1892–1910
84. William Bartram: Travels & Other Writings
85. John Dos Passos: U.S.A.
86. John Steinbeck: The Grapes of Wrath & Other Writings 1936–1941
87, 88, & 89. Vladimir Nabokov: Novels & Other Writings
90. James Thurber: Writings & Drawings
91. George Washington: Writings
92. John Muir: Nature Writings
93. Nathanael West: Novels & Other Writings
94 & 95. Crime Novels: American Noir of the 1930s, 40s, & 50s
96. Wallace Stevens: Collected Poetry & Prose
97. James Baldwin: Early Novels & Stories
98. James Baldwin: Collected Essays
99 & 100. Gertrude Stein: Writings
101 & 102. Eudora Welty: Novels, Stories, & Other Writings
103. Charles Brockden Brown: Three Gothic Novels
104 & 105. Reporting Vietnam: American Journalism
106 & 107. Henry James: Complete Stories 1874–1891
108. American Sermons
109. James Madison: Writings
110. Dashiell Hammett: Complete Novels
111. Henry James: Complete Stories 1864–1874
112. William Faulkner: Novels 1957–1962
113. John James Audubon: Writings & Drawings
114. Slave Narratives
115 & 116. American Poetry: The Twentieth Century
117. F. Scott Fitzgerald: Novels & Stories 1920–1922
118. Henry Wadsworth Longfellow: Poems & Other Writings
119 & 120. Tennessee Williams: Collected Plays
121 & 122. Edith Wharton: Collected Stories
123. The American Revolution: Writings from the War of Independence
124. Henry David Thoreau: Collected Essays & Poems
125. Dashiell Hammett: Crime Stories & Other Writings
126 & 127. Dawn Powell: Novels
128. Carson McCullers: Complete Novels
129. Alexander Hamilton: Writings
130. Mark Twain: The Gilded Age & Later Novels
131. Charles W. Chesnutt: Stories, Novels, & Essays
132. John Steinbeck: Novels 1942–1952
133. Sinclair Lewis: Arrowsmith, Elmer Gantry, Dodsworth
134 & 135. Paul Bowles: Novels, Stories, & Other Writings
136. Kate Chopin: Complete Novels & Stories
137 & 138. Reporting Civil Rights: American Journalism
139. Henry James: Novels 1896–1899
140. Theodore Dreiser: An American Tragedy
141. Saul Bellow: Novels 1944–1953
142. John Dos Passos: Novels 1920–1925
143. John Dos Passos: Travel Books & Other Writings
144. Ezra Pound: Poems & Translations
145. James Weldon Johnson: Writings
146. Washington Irving: Three Western Narratives
147. Alexis de Tocqueville: Democracy in America
148. James T. Farrell: Studs Lonigan Trilogy
149, 150, & 151. Isaac Bashevis Singer: Collected Stories
152. Kaufman & Co.: Broadway Comedies
153. Theodore Roosevelt: Rough Riders, An Autobiography
154. Theodore Roosevelt: Letters & Speeches
155. H. P. Lovecraft: Tales
156. Louisa May Alcott: Little Women, Little Men, Jo's Boys
157. Philip Roth: Novels & Stories 1959–1962
158. Philip Roth: Novels 1967–1972
159. James Agee: Let Us Now Praise Famous Men, A Death in the Family, Shorter Fiction
160. James Agee: Film Writing & Selected Journalism
161. Richard Henry Dana Jr.: Two Years Before the Mast & Other Voyages
162. Henry James: Novels 1901–1902
163. Arthur Miller: Plays 1944–1961
164. William Faulkner: Novels 1926–1929
165. Philip Roth: Novels 1973–1977

166 & 167. American Speeches: Political Oratory
168. Hart Crane: Complete Poems & Selected Letters
169. Saul Bellow: Novels 1956–1964
170. John Steinbeck: Travels with Charley & Later Novels
171. Capt. John Smith: Writings with Other Narratives
172. Thornton Wilder: Collected Plays & Writings on Theater
173. Philip K. Dick: Four Novels of the 1960s
174. Jack Kerouac: Road Novels 1957–1960
175. Philip Roth: Zuckerman Bound
176 & 177. Edmund Wilson: Literary Essays & Reviews
178. American Poetry: The 17th & 18th Centuries
179. William Maxwell: Early Novels & Stories
180. Elizabeth Bishop: Poems, Prose, & Letters
181. A. J. Liebling: World War II Writings
182. American Earth: Environmental Writing Since Thoreau
183. Philip K. Dick: Five Novels of the 1960s & 70s
184. William Maxwell: Later Novels & Stories
185. Philip Roth: Novels & Other Narratives 1986–1991
186. Katherine Anne Porter: Collected Stories & Other Writings
187. John Ashbery: Collected Poems 1956–1987
188 & 189. John Cheever: Complete Novels & Collected Stories
190. Lafcadio Hearn: American Writings
191. A. J. Liebling: The Sweet Science & Other Writings
192. The Lincoln Anthology
193. Philip K. Dick: VALIS & Later Novels
194. Thornton Wilder: The Bridge of San Luis Rey & Other Novels 1926–1948
195. Raymond Carver: Collected Stories
196 & 197. American Fantastic Tales
198. John Marshall: Writings
199. The Mark Twain Anthology
200. Mark Twain: A Tramp Abroad, Following the Equator, Other Travels
201 & 202. Ralph Waldo Emerson: Selected Journals
203. The American Stage: Writing on Theater
204. Shirley Jackson: Novels & Stories
205. Philip Roth: Novels 1993–1995
206 & 207. H. L. Mencken: Prejudices
208. John Kenneth Galbraith: The Affluent Society & Other Writings 1952–1967
209. Saul Bellow: Novels 1970–1982
210 & 211. Lynd Ward: Six Novels in Woodcuts
212. The Civil War: The First Year
213 & 214. John Adams: Revolutionary Writings
215. Henry James: Novels 1903–1911
216. Kurt Vonnegut: Novels & Stories 1963–1973
217 & 218. Harlem Renaissance Novels
219. Ambrose Bierce: The Devil's Dictionary, Tales, & Memoirs
220. Philip Roth: The American Trilogy 1997–2000
221. The Civil War: The Second Year
222. Barbara W. Tuchman: The Guns of August, The Proud Tower
223. Arthur Miller: Plays 1964–1982
224. Thornton Wilder: The Eighth Day, Theophilus North, Autobiographical Writings
225. David Goodis: Five Noir Novels of the 1940s & 50s
226. Kurt Vonnegut: Novels & Stories 1950–1962
227 & 228. American Science Fiction: Nine Novels of the 1950s
229 & 230. Laura Ingalls Wilder: The Little House Books
231. Jack Kerouac: Collected Poems
232. The War of 1812
233. American Antislavery Writings
234. The Civil War: The Third Year
235. Sherwood Anderson: Collected Stories
236. Philip Roth: Novels 2001–2007
237. Philip Roth: Nemeses
238. Aldo Leopold: A Sand County Almanac & Other Writings
239. May Swenson: Collected Poems
240 & 241. W. S. Merwin: Collected Poems
242 & 243. John Updike: Collected Stories
244. Ring Lardner: Stories & Other Writings
245. Jonathan Edwards: Writings from the Great Awakening
246. Susan Sontag: Essays of the 1960s & 70s

247. William Wells Brown: Clotel & Other Writings
248 & 249. Bernard Malamud: Novels & Stories of the 1940s, 50s, & 60s
250. The Civil War: The Final Year
251. Shakespeare in America
252. Kurt Vonnegut: Novels 1976–1985
253 & 254. American Musicals 1927–1969
255. Elmore Leonard: Four Novels of the 1970s
256. Louisa May Alcott: Work, Eight Cousins, Rose in Bloom, Stories & Other Writings
257. H. L. Mencken: The Days Trilogy
258. Virgil Thomson: Music Chronicles 1940–1954
259. Art in America 1945–1970
260. Saul Bellow: Novels 1984–2000
261. Arthur Miller: Plays 1987–2004
262. Jack Kerouac: Visions of Cody, Visions of Gerard, Big Sur
263. Reinhold Niebuhr: Major Works on Religion & Politics
264. Ross Macdonald: Four Novels of the 1950s
265 & 266. The American Revolution: Writings from the Pamphlet Debate
267. Elmore Leonard: Four Novels of the 1980s
268 & 269. Women Crime Writers: Suspense Novels of the 1940s & 50s
270. Frederick Law Olmsted: Writings on Landscape, Culture, & Society
271. Edith Wharton: Four Novels of the 1920s
272. James Baldwin: Later Novels
273. Kurt Vonnegut: Novels 1987–1997
274. Henry James: Autobiographies
275. Abigail Adams: Letters
276. John Adams: Writings from the New Nation 1784–1826
277. Virgil Thomson: The State of Music & Other Writings
278. War No More: American Antiwar & Peace Writing
279. Ross Macdonald: Three Novels of the Early 1960s
280. Elmore Leonard: Four Later Novels
281. Ursula K. Le Guin: The Complete Orsinia
282. John O'Hara: Stories
283. The Unknown Kerouac: Rare, Unpublished & Newly Translated Writings
284. Albert Murray: Collected Essays & Memoirs
285 & 286. Loren Eiseley: Collected Essays on Evolution, Nature, & the Cosmos
287. Carson McCullers: Stories, Plays & Other Writings
288. Jane Bowles: Collected Writings
289. World War I and America: Told by the Americans Who Lived It
290 & 291. Mary McCarthy: The Complete Fiction
292. Susan Sontag: Later Essays
293 & 294. John Quincy Adams: Diaries
295. Ross Macdonald: Four Later Novels
296 & 297. Ursula K. Le Guin: The Hainish Novels & Stories
298 & 299. Peter Taylor: The Complete Stories
300. Philip Roth: Why Write? Collected Nonfiction 1960–2013
301. John Ashbery: Collected Poems 1991–2000
302. Wendell Berry: Port William Novels & Stories: The Civil War to World War II
303. Reconstruction: Voices from America's First Great Struggle for Racial Equality
304. Albert Murray: Collected Novels & Poems
305 & 306. Norman Mailer: The Sixties
307. Rachel Carson: Silent Spring & Other Writings on the Environment
308. Elmore Leonard: Westerns

DATE DUE
